2nd Edition

Criminal Evidence

PRINCIPLES, CASES, AND READINGS

2nd Edition

Criminal Evidence

PRINCIPLES, CASES, AND READINGS

Thomas J. Gardner

WEST PUBLISHING COMPANY

ST. PAUL   NEW YORK   LOS ANGELES   SAN FRANCISCO

Copyediting by Chris Thillen

Artwork by Rolin Graphics

Text design by Rick Chafian

COPYRIGHT © 1978 By WEST PUBLISHING COMPANY
COPYRIGHT © 1988 By WEST PUBLISHING COMPANY
          50 W. Kellogg Boulevard
          P.O. Box 64526
          St. Paul, MN 55164–1003
Library of Congress Cataloging-in-Publication Data

Gardner, Thomas J., 1921–
  Criminal evidence.

  (West's criminal justice series)
  Includes index.
  1. Evidence, Criminal—United States—Cases.
I. Title. II. Series: Criminal justice series.
KF9660.A7G37 1988   345.73'06 87–13367
ISBN 0–314–34735–6   347.3056

To Eileen Gardner

West's Criminal Justice Series

Bennett & Hess *Criminal Investigation, Second Edition*

Blonien & Greenfield *California Law Manual for the Administration of Justice*

Burns *Corrections: Organization and Administration*

Cromwell & Keefer *Police-Community Relations, Second Edition*

Cromwell, Killinger, Kerper, Walker *Probation & Parole in the Criminal Justice System, Second Edition*

Cromwell, Killinger, Sarri & Solomon *Juvenile Delinquency: Readings*

Dix & Sharlot *Cases and Materials on Basic Criminal Law, Third Edition*

Dowling *Teaching Materials on Criminal Procedure*

Faust & Brantingham *Juvenile Justice Philosophy: Readings, Cases and Comments, Second Edition*

Felkenes *Michigan Criminal Justice Law Manual*

Ferdico *Criminal Procedure for the Law Enforcement Officer, Third Edition*

Ferguson *The Nature of Vice Control in the Administration of Justice*

Ferguson *Readings on Concepts of Criminal Law*

Gaines & Ricks *Readings on Police Organization and Management*

Gardner *Law of Criminal Evidence, Second Edition*

Gardner *Criminal Law, Third Edition*

Hess & Wrobleski *Introduction to Private Security, Second Edition*

Imwinkelried, et al. *Criminal Evidence*

Johnson *Elements of Criminal Due Process*

Johnson *An Introduction to the Juvenile Justice System*

Kenney & More *Principles of Investigation*

Kerper & Israel *Introduction to the Criminal Justice System, Second Edition*

Kerper & Kerper *Legal Rights of the Convicted*

Killinger & Cromwell *Corrections in the Community: Readings, Second Edition*

Killinger & Cromwell *Introduction to Corrections: Readings*

Killinger, Cromwell and Cromwell *Issues in Corrections and Administration*

Killinger, Cromwell and Wood *Penology: The Evolution of Corrections in America, Second Edition*

Klein *Law of Evidence for Police, Second Edition*

LaFave *Principles of Criminal Law*

Leonard *Fundamentals of Law Enforcement: Problems and Issues*

Lewis *Criminal Procedure: The Supreme Court's View-Cases*

Maddex *Constitutional Law: Cases and Comments, Second Edition*

Markle *Criminal Investigation and Presentation of Evidence*

More *The American Police: Text and Readings*

More *Criminal Justice Management: Text and Readings*

More *Effective Police Administration, Second Edition*

Parker & Meier *Interpersonal Psych. for Law Enforcement and Corrections*

Perrine, et al. *Administration of Justice: Principles and Procedures*

Reid, *Criminal Justice: Procedures and Issues*

Roberg *Police Management and Organizational Behavior*

Roberg & Webb *Critical Issues in Corrections: Problems, Trends and Prospects*

Samaha *Criminal Law, Second Edition*

San Diego Police Department *Police Tactics in Hazardous Situations*

Schwartz & Goldstein *Law Enforcement Handbook, Second Edition*

Senna & Siegel *Juvenile Law: Cases and Comments*

Senna & Siegel *Introduction to Criminal Justice System, Fourth Edition*

Siegel *Criminology, Second Edition*

Siegel & Senna *Juvenile Delinquency: Theory, Practice and Law, Third Edition*

Smith & Berlin *Introduction to Probation and Parole, Second Edition*

Souryal *Police Administration and Management*

Sutor *Police Operations: Tactical Approaches to Crimes in Progress*

Vetter & Territo *Crime & Justice in America: A Human Perspective*

Wadman, Paxman & Bentley *Law Enforcement Supervision: A Case Study Approach*

Wrobleski & Hess *Introduction to Law Enforcement and Criminal Justice, Second Edition*

Contents in Brief

Explanatory Note

The author has attempted to present the general principles of criminal evidence in this textbook. However, because of the variance in state statutes and court decisions from state to state, it is recommended that students and officers consult with legal advisers before assuming that principles of law applicable in other jurisdictions exist in their states.

Table of Contents

HIGHLIGHTS

HIGHLIGHTS

HIGHLIGHTS

HIGHLIGHTS

HIGHLIGHTS

HIGHLIGHTS

Fourth Amendment of the U.S. Constitution   314
"Urgent Need" as Defined by the Dorman Case in Justifying Exigency Entry   323
FBI Articles on Emergency Search of Premises   324

HIGHLIGHTS

HIGHLIGHTS

HIGHLIGHTS

HIGHLIGHTS

Part Four   Physical and Demonstrative Evidence

HIGHLIGHTS

HIGHLIGHTS

HIGHLIGHTS

HIGHLIGHTS

Table of Cases

Introduction

Today as we are preparing to celebrate the 200th anniversary of the American Bill of Rights in 1991, we continue to wrestle with the question of what is a fair trial for a person charged with a crime. Rules of evidence are important in protecting the fundamental rights of an accused, which are guaranteed by the Bill of Rights. But rules of evidence are also necessary to assure the interest of the public in the efficient and effective functioning of the American criminal justice system.

The question of what is a fair trial was probably debated centuries ago when European and English courts began functioning. Many changes have occurred as the years have gone by. Many medieval practices, such as holding animals criminally responsible for the harm they had done, were discontinued before the American Revolution.

Persons charged with crimes have a right to a fair trial. What is a fair trial is determined to a great extent by the rules of evidence used in the courts at that time. What was considered a fair trial in 1692 during the witchcraft trials in Salem, Massachusetts certainly was different than a fair trial today in the United States. In 1692, 19 persons were executed in Salem as witches and 150 more were jailed by evidence that would not be permitted in trials today in any democratic country in the world.

Ninety-nine years after the Salem witchcraft trials, the United States ratified the Bill of Rights (see appendix A). The ratification in 1791 of the first ten Amendments, which constitute the American Bill of Rights, established many of the requirements for the rules of evidence used today in our state and federal courts.

U.S. Supreme Court cases have always been important in establishing the rules and guidelines used in determining the requirements of a fair trial under the Bill of Rights. In recent years, U.S. Supreme Court cases have become much more important as voters in states such as Florida and California have amended the constitutions of their states and now require courts in those states to interpret questions involving the suppression of physical evidence "in conformity with the 4th Amendment ... as interpreted by the United States Supreme Court" (Florida Constitution).

Constitutional amendments, such as have been enacted in California and Florida, have eliminated to a large extent the state rules of evidence as to the suppression (keeping out) of physical evidence for use in criminal trials in those states.

An effort has been made to present all of the important U.S. Supreme Court criminal evidence cases in this textbook. Many of the cases are presented in the material within the chapters. Over thirty other U.S. Supreme Court cases are presented as problems at the end of many of the chapters. Because of the increased importance of these cases, it is hoped that this method will assist in providing a better understanding of the principles of the law of evidence.

2nd Edition

Criminal Evidence

PRINCIPLES, CASES, AND READINGS

PART ONE

Introduction to Criminal Evidence

1

Important Aspects of the American Criminal Justice System

HISTORY OF THE RULES OF EVIDENCE

Hundreds of years ago, English courts began developing rules of evidence as part of the English system of justice. Rules of evidence are rules which determine the use and admissibility of evidence in courts. The early judge-made rules of England were brought by settlers to the American colonies to be used in the colonial courts as common-law rules of evidence.

Rules of evidence are an important part of any criminal justice system. In a democracy, evidence rules are important both in safeguarding the rights of persons accused of crimes and also in assuring the interest of the public in the administration of criminal justice. There always have been debates and arguments over what the rules of evidence should be and what would best serve the needs of society.

Many changes have been made over the years in the law and rules of evidence. This can be seen by comparing the procedures used today with the practices of past centuries. The Salem witchcraft trials of 1692 are referred to in the introduction to this text. Under the rules of evidence used today, it would be impossible to obtain convictions to execute 19 persons and to imprison 150 others. This and other episodes caused concerned American colonists to request that a Bill of Rights be added to the Constitution adopted in 1787 at the Philadelphia Convention.

In tracing the history of the Fourth Amendment of the U.S. Constitution (part of the American Bill of Rights), the U.S. Supreme Court demonstrated why the right of privacy was protected by the search warrant requirement and the **probable cause** requirement, stating

Vivid in the memory of the newly formed independent Americans were those general warrants known as writs of assistance under which officers of the Crown had so bedeviled the Colonists. The hated writs of assistance had given customs officials blanket authority to search where they pleased for goods imported in violation of British tax laws. They were denounced by James Otis as "the worst instrument of arbitrary power, the most destructive of English liberty, and the fundamental principles of law, that ever was found in an English law book" because they placed "the liberty of every man in the hands of every petty officer." The historic occasion of that denunciation in 1761 at Boston, has been characterized as "perhaps the most prominent event which inaugurated the resistance of the colonies to the oppressions of the mother country." "Then and there," said John Adams, "was the first scene of the first act of opposition to the arbitrary claims of Great Britain. Then and there the child Independence was born." *Stanford v. Texas*, 379 U.S. 476, 85 S.Ct. 506 (1965).

Other examples can be seen in the history of early England. Before and after the Norman Conquest of England (1066), the guilt or innocence of an accused was often determined through trial by combat or ordeal. Trial by combat was ordinarily reserved for members of the nobility. The accused and his accuser often fought with arms to determine the guilt or innocence of the accused.

Other ordeals were also used to determine guilt or innocence. The accused might be required (if he said that he was innocent) to hold a piece of red-hot iron in his hands or to thrust his hands and arms into boiling water or oil. The theory was that if the accused was innocent, God would protect him. The famous English lawyer, Sir William Blackstone, wrote before the American Revolution that "(o)ne cannot but be astonished at the folly and impiety of pronouncing a man guilty, unless he was cleared by a miracle ..." [1]

Trial by the ordeal of water consisted of throwing the accused into a body of water. Floating was evidence of his guilt. Sinking was evidence of innocence. The English judge, Sir James Stephens, wrote in 1883 that

> In nearly every case, the accused would sink. This would prove his innocence, indeed, but there would be no need to take him out. He would thus die honourably. If by accident he floated, he would be put to death disgracefully. [2]

The American founding fathers were aware of the injustices of these practices of the past and set down principles in the U.S. Constitution conceived to afford an accused a fair trial. They borrowed much of their concept of fairness from the already established common law. In addition, early American judges and lawyers were strongly influenced by Blackstone's *Commentaries*, which were published in the 1760s and sold by the thousands throughout the United States in the years which followed.

Rules of evidence have always played a very important role in both civil and criminal trials. In modern times, there was a trend toward severely limiting evidence which could be admitted for use in trials. Legislation and court decisions in the 1970s, however, have reversed this trend toward limiting evidence which may be used in trials. For example, the Federal Rules of Evidence, which were enacted by the Congress of the United States and which became effective in 1975, reflect the tendency toward a greater admissibility of evidence. The Federal Rules and similar rules enacted by some of the state legislatures represent changes in federal and state practices.

Court decisions in the 1970s have also in some instances permitted greater admissibility of evidence. The question before the courts in all of these cases is that of defining and protecting the rights of defendants in criminal trials while at the same time maintaining an effective trial system capable of seeking and determining the truth. As an increasing number of criminal trials are brought before American courts, it is exceedingly important that law enforcement officers know and observe the rules of evidence used before these courts.

THE ACCUSED'S RIGHT TO A FAIR TRIAL

The U.S. Supreme Court and other courts in this country have repeatedly held that the "law does not require that a defendant receive a perfect trial, only a fair one." [3] It follows that if a defendant is to have a fair trial, which is his constitutional right, it is important to establish what is fair. Fairness in trials is determined to a great extent by rules of evidence because rules of evidence play an important role in the determination of guilt or innocence in criminal trials.

In the case of *Tehan v. Shott,* the U.S. Supreme Court stated that the "basic purpose of a trial is the determination of truth," [4] and in the case of *Berger v. United States,* that the dual aim of American criminal justice is "that the guilty shall not escape or the innocent suffer." [5] In Rule 102 of the Federal Rules of Evidence, the Congress of the United States stated that

> These rules shall be construed to secure fairness in administration, elimination of unjustifiable expense and delay, and promotion of growth and development of the law of evidence to the end that the truth may be ascertained and proceedings justly determined.
>
> (See the Federal Rules of Evidence in appendix B.)

Controlling the admission of evidence to assure a defendant accused of a crime of a "fair" trial are the following:

- The Constitution of the United States, which Article VI provides is "the supreme Law of the Land"; and in state trials, the constitution of the state wherein the trial is held.
- The rules of evidence of the state enacted by the state legislature and made part of the state statutes.
- Court decisions of the state interpreting applicable constitutional provisions and state statutes.

The Continuing Controversy Over What Constitutes a Fair Trial

Many persons in the United States are very upset over court decisions as to what is a fair trial. It is not uncommon to hear people say that criminal defendants have too many rights under our system.

Those who believe that the rules of evidence are hindering and hampering too severely the search for truth in criminal cases have several courses of action. Because we live in a democracy, they may urge their state legislators to make changes in the rules of evidence in their state. Because state judges are elected officials, voters can inform themselves so as to elect the best-qualified persons to serve as judges in their state. In state judicial elections, it is common for candidates to campaign on the slogan that they would be (or that they are) a "fair but firm" judge.

Probably the most significant change that has occurred in a number of states, including California and Florida, was brought about when voters in those states amended and changed their state constitutions in one of the following ways:

The American Adversary System (Called by some the "Set the Parties Fighting" System)

Judge Learned Hand observed in 1935 that "It is impossible to expect that a criminal trial shall be conducted without some showing of feeling; the stakes are high and participants are inevitably charged with emotion." [a]

RULINGS OF THE U.S. SUPREME COURT IN THE 1985 CASE OF U.S. v. YOUNG [b]

Prosecutor

"Nearly a half century ago this Court counselled prosecutors 'to refrain from improper methods calculated to produce a wrongful conviction . . . .' *Berger v. United States,* 295 U.S. 78, 88. The Court made clear, however, that the adversary system permits the prosecutor to 'prosecute with earnestness and vigor.' In other words, 'while he may strike hard blows, he is not at liberty to strike foul ones.'

The line separating acceptable from improper advocacy is not easily drawn; there is often a gray zone. Prosecutors sometimes breach their duty to refrain from overzealous conduct by commenting on the defendant's guilt and offering unsolicited personal views on the evidence. Accordingly, the legal profession, through its Codes of Professional Responsibility, and the federal courts, have tried to police prosecutorial misconduct. In complementing these efforts, the American Bar Association's Standing Committee on Standards for Criminal Justice has promulgated useful guidelines, one of which states that

> [i]t is unprofessional conduct for the prosecutor to express his or her personal belief or opinion as to the truth or falsity of any testimony or evidence or the guilt of the defendant. ABA Standards for Criminal Justice 3–5.8(b)(2d ed. 1980).

Defense Lawyer

". . . [t]he interests of society in the preservation of courtroom control by the judges are no more to be frustrated through unchecked improprieties by defenders. *Sacher v. United States,* 343 U.S. 1, 8. Defense counsel, like the prosecutor, must refrain from interjecting

- Proposition 8, passed by the California voters in 1982, added section 28(d) to article I of the California Constitution which "abrogated (cancelled)...a defendant's right to object to and suppress evidence seized in violation of the California but not the federal Constitution." [6]
- The voters of Florida amended the Florida Constitution (effective in 1983) so as to compel Florida courts to interpret questions involving the suppression of physical evidence "in conformity with the 4th Amendment...as interpreted by the United States Supreme Court." [7]

The effect of such constitutional amendments is to abolish state exclusionary rules in that state. The California exclusionary rule was once known as perhaps the strongest state exclusionary rule in the country. The California consti-

personal beliefs into the presentation of his case. ABA Standards for Criminal Justice p. 4–97 provides the following guideline:

> The prohibition of personal attacks on the prosecutor is but a part of the larger duty of counsel to avoid acrimony in relations with opposing counsel during trial and confine argument to record evidence. It is firmly established that the lawyer should abstain from any allusion to the personal peculiarities and idiosyncrasies of opposing counsel. A personal attack by the prosecutor on defense counsel is improper, and the duty to abstain from such attacks is obviously reciprocal. Defense counsel, like his adversary, must not be permitted to make unfounded and inflammatory attacks on the opposing advocate.

Judge

"We emphasize that the trial judge has the responsibility to maintain decorum in keeping with the nature of the proceeding; 'the judge is not a mere moderator but is the governor of the trial for the purpose of assuring its proper conduct.' *Quercia v. United States*, 289 U.S. 466, 469. The judge 'must meet situations as they arise and [be able] to cope with ... the contingencies inherent in the adversary process.' *Geders v. United States*, 425 U.S., at 86. Of course, 'hard blows' cannot be avoided in criminal trials; both the prosecutor and defense counsel must be kept within appropriate bounds."

> The prosecutor, the defense lawyer, and the trial judge each have duties and responsibilities that must be met if justice is to be attained. Former U.S. Supreme Court Chief Justice Burger compared the American adversary system to a three-legged stool. The judge, prosecutor, and defense lawyer all must be competent in performing their duties for the system to work. If any of the legs is weak or fails to render proper service, the system may not perform properly. A guilty person might not be convicted, or an innocent person might be found guilty.

a United States v. Wexler, 79 F.2d 526, 529 (2d Cir.1935), review denied 297 U.S. 703, 56 S.Ct. 384 (1936).

b United States v. Young, 470 U.S. 1, 105 S.Ct. 1038 (1985).

tutional amendment now forbids excluding "relevant evidence" unless federal law also requires suppression.

Under the federalist system used in the United States, each state may create their own rules of evidence as long as the minimum standards of a fair trial interpreted by the U.S. Supreme Court are complied with. Understanding the exclusionary rule of evidence in California and Florida is now much simpler since only the federal rule is used in both state and federal courts.

THE AMERICAN ADVERSARY SYSTEM

When a person is charged with a crime, the state (or government) in alleging his guilt becomes an adversary and is represented in court by a prosecutor.

The prosecutor is obligated to "seek justice, not merely to convict," [8] and attempts to have the defendant "found-guilty-beyond-a-reasonable-doubt-by-a-unanimous-jury-in-accordance-with-law-after-a-fair-trial."

The prosecutor's adversary (opponent) in a criminal trial is the defense attorney whose duty "is to represent his client (the defendant) zealously within the bounds of the law ...." [9] "The 'alter ego' concept of a defense lawyer, which sees him as a 'mouthpiece' for his client, is fundamentally wrong, unethical and destructive of the lawyer's image; more important to the accused, perhaps, this pernicious idea is destructive of the lawyer's usefulness. The lawyer's value to each client stems in large part from the independence of his stance, as a professional representative rather than as an ordinary agent." [10]

The trial judge neutrally presides at the criminal trial and "has the responsibility for safeguarding both the rights of the accused and the interests of the public in the administration of criminal justice. The adversary nature of the proceedings does not relieve the trial judge of the obligation of raising on his own initiative, at all appropriate times and in an appropriate manner; matters which may significantly promote a just determination of the trial. The only purpose of a criminal trial is to determine whether the prosecution has established the guilt of the accused as required by law, and the trial judge should not allow the proceedings to be used for any other purpose." [11]

The two adversaries (the prosecutor and the defense lawyer) approach the facts in the case from entirely different prospectives. Each advocate comes to the trial prepared to present his evidence and arguments. The trial judge and the jury come to the trial uncommitted. Within the framework of the rules of evidence and the rules of court procedure, witnesses and evidence are presented. Witnesses are cross-examined and evidence is challenged.

Because most of the weak cases and cases in which the defendant has a credible defense are filtered out of the system by plea bargaining, the cases that do go to trial are for the most part either strong cases for the government or cases involving serious criminal charges. For these reasons, it is commonly understood that the defense counsel cannot "win" often in the adversary contest.

Because a criminal trial "is in the end basically a fact-finding process," [12] questions of fact must be determined in all contested criminal cases.[13] The U.S. Supreme Court stated in the case of *Tehan v. U.S. ex rel. Shott* [14] that "(t)he basic purpose of a trial is the determination of truth." Therefore, after the adversaries (the prosecutor and the defense lawyer) have presented all of their evidence, and made all of their motions and arguments, the trier of fact must then make the determination as to whether the government has carried the burden of proving the defendant guilty beyond reasonable doubt.

THE AMERICAN ACCUSATORIAL SYSTEM

The United States and most of the English-speaking democracies in the world use the accusatorial system in criminal investigations and in criminal trials. The U.S. Supreme Court stated in the case of *Rogers v. Richmond* [15] that

> ours is an accusatorial and not an inquisitial system—a system in which the State must establish guilt by evidence independently and

Purposes of the Rules of Evidence

The Uniform Rules and the Federal Rules of Evidence state that the purposes of the rules are to "secure fairness in administration, elimination of unjustifiable expense and delay, and promotion of growth and development of the law of evidence to the end that the truth may be ascertained and proceedings justly determined."

In this highlight, some of the rules of evidence are categorized, with specific rule numbers noted in parentheses. These rules are included in their entirety in appendix B.

RULES THAT ARE MEANT TO ASSIST IN THE SEARCH FOR TRUTH AND ALSO TO EXPEDITE TRIALS

Rules meant to assist in the search for truth by guarding against unreliable evidence which could be prejudicial, misleading, inaccurate, or distracting:

- Rules requiring that evidence be relevant, material, and competent (Rules 401, 402, 403).
- The **opinion evidence** rule (Rule 701).
- The **hearsay evidence** rules (See chapter 7).

Rules which help forward trial processes and assist in expediting trials:

- Rules concerning **judicial notice** (Rule 201) which relieves a party of the necessity of proving something in court which is of common knowledge or the fact can be determined by "resort to sources whose accuracy cannot reasonably be questioned."
- Rules concerning presumptions and inferences which give directions to judges and juries and also determine in criminal and civil actions which of the parties has the burden of proof and the burden of coming forward with evidence (Rule 301).

RULES OF EVIDENCE WHICH ARE NOT DESIGNED TO BE OF ASSISTANCE IN THE SEARCH FOR TRUTH BUT HAVE OTHER PURPOSES. THESE RULES OF EVIDENCE COULD ACTUALLY HINDER THE SEARCH FOR TRUTH.

- Testimonial privilege rules (Rule 501) which have been created to protect relationships and interests such as husband-wife, lawyer-client, doctor-patient, clergyman-penitent relationships. These relationships have been determined by the common law and state legislators to be of such importance as to justify the sacrifices of preventing the use of what might be very reliable evidence from use in criminal and civil trials.
- The rule of exclusion of evidence (the **exclusionary rule**), which prevents the use of evidence that has been improperly or illegally obtained by law enforcement officers. The purpose of this rule is to discourage and deter improper or illegal conduct or procedure by law enforcement officers. The exclusionary rule is very controversial and was referred to as "that Draconian judicial doctrine" by Chief Justice Burger of the U.S. Supreme Court (*Brewer v. Williams,* 430 U.S. 387, 97 S.Ct. 1232 (1977).

freely secured and may not by coercion prove its charge against an accused out of his own mouth.

Under the accusatorial system, suspects and defendants have an absolute right to remain silent as to communications which could incriminate them. If a defendant chooses to remain silent, the state (or government) must carry the burden of proving him guilty beyond a reasonable doubt—using evidence obtained elsewhere in a manner which did not violate the rights of the suspect.

Most European countries and other democracies of the world do not use the accusatorial system, but use instead a system called the inquisitorial system. Under the inquisitorial system, defendants do not have an absolute right to remain silent.[16] In some European countries, special judges become responsible for the investigation of serious crimes and question witnesses and suspects.

While countries using the inquisitorial system rely more heavily on the obtaining of confessions in the solving of crimes, the U.S. Supreme Court expressed a different philosophy in the 1964 case of *Escobedo v. Illinois*,[17] where Justice Goldberg writing for the majority in a 5/4 decision held that

> We have learned the lesson of history, ancient and modern, that a system of criminal law enforcement which comes to depend on the "confession" will, in the long run, be less reliable and more subject to abuses than a system which depends on extrinsic evidence independently secured through skillful investigation .... This Court also has recognized that "history amply shows that confessions have often been extorted to save law enforcement officials the trouble and effort of obtaining valid and independent evidence ...." *Haynes v. Washington*, 373 U.S. 503, 519, 83 S.Ct. 1336, 1346.
>
> We have also learned the companion lesson of history that no system of criminal justice can, or should, survive if it comes to depend for its continued effectiveness on the citizens' abdication through unawareness of their constitutional rights. No system worth preserving should have to *fear* that if an accused is permitted to consult with a lawyer, he will become aware of, and exercise, these rights. If the exercise of constitutional rights will thwart the effectiveness of a system of law enforcement, then there is something very wrong with that system.

Some of the ways that criminal trials in the United States and the American criminal justice system differ from the criminal justice systems of other industrial democracies of the world are demonstrated in the following material:

ACCESS TO EVIDENCE BY DEFENDANTS

A Criminal Trial Is a Search for Truth, Not a Poker Game in Which Total Secrecy Is Maintained

Both the prosecutor representing the state and the defense attorney representing the defendant are concerned with the discovery of important facts concerning their cases. The prosecutor has available to him the evidence obtained by the investigating officers, who in most instances have brought the case into the prosecutor's office requesting that criminal charges be filed. A defense law-

Differences Between the American Criminal System and Systems Used in Other Democratic Countries

The United States:	While other industrial democracies:
Uses a plea bargaining system to dispose of the vast majority of criminal cases	Do not rely upon plea bargaining to the extent that it is used in the United States
Has totally rejected "the widespread practice in civil law countries of having career magistrates, selected as relative youths to function in the role of impartial adjudicators." (Federal Judge Marvin E. Frankel)	As a general rule do not use the American system of political appointment or election of judges
Places a great amount of discretion and responsibility in the hands of public prosecutors [a]	Do not place as much discretion and responsibility in the hands of prosecutors
Has created rules which make it more difficult to obtain confessions and admissions to use as evidence	Rely more heavily upon obtaining confessions and admissions for use as evidence in criminal trials
Has adopted the American exclusionary rule	Have not adopted the American exclusionary rule; therefore, much of the evidence which would be excluded from use in American criminal trials may be used in the courts of other countries
Has created rules which permit criminal trials to be much longer than similar American criminal trials in the 1950s and 1960s (see the book, *Helter Skelter,* relating the events in the California Manson trial, which ran for nine months with a sequestered jury)	Have not permitted the excesses seen in the Manson trial
In 1986–87, a New York narcotic trial lasted 17 months. Because pizza parlors were used as fronts to distribute drugs, newspapers referred to the trial as the "pizza trial".	

[a] See the article entitled "Court Reform: Not Plea Bargaining," written by California Judge Arthur L. Alarcon while he was chairman of the California Bar Association Committee on Criminal Justice. The article appears in the February 1976 issue of *Criminal Justice Digest*.

yer's first source of information is usually the defendant, who may or may not provide accurate information as to the facts leading to the criminal charges.

But what evidence is the state obligated to disclose to defendants prior to trial as to the case against them? What right of discovery should defendants have as to evidence and information in the possession of the prosecutor and

The Prosecutor's Duty Is to Seek Justice

THE AMERICAN PROSECUTOR IS UNIQUE IN THE WORLD

First, the American prosecutor is a public prosecutor representing the people in matters of criminal law. Traditionally, European societies viewed crimes as wrongs against an individual whose claims could be pressed through private prosecution. Second, the American prosecutor is usually a local official, reflecting the development of autonomous local governments in the colonies. Finally, as an elected official, the local American prosecutor is responsible only to the voters.

PROSECUTION IS THE FUNCTION OF REPRESENTING THE GOVERNMENT IN CRIMINAL CASES

After the police arrest a suspect, the prosecutor coordinates the government's response to crime—from the initial screening, when the prosecutor decides whether or not to press charges, through trial and, in some instances, at the time of sentencing, by the presentation of sentencing recommendations.

Prosecutors have been accorded much discretion in carrying out their responsibilities in that they make many of the decisions that determine whether or not a case will proceed through the criminal justice process.

THE DECISION TO CHARGE IS SOLELY AT THE PROSECUTOR'S DISCRETION

Once an arrest is made and the case is referred to the prosecutor, most prosecutors screen cases to determine whether the cases merit prosecution. The prosecutor can refuse to prosecute, for example, because of insufficient evidence. The decision to charge is not usually reviewable by any other branch of government. Some prosecutors accept almost all cases for prosecution; others screen out many cases.

THE OFFICIAL ACCUSATION IN FELONY CASES IS EITHER A GRAND JURY INDICTMENT OR A PROSECUTOR'S BILL OF INFORMATION

According to Jacoby, the accusatory process in a jurisdiction usually follows one of four paths:

the police? What right of discovery should be given to the state as to defendant's case? These questions are answered by the statutes of each state and by the cases interpreting the due process rights of defendants charged with criminal offenses.

Many cases have come before courts in recent years regarding the obligation to disclose (reveal) evidence and the right to discover facts and evidence prior to trial. In the 1973 case of *Wardius v. Oregon,* 412 U.S. 470, 93 S.Ct. 2208, 37 L.Ed.2d 82, the U.S. Supreme Court encouraged states to expand discovery procedures which "by increasing the evidence available to both parties, en-

- Arrest to preliminary hearing for bindover to grand jury for indictment
- Arrest to grand jury for indictment
- Arrest to preliminary hearing to a bill of information
- A combination of the above at the prosecutor's discretion.

PROSECUTING OFFICIALS INCLUDE LOCAL PROSECUTORS AND DISTRICT ATTORNEYS, STATE ATTORNEYS GENERAL, AND U.S. ATTORNEYS

Prosecution is predominantly a State and local function carried out by more than 8,000 State, county, municipal, and township prosecution agencies. In all but five States, local prosecutors are elected officials. Many small jurisdictions engage a part-time prosecutor who also maintains a private law practice. Prosecutors in urban jurisdictions often have offices staffed by many full-time assistants. Federal prosecution is the responsibility of 94 U.S. attorneys who are appointed by the President.

Whatever the method of accusation, the State must demonstrate at this stage that there is probable cause to support the charge.

Nineteen States require indictments in felony prosecutions unless waived by the accused. Five States require indictments only in cases that involve capital offenses.

THE GRAND JURY EMERGED FROM THE AMERICAN REVOLUTION AS THE PEOPLE'S PROTECTION AGAINST OPPRESSIVE PROSECUTION BY THE STATE

Today, the grand jury is a group of ordinary citizens, usually no more than 23, which has both accusatory and investigative functions. The jury's proceedings are secret and not adversarial so that most rules of evidence for trials do not apply. Usually, evidence is presented by the prosecutor who brings a case to the grand jury's attention. However, in some States, the grand jury is used primarily to investigate issues of public corruption and organized crime.

Source: Report to the Nation on Crime and Justice.

hances the fairness of the adversary system." The Court noted that while "the due process clause (of the U.S. Constitution) has little to say regarding the amount of discovery which the parties must be afforded ... it does speak to the balance between the accused and his accuser." The Court further held in that case that

> The State may not insist that trials be run as a "search for truth" so far as defense witnesses are concerned, while maintaining "poker game" secrecy for its own witnesses. It is fundamentally unfair to require a

defendant to divulge the details of his own case while at the same time subjecting him to the hazard of surprise concerning refutation of the very pieces of evidence which he disclosed to the State.

In the *Wardius* case, the defense was required by Oregon statute to give notice of the use of an alibi defense prior to trial. The U.S. Supreme Court held that such a statute violated due process unless reciprocal discovery rights were also given to defendants as to the state's case.

The Prosecutor's Ethical Responsibilities

The U.S. Supreme Court stated in the 1935 case of *Berger v. United States*, 295 U.S. 78, 55 S.Ct. 629 (1935), that

> The United States Attorney is the representative not of an ordinary party to a controversy, but of a sovereignty whose obligation to govern impartially is as compelling as its obligation to govern at all; and whose interest, therefore, in a criminal prosecution is not that it shall win a case, but that justice shall be done. As such, he is in a peculiar and very definite sense the servant of the law, the twofold aim of which is that guilt shall not escape or innocence suffer. He may prosecute with earnestness and vigor—indeed, he should do so. But, while he may strike hard blows, he is not at liberty to strike foul ones. It is as much his duty to refrain from improper methods calculated to produce a wrongful conviction as it is to use every legitimate means to bring about a just one.

The Circuit Court of Appeals stated in the 1969 case of *Taylor v. United States*, 413 F.2d 1095 (D.C.Cir.1969) that

> the prosecution has an obligation to set an example of professional conduct. The Government may prosecute vigorously, zealously with hard blows if the facts warrant, for a criminal trial is not a minuet. Nevertheless, there are standards which a Government counsel should meet to uphold the dignity of the Government.

The Prosecutor's Duty to Disclose Exculpatory Evidence

Exculpatory evidence is evidence that tends to show innocence. The following cases establish the well-recognized rule that a prosecutor has a duty to disclose evidence favorable (exculpatory) to an accused upon request where the evidence is material to guilt or innocence. Where such evidence is in the exclusive possession of the prosecution, it must be disclosed even when there is no request for disclosure by the defense if such evidence is "clearly supportive of a claim of innocence." It has been held that law enforcement officers are part of the prosecution and the duty of disclosure rests upon them also.

Brady v. Maryland

Supreme Court of the United States (1963)
373 U.S. 83, 83 S.Ct. 1194

The defendant testified that he participated in the robbery charged but stated that his accomplice had killed the victim. Despite a request for exculpatory evidence from the defense lawyer, the prosecutor withheld a statement by the accomplice admitting the killing but the accomplice claimed that the defendant had wanted to strangle the victim while the accomplice had wanted to shoot him. After the defendant was sentenced to death by a jury, the case was remanded for retrial on the question of punishment but not on the question of guilt. The U.S. Supreme Court quoted the Maryland Court of Appeals as saying that there was "considerable doubt" as to how much good the undisclosed statement would have done the defendant, but that it was "too dogmatic" to say that the jury would not have attached "any significance" to the evidence. The U.S. Supreme Court held that

> the suppression by the prosecution of evidence favorable to an accused upon request violates due process where the evidence is material either to guilt or to punishment, irrespective of the good faith or bad faith of the prosecution.

Giles v. Maryland

Supreme Court of the United States (1967)
386 U.S. 66, 87 S.Ct. 793

The defendant's conviction for rape was reversed and remanded for a further hearing because of failure by the prosecutor to disclose the following information regarding the complaining witness and alleged victim of the rape:

- One month after the crime charged and four months before the defendant's trial, the prosecutrix charged two other men with rape in an incident which occurred at a party and then retracted the charges.
- Within hours of the above incident, the prosecutrix attempted to commit suicide and was then hospitalized for psychiatric examination.

The U.S. Supreme Court held that

> In the end, any allegation of suppression boils down to an assessment of what the State knows at trial in comparison to the knowledge held by the defense. It would seem that the Maryland Court of Appeals would reverse as unconstitutional a conviction in a trial that included suppression of evidence tending to prove nymphomania, or more comprehensively, suppression of evidence concerning the mental condition of the complaining witness and the interrelated issues of her

consent and credibility. If such is the case, it would be helpful to have the Maryland Court of Appeals' views as to whether on this record the petitioners have been afforded a full and fair hearing on this issue.

Using Perjured Testimony and/or False Evidence to Obtain a Conviction

Mooney v. Holohan

Supreme Court of the United States (1935)
294 U.S. 103, 55 S.Ct. 340

The U.S. Supreme Court made it very clear that a conviction obtained by the knowing use of false testimony or false evidence is a denial of due process of law and will be reversed. The Court held that

if a state has contrived a conviction through the pretense of a trial which in truth is but used as a means of depriving a defendant of liberty through a deliberate deception of court and jury by the presentation of testimony known to be perjured. Such a contrivance by a state to procure the conviction and imprisonment of a defendant is as inconsistent with the rudimentary demands of justice as is the obtaining of a like result by intimidation.

Miller v. Pate

Supreme Court of the United States (1967)
386 U.S. 1, 87 S.Ct. 785

The U.S. Supreme Court reversed and remanded the defendant's murder and rape conviction. The prosecutor referred to and exhibited to the jury a pair of "blood-stained shorts" which were an important link in the chain of the circumstantial evidence case against the defendant. The prosecutor knew but did not tell the jury or defense lawyer that the reddish-brown stains on the shorts were not blood, but paint. The Supreme Court held that the prosecution "deliberately misrepresented the truth" and that

More than 30 years ago this Court held that the Fourteenth Amendment cannot tolerate a state criminal conviction obtained by the knowing use of false evidence .... There has been no deviation from that established principle .... There can be no retreat from that principle here.

Failure of the Defense Attorney to Make a Motion for Disclosure of Evidence Favorable to the Defendant

United States v. Agurs

Supreme Court of the United States (1976)
427 U.S. 97, 96 S.Ct. 2392

When the deceased and the defendant (Linda Agurs) registered in a motel, he was wearing a bowie knife and carried another knife in his pocket. Circumstantial evidence indicated that the parties completed an act of sexual intercourse and that the deceased had gone to a bathroom down the hall. The jury may have inferred that the defendant took $360, which it was reported that the deceased had in his pockets. When the deceased returned to the motel room, a fight started and the deceased was killed with multiple stab wounds, while a physical examination showed no cuts or bruises on Linda Agurs except for needle marks on her upper arm. In arguing self-defense, the defense lawyer showed that the defendant had screamed for help fifteen minutes after going into the motel room and that the deceased was on top of the defendant when employees of the motel forced their way into the room. However, the defense attorney did not make a motion or request the deceased's prior criminal record. His record showed two convictions for carrying a deadly weapon (knives) on prior occasions with one count combined with assault. In affirming the jury's verdict of second-degree murder, the U.S. Supreme Court pointed out the inconsistency of the multiple stab wounds with a theory of self-defense, holding that

> In many cases, ... exculpatory information in the possession of the prosecutor may be unknown to defense counsel. In such a situation he may make no request at all, or possibly ask for "all *Brady* material" or for "anything exculpatory." Such a request really gives the prosecutor no better notice than if no request is made. If there is a duty to respond to a general request of that kind, it must derive from the obviously exculpatory character of certain evidence in the hands of the prosecutor. But if the evidence is so clearly supportive of a claim of innocence that it gives the prosecution notice of a duty to produce, that duty should equally arise even if no request is made. Whether we focus on the desirability of a precise definition of the prosecutor's duty or on the potential harm to the defendant, we conclude that there is no significant difference between cases in which there has been merely a general request for exculpatory matter and cases, like the one we must now decide, in which there has been no request at all ....
>
> Since the arrest record was not requested and did not even arguably give rise to any inference of perjury, since after considering it in the context of the entire record the trial judge remained convinced of respondent's guilt beyond a reasonable doubt, and since we are satisfied that his firsthand appraisal of the record, was thorough and

entirely reasonable, we hold that the prosecutor's failure to tender Sewell's record to the defense did not deprive respondent of a fair trial as guaranteed by the Due Process Clause of the Fifth Amendment.

State Has Duty Under the Fourteenth Amendment to Preserve Potentially Exculpatory Evidence for Defendants

California v. Trombetta

Supreme Court of the United States (1984)
467 U.S. 479, 104 S.Ct. 2528

A number of California drunken driving cases were considered together. The drivers had submitted to a Intoxilyzer (breath-analysis) test and had registered a blood-alcohol concentration high enough to be presumed to be intoxicated under California law. It was technically feasible to preserve samples of the defendants' breath but the officers followed usual procedures and did not. In holding that there was no violation of due process in failing to preserve the evidence, the Court ruled that

To begin with, California authorities in this case did not destroy (defendants') breath samples in a calculated effort to circumvent the disclosure requirements established by *Brady v. Maryland* ... the officers here were acting "in good faith and in accord with their normal practices." ...

More importantly, California's policy of not preserving breath samples is without constitutional defect. Whatever duty the Constitution imposes on the States to preserve evidence, that duty must be limited to evidence that might be expected to play a significant role in the suspect's defense. To meet this standard of constitutional materiality, ..., evidence must both possess an exculpatory value that was apparent before the evidence was destroyed, and also be of such a nature that the defendant would be unable to obtain comparable evidence by other reasonably available means. Neither of these conditions is met on the facts of this case.

Although the preservation of breath samples might conceivably have contributed to respondents' defenses, a dispassionate review of the Intoxilyzer and the California testing procedures can only lead one to conclude that the chances are extremely low that preserved samples would have been exculpatory. The accuracy of the Intoxilyzer has been reviewed and certified by the California Department of Health. To protect suspects against machine malfunctions, the Department has developed test procedures that include two independent measurements (which must be closely correlated for the results to be admissible) bracketed by blank runs designed to ensure that the machine is purged of alcohol traces from previous tests. In all but a tiny fraction of cases, preserved breath samples would simply confirm the

---

Duty to Preserve Evidence

The state and the federal government have a duty to preserve evidence for possible use by a defendant if

- the "... exculpatory (tending to prove innocence) value ... was apparent."
- the evidence was "of such nature that the defendant would be unable to obtain comparable evidence by other reasonably available means."

In the case of *California v. Trombetta,* the U.S. Supreme Court noted that it was standard practice not to preserve samples of a drunk driver's breath and that the officers acted in "good faith" in not preserving the evidence.

Intoxilyzer's determination that the defendant had a high level of blood-alcohol concentration at the time of the test. Once the Intoxilyzer indicated that respondents were legally drunk, breath samples were much more likely to provide inculpatory than exculpatory evidence.

Even if one were to assume that the Intoxilyzer results in this case were inaccurate and that breath samples might therefore have been exculpatory, it does not follow that respondents were without alternative means of demonstrating their innocence. Respondents and *amici* have identified only a limited number of ways in which an Intoxilyzer might malfunction: faulty calibration, extraneous interference with machine measurements, and operator error .... Respondents were perfectly capable of raising these issues without resort to preserved breath samples. To protect against faulty calibration, California gives drunk driving defendants the opportunity to inspect the machine used to test their breath as well as that machine's weekly calibration results and the breath samples used in the calibrations. Respondents could have utilized this data to impeach the machine's reliability. As to improper measurements, the parties have identified only two sources capable of interfering with test results: radio waves and chemicals that appear in the blood of those who are dieting. For defendants whose test results might have been affected by either of these factors, it remains possible to introduce at trial evidence demonstrating that the defendant was dieting at the time of the test or that the test was conducted near a source of radio waves. Finally, as to operator error, the defendant retains the right to cross-examine the law enforcement officer who administered the Intoxilyzer test, and to attempt to raise doubts in the mind of the fact-finder whether the test was properly administered.

Probably all states have enacted statutes which provide procedures in which evidence is made available to defendants in criminal trials and their attorneys. Compliance with these discovery and disclosure statutes should be assured in all cases.

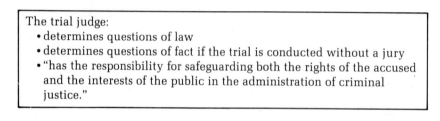

The trial judge:
- determines questions of law
- determines questions of fact if the trial is conducted without a jury
- "has the responsibility for safeguarding both the rights of the accused and the interests of the public in the administration of criminal justice."

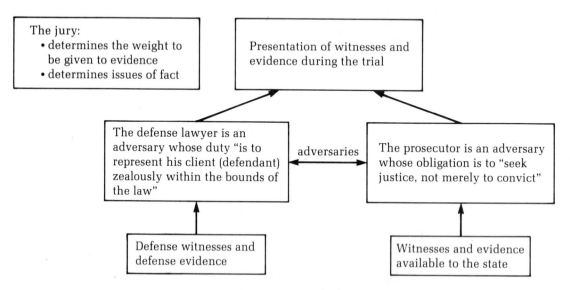

The jury:
- determines the weight to be given to evidence
- determines issues of fact

Presentation of witnesses and evidence during the trial

The defense lawyer is an adversary whose duty "is to represent his client (defendant) zealously within the bounds of the law"

adversaries

The prosecutor is an adversary whose obligation is to "seek justice, not merely to convict"

Defense witnesses and defense evidence

Witnesses and evidence available to the state

Figure 1.1   Presenting Evidence in a Courtroom

PROBLEMS

1. A videotape of a robbery enabled witnesses to identify the defendant as the person who committed the robbery. The police tried unsuccessfully to persuade the victims to turn over the tape and to photograph some frames in an effort to obtain and preserve evidence for use at trial. The police did not get the tape, which was later destroyed. The defense argues that testimony identifying the defendant as the person who committed the robbery should have been excluded and suppressed from use at the defendant's trial because of the failure of the police to seize the videotape. Should the police have seized the tape? Has the defendant's right to a fair trial been violated? Should the Supreme Court of California affirm or reverse the defendant's conviction? Explain. *In re Michael L.,* 39 Cal.3d 81, 216 Cal.Rptr. 140, 702 P.2d 222 (Cal.Sup.Ct.1985).

2. At the scene of a murder, police found the severed fingertip of the defendant. From the fingertip, a fingerprint and blood samples were obtained, which were found to match the defendant. However, the fingertip was later destroyed by the police. Because the fingertip was not available for examination by the defense, the trial court suppressed and excluded from use as

evidence "the fingertip and all evidence relating thereto, of whatever kind or nature" (fingerprint, blood samples, fact that defendant was missing a fingertip). The defendant moved for dismissal of the criminal charges, which was denied. The defendant was convicted of first-degree murder and conspiracy to commit first-degree murder using the remaining evidence. On appeal, defendant again argued for dismissal of all charges because of destruction of the fingertip. Should the Colorado Court dismiss the charges or affirm the conviction? Were the defendant's rights to a fair trial violated? Explain. *People v. Morgan,* 681 P.2d 970 (Colorado App.1984), certiorari denied 5/21/84.

NOTES

[1] Blackstone *Commentaries* 344.

[2] *A History of the Criminal Law of England,* Vol. 1, p. 73 (MacMillan & Co., 1883).

[3] Michigan v. Tucker, 417 U.S. 433, 94 S.Ct. 2357 (1974).

[4] 382 U.S. 406, 86 S.Ct. 459 (1966) rehearing den. 383 U.S. 931, 86 S.Ct. 925 (1966).

[5] 295 U.S. 78, 55 S.Ct. 629 (1935).

[6] See In re Lance W., 37 Cal.3d 873, 210 Cal.Rptr. 631, 694 P.2d 744 (1985).

[7] See State v. Cross, 487 So.2d 1056, 39 CrL 2174 (Fla.Sup.Ct.1986).

[8] ABA Standards Relating to the Prosecution Function and the Defense Function 1.1(c).

[9] ABA Code EC 7–1.

[10] P. 174 of the Commentary of the ABA Standards Relating to the Prosecution Function and the Defense Function.

[11] P. 167 of General Responsibility of the Trial Judge, ABA Standards Relating to the Administration of Criminal Justice.

[12] Herring v. New York, 422 U.S. 853, 95 S.Ct. 2550 (1975).

[13] Questions of fact are determined by the factfinder. This would be a jury in a jury trial or the trial judge when a case is tried without a jury. Questions of law are always determined by the trial judge.

[14] 382 U.S. 406, 416, 86 S.Ct. 459 (1966).

[15] 365 U.S. 534, 540–41, 81 S.Ct. 735, 739–40 (1961).

[16] In his book, *The Judicial Process* (Oxford University Press, 2d ed. 1975), Henry J. Abraham points out that probably no democratic criminal justice system operates on the presumption of "guilty-until-proven-innocent" as is sometimes suggested (see pages 100–102).

[17] 378 U.S. 478, 84 S.Ct. 1758 (1964).

Using Evidence in Determining
Guilt or Innocence

EVALUATION AND REVIEW OF EVIDENCE

A Lot of Judging Occurs before a Case Is Presented to a Judge

In most criminal cases, evidence is evaluated (judged) by many persons before it is presented in a courtroom to a judge. For example, consider a shoplifting case:

1. Store employees (or security persons) would ordinarily be the first to evaluate and judge the information and evidence available to them before detaining a person for shoplifting. Probable cause based upon firsthand information by a reliable adult employee is the usual standard required. Store employees are told "If you did not see it, it did not happen," and "When in doubt, let him go."

2. After a suspect is detained for shoplifting and the police (or sheriff) are called, the officer must then evaluate the available evidence before proceeding. If the evidence is insufficient, the suspect should be immediately released.

3. Evaluations made in points 1 and 2 are often reviewed immediately by superiors (store managers and police sargeants).

4. If the case is presented to a prosecutor (city attorney or district attorney), the prosecutor would review the available evidence to determine whether further proceedings are warranted.

5. If a charge or citation is issued, a defense lawyer in many cases would review the evidence looking for weaknesses in the case. Insufficient or questionable evidence, use of improper procedure, or lack of probable cause based upon firsthand information would be some of the weaknesses a defense lawyer would look for.

6. A motion to suppress evidence and dismiss could bring the matter before a judge. To rule on the motion, the judge would have to review the evidence.

7. Should the defense motion be denied, the case could then be tried before a jury, who would evaluate the evidence in determining guilt or innocence.

8. A convicted defendant can appeal his case and argue to an appellate court that the evidence was not sufficient to support a finding or a judgment of

guilt. The appellate court would then review the evidence. The defendant in the 1984 case of *Lee v. State* [1] did not argue insufficient evidence, but in his appeal argued instead that a shoplifter had to leave a store in order to be convicted of larceny (theft). The Maryland Court of Special Appeals, however, affirmed the defendant's conviction, holding that it was not necessary that a state show that a defendant leave a store to be convicted of shoplifting. Stating that they found no court decision holding otherwise, the Court held that once "a customer goes beyond the mere removal of goods from the shelf and crosses the threshold into the realm of behavior inconsistent with the owner's expectations, the circumstances may be such that a larcenous intent can be inferred."

Not only in shoplifting cases, but in most criminal cases, evidence is carefully evaluated (judged) by a number of persons before the evidence is presented to a judge.

In the process of review and evaluation of evidence, weaker cases are filtered out of the system or lesser charges are used. Not all cases go to court and trial. A merchant might recover his merchandise from a shoplifter and, after warning the person, take no further action. A police officer might take a teenaged shoplifter home to his or her parents. After the parents have been informed of the incident, the matter may be dropped.

THE REQUIREMENT OF COMPETENT, RELIABLE EVIDENCE TO CHARGE AND TRY A SUSPECT

The Authority to Commence Criminal Prosecutions

The U.S. Supreme Court pointed out in the 1986 case of *Holbrook v. Flynn* [2] that

> Central to the right to a fair trial, guaranteed by the Sixth and Fourteenth Amendments, is the principle that "one accused of a crime is entitled to have his guilt or innocence determined solely on the basis of the evidence introduced at trial, and not on grounds of official suspicion, indictment, continued custody, or other circumstances not adduced as proof at trial." *Taylor v. Kentucky,* 436 U.S. 478, 485 (1978).

Therefore, in order to charge a person with a crime, reliable and admissible evidence must be available to sustain the criminal charge.

Each state has authority to commence a criminal prosecution if sufficient evidence is available to justify the criminal charge. The U.S. Supreme Court pointed out that the authority of the states "derive from separate and independent sources of power and authority originally belonging to them before admission to the Union and preserved to them by the Tenth Amendment." [3]

Each state also "has the power, inherent in any sovereign, independently to determine what shall be an offense against its authority and to punish such offenses, and in doing so each 'is exercising its own sovereignty, not that of the other.' " [4]

When there is sufficient evidence to show that a defendant by a single act violates the peace and dignity of two sovereigns by violating the laws of each by his single act, he has committed two distinct crimes. The defendants in the following U.S. Supreme Court cases were prosecuted by two different sovereigns for the one crime committed in violation of both governments:

Heath v. Alabama

Supreme Court of the United States (1985)
474 U.S. 82, 106 S.Ct. 433

The defendant lived in Alabama, where he confessed that he hired two men in Georgia to kidnap his pregnant wife from their Alabama home and kill her. The murder took place in Georgia. After the defendant confessed to the crimes, he was convicted of "malice" murder in Georgia. Alabama then charged and convicted him of the capital offense of murder during a kidnapping. The U.S. Supreme Court affirmed both convictions under the dual sovereignty doctrine, holding that

> To deny a State its power to enforce its criminal laws because another State has won the race to the courthouse "would be a shocking and untoward deprivation of the historic right and obligation of the States to maintain peace and order within their confines." *Bartkus v. Illinois,* 359 U.S. at 137.

Bartkus v. Illinois

Supreme Court of the United States (1959)
359 U.S. 121, 79 S.Ct. 676

The defendant was tried in a Chicago federal court for the robbery of a federally insured bank. Because of problems, the defendant was acquitted of the charge. The State of Illinois then indicted the defendant and convicted him on substantially the same evidence used in the federal trial. Under the double jeopardy limitations, neither a state nor the federal government may try a person twice for the same offense. However under the dual sovereignty doctrine, this robbery violated both state and federal law and the defendant's conviction was affirmed by the U.S. Supreme Court.

The Dual Sovereignty Doctrine

The Fourteenth Amendment provides that "All persons born or naturalized in the United States and subject to the jurisdiction thereof, are citizens of the United States and of the State wherein they reside." The **dual citizenship** concept is part of the **dual sovereignty** doctrine.

Who Exercises Discretion in the Criminal Justice System?

DISCRETION IS EXERCISED THROUGHOUT THE CRIMINAL JUSTICE SYSTEM

Discretion is an authority conferred by law to act in certain conditions or situations in accordance with an official's or an official agency's own considered judgment and conscience. Traditionally, criminal and juvenile justice officials, in particular the police, prosecutors, judges, and paroling authorities, have been given a wide range of discretion.

Legislative bodies have recognized that they cannot foresee every possibility, anticipate local mores, and enact laws that clearly encompass all conduct that is criminal and all that is not. Therefore, those charged with the day-to-day response to crime are expected to exercise their own judgment within guidelines set by law.

Discretion is also necessary to permit the criminal and juvenile justice systems to function within available resources. The enforcement and prosecution of all laws against all violators is beyond the financial resources available. Therefore, criminal and juvenile justice officials must have the authority to allocate resources in a way that meets the most compelling needs of their own communities.

The limits of discretion vary from State to State and locality to locality.

For example, the range of options available to judges when they sentence offenders varies greatly. In recent years, some States have sought to limit the judges' discretion in sentencing by passing mandatory and determinate sentencing laws.

The *Heath* and *Bartkus* cases (just presented) demonstrate that states have extensive authority not only to create criminal laws, but also to punish conduct which violates those laws.

Under the American federal system, each state has its own constitution, court system, and other governmental units. States have the principal responsibility of maintaining public order within their boundaries. The U.S. Supreme Court stated in the case of *Heath v. Alabama* [5] that the U.S. Supreme Court

> has uniformly held that the States are separate sovereigns with respect to the Federal Government because each State's power to prosecute is derived from its own "inherent sovereignty," not from the Federal Government ....
>
> ... As stated in *Lanza,* 260 U.S., at 382, 43 S.Ct., at 142,
> "[e]ach government in determining what shall be an offense against its peace and dignity is exercising its own sovereignty ....
>
> "It follows that an act denounced as a crime by both national and state sovereignties is an offense against the peace and dignity of both and may be punished by each."

See also *Bartkus v. Illinois,* 359 U.S. 121, 79 S.Ct. 676, 3 L.Ed.2d 684 (1959); *Westfall v. United States,* 274 U.S. 256, 258, 47 S.Ct. 629, 71 L.Ed. 1036 (1927) (Holmes, J.) (the proposition that the State and Feder-

WHO EXERCISES DISCRETION?

These criminal justice officials...	...must often decide whether or not or how to:
Police	Enforce specific laws Investigate specific crimes Search people, vicinities, buildings Arrest or detain people
Prosecutors	File charges or petitions for adjudication Seek indictments Drop cases Reduce charges
Judges or magistrates	Set bail or conditions for release Accept pleas Determine delinquency Dismiss charges Impose sentence Revoke probation
Correctional officials	Assign to type of correctional facility Award privileges Punish for disciplinary infractions
Paroling authority	Determine date and conditions of parole Revoke parole

Source: Report to the Nation on Crime and Justice.

al Governments may punish the same conduct "is too plain to need more than statement").

The States are no less sovereign with respect to each other than they are with respect to the Federal Government. Their powers to undertake criminal prosecutions derive from separate and independent sources of power and authority originally belonging to them before admission to the Union and preserved to them by the Tenth Amendment .... The States are equal to each other "in power, dignity and authority, each competent to exert that residuum of sovereignty not delegated to the United States by the Constitution itself." *Coyle v. Oklahoma,* 221 U.S. 559, 567, ... Thus, "[e]ach has the power, inherent in any sovereign, independently to determine what shall be an offense against its authority and to punish such offenses, and in doing so each 'is exercising its own sovereignty, not that of the other.'" *Wheeler,* 435 U.S., at 320, 98 S.Ct., at 1084.

It is axiomatic that "[i]n America, the powers of sovereignty are divided between the government of the Union, and those of the States. They are each sovereign, with respect to the objects committed to it, and neither sovereign with respect to the objects committed to the other." *McCulloch v. Maryland,* 4 Wheat. 316, 410, 4 L.Ed. 579 (1819). It is as well established that the States, "as political communities, [are] distinct and sovereign, and consequently foreign to each other." *Bank of United States v. Daniel,* 12 Pet. 32, 54, 9 L.Ed. 989 (1838) .... The

---

Functions and Goals of the Criminal Justice System

The most basic function of any government is to provide for the security of the individual and his property. U.S. Supreme Court in *Lanzetta v. New Jersey,* 306 U.S. 451, 455.

The generally recognized overall goals of the criminal justice system are:

- To discourage and to deter persons from committing crimes.
- To protect society from dangerous and harmful persons.
- To punish persons who have committed crimes.
- To rehabilitate and reform persons who have committed crimes.

Constitution leaves in the possession of each State "certain exclusive and very important portions of sovereign power." The Federalist No. 9, p. 55 (J. Cooke ed. 1961). Foremost among the prerogatives of sovereignty is the power to create and enforce a criminal code . . . . To deny a State its power to enforce its criminal laws because another State has won the race to the courthouse "would be a shocking and untoward deprivation of the historic right and obligation of the States to maintain peace and order within their confines." *Bartkus,* 359 U.S., at 137, 79 S.Ct., at 685.

Persons living in the United States are protected under the U.S. Constitution and, also, under the constitution of the state in which they are residing. Each state has the authority to create their own rules of evidence as long as the rules of evidence conform to the basic requirements established by the U.S. Constitution.

Under the constitutions of their state, the Supreme Courts of each state may create their own state exclusionary rules of evidence. This has created some very complicated situations and has caused voters in California and Florida to amend their constitutions and require courts in those states to suppress "relevant evidence" only in situations "as interpreted by the U.S. Constitution."

PLEAS WHICH A DEFENDANT MAY ENTER TO A CRIMINAL CHARGE

After a defendant has been charged with a criminal offense, the defendant and his attorney must evaluate the evidence available to the state supporting its criminal charge. Their evaluation of the evidence could determine what defenses they will or will not use. Their evaluation of the evidence would determine what plea they will enter. The following pleas are available to defendants:

- *Not guilty.*
- *Guilty.* This may be made as an "Alford plea" in states permitting the use of the Alford plea.

- *An insanity plea (or defense).* The usual insanity plea is not guilty by reason of mental disease or defect. This plea may be joined with a plea of not guilty. If it is not joined with a not guilty plea, the defendant then admits committing the offense but pleads a lack of mental capacity.

   A jury or a judge may, if the evidence permits, find a defendant guilty but mentally ill under the statutes of eight states.[6] Such a person is not legally insane but at the time of the offense had serious mental or emotional problems. Under this verdict, prison authorities must provide necessary psychiatric or psychological treatment to restore the offender's mental and emotional health in an appropriate treatment setting.

- *No contest (nolo contendere).* If permitted by the statutes of a state which might allow the plea subject to the approval of the court. A defendant using this plea would seek to avoid admitting guilt in hopes that he could successfully deny the truth of the charges in a related civil action (or related hearings).

- *Standing mute or refusing to enter a plea.* This would ordinarily cause the court to direct the entry of a plea of not guilty on behalf of the defendant.

The Not Guilty Plea

All defendants in criminal cases are presumed innocent until proven guilty through the use of evidence and witnesses presented during the trial of the defendant. The burden of proof is always on the state (or government).

The level of proof required in criminal cases is **proof beyond a reasonable doubt.** This level of proof is the highest the law requires in any kind of case. It means that the evidence presented during the trial must convince the finder of fact (jury or judge) of the defendant's guilt to a moral certitude. It does not mean that the evidence must show that the defendant is guilty beyond *any* doubt, nor does it require evidence of absolute certainty of the defendant's guilt. The burden on the state is to prove the defendant guilty beyond any *reasonable* doubt.

Because of the constitutional presumption of innocence, the system of justice used in the United States is an accusatorial system. The accuser must bear the entire burden of proving the charge by the use of competent evidence. The defendant does not have to do anything. The burden is on the state to come forward with sufficient evidence to carry the burden of proof beyond reasonable doubt.

The defendant can remain silent and inactive. Or the defendant can appear as a witness on his own behalf and may present evidence showing or tending to show his innocence. The defendant may also very actively attack or seek to hinder and minimize the state's evidence and case by use of motions before, during, or after the trial.

The defendant can deny that he performed the acts charged or he can assert an affirmative defense. In an affirmative defense, a defendant in effect admits that he or she performed the acts charged, but claims that he or she had a lawful excuse for doing so, and thus is not guilty of the crime charged. To assert an affirmative defense, the defendant must come forward with evidence showing a basis for the affirmative defense.

An example of an affirmative defense is the defense of entrapment. The 1984 *De Lorean* case illustrates the use of this defense. During his five-month trial De Lorean did not take the witness stand on his own behalf but his lawyers, through lengthy cross-examination of government witnesses, presented enough evidence to raise a factual question as to whether entrapment had occurred. When the *De Lorean* case went to the jury to determine guilt or innocence, a jury instruction was presented to the jury on the issue of entrapment. The jury found that De Lorean was entrapped and he was therefore found not guilty. See chapter 4, "Cross-Examination of Witnesses," for a further discussion of the cross-examination results obtained in the *De Lorean* case.

The Guilty Plea

Many guilty pleas are entered in criminal cases in courts throughout the United States. Many of the guilty pleas result from the realization that the state has sufficient evidence to carry the burden of proof to obtain a conviction. In a small percentage of the cases, defendants are sorry and repentant for what they have done and express this in open court.

A good percentage of guilty pleas are the result of plea or sentence bargaining. In all guilty plea hearings, the U.S. Supreme Court has required in the case of *Boykin v. Alabama* [7] and other cases that the court record show that a defendant who pleads guilty does so after intelligently and voluntarily waiving his constitutional rights.

The so-called Alford Plea permits a defendant to acknowledge that there is sufficient reliable evidence in the hands of the state or government to convict him. The Alford Plea defendant can enter a guilty plea but at the same time maintain his innocence. Federal courts adopted this plea in the 1970 case of *North Carolina v. Alford,* [8] but the rule or doctrine has not been made mandatory for states. Not all of the state courts have adopted the rule.

The Insanity Plea

If an insanity plea were entered in a minor criminal matter, the state might agree and join the defendant in requesting the court to find the defendant legally insane. The defendant would very likely then be held for mental observations and treatment for a much longer period than he would have had he been convicted of the crime charged.

For these reasons, the insanity plea and defense is used by defendants primarily in murder cases, for which sentences are severe. In using the insanity defense, most defendants also enter a not guilty plea. The trial would then be bifurcated, with the first part determining guilt or innocence of the charge. The second part of the trial would determine the legal issue of whether the defendant was legally insane when he committed the criminal act.

Factors Ordinarily Considered in Plea Bargaining

- The strengths and weaknesses of the evidence in the case being considered
- Whether the court has a heavy and busy calendar of cases
- Whether the prosecutor has many cases pending
- The number of cases which the defense lawyer is handling at that time

A defendant who plea bargains waives his right to

- a jury trial
- confrontation of witnesses
- have the state carry the burden of proving him guilty beyond a reasonable doubt
- his privilege against self-incrimination

In return for a plea of guilt, the state may

- reduce the charge to a lesser or related charge, or
- drop other charges (and in many instances read them into the record), or
- agree to the imposition of a particular sentence, or
- the prosecutor, as a representative of the state, may agree to "go easy."

If a defendant will

- testify as a witness against other defendants or suspects, or
- provide law enforcement officials with information or evidence of other criminal activities.

The state may

- take any of the above actions, or
- drop all charges against a defendant, or
- not charge a suspect with any criminal offense if charges have not been filed.

Because there is a legal inference that all persons are sane and normal, most states place the burden on a defendant using the insanity plea to come forward with the necessary evidence showing that he or she as so mentally diseased or defective that he or she was unable to formulate the mental intent to commit the crime charged.

In 1981, John Hinckley was charged with attempting to kill the president of the United States. In a wild shooting spree in Washington, D.C., Hinckley killed one person and seriously wounded others, including the president. At the time of the Hinckley shooting, the lower federal courts had reversed the burden of coming forward with evidence and required the government to carry the burden of proving that Hinckley was sane and normal. The government could not produce evidence showing this, and Hinckley was therefore found not guilty because of insanity.

In 1984, the Congress of the United States passed legislation providing that the federal courts rejoin most of the state courts in requiring that defendants using the insanity plea to prove by clear and convincing evidence that the defendant was insane at the time of the crime. Studies show that the success rate by defense lawyers in using the defense of insanity is very low (less than 1 percent are successful).

Plea Bargaining

An extensive study of plea bargaining [1] in the United States was done by Professor William McDonald of Georgetown University under the support of the U.S. Department of Justice. In 1985, the results of the study were published in *Plea Bargaining: Critical Issues and Common Practices* [2]. The study is based upon structured interviews with over 200 officials and defendants; structured observations of over 700 guilty plea cases; statistical analysis of case file data from over 3,000 felony cases; and a plea bargain decision simulation administered to 138 prosecutors and 105 defense attorneys. The study makes the following observations:

- "The findings suggest that plea bargaining cannot be abolished but can be changed. The policy choices are: how much of a concession should be given to defendants; which criminal justice official should give it; and what procedures are necessary to safeguard against the institutional weaknesses of the plea bargaining system."

- Where plea bargaining is forbidden or severely restricted, judges have increased the size of the sentencing "discount" used to encourage guilty pleas. Defense lawyers soon get the message and pass it on to their clients. For example, when Alaska established a "no plea bargaining policy" for prosecutors, the study showed that defendants convicted after going to trial received more than double the sentence (138 percent) than did defendants who entered a guilty plea. (See p. 103 of the study.)

- "The practice of plea bargaining is neither as bad as its critics fear nor as good as its reformers hope. The decisions of prosecutors and defense counsel regarding whether to plea bargain a case and on what terms is not as haphazard as it may appear. There is considerable agreement among and between the two types of attorneys as to what factors are important and how much weight to attach to them in deciding the appropriate disposition of cases. Prosecutors systematically take into account the seriousness of the criminal and the crime as well as the evidentiary strength of the case. Defense counsel

DETERMINING GUILT OR INNOCENCE BY GOING TO TRIAL OR BY USING PLEA BARGAINING

It is estimated that guilt or innocence is determined by jury trials in about 8 percent of the criminal cases in the United States. Demands by defendants and their lawyers for a jury trial are many more times greater but most defendants waive their right to a jury before going to trial.

There are just not enough courts and other resources in the United States to handle double or triple the number of jury trials now being heard, unless dramatic changes are made in the American court system.

Bench trials (trials before a judge without a jury) are also alternatives available to defendants charged with crimes. But plea bargaining, or plea negotiation, is the most common method of determining guilt or innocence in the United States.

consider these same factors but also look for characteristics of their clients or the case upon which to base a special appeal for an even more lenient disposition. When presented with the same hypothetical cases prosecutors and defense counsel were in remarkable agreement in their estimates of the probability of conviction in those versions of the cases where the evidentiary strength of the case was strong. But in the weaker version there were significant differences among and between them."

■ "Prosecutors do not appear to engage in elaborate frauds or substantially deceptive practices in order to bluff defendants into pleading guilty. Defense attorneys do not engage in 'court busting.' [3] The 'overcharging' of prosecutors does not involve unethical or unlawful conduct. The problem lies with the concept of 'overcharging' [4] itself. Existing national standards for the charging decision require inconsistent purposes of the charging decision which can be regarded as 'overcharging.' Much of what is referred to as 'overcharging' involves cases in which there are accurate charges with supportable evidence, but as a matter of local policy these cases involve types of crimes or criminals who are regularly disposed of with less serious charges."

[1] Permission to print the quoted sections was given by Professor William F. McDonald, Deputy Director of the Institute of Criminal Law and Procedure, Georgetown University, Washington, D.C.

[2] For sale by the Superintendent of Documents, U.S. Government Printing Office, Washington, D.C. 20402.

[3] The term *court busting* means taking so many criminal cases to a jury or bench trial that the court calendar becomes congested to the point of "busting." Defense lawyers do not have the time in their busy schedules to do this, nor would it serve anyone's purposes. Defendants also do not have the funds to pay the extra costs of going to a jury trial.

[4] The term *overcharging* means to charge criminal offenses higher and greater than that justified by the available evidence.

Plea Bargaining or Plea Negotiation

In 1967 the President's Commission on Law Enforcement and Administration of Justice stated that "(w)hen a decision is made to prosecute, it is estimated that in many courts as many as 90 percent of all convictions are obtained by guilty pleas." [9]

In appraising the amount and quality of the evidence against his client, the American defense lawyer often turns to plea bargaining if the government has a strong case. He usually informs his client that there is a strong likelihood that he will be convicted and should consider "copping a plea."

However, not all guilty pleas are plea bargained. Some guilty pleas are simple acknowledgement of guilt without any assurance from a prosecutor as to the penalty. Plea bargaining, or sentence bargaining, implies a situation in which a defendant receives (or is assured of) a consideration in return for his guilty plea. [10] Considerations which could cause a defendant to plead guilty are

- Receiving an agreed-upon sentence or penalty instead of running the risk of a more severe sentence.

- Reaching an agreement in a case having multiple charges to drop one or more of the charges, which in most situations are then "read into the record" in court for sentencing consideration.[11]

- Permitting a defendant to plead guilty to a lesser charge.

- Recommending to the court that the defendant receive probation or a suspended sentence.

- Agreement by the prosecutor to drop charges against another person (such as the defendant's wife or girl friend).

- Reducing charges or dropping charges when the defendant agrees to testify as a state's witness (such as a burglar turning state's evidence against his "fence").

- Reducing charges or receiving probation or a suspended sentence when the defendant agrees to compensate the victim for damages or injuries which occurred.

- Receiving probation or a suspended sentence when the defendant agrees to undergo psychiatric, drug, or alcohol treatment when the criminal conduct was caused by any of these conditions (in some of these situations, the defendant agrees to commit himself to an institution for such treatment).

Urban prosecutors list the following reasons why plea bargaining—or negotiated pleas, or sentence pleading—has become a standard practice in most urban American communities:

- It clears the court calendar of that case with a rapid trial and punishment.

- The defendant participates and admits his guilt to the charge, to which he pleads guilty.

- The practice eliminates many appeals.

- The practice provides a certainty of adjudication.

- A guilty plea could be the first step toward genuine rehabilitation.

The President's Commission commented as follows in the 1967 report entitled "The Challenge of Crime in a Free Society":

> Many overburdened courts have come to rely upon these informal procedures to deal with overpowering caseloads, and some cases that are dropped might have been prosecuted had sufficient resources been available. But it would be an oversimplification to tie the use of early disposition solely to the problem of volume, for some courts appear to be able to deal with their workloads without recourse to such procedures. Furthermore, the flexibility and informality of these discretionary procedures make them more readily adaptable to efforts to individualize the treatment of offenders than the relatively rigid procedures that now typify trial, conviction, and sentence. It would require radical restructuring of the trial to convert sentencing procedures into a comparable opportunity for the prosecution and the defense to discuss dispositional alternatives. Moreover, by placing less emphasis on the issue of culpability, discretionary procedures may

enable the prosecutor to give greater attention to what disposition is most likely to fit the needs of those whose cases he considers. The pressures on the prosecutor to insist on a disposition that fits the popular conception of punishment are less before conviction, when the defendant has not officially and publicly been found guilty . . . .

The main dangers in the present system of nontrial dispositions lie in the fact that it is so informal and invisible that it gives rise to fears that it does not operate fairly or that it does not accurately identify those who should be prosecuted and what disposition should be made in their cases. Often important decisions are made without adequate information, without sound policy guidance or rules, and without basic procedural protections for the defendant, such as counsel or judicial consideration of the issues. Because these dispositions are reached at an early stage, often little factual material is available about the offense, the offender, and the treatment alternatives. No record reveals the participants, their positions, or the reason for or facts underlying the disposition. When the disposition involves dismissal of filed charges or the entry of a guilty plea, it is likely to reach court, but only the end product is visible, and that view often is misleading. There are disturbing opportunities for coercion and overreaching, as well as for undue leniency. The very informality and flexibility of the procedures are sources both of potential usefulness and of abuse.

Debates have continued over the years as to plea bargaining. The practice was denounced as early as 1875.[12] However, over the years, plea negotiation has continued. Some of the cases which received national attention are

- A former vice-president of the United States, Spiro Agnew, was convicted on the basis of a negotiated plea.

- John Hinckley, Jr. offered to plead to assault charges and would accept a single life sentence with parole eligibility after ten years. The government turned down Hinckley's offer only to find that Hinckley was able to obtain a verdict of "not guilty by reason of mental disease and defect," with release possible within a matter of years.

- Harry Douglas Seigler was charged with robbery and murder of a Richmond, Virginia man. While the jury was deliberating, Seigler accepted the state's offer to plead guilty to avoid a possible death sentence. Within minutes after Seigler accepted the plea bargain, the jury returned with a verdict of not guilty. Seigler received a sixty-year sentence. *Commonwealth v. Seigler,* ___ A.2d ___ (Va.1983).

- After James Earl Ray was charged with the murder of Rev. Martin Luther King, he entered a guilty plea to avoid the death penalty. As a result of the plea bargain, Ray received a ninety-nine-year sentence. Because Ray was stabbed by other inmates several times and also has tried to escape a number of times, he is held in solitary confinement for his own protection. In 1979, a Congressional committee investigating the assassinations of Rev. King and President Kennedy concluded that Ray probably killed Rev. King as part of a conspiracy but insufficient evidence is available as to who the conspirators might have been.

Minority View That the "Plea Bargaining System is an Unnecessary Evil That Should Be Abolished"

Different views on the American plea bargaining system were presented in a CBS "60 Minutes" show in January 1987. Judge Ralph Adam Fine, author of the book *Escape of the Guilty,* stated that "the plea bargaining system is an unnecessary evil that should be abolished." Harry Reasoner of the CBS program pointed out that Judge Fine represented "a minority voice." Other statements by Judge Fine as to plea bargaining were

- A defendant receiving a sentence based on plea bargaining will "walk out of the courtroom thinking he has gotten away with something."

- Elimination of plea bargaining would "let the criminal know that the system meant business."

- Even when the sentence is appropriate and is fair for the crime, the defendant "goes out into the community and says, 'Guess what. I got away with it.' "

- Harry Reasoner pointed out that after plea bargaining was discontinued in New Orleans there had been no drop in the crime rate. Judge Fine responded that this was all right because "they have restored honesty and justice to the system."

Proposed guidelines by the U.S. Sentencing Commission in 1986 would provide a 20-percent discount in sentences to defendants who enter guilty pleas. The authors of the guidelines, however, did not want this to be automatic but wanted the 20-percent sentencing discount attached to a defendant accepting responsibility for his (or her) criminal conduct. As it does today, larger sentencing discounts could be earned through cooperation with law enforcement agencies. (See 40 CrL 2226, dated 12/17/86.)

- Ivan Boesky, a prominent Wall Street speculator, entered a guilty plea to one felony count of criminal "inside trading" in November 1986. The federal prosecutor did not charge Boesky with additional felonies, in return for his agreement to pay $100 million in penalties for his ill-gotten gains and to cooperate in apprehending other offenders. A federal judge will then determine whether to impose a prison sentence upon Boesky. Boesky made the covers of both *Time* and *Newsweek.* The *Time* cover story was "Wall St. Scam: Making Millions with *Your* Money (Investor 'Ivan the Terrible' Boesky)."

- The most unusual plea bargain in Canadian history occurred when Clifford R. Olson provided the necessary evidence needed to convict him of the rape and murder of eleven children. In 1982, the Canadian Mounted Police established a trust fund of $90,000 for Olson's wife and son as payment for the evidence needed to prove Olson's guilt of the murders and rapes. See the Wall Street Journal's 1/27/82 article entitled "Paying a Murderer for Evidence" (also reprinted in the 86/87 *Criminal Justice* book published by Dushkin Publishing Group, Inc.).

Bluffing as to the Strength of Evidence or Ability of Witnesses

Prosecutors, defense lawyers, and law enforcement officers occasionally engage in "bluffing" either prior to trial or plea bargaining. The bluffing could be "mild puffery" or offhand remarks such as "We've got a solid case." The bluffing could be done to hide a weakness in the case, such as: the inability of star witness for the prosecution to pick the defendant out of a lineup; the loss of evidence; inability to contact (or failure to subpoena) an important witness. The defense case also could have become weaker or it could have improved by (for example) the discovery of a reliable alibi witness.

THE FOLLOWING ARE LEGAL LIMITS AND RESTRICTIONS ON BLUFFING BY PROSECUTORS:

- Criminal charges may not be filed against a defendant unless probable cause can be proven by the evidence and witnesses.

- Upon request of the defense, prosecutors must make available the results of ballistics tests, chemical analyses, lineup, statements made to police by the defendant, and other important evidence. *Brady v. United States,* 373 U.S. 83 (1963).

- Evidence showing (or tending to show) that the defendant is innocent of the charges (exculpatory evidence) must be immediately made available to the defense, even without a prior request. *United States v. Aqurs,* 427 U.S. 97 (1976).

Using a bluff to hide or suppress discoverable or exculpatory evidence is illegal and improper.

Using a Withdrawn Plea of Guilty as Evidence

Rule 410 of the Federal Rules of Evidence and Rule 11(6) of the Federal Rules of Criminal Procedure forbid the use of any of the following as evidence:

> ... evidence of a plea of guilty, later withdrawn, or a plea of nolo contendere, or of an offer to plead guilty or nolo contendere to the crime charged or any other crime, or of statements made in connection with any of the foregoing pleas or offers ....

The great majority of states follow this federal rule, which forbids the use of such statements as evidence. A few states, however, have held to the contrary in court decisions made many years ago. These old rulings are likely to be reversed, however, should new cases come before courts in the few states approving the use of such evidence.

CRIMINAL TRIAL PROCEDURE

With the issuance of a criminal complaint or a criminal indictment, the government has commenced a criminal action. By such formal charging, the govern-

Why Are Some Cases Rejected or Dismissed?

ONCE CHARGES ARE FILED, A CASE MAY BE TERMINATED ONLY BY OFFICIAL ACTION

The prosecutor can drop a case after making efforts to prosecute (*nolle prosequi*), or the court can dismiss the case on motion of the defense on grounds that the government has failed to establish that the defendant committed the crime charged. The prosecution may also recommend dismissal, or the judge may take the initiative in dismissing a case. A dismissal is an official action of the court.

WHAT ARE THE MOST COMMON REASONS FOR REJECTION OR DISMISSAL?

Many criminal cases are rejected or dismissed because of:

- *Evidence problems* that result from a failure to find sufficient physical evidence that links the defendant to the offense
- *Witness problems* that arise, for example, when a witness fails to appear, gives unclear or inconsistent statements, is reluctant to testify, or is unsure of the identity of the offender
- *Office policy,* wherein the prosecutor decides not to prosecute certain types of offenses, particularly those that violate the letter but not the spirit of the law (for example, offenses involving insignificant amounts of property damage)
- *Due process problems* that involve violations of the Constitutional requirements for seizing evidence and for questioning the accused
- *Combination with other cases,* for example, when the accused is charged in several cases and the prosecutor prosecutes all of the charges in a single case
- *Pretrial diversion* that occurs when the prosecutor and the court agree to drop charges when the accused successfully meets the conditions for diversion, such as completion of a treatment program.

ment has indicated that its resources will be used in an attempt to obtain a criminal conviction. The parties to a criminal action are the state (or other governmental unit such as the U.S. government) and the person charged, who is then called the defendant. If the criminal action is initiated by a state, the title of the action would be State, People, or Commonwealth versus the named defendant. For example:

Commonwealth of Pennsylvania vs. John Doe

If the action were initiated by the federal government, the title to the action would be:

United States of America vs. John Doe

**A PRIOR RELATIONSHIP BETWEEN VICTIM AND DEFENDANT
WAS A MAJOR CAUSE OF WITNESS PROBLEMS**

Williams found that problems with the complaining witness accounted for 61% of the refusals to prosecute violent crimes by nonstrangers and 54% of the dismissals. Conviction rates are commensurately lower in cases involving family acquaintances; Boland showed that, in New Orleans, the conviction rate for crimes by strangers was 48%, but only 30% for crimes by friends or acquaintances and 19% for crimes by family members.

**THE FOURTH AMENDMENT PROHIBITS UNREASONABLE
SEARCHES AND SEIZURES IN THE COLLECTION OF EVIDENCE**

Under the exclusionary rule evidence obtained in violation of the Fourth Amendment may not be used in criminal proceedings against the accused. Both the police and prosecutors drop cases based on what they find is improperly obtained evidence. An estimated 45,000 to 55,000 felony and serious misdemeanor cases were dropped by prosecutors during 1977.

**IMPROPERLY OBTAINED EVIDENCE AND RELATED PROBLEMS
APPEAR TO BE MAJOR CAUSES OF REJECTIONS AND
DISMISSALS IN DRUG CASES**

A recent report from the National Institute of Justice found that 70% of the felony cases rejected in California were drug cases. In two local prosecutor's offices in California, 30% of all felony arrests for drug offenses were rejected because of search and seizure problems.

Source: Report to the Nation on Crime and Justice.

The Criminal Complaint

A criminal complaint is a written document containing the essential facts constituting the offense charged. The criminal complaint must state

- What is being charged (the crime or crimes).
- Who is charged.
- Where the alleged offense was committed.
- How the complainant knows that the defendant is the person who did what is alleged in the charging portion of the complaint (this may be based upon firsthand knowledge by the person signing the complaint, or upon information and belief).

- When the alleged act took place.
- The possible penalties.

Initial Appearance Before a Court

Statutes and court rulings in many states require that an arrested person must be taken before a court within a reasonable time. Failure to take an arrested person before a court within a reasonable time could jeopardize the admissibility of any confession or statements obtained during an unreasonable detention.

The duties of the judge at the initial court appearance are to

- Inform the defendant of the criminal charge (or charges).
- Supply him with a copy of the complaint or indictment.
- Inform him of the possible penalties (in some jurisdictions, this would only be done in felony cases).
- Inform the defendant of his right to an attorney.
- Appoint counsel for an indigent defendant who is unable to pay for his own attorney.
- Inform the defendant as to whether he is entitled to a preliminary hearing in cases in which the defendant is charged with a felony.
- Set a trial date if the defendant is charged with a misdemeanor; or set a date for the preliminary hearing if the defendant is charged with a felony; or transfer the case to a court in the appropriate jurisdiction.
- Determine bail for the defendant.

The sufficiency of the complaint may be challenged at the initial appearance before a court. If the complaint is defective or insufficient, it must be amended or reissued, or the proceedings against the defendant must be dropped.

Preliminary Hearing or Examination

A preliminary examination is a hearing before a court for the purpose of determining whether the state has sufficient evidence to show that probable cause exists to believe that a felony has been committed by the defendant. Defendants charged with a misdemeanor do not have a right to a preliminary hearing. Nor do defendants who have been indicted by a grand jury have a right to a preliminary hearing unless the statutes or court decisions of the state grant this right. The burden of proof imposed upon the state at a preliminary hearing is that of probable cause. The evidence at a preliminary hearing need not be sufficient to prove the charge against the defendant beyond a reasonable doubt.

In commenting upon the importance of the preliminary hearing to the defendant, the American Civil Liberties book, *The Rights of Suspects*,[13] states on pages 84–85 that

> The value of a preliminary hearing to the defendant is enormous. It informs the defendant of the details of the state's case against him, it gives the defense an opportunity to see the demeanor and testimonial ability of the

prosecution witnesses and it provides an opportunity to size up the whole case: to establish whether a guilty plea would be appropriate, or what the chances are to win at trial. Preliminary hearings also have the effect of freezing the testimony of the prosecution witnesses. This means that if the prosecution witnesses testify differently at trial, they can be impeached by introducing into evidence their original testimony at the preliminary hearing. Inconsistencies in the testimony of witnesses at different times are sometimes the strongest part of the defense case. Generally the defendant does not take the stand at a preliminary hearing, since the only purpose this would serve would be to disclose the defense's case to the prosecutor. Preliminary hearings also have the effect of perpetuating testimony: that is, if a witness testifies at a preliminary hearing and subsequently leaves the state, becomes very ill or dies, the testimony of that witness at the preliminary hearing can be used at trial and the witness's presence at the trial will not be necessary. If it is suspected that a witness may not be present at a future trial, then it may be wisest to waive the preliminary hearing. Otherwise, preliminary hearings are very important. Their importance is emphasized here because many lawyers, particularly those in private practice, for whom time is money, do not tell their clients that they have a right to a preliminary hearing and they waive the hearing. The knowledgeable defendant should not permit this.

The duties of the trial judge at the preliminary hearing are

- To determine the plausibility of the state's case.
- To determine whether the state has carried the burden of showing probable cause to believe that the defendant had committed the felony of which he is charged.
- To determine whether probable cause has been shown for each count where more than one felony has been charged.
- To reduce the charge against the defendant from a felony to a misdemeanor if, after hearing the evidence, the judge concludes that only a misdemeanor was committed (this may only be done in states where judges are authorized to do so by state statutes or court decisions).
- To dismiss the complaint if the court finds that probable cause did not exist to believe that the defendant committed the felony charged. The prosecuting attorney may refile the charge if he has other or new evidence available.

Pretrial Motions

A motion is an application by an attorney for a court order. A motion may be a motion to dismiss for one of many reasons. Or, it may be a motion for discovery. Motions to suppress evidence based upon allegations of improper police or prosecution conduct are very common. Some of the many other motions that may be made are: motions to change venue, motions for adjournments, motions to sequester witnesses, and motions for speedy trial.

Arraignment

An arraignment is a short appearance by the defendant in the court in which his trial will be held. The arraignment is held in open court in the following manner:

Most Cases That are Prosecuted Result in Convictions

Most cases brought by prosecutor result in a plea of guilty.

MANY GUILTY PLEAS ARE THE RESULT OF PLEA NEGOTIATIONS

According to McDonald's recent study, a negotiated plea occurs when a defendant pleads guilty with the reasonable expectation that the State will give some consideration such as reduction in the number or severity of the charges and/or a more lenient sentence.

Guilty pleas are sometimes explicitly traded for a less severe charge or sentence, but they also result from a straightforward admission of guilt by a defendant. This may result from a hope or impression that such a plea will be rewarded by a lighter sentence or from a concern that a trial will reveal damaging evidence.

The predominance of guilty pleas is not new in the criminal justice system. A study in Connecticut covering the 84 years from 1880 to 1954 concludes that between 1880 and 1910 only 10% of all convictions were obtained by trial. In Boland's study of felony dispositions in 1979, the proportion of guilty pleas from all convictions in 13 jurisdictions ranged from 81% in Louisville to 97% in Manhattan Borough, New York.

MOST FELONY CASES THAT REACH TRIAL ARE TRIED BEFORE A JURY

A person accused of a crime is guaranteed a trial by jury. However, the accused may waive the right to trial by jury and be tried by a judge who serves as finder of fact and determines issues of law. Such trials are called bench trials. Brosi showed that the percentage of trials to felony filings was no more than 21% in all 12 jurisdictions studied.

- If the defendant appears without an attorney, the court advises him of his right to an attorney.
- The prosecutor or the court delivers a copy of the indictment or information in felony cases to the defendant and reads the indictment, information, or complaint to the defendant unless the defendant waives the reading.
- The court then asks the defendant what his plea is.
- The defendant then pleads not guilty, guilty, not guilty by reason of mental disease or defect, or any other plea which is authorized by the statutes or court decisions of that state.
- If the defendant refuses to plead or stands mute, the court enters a plea of not guilty into the record on the defendant's behalf.

A MAJOR REFORM HAS BEEN TO INCREASE THE RESPONSIBILITY OF JUDGES FOR ENSURING FAIRNESS IN PLEA NEGOTIATIONS

The judge does not examine the strength of the case against the defendant but does try to determine if unfair coercion was used to induce a plea.

The right that judges most commonly explain in open court to a defendant pleading guilty is the right to trial by jury. McDonald reports that about 30% of the time, judges asked the defendant if promises other than the plea agreement had been made; 65% of the time they asked if any threats or pressures had caused them to plead guilty. Judges rejected only 2% of the guilty pleas observed.

MOST CASES THAT GO TO TRIAL RESULT IN CONVICTION

The conviction rate at trial varies by jurisdiction because of:

- Differences in screening policy
- Pleas in strong cases resulting in a relatively weaker mix of cases going to trial.

18 STATES AND THE DISTRICT OF COLUMBIA REQUIRE A UNANIMOUS VERDICT IN ALL TRIALS

Currently, 45 States require unanimity in criminal verdicts, but 26 of these States do not require unanimity in civil verdicts. Five States (Louisiana, Montana, Oregon, Oklahoma, and Texas) do not require unanimous verdicts in criminal or civil trials.

The proportion of jury votes needed to convict varies among jurisdictions that do not require unanimity, ranging from two-thirds in Montana to five-sixths in Oregon.

All States require unanimity in capital cases, and the U.S. Supreme Court does not permit a criminal finding of guilt by less than a six-person majority. Thus, a six-person jury must always be unanimous in a criminal finding of guilty.

Source: Report to the Nation on Crime and Justice.

- A trial date is then set and if the defendant does not wish a jury trial, he waives his right to a jury trial at that time. The trial date would have to be within the limits set by the "speedy trial" requirement of that jurisdiction unless the defendant waives his right to a speedy trial.

The Right to a Jury Trial

The right to a trial by jury in criminal cases was established in Article III, Sec. 2 and the Sixth Amendment of the U.S. Constitution. Probably all state constitutions also guarantee this right.

Most defendants in criminal cases, however, waive their right to a jury trial. The reasons for this can probably be summarized as follows: (1) the defendant believes that he has as good (and sometimes even a better) chance of being found not guilty by a judge than by taking his case to a jury, (2) it is commonly believed that some judges will give greater sentences to defendants who request jury trials and are convicted, and (3) many defense lawyers do not often urge their clients to demand a jury trial for the reasons already given and because they may be too busy at that particular time to handle too many jury cases. Since jury trials take longer, they also require a larger legal fee.

The Criminal Trial

The Opening Statements

Both criminal and civil trials commence with the right of the attorneys to make opening statements. If the criminal trial is a bench trial (that is, without a jury), it is likely that both attorneys will waive their opening statements. However, in jury trials both attorneys usually make opening statements. The prosecutor will state the charge against the defendant and perhaps briefly outline the state's case against the defendant to aid the jury in understanding the evidence the state is about to present. The defense attorney may then present his opening statement, or may reserve his right to make his statement until after the state has rested its case.

The State's Case

After the opening statements, the state must then present its case. Witnesses are called and other types of evidence are presented. Chapter 4 presents material on the examination of witnesses, which briefly consists of

- The direct examination or questioning of the witness.
- Cross-examination by opposing counsel.
- Redirect examination by the attorney calling the witness.
- Re-cross-examination.

When the state has presented all of its available evidence and witnesses, it will rest its case. The defense attorney will then usually move for dismissal of the charges against the defendant.

The Defendant's Case

The defense attorney then presents his witnesses, who are subject to cross-examination by the prosecutor. The defendant may, if he wishes, appear as a witness in his own behalf. Chapter 3 (Using Presumptions and Inferences) presents material on the defendant as a witness. After the defense has presented all of the evidence and witnesses available in an attempt to prove that the defendant should not be convicted, it will rest its case.

Rebuttal

After the defense attorney has rested his case, the prosecutor may call rebuttal witnesses in an attempt to answer and refute testimony and evidence offered by the defense. After the state's rebuttal, the defense may then offer rebuttal witnesses and evidence to answer and refute evidence presented by the state in rebuttal. After both parties have completed their rebuttal, the defense attorney may again move for dismissal of the charges against the defendant.

Closing Arguments

After both sides have rested, the prosecutor and the defense attorney may make their closing arguments. Closing arguments are particularly important in jury cases in which the laymen sitting on the jury do not have the experience and training a trial judge would have. In closing arguments, the attorneys may summarize their cases and make persuasive arguments in an attempt to convince the trier of facts as to the merits of their particular case.

Unless state statutes or court decisions provide otherwise, the prosecutor will present his closing argument first. Though the prosecutor may use his skills as a speaker to reason and persuade, he must be very careful not to prejudice the defendant's right to a fair trial. Neither attorney may refer to facts which have not become part of the trial record as evidence. But the prosecutor must be much more careful than the defense attorney not to make statements which are inflammatory or prejudicial to the defendant's right to a fair trial. Such statements could cause the trial judge to declare a mistrial or could cause a conviction to be reversed upon appeal.

Instructions to the Jury

Before the case is given to the jury for its deliberations, the jury must be instructed as to the law to apply to the facts of the case. The usual jury charges would include an instruction as to the presumption of the defendant's innocence, the burdens of proof required of the state, a definition of the crime (or crimes) charged, and the essential elements of that crime which must be proved by the state.

The attorneys may request the judge to give other instructions in addition to those ordinarily given. However, the determination as to what instructions are given is made by the trial judge. His decision, of course, is subject to appeal to a higher court. Uniform standard jury instructions have been developed in many states to make this task easier for all concerned and to assure that the rights of defendants to a fair trial are uniformly observed.

Either attorney may enter an objection to the instructions which the trial judge has indicated that he will give. During jury deliberations, the jury may request further instructions or may request that the instructions (or part of them) be repeated. Again, the trial judge determines what additional instructions are given to the jury.

After the jury has been instructed, it goes to the jury room for deliberations. During deliberations, it is isolated from contact and communication with other persons. If the deliberations extend over one day, the jury may be sequestered; that is, spend the night in a hotel at state expense.

In the majority of states, a unanimous jury vote is required for a criminal conviction. Some states, however, have enacted statutes which permit a conviction on less than a unanimous vote. Such statutes have been held constitutional by the U.S. Supreme Court because the U.S. Constitution does not demand a unanimous jury vote. Should the jury indicate after a period of time

Use of Evidence in the Stages of the Criminal Process

Investigative Stage

Charging Stage

Investigation of criminal incident

Criminal charges would be determined (or refused) by a grand jury in states using the grand jury system (the grand jury system is used by the federal government).

Criminal charges would be determined (or refused) by a prosecutor (district attorney, state's attorney, city attorney, etc.) in states using this system.

If it is known (or suspected) that a crime or offense has been committed, law enforcement officers or private persons and investigators would seek evidence of the offense. If competent evidence exists amounting to probable cause to believe that

- a crime (or offense) has been committed, and
- that a specific person (persons) committed the offense,

the matter can then be taken to a prosecutor.

If it is determined that probable cause exists proving

- corpus delicti (that a crime has been committed), and
- that the suspect was a party to the crime,[a]

then a criminal charge or indictment can be issued (or charging the suspect with a crime or crimes).

[a] A party to a crime can be (a) the person (or persons) who actually committed the crime; or (b) a conspirator who hired, procured, planned, or counseled the crime; or (c) a person (or persons) who aided and abetted in the commission of the crime. Different evidence is required to carry the burden of proving each of the different categories of parties to a crime.

that it is deadlocked and cannot reach a verdict, the trial judge may consider giving the jury a charge or instructions urging it to make an additional effort to reach a verdict. The so-called dynamite charge, made in an effort to break a deadlock, has to be carefully worded so as to not infringe upon the defendant's right to a fair trial.

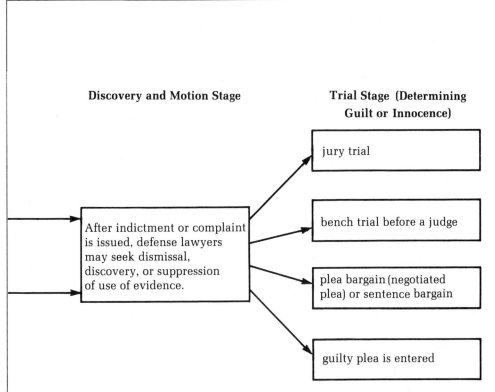

Discovery and Motion Stage

Trial Stage (Determining Guilt or Innocence)

> jury trial

> After indictment or complaint is issued, defense lawyers may seek dismissal, discovery, or suppression of use of evidence.

> bench trial before a judge

> plea bargain (negotiated plea) or sentence bargain

> guilty plea is entered

The defense lawyer will seek to discover and obtain evidence helpful to his client. He may also make some or all of the following motions [b] before the court:

- motion to dismiss because of insufficient evidence, etc.
- motion to dismiss because of improper procedure, or constitutionality of statute, etc.
- motion to suppress evidence (statements, physical evidence, identification evidence, or procedure, etc.)
- motion for discovery of evidence.

[b] A *motion* means an application for an order from the trial judge or other court.

The decision by the defense as to whether to try the case before a jury or judge is generally based upon the evaluation of the case and the evidence. As weaker cases are filtered out of the system or are charged as lesser offenses, most cases which reach the trial stage are strong governmental cases. In these cases, the defense may attempt to plea bargain or may enter a guilty plea. Should the state have a weakness in their case at this stage, they may attempt to plea bargain.

The Jury Verdict and the Judgment of the Court

Should the jury remain deadlocked, the jury will be excused and the case dismissed. In "hung" jury cases, the prosecuting attorney may reissue the criminal charge against the defendant and begin the process of trying the defendant again. The second (or third) trial is considered to be a continuation in legal contemplation of the criminal proceedings to determine the guilt or innocence of the defendant. The process of retrying a defendant may continue until the defendant is either found to be guilty or innocent by a jury of his peers.

Should the jury reach a finding, it is called back into the courtroom where it announces its finding to the court. If the finding and verdict is that of not guilty, the trial judge will enter a judgment of not guilty and the defendant is then free to leave. If the finding and verdict of the jury is that of guilty, the prosecuting attorney will make a motion that the court enter a judgment of guilty. The defense attorney will usually make a motion for a judgment of not guilty, notwithstanding the verdict.

For cases in which the trial is held without a jury, the trial judge will make the findings of fact. If the judge finds that the evidence presented by the state proves all of the essential elements of the crime charged and that the defendant committed the crime, he will enter a judgment of guilty. Should the state fail to prove any of the essential elements of the crime beyond a reasonable doubt, the judgment would then be not guilty.

Sentencing

When defendants are found guilty of the crimes of which they have been charged, the trial judge must then determine the sentence. All criminal laws have penalty sections. In some instances, mandatory penalties attach to the violation. In most offenses, however, the trial judge has considerable discretion. Factors which would affect the sentence determination include: the seriousness of the offense, the past criminal record of the defendant (if any), the age of the offender, the sentence usually given in that community for the offense, whether restitution has been made to the victim, and the likelihood of the defendant to commit other criminal violations.

NOTES

[1] 59 Md.App. 28, 474 A.2d 537, 35 CrL 2147 (1984).

[2] ___ U.S. ___, 106 S.Ct. 1340 (1986).

[3] Heath v. Alabama, 474 U.S. 82, 106 S.Ct. 433 (1985).

[4] See note 3 above.

[5] See note 3 above.

[6] The states using the verdict of guilty but mentally ill are Michigan, Indiana, Illinois, Georgia, Kentucky, New Mexico, Delaware, and Alaska.

[7] 395 U.S. 238, 89 S.Ct. 1709 (1969).

[8] 400 U.S. 25, 91 S.Ct. 160 (1970).

[9] Page 4 of Task Force Report: The Courts, The President's Commission on Law Enforcement and Administration of Justice, published by the U.S. Government Printing Office in 1967.

[10] As to the discretion vested in prosecutors, see the National District Attorneys Association booklet entitled "The Prosecutor's Screening Function." This booklet cites 27 Corpus Juris Secundum, p. 648, § 10, which summarizes the authority of prosecutors as follows:

> The prosecuting attorney has wide discretion in the manner in which his duty shall be performed, and such discretion cannot be interfered with by the courts unless he is proceeding or is about to proceed, without or in excess of jurisdiction. Thus, except as ordained by law, in the performance of official acts he may use his own discretion without obligation to follow the

judgment of others who may offer suggestions; and his conclusions in the discharge of his official liabilities and responsibilities are not in any wise subservient to the views of the judge as to the handling of the state's case.

11 "Read-in" plea bargains are used most often in property offenses such as burglary and forgery when there is repetitious conduct on the part of the defendant. An example of a read-in plea bargain occurred in Milwaukee in 1975. A woman was charged with forging 10 checks. She pleaded guilty to 2 of the charges. The other 8 charges were dismissed and information that she had forged 628 checks was read into the record. The judge sentenced her to the maximum 20 years. Time was saved, the cases were solved, and the woman paid her debt to society.

12 Golden v. State, 49 Ind. 424, 427 (1875), in which the Supreme Court of Indiana labeled a plea arrangement a "corrupt agreement" and compared the procedure to "corrupt purchasing of an indulgence."

13 Permission to reprint this paragraph was granted by the American Civil Liberties Union.

Evidence and the Burdens of Proof

EVIDENCE AND PROOF

What Is Evidence?

Evidence is ordinarily defined as the means of establishing and proving the truth or untruth of any fact which is alleged. Evidence can consist of the testimony of witnesses, physical objects, documents, records, fingerprints, photographs, etc. The famous English lawyer and writer, Sir William Blackstone, defined evidence in the 1760s as

Evidence signifies that which demonstrates, makes clear or ascertains the truth of the very fact or point in issue, either on the one side or other.

When the quality and quantity of the evidence presented is so convincing and is sufficient to prove the existence of the fact sought to be proved or disproved, the result is proof of the fact. Proof is therefore the result of evidence and evidence is the means of attaining proof. Whether a fact has been proved is determined by the trier of the facts (jury or judge).

Evidence can also be used to disprove a fact which the adversary (other lawyer) is seeking to prove. Defendants also present evidence in the form of testimony of witnesses, physical objects, etc. Witnesses can contradict one another, as often occurs in rape cases when the parties knew one another before the incident. The key witness for the state ordinarily testifies that the sex act occurred by use of threat or force, while the defendant will often testify that the act was consented to. Evidence of bruises (photographs) or other physical evidence of violence would be important to corroborate the testimony of the state's witness. The lack of bruises, torn clothing, or other physical evidence of a violent assault could create serious doubts in the minds of the jury as to the charges of the state.

Direct Evidence and Circumstantial Evidence

Evidence is either direct or circumstantial (indirect). Direct evidence is that evidence which proves a fact in issue directly without any reasoning or inferences being drawn on the part of the factfinder. Testimony of a witness that he

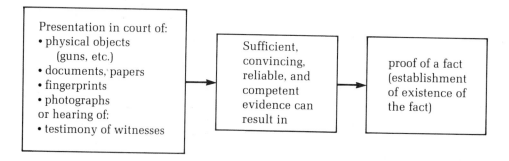

Figure 3.1   Use of Evidence to Establish Proof of a Fact

saw the defendant commit the crime or a confession by the defendant that he committed the crime would be examples of direct evidence.

However, persons committing crimes most often attempt to do so secretly. They often attempt to commit the crime in such a manner that they will not be observed and without leaving any incriminating evidence.[1] Because sufficient direct evidence is not available in many criminal cases, the state must often rely upon circumstantial evidence to assist in carrying the burden of proof.

Circumstantial evidence is that evidence which indirectly proves a fact in issue. The factfinder must draw an inference or reason from circumstantial evidence. Examples of circumstantial evidence which authorized Dallas police to seek to arrest Lee Harvey Oswald after the killing of President John Kennedy were

- Oswald worked in the Texas Book Depository, and was seen in the building on the day of the killing, and had access to the upper floors.

- It was known that the presidential motorcade would be passing the Book Depository building, so Oswald had the opportunity to plan the crime.

- Oswald qualified as a sharpshooter while in the U.S. Marine Corps, and was seen carrying a brown paper package into the building on the day of the assassination.

- Oswald was seen fleeing the building and also otherwise conducted himself in a guilty manner.

- Oswald killed a Dallas police officer who attempted to take him into custody. The killing occurred with a handgun.

- Oswald had a political motive to kill the president and was classified as a political extremist who left the United States and gave up his citizenship to live in the Soviet Union. An FBI man stationed in Dallas was quoted as saying, "We knew he was capable of assassinating the president, but we didn't dream he'd do it."

- After the shooting, an Italian-Manlicker-Carcano 6.5-millimeter rifle with three shell casings was found on the sixth floor of the depository building (it was later reported that Oswald's palm print was found on the barrel of the rifle).

Because no one saw the person actually firing the rifle, the evidence against Oswald up until the time that he killed the Dallas police officer was largely circumstantial. The U.S. Supreme Court stated in the case of *Holland v. United States* [2] that

> Circumstantial evidence in this respect is intrinsically no different from testimonial evidence. Admittedly, circumstantial evidence may in some cases point to a wholly incorrect result. Yet this is equally true of testimonial evidence. In both instances, a jury is asked to weigh the chances that the evidence correctly points to guilt against the possibility of inaccuracy or ambiguous inference. In both, the jury must use its experience with people and events in weighing the probabilities. If the jury is convinced beyond a reasonable doubt, we can require no more.

In most criminal cases, both direct and circumstantial evidence is presented by the government in obtaining a conviction. In the case of *United States v. Roustio* [3], the Federal Court of Appeals held that

> The law is well settled that a jury verdict must be sustained if there is substantial evidence, taking the view most favorable to the Government, to support it. Our review of the evidence, as hereinabove fully set out, leaves us with the clear conviction that the evidence was competent, relevant and substantial enough to support the jury's verdict and defendant's subsequent conviction. . . .
>
> The fact that defendant's conviction is based in part, at least, on circumstantial evidence, is of no moment to a decision concerning the sufficiency of the evidence. . . .
>
> We hold here that defendant's fingerprints had probative value and that it was for the jury to determine in light of all the other evidence, drawing upon their own common sense and general experience, whether such evidence permitted an inference to be drawn that beyond a reasonable doubt defendant robbed the bank in question. The jury was convinced beyond a reasonable doubt and "we can require no more." *Holland,* supra, 348 U.S. at 140, 75 S.Ct. 127.

Means-Opportunity-Motive as Circumstantial Evidence

When eyewitness identification evidence is not available, it has often been stated that investigators and officers should use, as a guideline in investigating crimes, the following questions:

- Who had the means of committing the crime?
- Who had the opportunity to commit the crime?
- Who had the motive to commit the crime?

Evidence that a person had one or all of the above could make the person suspect and justify further efforts to determine whether the person was involved in the offense. Strong circumstantial evidence justified the Dallas police to seek Oswald after the assassination of President Kennedy. The fact that Oswald fled, and then later killed a Dallas police officer, strengthened the circumstantial evidence against Oswald.

Example of Direct Evidence

a) X was seen committing the crime.
b) X was apprehended at the scene of the crime.

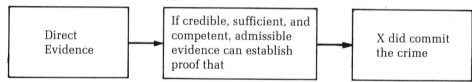

Example of Circumstantial (Indirect) Evidence

a) X was the only person who had an opportunity to commit the crime.
b) X had the means to commit the crime.
c) X's fingerprints were found at the scene of the crime.

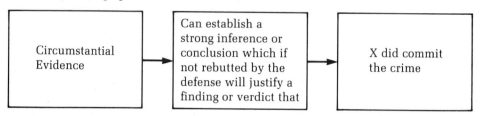

Figure 3.2   Direct Evidence and Circumstantial Evidence

Defendants may also use circumstantial evidence. A defendant may argue that he (or she) did not have one or more of the means-opportunity-motive to commit the crime. A defendant could by use of such evidence show (or raise a reasonable doubt) whether he (or she) committed the offense. The state and the government have the burden of coming forward with sufficient evidence to prove their accusations beyond a reasonable doubt.

Proving Corpus Delicti by Means of Circumstantial Evidence

In all criminal cases, the state must prove (1) that a crime has been committed (*corpus delicti*); and (2) that the defendant (or defendants) committed the offense.

Corpus delicti means the body or substance of the crime. The state must show that a crime has actually been committed before it may charge a person with committing the crime. If a state is unable to produce direct or circumstantial evidence proving corpus delicti, it may not then charge a person with a criminal offense. As an example, suppose that fire and police investigators suspect that a fire which completely burned out a building was arson, and deliberately started. The building housed a business which was in serious financial trouble. The building and its contents were a total loss and were heavily insured. It can be shown that the owner of the building had the means, opportunity, and motive for "torching" the building; but the state does not have

Table 3.1   Classifications of Evidence

CLASSIFICATION OF EVIDENCE	DIRECT EVIDENCE	CIRCUMSTANTIAL EVIDENCE
	Evidence which proves or disproves a fact in issue without any reasoning or inferences being drawn on the part of the factfinder	*Evidence which indirectly proves or disproves a fact in issue. The factfinder must reason or draw an inference from circumstantial evidence*
Types of Evidence		
Statements by a suspect or defendant	Statements that a suspect committed the crime would be direct evidence (*full* or *partial* confession).	Statements that the suspect was with the deceased victim a short time before the murder could be used as circumstantial evidence by the state (incriminating statements, but neither a full or partial confession).
Testimony of witnesses or the victim	Could identify the suspect as the person who committed the crime and be direct evidence.	Could incriminate the suspect by providing evidence which would link the suspect to the crime or would provide evidence showing motive, means, or opportunity for suspect to commit crime (suspect seen fleeing from crime scene).
Physical evidence	Contraband (drugs, stolen property, concealed weapons, etc.) is direct evidence when a suspect is charged with possession, etc., of such evidence.	Otherwise, physical evidence is generally circumstantial evidence (fingerprints, blood stains, weapon used to commit crime, bite marks, etc.).
Evidence obtained as a result of wiretapping or electronic surveillance	Statements directly showing who committed the crime would be direct evidence.	Statements which incriminate but do not directly show who committed the crime would be circumstantial evidence.

sufficient evidence to prove corpus delicti, and therefore cannot charge the owner with a criminal offense.

As a general rule, corpus delicti must be established beyond a reasonable doubt.[4] Corpus delicti may be proved by a combination of direct and circumstantial evidence or by either alone. When corpus delicti is attempted to be proven by circumstantial evidence, the general rule is that the evidence must be so conclusive as to eliminate all reasonable doubt in concluding that a crime was committed. The following case illustrates:

Epperly v. Commonwealth

Supreme Court of Virginia (1982)
294 S.E.2d 882

An eighteen-year-old college girl (Gina Hall) was last seen leaving a dance with the defendant. Her body was never found to conclusively prove that she was murdered. But her blood-soaked clothing was found. Her car was also found and there was evidence of a violent struggle at a house on Claytor Lake, where the defendant was seen after the dance. Dog-tracking evidence was admitted at the defendant's trial corroborating some of the allegations of the state as to her whereabouts after the dance. The defendant also made incriminating statements which were admitted as evidence. In holding that the state carried the burden of proving corpus delicti, the Supreme Court of Virginia affirmed the defendant's conviction, ruling that

> The court instructed the jury that the Commonwealth must first prove that Gina was dead and that her death was caused by criminal violence. The instruction told the jury that these elements might be proved "either by direct evidence or by proof so strong as to produce the full assurance of moral certainty." Defendant agrees that this instruction correctly states the law, but argues that the evidence was insufficient to warrant the jury's finding the existence of the *corpus delicti* ....

> In homicide cases, the *corpus delicti* must consist of proof (1) of the victim's death, and (2) that it resulted from the criminal act or agency of another .... Although this is the first such case to come to this Court in which the victim's body was not found, we have long held that the *corpus delicti* may be proven by circumstantial evidence.

> We think the evidence was sufficient to warrant the jury in finding, to the full assurance of moral certainty, that Gina Hall was dead as the result of the criminal act of another person. The jury was entitled to take into account, in this connection, her sudden disappearance, her character and personal relationships, her physical and mental health, the evidence of a violent struggle at the house on Claytor Lake, her hidden, blood-soaked clothing, and the defendant's incriminating statements—particularly his reference to "the body" before it was generally thought she was dead.

All cities in the United States have missing persons. Such persons may be living elsewhere in the world and have cut all ties with their family and friends. To charge a person with the murder of a missing person requires proof beyond reasonable doubt that (1) the missing person was murdered, and (2) that the defendant (person charged) committed the crime.

Can Circumstantial Evidence Alone Support a Criminal Conviction?

Any fact or issue in a trial may be proved by circumstantial evidence or may be proved by a combination of both circumstantial and direct evidence.[5] The U.S. Supreme Court stated that [6]

> ... direct evidence of a fact is not required. Circumstantial evidence is not only sufficient, but may also be more certain, satisfying and persuasive than direct evidence....

The Supreme Court of California held that [7]

> This was sufficient evidence to require the case to go to the jury. Had it been submitted to the jury, the rule is that: "[T]he jury properly may reject part of the testimony of a witness, though not directly contradicted, and combine the accepted portions with bits of testimony or inferences from the testimony of other witnesses thus weaving a cloth of truth out of selected available material ...." Furthermore, negligence may be proved circumstantially like any other issue of fact, and indirect evidence may outweigh direct evidence on the contested point.... "... direct evidence may be disbelieved and contrary circumstantial evidence relied upon to support a verdict or finding." (*Bruce v. Ullery,* 58 Cal.2d 702, 711, 25 Cal.Rptr. 841, 846, 375 P.2d 833, 838.) It also must be remembered that "[w]here reliance is placed on circumstantial evidence, it is not necessary that there be no possibility of deriving any other reasonable inference from the evidence." (*Varas v. Barco Mfg. Co.,* 205 Cal.App.2d 246, 262, 22 Cal.Rptr. 737, 746.)

The Supreme Court of Iowa held that [8]

> *In a criminal case* where circumstantial evidence alone is relied on to prove any one or more of the essential elements of the crime the evidence must be entirely consistent with defendant's guilt and wholly inconsistent with any rational hypothesis of defendant's innocence and so convincing as to exclude a reasonable doubt that defendant was innocent of the offense charged.

The Court of Special Appeals of Maryland held that [9]

> Circumstantial evidence alone is sufficient to support a verdict of guilty (except for the crime of treason and, in some jurisdictions, perjury) or it may be used in conjunction with direct evidence. It may corroborate other testimony and may be used to prove any element of the crime, such as the *corpus delicti* or the criminal agency of the accused.
>
> "The law makes no distinction between direct evidence of a fact and evidence of circumstances from which the existence of a fact may be inferred. No greater degree of certainty is required when the evidence is circumstantial than when it is direct, for in either case the trier of fact must be convinced beyond a reasonable doubt of the guilt of the accused."

Presenting a "web of circumstances" or "inference stacking" (building one inference on top of another) generally requires some physical evidence which links (or ties) the suspect to the crime charged. The linking evidence could be the murder weapon, it could be fingerprints, footprints, bite marks in a murder and rape case, or a witness who places the defendant in or near the crime scene.

The state must anticipate and attempt to answer all of the doubts in the minds of the jury (or judge). The defense lawyer's job is to act as the devil's advocate and to raise all the doubts he (or she) can.

Using the Battered Child Syndrome as Circumstantial Evidence

For cases in which parents and other persons are charged with the death of or injuries to children, circumstantial evidence in the form of the "battered child syndrome" has been permitted by many courts. Without the use of circumstantial evidence, it would be difficult or impossible to prove many of these cases. The Court of Appeals of New York described the battered child syndrome as follows in the case of *People v. Henson:* [10]

> Initially developed following extensive research more than a decade ago, "the diagnosis of the 'battered child syndrome' has become an accepted medical diagnosis." ... "A finding ... of the 'battered child syndrome' ", the court in *People v. Jackson* pointed out (18 Cal.App.3d at p. 507, 95 Cal.Rptr. at p. 921), "is not an opinion by the doctor as to whether any particular person has done anything" but, rather, it "simply indicates" that a child of tender years found with a certain type of injury "has not suffered those injuries by accidental means." Thus, although the decision to admit such expert testimony is within the discretion of the trial court ... there is little doubt of its relevancy in prosecutions of the kind before us.
> "As indicated, the diagnosis is used in connection with very young children, around three or four years old, and is based upon a finding that such a child exhibits evidence, among other injuries, of subdural hematoma, multiple fractures in various stages of healing, soft tissue swellings or skin bruising. Also pertinent to the diagnosis is evidence that the child is generally undernourished and that the severity and type of injury in evidence on his body is inconsistent with the parents' story of its occurrence.... This sort of expert medical testimony—that the victim is a "battered child"—coupled with additional proof—for instance, that the injuries occurred while the child was in the sole custody of the parents—would permit the jury to infer not only that the child's injuries were not accidental but that, in addition, they occurred at the culpable hands of its parents....

The Supreme Court of Minnesota held in the case of *State v. Loss* that [11]

> We hold that the establishment of the existence of a battered child, together with the reasonable inference of a battering parent, is sufficient to convict defendant herein in light of the other circumstantial evidence presented by the prosecution. It is very difficult in these prosecutions for injuries and death to minor children to establish the guilt of a defendant other than by circumstantial evidence. Normally,

as was the case here, there are no eyewitnesses. The establishment of the fact that the deceased child was a battered child was proper, and adequate foundation was laid for the introduction of the evidence which conclusively established a battered child syndrome. The prosecution properly presented to the jury the psychological framework which constitutes a battering parent. It did not attempt to point the finger of accusation at defendant as a battering parent by its medical testimony. Rather, it presented sufficient evidence from which the jury could reasonably conclude that defendant fit one of the psychological patterns of a battering parent . . . .

The applicable rule to determine the sufficiency of circumstantial evidence was set forth originally in *State v. DeZeler,* 230 Minn. 39, 52, 41 N.W.2d 313, 322 (1950), which held that circumstantial evidence will support a conviction only where the facts described by it . . . .

. . . form a complete chain which, in the light of the evidence as a whole, leads so directly to the guilt of the accused as to exclude, beyond a reasonable doubt, any reasonable inference other than that of guilt.

The "Sufficiency of Evidence" Requirement to Justify a Verdict or Finding of Guilt

One of the most common grounds for appeals from jury verdicts or a judge's finding of guilty is that of insufficiency of evidence. In this appeal, the defense argues that there was not sufficient evidence to support the verdict or finding of guilt beyond reasonable doubt.

A jury's verdict or a judge's finding must be supported and based upon legal and substantial evidence. Mere possibilities, suspicion, or conjecture will not support a verdict or finding of guilt. If the evidence is inherently incredible or is contrary to common knowledge and experience or established physical facts, it will not support a finding of guilt.

Either direct or circumstantial evidence will support a finding or verdict of guilt if the evidence is legally sufficient to prove all of the essential elements of the crime charged. The Court of Special Appeals of Maryland held in the case of *Metz v. State* [12] that

In short, we feel that the test for sufficiency is the same whether the evidence be direct, circumstantial, or provided by rational inferences therefrom.

The following cases illustrate questions of sufficiency of evidence issues which have come before appellate courts:

In re Woods

Court of Appeals of Illinois (1974)
20 Ill.App.3d 641, 314 N.E.2d 606

Identification evidence of the defendant's involvement in a robbery was suppressed and could not be used because of improper procedures. The only remaining evidence which could be used was evidence of his presence at the scene of the crime and the fact that he ran away. In holding that this evidence was insufficient to support defendant's conviction, the court ruled that

> Mere presence at the scene of the crime is insufficient to establish accountability ..., and we believe that presence at the scene together with flight, in the absence of other circumstances indicating a common design to do an unlawful act, does not establish accountability.

State v. Drake

Court of Appeals of Missouri (1974)
512 S.W.2d 166

The Court held that "association with a known criminal is not, standing alone, reasonable grounds for arrest," but pointed out that in this case, the following additional evidence existed:

- A felony had just been committed.
- The defendant was at the scene of the crime.
- The defendant had in his possession fruits of the crime.

In affirming the defendant's conviction and holding that sufficiency of evidence existed, the Missouri Court of Appeals held that

> In testing the sufficiency of evidence in a criminal prosecution, the court is to consider all evidence in the light most favorable to the State.... Defendant was found in possession of three rings identified as property belonging to the victim shortly after the crime had been committed. The unexplained possession of recently stolen property has been sufficient to sustain a conviction of stealing.... In *State v. Cobb,* 444 S.W.2d 408 (Mo. banc 1969), the court held that unexplained possession does not raise a presumption of guilt but it is a circumstance from which guilt may be inferred as a matter of fact with the jury entitled to draw an inference unfavorable to the defendant. The property here was in the unexplained sole and exclusive possession of defendant and it had been recently stolen. The evidence sufficiently supports the conviction.

Harmless Error as Distinguished From Reversible Error

The U.S. Supreme Court stated in the case of *Michigan v. Tucker* [13] that "the law does not require that a defendant receive a perfect trial, only a fair one." Errors occur in trials but appellate courts will not reverse and order a new trial if the error was a "harmless error." Many (if not all) states have developed tests for determining whether errors were harmless or prejudicial to the fundamental rights of a defendant. In the following cases, the U.S. Supreme Court established the current harmless error rule:

Chapman v. California

Supreme Court of the United States (1967)
386 U.S. 18, 87 S.Ct. 824

The U.S. Supreme Court held that a California prosecutor's repeated comments on the failure of defendants charged with robbery and murder to take the witness stand and testify was not harmless error. In holding that the prosecutor's comments might have contributed to the convictions of the defendants, the Court ruled

> We, therefore, ... hold ... that before a federal constitutional error can be held harmless, the court must be able to declare a belief that it was harmless beyond a reasonable doubt.

In the 1986 case of *Delaware v. Van Arsdall,* 475 U.S. 673, 106 S.Ct. 1431, the U.S. Supreme Court held that some constitutional errors, such as denial of the right to counsel are so fundamental that they cannot be harmless error. The Court pointed out that whether an error is harmless will depend upon such factors as "... the importance of the witness' testimony in the prosecutor's case (where defendant could not impeach a prosecution witness for bias), whether the testimony was cumulative, the presence or absence of evidence corroborating or contradicting the testimony of the witness on material points, the extent of cross-examination otherwise permitted, and, of course, the overall strength of the prosecution's case."

QUANTUMS OF EVIDENCE

The term *quantum* is used to measure amounts of evidence (information). Quantums of evidence are important because a given quantum of evidence could authorize a government official to act in a manner which would cause the restraint of freedom of movement of an individual, or could also result in a search or seizure.

Just as sugar is measured in stores by pounds and gasoline is measured in service stations by gallons, evidence is measured in our legal system in legally recognized quantums.

The quantums of evidence used in the American criminal justice system are

- **reasonable suspicion,** which is less than probable cause and which will authorize an investigative detention.
- **probable cause,** which is required to make an arrest, issue an arrest or search warrant, or to hold a person in custody.
- **proof beyond reasonable doubt,** which is the amount and quality of evidence necessary to convict a person of a crime after a trial has been held.

Voluntary Conversations Between Law Enforcement Officers and Private Citizens

Law enforcement officers can engage in voluntary conversations with persons in order to obtain information. This technique has been used by both law enforcement officers and private security persons as an investigative procedure.

Asking a motorist parked at the side of a road if there is anything wrong, or talking to a person on a street or in a public place, might produce information valuable to maintaining public order. The U.S. Supreme Court stated in 1983 that [14]

> law enforcement officers do not violate the Fourth Amendment by merely approaching an individual on the street or in another public place, by asking him if he is willing to answer some questions, by putting questions to him if the person is willing to listen, or by offering in evidence in a criminal prosecution his voluntary answers to such questions ....
>
> The person approached, however, need not answer any question put to him; indeed, he may decline to listen to the questions at all and may go on his way .... He may not be detained even momentarily without reasonable, objective grounds for doing so; and his refusal to listen or answer does not, without more, furnish those grounds. If there is no detention—no seizure within the meaning of the Fourth Amendment—then no constitutional rights have been infringed.

Reasonable Suspicion

To engage in a voluntary conversation with a private citizen requires no showing of authority by a law enforcement officer. The officer might only have a hunch, mere suspicion, or a gut reaction.

To detain a person, however, and to restrain the freedom of movement of a person requires that quantum of evidence known as reasonable suspicion. The test used to determine whether a person "has been 'seized' within the meaning of the Fourth Amendment (is) only if, in view of all of the circumstances surrounding the incident, a reasonable person would have believed that he was not free to leave." [15] The U.S. Supreme Court stated that [16]

> characterizing every street encounter between a citizen and the police as a "seizure," while not enhancing any interest secured by the Fourth Amendment, would impose wholly unrealistic restrictions upon a wide variety of legitimate law enforcement practices. The Court has on other occasions referred to the acknowledged need for police questioning as a tool in the effective enforcement of the criminal laws. "Without such investigation, those who were innocent might be falsely accused, those who were guilty might wholly escape prosecution, and many crimes would go unsolved. In short, the security of all would be diminished. *Haynes v. Washington,* 373 U.S. 503, 515 [83 S.Ct. 1336, 1344]."
>
> We conclude that a person has been "seized" within the meaning of the Fourth Amendment only if, in view of all of the circumstances

surrounding the incident, a reasonable person would have believed that he was not free to leave. Examples of circumstances that might indicate a seizure, even where the person did not attempt to leave, would be the threatening presence of several officers, the display of a weapon by an officer, some physical touching of the person of the citizen, or the use of language or tone of voice indicating that compliance with the officer's request might be compelled. In the absence of some such evidence, otherwise inoffensive contact between a member of the public and the police cannot, as a matter of law, amount to a seizure of that person.

If a person has been seized (detained of his freedom of movement) under the "free-to-leave test," the officer must be able to show that he had reasonable suspicion to believe that the person was committing a crime, had committed a crime, or was about to commit a crime. The U.S. Supreme Court has required "ample factual justification" to undertake "legitimate and restrained investigative conduct[17]

Chapter 10 contains further information and cases on the authority to make investigative detentions (or, as they are commonly called, *Terry* stops) when the officer is able to show that quantum of evidence known as reasonable suspicion.

Probable Cause, or Reasonable Grounds to Believe

Probable cause to arrest is that quantum of evidence which would cause a reasonable law enforcement officer to believe that the defendant probably committed a crime. The Supreme Court of Pennsylvania quoted the U.S. Supreme Court as follows in defining probable cause: [18]

> ... [p]robable cause means that "the facts and circumstances within their (arresting officers) knowledge and of which they had reasonably trustworthy information were sufficient in themselves to warrant a man of reasonable caution in the belief" that the suspect had committed a crime: *Carroll v. United States,* 267 U.S. 132, 162, 45 S.Ct. 280, 288, 69 L.Ed. 543 (1925).

The term *reasonable grounds to believe* means the same as *probable cause.* The U.S. Supreme Court also further explained probable cause in the case of *Brinegar v. United States* [19] as follows:

> In dealing with probable cause, ... as the very name implies, we deal with probabilities. These are not technical; they are the factual and practical considerations of everyday life on which reasonable and prudent men, not legal technicians, act.

We deal with probabilities almost every day in our lives. If, after hearing a weather forecaster state that there was a 90-percent chance of rain tomorrow, how would we respond when a friend asked what the weather forecast was for tomorrow? Would we answer that rain was possible, or that rain was probable, or that rain was certain? How would we respond if the weather forecast predicted a 10-percent possibility of rain?

Cases and additional material on probable cause are presented in chapter 10.

Police/Citizen Contact

To talk with a person on a voluntary basis	No showing of authority is necessary while the conversation is voluntary. "... a person has been 'seized' within the meaning of the Fourth Amendment *only* if, in view of all of the circumstances surrounding the incident, a reasonable person would have believed that he was *not* free to leave". (emphasis added) U.S. Supreme Court.
To make an investigative stop (*Terry* stop)	Reasonable suspicion to believe that the person has committed, is about to commit, or is committing a crime is needed.
To arrest a person, or to obtain an arrest or search warrant	Probable cause, or reasonable grounds to believe, that ▪ a specific crime or offense has been committed, and ▪ the suspect is the person who committed the crime, or is a party to the crime or offense must exist.

Proof Beyond Reasonable Doubt

A person charged with a crime has a right to be tried before a jury, has a right to cross-examine witnesses of the state, has a right to compel witnesses to appear in his behalf, and other rights to a fair trial as defined by the U.S. Constitution. There is presumption that all persons are innocent until proven guilty.

The burden of proving a defendant guilty of every element of a crime charged is upon the state or government. The amount of evidence must be sufficient to satisfy a jury or judge of the defendant's guilt beyond a reasonable doubt.

The term *reasonable doubt* means a doubt for which a reason can be given, after there has been a fair and rational consideration of the evidence (or the lack of evidence). Jury instructions inform jurors that the doubt must be such as would cause a person of ordinary prudence to hesitate or pause before concluding that the defendant was guilty.

The government does not have to prove guilt with absolute certainty. U.S. Supreme Court Justice Harlan commented on this in his concurring opinion in the 1970 case of *In re Winship*,[20] stating that

> the factfinder cannot acquire unassailably accurate knowledge of what happened. Instead, all the factfinder can acquire is a belief of what *probably* happened. The intensity of this belief—the degree to which a factfinder is convinced that a given act actually occurred—can, of course, vary ....

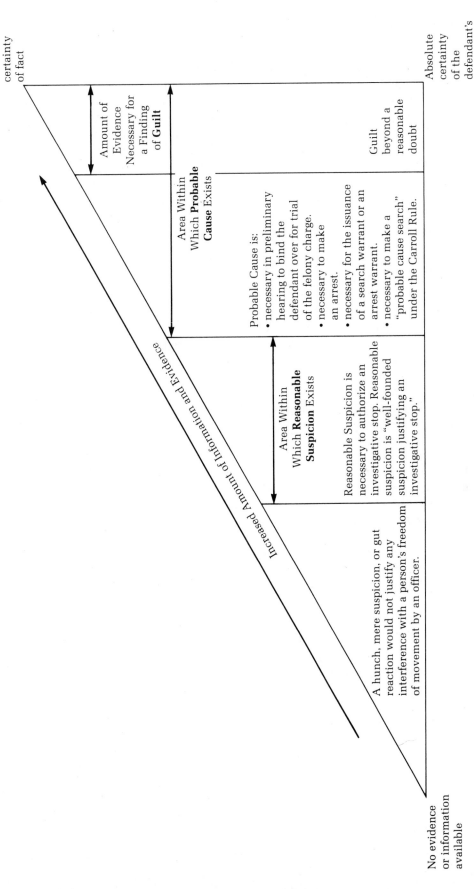

Figure 3.3 Standards of Proof Required in Criminal Cases

Justice Harlan also pointed out that if the burden of proof in criminal trials was less than proof beyond a reasonable doubt, then "there would be a smaller risk of factual errors that result in freeing guilty persons, but a far greater risk of factual errors that results in convicting the innocent." On the other hand, if the government were required to carry the burden of proving guilt with absolute certainty, many more guilty persons would be freed and probably no innocent person would ever be wrongfully convicted. The requirement of proof beyond a reasonable doubt is therefore a compromise between these two positions in "reducing the risk of convictions resting on factual error." [21]

BURDENS OF PROOF

A criminal trial commences with the burden on the government of producing sufficient admissible and credible evidence to support the charges which have been made against the defendant. In presenting its case against the defendant, the government must present evidence proving each of the essential elements of the crime charged beyond a reasonable doubt.

After the government has put on all of its witnesses and presented all of the available evidence, they will rest their case. Should the government fail to prove all of the essential elements of the crime charged in the presentation of their case, the charge (or charges) against the defendant will be dismissed on motion by the defense attorney, since the government has failed to present sufficient evidence to support its accusation against the defendant.

Because the government in the great majority of criminal cases carries the burden of proving all the essential elements of the crime charged beyond reasonable doubt, the motion to dismiss is generally refused. The defense then has the opportunity to present their case. Evidence is ordinarily presented in an effort to disprove the state's charges or an attempt is made to establish an affirmative defense.

After the defense rests its case, a motion for dismissal is also sometimes made. If this motion is denied, the case would then go to the jury. In determining the verdict, the jury must decide whether the evidence taken as a whole proves the defendant guilty beyond a reasonable doubt. In the 1971 case of *United States v. Vuitch,*[22] the U.S. Supreme Court held that courts should always set aside a jury verdict of guilty when there is not sufficient evidence from which a jury could find a defendant guilty beyond a reasonable doubt.

USING HEARSAY INFORMATION TO ESTABLISH PROBABLE CAUSE OR REASONABLE SUSPICION

Sources and Possible Uses of Hearsay Information

As human beings, we all rely upon our senses (hearing, seeing, smelling, etc.) for information. Such information, which we receive and obtain through our senses, is firsthand information and it is not hearsay information. **Hearsay** information is that information of which we do not have personal knowledge but which we have received from others. Hearsay information is therefore information of which we have "heard it said."

During the course of practically every day, we receive hearsay information. For example, much of the world and national news which we receive by means of newspapers, magazines, television, and radio is hearsay information relayed to us through news services and television networks. Because this information is for the most part very accurate, we generally accept it as trustworthy because of its source.

Law enforcement officers in the course of their official duties also receive much hearsay information from different sources. Some sources providing hearsay information to law enforcement officers are reliable and such information received by the officers may therefore be accepted as trustworthy. Other sources, however, have questionable reliability and tests have been developed in the law to test the reliability and credibility of this information. Other sources (such as rumors and anonymous tips) cannot be accepted as reliable and, other than providing a possible investigative lead, do not provide the officer with information he may accept as reliable and trustworthy.

The different sources from which law enforcement officers could receive hearsay information are

- Communications from their departments, from other law enforcement agencies, and from fellow officers.
- Communications from private persons and citizens (victims of crimes, witnesses to crimes) who have personal knowledge which they communicate to law enforcement officers.
- Information from "police informants".
- Information from anonymous sources, such as telephone calls and letters where the person supplying the information does not disclose his identity.

Hearsay Communications From Other Police Agencies

Law enforcement officers receive considerable amounts of information from their departments, from other law enforcement agencies, and from other law enforcement officers. Officers may rely upon such information as reliable and credible even though they may not have firsthand knowledge of the facts themselves. The following two U.S. Supreme Court cases concern police bulletins sent out to other departments:

Whiteley v. Warden

Supreme Court of the United States (1971)
401 U.S. 560, 91 S.Ct. 1031

Based upon an informant's tip and a sheriff's conclusion that the defendant and his companion had committed the crime of breaking and entering, an arrest warrant was issued by a magistrate. A Wyoming state police bulletin was issued and the defendant was arrested by Laramie, Wyoming police officers. In holding that probable cause to support the issuance of the arrest warrant did not exist, the U.S. Supreme Court ruled that

Other Classifications of Evidence

CORROBORATIVE EVIDENCE

Corroborative evidence is evidence which strengthens, adds weight or credibility. In many instances, corroborative evidence is the most important evidence in carrying the burden of persuasion in the minds of the factfinder. The state cannot obtain a conviction in a rape case without corroborative evidence because the testimony of the victim alone will not carry the burden of proof.

PRIMA FACIE EVIDENCE

The term *prima facie* is Latin for "at first sight," or "on the face of it." Prima facie evidence is that amount of evidence or that quality of evidence which is sufficient in itself to prove a case. When the state presents a prima facie case, the defense must respond or accept a very serious risk of conviction. A prima facie case is then a very strong case with sufficient evidence to obtain a conviction.

CONCLUSIVE EVIDENCE AND CONFLICTING EVIDENCE

Conclusive evidence is evidence from which only one reasonable conclusion may be drawn. The term *conclusive evidence* is sometimes used in statutes where the legislature requires evidence so strong as to conclusively prove the fact or issue. The term *conflicting evidence* is usually used to indicate a situation where evidence both proving and disproving a fact or issue has been presented; and, depending upon the weight and credibility accorded the evidence, the factfinder could find either way.

CUMULATIVE EVIDENCE

Cumulative evidence is additional evidence of the same kind which proves the same point as evidence already presented. However, evidence of a different type of source or evidence of a different kind is not cumulative even though it tends to prove or disprove the same fact or issue. See the U.S. Supreme Court case of *Hamling v. United States,* 418 U.S. 87, 94 S.Ct. 2887, discussing cumulative evidence.

We do not, of course, question that the Laramie police were entitled to act on the strength of the radio bulletin. Certainly police officers called upon to aid other officers in executing arrest warrants are entitled to assume that the officers requesting aid offered the magistrate the information requisite to support an independent judicial assessment of probable cause. Where, however, the contrary turns out to be true, an otherwise illegal arrest cannot be insulated from challenge by the decision of the instigating officer to rely on fellow officers to make the arrest.

In sum, the complaint on which the warrant issued here clearly could not support a finding of probable cause by the issuing magistrate. The arresting officer was not himself possessed of any factual data tending to corroborate the informer's tip that Daley and Whiteley

POSITIVE AND NEGATIVE EVIDENCE

Most evidence is positive evidence, in that it is presented in positive terms. Some evidence, however, is presented in negative terms and has been referred to as negative evidence. For example, a motorist testifying that he saw a "Construction Ahead" sign on the road would be positive evidence. However, another motorist testifying that he did not see any signs is negative evidence if the witness was not paying particular attention. See 32 C.J.S. Evidence 1079 for discussion and case citations.

TESTIMONIAL EVIDENCE

Testimony of a witness in court, under oath and subject to cross-examination.

TANGIBLE EVIDENCE

Tangible or physical evidence are objects such as weapons, drugs, or clothing, which are used as evidence. Some tangible evidence is contraband (that is, objects which are illegal to possess, such as illegal drugs, guns, or stolen property). Other physical or tangible evidence is what was formerly called *mere evidence.* The defendant lawfully owns the object, such as a ski mask, sunglasses, or a jacket; but the objects are used as evidence because the victim identifies the offender as wearing such objects at the time of the crime. Mere evidence is returned to the defendant after being used as evidence. Contraband is never returned to the defendant.

DEMONSTRATIVE EVIDENCE

See chapter 18 on demonstrative evidence and exhibits such as diagrams, charts, and photographs of a crime scene or traffic accident.

SCIENTIFIC EVIDENCE

See chapter 20 on scientific evidence, which is the product of crime laboratories and coroner's laboratories (such as dramatized by the TV series "Quincy").

committed the crime. Therefore, petitioner's arrest violated his constitutional rights under the Fourth and Fourteenth Amendments; the evidence secured as an incident thereto should have been excluded from his trial.

United States v. Hensley

Supreme Court of the United States (1985)
469 U.S. 221, 105 S.Ct. 675

(This case is also presented in chapter 12.)

Police in St. Bernard, Ohio had reasonable suspicion to believe that the defendant was involved in an armed robbery. However, a police bulletin was issued asking other departments to pick up the defendant and hold him for St. Bernard. When Hensley was stopped on the "wanted flyer," a concealed revolver was seen a minute or so after the stop. Hensley was arrested for the handgun violation. In affirming the stop and the conviction of the defendant, the Supreme Court held that

> The justification for a stop did not evaporate when the armed robbery was completed. Hensley was reasonably suspected of involvement in a felony and was at large from the time the suspicion arose until the stop by the Covington police. A brief stop and detention at the earliest opportunity after the suspicion arose is fully consistent with the principles of the Fourth Amendment.
>
> Turning to the flyer issued by the St. Bernard police, we believe it satisfies the objective test announced today. An objective reading of the entire flyer would lead an experienced officer to conclude that Thomas Hensley was at least wanted for questioning and investigation in St. Bernard. Since the flyer was issued on the basis of articulable facts supporting a reasonable suspicion, this objective reading would justify a brief stop to check Hensley's identification, pose questions, and inform the suspect that the St. Bernard police wished to question him. As an experienced officer could well assume that a warrant might have been obtained in the period after the flyer was issued, we think the flyer would further justify a brief detention at the scene of the stop while officers checked whether a warrant had in fact been issued. It is irrelevant whether the Covington officers intended to detain Hensley only long enough to confirm the existence of a warrant, or for some longer period; what matters is that the stop and detention that occurred were in fact no more intrusive than would have been permitted an experienced officer on an objective reading of the flyer.
>
> To be sure, the St. Bernard flyer at issue did not request that other police departments briefly detain Hensley merely to check his identification or confirm the existence of a warrant. Instead, it asked other departments to pick up and hold Hensley for St. Bernard. Our decision today does not suggest that such a detention, whether at the scene or at the Covington police headquarters, would have been justified. Given the distance involved and the time required to identify and communicate with the department that issued the flyer, such a detention might well be so lengthy or intrusive as to exceed the permissible limits of a *Terry* stop....
>
> The length of Hensley's detention from his stop to his arrest on probable cause was brief. A reasonable suspicion on the part of the St. Bernard police underlies and supports their issuance of the flyer. Finally, the stop that occurred was reasonable in objective reliance on the flyer and was not significantly more intrusive than would have been permitted the St. Bernard police. Under these circumstances, the investigatory stop was reasonable under the Fourth Amendment, and the evidence discovered during the stop was admissible.

Hearsay Statements From Private Citizens

Victims of crimes and witnesses to crimes report the incidents to law enforcement officers daily in cities and counties throughout the United States. Even though the officers may not have personal knowledge of any of the incidents reported, they may rely upon such hearsay information as reliable and trustworthy if the information appears reasonable.

If crime victims (or witnesses) are able to give specific descriptions of criminals or their vehicles which single them out or identify them in a manner establishing probable cause, such offenders may immediately be taken into custody.

If the description by crime victims or witnesses does not establish probable cause, but does establish reasonable suspicion, an investigative stop (*Terry* stop) may be made. See chapter 10 for cases and material on such stops.

Hearsay Information From Police Informants

Police informants differ from other persons providing hearsay information to law enforcement officers in that

- Police informers usually expect money or a concession for the information or "tip" they provide. For example, a heroin addict would expect to receive a reduction in charge or penalty, or not to be charged at all for providing information as to the suppliers of drugs.
- Many police informers have usually been in trouble with the law and therefore their motives for providing information to the police are viewed with suspicion.

Information from police informers and other persons may always be used as leads for further investigations regardless of the source of the information. But before hearsay information from a police informer may be used as an essential element of probable cause, the "totality of the circumstances" must demonstrate that reliable information establishes either probable cause or reasonable suspicion. The following U.S. Supreme Court cases concern police actions based upon information from police informants:

Adams v. Williams

Supreme Court of the United States (1972)
407 U.S. 143, 92 S.Ct. 1921

At 2:15 A.M., a police informant approached a police car and told a police sergeant who knew him that a man seated in a nearby car had narcotics and was carrying a gun at his waist. After calling for assistance, the sergeant approached the car and asked Williams to open the door. When Williams rolled down the window instead, the sergeant reached into the car and removed a fully loaded revolver from Williams' waistband. Because the gun was not visible before its removal, Williams was then arrested. In the search incident to the arrest, a substantial amount of heroin was found on Williams' person. The defendant argued that there was no showing of reliability of the informant nor corroboration of his information. In affirming the defendant's convictions, the U.S. Supreme Court held that

> While properly investigating the activity of a person who was reported to be carrying narcotics and a concealed weapon and who was sitting alone in a car in a high-crime area at 2:15 in the morning, Sgt. Connolly had ample reason to fear for his safety. When Williams rolled down his window, rather than complying with the policeman's request to step out of the car so that his movements could more easily be seen, the revolver allegedly at Williams' waist became an even greater threat. Under these circumstances the policeman's action in reaching to the spot where the gun was thought to be hidden constituted a limited intrusion designed to insure his safety, and we conclude that it was reasonable. The loaded gun seized as a result of this intrusion was therefore admissible at Williams' trial. . . .
>
> Once Sgt. Connolly had found the gun precisely where the informant had predicted, probable cause existed to arrest Williams for unlawful possession of the weapon. Probable cause to arrest depends "upon whether, at the moment the arrest was made . . . the facts and circumstances within [the arresting officers'] knowledge and of which they had reasonably trustworthy information were sufficient to warrant a prudent man in believing that the [suspect] had committed or was committing an offense." *Beck v. Ohio,* 379 U.S. 89, 91, 85 S.Ct. 223, 225, 13 L.Ed.2d 142 (1964). In the present case the policeman found Williams in possession of a gun in precisely the place predicted by the informant. This tended to corroborate the reliability of the informant's further report of narcotics and, together with the surrounding circumstances, certainly suggested no lawful explanation for possession of the gun. Probable cause does not require the same type of specific evidence of each element of the offense as would be needed to support a conviction.

McCray v. Illinois

Supreme Court of the United States (1967)
386 U.S. 300, 87 S.Ct. 1056

Two Chicago police officers were told by an informant that the defendant was selling heroin and had heroin in his possession. The informant stated that the defendant could be found at 47th and Calumet at that time. The officers drove to that vicinity and after the informant pointed out the defendant, the informant left on foot. The officers then arrested the defendant and found heroin in his possession. In holding that "the officers did rely in good faith upon credible information supplied by a reliable informant," the Court pointed out that

- One officer testified under oath that the informant had supplied him with accurate information "fifteen, sixteen times at least," and the other officer testified he had received accurate information from the informant "20 to 25 times."
- The officers corroborated (confirmed) the information given to them by the informant that the defendant was at 47th and Calumet at the time stated.

In holding that the identity of the informer did not have to be disclosed, the Supreme Court ruled that

> The arresting officers in this case testified, in open court, fully and in precise detail as to what the informer told them and as to why they had reason to believe his information was trustworthy. Each officer was under oath. Each was subjected to searching cross-examination. The judge was obviously satisfied that each was telling the truth, and for that reason he exercised the discretion conferred upon him by the established law of Illinois to respect the informer's privilege.

Draper v. United States

Supreme Court of the United States (1959)
358 U.S. 307, 79 S.Ct. 329

> An informant who was paid small amounts of money informed a federal narcotic agent in Denver that the defendant "was peddling narcotics to several addicts." During the prior six months, information from the informer was always found to be accurate and reliable. Four days later, the informer told the agent that Draper had made the trip from Denver to Chicago to obtain heroin and would be returning by train. The informer gave the narcotic agent a detailed physical description of Draper and the clothing he was wearing. The informer also told the agent that Draper would be carrying "a tan zipper bag" and that he habitually "walked real fast." The federal narcotic agent and a Denver police officer went to the Denver Union Station and kept watch over all incoming trains from Chicago on the days during which the informer had stated Draper would probably be returning. When they saw a man matching the description given by the informer, they arrested the man. A search of Draper incident to the arrest revealed heroin. In affirming Draper's conviction, the U.S. Supreme Court held that

> > The information given to narcotic agent Marsh by "special employee" Hereford may have been hearsay to Marsh, but coming from one employed for that purpose and whose information had always been found accurate and reliable, it is clear that Marsh would have been derelict in his duties had he not pursued it. And when, in pursuing that information, he saw a man, having the exact physical attributes and wearing the precise clothing and carrying the tan zipper bag that Hereford had described, alight from one of the very trains from the very place stated by Hereford and start to walk at a "fast" pace toward the station exit, Marsh had personally verified every facet of

the information given him by Hereford except whether petitioner had accomplished his mission and had the three ounces of heroin on his person or in his bag. And surely, with every other bit of Hereford's information being thus personally verified, Marsh had "reasonable grounds" to believe that the remaining unverified bit of Hereford's information—that Draper would have the heroin with him—was likewise true. . . .

We believe that, under the facts and circumstances here, Marsh had probable cause and reasonable grounds to believe that petitioner was committing a violation of the laws of the United States relating to narcotic drugs at the time he arrested him. The arrest was therefore lawful, and the subsequent search and seizure, having been made incident to that lawful arrest, were likewise valid. It follows that petitioner's motion to suppress was properly denied and that the seized heroin was competent evidence lawfully received at the trial.

Affirmed.

USING PRESUMPTIONS AND INFERENCES

Presumptions were created centuries ago to provide starting points in criminal trials and to permit the orderly functioning of civil and criminal trials. The best-known presumption (and probably the oldest) is the presumption of innocence until proven guilty. This presumption provides a starting point. The government must come forward with evidence and attempt to carry the burden of overcoming the presumption of innocence. The factfinder will then determine whether the government has presented evidence which carries the burden of proving the defendant guilty beyond reasonable doubt.

The Supreme Court of Pennsylvania [23] and the Supreme Court of Indiana [24] defined the legal significance and nature of a presumption as follows:

> . . . a presumption of law is not evidence nor should it be weighed by the factfinder as though it had evidentiary value. Rather, a presumption is a rule of law enabling the party in whose favor it operates to take his case to the jury without presenting evidence of the fact presumed. It serves as a challenge for proof and indicates the party from whom such proof must be forthcoming. When the opponent of the presumption has met the burden of production thus imposed, however, the office of the presumption has been performed; the presumption is of no further effect and drops from the case.

Inferences Distinguished From Presumptions

A **presumption** is a conclusion (deduction) which the law requires that the factfinder (jury or judge) *must* make. A jury and judge *must* presume that a defendant is innocent at the commencement of the trial.

If a presumption is not overcome by evidence showing otherwise, judges and jurors *must* accept the presumption as true. If the burden of overcoming

CIVIL LIABILITY OF LAW ENFORCEMENT OFFICERS FOR FALSE ARREST

The civil liability of the police officer does not turn on whether the arrest was in fact legal, but whether he reasonably believed the arrest to be legal, an obviously lesser standard (than the standard required for a lawful arrest).

(A) . . . policeman is protected from civil liability even in the absence of probable cause, so long as the officer had a good faith belief in the existence of probable cause. *FBI Law Enforcement Bulletin* article, "Probable Cause: The Officer's Shield to Suits Under the Federal Civil Rights Act," July 1976.

(In the 1986 case of *Malley v. Briggs*, the U.S. Supreme Court refused to give absolute immunity to a police officer who relied on a warrant holding that "a damage remedy for an arrest following an objectively unreasonable request for a warrant imposes a cost directly on the officer responsible for the unreasonable request, without the side effect of hampering a criminal prosecution." 475 U.S. 335, 106 S.Ct. 1092, 38 CrL 3169).

the presumption is met and the presumption is overcome with evidence, the presumption has no further effect and drops from the case.

Inferences are conclusions (or deductions) that a jury or judge *may* make from a fact or group of facts presented to them. For example, when evidence is presented showing that the defendant ran away and tried to conceal himself when a uniformed police officer approached, the jury or judge *may* draw an inference from these facts. If the defendant does not take the witness stand and explain or give reasons for his conduct, the jury or judge *may* (not *must*) draw an inference (conclusion) that the defendant's conduct showed a guilty mind.

In the 1979 case of *Sandstrom v. Montana*,[25] the U.S. Supreme Court held that an instruction to a jury that "the law presumes that a person intends the ordinary consequences of his voluntary acts" shifted the burden of proof in the criminal case to the defendant. Because the state must prove all of the essential elements of the crime charged, the burden-shifting presumption as to the intent of the defendant violated his due process rights.

Instead of the jury instruction which was given in the *Sandstrom* case, an instruction providing "the jury may infer that a person intends the ordinary consequences of his voluntary act" may be used.

In the 1983 case of *Connecticut v. Johnson*,[26] the defendant was charged with attempted murder, robbery, kidnapping, and first-degree sexual assault. The trial court instructed the jury that "a person's intention may be inferred from his conduct and every person is conclusively presumed to intend the natural and necessary consequences of his act."

In reversing and holding that the jury instruction in the case of *Connecticut v. Johnson* was in error, the U.S. Supreme Court ruled that

The conclusive presumption the jury was instructed to apply permitted the jury to convict respondent without ever examining the evidence concerning an element of the crimes charged. Such an error deprived respondent of "constitutional rights so basic to a fair trial that their infraction can never be treated as harmless error."

The Inference that Persons Are Sane and Normal

There is an inference that witnesses and defendants in civil and criminal cases are sane and normal. If a defendant in a criminal case seeks to use the insanity defense, who has the burden of coming forward with evidence showing otherwise?

Most states place the burden on the defendant to come forward with evidence demonstrating that he was so mentally diseased or defective that he could not formulate a criminal intent. Under the 1952 U.S. Supreme Court holding of *Leland v. Oregon*,[27] states may continue to use this practice if they wish.

At the time of the *Hinckley* case, the lower federal courts had placed the burden on the government to show that defendants such as *Hinckley* were sane and normal. In view of Hinckley's wild, bizarre behavior before and after the senseless shooting spree in Washington, D.C., where Hinckley killed one person and seriously wounded others, including the president, the jury could not find Hinckley sane and normal. In 1984 Congress corrected this problem, requiring that defendants seeking to use the insanity defense in a federal criminal court must now come forward with evidence showing clearly and convincingly that the defendant was insane at the time of the crime.

PROBLEMS

1. A New York State trooper saw a car traveling at an excessive rate of speed on the New York Thruway. The officer overtook the speeding vehicle and stopped it. Four men were in the vehicle (two in the front and two in the back seat). As the officer was asking the driver for his license and the vehicle registration, the officer smelled burnt marijuana. The officer then saw an envelope marked "Supergold" lying on the floor of the car between the two men in the front seat.

   The evidence which was available to the officer would permit him to draw an inference as to which of the men possessed the marijuana. Did the evidence and the inference drawn from the evidence establish probable cause to arrest the driver? Or the two men in the front seat? Can it be inferred from the evidence that probable cause existed to arrest all four men? Explain. *New York v. Belton,* 453 U.S. 454, 101 S.Ct. 2860 (1981).

2. A guard at the state prison in Walpole, Massachusetts heard loud voices coming from a walkway. The officer immediately opened the door to the walkway and saw "an inmate named Stephens bleeding from the mouth and suffering from a swollen eye. Dirt was strewn about the walkway which the officer viewed to be further evidence of a scuffle." The officer saw three inmates, including an inmate named Hill, jogging away together down the walkway. There were no other inmates in the area, which was enclosed by a chain-link fence. The officer concluded that the three men acted as a group in assaulting Stephens. There was no evidence as to who actually beat

Stephens. Was there sufficient evidence to punish Hill as one of the three men in the assault, by taking away "good-time credits" belonging to Hill? Explain. *Superintendent, Mass. Correctional Institution, Walpole v. Hill,* 472 U.S. 445, 105 S.Ct. 2768, 37 CrL 3108 (U.S.Sup.Ct.1985).

3. Kent Hansen was sitting on a public park bench close to a man who was smoking a marijuana cigaret. When an officer in plain clothes saw the marijuana cigaret and smelled burning marijuana, he arrested both men. The officer did not see Hansen holding or smoking the marijuana cigaret. Could the officer properly infer from the information he had that there was an active participation by Hansen in the use or possession of the marijuana? Should Hansen's conviction be affirmed? Give reasons for your answer. *State of Arizona v. Hansen,* 117 Ariz. 496, 573 P.2d 896 (App.Ct.1978).

4. An experienced law enforcement officer used the following incident as an example for classes. The officer's wife was babysitting for their five-year-old grandson while the parents were away. No one else was in the house when the grandmother put the child in a bed for an afternoon nap. A short time later while the grandmother was in the basement, she heard a crash and ran back upstairs. When she entered the child's room, she saw the window drapes lying across the bed and on the floor. Because the child had the means and opportunity of pulling the drapes down, the grandmother said to the child, "Why did you pull the drapes down?" The child looked his grandmother in the eye and replied, "You didn't see me do it and you can't prove that I did it."

   List the evidence available to the grandmother which caused her to conclude that the child pulled the drapes down. Indicate whether this was direct or circumstantial evidence.

   If this situation was presented to a jury, would they be justified in making the same conclusion that the grandmother made? Would the jury's verdict be sustained by the trial court and the appellate court in that there was sufficient evidence to sustain the jury's finding?

5. Can circumstantial evidence be used to convict a person of income tax evasion by use of the "net worth method"? The U.S. government showed Holland's opening net worth with reasonable certainty. A year later, Holland's net worth increased considerably but his income tax return showed a lesser amount. This was shown for a series of years. Can a jury draw an inference from this type of circumstantial evidence which would support a criminal conviction for tax fraud? *Holland v. United States,* 348 U.S. 121, 75 S.Ct. 127 (1954).

NOTES

[1] For example, a sixty-five-year-old woman told a panel on rape how the assault upon her was committed. Her assailant seized her at a time when help from other persons was not available. The man's face was covered so that she could not identify him. He wore gloves to assure that he would leave no fingerprints. He also used a condom so that he would not leave semen for use as evidence.

[2] 348 U.S. 121, 75 S.Ct. 127 (1954).

[3] 455 F.2d 366 (7th Cir.1972).

[4] 23 Corpus Juris Secundum, Criminal Law, 917.

[5] See 32a Corpus Juris Secundum (Evidence) § 1039.

[6] Michalic v. Cleveland Tankers, Inc., 364 U.S. 325, 81 S.Ct. 6 (1960).

[7] Kopfinger v. Grand Central Public Market, 60 Cal.2d 852, 37 Cal.Rptr. 65, 389 P.2d 529 (1964).

[8] State v. Williams, 179 N.W.2d 756 (Iowa 1970).

[9] Robinson v. State, 18 Md.App. 678, 308 A.2d 734 (1973).

[10] 33 N.Y.2d 63, 349 N.Y.S. 657, 304 N.E.2d 358 (1973).

[11] 295 Minn. 271, 204 N.W.2d 404 (1973).

[12] 9 Md.App. 15 at 23, 262 A.2d 331 at 335 (1970).

[13] 417 U.S. 433, 94 S.Ct. 2357 (1974).

[14] Florida v. Royer, 460 U.S. 491, 103 S.Ct. 1319 (1983).

[15] United States v. Mendelhall, 446 U.S. 544, 100 S.Ct. 1870 (1980).

[16] United States v. Mendelhall, see note 15 above.

[17] Terry v. Ohio, 392 U.S. 1, 88 S.Ct. 1868 (1968).

[18] Commonwealth v. Bishop, 425 Pa. 175, 228 A.2d 661 (1967).

[19] 338 U.S. 160, 60 S.Ct. 1302 (1949).

[20] 397 U.S. 358, 363, 90 S.Ct. 1068, 1072 (1970).

[21] See also Speiser v. Randall, 357 U.S. at 525–526, 78 S.Ct. at 1342 where the U.S. Supreme Court stated:

> "There is always in litigation a margin of error, representing error in factfinding, which both parties must take into account. Where one party has at stake an interest of transcending value—as a criminal defendant his liberty—this margin of error is reduced as to him by the process of placing on the other party the burden of ... persuading the factfinder at the conclusion of the trial of his guilt beyond a reasonable doubt. Due process commands that no man shall lose his liberty unless the Government has borne the burden of ... convincing the factfinder of his guilt."

[22] 402 U.S. 62, 91 S.Ct. 1294 (1971).

[23] Commonwealth v. Vogel, 440 Pa. 1, 17, 268 A.2d 89, 102 (1970).

[24] Sumpter v. State, 261 Ind. 471, 306 N.E.2d 95 (1974).

[25] 442 U.S. 510, 99 S.Ct. 2450.

[26] 32 CrL 3053.

[27] 343 U.S. 790, 73 S.Ct. 4 (1952).

PART TWO

Witnesses and the Use of Their Testimony as Evidence

Witnesses and the Examination of Witnesses

CHAPTER OUTLINE

Witnesses are essential in all cases because without witnesses neither civil nor criminal actions could be commenced and conducted. Most witnesses are very cooperative in performing their civic duty, but unfortunately some witnesses are not cooperative. The following boxed material summarizes why some witnesses are not cooperative.

QUALIFICATIONS NECESSARY TO BE A WITNESS

In order to be a witness, a person must satisfy the following requirements:

- *Requirement of personal knowledge.* The witness must have some personal knowledge of the matter before the court. If the governor of a state was in a bank at the time it was robbed, he (or she) would have enough personal knowledge to be subpoenaed if he was needed as a witness by either the state or the defense.

- *Requirement that every witness declare that he (or she) will testify truthfully.* Most witnesses will take an oath swearing that they will tell the truth. However, the Federal Rules of Evidence (Rule 602) and the Uniform Rules of Evidence also provide for an "affirmation," which, like the oath, requires "every witness . . . to declare that he will testify truthfully . . .".

- *Requirement of Competency.* The usual modern standard for determining the competency of a witness has been stated: "Competency depends upon the witness' capacity to observe, remember and narrate as well as an understanding of the duty to tell the truth." [1]

See Article VI of the Federal Rules of Evidence in appendix B of this text.

Is a Young Child Qualified to Appear as a Witness?

Of the three general requirements to be a witness, the question of the competency of young children presents the greatest problem. Many cases concerning the competency of young children to appear as witnesses have come before courts in recent years. The following cases received national attention:

Why Some Witnesses Are Not Cooperative

In one episode of the TV "All in the Family" series, the fictional Archie Bunker witnessed a mugging but did not stay at the scene to assist in identifying the offender. In explaining his action to his wife and his son-in-law, Archie expressed his concern for a long wait in the courthouse for the case to be called, which would be followed by "the other lawyer mak(ing) a monkey outta you." Other reasons given for a lack of cooperation by witnesses are as follows:

- *Threats against witnesses.* A former U.S. Department of Justice official stated that "I think that this factor alone might be responsible for half of the cases that have to be scrubbed. Not only are we unable to protect huge numbers of citizens from crimes in the first place, but we can't instill confidence in them that the law can protect them if they testify against the accused." [a]

- *Financial losses.* Most states pay up to $15 or $20 per day as witness fees. Unless vacation time is used or the employer makes up the difference, most witnesses who are working suffer some financial loss because of the time lost from their employment. A few witnesses have lost their jobs because they were obligated to spend time in courtrooms.

- *Delays and adjournments.* The National Advisory Committee on Criminal Justice Standards and Goals recognized that "delays are an accepted defense practice for wearing down the witness. Not infrequently, the financial and emotional costs become too much for the victim, and she asks to withdraw ...". [b]

- *Failure to inform as to outcome of case.* Plea bargaining is used to settle many criminal cases. The National Advisory Committee on Criminal Justice Standards concluded that "(m)ost victims strongly desire *official* notification of the disposition of their case, even if it ends in acquittal, rather than having to ask or find out from others. Failure to receive such feedback is often the victim's complaint ...". [c]

Victim assistance programs, law enforcement agencies, and prosecutors throughout the United States have made considerable efforts in recent years to correct the problems which have caused some witnesses to be less than cooperative.

[a] In the case of People v. Carradine, 52 Ill.2d 231, 287 N.E.2d 670 (1972), a Chicago mother of six children was sentenced to six months in jail for refusing to testify as a witness for the state in a murder prosecution. The woman stated that she was fearful for her life and the safety of her children because a well-known Chicago street gang had threatened her. The court held that such fear alone was not justification for refusal to testify, nor was her belief that the police could not effectively protect her from such danger.

[b, c] Both statements are taken from the "Report of the Task Force on Criminal Justice Research and Development."

- Charges were filed in 1984 against twenty-five adults accused of sexually abusing children in Jordan, Minn. After further investigation and review, the charges were dropped because of insufficient evidence.

- In Honolulu, Hawaii, James McKellar, a real estate salesman, was being tried in 1986 for kidnapping, rape, assault, sexual abuse, and promoting child abuse. The state's only two witnesses were four years old at the time of the alleged crimes. The defense challenged the competency of the girls to testify. A Minnesota psychologist compared the case to the Jordan, Minnesota case and testified that "highly coercive, highly pressurized" questioning by parents, by attorneys for the parents, police, and prosecutors had "a confounding and contaminating effect" on the girls recollections, rendering them "completely unreliable." The trial judge agreed and in a twenty-page ruling held that the girls were incompetent to testify in the trial of *State v. McKellar,* case number CR–85–0553. The judge's ruling left the state with no witnesses to present its case.[2]

Most witnesses take the witness stand and testify without being challenged. However, the opposing attorney could challenge a witness as not being competent. The trial court would then determine the competency of the witness. If a young child is called as a witness, most courts would question the child (**voir dire**) to determine whether the child is competent. The finding of the trial court as to competency will not be disturbed by appellate courts in the absence of abuse of discretion.[3] Cases illustrating competency follow:

State v. Schossow

Supreme Court of Arizona (1985)
145 Ariz. 504, 703 P.2d 448

During the defendant's trial on three counts of child molestation, four girls, aged 7 to 9½ years, testified against the defendant. The defense lawyer did not challenge the competency of the girls and the trial judge failed to conduct any preliminary examination to establish their competency to testify. The Supreme Court of Arizona held that Arizona statutes require trial judges to make inquiries on their own into the competency of children under 10 years, and that failure to do so "will be fundamental and prejudicial error ...". The Court did not reverse the conviction and reviewed the history of child witnesses as follows:

> At common law no child under fourteen years of age was eligible to testify as a witness. Annot., 81 A.L.R.2d 386, 389–90 (1962). It was not until 1779 that the law renounced the rule of absolute disqualification. In *Rex v. Brasier,* 1 Leach 199, 168 Eng.Rep. 202 (1779), the court held that a child less than seven years old was competent to testify "*provided* such infant appears, *on strict examination by the court,* to possess a sufficient knowledge of the nature and consequences of an oath ...." The United States Supreme Court followed the *Brasier* rule in *Wheeler v. United States,* 159 U.S. 523, 16 S.Ct. 93, 40 L.Ed. 244 (1895) and held that a five year old child was competent to testify in a criminal trial for murder. The Court stated that the
>> decision of this question rests primarily with the trial judge, who sees the proposed witness, notices his manner, his apparent possession or lack of intelligence, and *may resort to any examination* which will tend to disclose his capacity and intelligence ....

In response to the *Wheeler* decision, a large number of states enacted statutes similar to A.R.S. [Arizona Revised Statutes] § 12–2202, which states, in pertinent part:

Persons who may not be witnesses.

The following shall not be witnesses in a civil action: ...

2. Children under ten years of age who appear incapable of receiving just impressions of the facts respecting which they are to testify, or of relating them truly.

Statutes similar to A.R.S. § 12–2202 have been construed to posit a presumption that children under the age of ten (or, in some cases, twelve) are incompetent to testify; this presumption can be rebutted by a showing of competency sufficient to allow the trial judge to make a finding on the issue.

State v. Pettis

Supreme Court of Rhode Island (1985)
488 A.2d 704

The defendant was convicted of first-degree sexual assault upon the testimony of a mentally retarded thirteen-year-old girl. The girl, who was fourteen at the time of trial, stated that she did not understand the difference between telling the truth and a lie. The Supreme Court of Rhode Island affirmed the defendant's conviction, holding that

The trustworthiness of the testimony is the standard for determining the competency of a child to testify. "[T]he traditional test is whether the witness has intelligence enough to make it worthwhile to hear him at all and whether he feels a duty to tell the truth." *McCormick, Handbook of the Law of Evidence* § 62 at 156 (3d ed. Cleary 1984) . . . .

A child may not testify as a witness unless the child can demonstrate to the trial justice that he or she "can (1) observe, (2) recollect, (3) communicate (a capacity to understand questions and to furnish intelligent answers), and (4) appreciate the necessity of telling the truth." *Id.* at 629, 410 A.2d at 442. We further stated in *In Re Gerald*, R.I., 471 A.2d 219, 221 (1984), that the failure of a witness to state clearly the difference between a lie and the truth does not render the witness incompetent to testify.

In the case before us the trial justice concluded, after a full examination of the witness, that she was competent to testify. The trial justice reasoned that

"[he was] satisfied ... that this witness, despite her shortcomings, has indicated that she is able to tell us what did or did not take place .... [W]ith regard to the distinction that she is asked to make between the truth and a lie .... I'm satisfied that in her own humble way she appreciates the necessity for telling the truth ...."

Voir Dire

The phrase *voir dire* is French for "to speak the truth." The term is used to denote the preliminary examination to determine whether a witness or juror is competent or qualified.

The voir dire of a young child whom one of the parties seeks to use as a witness would be a series of questions to determine whether the child has the perception, memory, and ability to testify as a witness in that case. The voir dire of a person who one of the parties sought to use as an expert witness would be questions to determine whether that person qualifies as an expert witness. The voir dire of a juror would be questions to determine whether the person is competent and what his interest and bias are. For example, an old friend of the arresting officer or the neighbor of the defendant would not qualify to sit on the jury because of their interest and natural bias.

The questions asked during the voir dire must relate to the competency and qualifications of the person and cannot relate to the facts of the case. With witnesses, it is usually the attorney calling the person as a witness who will conduct the voir dire, although in many cases the trial judge will question a very young child to determine competency. In all instances, the opposing attorney would have an opportunity to cross-examine the witness during the voir dire if the competency or qualifications were still in doubt or in contest.

Unreliability as Distinguished From Incompetency

The issue of competency most often comes before courts when one of the parties seeks to use a very young child as a witness. It is very rare that the competency of an adult who appears as a witness will be challenged.

Although a witness may be found competent to testify, his subsequent statements may show that he is unreliable, or may even be deliberately false. Unreliability is sometimes related to physical, mental, or emotional disabilities of the witness. The identification testimony of a witness with poor eyesight may be shown to be unreliable. Such disabilities as poor hearing and senility could also cause a jury or a court to consider a witness' statements to be less reliable than that of witnesses with normal physical abilities.

A person who is a severe neurotic could be a competent witness and may be very reliable because a neurotic is by definition a person who is in touch with reality. But a psychopath is in most instances not to be trusted as a witness. A psychopath could make a fine appearance in court and be a very impressive witness, but with no conscience to keep him from saying anything he wants to, he experiences no conflict in regard to the moral rightness or wrongness of his statements.

Memories of witnesses could be severely impaired by the use of drugs, as could the moral compulsion to tell the truth. Courts differ in their attitude toward the drug-addicted witness. In some courts, proof of addiction to any drug can be introduced to impeach (cast doubt on) the credibility of a witness. In other courts, the drug involved must be shown to impair faculties of the witness before proof of addiction will be admitted for impeachment.

NIJ Study: "When the Victim is a Child" [a]

The National Institute of Justice (NIJ) has published a study of new methods for easing the trauma faced by child victims and witnesses who have to go through criminal proceedings. The report is designed for prosecutors, judges, police officers, and other professionals interested in improving the way the criminal justice system treats child abuse victims.

The study, "When the Victim is a Child," responds to an urgent need expressed by the Attorney General's Task Force on Family Violence, which called for research into the court treatment of child victims. It discusses the competency of child witnesses, child victim advocates, videotaping statements, and testimony,[b] as well as recommended changes in hearsay statutes. Included is a comparative survey of each State's legislation to protect child witnesses in sexual abuse.

After discussing in detail the various problems both the system and the child victim face, the report makes a number of recommendations for improvements. For example, it called for an end to State laws requiring that witnesses be at least a certain age. Many States bar or greatly curtail testimony from young witnesses, whereas Federal rules permit testimony from any competent witness irrespective of age.

In addition, the report recommends the adoption of State legislation to permit special exceptions to the hearsay rule for children. Such laws would admit certain out-of-court statements to counselors or prosecutors that might otherwise be ruled out because they are not available from the young witnesses during direct examination.

Other legal provisions examined in the report include proposals for:

- Permitting a child witness to have a support person during testimony;
- Offering services to explain the court procedures to the child and his or her family;
- Directing law enforcement officers, social service agencies, and prosecutors to conduct joint investigations in each child sexual abuse case using a single trained interviewer; and
- Scheduling trials to give priority to those involving young victims and discouraging postponements.

The study, which was conducted by a private research firm, also contains appendixes on interviewing child victims and videotaping a child's statement or testimony.

The publication is for sale from the Superintendent of Documents, U.S. Government Printing Office, Washington, DC (stock number 027–000–01248–5). The price is $3.25. Microfiche copies are available from the National Criminal Justice Reference Service, Box 6000, Rockville, MD 20850, telephone (301) 251–5500. The toll-free number is 800–851–3420.

[a] Taken from the November 1986 issue of *FBI Law Enforcement Bulletin.*

[b] The U.S. Supreme Court has held that the loss of eye contact in televised or videotaped testimony does not violate the Sixth Amendment and that eye contact is a "trivial adjunct to the right of cross-examination." Davis v. Alaska, 415 U.S. 308 (1974). The Pennsylvania Superior Court held to the contrary in the 1986 case of Commonwealth v. Ludwig, ___ A.2d ___, 40 CrL 2166. In the *Ludwig* case, a five-year-old girl, who had accused her father of sexual abuse, had "frozen" at the preliminary hearing. At the trial, the girl was permitted to testify by use of a closed-circuit TV. The Superior Court reversed, holding that not only cross-examination but also eye-to-eye contact with one's accuser is guaranteed by the Sixth Amendment.

CREDIBILITY OF WITNESSES

Methods Used to Keep Witnesses Honest

Witnesses have a serious responsibility to tell the truth. In order to encourage witnesses to tell the truth, and to bring before the court and the jury the facts pertaining to the issues of the case, the following procedures are used:

- Witnesses must take an oath (or affirmation) that they will tell the truth.
- Witnesses must be personally present at the trial (the defendant's Sixth-Amendment right to confront witnesses against him must be complied with).
- Witnesses are subject to cross-examination.

In addition, witnesses who do not tell the truth run the risk of being charged with perjury. If they refuse to testify or refuse to answer questions which are not privileged, they could be found in contempt of court and punished.

Credibility and the Weight of Evidence

The determination as to whether statements made by witnesses are to be believed (credibility) and the weight to be given to a witness' testimony are made by the trier of fact. When a jury is sitting in a case, they are the trier of fact. If a case is tried without a jury (bench trial), the judge is then the trier of fact.

In determining the credibility and the weight to be given to the testimony of witnesses, the following factors should be used by factfinders:

- *Perception.* Did the witness perceive (see, hear, smell, etc.) accurately? Did he or she have an opportunity to observe and perceive?
- *Memory.* Has the witness retained an accurate impression of what he or she saw, heard, smelled, etc.? Is his memory of the events accurate?
- *Narration by the witness.* Do the testimony of the witness and the language he uses accurately describe the events which occurred?

In determining the weight and the credit to be given to the testimony of each witness, juries and judges as the triers of fact also use their common knowledge and experience. Statements of witnesses which are incredible or contrary to commonly known facts do not have to be believed by juries or judges. The "Incontrovertible Physical Facts" rule (or the Physical Facts rule) holds that the fact-finding body (jury or judge) will give no weight to statements by witnesses which are so inherently incredible, unbelievable and contrary to physical facts, known physical laws, general knowledge or human experience.[4]

The reasonableness of a witness' testimony, his interest or lack of interest in the results of the trial, his bias or prejudice (if any are shown), his clearness or lack of clearness of recollection, and the overall impression obtained by the jury are factors used in determining the weight and credit to be given to the testimony of a witness. The following example is used to illustrate weight of

Permitting a Witness to Testify Without Disclosure of Identity Because of Threats of Physical Harm

Authority for permitting a witness to testify without disclosing his (or her) identity is given in the *FBI Law Enforcement Bulletin* article entitled "The Informer-Witness," published in May 1977. The article states that

appellate courts frequently have supported a trial judge's decision to allow a witness to testify without divulging his name,[5] present address,[6] or place of employment,[7] if disclosure would jeopardize the safety of the witness or possibly his family. In order to establish the existence of danger, the government bears the burden of demonstrating a factual basis for its concern. Mere conjecture that physical harm might result if the informer identified himself on the witness stand is not sufficient.[8] (An exception might exist in the narcotics field where at least one court has taken notice of the fact that "[u]ndercover work, particularly in the narcotics area, is a dangerous business . . . ."[9]) In order to satisfy this burden, it seems likely that prosecutors will rely on the officer and the witness to document previous threats received by the informant. Some courts have suggested that information concerning the threats might be submitted to the trial judge in chambers, out of the presence of the jury.[10] Law enforcement officers who have regular contact with informers would thus be well advised to record, either in the informant's file or the substantive case file, any threats received by the informer himself or other members of his family.

Caveat: The courts have limited the exception discussed above to situations in which physical safety is threatened. Thus, fear that an informer's employment might be jeopardized is not sufficient to override the defendant's right to cross-examination.[11]

[5] United States v. Ellis, 468 F.2d 638 (9th Cir.1972); United States v. Crovedi, 467 F.2d 1032 (7th Cir.1972), cert. denied, 410 U.S. 982 (1973); United States v. Palermo, 410 F.2d 468 (7th Cir.1969).

[6] United States v. Crockett, 506 F.2d 759 (5th Cir.1975); United States v. Smaldone, 484 F.2d 311 (10th Cir.1973), cert. denied, 415 U.S. 915 (1974); Richardson v. State, 508 S.W.2d 380 (Tex.Crim.App.1974) (also withheld were the witness' wife's name, name of bank, and names and addresses of associates). Contra, Hassberger v. State, 321 So.2d 577 (Fla.Dist.Ct.App.1975).

[7] People v. Durley, 51 Ill.2d 590, 283 N.E.2d 882 (1972).

[8] United States v. Palermo, 410 F.2d 468, 472 (7th Cir.1969).

[9] United States v. Alston, 460 F.2d 48, 53 (5th Cir.1972), cert. denied, 409 U.S. 871 (1972). The *Alston* court drew a distinction between a law enforcement employee working undercover and an informer "whose motives or background might be subject to considerably less supervision and correspondingly greater doubt." Id. at 53. There is less need for the background information of an undercover employee because he can be "placed" within a milieu of supervision, training, and authority for purposes of cross-examination.

[10] United States v. Varelli, 407 F.2d 735 (7th Cir.1967), cert. denied sub nom. Saletko v. United States, 405 U.S. 1040 (1972); Beasley v. State, 318 A.2d 501 (Md.Ct.App.1974).

[11] United States v. Ott, 489 F.2d 872 (7th Cir.1973).

evidence. A defendant is charged with armed robbery after being positively identified by two eye-witnesses. The defendant uses an alibi defense, stating that he was attending a college class on the evening and time of the robbery. The following witnesses verify his alibi:

The 1670 Trial of William Penn (Founder of Pennsylvania)

An important case in the historic development of the power and authority of the jury to independently determine the credibility of witnesses and the weight to be given to their testimony occurred in London in 1670. William Penn (the founder of Pennsylvania) was a peaceful and non-violent man but he was charged with preaching to an unlawful assembly. The basis for the charge was that Penn had addressed his religious group in an orderly church meeting in London. Penn was not of the same religious faith as the King of England and all of the governmental officials. After the trial, the English jury refused to convict Penn. They were ordered to reconsider their finding but the jury continued to refuse to convict. The jury was held for two days without food or water and other accommodations (fire or a chamberpot which they requested). When this did not break them, they were released after being fined for their final verdict of not guilty. A plaque can be found today in Old Bailey (the central criminal justice building in London) commemorating the "courage and endurance" of that jury. An appellate court sustained Penn and the jury in a writ of Habeas Corpus holding that juries were not to be punished for failing to make findings as ordered by the trial court.

- The defendant's girlfriend, who stated that she went to class with him. Because a girlfriend could be a very biased witness, a judge or a jury could give little weight to the testimony of such a witness.

- The college instructor, who was a disinterested witness, testified that the defendant was in the classroom on the night and at the time of the crime. Because the instructor was a disinterested witness, his testimony would ordinarily be given greater weight.

The weight and credibility to be given evidence is not necessarily determined by the number of witnesses or the amount of evidence available. Factfinders could find that the testimony of one witness was more credible and carried more weight than five witnesses. In making this determination, the factfinder would have to judge the perception, memory, and narration of the witness in ascertaining the truth of the matter.

Demeanor as Evidence in Judging Witnesses

Not only are the words of a witness evidence in a trial, but the demeanor of the witness has been held also to be evidence which may be used in determining credibility. In everyday life, we judge other persons not only by what they say, but also to some extent by their appearances and their conduct. The following ruling in the 1952 case of *Dyer v. MacDougall* [5] by Judge Learned Hand is sometimes quoted by other courts:

> It is true that the carriage, behavior, bearing, manner and appearance of a witness—in short, his "demeanor"—is a part of the evidence. The words used are by no means all that we rely on in making up our

minds about the truth of a question that arises in our ordinary affairs, and it is abundantly settled that a jury is as little confined to them as we are. They may, and indeed they should, take into consideration the whole nexus of sense impressions which they get from a witness.... Moreover, such evidence may satisfy the tribunal, not only that the witness' testimony is not true, but that the truth is the opposite of his story; for the denial of one, who has a motive to deny, may be uttered with such hesitation, discomfort, arrogance or defiance, as to give assurance that he is fabricating, and that, if he is, there is no alternative but to assume the truth of what he denies.

The Jury, Not the Trial Judge, Determines the Credibility of Witnesses

A defendant charged with a crime has a constitutional right to trial by jury. If a jury is sitting on a case, it is the jury that determines the credibility (believability) of witnesses. The following case illustrates:

United States v. Bates

U.S. Court of Appeals, Fifth Circuit (1972)
468 F.2d 1252

A witness (Jackson) changed his story after a noon recess in a trial. The appellate Court held that

At that point the jury was faced with a choice of believing one of two conflicting statements by the same witness. By instructing the marshal to arrest Jackson on a charge of perjury committed "this morning" the trial judge was in effect telling the jury that Jackson was lying in his initial testimony and being truthful in his recanted testimony. It was for the jury to determine which of the witness' stories would be given credence, or indeed whether the witness would be believed at all. The comments by the trial judge clearly infringed upon the jury's credibility determining process and appellant was thereby deprived of a fair trial.... "It is well known, as a matter of judicial notice, that juries are highly sensitive to every utterance by the trial judge, the trial arbiter, and that some comments may be so highly prejudicial that even a strong admonition by the judge to the jury, that they are not bound by the judge's views, will not cure the error." *Bursten v. United States,* 395 F.2d at 983. Accordingly, Bates' conviction on both counts must be reversed and the case remanded for a new trial.

THE CONSTITUTIONAL RIGHTS OF DEFENDANTS REGARDING WITNESSES

Defendant's Right to Compel the Attendance of Witnesses

The Sixth Amendment of the U.S. Constitution provides that "In all criminal prosecutions the accused shall enjoy t he right . . . to have compulsory process for obtaining witnesses in his favour . . . ."

In order to assure the attendance of a witness, a **subpoena** must be issued. A subpoena is a command to the person to whom it is directed to appear on a specified date at a given time and place for the purpose of testifying. In addition, the person may be required to bring with him documents or other materials that are expected to be useful in the proceedings to which he is summoned. A **subpoena duces tecum** would describe the material which the witness is to bring with him.

The right to the compulsory process to obtain the attendance of witnesses does not mean that the defendant can subpoena any and all persons he wishes in order to delay the case and to make his trial a cumbersome process. He may subpoena only competent persons who have a personal knowledge of facts relevant to his case.

Defendant's Right to Confront and Cross-Examine Witnesses

Not only does the Sixth Amendment give defendants the right to compel witnesses to appear on his behalf but it also provides that "the accused shall enjoy the right to be confronted by the witnesses against him . . . ." The U.S. Supreme Court held in the 1965 case of Pointer v. Texas [6] that

> We hold today that the Sixth Amendment's right of an accused to confront the witnesses against him is likewise a fundamental right and is made obligatory on the States by the Fourteenth Amendment.
>
> It cannot seriously be doubted at this late date that the right of cross-examination is included in the right of an accused in a criminal case to confront the witnesses against him. And probably no one, certainly no one experienced in the trial of lawsuits, would deny the value of cross-examination in exposing falsehood and bringing out the truth in the trial of a criminal case. . . .
>
> Under this Court's prior decisions, the Sixth Amendment's guarantee of confrontation and cross-examination was unquestionably denied petitioner in this case. As has been pointed out, a major reason underlying the constitutional confrontation rule is to give a defendant charged with crime an opportunity to cross-examine the witnesses against him.

For centuries, cross-examination has been considered to be one of the essential safeguards of the accuracy and completeness of testimony given by a witness. In the 1974 case of *Davis v. Alaska*,[7] Chief Justice Burger, writing for the U.S. Supreme Court, held that

Cross-examination is the principal means by which the believability of a witness and the truth of his testimony are tested. Subject always to the broad discretion of a trial judge to preclude repetitive and unduly harassing interrogation, the cross-examiner is not only permitted to delve into the witness' story to test the witness' perceptions and memory, but the cross-examiner has traditionally been allowed to impeach, i.e., discredit, the witness. One way of discrediting the witness is to introduce evidence of a prior criminal conviction of that witness. By so doing the cross-examiner intends to afford the jury a basis to infer that the witness' character is such that he would be less likely than the average trustworthy citizen to be truthful in his testimony. The introduction of evidence of a prior crime is thus a general attack on the credibility of the witness. A more particular attack on the witness' credibility is effected by means of cross-examination directed toward revealing possible biases, prejudices, or ulterior motives of the witness as they may relate directly to issues or personalities in the case at hand. The partiality of a witness is subject to exploration at trial, ... We have recognized that the exposure of a witness' motivation in testifying is a proper and important function of the constitutionally protected right of cross-examination.

After a brutal murder, two suspects were arrested. Each was charged and tried separately, allowing juries to decide which of the two men was the killer. One man was acquitted and the case of the convicted man (which follows) came before the U.S. Supreme Court in 1986:

Delaware v. Van Arsdall

Supreme Court of the United States (1986)
475 U.S. 673, 106 S.Ct. 1431

A New Year's party started on the morning of 31 December 1981 in the adjacent apartments of Daniel Pregent and Robert Fleetwood. Dozens of people came and went from the party, which went on all afternoon and evening. A great deal of drinking occurred and fights broke out periodically. Doris Epps became intoxicated and, after passing out, was placed on a sofa bed in Pregent's apartment. After a fight at 11 P.M., Fleetwood closed the party in his apartment to all but a few people. At about 1 A.M., Doris Epps' body was found lying in a pool of blood on the kitchen floor in Pregent's apartment. The two men (Daniel Pregent and Robert Van Arsdall), who were with Epps at the time she was killed, were both arrested. They were each charged with the murder in separate trials. Pregent was acquitted and Van Arsdall (defendant in this case) was convicted. The appeal in this case concerns the trial judge's refusal to allow the defendant's attorney to cross-examine Fleetwood about the dismissal of a criminal charge against him (being drunk on a public highway) in return for Fleetwood agreeing to speak to the prosecutor about Epps' murder. Fleetwood was the tenth of sixteen prosecution witnesses who testified in the defendant's trial. The Supreme Court held that the restriction on cross-examination was improper since it was in violation of defendant's Sixth-Amendment right to confront witnesses against him. But the question of whether the error was reversible ("harmless beyond a reasonable doubt") was left to the Delaware Supreme Court.

TYPES OF WITNESSES AND OPINION EVIDENCE

Ordinary (or Lay) Witnesses and Expert Witnesses

Most witnesses are **ordinary, or lay, witnesses** who are called to testify as to the firsthand information they have regarding the case before the court. Their testimony is ordinarily limited to what they have seen, heard (hearsay is in most instances excluded), smelled, and on rare occasions tasted. Law enforcement officers appear in most instances as ordinary witnesses, although some officers also appear as expert witnesses when they qualify and appear to testify as to fingerprinting, traffic matters, weapons, etc.[8]

An **expert witness** is a person who has had special training, education, or experience. Because of his experience and background, the expert witness may be able to assist the jury and the court in resolving the issues before them. The party offering a witness as an expert must lay a foundation (that is, ask a series of questions) establishing his witness as an expert in the field for which he will testify and offer opinions.

Three questions are presented to a trial court when one of the parties seeks to introduce an expert witness:

- Is the subject upon which the expert witness will testify one for which the court can receive the opinion of an expert?
- What qualifications are necessary to qualify the witness as an expert?
- Does the witness meet these qualifications?

When there is a subject upon which an expert witness may testify, the determination as to whether a witness qualifies as an expert is made by the trial judge. The trial judge is given a great deal of latitude and discretion in determining whether a witness qualifies as an expert witness. To qualify as an expert in some fields (a medical expert, for example) requires years of formal education, training, and a license. Other subject matters such as fingerprinting, handwriting, etc., require other types of training, skills, qualifications, and experiences. Rule 702 of the Federal Rules of Evidence and the Uniform Rules of Evidence provides that

If scientific, technical, or other specialized knowledge will assist the trier of fact to understand the evidence or to determine a fact in issue, a witness qualified as an expert by knowledge, skill, experience, training, or education, may testify thereto in the form of an opinion or otherwise.

As to the qualifications necessary to be a handwriting expert, the Court in the case of *First Galesburg National Bank & Trust Company v. Federal Reserve Bank,*[9] stated that

> There is no test by which it can be determined with mathematical certainty how much experience or knowledge of handwriting a witness must have in order to qualify as an expert for comparison.... In order that a witness be competent as an expert in respect to handwriting, it is not necessary that he should belong to any particular calling or profession; it is only necessary that the business opportunities and intelligence of the witness should be such as to enable him to have reasonable skill in judging of handwriting.

In footnote 12 of the case of *Miller v. California,* 413 U.S. 15, 93 S.Ct. 2607, the U.S. Supreme Court held that a police officer qualified as an expert witness as to "community standards" in an obscenity case, stating that

> The record simply does not support appellant's contention, belatedly raised on appeal, that the State's expert was unqualified to give evidence on California "community standards." The expert, a police officer with many years of specialization in obscenity offenses, had conducted an extensive statewide survey and had given expert evidence on 26 occasions in the year prior to this trial. Allowing such expert testimony was certainly not constitutional error.

The weight and effect to be accorded testimony of opinion or judgments of expert witnesses are for the trier of fact (jury or judge) to determine as to the value which will be accorded. The credibility of expert witnesses is also determined by the jury or judge as the trier of fact.[10]

Opinion Evidence by Ordinary Witnesses

An ordinary witness is qualified to testify because he has firsthand knowledge of an issue before the court. The expert witness has something different to contribute in assisting the trier of fact. Neither witness would be permitted to give his opinion as to whether the defendant is guilty or innocent because this determination is for the factfinder to decide based upon the evidence presented.

The testimony of ordinary witnesses is usually statements of fact as to what he has seen, heard, etc., but he may give his opinions and conclusions as to common things which are within the knowledge of the average layman. He may give his opinion and conclusion, for example, that the defendant was intoxicated, that the defendant was angry, or as to the value of his property which was stolen or destroyed. Rule 701 of the Federal Rules of Evidence, and the Uniform Rules of Evidence, provide that

> If the witness is not testifying as an expert, his testimony in the form of opinions or inferences is limited to those opinions or inferences which are (a) rationally based on the perception of the witness and (b) helpful to a clear understanding of his testimony or the determination of a fact in issue.

Opinion Evidence by Expert Witnesses

The expert witness ordinarily testifies as to matters which are complicated and outside the knowledge of the average person. To do this, the expert witness must have sufficient skill, knowledge, or experience in the field about which he is testifying. If the expert witness has personal knowledge of facts concerning the case, he may testify to them. The expert witness may also give his opinion based upon facts or data obtained from one of the following possible sources:

- The expert witness gives opinions based upon his or her firsthand observations. This is the usual manner in which expert witnesses testify. Physicians, ballistic experts, fingerprint experts, traffic experts, etc. in most instances base their opinions upon firsthand observations they have made.

- The expert attends the trial and hears the testimony that establishes the facts upon which the expert's opinion will be based.

- A hypothetical question is posed, made up of a combination of assumed or proven facts and circumstances upon which the opinion of the expert is asked. The hypothetical question can be based upon any theory reasonably deduced from the evidence. It must, however, select and present the facts fairly and may not assume facts not already proven. The danger with long and confusing hypothetical questions is that the jury may simply ignore the answer of the expert witness, as they may ignore the testimony of any witness.

- Information is presented to the expert outside of the courtroom upon which the expert will base his opinion to be used as evidence in court. The opinion in this situation would not be based upon firsthand observation.

THE DEFENDANT AS A WITNESS

Under the old common law, defendants in criminal cases were not competent to testify at their own trial. Only in a few types of charges (such as treason) were defendants able to defend themselves by appearing as a witness, and then only by making an unsworn statement.

Today, all defendants are competent to appear as witnesses in their trials. A defendant may appear as a witness in his own behalf or he may choose to exercise his right to remain silent. If a defendant decides not to appear as a witness in his trial, he may increase the risk of being convicted. If a defendant voluntarily offers himself as a witness in his own behalf and testifies,

- He waives his constitutional privilege of not answering proper questions which may tend to incriminate him of the crime for which he is on trial, and

- He subjects himself to cross-examination and possible impeachment,

- Which may "open the door to otherwise inadmissible evidence which is damaging to his case." *McGautha v. California,* 402 U.S. 183, 91 S.Ct. 1454 (1971) (for example, see the case of *Harris v. New York,* 401 U.S. 222, 91 S.Ct. 643, in which the Supreme Court permitted statements from an otherwise excluded confession to be used for impeachment purposes).

Additional Classifications of Witnesses

MATERIAL WITNESS

A material witness is one whose testimony is important to a fair determination of a case.

RES GESTAE WITNESS

The Latin phrase *res gestae* means "things done." A res gestae witness testifies as to the things done and facts, circumstances, and statements made concerning the crime committed.

CORPUS DELICTI WITNESS

A corpus delicti witness will testify that the crime charged was committed. In many of the crimes against a person, the victim will testify as both a res gestae and a corpus delicti witness. However, in criminal homicide, the victim is not available and an expert witness (medical doctor) testifies as a corpus delicti witness in most cases.

ALIBI WITNESS

An alibi witness will testify that the defendant could not have committed the crime of which he is charged, because the defendant was in another place at the time the crime was committed.

REBUTTAL WITNESS

A rebuttal witness is called to rebut (contradict) evidence or testimony presented by the opposing party.

CHARACTER WITNESS

A character witness will testify as to the good character of the defendant. After the defense has made an issue of the character of the accused, the prosecutor may then produce evidence or a witness who will testify as to the bad character of the accused.

HOSTILE WITNESS AS DISTINGUISHED FROM A FRIENDLY WITNESS

A hostile witness is a witness who is hostile to the attorney questioning him. Because the hostile witness is uncooperative, and not ordinarily susceptible to questions for which the

To a defendant with a criminal record or a defendant who faces the risk of impeachment by other means, the choice of taking the witness stand to testify presents serious dangers to his case. However, the U.S. Supreme Court stated in the 1971 *McGautha v. California* case (402 U.S. at 215, 216, 91 S.Ct. at 1471) that "it is not thought inconsistent with the enlightened administration of criminal justice to require the defendant to weigh such pros and cons in deciding whether to testify."

In the 1972 case of *Brooks v. Tennessee*,[11] the defendant who wanted to testify on his own behalf was required by a Tennessee statute "to testify ...

answer is suggested in the question, trial judges will ordinarily permit leading questions to be asked of hostile witnesses.

CORROBORATIVE WITNESS

A corroborative witness is one who affirms, strengthens, and adds weight to the testimony of another witness; or who affirms and corroborates other evidence which has been presented. A doctor who examined a woman who was raped would ordinarily testify to corroborate the commission of the crime.

ACCOMPLICE WITNESS

An accomplice witness testifies that he participated in the crime charged. The accomplice witness may be one of the defendants charged with the crime, or he may be a witness for the state after being granted immunity or assured that he will not be charged (or charged with a lesser offense). Because the testimony of accomplice witness is highly incriminating, defense attorneys must make an attempt to discredit the testimony and/or the witness. The Federal Court of Appeals, in the 1984 case of *United States v. Harris*, 738 F.2d 1068 (9th Cir.1984), approved of the following jury instruction on accomplice witnesses who in this case was a ''confessed codefendant'':

> The testimony of . . . a confessed codefendant who provides evidence against a defendant for . . . immunity from punishment . . . must be examined and weighed by the jury with greater care than the testimony of an ordinary witness. The jury must determine whether the informer's testimony has been affected by interest or by prejudice against the defendant.

PROSECUTING WITNESS

A prosecuting witness is a person who instigates the prosecution and causes the accused to be arrested or charged. A *prosecutrix* would be a female who causes criminal charges to be issued. For a discussion of the term, see *State v. Campbell*, 299 Or. 633, 705 P.2d 694 decided in 1985 by the Supreme Court of Oregon.

before any other testimony for the defense is heard by the court trying the case." [12] In holding that the defendant "was deprived of his constitutional rights when the trial court excluded him from the stand for failing to testify first," the U.S. Supreme Court stated that

> Although a defendant will usually have some idea of the strength of his evidence, he cannot be absolutely certain that his witnesses will testify as expected or that they will be effective on the stand. They may collapse under skillful and persistent cross-examination, and through no fault of their own they may fail to impress the jury as

honest and reliable witnesses. In addition, a defendant is sometimes compelled to call a hostile prosecution witness as his own. Unless the State provides for discovery depositions of prosecution witnesses, which Tennessee apparently does not, the defendant is unlikely to know whether this testimony will prove entirely favorable.

Commenting on the Failure of a Defendant to Take the Witness Stand

When the government presents its evidence and case in a criminal trial, the serious accusations in many cases naturally raise many questions in the minds of the jury. They look to the defense table and the defendant sitting at that table to see how the defense is going to answer the charges which have been made. If the defendant does not take the stand in his own behalf, this failure could seriously injure his case.

Before 1965, it was a very common practice for prosecutors and judges to comment to the jury on the failure of the defendant to take the witness stand to give his explanation of what happened. In the 1965 case of *Griffin v. California*,[13] the U.S. Supreme Court held that such comments by prosecutors and judges on the failure of the defendant to take the witness stand in his own behalf violated the Fifth Amendment right of defendants to remain silent.

DIRECT EXAMINATION OF WITNESSES [14]

The Question-and-Answer Method

In criminal cases, the government has the burden of proving the charges made against the defendant beyond a reasonable doubt. The state also has the burden of coming forward first with evidence showing that the defendant committed the offenses with which he is charged. Therefore, the first witnesses to appear in criminal cases are government witnesses called by the prosecutor to support the state's case.

In most instances, the government's case is presented by testimony as to the chronological order of events as they occurred. Usually an attempt is made to let the witness tell his story first with as few interruptions as possible, by using such questions as

"Where were you on the night of June 23d?"
"Will you tell the court and jury what you saw and heard at that time?"

The **question-and-answer method** must be used in American courtrooms so that the opposing lawyer may object to the question before the answer is in evidence. However, by the use of short general questions such as "What did you see?", "What did you do?", and "What happened next?", the witness is able to tell his story and at the same time is kept to the point. After the witness has presented a general account of the facts known to him, the prosecutor may then go back and fill in or emphasize details with more specific questions.

Witnesses and Their Testimony

In order to qualify as a witness, a person:

- Must have relevant information.
- Must be competent.
- Must declare that he will testify truthfully.

    To be competent, a witness:

- Must be able to remember and relate.
- Must be able to distinguish fact from fantasy.
- Must know that they must tell the truth.

    In evaluating a witness' testimony, the following factors should be considered by the factfinder:

- Accuracy of perception.
- Accuracy of memory and recall.
- Accuracy of narration.

    In an attempt to keep witnesses honest, Anglo-Saxon law has developed the following conditions under which witnesses would ideally be required to testify:

- Under oath (or affirmation).
- In the presence of the factfinder and the accused.
- Subject to cross-examination.
- Subject to possible perjury charges for failure to tell the truth.

The Forgetful Witness

Witnesses sometimes either forget a fact (name, address, type of vehicle, etc.) or forget to include an important fact in the presentation of their testimony. The following methods can be used to help the forgetful witness:

- *Jogging the memory of the witnesses.* To jog their memory and to remind them of any facts they may have omitted, signals in the form of questions may be used by prosecutors and lawyers. Examples of such questions are

    "What, *if anything else,* happened at this point?"
    "When you looked (*place*), did you see anything?"

    These questions are used in an attempt to make the witness realize that he has forgotten to testify as to an important fact. If the witness has been informed in advance that such signals will be used, he is more likely to search his mind for the fact which the prosecutor seeks to have him include in his testimony.

Qualification and Competency of a Witness

The Trial Judge Determines:

- The Qualification of a Witness
  The requirement of personal knowledge to appear as an ordinary witness.
  The requirement of skill, training, knowledge, or experience to appear as an expert witness.

- The Competency of a Witness
  Ability to perceive.
  Ability to remember and recall.
  Ability to testify and communicate under oath or affirmation.

- Questions of Law
  Rules on motions.
  Rules on objections by attorneys.
  Instructs the jury.
  Safeguards both the rights of the accused and the interest of the public in the administration of criminal justice.

As Factfinders, the Jury:

- Determines the credibility of the testimony of all witnesses. The factfinders may believe one witness as against many.

- Passes upon and resolves conflicts in the testimony of witnesses.

- Determines the weight to be given all evidence (statements of witnesses, physical evidence, etc.)

- Determines whether sufficient evidence exists to justify a verdict of guilty. (However, a guilty verdict is subject to review by the trial judge and appellate courts, who determine as a matter of law whether sufficient evidence exists to sustain the guilty verdict.)

- *Refreshing recollection (memory).*[15] Witnesses, whether lay or expert, who are going to testify about detailed information ordinarily will refresh their memory prior to taking the witness stand by reviewing notes, case files, reports, etc. Law enforcement officers, for example, should review their written reports or notes very carefully prior to a trial in which they will appear as a witness.

  If, while on the witness stand, a witness is not able to recall a fact which the questioning attorney seeks to place in evidence, his memory can be refreshed by showing (a) that the witness does not remember the fact, and (b) that something exists which can refresh his (or her) memory. The item is then handed to the witness, who reads the item to himself and returns the item to the prosecutor. The witness then testifies as to his refreshed recollection.

- *Past recollection recorded.* When a witness' memory is not refreshed after reading a document or item handed to him in an attempt to refresh his recollection, the witness' memory cannot then be used as evidence. Unless a document or writing exists which states the fact that the questioning attorney seeks to have admitted into evidence, the attorney will fail to have this evidence presented. However, if such a document or writing does exist, the document or writing may be admitted into evidence and the witness may read the document or writing to the jury. In **past recollection recorded,** the writing (or document) is the evidence. In **refreshing memory** (or recollection), the witness' memory and testimony is the evidence.

The Requirements of Relevancy, Materiality, and Competency [16]

Without the controls and limits that are set on information or testimony presented in court, trials would be much longer than they are now. Testimony about unrelated matters would also cause confusion and would clutter the factfinding process. To minimize clutter and to avoid confusion, a number of valves control the flow of trial evidence. All evidence must be relevant, material, and competent in order to be admitted into evidence. To introduce facts, testimony, or a physical object as evidence,

- The evidence must address a *material* fact.
- It must be *relevant* to that fact.
- It must be able to affect the probable truth or falsity of that fact by being *competent*.

A fact is **material** if it will affect the result of a trial. For example, the defendant is charged with a crime committed in a tavern at ten o'clock at night. State witnesses testifying that they saw the defendant in a tavern at that time would be *relevant* and *material*. Defense witnesses testifying that the defendant was at another place five miles away would also be relevant and material to the fact in issue.

Evidence is **relevant** if it has a tendency to make a material fact more or less probable. Testimony by a witness that he saw the defendant in the tavern at ten o'clock would be *relevant* evidence. However, testimony that the tavern was hit by lightning and burnt down a week later would not be relevant as the fire is not material to the case. The questions which must be asked are

- Is the fact *material* to the dispute?
- If so, does the proposed evidence have any tendency to make that more or less probable (*relevant*)?

After a witness had testified that the defendant was in the tavern at the time the crime was committed, the questioning continues:

Q: "Were you in the tavern that night?"
A: "No, I wasn't."
Q: "How do you know the defendant was in the tavern?"
A: "John told me."

The testimony is *relevant* to the *material* issue in dispute but is not **competent** because the personal knowledge foundation required by Rule 6.02 of the Uniform Evidence Code has not been satisfied. However, changing the example slightly would make the testimony non-hearsay:

Q: "How do you know the defendant was in the tavern?"
A: "The defendant told me he was in the tavern."

Since the defendant is the opposing party in the criminal action, the matter about which the witness has personal knowledge is the defendant's incriminating admission. The testimony is now competent, relevant, and material. It is not forbidden by the hearsay rule.

Objections

Under the adversary system, **objections** are the first line of defense during a trial to the evidence which the opposing party seeks to use to establish its case. The initiative and responsibility to object is placed on the opposing lawyers and not the judge. Failure to object, in most instances, is a waiver upon appeal of any ground to complain of the admissibility of the evidence.[17] The exception to this is the doctrine of plain error, which would permit an appeal when the admission of the evidence was an obvious or plain error. Objections are classified as follows:

- *Objections to the substance of the question.* These objections go to the answer called for by the question. Usual objections in this area would be irrelevant, immaterial, incompetent, hearsay, etc.

- *Objections to the form of the question.* These objections go to the manner in which the question is worded. In most instances, the question may be rephrased and asked again in a form in which both the question and answer will be admissible. Usual objections to the form of a question are that the question is leading, argumentative, calls for speculation, misstates a fact in evidence, etc.

- *Objections to the answer.* If an attorney is slow in objecting, he usually pays the penalty and is told to object faster. In this situation and otherwise, a lawyer can object to an answer and ask that the answer be stricken from the record because: (a) The answer is unresponsive to the question.[18] This most often occurs when the witness volunteers additional information beyond the scope of the question asked. (b) The answer contains an inadmissible opinion. (c) Inadmissible hearsay statements are included in the answer.

Leading Questions

Leading questions are the most frequent reason for objecting to the form of the question. A leading question is one which suggests to the witness the answer desired by the attorney asking the question. The general rule is that a lawyer cannot lead his own witness (that is, a witness he has called). Therefore, on direct examination, leading questions cannot generally be used.

However, in identifying witnesses on direct examination, leading questions are sometimes used without objections from the opposing counsel. Ques-

---

Objections to Questions

OBJECTIONS TO THE FORM OF THE QUESTION

- Leading
- Calls for speculation
- Argumentative
- Misstates facts in evidence
- Assumes facts not in evidence
- Vague and ambiguous
- Repetitive or cumulative
- Misleading

OBJECTIONS TO THE SUBSTANCE OF THE QUESTION

- Irrelevant
- Immaterial
- Incompetent
- Calls for hearsay
- Insufficient foundation
- Calls for inadmissible opinion answer
- Beyond the scope of the direct examination

OBJECTIONS TO THE ANSWER

- Unresponsive
- Inadmissible opinion
- Inadmissible hearsay statement

---

tions such as "Your name is John Smith?" present little danger of improper suggestiveness and such questions are sometimes used to get the preliminaries over quickly.

The trial judge has a great deal of discretion regarding the use of leading questions on direct examination. If the witness appears to be hostile to the attorney who is questioning him, judges will generally permit leading questions to be asked. Leading questions are also permitted in many instances on the direct examination of children, or with witnesses who are having difficulty in understanding the questions or in framing their answer. The danger of suggestion is apparent in these situations, but it is a risk that is taken and the testimony may be weighed with this factor in mind.

On cross-examination, the danger of suggestion does not ordinarily exist and leading questions are commonly used in order to test statements made on the direct examination and to test the credibility of the witness. However, there have been situations in which trial judges have forbidden the use of leading questions on cross-examination because the witness appeared to be biased in favor of the attorney who was cross-examining them.[19]

CROSS–EXAMINATION OF WITNESSES

After the direct examination, the witness may then be **cross-examined** [20] by the opposing attorney. For centuries, cross-examination has been considered one of the essential safeguards of the accuracy and completeness of testimony given by a witness. The U.S. Supreme Court held in the case of *Davis v. Alaska* that [21]

> Cross-examination is the principal means by which the believability of a witness and the truth of his testimony are tested. Subject always to the broad discretion of a trial judge to preclude repetitive and unduly harassing interrogation, the cross-examiner is not only permitted to delve into the witness' story to test the witness' perceptions and memory, but the cross-examiner has traditionally been allowed to impeach, i.e., discredit, the witness.

Purposes of Cross-Examination

The most effective defense to cross-examination is for a witness to testify truthfully and simply in answering all questions, even though the answers may sometimes be embarrassing or harmful. The purposes of cross-examination are

- To test the "believability of a witness and the truth of his testimony" (the U.S. Supreme Court in *Davis v. Alaska,* supra).
- To bring out facts supporting the cross-examiner's case.
- To impeach (discredit) the witness (which also is a means of testing the "believability of a witness and the truth of his testimony").

If a witness has not hurt the opposing party's case, there usually is no reason to cross-examine him unless there is a possibility of bringing out facts which might help the case of the cross-examiner.

Cross-examination is often exploratory, and for that reason it is risky because in cross-examination the cross-examiner can further hurt his case. In the 1931 case of *Alford v. United States,*[22] the U.S. Supreme Court stated that

> Counsel often cannot know in advance what pertinent facts may be elicited on cross-examination. For that reason it is necessarily exploratory; and the rule that the examiner must indicate the purpose of his inquiry does not, in general, apply. It is the essence of a fair trial that reasonable latitude be given the cross-examiner, even though he is unable to state to the court what facts a reasonable cross-examination might develop. Prejudice ensues from a denial of the opportunity to place the witness in his proper setting and put the weight of his testimony and his credibility to a test, without which the jury cannot fairly appraise them.

Impeachment is another aspect of cross-examination and in criminal cases is probably the most effective cross-examination technique. By use of impeach-

---

The *De Lorean Case* as an Example of Bringing Out Facts Supporting the Cross-Examiner's Case

In the 1984 *De Lorean case,* which lasted five months in California, De Lorean did not take the witness stand in his own defense. It was through lengthy cross-examination of government witnesses that evidence supporting De Lorean's defense of entrapment was made part of the trial record. Through cross-examination, lawyers for De Lorean were able to show that potential evidence was destroyed, that investigative guidelines of the governmental agency were violated, and that government agents failed to keep a proper rein on their paid informant. When De Lorean backed out of the drug deal because of a lack of cash, it was government agents who called him back, suggesting the use of collateral. When the government's chief prosecutor and the drug agents had drinks together, the defense presented the meeting as a boozy celebration of De Lorean's imminent arrest. On cross-examination, government agents admitted that they speculated as to whether they would make the cover of *Time* magazine.

With this evidence on the trial record as the result of cross-examination, the jury found De Lorean not guilty of all eight criminal charges after seven days of deliberation. The decision to not put De Lorean on the witness stand and subject him to lengthy cross-examination was probably not made until after the defense saw how successful their cross-examination had been.

---

ment, "the cross-examiner intends to afford the jury a basis to infer that the witness' character is such that he would be less likely than the average trustworthy citizen to be truthful in his testimony." [23] Impeachment may be accomplished by cross-examination and also by the introduction of other evidence. The function of impeachment may be classified as follows:

- An attack on the witness' credibility and qualifications to testify truthfully because of prior criminal conviction (and in some jurisdictions and some instances, a showing of prior bad conduct).

- An attack on the testimony given by the witness on direct examination by a showing of prior inconsistent statements.

- An attack on the witness' credibility by showing bias, prejudice, or ulterior motives of the witness.

Limiting Cross-Examination by Rape-Shield Laws

Women's groups throughout the United States have deeply resented the probing into the past sex lives of the victims of sex crimes as part of cross-examination by defense lawyers. Because of this, and in an effort to encourage the reporting of rape, most states have enacted **rape shield laws,** [24] limiting cross-examination of witnesses who have been the victims of rape and sexual assault.

For example, the Ohio rape shield statute (RC 2907.02(D)) provides that "evidence of specific instances of the victim's sexual activity, opinion evidence of the victim's sexual activity and reputation evidence of the victim's sexual

Methods of Impeaching a Witness

- By showing through cross-examination:
  Prior convictions
  Previous bad conduct
  Ulterior motive or state of mind
  Bias or prejudice
  Reputation evidence of character
  Prior inconsistent statements or writings
  Physical deficiencies (poor eyesight, bad hearing, etc.)

- By introducing extrinsic (other) evidence showing:
  Any of the faults and shortcomings listed above

- By showing through both cross-examination and the introduction of additional evidence:
  Any of the faults and shortcomings listed above

activity shall not be admitted under this section unless it involves evidence of ... the victim's prior sexual activity with the offender."

Therefore, under this type of rape shield statute, a defense lawyer may ask the state's witness if she has ever had sexual relations with the defendant. If the witness who is alleging sexual assault answers no, then no further cross-examination along this line may occur. If the witness answers yes to the question, it would then be relevant and proper for the defense lawyer to ask further questions as to how many times, over what period of time, and under what circumstances.

The following illustrate a few of the cases appearing before appellate courts in the United States:

State v. Vaughon

Supreme Court of Louisiana (1984)
448 So.2d 1260, 35 CrL 2064

The defendant was convicted of the forcible rape of a fifteen-year-old runaway girl. On cross-examination at the trial of the defendant, the girl admitted that she had voluntarily consented to sexual intercourse with the defendant both before and after the alleged rape. When the defense lawyer attempted to get into evidence facts regarding a night she had spent in a cabin with a man with whom she and another girl had been hitchhiking, the trial judge sustained the state's objection, holding that such questions violated Louisiana's rape shield law. In affirming the trial judge's ruling and defendant's conviction, the Supreme Court of Louisiana held that

> We conclude that evidence of a single instance of sexual intercourse between the victim and another individual days prior to the rape is not relevant to a determination of whether the act with defendant was

Targets of Cross-Examination

When the testimony of a witness has hurt his case, a cross-examining attorney is likely to concentrate on some or all of the following points:

1. Known or suspected biases or prejudices of a witness.

2. Motives which could cause a witness to exaggerate or distort his testimony.

3. Indications that the memory of the witness is not accurate or that his (or her) memory of the event is not certain.

4. Showing that the eyesight or hearing of the witness is deficient or defective (for example, showing that the witness did not have his glasses on at the time of the event).

5. Questioning the opportunity of the witness to make observations.

6. Criminal record of witness (if such evidence is admissible in that jurisdiction).

7. Prior misconduct of the witness for which there has been no conviction (if admissible in that jurisdiction).

8. Reputation evidence concerning the witness' character for untruthfulness (if admissible in that jurisdiction).

9. Inconsistent testimony of witness at preliminary hearing, at motion to suppress hearing, or at other times.

10. Prior inconsistent statements of witness made to police, prosecutor, or other persons.

11. Omitted facts which are favorable to the cross-examining attorney's case.

12. Bringing out greater detail on facts testified to by witness which are favorable to the cross-examining attorney's case.

13. Records, reports, or memoranda used by the witness.

consensual. The fact that the victim consented to intercourse with another man is not probative of her subsequent conduct with defendant. Rather, were the evidence to be admitted, the victim would be confronted with the accusations of her own chastity, which cannot be shown to have any relation to the crime of rape.

State v. Williams

Supreme Court of Ohio (1986)
487 N.E.2d 560, 38 CrL 2341

The Supreme Court of Ohio held that an alleged rape victim who testified on direct examination that she was homosexual thereby waived the protection of the Ohio rape shield law. Because the woman's statement was that she would not have sex with a male person, the defense was allowed to rebut the inference on cross-examination. However, the court did not permit another defense witness to testify as to his prior sexual relations with the victim and also would not permit evidence of the victim's reputation as a prostitute. The Supreme Court of Ohio stated that

> The major reasons behind the enactment of the rape shield law are to guard the complainant's sexual privacy and protect her from undue harassment, to discourage the tendency in rape cases to try the victim rather than the defendant (thereby encouraging the reporting of rape), and to aid in the truth-finding process by excluding evidence that is unduly inflammatory and prejudicial while being only marginally probative . . . .
>
> In State v. Leuin, 11 Ohio St.3d 172 (1984), a dentist was charged with gross sexual imposition for activity with two former patients. At trial, a dental assistant testified that she never had sexual relations with the dentist at the office. The state offered rebuttal testimony by a former employee of the dentist who claimed she inadvertently observed the assistant and the dentist engaged in sexual activity at the office. We held the testimony inadmissible under Rule 608(B) as extrinsic evidence offered to impeach a witness' credibility on a purely collateral matter. See also State v. Kamel, 12 Ohio St.3d 306 (1984).

REDIRECT EXAMINATION AND RE–CROSS– EXAMINATION

After the cross-examination, the lawyer who produced the witness may then conduct a **redirect examination** of his witness. Questions on redirect examination are generally limited to new matters drawn out on the cross-examination and in refuting and explaining impeachment issues. The purposes of redirect examination can be defined as follows:

- Rehabilitating a witness who has been impeached on cross-examination by explanations of matters upon which the cross-examiner sought to impeach the witness. Questions such as the following may be asked: "Officer Smith, why did you _____?" and "Officer Smith, what did you mean when you stated _____?"

- Rehabilitating by means of prior consistent statements when the impeachment was made by means of prior inconsistent statements.

During the redirect examination, witnesses may be brought to rebut the cross-examination and assist in rehabilitation. New evidence may also be presented if the cross-examiner has opened the door to new matters.

Re-cross-examination is the fourth and usually the last stage of the examination of the witness. With many witnesses, the questioning has been completed before reaching this stage. The re-cross-examination is usually confined to matters dealt with on the redirect examination.

THE ROLE OF THE TRIAL JUDGE IN EXAMINING WITNESSES

The duty of the trial judge is to neutrally preside at the criminal trial in determining questions of law and assuring the defendant of a fair trial.[25] Under the old common law, and at present in probably all jurisdictions, the trial judge may, in both civil and criminal cases,

- interrogate witnesses;
- call witnesses, either on his own motion or at the request of one of the parties.

In Most States, Trial Judges May Not Comment on the Evidence

In the great majority of jurisdictions in the United States, the trial judge may not comment on the weight of the evidence. Juries are usually instructed on the manner in which they may determine the weight of the evidence, that is, the credibility of witnesses and the weight that they may decide should be given to real and physical evidence. In only a very few jurisdictions in the United States may the trial judge comment on the weight of the evidence presented in a trial.

Interrogation of Witnesses by the Trial Judge

The authority of the trial judge to question witnesses is well established in the law. Examination of witnesses by the trial judge is necessary to bring out needed facts which were not brought out by the lawyers. McCormick on *Evidence* (2d ed., page 12) also cites cases in which jurors, with the permission of the judge, have also questioned witnesses.

Because the trial judge must remain neutral and impartial, he must be careful in the use of leading questions in those jurisdictions which forbid the judge from commenting on the weight of the evidence. The improper use of leading questions could suggest and indicate to the jury that the judge believed that the witness was lying, which would violate the rule against commenting on the evidence held in the majority of American jurisdictions. In the case of *Commonwealth v. Butler,*[26] the Supreme Court of Pennsylvania disapproved of a practice of a trial judge of questioning only the witnesses he suspected of untruthfulness, while not questioning other witnesses. The court held that

> We do not agree with the trial court's interpretation of his powers in the trial of a case. If a judge followed the practice which this judge advocated here, a practice of questioning every witness whom the judge did not believe to be telling the truth, while questioning no other witnesses, it would be tantamount to telling the jury his views of which witnesses were to be believed. Credibility is solely for the jury. Just as a trial judge is not permitted to indicate to the jury his views on the verdict that they should reach in a criminal case, ... similarly he is not permitted to indicate to a jury his views on whether particular witnesses are telling the truth.

The Authority of a Trial Judge to Call Witnesses

Whereas questioning witnesses is a very common practice by trial judges, the calling of witnesses by judges is not. However, the authority of a trial judge to call witnesses whom the parties might not have chosen to call is commonly vested in the trial judge. Again, the purpose is to bring out needed facts which should be presented.

Juries tend to associate a witness with the party calling him. Because of this, and because a prosecutor might expect a necessary witness to be hostile to him, the prosecutor might then request the judge to call the witness as the judge's witness. The witness might then be questioned and, if necessary, impeached. This practice was probably used more frequently when the rule against impeaching one's own witness was strictly enforced.

HYPNOSIS OF WITNESSES

Hypnosis of witnesses is sometimes used to improve their memories of criminal incidents. On occasions, remarkable results are obtained. The following example received national attention. In 1976, children in a school bus were kidnapped in Chowchilla, California. The school bus, with the twenty-six children and driver, were buried in the ground while a ransom attempt was made. After the children and the bus driver were rescued from their underground prison, police sought information regarding the three armed, masked abductors. The bus driver volunteered to be placed under hypnosis and was able to recall all but one digit of the license plate of the kidnappers' car. This information aided in the apprehension of the kidnappers, who were tried and convicted.

Since the Chowchilla incident, the use of hypnosis in criminal cases has increased considerably in the United States. Hypnosis is used for the following three purposes:

1. As an investigative technique to uncover more facts, as in the Chowchilla case.

2. As a therapeutic and diagnostic tool to help victims of crime to recover from the effects of the crime.

3. As a way to enhance the victim's (or witness's) recall for the purposes of testifying during the criminal trial.

Many cases have come before courts in the United States presenting the issue of whether a witness may testify when the recollection (memory) of the witness has been "hypnotically induced recollection." The Supreme Court of Hawaii, in the 1985 case of *State v. Moreno,*[27] listed rules which have been established by courts hearing this issue:

(1) Some states have ruled that the testimony is admissible, with the weight for the trier of the facts. Such a ruling was made in Harding v. State, 5 Md.App. 230, 246 A.2d 302 (1968) (since overruled).

(2) In New Jersey, a variant rule was adopted, under which the testimony was admissible provided that certain stringent criteria laid down by the court were met. State v. Hurd, 432 A.2d 86, 29 CrL 2398 (N.J.1981). (On a review of the record, it is apparent that the Hurd criteria were not met in this case.)

(3) The courts in certain states have permitted the witness to testify as to those facts which can be shown to have been recalled prior to

hypnosis. People v. Hughes, 59 N.Y.2d 523, 453 N.E.2d 484, 466 N.Y.S.2d 255, 33 CrL 2341 (Ct.App.1983); Commonwealth v. Kater, 388 Mass. 519, 447 N.E.2d 1190, 33 CrL 2048 (1983); State v. Collins, 132 Ariz. 180, 644 P.2d 1266, 30 CrL 2348, modified 31 CrL 2155 (1982).

(4) Finally, certain courts have ruled a witness incompetent to testify as to any matters covered during the hypnotic sessions regardless of prior recorded memory with respect thereto. People v. Shirley, 31 Cal.3d 18, 181 Cal.Rptr. 243, 641 P.2d 775, 30 CrL 2485, modified 31 CrL 2398 (1982).

The Supreme Court of Hawaii followed rule (3) above in the first-degree rape case of *State v. Moreno,*[28] holding that

> it is apparent, in this case, that the victim's testimony that appellant had sexual intercourse with her, was an hypnotically induced recollection, and we therefore hold that the testimony was, per se, inadmissible.
>
> We adopt the rule that a witness may testify as to matters which can be known to have been recollected, by that witness, prior to hypnosis. (We recognize, as did the courts in New York, Massachusetts and Arizona, that separating the wheat of prior recollection, from the chaff of hypnotically induced recollection, may be a difficult task for the trial court in any case and that circumstances will vary from case to case. We also recognize that in the event of the admission of such testimony, the defense may, on cross-examination and at its peril, go into the fact of hypnosis and the changed recollection resulting therefrom.)

The Supreme Courts of Alaska and Arkansas joined the Hawaiian courts in holding that once a person has been hypnotized, he (or she) should be permitted to testify *only* about what he remembered prior to the hypnosis session. In adopting rule (3), they turned down what was called the "middle of the road" (rule (2)), adopted by the New Jersey courts.

The Arizona Supreme Court held in the assault and disorderly conduct case of *State v. Mena*[29] that a "witness who has been under hypnosis ... should not be allowed to testify ..." The Court stated that

> It is generally agreed that hypnosis is a state of altered consciousness and heightened suggestibility in which the subject is prone to experience distortions of reality, false memories, fantasies and confabulation (the "filling in of memory gaps with false memories of inaccurate bits of information"). Dilloff, The Admissibility of Hypnotically Influenced Testimony, 4 Ohio N.U.L.Rev. 1, 5 (1977). See 9 Encyclopedia Britannica 133 (1974) .... In the context of pretrial interrogation under hypnosis, these distortions, delusions and confabulations are apparently aggravated by the tendency of a subject to respond in a way he believes is desirable to the hypnotist. This may happen even without any intent or awareness on the part of the hypnotist or the subject. For example, Spector & Foster state, at page 578: "The hypnotized subject may respond to implicit stimuli unintentionally emanating from the hypnotist, and unrecognized by him. The desire to please the hypnotist may induce the subject to mirror the attitude detected in the hypnotist's questions and in his behavior." ...

We realize that it will often be difficult to determine whether proffered testimony has been produced by hypnosis or has come from the
witness' own memory, unaffected by hypnotic suggestion. In order to
ensure against the dangers of hypnosis, therefore, this Court will consider testimony from witnesses who have been questioned under hypnosis regarding the subject of their offered testimony to be inadmissible in criminal trials from the time of the hypnotic session forward.

The first hypnosis case to be heard by the U.S. Supreme Court was argued
in 1987. The defendant in the case of *Rock v. Arkansas*[30] was in a different
position than defendants in most hypnosis cases. She alleged that she could
not remember anything about the killing with which she was charged. After
she underwent hypnosis to induce recollection, the trial court permitted her to
testify only as to what she had been able to remember before being hypnotized.

Because the defendant's hypnotically induced account of the incident was
favorable to her defense, she appealed the lower court rulings to the U.S.
Supreme Court, arguing that the lower court rulings violated her constitutional
right to testify in her own behalf. As of the date of the printing of this textbook,
a decision has not been handed down by the U.S. Supreme Court.

PROBLEMS

1. Fifteen years after the gangland killing of two men in Providence, Rhode
   Island, the defendant (who had escaped from custody) was tried on murder
   charges. The state's key witness was a sixty-eight-year-old man. This witness was the only person able to connect the defendant with the two
   murders which had occurred fifteen years earlier. The witness had prema-
   ture Alzheimer's disease and other medical problems. The defense lawyer
   attempted on cross-examination to show that the witness was suffering
   from a disease that affected his memory. However, the trial judge sustained
   all of the prosecutor's objections to such questions, and the only evidence
   the defense lawyer was able to place before the jury was that the witness
   had a "problem" with his memory. Was the defendant's Sixth Amendment
   right to cross-examine the witness violated? Explain. *State v. Manocchio,*
   ___ R.I. ___, 496 A.2d 931 (R.I.Sup.Ct.1985).

2. After the body of a young woman was found, investigating officers developed a strong circumstantial evidence case against Bruce Curtis. Curtis was
   arrested and charged with first-degree murder. To corroborate the significant amount of physical evidence, which suggested that the killing occurred
   during the course of a rape or attempted rape, the government subpoenaed
   an acquaintance of Curtis. The man testified that a few weeks before the
   murder Curtis had said that "if he ever took a lady out and she didn't give
   him what he wanted, he'd kick their (expletive deleted) and take it." The
   trial judge permitted the statements and testimony as evidence. However,
   the defense lawyer objected to the testimony as being unduly prejudicial
   and irrelevant. Is the testimony and evidence relevant? Should Curtis' con-

viction be reversed or affirmed? Explain. *United States v. Curtis,* 568 F.2d 643 (9th Cir.1978).

3. The defendant was charged with fondling and engaging in sexual intercourse with a twelve-year-old girl. Through cross-examination and witnesses, he wishes to use the defenses that the girl consented to the acts and was previously unchaste. There is no dispute to the fact that the girl consented, and she has had previous sexual experience. Would these defenses be permitted under the statutes of the criminal code and the code of evidence in your state? Explain. *State v. Lanier,* 464 So.2d 1192 (Fla.Sup.Ct.1985).

NOTES

[1] This statement was used in the cases of United States v. Benn, 476 F.2d 1127 (D.C.Cir.1972) and State v. Manning, 162 Conn. 112, 291 A.2d 750 (1971). Standards used years ago in the United States provided that "(a) man is competent to testify who believes in the existence of God, and that divine punishment either in this life or in the life to come, will be the consequence of perjury." Free v. Buckingham, 4 N.H. 44 (1828). In the 20th Century, the religious requirement of the oath requirement was changed by all states allowing a witness to qualify by a simple affirmation that he would tell the truth. McCormick on Evidence, 71 at p. 150 (1954) states:

"The rules which disqualify witnesses who have knowledge of relevant facts and mental capacity to convey that knowledge are serious obstacles to the ascertainment of truth. For a century the course of legal evolution has been in the direction of sweeping away these obstructions."

[2] The accusations commenced when the younger girl's mother (the child was a few months younger than the second girl) asked about marks which appeared to be burns on her daughter's arms and legs. The child said the marks were mosquito bites. The mother continued to question the girl, who then said the marks were inflicted by a gun-shaped cigarette lighter by a man (the defendant) who took her home from school. The mother then reported the matter to the police. Over the next few days, as questioning continued, the girl's account became more elaborate. She told of the other girl's presence. The second girl joined in the stories in what the judge termed "cross-germination of information." The girls stated that a five-year-old boy was also subjected to sexual abuse, but the boy denied having been a part of any such incidents. The judge concluded that the girls' accounts were likely to be the result of "layers and layers of interviews, questions, examinations, etc. which were fraught with textbook examples of poor interview techniques."

[3] See 24A Corpus Juris Secundum 1869. In People v. Sims, 113 Ill.App.2d 58, 251 N.E.2d 795 (1969), the Illinois Appellate Court held that "(a) decision of the trial judge may be reviewed, but, because of his unique position and the latitude of his discretion in this matter, his decision will not be reversed unless there has been an abuse of discretion or a manifest misapprehension of a legal principle."

[4] See 32A Corpus Juris Secundum, Evidence 1031 and State v. Davis, 504 S.W.2d 221 (Mo.App.1973). See also the case of Chapman v. State, 69 Wis.2d 581, 230 N.W.2d 824 (1975), in which the Supreme Court of Wisconsin in quoting other cases held that

... This court will not upset a jury's determination of credibility "... unless the fact relied upon is inherently or patently incredible." To be incredible as a matter of law, evidence must be " '... in conflict with the uniform course of nature or with fully established or conceded facts.' " ... There is nothing inherently incredible about a participant in a crime telling others what he did. This is particularly so where his expressed complaint is that he received none of the proceeds of the joint criminal venture. The determination of this witness' credibility and the weight to be given his testimony was "... properly a function of the trier of facts."

[5] 201 F.2d 265, 268 (2d Cir.1952).

[6] 380 U.S. 400, 85 S.Ct. 1065 (1965).

[7] 415 U.S. 308, 94 S.Ct. 1105 (1974). In the case of Davis v. Alaska, the defendant was convicted of burglary and grand larceny. A crucial witness for the prosecution (Richard Green) was a sixteen-year-old juvenile who was on probation for burglarizing two cabins. The state obtained a protec-

tive order forbidding the disclosure of Green's juvenile record during his testimony in the trial of Davis. In reversing and remanding Davis' conviction for a new trial, the U.S. Supreme Court held that "The State's policy interest in protecting the confidentiality of a juvenile offender's record cannot require yielding of so vital a constitutional right as the effective cross-examination for bias of an adverse witness. The State could have protected Green from exposure of his juvenile adjudication in these circumstances by refraining from using him to make out its case; the State cannot, consistent with the right of confrontation, require the petitioner to bear the full burden of vindicating the State's interest in the secrecy of juvenile criminal records. The judgment affirming petitioner's convictions of burglary and grand larceny is reversed and the case is remanded for further proceedings not inconsistent with this opinion."

[8] See Article VII of the Federal Rules of Evidence in appendix B.

[9] 295 Ill.App. 524, 15 N.E.2d 337 (1938).

[10] See 32 Corpus Juris Secundum 569(10).

[11] 406 U.S. 605, 92 S.Ct. 1891 (1972).

[12] Tenn.Code Ann. § 40–2403 (1955).

[13] 380 U.S. 609, 85 S.Ct. 1229 (1965).

[14] See Rule 611 of the Federal Rules of Evidence in appendix B.

[15] See Rule 612 of the Federal Rules of Evidence in appendix B.

[16] See Rules 401, 402, and 403 of the Federal Rules of Evidence in appendix B.

[17] An "offer of proof" is often made to a ruling on an important ruling on an objection or to the admission of evidence. The purpose of the offer of proof is (a) to present proof to the judge in an effort to have the judge reverse his (or her) ruling; and (b) to preserve the right to appeal to a higher court on the issue.

[18] See the 1975 case of State v. Foss, 310 So.2d 573 (La.1975) where the Supreme Court of Louisiana reversed a conviction because of an unresponsive answer by a police officer. In answering a question on cross-examination, the officer stated that the defendant had bragged to the police officer that another police officer thought that the defendant was the "king pin" of a burglary operation.

[19] See pages 9–10 of McCormick on *Evidence,* 2nd ed., and the cases cited there.

[20] See Federal Rule 611(b) in appendix B.

[21] 415 U.S. 308, 94 S.Ct. 1105 (1974).

[22] 282 U.S. 687, 51 S.Ct. 218 (1931). In the case of Alford v. United States, the U.S. Supreme Court reversed the defendant's conviction because during cross-examination "questions seeking to elicit the witness' place of residence were excluded on the government's objection that they were immaterial and not proper cross-examination."

However, for more recent cases, in which witnesses were not required to disclose their names, present address, or place of employment, see the 1977 FBI article entitled "The Informer-Witness."

[23] See note 22 above.

[24] See Federal Rule 412 in appendix B.

[25] See Federal Rule 613 in appendix B.

[26] 448 Pa. 128, 291 A.2d 89 (1972). See also the 1985 case of State v. Fernandez, 198 Conn. 1, 501 A.2d 1195 (1985), in which the Connecticut Supreme Court held that the trial judge "implicated the witness' credibility in the eyes of the jury . . . this cast doubt upon the defense theory of the case." It was held that this conduct was reversible error.

[27] ___ Hawaii ___, 709 P.2d 103, 38 CrL 2209 (Hawaii Sup.Ct.1985).

[28] See note 27 above.

[29] 128 Ariz. 226, 624 P.2d 1274, 28 CrL 2518 (Ariz.Sup.Ct.1981).

[30] The U.S.Sup.Ct. reversed Rock v. Arkansas holding that "wholesale inadmissibility" defendant's testimony was arbitrary (41 CrL 4126).

Using Confessions and Statements as Evidence

Incriminating statements are often offered for use as evidence in criminal cases. However, to be admitted for use in a courtroom as evidence, the statement must not only be relevant and material to the issues before the court, but the statements must also be obtained in a manner that is not in violation of the exclusionary rule. This chapter outlines the tests and requirements used by courts to determine the admissibility of statements in criminal cases.

THE DIFFERENCE BETWEEN A CONFESSION AND AN ADMISSION

A defendant charged with purse snatching in Tulsa, Oklahoma acted as his own attorney. While cross-examining the victim he asked, "Did you get a good look at my face when I took your purse?" Was this question made, on the record in court, a confession or an admission of guilt?

A confession ordinarily consists of statements acknowledging guilt and tending to provide proof of all the essential elements of the crime. An admission ordinarily furnishes only evidence tending to prove one or more of the essential elements of the crime, and does not acknowledge guilt. While an admission implicates the suspect but does not directly incriminate him, a confession fully incriminates a suspect.

The Supreme Court of Illinois stated in the case of *People v. Stanton* [1] that

> There is a distinction between a statement which is only an admission and one which constitutes a confession of guilt of the crime charged. A confession is a voluntary acknowledgment of guilt after the perpetration of an offense, and it does not embrace mere statements or declarations of independent facts from which guilt may be inferred, while an admission is any statement or conduct from which guilt of the crime may be inferred but guilt does not necessarily follow.

The following examples are used to illustrate:

- *An admission:* A statement by a suspect that he knows who committed the burglary which is being investigated and that he was with these persons on the night that the burglary was committed.

- *A confession:* A statement by the defendant that he committed the burglary of which he is suspected.

117

- *A full confession:* Statements by the defendant that he committed the burglary with which he is charged, with full information as to details; the name of his accomplice, the name of his fence, and other information which could be used for further investigations.

Confessions are often the prime source of other evidence in that they sometimes provide officers with information which might not otherwise be available. Confessions can clear a series of crimes, such as burglaries. They can provide leads and evidence which could lead to the convictions of the suspect's accomplices and other persons. Confessions can also provide investigating officers with information as to the extent and scope of conspiracies and continuous criminal activities.

THE REQUIREMENT OF CORROBORATION IN USING CONFESSIONS AND ADMISSIONS AS EVIDENCE

In using confessions and admissions as evidence, corroborating evidence proving corpus delicti (that a crime was committed) must be introduced. The following examples illustrate this requirement:

- A man walks into a police station and makes a full confession that he has just killed his wife. Investigating officers obtain corroborating evidence of the confession when they discover the wife's body as described by the man. The confession and the corroborating evidence would ordinarily be sufficient to sustain a conviction even for situations in which the man later denied his guilt.
- The situation is the same as the example above, except that no body is found and no evidence corroborating the man's confession can be obtained. Even if the man was married and his wife could not be found, he could not be convicted of murder unless the state can establish and prove the corpus delicti of the crime with evidence other than the man's confession (see *Ex parte Flodstrom,* 45 Cal.2d 307, 288 P.2d 859 (1955), in which a mother confessed that she caused the death of her baby by smothering. However, doctors could not determine whether the baby died of natural causes or by the confessed criminal acts of the mother. Because the State of California could not prove corpus delicti from evidence other than the mother's confession, the proceedings were dismissed).

In writing of the origins of the corroboration rule and its application to a criminal tax evasion case, the U.S. Supreme Court held in the case of *Smith v. United States* [2] that

> The corroboration rule, at its inception, served an extremely limited function. In order to convict of serious crimes of violence, then capital offenses, independent proof was required that *someone* had indeed inflicted the violence, the so-called *corpus delicti.* Once the existence of the crime was established, however, the guilt of the accused could be based on his own otherwise uncorroborated confession. But in a crime such as tax evasion there is no tangible injury which can be isolated as a *corpus delicti.* As to this crime, it cannot be shown that the crime has been committed without identifying the accused. Thus

we are faced with the choice either of applying the corroboration rule to this offense and according the accused even greater protection than the rule affords to a defendant in a homicide prosecution, ... or of finding the rule wholly inapplicable because of the nature of the offense, stripping the accused of this guarantee altogether. We choose to apply the rule, with its broader guarantee, to crimes in which there is no tangible *corpus delicti,* where the corroborative evidence must implicate the accused in order to show that a crime has been committed.

THE VOLUNTARINESS TEST

Prior to 1964, the only test (other than relevancy, materiality, and competency) used to determine the admissibility of confessions and admissions was the **voluntariness test.**[3] The voluntariness test derives from the due process (fundamental fairness) requirement of the Fifth and Fourteenth Amendments to the U.S. Constitution. The voluntariness test requires that the confession or admission be voluntarily given and is not the result of coercion or duress. Coercion and duress can be physical, mental, or otherwise. The following 1936 U.S. Supreme Court case illustrates an early use of the voluntariness test:

Brown v. Mississippi

Supreme Court of the United States (1936)
297 U.S. 278, 56 S.Ct. 461

When a murder occurred in Mississippi in 1934, the defendants, three black men, were taken into custody by law enforcement officers. By means of whippings, beatings, and the actual hanging of one of the defendants by a rope to the limb of a tree, confessions to the murder were obtained from the defendants. With practically no other evidence and with the rope mark "plainly visible" on the neck of the defendant who was hung, the criminal trial charging the defendants of murder began. The defendants were convicted despite the fact that a state witness (a deputy sheriff) admitted that brutality and violence were used to obtain the confessions. In reversing the convictions, the U.S. Supreme Court held that

> The question in this case is whether convictions, which rest solely upon confessions shown to have been extorted by officers of the state by brutality and violence, are consistent with the due process of law required by the Fourteenth Amendment of the Constitution of the United States ....
> ... The rack and torture chamber may not be substituted for the witness stand ....
> In the instant case, the trial court was fully advised by the undisputed evidence of the way in which the confessions had been procured. The trial court knew that there was no other evidence upon which conviction and sentence could be based. Yet it proceeded to permit conviction and to pronounce sentence. The conviction and sentence

were void for want of the essential elements of due process, and the proceeding thus vitiated could be challenged in any appropriate manner.

The Practical Need for Police Questioning

The U.S. Supreme Court has acknowledged the practical need "for police questioning as a tool for the effective enforcement of criminal laws." [4] The U.S. Supreme Court further stated that [5]

> Without such investigation, those who were innocent might be falsely accused, those who were guilty might wholly escape prosecution, and many crimes would go unsolved. In short, the security of all would be diminished . . . . At the other end of the spectrum is the set of values reflecting society's deeply felt belief that the criminal law cannot be used as an instrument of unfairness, and that the possibility of unfair and even brutal police tactics poses a real and serious threat to civilized notions of justice. "[I]n cases involving involuntary confessions, this Court enforces the strongly felt attitude of our society that important human values are sacrificed where an agency of the government, in the course of securing a conviction, wrings a confession out of an accused against his will."
>
> This Court's decisions reflect a frank recognition that the Constitution requires the sacrifice of neither security nor liberty. The Due Process Clause does not mandate that the police forego all questioning, or that they be given carte blanche to extract what they can from a suspect. "The ultimate test remains that which has been the only clearly established test in Anglo-American courts for two hundred years: the test of voluntariness. Is the confession the product of an essentially free and unconstrained choice by its maker? If it is, if he has willed to confess, it may be used against him. If it is not, if his will has been overborne and his capacity for self-determination critically impaired, the use of his confession offends due process." *Culombe v. Connecticut,* supra, 367 U.S., at 602, 81 S.Ct., at 1879.

The Test of the "Totality of All the Surrounding Circumstances"

In the U.S. Supreme Court case of *Rogers v. Richmond,* [6] the defendant was interrogated for six hours by at least three police officers. When the chief of police indicated that he was about to have the defendant's wife taken into custody, the defendant announced his willingness to confess. The Supreme Court reversed, holding that the trial court admitted into evidence an involuntary confession. The test for determining whether a confession is voluntary was stated by the U.S. Supreme Court as follows: [7]

> In determining whether a defendant's will was overborne in a particular case, the (Supreme) Court has assessed the totality of all surrounding circumstances—both the characteristics of the accused and the

details of the interrogation. Some of the factors taken into account have included

the youth of the accused, ...[8]

his lack of education, ...[9]

or his low intelligence, ...[10]

the lack of any advice to the accused of his constitutional rights, ...[11]

the length of detention, ...[12]

the repeated and prolonged nature of the questioning, ...[13]

and the use of physical punishment such as the deprivation of food or sleep, ...[14]

In all of these cases, the Court determined the factual circumstances surrounding the confession, assessed the psychological impact on the accused, and evaluated the legal significance of how the accused reacted.

The significant fact about all of these decisions is that none of them turned on the presence or absence of a single controlling criterion; each reflected a careful scrutiny of all the surrounding circumstances.

Because of its nature, a confession usually has an overwhelming weight in the eyes of a jury. In most cases, there is little difference in the outcome between a case in which a prosecutor comes into court armed with a full confession and a plea-bargained case in which the defendant has admitted his guilt. In both types of cases, the court must determine whether the defendant freely, voluntarily, and knowingly waived his rights before incriminating himself.

Promises

Promises may render a confession inadmissible. The test usually applied is whether the promise by a law enforcement officer was of such a nature that it caused the defendant to make the confession. Promises which could cause a confession to be held inadmissible are promises: (1) not to prosecute; (2) to release the defendant from custody; (3) of a lighter sentence; (4) to drop one or more of the charges; and (5) not to arrest a wife, friend, or other person. When deception occurs or when a promise is not kept, defense lawyers are more likely to move the court to have the confession held to be involuntary. The following cases illustrate:

United States v. Springer

U.S. Court of Appeals, Seventh Circuit (1972)
460 F.2d 1344

The FBI agent who had done most of the questioning testified that he had informed Springer "that if he were to cooperate, no promises of any kind would be made to him; however, the United States Attorney would know of the fact that he had cooperated, and the Court would also be aware of the fact that he had cooperated." In affirming the conviction, the court held that

No public policy should castigate confession of crime merely because it may have been prompted by the hope that cooperation might achieve or increase the chances of a lenient sentence. *United States v. Drummond,* 354 F.2d 132, 144, 149 (2d Cir. En Banc 1965), cert. denied, 384 U.S. 1013 (1966).

Wallace v. State

Supreme Court of Alabama (1973)
290 Ala. 201, 275 So.2d 634

The following statement made to the defendant was held not to be an expressed or implied promise. The officer said, "... if the probation officer asked if you give (sic) a statement and told the truth that we could tell him that you did." The defendant was also told that the officers could not promise him anything.

United States v. Bailey

U.S. Court of Appeals, Fifth Circuit (1972)
468 F.2d 652

The trial court found that a police officer had "pled with appellant to give himself up if he was guilty, saying it would be better for all concerned if he would do so." In sustaining the admission of the confession, the appellate court held that

from the totality of the circumstances found to have occurred in the instant case, we are unable to say that appellant's confession was involuntary as a matter of law due to psychological coercion.

Wasilowski v. Dietz

U.S. District Court, N.J. (1981)
____ F.Supp.2d ____, 30 CrL 2074, conviction affirmed 681 F.2d 811

The defendant was living with a woman, his mother, and four children. Police arrested the defendant in connection with the disappearance of one of the children. After the defendant had been given the *Miranda* warnings three times, he told the police that he would make a statement about the disappearance of the child if the woman's three other children were transported to Massachusetts to live with their grandmother. With the evidence which then became available, the defendant was convicted in New Jersey of manslaughter, unlawfully disposing of a body, and child abuse. The defendant argued that the police made a false promise because the children were not placed in the custody of their grandmother. The court affirmed the convictions, holding that

> A promise which indicates to a suspect that his legal position in the criminal justice system will be improved if he confesses is particularly offensive and likely to exert impermissible pressure on the suspect. ... A promise of benefits which in no way relates to the suspect's status in the criminal justice system may be equally coercive .... Such promises are similar to threats in that they invariably exert a degree of pressure on the suspect to speak when he would otherwise remain silent. As such, their effect is coercive. A different situation is presented, however, when the suspect initiates the exchange of promises .... A suspect willing to make a statement in exchange for a benefit, particularly when that benefit is unrelated to his status in the criminal justice system, cannot complain that he was tricked or coerced, or that his will was overborne in any way. Because it is undisputed that the agreement was reached at the initiation of petitioner, and because the promise by the police did not relate to his legal status, the court finds that his statements were made freely and voluntarily.
>
> The failure of the state officers to perform their agreement with petitioner does not affect the voluntariness of his statements. A statement which is made voluntarily is not rendered involuntary by subsequent events.

State v. Ware

Supreme Court of Iowa (1973)
205 N.W.2d 700

The Supreme Court of Iowa held that the defendant was deprived of due process of law and a fair trial when the arresting officer testified that the defendant admitted that he and two others intended to commit a robbery after the officer had told him "it would go easier if he wanted to tell us anything." The court held that the error was not cured by the trial court's instruction to the jury to disregard the testimony.

> ... we are satisfied the aforesaid "not so subtle" promissory leniency expressed by officers Booth and Foster induced the then frightened defendant to incriminate himself. ... In other words it cannot be said defendant's statement was the product of a "rational intellect and free will" ....
>
> We now hold Ware's incriminating statement was impermissibly induced. Therefore its admission in evidence served to deny defendant due process of law. By the same token he was not accorded a fair trial.

What Can a Law Enforcement Officer Promise?

When dealing with informants or other persons charged with a crime, law enforcement officers should not make promises.

- If a promise is made, it should be no more than that the law enforcement officer will inform the prosecutor that the person has cooperated.
- To avoid accusations that promises were made, law enforcement officers should attempt to have other persons present when talking to arrested persons or informants.

If an unkept promise caused or substantially contributed to a confession or guilty plea being made, the guilty plea or confession could be suppressed or withdrawn.

State v. Oyarzo

Supreme Court of Florida (1973)
274 So.2d 519

The defendant, who was a Mexican, was convicted by a jury on the charge of possession and sale of cocaine. One of the arresting officers who was a friend of the defendant testified that "... observing that the defendant was in fear, I explained to him that he had nothing to fear, that we would protect him, that we would take care of him, and I would. And I explained to him our system under American laws as far as his rights, being a foreigner."

The appellate court affirmed the conviction, holding that

The trial court and the jury were entitled to find, on the evidence presented, that one statement by a law enforcement agent expressing friendship for the defendant, was not sufficient to render involuntary defendant's incriminating statements given after proper *Miranda* warnings.

Deception and Misrepresentation

The conclusion to the April 1982 article in the *FBI Law Enforcement Bulletin* entitled "Confessions and Interrogation: The Use of Artifice, Strategem, and Deception" is as follows:

As a general rule, the courts have found that the use of artifice, stratagem, and deception by law enforcement officers does not, standing alone, render an otherwise voluntary confession inadmissible. However, the use of certain extreme forms of deception, for example, the "reverse lineup" [15] technique discussed by the Supreme Court in *Miranda v. Arizona,* could result in a finding of inadmissibility by the courts on grounds that they render a confession unreliable, violate the

---

Promises

Promises that induce

- *a confession* could provide grounds for a defense lawyer to seek suppression of the confession or incriminating admission. "Additionally, when deception takes the form of a promise of leniency ... the chances that the confession will be found involuntary, and therefore inadmissible, are greatly increased." *FBI Law Enforcement Bulletin,* April 1982.

- *a guilty plea* require that the promise be fulfilled. The U.S. Supreme Court held that "when a plea rests in any significant degree on a promise or agreement of the prosecutor, so that it can be said to be part of the inducement or consideration, such promise must be fulfilled." *Santobello v. New York,* 404 U.S. at 262, 92 S.Ct. at 499.

When a confession is used as evidence or a guilty plea is entered by a defendant, the trial court must determine in both cases that the defendant freely, voluntarily, and knowingly waived his rights before incriminating himself. The government must prove that a confession is voluntary by a preponderance of the evidence. *Lego v. Twomey,* 404 U.S. 477, 489, 92 S.Ct. 619, 627 (1972).

---

constitutional doctrine of "fundamental fairness," or have the effect of overbearing a defendant's right of "free and rational choice." Additionally, when deception takes the form of a promise of leniency or assistance in return for a confession, or is used to make such a promise more plausible, the chances that the confession will be found involuntary, and therefore inadmissible, are greatly increased. Finally, a misrepresentation of constitutional rights, such as telling a defendant he is required to give a statement, can be expected to result in suppression of the confession.

Although court decisions appear to leave considerable room for the legitimate use of artifice, strategem, and deception by law enforcement officers, the following factors should be considered before such techniques are used.

First, it is important to reiterate that while the use of deception, without more, will generally not result in a confession being found involuntary, the fact that deception was used, coupled with other factors present in a case, could have this result. Therefore, if other circumstances known to the interrogator suggest that a confession, if obtained, could be successfully challenged on voluntariness grounds, deception should be avoided. Such a case would be the questioning of a suspect particularly vulnerable due to age, experience, naivete, or mental or physical impairment.

Second, though a court may find a confession obtained through the use of deception to be voluntary and therefore admissible, the officer who obtains the confession and offers it in evidence at trial must understand that the fact of deception will probably be brought out during cross-examination. This could impact on how much weight the court or jury ultimately places on the confession and the officer's other testimony.

Finally, notwithstanding the fact that a confession obtained through the use of deception has been found voluntary by the trial court, a prosecutor may be reluctant to offer it into evidence unless its admission is deemed essential to obtain a conviction. The reason is that should the confession be found involuntary on appeal, the government is precluded from arguing that the error was harmless. Therefore, the conviction must be reversed even though the other evidence admitted at trial was sufficient to warrant the conviction.

Some of the cases appealed on grounds of deception and misrepresentation are cases in which the defendant was falsely told that

- The weapon used in the crime had been recovered.[16]
- He had been identified by witnesses.[17]
- His polygraph test showed he was lying.[18]
- His fingerprints or other evidence were found at the crime scene.[19]
- His polygraph test showed gross deceptive patterns.[20]
- Another suspect had named the defendant as the triggerman.[21]
- The test of the clothing showed defendant was untruthful.[22]
- Police concealed the fact that the victim had died.[23]
- A New York detective presented himself to the defendant (a soldier) as an army officer, stating "The Army and I want to help you." [24]

In all of the cases, the appellate courts held under the **totality of the circumstances test** that the confessions and admissions were voluntarily given. The following U.S. Supreme Court case also illustrates:

Frazier v. Cupp

Supreme Court of the United States (1969)
394 U.S. 731, 89 S.Ct. 1420

The defendant was falsely told that his codefendant had confessed, after which the accused made a full confession. Holding that the confession was admissible, the U.S. Supreme Court ruled that

> The questioning was of short duration, and petitioner was a mature individual of normal intelligence. The fact that the police misrepresented the statements that Rawls had made is, while relevant, insufficient in our view to make this otherwise voluntary confession inadmissible. These cases must be decided by viewing the "totality of the circumstances," . . . and on the facts of this case we can find no error in the admission of petitioner's confession.

Threats

Threats, by their very nature, are coercive and evidence that a threat was made by a law enforcement officer would have to be considered by a court in

Tricking Defense Lawyers

Rhode Island police were investigating the brutal beating and slaying of Mary Jo Hickey, who was found in a factory parking lot in Providence. Several months later, defendant Burbine was arrested on other charges and was believed to have been involved in the killing. Burbine's sister contacted a lawyer to represent Burbine while he was in custody. The attorney telephoned the police department and was assured that Burbine would not be questioned until the next day. However, questioning began that evening. Burbine was given the *Miranda* warnings and executed a series of written waivers. He then confessed to the murder of the young woman. Burbine was not informed that his sister had contacted a lawyer to represent him and that the attorney had telephoned the police station. The U.S. Supreme Court affirmed the conviction in the case of *Moran v. Burbine,* 475 U.S. 412, 106 S.Ct. 1135, 38 CrL 3182 (1986), holding that

> No doubt the additional information would have been useful to respondent; perhaps even it might have affected his decision to confess. But we have never read the Constitution to require that the police supply a suspect with a flow of information to help him calibrate his self interest in deciding whether to speak or stand by his rights. Once it is determined that a suspect's decision not to rely on his rights was uncoerced, that he at all times knew he could stand mute and request a lawyer, and that he was aware of the state's intention to use his statements to secure a conviction, the analysis is complete and the waiver is valid as a matter of law. The Court of Appeals' conclusion to the contrary was in error. . . .
>
> At the outset, while we share respondent's distaste for the deliberate misleading of an officer of the court, reading *Miranda* to forbid police deception of an *attorney* "would cut [the decision] completely loose from its own explicitly stated rationale." *Beckwith v. United States,* 425 U.S. 341, 345 (1976). As is now well established, "[t]he . . . *Miranda* warnings are 'not themselves rights protected by the Constitution but [are] instead measures to insure that the [suspect's] right against compulsory self-incrimination [is] protected.' " *New York v. Quarles,* 467 U.S. 649, 654 (1984), quoting *Michigan v. Tucker,* 417 U.S. 433, 444 (1974). Their objective is not to mold police conduct for its own sake. Nothing in the Constitution vests in us the authority to mandate a code of behavior for state officials wholly unconnected to any federal right or privilege. The purpose of the *Miranda* warnings instead is to dissipate the compulsion inherent in custodial interrogation and, in so doing, guard against abridgement of the suspect's Fifth Amendment rights. Clearly, a rule that focuses on how the police treat an attorney—conduct that has no relevance at all to the degree of compulsion experienced by the defendant during interrogation—would ignore both *Miranda*'s mission and its only source of legitimacy.

The U.S. Supreme Court noted that a number of state courts reached a contrary conclusion. See State v. Jones, 19 Wash.App. 850, 578 P.2d 71 (1978) and State v. Beck, 687 S.W.2d 155 (Mo.1985).

assessing "the psychological impact on the accused, and evaluat(ing) the legal significance of how the accused reacted" (the U.S. Supreme Court in *Schneckloth v. Bustamonte,* 412 U.S. 218, 93 S.Ct. 2041 (1973)). Confessions were held to be involuntary in several U.S. Supreme Court cases, in which the following threats were made:

- That the defendant's wife would be taken into custody if he did not confess. *Rogers v. Richmond,* 365 U.S. 534, 81 S.Ct. 735 (1961).

- That a friend would lose his job if the defendant did not confess. *Spano v. New York,* 360 U.S. 315, 79 S.Ct. 1202 (1959).

- In the 1963 case of *Lynumn v. Illinois,* 372 U.S. 528, 83 S.Ct. 917 (1963), the U.S. Supreme Court reversed and remanded the defendant's conviction, ruling that

  > It is thus abundantly clear that the petitioner's oral confession was made only after the police had told her that state financial aid for her infant children would be cut off, and her children taken from her, if she did not "cooperate." These threats were made while she was encircled in her apartment by three police officers and a twice convicted felon who had purportedly "set her up." There was no friend or adviser to whom she might turn. She had had no previous experience with the criminal law, and had no reason not to believe that the police had ample power to carry out their threats.
  >
  > We think it clear that a confession made under such circumstances must be deemed not voluntary, but coerced. That is the teaching of our cases. We have said that the question in each case is whether the defendant's will was overborne at the time he confessed. . . . If so, the confession cannot be deemed "the product of a rational intellect and a free will." *Blackburn v. Alabama,* 361 U.S. 199, 208, 80 S.Ct. 274, 280, 4 L.Ed.2d 242.

Threats of Loss of Job or Professional License as Affecting Statements and Admissions

The following cases illustrate situations in which the threat of losing their job or professional license faced persons who were requested to make statements which could incriminate them.

Garrity v. New Jersey

Supreme Court of the United States (1967)
385 U.S. 493, 87 S.Ct. 616

New Jersey police officers under investigation were given the choice of incriminating themselves or forfeiting their jobs. The officers chose to confess and were charged and convicted of conspiracy to obstruct justice. Statements from their reports were used in the criminal trials. In reversing the convictions, the U.S. Supreme Court held that

> The choice given petitioners was either to forfeit their jobs or to incriminate themselves. The option to lose their means of livelihood or to pay the penalty of self-incrimination is the antithesis of free choice to speak out or to remain silent. That practice, like interrogation practices we reviewed in *Miranda v. State of Arizona,* 384 U.S. 436, 464–465 . . . is "likely to exert such pressure upon an individual as to disable him from making a free and rational choice." We think the statements were infected by the coercion inherent in this scheme of

Do the Police Trick a Suspect When They Fail to Inform Him of All the Crimes He May Be Questioned About?

Bureau of Alcohol, Tobacco, and Firearms (ATF) officers received information from an informant that John Spring was engaged in the interstate transportation of stolen firearms, and that Spring had murdered a man during a Colorado hunting trip and had hidden the body. The ATF officers then set up an undercover operation to purchase firearms from Spring. Spring was arrested when he sold firearms in the undercover purchase. Spring was advised twice of his *Miranda* rights and signed a statement that he understood and waived his rights. Spring was first questioned as to the firearms violations which led to his arrest. He was then asked other questions and admitted that he had shot his aunt when he was ten years old and also admitted that he had "shot another guy once." Six weeks later, Colorado law enforcement officers went to the jail where Spring was being held in Kansas City and gave Spring the *Miranda* warnings. Spring again signed a waiver form that he understood his rights and was willing to waive them. The officers questioned Spring as to the Colorado homicide and Spring stated that he "wanted to get it off his chest." Spring then confessed to the murder and provided information in an interview that lasted approximately 1½ hours. Officers then prepared a written statement summarizing the interview which Spring read, edited, and signed. The U.S. Supreme Court held that Spring's oral and written statements were admissible and affirmed his murder conviction, holding that

> We note first that the Colorado courts made no finding of official trickery. In fact, as noted above, the trial court expressly found that "there was no element of duress or coercion used to induce Spring's statements." Spring nevertheless insists that the failure of the ATF agents to inform him that he would be questioned about the murder constituted official "trickery" sufficient to invalidate his waiver of his Fifth Amendment privilege, even if the official conduct did not amount to "coercion." Even assuming that Spring's proposed distinction has merit, we reject his conclusion. This Court has never held that mere silence by law enforcement officials as to the subject matter of an interrogation is "trickery" sufficient to invalidate a suspect's waiver of *Miranda* rights, and we expressly decline so to hold today . . . .
>
> . . . We have held that a valid waiver does not require that an individual be informed of all information "useful" in making his decision or all information that "might . . . affec[t] his decision to confess." *Moran v. Burbine,* 475 U.S., at ___. "[W]e have never read the Constitution to require that the police supply a suspect with a flow of information to help him calibrate his self-interest in deciding whether to speak or stand by his rights." Here, the additional information could affect only the wisdom of a *Miranda* waiver, not its essentially voluntary and knowing nature. Accordingly, the failure of the law enforcement officials to inform Spring of the subject matter of the interrogation could not affect Spring's decision to waive his Fifth Amendment privilege in a constitutionally significant manner.
>
> This Court's holding in *Miranda* specifically required that the police inform a criminal suspect that he has the right to remain silent and that *anything* he says may be used against him. There is no qualification of this broad and explicit warning. The warning, as formulated in *Miranda,* conveys to a suspect the nature of his constitutional privilege and the consequences of abandoning it. Accordingly, we hold that a suspect's awareness of all the possible subjects of questioning in advance of interrogation is not relevant to determining whether the suspect voluntarily, knowingly, and intelligently waived his Fifth Amendment privilege.

Colorado v. Spring, ___ U.S. ___, 107 S.Ct. 851, 40 CrL 3194 (U.S.Sup.Ct.1987).

questioning and cannot be sustained as voluntary under our prior decisions ....

We conclude that policemen, like teachers and lawyers, are not relegated to a watered-down version of constitutional rights. ....

... We now hold the protection of the individual under the Fourteenth Amendment against coerced statements prohibits use in subsequent criminal proceedings of statements obtained under threat of removal from office, and that it extends to all, whether they are policemen or other members of our body politic.

Reversed.

Gardner v. Broderick

Supreme Court of the United States (1968)
392 U.S. 273, 88 S.Ct. 1913

In a proceeding to review the discharge of a New York City police officer, the U.S. Supreme Court reversed the lower courts, holding that the discharge was lawful. The officer was subpoenaed to appear before a grand jury investigating bribery and police corruption. The officer was asked to sign a "waiver of immunity" after being told that he would be fired if he did not sign. When he would not sign the waiver, he was discharged from his job. In reversing, the Supreme Court held that

> Here, petitioner was summoned to testify before a grand jury in an investigation of alleged criminal conduct. He was discharged from office, not for failure to answer relevant questions about his official duties, but for refusal to waive a constitutional right. He was dismissed for failure to relinquish the protections of the privilege against self-incrimination. The Constitution of New York State and the City Charter both expressly provided that his failure to do so, as well as his failure to testify, would result in dismissal from his job. He was dismissed solely for his refusal to waive the immunity to which he is entitled if he is required to testify despite his constitutional privilege.

Spevack v. Klein

Supreme Court of the United States (1967)
385 U.S. 511, 87 S.Ct. 625

A lawyer was disbarred for refusing to produce demanded financial records when served with a subpoena duces tecum and for refusing to testify at judicial inquiry. In reversing, the U.S. Supreme Court held that the documents had no "public aspects" but were "private papers." The Court stated that

> Lawyers are not excepted from the words "No person ... shall be compelled in any criminal case to be a witness against himself"; and we can imply no exception. Like the school teacher in *Slochower v.*

> *Board of Higher Education of City of New York,* 350 U.S. 551, ... and
> the policemen in *Garrity v. State of New Jersey* ... lawyers also enjoy
> first-class citizenship.

Broderick v. Police Commissioner of Boston

Supreme Judicial Court of Massachusetts (1975)
368 Mass. 33, 330 N.E.2d 199

Approximately ninety police officers from Boston spent a weekend in Newport, Rhode Island, participating in a Law Day celebration. A few days later, the Boston Police Commissioner began to receive complaints regarding the conduct of some of the officers. The manager of a Ramada Inn complained of skinny-dipping in the motel pool, and screaming, yelling, and foul language. Local police were called to the Inn twice and state police once. Other complaints had to do with the conduct of some of the officers during the parade on Saturday. The commissioner's office prepared a questionnaire of fifteen specific questions which were sent to over a hundred officers listed as being absent from duty on the days in question. "As required by *Gardner* and *Garrity* (cases) ... the questionnaire provided that the officers' answers could not be used in evidence in criminal prosecutions against them." The Supreme Judicial Court of Massachusetts held that the "inquiry was reasonably related to determining the judgment and 'fitness' of these men as police officers and violated none of the constitutional rights."

The McNabb-Mallory Rule

The **McNabb-Mallory Rule** [25] is a rule applicable only to federal courts which forbids the use of statements and confessions procured as a result of delay in arraignments. Because the rule is nonconstitutional in scope, it is not applicable to state courts. However, state courts or state statutes have established local rules of evidence governing situations in which unreasonable delays occur in arraigning a defendant or in taking a defendant before a court after his arrest. [26]

Long detentions between the time of arrest and the defendant's initial appearance before a court, or his arraignment, are generally looked upon with disfavor by courts. Courts which exclude confessions or statements obtained during a period of unreasonable detention state that the rule has been established "to prevent the weakening of the resistance of an accused by the psychological pressure of being held in custody and 'worked upon' by the police in order to obtain evidence." [27]

Law enforcement officers who have made an arrest should very carefully comply with the statutes or court rulings in their jurisdiction as to the taking of the arrested person before a court for his initial appearance or for his arraignment. Failure to do so could jeopardize any confessions or statements obtained during the unreasonable delay since the statements could be held to be involuntarily obtained.

THE *MIRANDA* TEST AND REQUIREMENTS

In 1964 and again in 1966, the U.S. Supreme Court created additional tests and requirements for determining the admissibility of testimonial evidence obtained from a suspect in custody. The voluntariness test continues to be used, but today it is only one of several tests determining the admissibility of confessions and incriminating statements as evidence in a criminal trial.

In the 1964 case of *Escobedo v. Illinois*,[28] the U.S. Supreme Court did not follow the totality of the circumstances approach but instead used one relevant factor among many in the case as the single determining factor of their ruling. In reversing and remanding the murder conviction of Danny Escobedo, the Court held that a confession taken from a suspect in custody is inadmissible because the defendant requested and was denied an opportunity to consult with his lawyer.

Two years later, in the well-known 1966 case of *Miranda v. Arizona*,[29] the U.S. Supreme Court made a dramatic change in the law governing the admissibility of confessions and other testimonial evidence by requiring that

> the prosecution may not use statements, whether exculpatory or inculpatory, stemming from custodial interrogation of the defendant unless it demonstrates the use of procedural safeguards effective to secure the privilege against self-incrimination.

The *Miranda* doctrine came into existence through a divided court in a 5/4 decision. A multitude of cases since 1966 (both federal and state) have concerned themselves with interpreting *Miranda*. The following two essential requirements must exist before the *Miranda* doctrine becomes applicable:

- The requirement that a custodial situation exists (*custody* is defined as "the functional equivalent of formal arrest").
- The requirement that *interrogation* occur ("questioning initiated by a law enforcement officer after a person has been taken into custody or otherwise deprived of his freedom of action in any significant way").

When a prosecutor seeks to use statements as evidence which are the product of "custodial interrogation," the prosecutor must demonstrate the following procedural safeguards in order to have the statements used as evidence:

- That sufficient and adequate warnings were given to the suspect.
- That the suspect understood the warnings.
- That the suspect waived his (or her) rights to remain silent and to have an attorney present during the questioning.

When *Miranda* Warnings Are Not Required

1. *Miranda* is not required when a person volunteers information. The U.S. Supreme Court held that "There is no requirement that police stop a person

who enters a police station and states that he wishes to confess to a crime, or a person who calls the police to offer a confession or any other statement he desires to make. Volunteered statements of any kind are not barred by the Fifth Amendment and their admissibility is not affected by our holding today." *Miranda v. Arizona*, 384 U.S. 436, 86 S.Ct. 1602 (1966). As an example, a deputy sheriff asked a prisoner awaiting trial, "How's it going, Ashford?" Ashford answered with a statement which incriminated him. The court held that the deputy could testify as to Ashford's incriminating statement.[30]

2. "General-on-the-scene questioning as to facts surrounding a crime or other general questioning of citizens in the fact-finding process is not affected by our holding. It is an act of responsible citizenship for individuals to give whatever information they may have to aid in law enforcement. In such situations the compelling atmosphere inherent in the process of in-custody interrogation is not necessarily present." *Miranda v. Arizona*, 384 U.S. at 477, 86 S.Ct. at 1629. Consider the following examples:

   - When a deputy sheriff working in a jail saw one of two men held in a drunk tank lying on the floor in a pool of blood, he asked the other man sleeping on a wall bench, "What happened?" The man answered, "I killed the son of a bitch last night; he would not shut up." The Supreme Court of Utah held that the defendant's response was properly admitted in evidence.[31]

   - Minutes after a shooting occurred on a street, a police officer arrived at the scene. A young boy at the scene told the officer that the assailant had run away between two houses. The officer proceeded in that direction and saw a man step out of a doorway. The officer (who had his revolver out) asked the man if he had been involved in the shooting. The man answered, "Yeh, I shot him." After the man was arrested, the murder weapon was found in his pocket. The statement of the defendant and the weapon were held to be properly admitted in evidence by the Wisconsin Supreme Court.[32]

3. Miranda is not required for investigative detentions based upon reasonable suspicion to believe the person is committing, has committed, or is about to commit a crime. In 1984, the U.S. Supreme Court stated this rule again as follows:[33]

   Under the Fourth Amendment, we have held, a policeman who lacks probable cause but whose "observations lead him reasonably to suspect" that a particular person has committed, is committing, or is about to commit a crime, may detain that person briefly in order to "investigate the circumstances that provoke suspicion." *United States v. Brignoni-Ponce*, 422 U.S. 873, 881, 45 L.Ed.2d 607, 95 S.Ct. 2574 (1975). "[T]he stop and inquiry must be 'reasonably related in scope to the justification for their initiation.'" Ibid. (quoting *Terry v. Ohio,* supra, at 29, 20 L.Ed.2d 889, 88 S.Ct. 1868.) Typically, this means that the officer may ask the detainee a moderate number of questions to determine his identity and to try to obtain information confirming or dispelling the officer's suspicions. But the detainee is not obliged to respond. And, unless the detainee's answers provide the officer with

---

A Principal Advantage of *Miranda*

In 1984, the U.S. Supreme Court again stated one of the "principal advantages" of *Miranda*: [a]

> One of the principal advantages of the doctrine that suspects must be given warnings before being interrogated while in custody is the clarity of that rule.
> "Miranda's holding has the virtue of informing police and prosecutors with specificity as to what they may do in conducting custodial interrogation, and of informing courts under what circumstances statements obtained during such interrogation are not admissible. This gain in specificity, which benefits the accused and the State alike, has been thought to outweigh the burdens that the decision in Miranda imposes on law enforcement agencies and the courts by requiring the suppression of trustworthy and highly probative evidence even though the confession might be voluntary under traditional Fifth Amendment analysis." *Fare v. Michael C.,* 442 U.S. 707, 718, 61 L.Ed.2d 197, 99 S.Ct. 2560 (1979).

[a] Berkemer v. McCarty, 468 U.S. 420 at 430, 104 S.Ct. 3138 at 3145 (1984).

---

probable cause to arrest him, he must then be released. The comparatively nonthreatening character of detentions of this sort explains the absence of any suggestion in our opinions that *Terry* stops are subject to the dictates of *Miranda.*

4. *Miranda* is not required in "ordinary traffic stops." The U.S. Supreme Court ruled in the 1984 case of *Berkemer v. McCarty* [34] that both the investigative stop and a traffic stop are similar in that both have "noncoercive aspect(s)," with traffic stops usually being temporary, brief, and public. The Court ruled that "persons temporarily detained pursuant to (traffic) stops are not 'in custody' for the purposes of *Miranda.*" The reasons for this ruling were explained as follows by the U.S. Supreme Court:

> Two features of an ordinary traffic stop mitigate the danger that a person questioned will be induced "to speak where he would not otherwise do so freely," *Miranda v. Arizona,* . . . First, detention of a motorist pursuant to a traffic stop is presumptively temporary and brief. The vast majority of roadside detentions last only a few minutes. A motorist's expectations, when he sees a policeman's light flashing behind him, are that he will be obliged to spend a short period of time answering questions and waiting while the officer checks his license and registration, that he may then be given a citation, but that in the end he most likely will be allowed to continue on his way. In this respect, questioning incident to an ordinary traffic stop is quite different from stationhouse interrogation, which frequently is prolonged, and in which the detainee often is aware that questioning will continue until he provides his interrogators the answers they seek.
>
> Second, circumstances associated with the typical traffic stop are not such that the motorist feels completely at the mercy of the police.

To be sure, the aura of authority surrounding an armed, uniformed officer and the knowledge that the officer has some discretion in deciding whether to issue a citation, in combination, exert some pressure on the detainee to respond to questions. But other aspects of the situation substantially offset these forces. Perhaps most importantly, the typical traffic stop is public, at least to some degree. Passersby, on foot or in other cars, witness the interaction of officer and motorist. This exposure to public view both reduces the ability of an unscrupulous policeman to use illegitimate means to elicit self-incriminating statements and diminishes the motorist's fear that, if he does not cooperate, he will be subjected to abuse. The fact that the detained motorist typically is confronted by only one or at most two policemen further mutes his sense of vulnerability. In short, the atmosphere surrounding an ordinary traffic stop is substantially less "police dominated" than that surrounding the kinds of interrogation at issue in *Miranda* itself, and in the subsequent cases in which we have applied *Miranda*.

However, if a motorist (or a passenger in a vehicle) is arrested or taken into custody, *Miranda* becomes applicable. In the *Berkemer v. McCarty* case, the defendant should have been given the *Miranda* warnings after his arrest for drunken driving and before police interrogation after his arrest.

5. *Miranda* is not required for booking questions, such as "What is your name? Where do you live?" Such questions do not seek incriminating answers.

6. *Miranda* is not required of private persons (although a few states do impose the requirement on private security officers). Employers and other private persons could ask questions which could produce incriminating answers. Since *Miranda* is not required of private persons, such confessions and incriminating admissions would be admitted as evidence in both civil and criminal cases.[35] The issue of whether a parole officer was obligated to give *Miranda* warnings was brought before the U.S. Supreme Court in 1984: Murphy was convicted in Minnesota for false imprisonment (criminal sexual conduct). His prison term of sixteen months was suspended and Murphy's punishment was three years of probation.

> The terms of Murphy's probation required, among other things, that he participate in a treatment program for sexual offenders at Alpha House, report to his probation officer as directed, and be truthful with the probation officer "in all matters." Failure to comply with these conditions, Murphy was informed, could result in his return to the sentencing court for a probation revocation hearing.

During the course of treatment, Murphy told a counselor that he had raped and murdered another woman eight years earlier. The counselor reported this to the probation officer. The probation officer determined that this information had to be given to the police, but she wanted to confront Murphy and discuss the new problem with him. She wrote to Murphy asking him to come to her office to discuss another matter. When Murphy met with the probation officer in her office, she immediately told him of the information regarding the rape and murder. Murphy became angry about what he considered a breach of confidence and stated that he "felt like calling a lawyer." He then denied the false imprisonment charge but admitted the murder and rape. Murphy's probation was then revoked and he was charged with first-degree murder. His incriminating statements were used in evidence at his trial. He appealed his conviction to the U.S. Supreme Court. The Court affirmed the conviction, holding that the probation officer was not obligated to give the *Miranda* warnings and that Murphy could have asserted his right to remain silent even though this would have meant revocation of his probation. *Minnesota v. Murphy,* 465 U.S. 420, 104 S.Ct. 1136 (1984).

Exceptions to the *Miranda* Requirements

The *Miranda* requirements should be complied with if a suspect is in custody and questioned by a law enforcement officer in a manner which would produce incriminating statements. The following exceptions to this requirement have been recognized by some courts in the United States

1. The **public safety** exception, recognized by the U.S. Supreme Court in the following case: [36]

New York v. Quarles

Supreme Court of the United States (1984)
467 U.S. 649, 104 S.Ct. 2626

A young woman approached a police squad car shortly after midnight in New York City. She told the officers that she had just been raped. She described the man, stating that he had just entered an A & P supermarket nearby, and that he was carrying a gun. The officers drove to the supermarket with the woman and spotted the man in the store. Upon seeing an officer, the man turned and ran to the rear of the store.

The officers, after losing sight of the man for a few seconds, ordered the man to stop and put his hands over his head. Four police officers surrounded Quarles. In frisking him, they discovered that he was wearing an empty shoulder holster. After Quarles was handcuffed, he was asked where the gun was. Quarles nodded in the direction of some empty cartons and answered, "the gun is over there." The police found a loaded .38 caliber revolver and formally arrested Quarles. *Miranda* warnings were then read to him from a card and Quarles agreed to answer questions. Quarles was charged with criminal possession of a weapon. Upon motion, the trial court suppressed the use of the gun and statement for use as evidence because they were obtained prior to compliance with *Miranda*. The U.S. Supreme Court reversed, creating the "public safety" exception to *Miranda*. The Court held that

> we recognize here the importance of a workable rule "to guide police officers, who have only limited time and expertise to reflect on and balance the social and individual interests involved in the specific circumstances they confront." *Dunaway v. New York,* 442 U.S. 200, 213–214 (1979). But as we have pointed out, we believe that the excep-

tion which we recognize today lessens the necessity of that on-the-scene balancing process. The exception will not be difficult for police officers to apply because in each case it will be circumscribed by the exigency which justifies it. We think police officers can and will distinguish almost instinctively between questions necessary to secure their own safety or the safety of the public and questions designed solely to elicit testimonial evidence from a suspect.

The facts of this case clearly demonstrate that distinction and an officer's ability to recognize it. Officer Kraft asked only the question necessary to locate the missing gun before advising respondent of his rights. It was only after securing the loaded revolver and giving the warnings that he continued with investigatory questions about the ownership and place of purchase of the gun. The exception which we recognize today, far from complicating the thought processes and the on-the-scene judgments of police officers, will simply free them to follow their legitimate instincts when confronting situations presenting a danger to the public safety.

2. The **rescue doctrine** adopted in California in the 1965 case of *People v. Modesto*.[37] The doctrine, which appears to be explicitly adopted only in California, allows statements of the defendant to be used in evidence when law enforcement officers were concerned about the safety of a missing or kidnapped victim. Because the principal concern is to rescue and save the life of the victim, this doctrine has long been recognized as an exception to *Miranda* in California.

When Is a Person in Custody for the Purposes of *Miranda*?

The U.S. Supreme Court held in the *Miranda* case that "By custodial interrogation, we mean questioning initiated by law-enforcement officers after a person has been taken into custody or otherwise deprived of his freedom of action in any significant way." *Miranda*, 384 U.S. at 444. **Custody** is also defined as "the functional equivalent of formal arrest." [38]

To determine whether custody exists, most American courts use the "objective test." The U.S. Supreme Court repeated its approval of the objective test of custody in 1984, holding that the "only relevant inquiry is how a reasonable man in the suspect's position would have understood his situation." *Berkemer v. McCarty*.[39]

An investigation detention (*Terry* stop) by a law enforcement officer does not ordinarily create an in-custody situation. The U.S. Supreme Court explained that the nonthreatening character of an investigative detention explains why *Terry* stops (investigative detentions) are not subject to the requirements of *Miranda*.

The typical and usual traffic stop also does not have the police-dominated atmosphere which is the concern of *Miranda*. Therefore, traffic stops, like investigative detentions, are not subject to the dictates of *Miranda*. However, the U.S. Supreme Court added in the *Berkemer* case, "If a motorist who has been detained pursuant to a traffic stop thereafter is subjected to treatment

The U.S. Supreme Court's Record In Refusing to Expand the *Miranda* Doctrine [1]

REFUSALS BY COURT

- *Minnesota v. Murphy* (1984) 465 U.S. 420—Refusal to extend *Miranda* requirements to interviews with probation officers
- *Fare v. Michael C.* (1979) 442 U.S. 707—Refusal to equate request to see a probation officer with request to see a lawyer for *Miranda* purposes
- *Beckwith v. United States* (1976) 425 U.S. 34—Refusal to extend *Miranda* requirements to questioning in noncustodial circumstances

ONLY EXCEPTION MADE

- *New York v. Quarles* (1984) 467 U.S. 649—"Public safety," exception, which permits custodial interrogation by law enforcement officers "to secure their own safety or the safety of the public"

[1] This material was presented by the Supreme Court in the case of New York v. Quarles, 467 U.S. 649, 104 S.Ct. 2626, 35 Cr.L. 31338.

Different Views on the *Miranda* Ruling

VIEW THAT THE *MIRANDA* RULING IS A GOOD RULING

Defense lawyers and civil libertarians generally believe that the *Miranda* ruling was a great idea which should be expanded. However, the U.S. Supreme Court has held that *Miranda* is a "prophylactic" safeguard against police abuse and is not an integral part of the Fifth Amendment.

VIEW THAT THE ORIGINAL *MIRANDA* DECISION WAS WRONG, BUT THAT IT SHOULD NOT BE OVERRULED

Persons who take this view point out that the U.S. Supreme Court is generally reluctant to overturn its own precedents. They often agree that the original *Miranda* decision was wrong but believe that *Miranda* has not imposed such a tremendous obstacle to effective law enforcement as to give the Supreme Court an important reason to overrule *Miranda*.

VIEW THAT THE *MIRANDA* RULING WAS WRONG AND SHOULD BE OVERRULED

Attorney General Edwin Meese has denounced *Miranda* as "infamous" and "wrong." In 1987, the U.S. Dept. of Justice released a 115-page report arguing that "we should seek to have *Miranda* overruled." Because the Reagan Administration will go out of office in 1989, they will have to move fast to attempt to overrule the 22-year-old *Miranda* Doctrine.

that renders him 'in custody' for practical purposes, he will be entitled to the full panoply of protection prescribed by *Miranda.*"

While most courts use the "objective" test, some courts use the "subjective" test to determine whether a person was in custody. The U.S. Supreme Court has rejected the "subjective" test. The following ruling from the 1984 case of *Berkemer v. McCarty* [40] illustrates the difference between the objective and the subjective tests.

An Ohio State Highway Patrol officer (Trooper Williams) saw McCarty's car weaving in and out of a lane on an Ohio highway. The officer stopped the vehicle and asked McCarty to get out of his car. When the officer saw that McCarty was having difficulty standing, McCarty was asked to take the balancing test (a field sobriety test). McCarty could not perform the test without falling. When the officer asked McCarty if he had been using intoxicants, McCarty responded that "he had consumed two beers and had smoked several joints of marijuana a short time before." McCarty's speech was so slurred that the officer had difficulty understanding him. McCarty was then placed under arrest and transported to a jail. The U.S. Supreme Court held that

> we find nothing in the record that indicates that respondent should have been given *Miranda* warnings at any point prior to the time Trooper Williams placed him under arrest. For the reasons indicated above, we reject the contention that the initial stop of respondent's car, by itself, rendered him "in custody." And respondent has failed to demonstrate that, at any time between the initial stop and the arrest, he was subjected to restraints comparable to those associated with a formal arrest. Only a short period of time elapsed between the stop and the arrest. At no point during that interval was respondent informed that his detention would not be temporary. Although Trooper Williams apparently decided as soon as respondent stepped out of his car that respondent would be taken into custody and charged with a traffic offense, Williams never communicated his intention to respondent. A policeman's unarticulated plan has no bearing on the question whether a suspect was "in custody" at a particular time; the only relevant inquiry is how a reasonable man in the suspect's position would have understood his situation. Nor do other aspects of the interaction of Williams and respondent support the contention that respondent was exposed to "custodial interrogation" at the scene of the stop. From aught that appears in the stipulation of facts, a single police officer asked respondent a modest number of questions and requested him to perform a simple balancing test at a location visible to passing motorists. Treatment of this sort cannot fairly be characterized as the functional equivalent of formal arrest.
>
> We conclude, in short, that respondent was not taken into custody for the purposes of *Miranda* until Williams arrested him. Consequently, the statements respondent made prior to that point were admissible against him.

Because most traffic stops are temporary, brief, and public, courts using the objective test will hold that motorists are not in custody situations. However, courts using the subjective test would conclude that McCarty was in custody at the time the police officer decided in his mind that he would take McCarty into custody.

The "Bright-line Rules" of *Miranda* and *Edwards*

The **bright-line rules** of *Miranda* [41] and *Edwards* [42] are

- "The prosecution may not use statements, whether exculpatory or inculpatory, stemming from custodial interrogation of a defendant unless it demonstrates the use of procedural safeguards (warnings) effective to secure the privilege against self-incrimination." *Miranda v. Arizona,* 384 U.S. 436, 86 S.Ct. 1602 (1966).

- "... once a suspect invokes his right of counsel, he may not be subjected to further interrogation until counsel is provided unless the suspect himself initiates the dialogue with the authorities." *Edwards v. Arizona,* 451 U.S. 477, 101 S.Ct. 1880 (1981).

In the 1984 case of *Smith v. Illinois,*[43] the U.S. Supreme Court further defined the bright-line rule, holding that

> *Edwards* set forth a "bright-line rule" that *all* questioning must cease after an accused requests counsel .... In the absence of such a bright-line prohibition, the authorities through "badger[ing]" or "overreaching"—explicit or subtle, deliberate or unintentional—might otherwise wear down the accused and persuade him to incriminate himself notwithstanding his earlier request for counsel's assistance. *Oregon v. Bradshaw,* 462 U.S. 1039, ——, 103 S.Ct. 2830, 2835, 77 L.Ed.2d 405 (1983) .... With respect to the waiver inquiry, we accordingly have emphasized that a valid waiver "cannot be established by showing only that [the accused] responded to further police-initiated custodial interrogation." *Edwards v. Arizona,* 451 U.S., at 484, 101 S.Ct., at 1885. Using an accused's subsequent responses to cast doubt on the adequacy of the initial request *itself* is even more intolerable. "No authority, and no logic, permits the interrogator to proceed ... on his own terms and as if the defendant had requested nothing, in the hope that the defendant might be induced to say something casting retrospective doubt on his initial statement that he wished to speak through an attorney or not at all." 102 Ill.2d, at 376, 80 Ill.Dec., at 789, 466 N.E.2d, at 241 (Simon, J., dissenting).

The following is from the *FBI Law Enforcement Bulletin* article entitled "Interrogation after Assertion of Rights" in the June 1984 issue:

Interrogation Under *Miranda*

A suspect could assert his right to remain silent or ask to have a lawyer present during custodial interrogation. When a suspect asserts one right or the other, or asserts both rights, the police are obligated to "scrupulously honor" the suspect's request and interrogation must cease.

The U.S. Supreme Court made it clear in *Rhode Island v. Innis* [44] that interrogation under *Miranda* includes not only verbal and express questioning, but also any actions or words that the law enforcement officer should know are likely to elicit or cause an incriminating response. In reviewing cases, the focus used by the courts is whether the police should have known that their conduct would lead or cause a suspect to incriminate himself.

Rhode Island v. Innis

Supreme Court of the United States (1980)
446 U.S. 291, 100 S.Ct. 1682

Five days after a cab driver was killed with a shotgun blast to the head, another cab driver reported that he was robbed by a man with a sawed-off shotgun. The cab driver was able to identify the defendant as the robber from photos. From this information, the defendant was arrested in the area of the robbery. Defendant was given his *Miranda* warnings three times by three different officers. He was unarmed and stated that he wanted to speak with a lawyer. While the defendant was being transported to the police station, two of the officers talked between themselves of the handicapped children's school in the area and the fear that one of the children would find the loaded shotgun and hurt themselves. The defendant interrupted the conversation between the police officers and asked them to turn the car around so that he could show them where the gun was located. Defendant was again given the *Miranda* warnings and responded that he understood the rights but that he "wanted to get the gun out of the way because of the kids in the area in the school." The defendant showed the police where the gun was hidden under some rocks off a road. Using the shotgun as evidence, defendant was charged and convicted of the murder and robbery of the deceased cab driver. In affirming the conviction of the defendant, the U.S. Supreme Court held that

> We conclude that the *Miranda* safeguards come into play whenever a person in custody is subjected to either express questioning or its functional equivalent. That is to say, the term "interrogation" under *Miranda* refers not only to express questioning, but also to any words or actions on the part of the police (other than those normally attendant to arrest and custody) that the police should know are reasonably likely to elicit an incriminating response from the suspect. The latter portion of this definition focuses primarily upon the perceptions of the suspect, rather than the intent of the police. This focus reflects the fact that the *Miranda* safeguards were designed to vest a suspect in custody with an added measure of protection against coercive police practices, without regard to objective proof of the underlying intent of the police. A practice that the police should know is reasonably likely to evoke an incriminating response from a suspect thus amounts to interrogation. But, since the police surely cannot be held accountable for the unforeseeable results of their words or actions, the definition of interrogation can extend only to words or actions on the part of police officers that they *should have known* were reasonably likely to elicit an incriminating response.
>
> Turning to the facts of the present case, we conclude that the respondent was not "interrogated" within the meaning of *Miranda*. It is

Interrogation After Assertion of Rights [1]

**IF A SUSPECT INVOKES HIS RIGHT TO REMAIN SILENT, OR
THAT INTERROGATION STOP**

Based on the Supreme Court's decision in *Mosley,* the lower court decisions applying the *Mosley* rule, it was concluded that second custodial interrogations, conducted after a subject has invoked his right to remain silent, will not be found to violate *Miranda* so long as the following guidelines are met:

- The subject's initial invocation of his right to remain silent is immediately honored;

- A significant period of time elapses before a second custodial interrogation is attempted; and

- The subject is readvised of his rights and provides a waiver at the beginning of the second interrogation.

**IF A SUSPECT INVOKES HIS RIGHT TO A LAWYER RATHER
THAN HIS RIGHT TO REMAIN SILENT**

Where a subject invokes the right to counsel rather than the right to remain silent, the Supreme Court's decision in *Edwards* provides that a police-initiated second custodial interrogation cannot be attempted until counsel has been made available to the defendant. Although the Supreme Court has not clarified what it meant by counsel being "made available," the following suggestions are offered to investigators:

- *Edwards* does not prevent a police officer from recontacting a subject for the limited purpose of determining whether he has had access to an attorney;

- If during such a recontact the accused says that either he has not had the opportunity to consult with counsel or he has done so and decided not to answer questions, all efforts to seek a waiver of rights and to interrogate should cease; and

- If during the limited recontact the accused states that either he has consulted with counsel or he has had the opportunity to do so but decided not to take advantage of it, a

undisputed that the first prong of the definition of "interrogation" was not satisfied, for the conversation between Patrolmen Gleckman and McKenna included no express questioning of the respondent. Rather, that conversation was, at least in form, nothing more than a dialogue between the two officers to which no response from the respondent was invited.

Moreover, it cannot be fairly concluded that the respondent was subjected to the "functional equivalent" of questioning. It cannot be said, in short, that Patrolmen Gleckman and McKenna should have known that their conversation was reasonably likely to elicit an incriminating response from the respondent. There is nothing in the record to suggest that the officers were aware that the respondent was peculiarly susceptible to an appeal to his conscience concerning the safety of handicapped children. Nor is there anything in the record to

second interrogation can be conducted, so long as the subject is willing to waive his rights and answer questions.

WHEN A SUSPECT INITIATES A SECOND INTERROGATION

- The special rules announced by the Supreme Court in *Mosley* and *Edwards* do not apply where the subject initiates the second interrogation.

- A subject will not be found to have initiated a second interrogation where the initiation is preceded by police actions or comments that equate with interrogation. General conversations with a subject about matters unrelated to his case do not constitute interrogation. Where these conversations relate to the subject's case, the courts differ as to how far the police can go before the conversation is found to be interrogation. Because of this uncertainty, officers should refrain from making any statements that could later be interpreted as an attempt to elicit an incriminating response from the subject.

- Not all statements will be interpreted as showing a willingness on the part of the defendant to resume questioning, i.e., a request to use the telephone or for a glass of water will not be viewed as a desire on the part of the defendant to continue the interrogation.

- Before proceeding with a subject-initiated second interrogation, the subject should be readvised of his rights and a waiver obtained.

- If the subject again invokes his rights, the second interrogation must cease.

[1] This material is taken from the June 1984 issue of the *FBI Law Enforcement Bulletin*. Cases cited are Michigan v. Mosley, 423 U.S. 96, 96 S.Ct. 321 (1975), and Arizona v. Edwards, 451 U.S. 477, 101 S.Ct. 3128 (1981).

suggest that the police knew that the respondent was unusually disoriented or upset at the time of his arrest.

State v. Young

Court of Appeals of North Carolina (1983)
65 N.C.App. 346, 309 S.E.2d 268

After the defendant was arrested on an unrelated charge, but before he was given the *Miranda* warnings, a deputy sheriff walked into the room where defendant was being held, holding up a pocketbook.

> Officer: "I wonder whose this is."
> Defendant: "It ain't mine. You didn't get it from me."
> Officer: "I wonder whose this is."
> Defendant: "It ain't mine."
> Officer: "It's yours or Duke's one."
> Defendant: "It's mine, I'm not going to get Duke in trouble."

The officer then searched the pocketbook and found LSD and marijuana. Defendant's conviction for possession of these drugs was reversed, holding that neither the drugs nor the statement admitting ownership could be used as evidence. The court held that the statement by the officer "was such that there was a reasonable possibility that they might invoke a response from the defendant.

State v. Uganiza

Supreme Court of Hawaii (1985)
___ Hawaii ___, 702 P.2d 1352

The defendant had asserted his right to remain silent and was being held in jail. He asked the sergeant (turnkey) of the jail why he was being held. The sergeant showed the defendant the written statements of several witnesses and explained how they incriminated the defendant. The defendant stated that he wished to explain. He was given *Miranda* warnings again, waived his rights, and made a formal confession. The Court held that this confession could not be used in evidence, ruling that

> It is uncontradicted that the Defendant told the turnkey that he did not wish to make a statement thereby invoking his right to remain silent. The issue presented is whether subsequent interrogation ceased. The test to determine interrogation is whether the police officer should have known that his questions, words, or actions were reasonably likely to elicit an incriminating response ....
> Here, the police officer should have known that the presentation of apparently overwhelming inculpatory evidence in the form of written witnesses' statements and oral explanations of them was reasonably likely to elicit such a response from the Defendant. This conduct constituted interrogation, thus violating Defendant's asserted constitutional rights.

(For a similar case, see *State v. Quinn,* 64 Md.App. 668, 498 A.2d 676 (1985); in which, after the defendant asked for an attorney, the officer showed him an "Application for Statement of Charges," which stated that several codefendants of Quinn had implicated him as the instigator of the robbery." In holding that the following confession could not be used as evidence, the court stated, "What the trooper did was innovative; it was also impermissible.")

The Cat-Out-of-the-Bag Problem

A suspect in custody answers a question during police interrogation and "lets the cat out of the bag" as to his guilt. The confession or incriminating statements are voluntarily given, but the suspect has not been given the *Miranda* warnings. The suspect has not asked for a lawyer or stated that he wishes to remain silent.

Can *Miranda* warnings then be given after the cat is out of the bag? If the suspect then waives his rights (after stating that he understands his rights), would the second confession be admissible as evidence? The following cat-out-of-the-bag case was argued before the U.S. Supreme Court in 1985:

Oregon v. Elstad

Supreme Court of the United States (1985)
470 U.S. 298, 105 S.Ct. 1285

Deputy sheriffs had a warrant to arrest Michael Elstad for burglary. They went to his parent's home, where the eighteen-year-old lived. After they had arrested Michael and asked him to get dressed, they questioned him in regard to the burglary without first giving him the *Miranda* warnings. Elstad admitted being party to the crime of burglary by stating, "Yes, I was there." An hour after arriving at the sheriff's department, Elstad was given the *Miranda* warnings for the first time. Elstad gave a full statement of his involvement in the burglary of $150,000 in goods. After Elstad's confession was typed, he reviewed the document, made corrections, and signed it. Elstad was charged and convicted of first-degree burglary. However, the conviction was reversed because the signed confession was used as evidence. The Court of Appeals held that the second confession was tainted by the improperly obtained first admission. The U.S. Supreme Court reversed, holding that

> Far from establishing a rigid rule, we direct courts to avoid one; there is no warrant for presuming coercive effect where the suspect's initial inculpatory statement, though technically in violation of *Miranda,* was voluntary. The relevant inquiry is whether, in fact, the second statement was also voluntarily made. As in any such inquiry, the finder of fact must examine the surrounding circumstances and the entire course of police conduct with respect to the suspect in evaluating the voluntariness of his statements. The fact that a suspect chooses to speak after being informed of his rights is, of course, highly probative. We find that the dictates of *Miranda* and the goals of the Fifth Amendment proscription against use of compelled testimony are fully satisfied in the circumstances of this case by barring use of the unwarned statement in the case in chief. No further purpose is served by imputing "taint" to subsequent statements obtained pursuant to a voluntary and knowing waiver. We hold today that a suspect who has once responded to unwarned yet uncoercive questioning is not there-

by disabled from waiving his rights and confessing after he has been given the requisite *Miranda* warnings.

The judgment of the Court of Appeals of Oregon is reversed, and the case is remanded for further proceedings not inconsistent with this opinion.

It is so ordered.

THE *MASSIAH* LIMITATION

The Case of *Massiah v. United States*

Law enforcement officers may continue investigations after a defendant has been charged with a crime or indicted. The purpose of such investigations would be to develop further evidence of the crime with which the defendant is charged or evidence of other crimes which the defendant may also have committed.

In the 1964 case of *Massiah v. United States,* the U.S. Supreme Court imposed constitutional limitations upon the manner in which such investigations are conducted after a defendant has been charged or indicted.

The facts and ruling in the *Massiah* case are as follows:

Massiah v. United States

Supreme Court of the United States (1964)
377 U.S. 201, 84 S.Ct. 1199

The defendant (a merchant seaman) and a man named Colson were charged with importing, concealing, and facilitating the sale of cocaine. The defendants were indicted for these offenses and released on bail. A few days later, and without Massiah's knowledge, Colson agreed to cooperate with the federal agents and permitted a radio transmitter to be installed under the front seat of his automobile. Then, according to a prearranged plan, Colson carried on a lengthy conversation with Massiah while federal agents listened in another car a short distance away. At Massiah's trial, one of the federal agents testified as to the incriminating statements he overheard by means of the radio transmitter. Although this investigative technique and procedure is a permissible means of obtaining evidence before suspects are indicted or charged (see chapter 15), the U.S. Supreme Court held that Massiah's Fifth and Sixth Amendment rights were violated, because he had already been indicted and was awaiting trial. In reversing Massiah's conviction, the Court held that

Here we deal not with a state court conviction, but with a federal case, where the specific guarantee of the Sixth Amendment directly applies: We hold that the petitioner was denied the basic protections of that guarantee when there was used against him at his trial evidence of his own incriminating words, which federal agents had deliberately elicited from him after he had been indicted and in the absence of his counsel. . . .

. . . We do not question that in this case, as in many cases, it was entirely proper to continue an investigation of the suspected criminal activities of the defendant and his alleged confederates, even though the defendant had already been indicted. All that we hold is that the defendant's own incriminating statements, obtained by federal agents under the circumstances here disclosed, could not constitutionally be used by the prosecution as evidence against *him* at his trial.

Reversed.

Brewer v. Williams [45]

Supreme Court of the United States (1977)
430 U.S. 387, 97 S.Ct. 1232

Soon after a ten-year-old Des Moines (Iowa) girl disappeared after going to a washroom in a YMCA, the defendant became the prime suspect. The defendant lived in the YMCA and had recently escaped from a mental hospital. A fourteen-year-old boy had seen the defendant carrying a bundle wrapped in a blanket and had held the YMCA door open for the defendant. The boy also opened the door to the defendant's automobile for him and stated that he "saw two legs in it (the bundle) and they were skinny and white." Before any action could be taken, Williams drove away and the next day his car was found abandoned in Davenport, Iowa, 160 miles from Des Moines. A warrant was then issued for his arrest on the charge of abduction.

When the defendant surrendered to the police through a lawyer, he was charged, arraigned, and committed to jail in Davenport. Before being transported back to Des Moines, he was advised by two attorneys not to make any statements to the police. The Des Moines police officers who transported the defendant by car were reported to have agreed not to question Williams during the trip.

During the 160-mile trip, Williams stated that "(w)hen I get to Des Moines and see Mr. McKnight (lawyer), I am going to tell you the whole story." One officer, however, delivered what is called the "Christmas burial speech," which said in part

since we will be going right past the area on the way into Des Moines, I feel that we could stop and locate the body, that the parents of this little girl should be entitled to a Christian burial for the little girl who was snatched away from them on Christmas Eve and murdered.

Williams then directed the officers to the spot where the victim's body was buried. In Williams' trial for murder, all of the evidence obtained during the automobile trip was permitted to be used as evidence. The trial judge and the Supreme Court of Iowa held that Williams had "waived his right to have an attorney present during the giving of such information." A federal district court, however, disagreed and the U.S. Supreme Court also held that it was error to use the evidence of how the girl's body was recovered. In ordering a new trial, the Court held that

The circumstances of this case are ... constitutionally indistinguish-able from those presented in *Massiah v. United States.* The petitioner in that case was indicted for violating the federal narcotics law. He retained a lawyer, pleaded not guilty, and was released on bail. While he was free on bail a federal agent succeeded by surreptitious means in listening to incriminating statements made by him. Evidence of these statements was introduced against the petitioner at his trial, and he was convicted. This Court reversed the conviction, holding "that the petitioner was denied the basic protections of that guarantee [the right to counsel] when there was used against him at his trial evidence of his own incriminating words, which federal agents had deliberately solicited from him after he had been indicted and in the absence of his counsel." 377 U.S., at 206.

That the incriminating statements were elicited surreptitiously in the *Massiah* case, and otherwise here, is constitutionally irrele-vant.... Rather, the clear rule of *Massiah* is that once adversary proceedings have commenced against an individual, he has a right to legal representation when the government interrogates him. It thus requires no wooden or technical application of the *Massiah* doctrine to conclude that Williams was entitled to the assistance of counsel guaranteed to him by the Sixth and Fourteenth Amendments.

The *Massiah* Problem

The *Massiah* problem (and violation) occurs under the following circumstances:

- The defendant has been formally charged with a crime and is waiting for the date of his trial (he is either out on bail or is being held in custody).
- Law enforcement officers seek further evidence in the form of incriminating statements.
- If the government interrogates him without legal representation, the state-ment obtained under these circumstances cannot be used as evidence.

IMPEACHMENT AND *MIRANDA*

A Defendant Does Not Have a Right to Commit Perjury

In 1971 the case of *Harris v. New York* [46] came before the U.S. Supreme Court. In that case, the defendant was charged with "twice selling heroin to an undercover police officer." After the defendant's arrest, he made incriminating statements which were held to be inadmissible under the *Miranda* doctrine. At the defendant's trial, the statements were not used in the presentation of the state's case but the police officer testified in detail as to the two purchases of heroin he made from the defendant. The defendant took the stand in his own defense and claimed that the substance he sold the officer was "baking pow-der and part of a scheme to defraud the purchaser."

The trial judge permitted the prosecutor to use statements made by the defendant after his arrest to impeach his testimony before the jury, and in-structed the jury that the statements "could be considered only in passing on petitioner's credibility and not as evidence of guilt." The U.S. Supreme Court affirmed the use of the statements for impeachment purposes, holding that [47]

> Every criminal defendant is privileged to testify in his own defense, or to refuse to do so. But that privilege cannot be construed to include the right to commit perjury.... Having voluntarily taken the stand, petitioner was under an obligation to speak truthfully and accurately, and the prosecution here did no more than utilize the traditional truth-testing devices of the adversary process. Had inconsistent statements been made by the accused to some third person, it could hardly be contended that the conflict could not be laid before the jury by way of cross-examination and impeachment.
>
> The shield provided by *Miranda* cannot be perverted into a license to use perjury by way of a defense, free from the risk of confrontation with prior inconsistent utterances. We hold, therefore, that petitioner's credibility was appropriately impeached by use of his earlier conflicting statements.
>
> Affirmed.

Oregon v. Hass

Supreme Court of the United States (1975)
420 U.S. 714, 95 S.Ct. 1215

> The defendant was arrested at his home for burglary. He was given the *Miranda* warnings and made an incriminating statement before he stated that he was in "a lot of trouble" and would like to telephone his attorney. The officer told him that he could telephone the lawyer "as soon as we got to the office." Before arriving at the police station, the defendant made other incriminating statements. The trial court ruled that these later incriminating statements were inadmissible. In his testimony as a witness in his trial, the defendant made statements contrary to the inadmissible statements. Holding that the inadmissible statements were admissible solely for impeachment purposes, the U.S. Supreme Court ruled that

> We are, after all, always engaged in a search for truth in a criminal case so long as the search is surrounded with the safeguards provided by our Constitution. There is no evidence or suggestion that Hass' statements to Officer Osterholme on the way to Moyina Heights were involuntary or coerced. He properly sensed, to be sure, that he was in "trouble"; but the pressure on him was no greater than that on any person in like custody or under inquiry by any investigating officer....
>
> We therefore hold that the Oregon appellate courts were in error when they ruled that Officer Osterholme's testimony on rebuttal was inadmissible on Fifth and Fourteenth Amendment grounds for purposes of Hass' impeachment. The judgment of the Supreme Court of Oregon is reversed.
>
> It is so ordered.
>
> Reversed.

Using a Defendant's Silence to Impeach His Credibility

After a person has been taken into custody or is under arrest, he has a Fifth Amendment right to remain silent and has no duty or obligation to speak. For example, in the 1965 case of *Griffin v. California*,[48] the U.S. Supreme Court held that comments by the prosecutor and the trial judge on the failure of the defendant to take the witness stand and to testify in his criminal case was a violation of the self-incrimination clause of the Fifth Amendment. Other cases having to do with defendant remaining silent are as follows:

United States v. Hale

Supreme Court of the United States (1975)
422 U.S. 171, 95 S.Ct. 2133

The defendant was arrested for robbery and identified by the victim as one of the robbers. The defendant was taken to the police station, given the *Miranda* warnings and searched. The sum of $158 in cash was found in his possession. Because the victim had lost $96, an officer asked the defendant, "Where did you get the money?" The defendant made no response to the officer's question. At his trial, the defendant stated on the witness stand that he ran when police officers approached him on the day of the robbery because he had narcotics in his possession, and that his estranged wife had given him $150 from her welfare check to purchase money orders for her. On cross-examination, the prosecutor caused the defendant to admit that he had not offered this explanation of his possession of the money to the police at the time of his arrest. The U.S. Supreme Court ordered a new trial, holding that the defendant's silence could not be used to impeach him, stating that

> A basic rule of evidence provides that prior inconsistent statements may be used to impeach the credibility of a witness. As a preliminary matter, however, the court must be persuaded that the statements are indeed inconsistent.... If the Government fails to establish a threshold inconsistency between silence at the police station and later exculpatory testimony at trial, proof of silence lacks any significant probative value and must therefore be excluded.
>
> In most circumstances silence is so ambiguous that it is of little probative force. For example, silence is commonly thought to lack probative value on the question of whether a person has expressed tacit agreement or disagreement with contemporaneous statements of others.... Silence gains more probative weight where it persists in the face of accusation, since it is assumed in such circumstances that the accused would be more likely than not to dispute an untrue accusation. Failure to contest an assertion, however, is considered evidence of acquiescence only if it would have been natural under the circumstances to object to the assertion in question ... the situation of an arrestee is very different, for he is under no duty to speak and, as in this case, has ordinarily been advised by government authorities

only moments earlier that he has a right to remain silent, and that anything he does say can and will be used against him in court . . . .

Not only is evidence of silence at the time of arrest generally not very probative of a defendant's credibility, but it also has a significant potential for prejudice. The danger is that the jury is likely to assign much more weight to the defendant's previous silence than is warranted. And permitting the defendant to explain the reasons for his silence is unlikely to overcome the strong negative inference that the jury is likely to draw from the fact that the defendant remained silent at the time of his arrest.

In the 1980 case of *Jenkins v. Anderson*,[49] the U.S. Supreme Court permitted a prosecutor to use silence to impeach a defendant charged with murder when he took the witness stand in his own defense. The Court held that

> Our decision today does not force any state court to allow impeachment through the use of prearrest silence. Each jurisdiction remains free to formulate evidentiary rules defining the situations in which silence is viewed as more probative then prejudicial. We merely conclude that the use of prearrest silence to impeach a defendant's credibility does not violate the Constitution. The judgment of the Court of Appeals is Affirmed.

THE *BRUTON* RULE

Witnesses May Use Their Privilege Against Self-Incrimination While on the Witness Stand

A witness (other than the defendant) may assert his or her privilege to remain silent while on the witness stand if the answer to a question would tend to incriminate them. Prosecutors should not call a witness who he (or she) knows will claim their Fifth Amendment privilege. The American Bar Association Standards provide that [50]

> A prosecutor should not call a witness who he knows will claim a privilege not to testify, for the purpose of impressing upon the jury the fact of the claim of privilege. In some instances, as defined in the Code of Professional Responsibility, doing so will constitute unprofessional conduct.

The following cases illustrate:

Douglas v. Alabama

Supreme Court of the United States (1965)
380 U.S. 415, 85 S.Ct. 1074

A man by the name of Lloyd had told police officers that Douglas had fired a shotgun at another man. However, after Lloyd was also charged with the

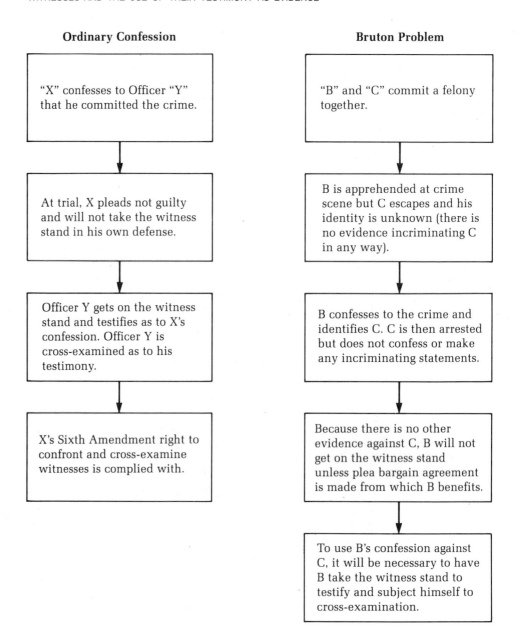

**Figure 5.1   Examples of an Ordinary Confession and
the Bruton Problem**

offense, he denied his confession. With no other direct evidence incriminating Douglas, the state proceeded but charged Douglas and Lloyd separately. When the state called Lloyd as a witness in Douglas' trial, Lloyd invoked his Fifth Amendment privilege and refused to answer any questions. The U.S. Supreme Court reversed and remanded Douglas' conviction, holding that

In the circumstances of this case, petitioner's inability to cross-examine Lloyd as to the alleged confession plainly denied him the right of cross-examination secured by the Confrontation Clause. Lloyd's alleged statement that the petitioner fired the shotgun constituted the only direct evidence that he had done so; coupled with the description of the circumstances surrounding the shooting, this formed a crucial link in the proof both of petitioner's act and of the requisite intent to murder. Although the Solicitor's reading of Lloyd's alleged statement, and Lloyd's refusals to answer, were not technically testimony, the Solicitor's reading may well have been the equivalent in the jury's mind of testimony that Lloyd in fact made the statement; and Lloyd's reliance upon the privilege created a situation in which the jury might improperly infer both that the statement had been made and that it was true.

Bruton v. United States

Supreme Court of the United States (1968)
391 U.S. 123, 88 S.Ct. 1620

The defendant (Bruton) and a codefendant (Evans) were tried together and convicted of armed postal robbery. Evans had confessed and admitted that he had an accomplice whom he would not name. The confession was used as evidence against Evans and the trial judge "instructed the jury that although Evans' confession was competent evidence against Evans it was inadmissible hearsay against petitioner (Bruton) and therefore had to be disregarded in determining petitioner's (Bruton's) guilt or innocence." In reversing Bruton's conviction, the U.S. Supreme Court held that

Here the introduction of Evans' confession posed a substantial threat to petitioner's right to confront the witnesses against him, and this is a hazard we cannot ignore. Despite the concededly clear instructions to the jury to disregard Evans' inadmissible hearsay evidence inculpating petitioner, in the context of a joint trial we cannot accept limiting instructions as an adequate substitute for petitioner's constitutional right of cross-examination. The effect is the same as if there had been no instruction at all. . . .
Reversed.

Solutions to the *Bruton* Problem

Law enforcement officers and prosecutors who have a *Bruton* problem have the following options available to them:

- If there is sufficient reliable evidence to convict all of the defendants without using one of the defendants as a witness, go to trial on that basis.

The Four Major Tests and Requirements Controlling the Admissibility of Statements

In addition to the requirements of relevancy, materiality, and competency, the major tests controlling the admissibility of statements as evidence are

- *Voluntariness test* which requires that statements or a guilty plea be freely and voluntarily given. This test and requirement exists during all stages of criminal proceedings.

- *Miranda requirements* become applicable only after a suspect is in custody, and before police interrogation.

- A *Massiah violation* occurs if a suspect charged with a crime is questioned in violation of his or her Sixth Amendment right to an attorney.

- A *Bruton violation* occurs if an incriminating statement is admitted for use during a criminal trial without permitting the incriminated person his or her Sixth Amendment right to cross-examine the source of the statement.

- If a confession (or an incriminating statement) from one of the defendants is required, charge and try the defendants separately in separate trials. In the *Bruton* case, Evans' confession could then be used against Evans if it was needed to obtain a conviction of Evans.

- In the case of *Douglas v. Alabama,* there was not enough evidence to convict both defendants. The state would have to determine which of the two defendants they wanted to convict of the felony charges and then plea bargain to get the cooperation of the other man as a witness.

RESULTS OF POLYGRAPH TESTS AS EVIDENCE

It is reported that more than 2 million polygraph (lie detector) tests are given every year in the United States and that 98 percent of the tests are administered in private industry.

Many persons in private industry argue that polygraph testing is needed for screening employees in positions of trust, since the U.S. Commerce Department estimates that employee theft annually inflates product costs in America by $40 billion to $50 billion.

Persons who oppose the use of polygraph tests refer to the tests as degrading and humiliating. The late Senator Sam Ervin reportedly called the tests "20th-century witchcraft." Criminal defense lawyer F. Lee Bailey testified before Congress in 1986 stating that polygraph tests are "useful investigative tools" and that when "properly run in good hands, it is a good test." Congress had a bill before it in 1986 which would have severely limited the use of polygraph tests in private industry.

Using the Results of Polygraph Tests as Evidence in Court

Persons charged or suspected of a crime cannot be compelled to take a polygraph test, because such compulsion would violate their Fifth Amendment privilege against self-incrimination. However, persons may voluntarily agree to take a polygraph test to affirm statements they have made or to demonstrate their innocence.

Most American courts, however, forbid the use of "any evidence of polygraph results and testimony of polygraph examiners" in criminal trials. In 1985, the Supreme Court of Colorado gave the following reasons for forbidding the use of polygraph evidence:

- "The inherent unreliability of polygraph results"
- "The inability of trial courts to judge the competency of polygraph examiners"
- "The tendency of juries to rely too heavily on 'expert' testimony of truthfulness" [51]

Admissions and Confessions Made by Persons Before, During, or After a Polygraph Test

In some instances, persons make incriminating admissions or confessions either before, during, or after a polygraph test is given.[52] The polygraph operator or examiner may testify as to these statements if

- the statements were voluntarily made, and
- the *Miranda* warnings were given and a waiver obtained in situations where the polygraph operator is a law enforcement officer. The *Miranda* warnings should also be given by private polygraph examiners if the suspect is in police custody.

Cases involving incriminating statements made before, during, or after polygraph tests included the following:

State v. Fields

Missouri Court of Appeals (1976)
538 S.W.2d 348

Incriminating statements of a soldier charged with rape which were made to law enforcement officers after taking a polygraph test were held to be admissible.

State v. Franks

Supreme Court of Iowa (1976)
239 N.W.2d 588

> A new trial was ordered by the Supreme Court of Iowa to determine whether statements which the defendant made to a polygraph operator who was a police detective were voluntary.

State v. McDowell

Supreme Court of South Carolina (1976)
266 S.C. 508, 224 S.E.2d 889

> In a murder trial, the trial court permitted the defendant's former jail cell mate to testify that
>
> - The defendant had told him that he and a partner had killed two men with a shotgun and had taken over $1,000 from the victims.
> - The defendant had asked him how to beat the polygraph test.
>
> The use of this evidence and the defendant's conviction was affirmed.

Sotelo v. State

Supreme Court of Indiana (1976)
264 Ind. 298, 342 N.E.2d 844

> In affirming the defendant's conviction for murder, the Supreme Court of Indiana held that a confession obtained after the defendant took a polygraph test did not by itself make the confession involuntary.

United States v. Randles

U.S. Court of Appeals, Sixth Circuit (1985)
765 F.2d 147, review denied 106 S.Ct. 406 (U.S.Sup.Ct.1985)

> Incriminating statements made by the defendant after she signed a *Miranda* waiver and took polygraph examination were properly held to be admissible in criminal trial. The trial court held that the defendant was not in custody at the time of her statements, but even if she were it was held that her waiver of rights under *Miranda* carried over and covered questioning that followed the polygraph examination.

PROBLEMS

1. Federal Internal Revenue agents from the Intelligence Division met with the defendant at a private home where the defendant occasionally stayed. The agents identified themselves and their function of investigating his federal income tax liability. The agents read a statement to the defendant from a printed card, but they did not give the defendant the *Miranda* warnings and receive a waiver of his rights. For about three hours the agents conversed with the defendant in what they described as a "friendly" and "relaxed" manner. In separate cars, the parties then went to the defendant's place of business where the defendant supplied his books to the agents after being informed that he was not required to furnish any books or records. The defendant was not arrested at the time but was later charged with criminal tax fraud. Were the statements and other evidence which the tax agents obtained at the voluntary meeting at the private home and then at defendant's place of business properly obtained and properly used as evidence in defendant's criminal trial? *Beckwith v. United States,* 425 U.S. 341, 96 S.Ct. 1612 (1976).

2. "An officer of the State Police investigated a theft at a residence near Pendleton. He asked the lady of the house which had been burglarized if she suspected anyone. She replied that the defendant was the only one she could think of. The defendant was a parolee and a 'close associate' of her son. The officer tried to contact defendant on three or four occasions with no success. Finally, about 25 days after the burglary, the officer left his card at defendant's apartment with a note asking him to call because 'I'd like to discuss something with you.' The next afternoon the defendant did call. The officer asked where it would be convenient to meet. The defendant had no preference; so the officer asked if the defendant could meet him at the state patrol office in about an hour and a half, about 5:00 P.M. The patrol office was about two blocks from defendant's apartment. The building housed several state agencies.

    The officer met defendant in the hallway, shook hands and took him into an office. The defendant was told he was not under arrest. The door was closed. The two sat across a desk. The police radio in another room could be heard. The officer told defendant he wanted to talk to him about a burglary and that his truthfulness would possibly be considered by the district attorney or judge. The officer further advised that the police believed defendant was involved in the burglary and [falsely stated that] defendant's fingerprints were found at the scene. The defendant sat for a few minutes and then said he had taken the property. This occurred within five minutes after defendant had come to the office. The officer then advised defendant of his *Miranda* rights and took a taped confession.

    At the end of the taped conversation the officer told defendant he was not arresting him at this time; he was released to go about his job and return to his family. The officer said he was referring the case to the district attorney for him to determine whether criminal charges would be brought. It was 5:30 P.M. when the defendant left the office.

    The defendant was then charged days later with burglary. Can all of the incriminating statements which defendant made be used in evidence against him? Were any improper promises made to the defendant? Did the officer's false statement that the defendant's fingerprints were found at the scene of the burglary prevent the use of any of the evidence? Were the defendant's confessions made voluntarily? Was *Miranda* properly complied with? *Oregon v. Mathiason,* 429 U.S. 492, 97 S.Ct. 711 (1977)"

3. Neville was stopped for running a stop sign. When he got out of his car, he stumbled and staggered. Based upon their observations of Neville, the police concluded he had been driving while under the influence. Neville was then placed under arrest and informed that he had a choice of submitting to a blood alcohol content test (BAC) or facing automatic revocation of his driver's license. When told of the choice, Neville responded, "I'm too drunk, I won't pass the test." Neville's response was viewed as a refusal to submit to a BAC test, and his driver's license was revoked. Neville contested the revocation on the grounds that he should have been warned that evidence of refusal could be used against him in court. Was Neville correct, and should such warnings be required? Explain your answer.

4. Police were investigating a shooting death outside a cafe in Dallas, Texas. Defendant and petitioner Orozco left the scene and returned to his boardinghouse to sleep. At about 4 a.m. four police officers arrived at petitioner's boardinghouse, were admitted by an unidentified woman, and were told that petitioner was asleep in the bedroom. All four officers entered the bedroom and began to question petitioner. From the moment he gave his name, according to the testimony of one of the officers, petitioner was not free to go where he pleased but was "under arrest." The officers asked him if he had been to the El Farleto restaurant that night and when he answered "yes" he was asked if he owned a pistol. Petitioner admitted owning one. After being asked a second time where the pistol was located, he admitted that it was in the washing machine in a backroom of the boardinghouse. Ballistics tests indicated that the gun found in the washing machine was the gun that fired the fatal shot.

Should the statements of the defendant be admitted as evidence? Should the gun be admitted as evidence? Explain your answer. *Orozco v. Texas,* 394 U.S. 324, 89 S.Ct. 1095 (1969).

5. Shortly after his arrest, eighteen-year-old Steven Smith was taken to an interrogation room at the Logan County Safety Complex for questioning by two police detectives. The session began as follows:

Q. "Steve, I want to talk with you in reference to the armed robbery that took place at McDonald's restaurant on the morning of the 19th. Are you familiar with this?"
A. "Yeah. My cousin Greg was."
Q. "Okay. But before I do that I must advise you of your rights. Okay? You have a right to remain silent. You do not have to talk to me unless you want to do so. Do you understand that?"
A. "Uh. She told me to get my lawyer. She said you guys would railroad me."
Q. "Do you understand that as I gave it to you, Steve?"
A. "Yeah."

Q. "If you do want to talk to me I must advise you that whatever you say can and will be used against you in court. Do you understand that?"

A. "Yeah."

Q. "You have a right to consult with a lawyer and to have a lawyer present with you when you're being questioned. Do you understand that?"

A. *"Uh, yeah. I'd like to do that."*

Q. "Okay." ... the interrogating officers proceeded to finish reading Smith his *Miranda* rights and then pressed him again to answer their questions:

Q. "... If you want a lawyer and you're unable to pay for one a lawyer will be appointed to represent you free of cost, do you understand that?"

A. "Okay."

Q. "Do you wish to talk to me at this time without a lawyer being present?"

A. *"Yeah and no, uh, I don't know what's what, really."*

Q. *"Well. You either have to talk to me this time without a lawyer being present* and if you do agree to talk with me without a lawyer being present you can stop at any time you want to."

Q. "All right. I'll talk to you then."

Smith then told the detectives that he knew in advance about the planned robbery, but contended that he had not been a participant. After considerable probing by the detectives, Smith confessed that "I committed it," but he then returned to his earlier story that he had only known about the planned crime. Upon further questioning, Smith again insisted that "I wanta get a lawyer." This time the detectives honored the request and terminated the interrogation.

Was Smith's confession to the armed robbery properly admitted as evidence against him? Should his conviction be affirmed? *Smith v. Illinois,* 469 U.S. 91, 105 S.Ct. 490 (1984).

6. The defendant, who was charged with a robbery and murder, was placed in a jail cell with a police informant. The informant overheard the defendant make incriminating statements which he passed on to the police. Can the informant appear as a witness and testify as to the statements he heard if he took no action other than merely listening to what the defendant had to say? Should the evidence of the defendant's statements be admissible if there was a prior arrangement of the police to put the informant in a position where he could overhear the defendant's statements? If the informant "deliberately elicited" the statements from the defendant by questions and conversation, should the evidence be admissible? Explain. *Kuhlmann v. Wilson,* ___ U.S. ___, 106 S.Ct. 2616 (U.S.Sup.Ct.1986).

7. The defendant approached a uniformed police officer in downtown Denver and stated that he had murdered someone and wanted to talk about it. The officer advised the defendant of his *Miranda* rights and the defendant stated that he understood those rights but still wanted to talk about the murder. A detective, who arrived a short time later, also advised the defendant of his rights. The defendant stated that he had come all the way from Boston to confess to the murder. After the defendant was taken to police headquar-

ters, he told his story to the police and took the police to the exact location of the murder. After being held overnight, the next day the defendant became disoriented while talking with a public defender. He was then sent to a state hospital and for the first time revealed to a psychiatrist that he was following the "voice of God" in confessing to the murder. A psychiatrist testified that the defendant was suffering from a psychosis which prevented him from understanding his rights and motivated his confession. The confession was suppressed and the Colorado Supreme Court held that the defendant's mental state, at the time of his confession, interfered with his "rational intellect" and his "free will." Does the federal constitution require that a state carry the burden of proving by "clear and convincing evidence" that the defendant waived his *Miranda* rights and that the defendant's confession was a product of his "free will"? Can confessions from defendants who are mentally ill be used against them in criminal actions? In civil actions? *Colorado v. Connelly*, ___ U.S. ___, 107 S.Ct. 515 (U.S.Sup.Ct.1986).

NOTES

[1] 16 Ill.2d 459, 158 N.E.2d 47 (1959).

[2] 348 U.S. 147, 75 S.Ct. 194 (1954).

[3] The Michigan Court of Appeals, in the case of People v. Switzer, 135 Mich.App. 779, 355 N.W.2d 670 (1984) held that the voluntariness test also applies to private persons and suppressed a confession obtained by force. The court held that "It is clear that confessions made involuntarily to the police may never be used against a criminal defendant, not only because the police broke the law, but more importantly because an involuntary confession is always of questionable trustworthiness.... We are persuaded that it should make no difference whether an involuntary statement is coerced by a police officer or a private citizen."

[4] Culombe v. Connecticut, 367 U.S. 568 at 578–580, 81 S.Ct. 1860 at 1865–1866 (1961).

[5] Schneckloth v. Bustamonte, 412 U.S. 218, 93 S.Ct. 2041 (1973).

[6] 365 U.S. 534, 81 S.Ct. 735 (1961).

[7] Schneckloth v. Bustamonte, see note 5 above.

[8] Haley v. Ohio, 332 U.S. 596, 68 S.Ct. 302 (1948).

[9] Payne v. Arkansas, 356 U.S. 560, 78 S.Ct. 844 (1958).

[10] Fikes v. Alabama, 352 U.S. 191, 77 S.Ct. 281 (1957).

[11] Davis v. North Carolina, 384 U.S. 737, 86 S.Ct. 1761 (1966).

[12] Chambers v. Florida, 309 U.S. 227, 60 S.Ct. 472 (1940).

[13] Ashcraft v. Tennessee, 322 U.S. 143, 64 S.Ct. 921 (1944).

[14] Reck v. Pate, 367 U.S. 433, 81 S.Ct. 1541 (1961).

[15] The term "reverse lineup" was discussed by the U.S. Supreme Court as follows in the case of Rhode Island v. Innis, 446 U.S. 291, 100 S.Ct. 1682: "For example, one of the practices discussed in *Miranda* was the use of line-ups in which a coached witness would pick the defendant as the perpetrator. This was designed to establish that the defendant was in fact guilty as a predicate for further interrogation. *Id.,* at 453, 86 S.Ct., at 1602. A variation on this theme discussed in *Miranda* was the so-called 'reverse line-up' in which a defendant would be identified by coached witnesses as the perpetrator of a fictitious crime, with the object of inducing him to confess to the actual crime of which he was suspected in order to escape the false prosecution. *Ibid.* The Court in *Miranda* also included in its survey of interrogation practices the use of psychological ploys, such as to 'posi[t]' 'the guilt of the subject,' to 'minimize the moral seriousness of the offense,' and 'to cast blame on the victim or on society.' *Id.,* at 450, 86 S.Ct., at 1615. It is clear that these techniques of persuasion, no less than express questioning, were thought, in a custodial setting, to amount to interrogation."

[16] Moore v. Hopper, 523 F.2d 1053 (5th Cir.1975).

[17] United States ex rel. Caminito v. Murphy, 222 F.2d 698 (2d Cir.1955), cert. denied 350 U.S. 896, 76 S.Ct. 155 (1955).

[18] Canada v. State, 56 Ala.App. 722, 325 So.2d 513 (1975).

[19] Roe v. People, 363 F.Supp. 788 (W.D.N.Y.1973) and Oregon v. Mathiason, 429 U.S. 492, 97 S.Ct. 711 (1977).

[20] State v. Kroupa, 16 Ariz.App. 254, 492 P.2d 750 (1972).

[21] Commonwealth v. Baity, 428 Pa. 306, 237 A.2d 172 (1968).

[22] McGee v. State, 2 Tenn.Crim.App. 100, 451 S.W.2d 709 (1970).

[23] People v. Smith, 246 N.E.2d 689 (1969), cert. denied 397 U.S. 1001, 90 S.Ct. 1150 (1970).

[24] United States ex rel. Lathan v. Deegan, 450 F.2d 181 (2d Cir.1971).

[25] McNabb v. United States, 318 U.S. 332, 63 S.Ct. 608 (1943) and Mallory v. United States, 354 U.S. 449, 77 S.Ct. 1356 (1957).

[26] A few of the state cases governing this situation are Vorhauer v. State, 212 A.2d 886 (Del.1966); Jacobs v. State, 248 So.2d 515 (Fla.App.1971); Oliver v. State, 250 So.2d 888 (Fla.1971); Phillips v. State, 29 Wis.2d 521, 139 N.W.2d 41 (1966).

[27] Embry v. State, 46 Wis.2d 151, 174 N.W.2d 521 (1970).

[28] 378 U.S. 478, 84 S.Ct. 1758 (1964).

[29] 384 U.S. 436, 86 S.Ct. 1602 (1966).

[30] People v. Ashford, 265 Cal.App.2d 673, 71 Cal.Rptr. 619 (1968).

[31] State v. Bennett, 30 Utah 2d 343, 517 P.2d 1029 (1973).

[32] Britton v. State, 44 Wis.2d 109, 170 N.W.2d 785 (1969).

[33] 468 U.S. 420, 104 S.Ct. 3138 (1984).

[34] See note 32 above.

[35] Exceptions to this rule are found in the following U.S. Supreme Court cases in this chapter: Garrity v. New Jersey, Gardner v. Broderick, and Spevack v. Klein.

[36] Courts which have adopted similar personal safety or public safety rules are People v. Toler, 45 Mich.App. 156, 206 N.W.2d 253 (1973), Ballew v. State, 246 Ark. 1191, 441 S.W.2d 453 (1969), People v. Chesnut, 51 N.Y.2d 14, 409 N.E.2d 958, 431 N.Y.S.2d 485 (1980), State v. Roadenbaugh, 234 Kan. 474, 673 P.2d 1166, 34 Cr.L. 2235 (Kan.Sup.Ct.1984). For a case holding that the "officer's safety was not in jeopardy sufficiently to allow questioning before giving the *Miranda* warnings," see State v. Hein, 138 Ariz. 360, 674 P.2d 1358, 34 Cr.L. 2235 (Ariz.Sup.Ct.1984).

[37] 62 Cal.2d 436, 42 Cal.Rptr. 417, 398 P.2d 753 (1965).

[38] Berkemer v. McCarty, see note 33 above.

[39] See note 33 above.

[40] See note 33 above.

[41] Miranda v. Arizona, 384 U.S. 436, 86 S.Ct. 1602 (1966).

[42] Edwards v. Arizona, 451 U.S. 477, 101 S.Ct. 1880 (1981).

[43] 469 U.S. 91, 105 S.Ct. 490 (1984).

[44] 446 U.S. 291, 100 S.Ct. 1682 (1980).

[45] This case was also before the U.S. Supreme Court in 1984. The second appearance was under the name of Nix v. Williams. Williams was in prison for kidnapping and in Nix v. Williams, 35 Cr.L. 3119, was convicted of the murder charge in the second trial. The Supreme Court affirmed the conviction under the "inevitable discovery" doctrine. See chapter 8 for the case.

[46] 401 U.S. 222, 91 S.Ct. 643 (1971).

[47] The Supreme Court cited the 1954 case of Walder v. United States, 347 U.S. 62, 74 S.Ct. 354, where "the Court permitted physical evidence, inadmissible in the case in chief, to be used for impeachment purposes."

[48] 380 U.S. 609, 85 S.Ct. 1229 (1965). In the Griffin case, the defendant had been seen with the murder victim on the evening of her death and the evidence placed him in the alley where her body was found. Prior to 1965, the practice of commenting on the defendant's failure to take the stand

and explain such circumstances was sanctioned by the American Bar Association, the American Law Institute, the Uniform Code of Evidence and the Model Code of Evidence.

[49] 447 U.S. 231, 100 S.Ct. 2124 (1980).

[50] ABA Standards for Criminal Justice (Sec. 5.7, p. 97). In the comments to the ABA Standards Relating to the Prosecution Function and the Defense Function (section 5.7(c), pp. 122–23) it is stated that "if the prosecutor is informed in advance that the witness will claim a privilege and he wishes to contest the claim, the matter should be treated without the presence of the jury and a ruling obtained."

[51] People v. Cummings, 706 P.2d 766 (Colo.1985) Review denied, ___ U.S. ___, 39 Cr.L. 4060 (1986) and People v. Anderson, 637 P.2d at 358.

[52] In the 1977 case of Sandlin v. Oregon Women's Correctional Center, 28 Or.App. 519, 559 P.2d 1308 (1977), the defendant argued that she had a right to a polygraph test. However, a test was not given to her. In affirming the defendant's conviction, the Court held that due process did not require the state to grant the defendant's request for a polygraph test. The Court also noted that this issue had not been decided by any other court.

Judicial Notice and Privileges Witnesses May Use

JUDICIAL NOTICE

If the parties in a civil or criminal action had to prove every fact and define every term they sought to use, the cost would be considerable not only in time but also in effort and in money. The doctrine of **judicial notice** [1] excuses parties in some instances of the burden of establishing facts and the burden of producing formal proof of facts by witnesses, documents, or other means.

In 1919 the California Supreme Court stated that "Judicial notice is a judicial short cut, a doing away ... with the formal necessity of evidence (where) there is no real necessity for it." [2]

Judicial Notice of Matters of Common Knowledge

Judicial notice is the recognition and acceptance of certain facts commonly known in the community by judges and jurors without further proof. Judicial notice of matters of common knowledge is probably the oldest form of the doctrine of judicial notice. Because the doctrine permits judges and jurors to recognize facts commonly known to them without the formal necessity of evidence proving the fact, judicial notice can be considered a practical form of a judicial short cut of getting on with the business at hand.

Judicial notice should not be taken of facts which are not capable of immediate and accurate determination by reference to easily accessible sources of information. A party contesting a fact to which judicial notice has been taken could therefore easily check these sources to determine the accuracy of the fact of which judicial notice was taken.

Examples of some of the facts which may be received by judicial notice are

- *The date on which a state ratified* a proposed constitutional amendment; U.S. Supreme Court stated they would take judicial notice: *Dillon v. Gloss,* 256 U.S. 368, 41 S.Ct. 510 (1921).

- *The meaning of words, phrases, or abbreviations.* The meanings of the word *fix* or the phrase *turning a trick.*

- *The sex of a witness or defendant.* The Supreme Court of Indiana held that [3]
  The sex of a human being is generally its most obvious characteristic. We can look at another human being and, with a very high degree of

certainty, ascertain his or her sex. Therefore, why couldn't a presiding judge take judicial notice of a defendant's sex? We believe he can and should.

- *Dates, days, and time*—the fact that the 4th of July was on a Friday in 1986 or the end of daylight on a given day.

The fact that the information was within the personal knowledge of the judge but was not a matter of common and general knowledge was held in Illinois not to qualify for judicial notice, as indicated in Palmer v. Mitchell: [4]

> Finally, it was error for the trial judge to take judicial notice of certain evidence which had been heard in the trial of the principal case. The doctrine of judicial notice operates to admit into evidence, without formal proof, those facts which are a matter of common and general knowledge and which are established and known within the limits of the jurisdiction of the court .... The facts of which the trial judge took judicial notice do not meet this requirement; indeed the facts which the trial judge had heard in the trial of the principal case were not a matter of common and general knowledge, but were within his personal knowledge only. Moreover, while courts take judicial notice of their records in a pending case, they cannot do so with respect to records of other proceedings.

Judicial notice is regulated by statutes in many states, as indicated by the Supreme Court of California in the case of *Barreiro v. State Bar of California* : [5]

> Judicial notice may not be taken of any matter unless authorized or required by law. (Evid.Code, § 452). This court is compelled to take judicial notice only of facts and propositions of generalized knowledge that are so universally known that they cannot reasonably be the subject of dispute. (Evid.Code, § 451.) If there is any doubt whatever either as to the fact itself or as to its being a matter of common knowledge, evidence should be required.

Judicial Notice of Scientific Facts

The well-known text, *McCormick on Evidence,*[6] commented that the most frequent shortcoming of the courts in dealing with the doctrine of judicial notice is their failure "to employ the doctrine of judicial notice in this field (scientific and technological facts) to the full measure of its usefulness." The following cases indicate that judicial notice is being used more extensively by courts in the area of scientific and technological facts.

State v. Brock

Court of Appeals of Ohio (1973)
34 Ohio App. 175, 296 N.E.2d 837

> "The sole question presented in this appeal is whether the trial court is permitted to take judicial notice of the fact that heroin is a habit forming drug within the meaning of R.C. 3917.17.2.

We conclude that the courts may take judicial notice of any scientific fact which may be ascertained by reference to a standard dictionary or is of such general knowledge that it is known by any judicial officer. 21 Ohio Jurisprudence 2d 76, Evidence, Section 63.

Since history has been recorded, heroin has been known as a crystalline narcotic made from morphine, but more potent than morphine because of its addictive properties ....

In the instant case, the trial court was correct in taking judicial notice of the fact that heroin is a narcotic drug and is habit forming."

State v. Finkle

Superior Court of New Jersey (1974)
128 N.J.Super. 199, 319 A.2d 733

The defendant was convicted of going twenty miles per hour over the speed limit. The sole evidence of his guilt was a reading from a VASCAR device operated by a state trooper. The state produced evidence showing that the instrument was accurate and that the trooper operating it was fully qualified. The trial court took judicial notice of the scientific reliability of the VASCAR device. In affirming the conviction of the defendant, the Superior Court of New Jersey also took judicial notice of the scientific reliability of VASCAR, holding that

We find that the conviction of defendant in the County Court of exceeding the speed limit is sustainable on the evidence adduced. In doing so, however, we point out that the factor of potential margin for error in VASCAR readings inherent in the intervention of the mental and physical processes of the operator of the device may well justify a court in declining to find guilt beyond a reasonable doubt where the reading is relatively close to the legal speed limit. But here there is no such problem in view of the wide disparity between the 55 m.p.h. limit and the 75.3 m.p.h. VASCAR reading. We also emphasize that in every future case there must be satisfactory proof of the good working order of the particular VASCAR instrument used and of the qualifications of the operator.

Affirmed; no costs on this appeal.

Judicial Notice of Statutes, Ordinances, Bylaws, and Resolutions

Courts may generally take judicial notice of statutes, ordinances, bylaws, and resolutions which they are obligated to enforce. Statutes in many states specifically authorize the extent of the use of judicial notice in this area. However, the general rule is that courts may not take judicial notice of statutes, ordinances, bylaws, or resolutions which they have no special function to enforce.[7]

State statutes, however, could give courts authority to take judicial notice of all legislation in that state and also the legislation of other states.

THE PRIVILEGE AGAINST SELF–INCRIMINATION

"The Public ... Has a Right to Every Man's Evidence." [8]

In the case of *United States v. Bryan*,[9] the U.S. Supreme Court held that "there is a general duty to give what testimony one is capable of giving and that any exemptions which may exist are distinctly exceptional." The Court also stated in the *Bryan* case that

> persons summoned as witnesses by competent authority have certain minimum duties and obligations which are necessary concessions to the public interest in the orderly operation of legislative and judicial machinery. A subpoena has never been treated as an invitation to a game of hare and hounds, in which the witness must testify only if cornered at the end of the chase. If that were the case, then, indeed, the great power of testimonial compulsion, so necessary to the effective functioning of courts and legislatures, would be a nullity. We have often iterated the importance of this public duty, which every person within the jurisdiction of the Government is bound to perform when properly summoned.

In the case of *Branzburg v. Hayes*,[10] the U.S. Supreme Court stated that "the longstanding principle (is) that 'the public ... has a right to every man's evidence' except for those persons protected by a constitutional, common-law, or statutory privilege."

Witnesses have an obligation to testify. They may, however, claim their privilege against self-incrimination or other privileges if these privileges are applicable and can lawfully be used.[11] The remainder of this chapter presents material on privileges which exist in the law.

The Constitutional Privilege Against Self-incrimination

The only privilege which has constitutional origins is the Fifth Amendment privilege against self-incrimination. The historic right of defendants and other persons not to testify as to facts which could incriminate them has been embodied in the Fifth Amendment provision that

> No person ... shall be required in any criminal case to be a witness against himself ....

A discussion of the privilege against self-incrimination has been presented in the section on the Accusatorial System of chapter 1 and further material is presented in chapter 5, Using Admissions and Confessions as Evidence.

THE ATTORNEY–CLIENT PRIVILEGE

The U.S. Supreme Court pointed out in the 1981 case of *Upjohn Company et al. v. United States et al.*[12] that the "attorney-client privilege [13] is the oldest of the

Where the Fifth Amendment Privilege Against Self-incrimination Does and Does Not Apply

The Fifth Amendment privilege against self-incrimination does *not* apply:

- When physical evidence is sought and obtained. See:
  Holt v. United States, 218 U.S. 245 (1910) (blouse)
  Schmerber v. California, 384 U.S. 757 (1965) (blood)
  Gilbert v. California, 388 U.S. 263 (1967) (handwriting exemplar)
  United States v. Wade, 388 U.S. 218 (1967) (compelling the accused to exhibit his person for observation)
  United States v. Dionisio, 410 U.S. 10 (1973) (voice exemplar)

- To corporations and other impersonal entities.
  Campbell Painting Corp. v. Reid, 392 U.S. 286 (1968), *United States v. Doe,* 465 U.S. 605, 104 S.Ct. 1237 (1984)
  United States v. White, 322 U.S. 694 (1944) (held that an unincorporated union did not have the privilege against self-incrimination)

- To records required for the benefit of the public or for public inspection.
  Shapiro v. United States, 335 U.S. 1 (1948) (where the public record was of lawful activities)
  Marchetti v. United States, 390 U.S. 39 (1968) (because wagering and gambling are usually unlawful, it was held that the federal registration requirement violated the Fifth Amendment privilege against self-incrimination)

- Where immunity has been granted.

- Where the incrimination is of others and is not self-incrimination.
  Bursey v. United States, 466 F.2d 1059 (9th Cir. 1972)

- Where there has been a voluntary, intelligent waiver of the privilege.

The Fifth Amendment privilege against self-incrimination does apply:

- When the evidence sought and obtained is of a testimonial or communicative nature.

- Where the recollection faculty of the brain is used.

privileges for confidential communications known to the common law." In holding that communications by Upjohn employees to corporate lawyers as to illegal payments made to foreign government officials were covered by the attorney-client privilege, the Court stated that the purpose of the privilege is

> to encourage full and frank communication between attorneys and their clients and thereby promote broader public interests in the observance of law and administration of justice. The privilege recognizes that sound legal advice or advocacy serves public ends and that such advice or advocacy depends upon the lawyer being fully informed by the client. As we stated last Term in *Trammel v. United States,* 445 U.S. 40, 51 (1980), "The attorney-client privilege rests on the need for the advocate and counselor to know all that relates to the client's reasons for seeking representation if the professional mission

is to be carried out." And in *Fisher v. United States,* 425 U.S. 391, 403 (1976), we recognized the purpose of the privilege to be "to encourage clients to make full disclosures to their attorneys." This rationale for the privilege has long been recognized by the Court, see *Hunt v. Blackburn,* 128 U.S. 464, 470 (1888) (privilege "is founded upon the necessity, in the interest and administration of justice, of the aid of persons having knowledge of the law and skilled in its practice, which assistance can only be safely and readily availed of when free from the consequences or the apprehension of disclosure"). Admittedly complications in the application of the privilege arise when the client is a corporation, which in theory is an artificial creature of the law, and not an individual; but this Court has assumed that the privilege applies when the client is a corporation, and the Government does not contest the general proposition.

The privilege belongs to the client, who has always had every right to expect that his attorney will not disclose or discuss the client's private legal matters with others. Lawyers are also bound by legal canons of ethics not to disclose such information to others.

Defendants who are charged with a crime or other persons who have legal problems must seek the advice and assistance of persons skilled in the practice of the law. Because neither criminal nor civil lawyers can function efficiently without adequate information from their clients,[14] the privilege protects disclosures made during confidential communications between the client and the lawyer. Because of the privilege, the client can be assured that any such confidential communications which he makes to his lawyer will not be used against him. As an example, a prosecutor could not call a defense lawyer as a witness and question him as to privileged communications with the defendant even though such information might be relevant and material evidence.

Since the privilege belongs to the client, it may also be waived by the client should this be in the client's best interest. The attorney cannot waive the privilege because it is not his to waive. The privilege is reported to exist in all of the jurisdictions of the United States. Some states continue to use the privilege in its common-law form while other states now have the privilege in the form of a statute.

The Requirement of an Attorney-Client Relationship

To have an attorney-client relationship, the attorney must be licensed to practice law or the client must be reasonably lead to believe that the person in whom he has confided is properly licensed to practice law in that jurisdiction. The privilege would exist even if the lawyer rejected the case, was not paid for his services, was fired by the client, or withdrew from the case before the matter was concluded.

The client must be seeking the professional legal services of the attorney and have the intention of establishing an attorney-client relationship. Consulting with an attorney for services which are nonlegal has been held not to fall within the privilege,[15] as have been situations in which a person informally seeks free legal advice or an opinion. Such situations could occur at luncheons, dinners, cocktail parties, etc.

The Requirement of Confidential or Private Communications

While state statutes and court decisions governing and interpreting the attorney-client privilege vary somewhat, it is generally held that the privilege applies only to confidential communications made within the lawyer-client relationship. Should a client discuss his legal business with his attorney in the presence of other persons at a cocktail party or in the steam room of a health club, such communications which were overheard by other persons would not fall within the privilege.

However, the necessary presence of the attorney's secretary, law clerk, or other employee during a conference in the lawyer's office would not cause a court to hold that the communications were not privileged. The privilege would also probably hold for most situations in which the client brought another person with him to the lawyer's office for a conference. The presence of a father, mother, or wife in a conference just before a trial or hearing is not uncommon and there is every reason to believe that the privilege would apply to such communications. The following 1985 case illustrates:

United States v. Lopez

U.S. Court of Appeals, Tenth Circuit (1985)
777 F.2d 543, 38 CrL 2208

Lopez and Jaramillo were both arrested for the possession of cocaine. Both men had separate attorneys. Jon Kwako represented Jaramillo and David Norveil represented Lopez. Attorney Kwako met with Lopez and Jaramillo at the detention center where both defendants were being held. Because there was no evidence to show that the meeting was held to plan a joint defense, the court held that the presence of Lopez at the meeting takes the statements made outside of the attorney-client privilege. In holding that Attorney Kwako can be called as a witness to testify as to the statements made, the Court ruled that

> There is no evidence that the meeting between Jaramillo, Kwako, and Lopez was held to plan a joint defense. It was called at Kwako's request after Lopez had already retained separate counsel who not present. These facts are analogous to U.S. v. Simpson, 475 F2d 934 (CADC 1973), where the codefendant's attorney attended a meeting between Simpson and his counsel. The court permitted the codefendant's counsel to testify to Simpson's statements at the meeting on the ground that the codefendant's attorney had interests adverse to those of Simpson and his counsel and his presence at the meeting precluded a finding of confidentiality. Accord, U.S. v. Melvin, 650 F2d 641 (CA5 1981).
>
> Unfortunately the record in this case does not indicate why and how Lopez became a participant in a meeting between Jaramillo and his attorney. What is clear, however, is that Lopez was represented by separate counsel who was not present. Furthermore, he maintained potentially adverse interests to those of Jaramillo as is shown by retention of separate counsel. Under the circumstances, one could not

Attorney-Client Privilege

The general rule is that the attorney-client privilege does not protect the name and identity of a client and the amount of the attorney fee.

> ... the identity of a client is a matter not normally within the privilege ... nor are matters involving the receipt of fees from a client usually privileged. *United States v. (Under Seal),* 774 F.2d 624, 628 (4th Cir.1985), review denied ___ U.S. ___, 106 S.Ct. 1514 (U.S.Sup.Ct.1986).

An exception to this rule exists when the disclosure of the identity of a client would implicate the client for a crime being investigated. The following example illustrates: An attorney made tax payments to the Internal Revenue Service on behalf of several clients. The IRS wanted the names of the clients but the court held that disclosure of their names would establish their guilt for the IRS charges under investigation. Disclosure was held to violate the Fifth Amendment and was not ordered. *Baird v. Koerner,* 279 F.2d 623 (9th Cir.1960).

reasonably assume that the disclosures at the meeting would remain in confidence. In view of the general rule that an attorney may testify about non-confidential communications, Kwako should have been permitted to testify.

The Presence of a Police Agent at a Lawyer-Client Conference

A person accused of a crime has a Sixth Amendment right to an attorney. In order for an attorney to provide effective assistance, there must be an opportunity to confer privately with his client out of the presence of other persons. If a law enforcement agency were to bug a jail conference room used by lawyers and their clients, this could be a violation of a defendant's Sixth Amendment right to an attorney.

A number of U.S. Supreme Court cases reviewed the problem which exists when a government agent is present during conversations between lawyers and their clients. In the case of *Hoffa v. United States,*[16] a paid government informer was engaged by James Hoffa in an attempt to bribe a member of the jury sitting in a criminal trial in which Hoffa was the defendant. The informer testified with respect to conversations which he overheard in Hoffa's hotel suite, but he did not testify as to Hoffa's conversations with his lawyer. The U.S. Supreme Court held that there was no violation of Hoffa's Sixth Amendment right to confer privately with his attorney. The following case also came before the U.S. Supreme Court:

Weatherford v. Bursey

Supreme Court of the United States (1977)
429 U.S. 545, 97 S.Ct. 837

Weatherford was working as an undercover officer. In order to maintain his cover, he was arrested at the same time that Bursey was arrested. Bursey and his lawyer invited Weatherford to meet with them because they believed that Weatherford could be of assistance. Bursey was convicted in his criminal trial. Weatherford did not expect to testify as a witness, but on the day of the trial it was decided to have Weatherford testify. None of the government's evidence was obtained as a result of Weatherford's participation at the meetings between Bursey and his lawyer. Bursey then commenced a civil suit, alleging that his civil rights had been violated. The U.S. Supreme Court held that none of Bursey's rights had been violated, ruling that

> There being no tainted evidence in this case, no communication of defense strategy to the prosecution, and no purposeful intrusion by Weatherford, there was no violation of the Sixth Amendment insofar as it is applicable to the States by virtue of the Fourteenth Amendment. The proof in this case thus fell short of making out a § 1983 claim .... There is no indication that any of (Weatherford's) testimony was prompted by or was the product of those meetings. Weatherford's testimony was surely very damaging, but the mere fact that he had met with Bursey and his lawyer prior to trial did not violate Bursey's right to counsel any more than the informant's meetings with Hoffa and Hoffa's lawyers rendered inadmissible the informer's testimony having no connection with those conversations.

THE HUSBAND–WIFE PRIVILEGE

The husband-wife privilege (marital privilege) is another privilege with ancient roots, going back hundreds of years in the law. Both the husband-wife and the lawyer-client privileges existed before the writing of the Bill of Rights and the creation of the United States as a country.

The U.S. Supreme Court pointed out in the case of *Trammel v. United States* [17] that when the husband-wife privilege came into use, women were "regarded as chattel or demeaned by denial of a separate legal identity and the dignity associated with recognition as a whole human being." The Court stated that because the "ancient foundations for so sweeping a privilege have long since disappeared," changes in the privilege have been made. In footnote 8 of the *Trammel* case, the U.S. Supreme Court lists the following four husband-wife privilege rules used in the United States:

Rule 1:   Eight States provide that one spouse is incompetent to testify against the other in a criminal proceeding: see Haw.Rev.Stat. § 621–18 (1976);

Iowa Code § 622.7 (1979); Miss.Code Ann. § 13–1–5 (Supp.1979); N.C. Gen.Stat. § 8–57 (Supp.1977); Ohio Rev.Code Ann. § 2945.42 (Supp. 1979); Pa.Stat.Ann., Tit. 42, §§ 5913, 5915 (Purdon Supp.1979); Tex. Crim.Proc.Code Ann. Art. 38.11 (Vernon 1979); Wyo.Stat. § 1–12–104 (1977).

Rule 2:   Sixteen States provide a privilege against adverse spousal testimony and vest the privilege in both spouses or in the defendant-spouse. alone: see Alaska Crim.Proc.Rule 26(b)(2); Colo.Rev.Stat. § 13–90–107 (1973); Idaho Code § 9–203 (Supp.1979); Mich.Comp.Laws § 600.2162 (Mich.Stat.Ann. § 27A.2162) (1968); Minn.Stat. § 595.02 (1978); Mo. Rev.Stat. § 546.260 (1978); Mont.Code Ann. § 46–16–212 (1979); Neb. Rev.Stat. § 27–505 (1975); Nev.Rev.Stat. § 49.295 (1977); N.J.Stat.Ann. § 2A:84A–17 (West 1976); N.M.Stat.Ann. § 20–4–505 (Supp.1977); Ore.Rev.Stat. § 44.040 (1977); Utah Code Ann. § 78–24–8 (1977); Va. Code § 19.2–271.2 (Supp.1979); Wash.Rev.Code § 5.60.060 (Supp. 1979); W.Va.Code § 57–3–3 (1966).

Rule 3:   Nine States entitle the witness-spouse alone to assert a privilege against adverse spousal testimony: see Ala.Code § 12–21–227 (1975); Cal.Evid.Code Ann. §§ 970–973 (West 1966 and Supp.1979); Conn. Gen.Stat. § 54–84 (1979); Ga.Code § 38–1604 (1978); Ky.Rev.Stat. § 421.210 (Supp.1978); La.Rev.Stat.Ann. § 15:461 (West 1967); Md.Cts. & Jud.Proc.Code Ann. §§ 9–101, 9–106 (1974); Mass.Gen.Laws Ann., ch. 233, § 20 (West Supp.1979); R.I.Gen.Laws § 12–17–10 (1970).

Rule 4:   The remaining 17 States have abolished the privilege in criminal cases: see Ariz.Rev.Stat.Ann. § 12–2231 (Supp.1978); Ark.Stat.Ann. § 28–101, Rules 501 and 504 (1979); Del.Code Ann., Tit. 11, § 3502 (1975); Fla.Stat. §§ 90.501, 90.504 (1979); Ill.Rev.Stat., ch. 38, § 155–1 (1977); Ind.Code §§ 34–1–14–4, 34–1–14–5 (1976); Kan.Stat.Ann. §§ 60–407, 60–428 (1976); Maine Rules of Evidence 501, 504; N.H.Rev. Stat.Ann. § 516:27 (1974); N.Y.Crim.Proc.Law § 60.10 (McKinney 1971); N.Y.Civ.Proc.Law §§ 4502, 4512 (McKinney 1963); N.D.Rules of Evidence 501, 504; Okla.Stat., Tit. 12, §§ 2103, 2501, 2504 (West Supp. 1979); S.C.Code § 19–11–30 (1976); S.D.Comp.Laws Ann. §§ 19–13–1, 19–13–12 to 19–13–15 (1979); Tenn.Code Ann. § 40–2404 (1975); Vt. Stat.Ann., Tit. 12, § 1605 (1973); Wis.Stat. §§ 905.01, 905.05 (1975).

The U.S. Supreme Court modified the federal husband-wife privilege rule in the following case:

Trammel v. United States

Supreme Court of the United States (1980)
445 U.S. 40, 100 S.Ct. 906

The defendant was involved with his wife and two other men in importing heroin illegally into the United States. After the defendant's wife was apprehended in a routine customs search in Hawaii, she agreed to cooperate with the government in return for lenient treatment. After being granted immunity, Mrs. Trammel testified in detail as to her husband's illegal activities. The defendant objected to his wife appearing as a witness against him, citing *Hawkins v. United States,* 358 U.S. 74, 79 S.Ct. 136, which adopted Rule 2. The U.S. Supreme Court modified the federal husband-wife privilege rule in federal courts and moved to Rule 3. In affirming the defendant's conviction, the Court stated that

> Our consideration of the foundations for the privilege and its history satisfy us that "reason and experience" no longer justify so sweeping a rule as that found acceptable by the Court in *Hawkins.* Accordingly, we conclude that the existing rule should be modified so that the witness-spouse alone has a privilege to refuse to testify adversely; the witness may be neither compelled to testify nor foreclosed from testifying. This modification—vesting the privilege in the witness-spouse—furthers the important public interest in marital harmony without unduly burdening legitimate law enforcement needs.
>
> Here, petitioner's spouse chose to testify against him. That she did so after a grant of immunity and assurances of lenient treatment does not render her testimony involuntary. Cf. *Bordenkircher v. Hayes,* 434 U.S. 357, 98 S.Ct. 663, 54 L.Ed.2d 604 (1978). Accordingly, the District Court and the Court of Appeals were correct in rejecting petitioner's claim of privilege, and the judgment of the Court of Appeals is
> Affirmed.

(See Rule 501 in appendix B, which is the present Privilege rule used in federal courts.)

The Crime Fraud or Joint Participant Exception to the Husband-Wife and Attorney-Client Privileges

A well-recognized exception to the attorney-client privilege is the exception made when the communications are made to an attorney for the purposes of advancing a crime or criminal ends.[18]

However, the husband-wife privilege is looked upon as having greater social importance than the attorney-client privilege. The U.S. Supreme Court stated, regarding the husband-wife privilege, that [19]

> We deal with a right of privacy older than the Bill of Rights .... Marriage is a coming together for better or for worse, hopefully enduring, and intimate to the degree of being sacred. It is an association that promotes a way of life, not causes; a harmony in living, not political faiths; a bilateral loyalty, not commercial or social projects.

Some states have abolished the husband-wife privilege in criminal cases (Rule 4) while others permit a willing spouse to testify if they wish (see *Trammel v. United States*).

In all states, both husband and wife may be charged and tried for crimes. But not all states and courts will compel a witness to testify against their spouse. In 1985, the U.S. Court of Appeals for the Second Circuit refused to create the exception forcing a wife to testify against her husband, stating that

> The marital privilege rests upon "its perceived role in fostering the harmony and sanctity of the marriage relationship," *Trammel,* 445 U.S. at 44, 100 S.Ct. at 909, ... and the "*natural repugnance* in every fair-minded person to compelling a wife or husband to be the means of the other's condemnation, and to compelling the culprit to the humiliation of being condemned by the words of his intimate life partner," 8 Wigmore, *Evidence* § 2228 at 217, (emphasis in original), forced from her by governmental compulsion. In light of its existence since the early days of the common law and of the importance of the interests which the marital privilege serves, we would leave the creation of exceptions to the Supreme Court or to Congress.[20]

THE PHYSICIAN–PATIENT PRIVILEGE

The physician-patient privilege did not exist at common law and therefore exists only in states which have created such a privilege by statutes. The state statutes define the extent and the limitations of the privilege. In the absence of a statute, there would be no privilege as to information obtained by a nurse, a dentist, a druggist, an orthopedist, a chiropractor, a Christian Science practitioner, or a veterinary surgeon. All of these professions, however, have codes of ethics and would ordinarily be reluctant to reveal information obtained in a professional relationship unless compelled to do so.

Because state statutes control the privilege if it does exist, physicians would have had to comply with the statutory requirements of their state. If the statutes of the state require the reporting of the treatment of persons treated for gunshot wounds, physicians would have to comply with this requirement. If the statutes required the reporting of persons treated for venereal disease, this requirement would have to be complied with.

The physician-patient privilege is considered to be a very limited privilege subjected to the interpretation of the statutes of each state. The privilege, where it does exist, is for the protection of the patient and not the physician. Where the privilege does exist, it may be waived only by the patient. It has been held that the privilege ends when the patient dies and that an autopsy does not create a physician-patient relationship between the body of the dead person and surgeon.[21] In states where the privilege does not end with the death of the patient, the death certificate is available upon which the attending physician is required by law to give his opinion as to the cause of death.

The Requirement of a Physician-Patient Relationship

For the privilege to exist, the patient must have consulted the physician for treatment or diagnosis for possible treatment. Where such conditions exist, it is immaterial by whom the doctor is employed or paid. If the physician under these circumstances calls in other medical doctors to aid in the treatment or diagnosis, any disclosures made to any of the doctors are also privileged.

The general rule is that a physician-patient privilege does not exist when a suspect or a defendant is being examined at the request of law enforcement officers, a court, or a prosecutor. Such situations could occur when law enforcement officers had probable cause to believe that the suspect was driving a motor vehicle under the influence of a drug or alcohol, or when a court or prosecutor wanted a defendant examined for the purpose of determining his mental or physical condition.[22]

Must the Communication Be Confidential?

If the statute creating the physician-patient privilege does not use the word *confidential,* should courts read this requirement into the requirement for the privilege? Whereas the presence of employees of the doctor or professional associates of the doctor would not affect the privileged relationship, would the presence of other persons during disclosures cause a court to hold that no privilege existed? Persons present while disclosures and statements are made may testify as to what they heard, but the ability of the physician to testify would depend upon the court's ruling as to whether a privilege existed.[23] As an *example,* a law enforcement officer is properly present when a family doctor is attending a critically injured suspect. The officer may testify as to statements which the suspect made to his doctor. Whether the doctor could testify as to these statements would depend upon the ruling of the trial court.

PSYCHOTHERAPIST–PATIENT PRIVILEGE

Although no psychotherapist-patient privilege existed at common law, many states have created this privilege by statutes. For a patient to qualify for this privilege, he (or she) would have to seek the treatment or diagnosis of a licensed psychotherapist for treatment of mental or emotional conditions, including drug addiction. The definition of a psychotherapist ordinarily includes licensed physicians and psychologists, or persons reasonably believed by the patient to be so licensed. The conditions and limitations of this privilege are ordinarily similar to the physician-patient privilege.

CLERGYMAN–PENITENT PRIVILEGE

About two-thirds of the states are reported to have statutes defining the clergyman-penitent privilege, with a few other states recognizing the privilege by court decisions. No clear-cut privilege emerged from the old common law protecting confidential communications with clergymen.

Statutes ordinarily define a clergyman as a minister, priest, rabbi, or other similar functionary of a religious organization, or a person reasonably believed to be so by the penitent consulting him. A clergyman would not have to be engaged full-time in his profession, but the definitions are not so broad as to include all self-denominated "ministers."

Clergy would not ordinarily reveal confessions and confidential disclosures made to them because of moral and ethical reasons. The privilege establishes a legal basis for preventing such disclosures. Very few cases exist illustrating the privilege and its use. The following is one of the few available cases:

In the Matter of Keenan v. Gigante

Court of Appeals of New York (1979)
47 N.Y.2d 160, 417 N.Y.S.2d 231, 390 N.E.2d 1151

Reverend Louis Gigante was a New York City Councilman and also a Roman Catholic priest. He was subpoenaed to appear before a grand jury investigating abuses and preferential treatment within the New York City Department of Corrections. Father Gigante was questioned in regard to his relationship with a prisoner named James Napoli and whether Father Gigante had sought to obtain a Christmas furlough for Napoli and attempted to get Napoli into a work-release program. Father Gigante refused to answer, stating that the "questions attempt to infringe upon my practicing my ministry, which is protected by the First Amendment of the Constitution." In holding that the clergyman-penitent privilege did not protect the conversations involved, the Court ruled that:

> On the record before us, appellant raises no colorable First Amendment right, his right to practice his ministry cannot serve to shield him from shedding light upon whether or not any unlawful efforts were undertaken to assist those confined in New York City penal institutions to obtain special privileges and entrance into work release programs or to obtain a transfer to less secure institutions. In so holding, we observe that the statutory privilege (CPLR 4505) affords appellant any necessary protection against infringement of freedom of religion by Grand Jury investigations, and we reject his contention that the right to practice his ministry bestows more extensive protection beyond the scope of the priest-penitent privilege accorded by statute.
> . . .
> Absent a showing that the conversations sought to be disclosed are embraced by the priest-penitent privilege, appellant, even though a clergyman, is, like all citizens, obligated to respond to those questions relevant to the Grand Jury's investigation.

THE PRIVILEGE OF A NEWSPERSON NOT TO REVEAL THE SOURCE OF HIS (OR HER) INFORMATION

At common law there was no privilege for a newsperson or a journalist to refuse to reveal the source of his information if requested to do so by an authorized legislative or judicial body. Some states (fewer than twenty) have provided some type of statutory protection for a newsperson's confidential sources.

In all other states, the rule remains that the public's right to know outweighs the private interest of newspersons not to reveal sources of their information unless a First Amendment interest exists.

Obtaining Information Needed in a Criminal Investigation

In the following U.S. Supreme Court case, the Court held that the First Amendment does provide "some protection for seeking out the news," but held that the First Amendment does not protect a newsman's agreement to conceal the criminal conduct of his source or evidence thereof:

Branzburg v. Hayes

Supreme Court of the United States (1972)
408 U.S. 665, 92 S.Ct. 2646

Three separate cases from different states were consolidated and heard together. Reporters were brought before grand juries and requested to testify as to the sources of stories which they had written regarding "traffic in illegal drugs . . . assassination attempts on the President and . . . (it was assumed) violent disorders endangering persons and property." The journalists objected on the ground that requiring them to testify would "drive a wedge of distrust and silence between the news media" and their confidential informants. Because none of the jurisdictions had statutes extending a privilege to newspersons not to reveal the source of their information, the Supreme Court affirmed orders that the newspersons must appear and reveal sources of their information.

> . . . the press may not circulate knowing or reckless falsehoods damaging to private reputation without subjecting itself to liability for damages, including punitive damages, or even criminal prosecution . . . .
>
> It has generally been held that the First Amendment does not guarantee the press a constitutional right of special access to information not available to the public generally . . . .
>
> Newsmen have no constitutional right of access to the scenes of crime or disaster when the general public is excluded, and they may be prohibited from attending or publishing information about trials if such restrictions are necessary to assure a defendant a fair trial before an impartial tribunal . . . .
>
> It is thus not surprising that the great weight of authority is that newsmen are not exempt from the normal duty of appearing before a grand jury and answering questions relevant to a criminal investigation. At common law, courts consistently refused to recognize the existence of any privilege authorizing a newsman to refuse to reveal confidential information to a grand jury.

Official Harassment of the Press or Use of the Press as an Investigative Tool

If information is needed from a newsperson for criminal investigation, the newsperson would be obligated to provide the information unless protected by a statutory privilege. Disclosure, however, would generally not be required unless such information were necessary in the investigation of criminal activity. The following cases illustrate:

Morgan v. State

Supreme Court of Florida (1976)
337 So.2d 951

A Miami grand jury investigating charges of official corruption in Dade County issued a sealed presentment. A woman news reporter obtained a copy of the document and published information on the secret report under her byline. When questioned as to the source of her information, she declined to answer. She was sentenced to a five-month jail sentence on contempt, although what she had done was not a crime and the information was not needed as part of a criminal investigation. In reversing the contempt order, the Supreme Court of Florida held that

The First Amendment is clearly implicated when government moves against a member of the press because of what she has caused to be published. These contempt proceedings were not brought to punish violation of a criminal statute and were not part of an effort to obtain information needed in a criminal investigation. Their purpose was to force a newspaper reporter to disclose the source of published information, so that the authorities could silence the source. The present case falls squarely within this language in the *Branzburg* plurality opinion: "Official harassment of the press undertaken not for purposes of law enforcement but to disrupt a reporter's relationship with his news sources would have no justification." 408 U.S. at 707–8, 92 S.Ct. at 2670.

State ex rel. Green Bay Newspaper Co. v. Circuit Court, Branch 1, Brown County

Supreme Court of Wisconsin (1983)
113 Wis.2d 411, 335 N.W.2d 367

As a result of a John Doe investigation, two Wisconsin men were charged with first-degree murder. Their lawyers filed motions for a change of venue. In order to determine whether a change of venue should be ordered, all news media were ordered to provide copies of newspaper articles on the murder and the John Doe investigation. Several articles had been written noting that the information was obtained from unnamed sources. Defendant Phillips and his attorney requested the identity of the unnamed sources to defend Phillips against the charge of murder. When the reporters would not disclose the information, they were held in contempt. In reversing and holding that the contempt order was not proper, the Supreme Court of Wisconsin ruled that

We agree with the Supreme Court of Virginia in *Brown v. Commonwealth*, 214 Va. 755, 204 S.E.2d 429, 431 (1974), that the journalist's privilege "is a *privilege* related to the First Amendment and not a First Amendment *right,* absolute, universal, and paramount to all other rights." (Emphasis in original.) We believe this conclusion is equally applicable to the journalist's privilege under the Wisconsin Constitution . . . .

A defendant has no constitutional right to compulsory process to obtain information that is not material. Evidence which is inadmissible at trial and which has not been shown to have a reasonable probability of leading to competent, relevant, material and exculpatory evidence is clearly immaterial to the defendant's defense . . . .

The defendant has a constitutional right to discover the existence of potential witnesses. This right includes the right to use compulsory process to obtain information which will lead to competent, relevant, material and exculpatory evidence. Information, such as the names of the reporters' sources, which might lead to exculpatory evidence would meet the requirements for compulsory process to issue. Because a journalist's privilege of nondisclosure is claimed, before a subpoena would be enforced the procedure set out herein would have to be followed.

In the present case, the defendant has not yet made a showing that there is a reasonable probability that the reporters' testimony will lead to competent, relevant, material and exculpatory evidence from witnesses apart from representatives of the state or witnesses at the John Doe . . . .

The reporters testified that their articles contained everything substantive that their sources had revealed to them. The news articles involved in this case contain no suggestion that the unnamed sources have any knowledge whatsoever about the crime for which the defendant is charged . . . .

In addition, nothing in the testimony of the reporters at the hearing on the motion to quash the subpoenas suggested that any of their sources might be able to provide exculpatory evidence.

Because the defendant Phillips has not made a showing, sufficient to require the denial of the reporters' motion to quash, the trial court erred in denying the motion and ordering *in camera* disclosure of the reporters' sources.

Since we determine that Phillips failed to make a *prima facie* case for the issuance of the subpoenas, the trial court's finding of contempt was not proper. We therefore reverse the contempt order entered by the court.

IS THERE A PARENT–CHILD PRIVILEGE?

Can a parent be compelled to testify against a child? Could a child be compelled to testify against a parent? Or could either voluntarily testify in a criminal case against the other?

The question of whether a privilege exists based solely on the parent-child relationship has come before many courts in recent years. The Seventh Circuit Court of Appeals reviewed these cases in the following case and found that only one federal trial court and only one state appellate court have recognized some type of parent-child privilege.[24] Most courts have refused to recognize a parent-child privilege.

In rejecting the rulings of the two American courts that recognized a parent-child privilege, the following court refused to recognize such a privilege:

United States v. Davies and Kaprelian

U.S. Court of Appeals, Seventh Circuit (1985)
768 F.2d 893

While a jewelry salesman was paying for gasoline at a self-service station, another man got into his Cadillac and drove away with the car and sample cases filled with jewelry. The Cadillac was driven to another state, where a witness and other information lead the FBI to believe that Kaprelian was involved in the theft. While agents had Kaprelian's house under surveillance, Kaprelian's teenaged daughter left the house on her bike. Agents followed her a few blocks and asked to talk to her after identifying themselves. The daughter stated that Davies was her father's girlfriend and gave the agents Davies' telephone number (where Kaprelian was living). From the number, the agents obtained the address, and by placing Davies' apartment under surveillance, they were able to arrest Davies as she was transporting the jewelry in a tote bag. In rejecting Kaprelian's claim of parent-child privilege forbidding the use of the evidence, the Court held that

> Even were there some substantial support for the defendant's proposition that there is a parent-child privilege this case would not be one in which it could be applied. Privileges apply only to prevent the use of testimony in a judicial proceeding. Kaprelian's daughter gave the F.B.I. agent his telephone number during the F.B.I.'s investigation of the jewel robbery. As the Supreme Court has noted, "[n]either *Hawkins* [*v. United States,* 358 U.S. 74, 79 S.Ct. 136, 3 L.Ed.2d 125 (1958)], nor any other privilege, prevents the Government from enlisting one spouse to give information concerning the other to aid in the other's apprehension." *Trammel,* 445 U.S. at 52 n. 12, 100 S.Ct. at 913 n. 12. Kaprelian makes no assertion that the government ever intended to call his daughter at the trial; his assertions of privilege are based solely on her questioning during the investigation. Thus neither this phone number nor any other evidence obtained through this critical investigative lead are subject to suppression by the district court.
>
> We thus reject Kaprelian's claim that there exists a privilege for communications between parents and their children in criminal cases and find no error in the admission of evidence developed as a result of obtaining Kaprelian's telephone number from his daughter.

THE PRIVILEGE OF A WITNESS NOT TO REVEAL HOW HE (OR SHE) VOTED

Because secrecy in voting is an essential element of the democratic process, many states have enacted statutes ensuring the secrecy of a witness' ballot.

Questions as to how a witness voted would ordinarily not be relevant or material to the issues before a court. However, in cases having to do with vote fraud or election law violations, the question might be relevant and material. In these situations, the state statutes would determine whether a privilege existed under which the witness might refuse to answer. The Uniform Rules of Evidence suggest the following statutory exception:

> This privilege does not apply if the court finds that the vote was cast illegally or determines that the disclosure should be compelled pursuant to the (election laws of the state).

THE PRIVILEGE OF THE GOVERNMENT NOT TO REVEAL STATE OR GOVERNMENTAL SECRETS

The question of what secrets the federal and state governments are privileged from revealing has been presented to many courts. For example, grand jury proceedings have traditionally been kept secret under the authority of old common law and modern statutes. As to military secrets and secrets of state, the privilege not to reveal such matters has been held by the U.S. Supreme Court to be "well established in the law of evidence." [25] The following case came before the U.S. Supreme Court in 1953:

United States v. Reynolds

Supreme Court of the United States (1953)
345 U.S. 1, 73 S.Ct. 528

Widows of civilians killed in the crash of a U.S. Air Force plane attempted to obtain the Air Force's official accident report for use in a civil suit. The Secretary of the Air Force wrote a letter to the trial judge stating that to make the document public was against public interest because the report contained information on secret electronic devices. In holding that the government had a privilege not to reveal such information, the Supreme Court ruled that

> In the instant case we cannot escape judicial notice that this is a time of vigorous preparation for national defense. Experience in the past war has made it common knowledge that air power is one of the most potent weapons in our scheme of defense, and that newly developing electronic devices have greatly enhanced the effective use of air power. It is equally apparent that these electronic devices must be kept secret if their full military advantage is to be exploited in the national interests. On the record before the trial court it appeared that this accident occurred to a military plane which had gone aloft to test secret electronic equipment. Certainly there was a reasonable danger that the accident investigation report would contain references to the secret electronic equipment which was the primary concern of the mission.
> Of course, even with this information before him, the trial judge was in no position to decide that the report was privileged until there had been a formal claim of privilege. Thus it was entirely proper to rule initially that petitioner had shown probable cause for discovery of the

Privileged Communications

ARE THE FOLLOWING EXCEPTIONS RECOGNIZED IN YOUR STATE?

Husband-Wife Privilege (Statute #_____)

- Where one spouse commits a crime against the other?_____
- Where one (or both) spouse commits a crime against a child of one (or both)?_____
- Where both spouses are parties to the action (divorce, for example)?_____
- Where a spouse is charged with prostitution or pandering?_____
- Other?_____

Doctor-Patient Privilege (Statute #_____)

- Are any other medical professionals included in the statute?_____
- Must gunshot wounds be reported?_____
- Must venereal disease be reported? Which diseases?_____
  _____
- Must "suspicious" or "reasonable grounds" child abuse be reported?_____
- Must evidence of homicide be reported?_____
- Does the privilege protect chemical (or blood) tests for intoxication?_____
- Does the privilege protect evidence in paternity proceedings?_____
- Can the privilege be used when the patient is suing the doctor for malpractice?_____
- Can the privilege be used when a judge ordered the physical, mental exam?_____
- Other?_____

Lawyer-Client Privilege (Statute #_____)

- Where the services of the lawyer are sought to aid and further a crime or fraud?_____
- Where the client will commit (or has committed) perjury?_____
- Where there has been a breach of duty by the client to the lawyer or by the lawyer to the client?_____
- Other?_____

Informant-Government Privilege (Statute #_____)

- This privilege belongs to? (Who may exercise the privilege?)_____
  _____
- Can identity of informant be ordered if the informant participated in crime?_____
- Can identity of informant be ordered if informant was present at crime?_____
- Can identity of informant be ordered if informant was present at time of arrest?_____
- Other?_____

documents. Thereafter, when the formal claim of privilege was filed by the Secretary of the Air Force, under circumstances indicating a reasonable possibility that military secrets were involved, there was certainly a sufficient showing of privilege to cut off further demand for the document on the showing of necessity for its compulsion that had then been made.

THE PRIVILEGE OF THE GOVERNMENT NOT TO REVEAL THE IDENTITY OF INFORMANTS

Courts in all states and the federal government recognize the privilege of the government not to reveal the identity of an informer who is not appearing as a witness. Should an informer or another person appear as a witness, they must reveal their true identity.[26]

An informer can be a private citizen who has provided information useful in developing the case against a defendant. An informer can also be a person receiving money or other considerations from a law enforcement agency for the information he provides.

In some situations, the government may be ordered by a court to reveal the identity of an informer. When confronted with a court order to reveal the name of an informer, the government must then make the choice of either:

- Revealing the identity of the informer
- Requesting the court to dismiss the criminal charge (or charges) against the defendant

Disclosing and Revealing the Identity of an Informant

Courts have long recognized that informants and undercover agents must be used in some criminal investigations. The U.S. Supreme Court stated in 1966 that:[27]

> it has long been acknowledged by the decisions of this Court ... that, in the detection of many types of crime, the Government is entitled to use decoys and to conceal the identity of its agents.

The *FBI Law Enforcement Bulletin* article entitled "The Informer's Identity at Trial" (February 1975) states the following in regard to disclosing and revealing the identity of an informant:

> In considering cases in which the informer is a witness, one writer has asserted that "disclosure will be compelled if the informer is a material witness on the issue of guilt."[28] The Court of Special Appeals of Maryland in *Nutter v. State*[29] carefully assessed the disclosure probabilities of an informant who was merely a witness to the criminal offense and not a participant or accessory. In noting that a "material witness" is one whose testimony is important to a fair determination of the cause, the court said:
> > "... although an eyewitness to a crime is clearly a 'material' witness as that word is ordinarily used, if he is an informer,

simply observing an illegal transaction but not participating in it, the fact that he observes the transaction does not necessarily make his possible testimony so important as to compel disclosure of his identity in the face of the rationale of the nondisclosure privilege."

State v. Booker,[30] a 1965 New Jersey case, offers a typical factual situation wherein the informant's role is limited to that of a mere witness. The informer was with a narcotics agent when the defendant approached their vehicle and initiated what resulted in a sale of narcotics to the agent. The court held that the mere presence of the informer during the commission of the illegal act did not remove him from the protection of the privilege.

Presence is only one fact to consider with all the other facts in determining whether disclosure of his identity is essential to assure a fair determination of the issues.[31] It appears, then, that when the informer merely witnesses the allegedly illegal act his identity normally will be protected.[32]

PROBLEMS

1. When a thirteen-year-old California girl became aware that her parents were using marijuana and cocaine, she pleaded with them to quit. They continued using drugs. After attending a church lecture by a policeman on the effects of drugs, Deanna Young decided to do something about the drugs in her home. While her parents were not home, she collected drugs and drug packaging equipment in a trash bag and turned everything over to the police. The cocaine had an estimated value of $2,800. Could the girl appear as a witness against her parents if the case went to trial?

2. Just before midnight, defendant Jerry Miller of Oregon called his brother in California and told him that he had just "strangled a kid." The defendant's brother advised him to call a mental hospital or to talk to someone who could help him with his problem. The defendant then called a state hospital and, after giving a false name, asked to speak to a doctor. When the secretary-receptionist asked what the problem was, the defendant replied, "Murder. I just killed a man." Before letting the defendant speak with a psychiatrist, the secretary obtained the telephone number from which the defendant was calling. While the defendant was speaking with the psychiatrist on duty, the sheriff was called. The defendant was taken into custody in a public phone booth as he was talking to the psychiatrist. The defendant was questioned without advising him of his *Miranda* rights. The defendant admitted that he had "hurt someone." The deceased victim's body was found in the defendant's hotel room. Which of the following persons could testify in the criminal homicide trial as to the statements made by the defendant? (a) the brother? (b) the secretary-receptionist at the hospital? (c) the psychiatrist who talked to the defendant for ten to fifteen minutes? (d) the police officer who took the defendant into custody? Explain the reasons for your answer. *State v. Miller*, 300 Or. 203, 709 P.2d 225 (Or.Sup.Ct.1985).

3. In the presence of one or more children, a husband (defendant) told his wife that he was planning a robbery. Late that night, while no other persons were

present, the husband gave his wife a ring and a watch taken in the robbery. A number of hours later, in the presence of three children, the husband told the wife that he had hit the victim with a brick and then robbed the victim. He told the wife that the watch and ring were obtained in the robbery. The ages of the children were thirteen, ten, and eight. The oldest child was from the wife's first marriage and the other two children were from the defendant's marriage. The robbery victim died and the wife testified as to the three conversations in the defendant's trial for murder and armed robbery. The state argued that the first and third conversations were not privileged since they could not be confidential in the presence of the children. The State also argued that the second conversation was not confidential and privileged because the husband gave his wife the watch and ring which he expected her to wear in public. Did the Supreme Court of Illinois hold that all or some of the conversations could not be used as evidence under the husband-wife privilege? Give reasons for your answer. Could the thirteen-year-old child appear as a witness? *People v. Sanders,* 99 Ill.2d 262, 75 Ill. Dec. 682, 457 N.E.2d 1241 (1983).

NOTES

[1] See Article II of the Federal Rules of Evidence in appendix B.

[2] Varcoe v. Lee, 180 Cal. 338, 181 P. 223, 226 (1919).

[3] Sumpter v. State, 261 Ind. 471, 306 N.E.2d 95 (1974).

[4] 57 Ill.App.2d 160, 206 N.E.2d 776 (1965).

[5] 2 Cal.3d 912, 88 Cal.Rptr. 192, 471 P.2d 992 (1970).

[6] West Publishing Co., 1954.

[7] See 31 Corpus Juris Secundum (Evidence) § 27, p. 872.

[8] The U.S. Supreme Court in Trammel v. United States, 445 U.S. 40, 100 S.Ct. 906, quoting other cases.

[9] 339 U.S. 323, 70 S.Ct. 724 (1950).

[10] 408 U.S. 665, 92 S.Ct. 2646 (1972). Within their statement, the Supreme Court quoted 8 J. Wigmore, Evidence, sec. 2192.

[11] As to the amount of judicial inquiry a trial court should make in determining whether a witness is lawfully and properly using his 5th Amendment privilege against self-incrimination, the U.S. Supreme Court stated in United States v. Reynolds, 345 U.S. 1, 73 S.Ct. 528 (1953) that "The privilege against self-incrimination presented the courts with a similar sort of problem. Too much judicial inquiry into the claim of privilege would force disclosure of the thing the privilege was meant to protect, while a complete abandonment of judicial control would lead to intolerable abuses. Indeed, in the earlier stages of judicial experience with the problem, both extremes were advocated, some saying that the bare assertion by the witness must be taken as conclusive, and others saying that the witness should be required to reveal the matter behind his claim of privilege to the judge for verification. Neither extreme prevailed, and a sound formula of compromise was developed. This formula received authoritative expression in this country as early as the Burr trial. There are differences in phraseology, but in substance it is agreed that the court must be satisfied from all the evidence and circumstances, and 'from the implications of the question, in the setting in which it is asked, that a responsive answer to the question or an explanation of why it cannot be answered might be dangerous because injurious exposure could result.' Hoffman v. United States, 341 U.S. 479, 486–487, 71 S.Ct. 814, 818 (1951). If the court is so satisfied, the claim of the privilege will be accepted without requiring further disclosure."

[12] 449 U.S. 383, 101 S.Ct. 677 (1981).

[13] The "work-product" doctrine is closely related to the attorney-client privilege. The U.S. Supreme Court stated in Upjohn Co. v. United States, 449 U.S. 383, 101 S.Ct. 677 (1981), that

This doctrine was announced by the Court over 30 years ago in Hickman v. Taylor, 329 U.S. 495 (1947). In that case the Court rejected "an attempt, without purported necessity or justification, to secure written statements, private memoranda, and personal recollections prepared or formed by an adverse party's counsel in the course of his legal duties." *Id.*, at 510. The Court noted that "it is essential that a lawyer work with a certain degree of privacy" and reasoned that if discovery of the material sought were permitted

> "much of what is now put down in writing would remain unwritten. An attorney's thoughts, heretofore inviolate, would not be his own. Inefficiency, unfairness and sharp practices would inevitably develop in the giving of legal advice and in the preparation of cases for trial. The effect on the legal profession would be demoralizing. And the interests of the clients and the cause of justice would be poorly served." *Id.*, at 511.

The "strong public policy" underlying the work-product doctrine was reaffirmed recently in United States v. Nobles, 422 U.S. 225, 236–240 (1975), and has been substantially incorporated in Federal Rule of Civil Procedure 26(b)(3).

As we stated last Term, the obligation imposed by a tax summons remains "subject to the traditional privileges and limitations." United States v. Euge, 444 U.S. 707, 714 (1980). Nothing in the language of the IRS summons provisions or their legislative history suggests an intent on the part of Congress to preclude application of the work-product doctrine. Rule 26(b)(3) codifies the work-product doctrine, and the Federal Rules of Civil Procedure are made applicable to summons enforcement proceedings by Rule 81(a)(3). See Donaldson v. United States, 400 U.S. 517, 528 (1971). While conceding the applicability of the work-product doctrine, the Government asserts that it has made a sufficient showing of necessity to overcome its protections. The magistrate apparently so found, Pet.App. 30a. The Government relies on the following language in *Hickman:*

> "We do not mean to say that all written materials obtained or prepared by an adversary's counsel with an eye toward litigation are necessarily free from discovery in all cases. Where relevant and nonprivileged facts remain hidden in an attorney's file and where production of those facts is essential to the preparation of one's case, discovery may properly be had .... And production might be justified where the witnesses are no longer available or may be reached only with difficulty." 329 U.S., at 511.

[14] In criminal cases, many defendants tell their attorneys only what the defendant believes is best for the attorney to know. Unless the defense attorney is able to obtain a broader picture of the events which occurred, his only information is his client's side of the story as presented to him by his client.

[15] See Chapter 10 of *McCormick on Evidence* (West Publishing Co., 1972).

[16] 385 U.S. 293, 87 S.Ct. 408 (1966).

[17] 445 U.S. 40, 100 S.Ct. 906 (1980).

[18] See In re John Doe Corp., 675 F.2d 482, 491 (2d Cir.1982).

[19] Griswold v. Connecticut, 381 U.S. 479, 486, 85 S.Ct. 1678, 1682 (1965).

[20] In re Grand Jury Subpoena U.S., 755 F.2d 1022 (2d Cir.1985).

[21] See 97 Corpus Juris Secundum (Witnesses) § 294.

[22] See State v. Shaw, 106 Ariz. 103, 471 P.2d 715 (1970) cert. denied by the U.S. Supreme Court, 400 U.S. 1009, 91 S.Ct. 569 (1971).

[23] See pages 216–217 of *McCormick on Evidence,* 2d ed. (West Publishing Co., 1972).

[24] The courts and cases holding a parent-child privilege exist are: In re Agosto, 553 F.Supp. 1298 (D.Nev.1983) and In re Application of A & M, 61 App.Div.2d 426, 403 N.Y.S.2d 375 (1975).

[25] United States v. Reynolds, 345 U.S. 1, 73 S.Ct. 528 (1953). Dean Wigmore in 8 Wigmore § 2378 stated that the privilege not to reveal military and state secrets was a privilege "the existence of which has never been doubted."

[26] See Smith v. Illinois, 390 U.S. 129, 88 S.Ct. 748 (1968) where the principal witness for the State did not use his true name. The U.S. Supreme Court reversed the defendant's conviction, holding that the defendant "was denied a right guaranteed to him under the Sixth and Fourteenth Amendments of the Constitution."

[27] Lewis v. United States, 385 U.S. 206, 208, 209, 87 S.Ct. 424, 426 (1966).

[28] Wigmore, supra footnote 5 at 769.

[29] 8 Md.App. 635, 262 A.2d 80 (1970).

[30] 86 N.J.Super. 175, 206 A.2d 365 (1965).

[31] Accord, Miller v. United States, 273 F.2d 279 (5th Cir.1959), cert. denied 362 U.S. 928, 80 S.Ct. 756 (1960); State v. Oliver, 50 N.J. 39, 231 A.2d 805 (1967).

[32] Estevez v. State, 130 Ga.App. 215, 202 S.E.2d 686 (1973); State v. Oliver, 50 N.J. 39, 231 A.2d 805 (1967); Kovash v. State, 519 P.2d 517 (Okla.Crim.App.1974). Contra, People v. McShann, 50 Cal.2d 802, 330 P.2d 33 (1958) (where the court indicated an eyewitness-nonparticipant informer's testimony that would vindicate the accused or lessen the risk of false testimony would be relevant); James v. State, 493 S.W.2d 201 (Tex.Crim.App.1973).

The Use of Hearsay in the Courtroom

This chapter was written by Attorney Michael Ash. Mr. Ash is a former assistant and deputy district attorney in Milwaukee County. He holds a Master's degree in Government and a law degree from Harvard University. Mr. Ash is now in the private practice of the law with the Milwaukee firm of Godfrey and Kahn.

THE HEARSAY RULE

Hearsay information in general is information of which we have "heard it said." Grandma receives a telephone call from dad that her new grandson has thick, wavy, red hair. Grandma boasts to friends of her infant grandson's thick, wavy, red hair. Not having seen the boy, she is relying upon and speaking on the basis of hearsay information, that is, what her son-in-law told her about the boy's hair. Until she has seen the child's head, she has only information of which "she has heard it said."

All American jurisdictions restrict considerably the admissibility at trial of evidence based on hearsay information, whether the evidence be oral or written. This chapter concerns itself with the extent to which such information is admissible in the trial of criminal and civil cases. Although admissibility rules may differ somewhat between criminal and civil cases, the hearsay rules as such do not. Admissibility rules differ in criminal cases because of constitutional issues that would not be present in civil cases.

The chapter concerns itself with the use of hearsay in the courtroom *at trial*. The extent to which hearsay rules apply at various types of courtroom hearings prior to trial varies considerably from jurisdiction to jurisdiction. In some states, for example, a "preliminary examination" may consist merely of the testimony of a police officer who reads police reports replete with hearsay information. Such testimony will be deemed admissible and will be held to justify a probable cause determination. In other jurisdictions, preliminary examinations will be miniature trials with numerous witnesses and hearsay rules strictly adhered to. Thus, it is necessary to consult the laws of your particular jurisdiction about the extent to which the following trial rules apply at various types of pretrial hearings at which evidence may be taken.

Hearsay is defined as "evidence of a statement made out of court, the statement being offered as an assertion to show the truth of matters asserted therein and thus resting for its value upon the credibility of the out-of-court assertor." [1] Rule 801(c) of the Federal Rules of Evidence defines hearsay as "a statement, other than one made by the declarant while testifying at the trial or hearing, offered in evidence to prove the truth of the matter asserted."

The hearsay rule of evidence is to the layman at once the most familiar and the least understood of all the rules of evidence. Even knowledgable laypersons, like police officers, are frequently puzzled by rulings that may not square with what they learned in classrooms. A lawyer's objection on hearsay grounds and the trial judge's exclusion of evidence on that basis may be mystifying and apparently unexplainable.

Partly, this results from the niceties of distinction which characterize hearsay law. These niceties are not easily capsulized and simplification of them may sacrifice accuracy and precision and may lead to misunderstandings. Lawyers and judges themselves may not understand the law of hearsay completely. It is a myth that judges are oracular fonts of perfect knowledge concerning the law. They are often average lawyers (or worse) who have been elevated to their positions by politics or happenstance.

Moreover, courtroom lawyers are advocates. They are ethically bound to advance any honestly defensible position that they believe to be to the advantage of their client. They may and frequently do make objections in the courtroom which they would not sustain if they were judges.

Furthermore, the progress of the trial (and the need to minimize inconvenience to jurors, witnesses, and other participants) requires that most evidentiary objections be ruled upon from the bench in almost reflexive fashion. The judge who frequently asks attorneys for argument on their objections or, worse, goes running into chambers to consult law books or chat with counsel, slows the trial, tries the patience of all participants, and acts to the detriment of the factfinding process.

Impromptu rulings, however, may not be sufficiently thought out and may therefore be "wrong," even though the judge, if he had time to reflect, might well have ruled correctly.

It is hard, finally, to exaggerate the impact of local customs and understandings on actual trial court practice. Significant variances in customs and understanding may occur from city to city within the same state and even from court to court or judge to judge within the same city. Sometimes such customs and understandings will result in marked discrepancy between actual practice in a given courtroom and those described as "correct" in this chapter. Hence, it is always important to find out and know what a given judge's attitude is likely to be toward an evidentiary question, especially when the "correct" rule is hard to determine or when the precise question falls within the numerous gray areas of hearsay law where the answer is not quite clear.

REASONS FOR HEARSAY RULE

Why is there a hearsay rule at all? Understanding the policies behind the rule is exceptionally important to an understanding of the rule itself.

In general, hearsay evidence is suspect. In many circumstances, it is deemed so unworthy of credit that even though relevant and material it will not be admitted and not brought to the jury's attention.

Three reasons are generally advanced for the existence of rules barring or limiting the admissibility of hearsay evidence:

- The source of the information has *not* been sworn and hence his assertion, unsupported by oath, is to that extent unworthy of acceptance.

- The assertor is *not* subject to cross-examination and therefore his assertion cannot be tested adequately. Cross-examination, it is believed, would result in testing the assertor's memory, ability to perceive, bias, truthfulness, and the like.

- The assertor is *not* present in the courtroom, and therefore, the trier of fact cannot observe his demeanor and appearance. The assertor reliability (and the credibility of his assertion) cannot therefore be tested by the kind of eyeball contact that courtroom testimony has traditionally provided.

Having evolved against this background and in light of these considerations, the law of hearsay typically permits the use of hearsay when there are "indications of reliability" in the assertion sufficient to compensate for the lack of (1) an oath, (2) cross-examination, and (3) the personal appearance of the assertor before the court.

HEARSAY RULE: EXCLUDES *ONLY* STATEMENTS OFFERED TO PROVE THE TRUTH OF MATTERS ASSERTED

Professor McCormick states that

> The hearsay rule forbids evidence of out-of-court assertions *to prove the facts asserted in them.* Manifestly, proof of utterances and writings may be made with an almost infinite variety of other purposes, not resting for their value upon the veracity of the out of court declarant and hence falling outside the hearsay classification. *McCormick on Evidence* (2nd Ed.), supra, § 249, p. 588.

The Federal Rules of Evidence are virtually identical. Statements of a person offered through another person (the witness) when not offered to prove the truth of the matter asserted are always held to be outside the scope of the hearsay rule and not objectionable on hearsay grounds. If the out-of-court assertion is not offered to prove the truth of the matter asserted, no need exists to have the assertor (1) sworn, (2) cross-examined, or (3) brought before the trier of fact. The assertor's credibility is not at issue, only the fact of the assertion having been made. On that issue, the witness on the stand testifying that the assertion was made can be (1) sworn, (2) cross-examined, and (3) before the tribunal. Thus, the purposes of the hearsay rule are sufficiently accomplished.

For example, A testifies that B said, "I saw C stab D five times with a knife." In the trial of C for the murder of D, such evidence would evidently be used to prove the fact of C's having stabbed D. Thus, A's testimony as to B's statement would be offered for the truth of what B asserted and should be excluded as inadmissible hearsay.

On the other hand, suppose Bob Buyer is being sued by Victor Victim in connection with an auto accident in which he rear-ended Victim's vehicle. Evidence at the trial has shown that the accident occurred one half hour after Buyer purchased the car he was driving from Sam Seller. Fred Friend testifies that at or about the time of the sale, Seller said, "The brakes in this car are defective." A lawyer objects on grounds of hearsay. What is the correct ruling?

The correct ruling depends on what Friend's testimony will be used to prove. If Friend's testimony were offered by Seller and used to prove that the brakes on Seller's car were defective, and therefore that he was not negligent, Friend's testimony would have to be excluded upon timely objection by Victim's attorney. Friend's testimony as to Seller's assertion would be used to prove the truth of the assertion and would therefore be inadmissible hearsay.

If, on the other hand, Friend testified that Buyer was standing next to Seller when Seller's assertion was made, and if Friend's testimony were offered by Victim to show that Buyer *knew* of the condition of the brakes when he took the wheel, the evidence would be admissible, and Buyer's attorney's objection should be overruled. The out-of-court assertion of Seller is not being offered to prove the truth of the matter asserted, but rather to prove something else. In this instance, that Buyer heard about a problem with the brakes and therefore failed to exercise due care in taking the vehicle on the road.

There are many ways in which an out-of-court assertion may be offered to prove something other than the truth of the matter asserted. Only a few of numerous possible examples follow:

- *Knowledge.* William Witness testifies that Fred Firebug told him that a can of gasoline was in the attic of the house the day before the fire occurred. Witness's testimony would *not* be admissible to prove that there was gasoline in the attic the day before the fire. It would be admissible to show that Firebug *knew* that there was gasoline in the attic before the fire.

- *Feelings or state of mind.* William Witness testifies that Fred Firebug had said, "Bobby Burnout took my money, stole my girl, and wrecked my car on the night of the senior prom." This testimony would not be admissible to show that Burnout had taken Firebug's money, or stolen his girlfriend, or wrecked his car. It would be admissible to show Firebug's feelings or state of mind about Burnout.

- *Insanity.* William Witness testifies that Charles Crazy had said, "I am Napoleon Bonaparte, Emperor of All France." Witness's testimony would not be admissible to show that Crazy was in fact a person named Napoleon Bonaparte. It would, however, be admissible to show circumstantially that Crazy was insane.

- *Effect on hearer.* William Witness testifies that he heard Bill Bully say to Tom Timid, "No one better mess with me. I am carrying a loaded .38." The testimony would not be admissible to show that Bully was carrying a gun. It would be admissible to show the effect on Timid's state of mind.

- *Verbal acts or verbal conduct.* William Witness testifies that he saw Betty Bargainer say to Charles Chiseler, "I accept your offer to buy my jewels for

$1,000." These are words to which the law attaches significance; in this case, the acceptance of an enforceable contract; and would be admissible to show the existence of such a contract. Witness testifies that he heard Farrah Fixer say to a police officer, "I have got 50 bucks in my purse for you if you'll tear up that traffic ticket." This verbal act constitutes the offering of a bribe and should be considered admissible.

- *Impeachment.* At a trial, A has testified at length and in detail about the circumstances of a barroom shooting. Witness testifies that A had told him, "I was in the men's room at the time of the shooting and didn't see anything." This prior inconsistent statement would be admissible as bearing on A's veracity and credibility and would be admissible for that purpose.

It frequently happens that an out-of-court statement could be relevant and used to prove both (1) the truth of the matter asserted and (2) something else. If offered to prove the truth of the matter asserted, a hearsay objection is well taken and should be sustained. On the other hand, if offered to prove something else, the hearsay objection is not well taken and should be overruled.

The device courts have employed to solve this problem is that of "limited admissibility" or "admissibility for a limited purpose." What this means is that the judge may admit the evidence "for a limited purpose," that is, the purpose consistent with admissibility under the hearsay rule, and instruct the jury that the evidence may not be considered for the improper purpose. If the case is being tried without a jury, the judge is supposed to consider the evidence for the proper purposes, but only for the proper purposes.

Using the example above, the scenario in a jury trial would go something like this. Victim's attorney would propound a number of preliminary questions to Friend, and then ask:

> Question: "What, if anything, did Seller say about the condition of the vehicle?"
> Buyer's attorney: "Objection, Your Honor, the question calls for hearsay."
> Victim's attorney: "Your Honor, the hearsay objection goes only to statements offered to prove the truth of the matter stated. In this instance, I am offering Friend's testimony as to Seller's assertion only for a limited purpose, that is, to show that Buyer knew the condition of the brakes and therefore was careless in driving the car on a highway without first having them repaired or checked."
> The Court: "Very well, counsel, the statement will be admitted for that purpose."

The court should tell the jury that it is to consider the evidence only for the allowable purpose. In this example, the court should say, "You are not allowed to consider Seller's statement on the question of the actual condition of the brakes, but only as bearing on Buyer's knowledge or belief."

Professor McCormick states, "Such an instruction may not always be effective, but admission of the evidence with a limiting instruction is normally the best available reconciliation of the respective interests." *McCormick on Evidence,* supra, § 59, p. 136.

Situations arise in which the danger of the jury's misusing the evidence is great. This could occur when the jury may be unduly confused by the judge's instructions or it could occur when the value of the evidence for its legitimate purpose is slight and the point for which it is competent can otherwise easily be proven. Under these circumstances, the trial judge has discretionary authority to exclude the evidence which is offered. However, "The normal practice is to admit the evidence." *McCormick on Evidence,* supra, § 59, pp. 135–36.

HEARSAY RULE: *NEVER* EXCLUDES ADMISSIONS OF A PARTY–OPPONENT

A **party** to a lawsuit is a person named in the pleadings whose rights will be determined by the outcome of the case. Suppose A is suing B for damages arising from an automobile accident allegedly caused by B's negligence. The caption of the case used in all official court documents is "A v. B." "A" and "B" are named in the pleadings. If A wins, B will have to pay A money. If A loses, A will have to pay costs to B. Rights of A and B will be determined by the outcome of the lawsuit. Hence, A and B are parties to the lawsuit.

Suppose William Witness takes the stand at B's request and testifies that A told him, "I was blind drunk and speeding when I crashed into B's car." A's attorney had objected on grounds of hearsay. Was Witness's testimony properly admitted?

The answer is, clearly, yes. Some authorities adopt a definition of the hearsay which excludes admissions of parties from the scope of the definition. Others speak of "admissions of a party opponent" as one of the exceptions to the hearsay rule (of which there are many).

Of this doctrine, Professor McCormick states that

Admissions are the words or acts of a party-opponent, or of his ... representative, offered as evidence against him ....

Regardless of the precise theory of admissibility, it is clear today that admissions of a party come in as substantive evidence of the facts admitted.

McCormick on Evidence (2nd Ed.), supra, § 262, pp. 628–29.

In criminal cases, one party (the plaintiff) is a governmental entity— "United States of America," "State of Florida," "People of California"—and the other is the accused person—the party defendant or, simply, the defendant. Statements of the defendant offered by the plaintiff, for example, "the State," will not be excluded by the hearsay rule. They are admissions of a party opponent and are admissible in evidence.

A confession is, of course, one kind of admission, usually the most incriminating. Confessions will not be excluded under the hearsay rule and will be deemed admissible if offered against the confessor.

Suppose A is charged with the murder of B on January 1, 1977. A offers the testimony of C, an inmate of the state prison, who testifies that D said to him, "I killed B all by myself on January 1, 1977." D does not testify. The state's attorney objected to C's testimony on grounds of hearsay. A's attorney replies that the statement at issue was an admission and is therefore admissible under an exception to the hearsay rule. Who is right?

On the arguments presented, the state's attorney is correct. The statement is undoubtedly a kind of admission but is not one "by a party opponent" to the lawsuit.[2] Because it is an out-of-court statement used to prove the truth of the matter asserted, it is hearsay and should be excluded.

HEARSAY RULE: EXCLUDES PRIOR TESTIMONY UNLESS WITNESS IS DEAD OR UNAVAILABLE AND PARTY AGAINST WHOM TESTIMONY IS OFFERED HAS HAD ADEQUATE OPPORTUNITY TO CROSS–EXAMINE

In General

Brenda Bandit is on trial for the armed robbery of George Grocer's store on May 1, 1987. At the trial, Grocer testifies at length about how he saw Bandit enter the store, point a sawed-off shotgun at his head, demand money, take cash from the register, and run from the store with the loot. Bandit's attorney extensively cross-examines Grocer about the incident and his identification of Ms. Bandit. A mistrial occurs and the state elects to try Bandit again. Prior to the second trial, Grocer dies. Can the state introduce at the second trial evidence as to Grocer's testimony at the first trial?

Clearly, the evidence falls within the scope of the hearsay rule. The state would call a witness, perhaps a court reporter, who would testify that Grocer was sworn, was asked certain questions, and gave certain answers. These answers would be used to prove the truth of matters asserted in the answers, that is, that Brenda Bandit came to George's grocery, pointed a sawed-off shotgun at Grocer, demanded money, took cash from the cash register, and fled.

Nevertheless, authorities are unanimous in saying that under such circumstances, the former testimony of Grocer is admissible. Some authorities adopt a definition of hearsay which excludes sworn, cross-examined past assertions from the definition of hearsay evidence. Others describe such assertions as simply being one of the numerous exceptions to the hearsay rule. One way or another, the testimony will normally be admitted.

Once past the simple example set forth above, the boundaries of the principle become comparatively hard to pinpoint. There is considerable difference between jurisdictions as to precisely what types of prior testimony are admissible and which are barred. This is an area in which it is especially important to consult the law of your own jurisdiction.

Professor McCormick, who treats prior testimony as an exception to the hearsay rule, summarizes the general scope of the exception as follows:

> The former testimony, to be admitted under this exception to the hearsay rule, must have been given under the sanction of the oath or such form of affirmation as is accepted as legally sufficient. More important, because more often drawn in question, is the requirement that the party against whom the former testimony is now offered, or a party in like interest, must have had a reasonable opportunity to cross-examine. Actual cross-examination, of course, is not essential, if the opportunity was afforded and waived. The opportunity must have been such as to render the conduct of the cross-examination or the decision not to cross-examine meaningful in the light of the circum-

stances which prevail when the former testimony is offered .... *McCormick on Evidence* (2nd Ed.), supra, § 255, p. 616.

He also points out that the witness must be shown to be unavailable before the exception can be relied upon:

> If former testimony is offered under the former testimony exception to the hearsay rule, then it is offered as a substitute for testimony given in person in open court, and the strong policy favoring personal presence requires that unavailability of the witness be shown, before the substitute is acceptable.
> *McCormick on Evidence* (2nd Ed.), supra, § 255, p. 617.

Some courts require in addition that the prior testimony be given under circumstances in which both the issues and the parties are identical.

The Impact of the Sixth Amendment Upon Hearsay Testimony

The Sixth Amendment to the United States Constitution provides: "In all criminal prosecutions, the accused shall enjoy the right ... to be confronted with the witnesses against him."

Obviously, this provision has a potential impact on the use of any hearsay evidence against a criminal defendant because hearsay is the assertion of a person not in court to confront the accused. Nevertheless, the confrontation issue has tended to arise especially frequently in "prior testimony" cases. The following case came before the U.S. Supreme Court:

Barber v. Page

Supreme Court of the United States (1968)
390 U.S. 719, 88 S.Ct. 1318

The defendant was charged with armed robbery in Oklahoma. The principal evidence against him was the testimony of an accomplice in the robbery, who had testified in person at the preliminary hearing. At the time of the trial, the accomplice witness, named Woods, was in a Texas prison 225 miles from the trial court. Instead of transporting the witness to testify in person, the state argued that he was unavailable, and read a transcript of his testimony from the preliminary hearing to the trial court. In reversing the conviction and ordering a new trial, the Supreme Court held that

> Here the State argues that the introduction of the transcript is within that exception on the grounds that Woods was outside the jurisdiction and therefore "unavailable" at the time of trial, and that the right of cross-examination was afforded petitioner at the preliminary hearing
> ...
> We start with the fact that the State made absolutely no effort to obtain the presence of Woods at trial other than to ascertain that he was in a federal prison outside Oklahoma. It must be acknowledged

that various courts and commentators have heretofore assumed that the mere absence of a witness from the jurisdiction was sufficient ground for dispensing with confrontation on the theory that "it is impossible to compel his attendance, because the process of the trial Court is of no force without the jurisdiction, and the party desiring his testimony is therefore helpless." 5 Wigmore, Evidence § 1404 (3d ed. 1940).

Whatever may have been the accuracy of that theory at one time, it is clear that at the present time increased cooperation between the States themselves and between the States and the Federal Government has largely deprived it of any continuing validity in the criminal law ....

In short, a witness is not "unavailable" for purposes of the foregoing exception to the confrontation requirement unless the prosecutorial authorities have made a good-faith effort to obtain his presence at trial. The State made no such effort here, and, so far as this record reveals, the sole reason why Woods was not present to testify in person was because the State did not attempt to seek his presence. The right of confrontation may not be dispensed with so lightly ....

... The right to confrontation is basically a trial right. It includes both the opportunity to cross-examine and the occasion for the jury to weigh the demeanor of the witness. A preliminary hearing is ordinarily a much less searching exploration into the merits of a case than a trial, simply because its function is the more limited one of determining whether probable cause exists to hold the accused for trial. While there may be some justification for holding that the opportunity for cross-examination of a witness at a preliminary hearing satisfies the demands of the confrontation clause where the witness is shown to be actually unavailable, this is not, as we have pointed out, such a case.

HEARSAY RULE: SEVEN MAJOR EXCEPTIONS

Spontaneous Declarations and Excited Utterances

All courts recognize an exception to the hearsay rule for spontaneous statements and excited utterances. The ultimate question is whether the statement was the result of reflective thought (in which case it may be inadmissible) or whether it was truly spontaneous. If the former, the hearsay rule may operate to exclude the statement. If the latter, the statement will be admitted under the exemption.

Spontaneous statements have been thought by judges and scholars to bear special indicia of reliability. Police officers have long recognized that the blurted out, tearful admission of a murderer at the scene of the crime is often a truer indication of what really happened than his carefully thought out reconstruction many months later at the time of his trial.

The boundaries of the law relating to the admissibility of various types of spontaneous declarations are murky and vary considerably from jurisdiction to jurisdiction. By far the broadest spontaneous declarations exception is set forth in the Federal Rules of Evidence Rule 803. Rule 803 provides in part that

The following are not excluded by the hearsay rule, even though the declarant is available as a witness:

(1) *Present sense impression.* A statement describing or explaining an event or condition made while the declarant was perceiving the event or condition, or immediately thereafter.

(2) *Excited utterance.* A statement relating to a startling event or condition made while the declarant was under the stress of excitement caused by the event or condition.

(3) *Then existing mental, emotional, or physical condition.* A statement of the declarant's then existing state of mind, emotion, sensation, or physical condition (such as intent, plan, motive, design, mental feeling, pain, and bodily health), but not including a statement of memory or belief to prove the fact remembered or believed unless it relates to the execution, revocation, identification, or terms of declarant's will.

(4) *Statements for purposes of medical diagnosis or treatment.* Statements made for purposes of medical diagnosis or treatment and describing medical history, or past or present symptoms, pain, or sensations, or the inception or general character of the cause or external source thereof insofar as reasonably pertinent to diagnosis or treatment.

Most jurisdictions have evolved rules that define more narrowly the spontaneous declarations and excited utterances that are exceptions to the hearsay rule. All jurisdictions, however, will admit statements for the truth of the matter asserted if

- there was an event or occurrence sufficiently startling to render normal reflective thought processes inoperative, and

- the statement was a spontaneous reaction to the occurrence or event and not the result of reflective thought.

Suppose Henry Hateful is accused of pushing his wife off the roof of a ten-story apartment building. At the time of the trial, Hateful's attorney calls Don Driver, a paramedic, to the stand. Driver testifies that he was at the scene of the incident within moments after being called and found Hateful's wife lying flat on the sidewalk in a pool of her own blood. He testifies that Sam Samaritan was bending over the body crying and frantically trying to stop the bleeding with a shirt that had been torn into pieces. Driver testifies that Samaritan, as soon as he saw the paramedic unit arrive, screamed out "Help her, help her, my God, she jumped, she jumped from that building."

This testimony would clearly be admissible to help Hateful establish that his spouse had in fact jumped and was not pushed from the top of the apartment building.

Suppose (to continue the example above), the police arrived shortly after the paramedic unit, and after taking Samaritan's name and address, asked him to come to the police station the next day to make a statement. At the station the next day, Samaritan gave a detailed, written, signed statement. Samaritan stated that while he was walking along, he looked up and saw a woman standing on the ledge of the roof of the ten-story apartment building. As he watched, she suddenly coiled and did a perfect swan dive to the ground ten stories below. Would the police officer who took the statement be permitted to testify at the trial as to what Samaritan told him at the station?

The answer is no. This testimony would be inadmissible because of the time factor. McCormick states that

> if the statement occurs while the exciting event is still in progress, courts have little difficulty finding that the excitement prompted the statement. But as the time between the event and the statement increases, so does the reluctance to find that the statement is an excited utterance ... perhaps an accurate rule of thumb might be that where the time interval between the event of the statement is long enough to permit reflective thought, the statement will be excluded in the absence of some proof that the declarant did not in fact engage in reflective thought process. Testimony that the declarant still appeared "nervous" or "distraught" and that there was a reasonable basis for continuing emotional upset will often suffice.

McCormick on Evidence (2nd Ed.), supra, § 297, p. 706.

Dying Declarations

Deathbed statements, like spontaneous declarations, have long been assumed to have their special indicia of reliability. A person about to go before his Maker and account for his life is, the theory goes, not likely to lie. Accordingly, dying declarations have long been recognized as exceptions to the hearsay rule. To lay the foundation for the admission of a dying declaration, it must be shown that

- the speaker believed that death was near and certain (not merely probable); and
- the speaker must be dead when the evidence is offered.

It is not required that the declarant actually die soon after the statement. It is enough if he is dead at the time the testimony is offered. The test is, as Professor McCormick puts it, "not the actual swiftness with which death ensued, but the declarant's belief in the nearness of death when he made the statement." *McCormick on Evidence* (2nd Ed.), § 282, p. 681.

Most courts in the United States also require that the use of dying declarations be limited to criminal prosecutions for homicide in which the defendant in the trial is charged with the death of the declarant. Many courts have also held that the declarations are admissible only insofar as they relate to the circumstances of the killing and to the event immediately preceding it. However, Federal Rule of Evidence 804(b)(2) provides that "in a prosecution for homicide or in a civil action or proceeding, a statement made by a declarant while believing that his death was imminent concerning the cause or circumstances of what he believed to be his impending death" is admissible.

Because dying declarations can be very important evidence and are ordinarily given great weight by a judge or jury, the following procedures should be used by officers investigating crimes involving seriously injured persons:

- Determine whether the victim is in serious danger of dying.
- If the victim is in critical condition, lose no time in speaking to him (or her).

- Determine whether the victim knows that he is dying and has given up all hopes of recovering.

- Obtain as clear and definite a statement as possible concerning the identity of the victim's assailant and the circumstances surrounding the crime. The statement may be oral or in writing. It need not be under oath.

- Obtain the names and addresses of other persons who heard the dying declaration.

Declarations Against Interest

Admissions of a party opponent are, of course, admissible notwithstanding any hearsay-based objections. This subsection deals with an exception applicable *only* to non-parties, that is, persons whose rights will not be determined by the lawsuit. Such persons are not named in the pleadings. Professor McCormick states the "declarations against interest" exception to the hearsay rule as follows:

> To satisfy the instant exception to the hearsay rule in its traditional form, two main requirements must be met: first, the declaration must state facts which are against the *pecuniary* or *proprietary* interest of the declarant, or the making of the declaration itself must create evidence which would endanger his *pocketbook* if the statement were not true; second, the declarant must be unavailable at the time of trial, ... minor qualifications may be added. The interest involved must not be too indirect or remote. The declarant ... must, so far as appears, have had the opportunity to observe the facts, as witnesses must have. *McCormick on Evidence* (2d Ed.), § 276, p. 670.

Suppose Fred Firebug were charged with incinerating an abandoned building which his sister claims to own. Firebug produces, at his trial, a butler to his now deceased mother who testifies that the mother told him, "I owned the property and the building on it, but I have turned it over to my son, Fred." This statement would be admissible to show that Fred owned the building in question because it would be held to be a declaration against proprietary or pecuniary interest on the part of Fred's mother.

Nearly all American courts have held the declarations against interest rule to apply only to declarations against proprietary or pecuniary interest. A minority of courts have permitted the exception to extend to declarations against *penal* interest. Under this theory, a confession by a non-party might be introduced into evidence through a witness since the statement would be detrimental to his penal interest and would make him liable to accusation, prosecution, and punishment.

No courts extend the so-called declarations against interest exception to declarations against interest across the board. The declaration must be shown to be against proprietary and, in some jurisdictions, penal interest.

Family History

A is charged with having sexual intercourse with a fourteen-year-old girl in a state in which the age of consent is sixteen. At issue is the age of the girl.

Neither her parents nor anyone present at or about the time she was born are available to testify. The girl herself, of course, has no personal knowledge of the date of her birth, but knows it only from what others have told her. Two questions raising the applicability of the hearsay rule present themselves:

- May the girl herself testify? ("I was born on January 1, 19__ and am therefore now fourteen years old.")
- May a neighbor of the girl's family testify? ("The girl's mother told me before all this (the alleged offense) that she was born on January 1, 19__ and so she is now fourteen years old.")

The answer to both questions is yes.

The "family history" or, as it is sometimes called, the "pedigree exception" to the hearsay rule is a well-recognized exception. The rule permits proof of matters of family history, relationship, and pedigree, such as birth, age, and race. To lay a foundation for the admission of testimony under the family history exception, it must be shown that

- It is impossible to produce the declarant (the person making the statements) as a witness because he has died or is otherwise unavailable.
- The declarant was related by blood or affinity (marriage) to the family. Some cases have held that other persons closely connected with such family may be the declarant.
- The statements or declarations must have been made before the filing of the suit and at a time when the declarant had no motive to distort the truth.

Age, marriages, deaths, births, relationship within the family, and other intrafamily circumstances fall within this exception to the hearsay rule.

Regularly Kept Records

The statutes and rules of evidence of virtually all states now provide for the admissibility of regularly kept written records. This exception to the hearsay rule is often called the "business records exception," but it should be remembered that the exception extends to regularly kept records of all types. These records could be kept in a hospital, a private club, a church, or any other organization which maintains regularly kept records.

Such regularly kept records commonly contain information written by unidentified or even unknown persons. Under this exception to the hearsay rule, these persons need not be called to the witness stand nor even identified. However, the regularly kept records may be admitted for use as evidence and the written information in the records may be used to prove or to disprove issues before the court.

Federal Rule of Evidence 803(6) and (7) defines the "regularly kept record" exception to the hearsay rule as follows:

(6) *Records of regularly conducted activity.* A memorandum, report, record, or data compilation, in any form, of acts, events, conditions, opinions, or diagnoses, made at or near the time by, or from information transmitted by, a person with knowledge, if kept in the course of

a regularly conducted business activity, and if it was the regular practice of that business activity to make the memorandum, report, record, or data compilation, all as shown by the testimony of the custodian or other qualified witness, unless the source of information or the method or circumstances of preparation indicate lack of trustworthiness. The term "business" as used in this paragraph includes business, institution, association, profession, occupation, and calling of every kind, whether or not conducted for profit.

(7) *Absence of entry in records kept in accordance with the provisions of paragraph (6).* Evidence that a matter is not included in the memoranda, reports, records, or data compilations, in any form, kept in accordance with the provisions of paragraph (6), to prove the nonoccurrence or nonexistence of the matter, if the matter was of a kind of which a memorandum, report, record, or data compilation was regularly made and preserved, unless the sources of information or other circumstances indicate lack of trustworthiness.

Professor McCormick writes as follows of the regularly kept record exception to the hearsay rule:

The exception is justified on grounds analogous to those underlying other exceptions to the hearsay rule. Unusual reliability is regarded as furnished by the fact that in practice regular entries have a comparatively high degree of accuracy (as compared to other memoranda) because such books and records are customarily checked as to correctness by systematic balance-striking, because the very regularity and continuity of the records is calculated to train the recordkeeper in habits of precision, and because in actual experience the entire business of the nation and many other activities constantly function in reliance upon entries of this kind .... Today, the inconvenience of calling those with firsthand knowledge and the unlikelihood of their remembering accurately the details of specific transactions convincingly demonstrate the need for recourse to their written records, without regard to physical unavailability.

McCormick on Evidence (2nd Ed.), supra, § 306, p. 720.

To lay the foundation necessary for the admission of regularly kept records as an exception to the hearsay rule, it must be shown that:

- The entry into the regularly kept records was made about the time of the event or transaction which is sought to be proved or disproved.
- Such events and transactions were regularly recorded by the organization maintaining the regularly kept records.
- If the witness testifying as to the entry into the records did not have personal knowledge of the event or transaction, that he did have knowledge that the entry was made in the ordinary course of the regular bookkeeping and record keeping procedure.

Official Written Statements and Public Records

There is a generally recognized exception to the hearsay rule for "written statements of public officials made by officials with a duty to make them, made upon firsthand knowledge of the facts. These statements are admissible as evidence of the facts recited in them." *McCormick on Evidence* (2nd Ed.), § 315, p. 735. Not every memo or piece of correspondence comes within this hearsay exception, but only those made in the course of official business and those required by law to be kept.

Court records, prison records, motor vehicle department records, and weather reports, are commonly admitted under this exception to the hearsay rule. Professor McCormick writes as follows of this exception:

> The special trustworthiness of official written statements is found in the declarant's official duty and the high probability that the duty to make an accurate report has been performed. The possibility that public inspection of some official records will reveal any inaccuracies and cause them to be corrected (or will deter the official from making them in the first place) has been emphasized . . . .
>
> A special need for this category of hearsay is found in the inconvenience of requiring public officials to appear in court and testify concerning the subject matter of their statements. Not only would this disrupt the administration of public affairs, but it almost certainly would create a class of official witnesses. Moreover, given the volume of business of public officers, the official written statement will usually be more reliable than the official's present memory. For these same reasons, there is no requirement that the declarant be shown to be unavailable as a witness.
>
> *McCormick on Evidence* (2d Ed.), § 315, pp. 735–36.

Efforts have been made by imaginative attorneys to have police reports admitted under this exception. In general, these efforts have not met with much success.[3] In most instances, courts refused to admit police reports as evidence because they contained hearsay and inadmissible conclusions. In refusing to admit a police accident report for use as evidence, the Supreme Court of Maryland held in the case of *Holloway v. Eich* [4] that

> A growing number of courts have held, however, that the portion of an accident report based on the officer's first-hand knowledge is admissible as proof of the facts recorded therein upon the ground that it is either a public record or a record made in the regular course of business. Thus, the officer's notations of the length of the skid marks, the dimensions of the road, the make of the vehicles involved, visibility and the weather would be admissible under the latter view, while his notation of how the accident occurred and who was responsible for the injury or damage would be excluded if he had not been at the scene at the time of the accident.

Virtually every jurisdiction now has a statute or court rule which governs the admissibility of public records. Because such statutes and rules are ordinarily very specific, it is always necessary to consult them on matters concerning the admissibility of official written statements and public records.

Statutes also commonly provide that copies of public records certified by the custodian to be true copies are admissible to the same extent as the originals.

The Hearsay Rule

Testimony Which is Not Hearsay

Testimony of matters of which the witness has first hand knowledge. Such evidence is always admissible if relevant, material, and competent. Includes testimony as to what the witness himself:

- saw
- heard
- smelled (if the witness is qualified to identify the smell)
- felt
- tasted

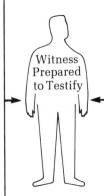

Witness Prepared to Testify

Hearsay Testimony

Testimony which is only admissible under one of the exceptions to the hearsay rule. Includes what other persons:

- saw
- heard
- smelled
- felt
- tasted

and communicated to the witness.

Hearsay upon hearsay is information communicated from other persons to a person who communicates to the witness. Hearsay upon hearsay is admissible only under a limited number of exceptions. These exceptions are:

- reputation evidence
- testimony as to date of birth, age, family relationship, etc.

Statements which are not hearsay under Rule 801 of the Federal Rules of Evidence and the Uniform Rules of Evidence include:

- Prior statements of a witness which are
  a. inconsistent with testimony and are given under oath
  b. consistent with his testimony and offered to rebut a charge against him, of recent fabrication or improper influence or motive.
- Admissions of a party-opponent (confessions and incriminating statements of a defendant in a criminal case would fall under this category).

The hearsay rule excludes *only* statements offered to prove the truth of the matter asserted. Therefore, out-of-court statements and assertions may be offered and will be admitted to prove something other than the truth of the matter asserted. Examples are:

- to show knowledge on the part of a defendant, witness or other persons
- to show feeling or state of mind
- to show insanity, mental disease, or mental defect
- to show the effect of a statement or assertion on the hearer
- to show a verbal act or verbal conduct
- for impeachment purposes

Exceptions to the hearsay rule which are listed in Rule 803 of the Federal Rules of Evidence and the Uniform Rules of Evidence apply where the availability of the declarant is immaterial (Rule 803):

- Present sense impression.
- Excited utterance.
- Then-existing mental, emotional, or physical condition.
- Statements for purposes of medical diagnosis or treatment.
- Recorded recollection.
- Records of regularly conducted activity.
- Absence of entry in records kept in accordance with 6.
- Public records and reports.
- Records of vital statistics.
- Absence of public record or entry.
- Records of religious organizations.
- Marriage, baptismal, and similar certificates.
- Family records.
- Records of documents affecting an interest in property.
- Statements in documents affecting an interest in property.
- Statements in ancient documents.
- Market reports, commercial publications.
- Learned treatises.
- Reputation concerning personal or family history.
- Reputation concerning boundaries or general history.
- Reputation as to character.
- Judgment of previous conviction.
- Judgment as to personal, family, or general history, or boundaries.
- Other exceptions.

Exceptions to the hearsay rule also apply where it must be shown that the declarant is unavailable (Rule 804):

- Former testimony of a witness.
- Statement made under belief of impending death.
- Statement against interest.
- Statement of personal or family history.
- Other exceptions.

Record of Past Recollection

Witnesses frequently are called to testify regarding events that may have occurred weeks and months before.[5] It is not surprising that they cannot always remember as much at the time of trial as they could relate at the time of the occurrence. Recollections may be refreshed by documents including their own written statements, but efforts at refreshment may be unsuccessful.

If the effort to refresh the recollection (memory) of the witness is unsuccessful, the written record or statements of the witness may be admitted under the law of all American jurisdictions. To introduce such evidence, the following criteria must be met:

- The witness must be shown to lack a present recollection of the event.
- The witness must be shown to have had firsthand knowledge of the event.
- The written statement has to have been made at or near the time of the event.
- The written statement has to have been made at a time when the witness's recollection was clear and accurate.
- The witness must testify that the written statement was true and accurate when made.

Other Exceptions to the Hearsay Rule

There are other exceptions to the hearsay rule which are not presented in this chapter. These exceptions are not presented in this text because they are not frequently encountered. However, it is important for students and law enforcement officers to be aware that additional exceptions to the hearsay rule do exist.

The exceptions to the hearsay rule which are presented in this chapter are sometimes identified by different names and phrases than those used in this chapter. Such local usage of names and phrases can be brought to the attention of students by instructors and teachers.

A WORD OF WARNING

In focussing upon the use of hearsay in the courtroom, it is easy to forget that other rules of evidence besides the hearsay rule may result in the exclusion of evidence. A piece of evidence may withstand hearsay-based objections and may fit within one of the exceptions of the hearsay rule. However, it may be excluded for use as evidence by other rules of evidence.

Written statements or records, for example, may be admissible under one of several exceptions to the hearsay rule. But if the document to be admitted contains opinions or conclusions, accounts of other persons' statements (hearsay), privileged communications, or irrelevant and prejudicial material, it will *not* be admitted at all or will be admitted only to the extent that the objectionable material can be conveniently edited out.

A WORD OF ADVICE

The trend of the law seems to be in the direction of making more hearsay information admissible as evidence than would have been admitted in the past. Indicative of this is Federal Rule of Evidence 803(24), which in strikingly broad terms provides for "other exceptions" to the hearsay rule for any

> statement not specifically covered by any of the foregoing exceptions but having equivalent circumstantial guarantees of trustworthiness, if the court determines that (A) the statement is offered as evidence of a material fact; (B) the statement is more probative on the point for which it is offered than any other evidence which the proponent can procure through reasonable efforts; and (C) the general purposes of these rules and the interests of justice will best be served by admission of the statement into evidence.

If a vital link in a chain of evidence is of a kind that would traditionally have been excluded from evidence under the hearsay rule, hope should not be abandoned. An imaginative lawyer may be able to develop a theory that will result in the admissibility of the evidence in question and even a change in the law of your jurisdiction. Here's hoping it's you that has the good lawyer.

NOTES

[1] *McCormick on Evidence* (2nd Ed., 1972), p. 584. Permission to quote from *McCormick on Evidence* was granted by the West Publishing Company of St. Paul, Minnesota.

[2] In some jurisdictions, the statement would be held to fall within the "declarations against interest" exception to the hearsay rule and be deemed admissible on that theory. The declarations against interest exception, which is quite narrow and comparatively unimportant, must be distinguished sharply from the admissions of a party-opponent exception discussed here.

[3] See 69 A.L.R.2d 1148 (1960).

[4] 255 Md. 591, 258 A.2d 585, 588 (1969).

[5] See also "Past Recollection Recorded" in chapter 4.

PART THREE

The American Exclusionary Rule

The Rule of Exclusion of Evidence

THE EXCLUSIONARY RULE

The Origins and Purpose of the Exclusionary Rule

Under the old common law, evidence obtained in an improper or illegal manner could be used in a criminal trial against a defendant. For example, if a police officer burglarized a suspect's home to obtain evidence to arrest and charge the suspect with a crime, the evidence obtained in the burglary could be used in the criminal trial.

The defendant's only remedy under the old common law in the above example would be to bring a civil law suit against the police officer, or to get the prosecutor to charge the officer with a criminal offense.

In an effort to discourage and stop improper and illegal police conduct, the exclusionary rule of evidence was created by the U.S. Supreme Court. The rule excludes (keeps out) and forbids the use of evidence in criminal cases if the evidence was obtained by governmental officials in a manner which violates the constitutional rights of suspects, a statute, or a court rule. The Supreme Court of the United States stated that [1]

> The deterrent purpose of the exclusionary rule necessarily assumes that the police have engaged in willful, or at the very least negligent, conduct which has deprived the defendant of some right. By refusing to admit evidence gained as a result of such conduct, the courts hope to instill in those particular investigating officers, or in their future counterparts, a greater degree of care toward the rights of an accused. Where the official action was pursued in complete good faith, however, the deterrence rationale loses much of its force.

The American exclusionary rule is a relatively new evidence rule. It was first used in federal courts in 1914 [2] but many states courts did not use the rule until it was made mandatory in 1961. [3] The rule is unique to the United States; no other country in the world has adopted or uses a rule comparable to the American exclusionary rule. Before becoming Chief Justice of the U.S. Supreme Court, Judge Warren Burger wrote in 1964 that "(u)nlike so many of our basic concepts of law this one has little or no linkage with past in terms of either Roman Law, Napolenonic Law or even with the Common Law of England." [4]

213

The Supreme Court of the United States has enforced the exclusionary rule over the years since 1914 (when it was made applicable to the federal courts) and 1961 (when it was made mandatory in state courts) based upon the following two assumptions:

- That the exclusion of evidence obtained in an improper or illegal method would discourage and deter future police investigative methods and procedures which were improper or illegal.
- That there are no other practical alternatives for the "policing of the police" and discouraging improper or illegal police conduct.

Opponents of the exclusionary rule argue against both of the above assumptions upon which the rule is based. They argue that the rule has not had a deterrent effect upon improper or illegal police searches and seizures and that alternative methods are available to the courts. Former Chief Justice Burger stated in his dissenting opinion in the case of *Bivens v. Six Unknown Named Agents* [5] that

> Suppressing unchallenged truth has set guilty criminals free but demonstrably has neither deterred deliberate violations of the Fourth Amendment nor decreased those errors in judgment that will inevitably occur given the pressure inherent in police work having to do with serious crimes.

One of the most widely quoted criticisms of the exclusionary rule can be found in the 1926 case of *People v. Defore,* [6] in which, in declining to adopt the exclusionary rule in New York State, Judge (later U.S. Supreme Court Justice) Cardozo wrote:

> The criminal is to go free because the constable has blundered .... A room is searched against the law, and the body of a murdered man is found .... The privacy of the home has been infringed, and the murderer goes free.

Since 1961, the rules governing the manner and method in which evidence may be obtained by law enforcement officers through search and seizure have become complex and difficult to understand. At the same time, crime has become a very serious national problem in the United States. Because of the rigidity of the American exclusionary rule, the American Law Institute (ALI) has recommended since 1971 that the rule be modified. Instead of the automatic suppression (or exclusion) of evidence, the ALI recommends that evidence should be excluded and suppressed from use in a criminal court "only if the court finds that such violation was substantial."

The 1961 Case of *Mapp v. Ohio*

Before 1961, about half of the states had state exclusionary rules forbidding the use of evidence obtained by improper or illegal police conduct. The other half of the states did not have exclusionary rules which would prevent the use of evidence resulting from police misconduct or police negligence.

When the Ohio courts used evidence obtained as a result of police misconduct in the criminal case of *Mapp v. Ohio,* the issue of whether use of such

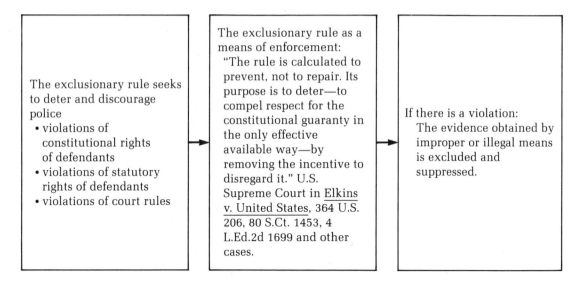

Figure 8.1   The Function of the Exclusionary Rule

evidence violated the U.S. Constitution was presented to the Supreme Court of the United States. The case is as follows:

Mapp v. Ohio

Supreme Court of the United States (1961)
367 U.S. 643, 81 S.Ct. 1684

Cleveland police officers heard that a fugitive was hiding in Miss Mapp's house. They demanded entrance but Miss Mapp refused. After keeping the house under surveillance for three hours, the officers again knocked at the door. When Mapp did not answer immediately, one of the several doors to the house was forcibly opened. The police stated that they had a warrant, which Miss Mapp demanded to see. Miss Mapp placed the paper "claimed to be a warrant" in her bosom. The police recovered the paper and began searching the entire home. Miss Mapp was placed in handcuffs and forcibly taken up to her bedroom. Neither the fugitive nor evidence of the fugitive were found. Obscene material was found in a trunk in the basement. Miss Mapp was convicted of the possession of the obscene material. "At the trial no search warrant was produced by the prosecution, nor was the failure to produce one explained or accounted for."

In making the federal exclusionary rule applicable to all of the states, the U.S. Supreme Court held that the Fourth Amendment right of privacy is enforceable against the states through the due process clause of the Fourteenth Amendment. The Court stated that

Having once recognized that the right to privacy embodied in the Fourth Amendment is enforceable against the States, that the right to be secure against rude invasions of privacy by state officers is, therefore, constitutional in origin, we can no longer permit that right to remain an empty promise. Because it is enforceable in the same manner and to like effect as other basic rights secured by the Due Process Clause, we can no longer permit it to be revocable at the whim of any police officer who, in the name of law enforcement itself, chooses to suspend its enjoyment. Our decision, founded on reason and truth, gives to the individual no more than that which the Constitution guarantees him, to the police officer no less than that which honest law enforcement is entitled, and, to the courts, that judicial integrity so necessary in the true administration of justice . . . .

. . . Today, we once again examine . . . the right of privacy free from unreasonable state intrusion . . . by official lawlessness in flagrant abuse of that basic right, reserved to all persons as a specific guarantee against that very same unlawful conduct. We hold that all evidence by searches and seizures in violation of the Constitution is, by the same authority, inadmissible in a State court.

The 1961 case of *Mapp v. Ohio* is important because for the first time in the history of the United States, the federal exclusionary rule was imposed upon state courts.

Many States Now Have Two Sets of Exclusionary Rules

The federal exclusionary rule has become very complex since the 1961 *Mapp v. Ohio* case. All states must follow the federal *Mapp* rule in determining the admissibility of evidence. However, it is not uncommon for state courts to impose additional requirements in interpreting the constitution or statutes of that state. State statutes, by themselves, could also alter the federal *Mapp* rule and impose a stricter standard in a given area of the law.

Therefore, two sets of exclusionary rules exist in many states. The federal rule is defined by the U.S. Supreme Court and other federal courts while the state exclusionary rule is defined and required by the state supreme court (and sometimes by state statutes). State law enforcement officers would be required to comply with the state requirements, which could be more stringent than those required by the federal *Mapp* rule. However, evidence to be used in criminal cases in federal courts in all states would be judged by the federal *Mapp* rule. Because most crimes are violations of state criminal codes, most criminal cases go into state criminal courts.

Some states have simplified this situation by eliminating, to a large extent, their state exclusionary rule. California and Florida are among the states which have enacted sections to their state constitutions requiring state courts in that state to determine the admissibility of evidence "in conformity with the 4th Amendment . . . as interpreted by the U.S. Supreme Court," Florida Constitution. (For the California change, see *In re Lance W.*, 210 Cal.Rptr. 631, 694 P.2d 744 (1985).)

THE FRUIT OF THE POISONOUS TREE DOCTRINE
(THE DERIVATIVE EVIDENCE RULE)

The exclusionary rule forbids the use of evidence which is directly obtained by improper or illegal police conduct. In the *Mapp* case, the entrance by the police into the home and the search of the home were improper and illegal. The police did not have a search warrant and did not have probable cause to obtain a search warrant. The obscene material was evidence found as a result of the police misconduct.

Not only is the use of evidence *directly* obtained from improper conduct prohibited, but also the use of evidence *indirectly* obtained from improper conduct. If the indirect evidence is derived and is the indirect result of an improper or illegal act, it will ordinarily be excluded. The rule forbidding the use of evidence derived indirectly from a wrong is known as the **derivative evidence rule,** or the **fruit of the poisonous tree doctrine.**

The derivative evidence rule states that unlawfully obtained information cannot be the lead or the basis for further investigation which then develops other evidence. The new evidence could be tainted, or the "fruit of the poisonous tree" (this phrase was first used in the 1939 case of *Nardone v. United States* by Justice Frankfurter).

The fruit of the poisonous tree doctrine is applicable if illegally obtained evidence is the basis for the discovery of

- other evidence which otherwise would not have been found;
- a witness who otherwise might not have been found;
- a confession or admission which would not have been made if the suspect or defendant were not confronted with tainted (illegally obtained) evidence.

When a defense lawyer makes a motion in a criminal case to suppress under the derivative evidence rule, the trial court would then have to determine whether the evidence which the state seeks to use was the direct or indirect product and result of improper or illegal police conduct. The court would have to determine whether the evidence was tainted (and to what extent it was tainted) by the illegally seized evidence. The following U.S. Supreme Court case illustrates:

Fahy v. Connecticut

Supreme Court of the United States (1963)
375 U.S. 85, 84 S.Ct. 229

A police officer saw a car driving slowly in downtown Norwalk, Connecticut at about 4:40 in the morning. He stopped the car and questioned the two men in the car. In checking the car, the officer found a can of black paint and a paint brush under the front seat. Fahy (the driver of the car) then drove his car home. A short time later, the police officer found that someone had painted swastikas on a synagogue a short distance from where he had stopped Fahy's car. Without a warrant, the officer went to Fahy's home, entered the garage, and removed the paint and brush from Fahy's car. After determining that the paint and brush fit the markings on the Jewish synagogue, the officer obtained an arrest warrant. When arrested, Fahy made incriminating statements; and later, at the police station, Fahy made a full confession. All the evidence was used in obtaining a conviction of Fahy and his companion. In reversing, the U.S. Supreme Court held that

> petitioner (Fahy) should have had a chance to show that his admissions were induced by being confronted with the illegally seized evidence.
>
> Nor can we ignore the cumulative prejudicial effect of this evidence upon the conduct of the defense at trial. It was only after admission of the paint and brush and only after their subsequent use to corroborate other state's evidence and only after introduction of the confession that the defendants took the stand, admitted their acts, and tried to establish that the nature of those acts was not within the scope of the felony statute under which the defendants had been charged. We do not mean to suggest that petitioner has presented any valid claim based on the privilege against self-incrimination. We merely note this course of events as another indication of the prejudicial effect of the erroneously admitted evidence.

EXCEPTIONS TO THE FRUIT OF THE POISONOUS TREE DOCTRINE

The Three Exceptions to the Fruit of the Poisonous Tree Doctrine Recognized by the U.S. Supreme Court

The U.S. Supreme Court has recognized three exceptions to the fruit of the poisonous tree doctrine. Situations in which evidence would *not* be suppressed and could be used in a criminal trial are

1. When the connection between the improper or lawless conduct of the police and the discovery of the challenged evidence had "become so attenuated as to dissipate the taint." *Nardone v. United States,* 308 U.S. 338, 60 S.Ct. 266 (1939).

2. The exclusionary rule and the fruit-of-the-poisonous-tree doctrine would have no application when the government learns of the evidence "from an independent source." *Silverthorne Lumber Company v. United States,* 251 U.S. 385, 40 S.Ct. 182 (1920).

3. When the normal course of police investigation would inevitably have led to the discovery of the evidence in question (inevitable discovery).

Lessening of the Impact of the Wrong by Time and an Act of the Defendant or a Third Party

The effect of the wrong may be attenuated (lessened) by the passage of time and the independent act of the defendant or another person. Such act (or acts) and the passing of time may break the causal chain linking the illegality and the evidence.

The case of *Wong Sun v. United States* is an example. After the defendant was arrested, he was released. Days later, he voluntarily returned to the federal agents' office. The U.S. Supreme Court held that because there was a passage of time and a significant act, the oral confession which the defendant made on his visit to the federal office was sufficiently free of the taint of the prior illegal acts of the agents to be admissible evidence. The case follows.

Wong Sun v. United States

Supreme Court of the United States (1963)
371 U.S. 471, 83 S.Ct. 407

At about 2 A.M. federal narcotic agents in San Francisco lawfully arrested one Hom Way and found heroin in his possession. Hom Way, who had not previously been an informant, stated that he purchased the heroin from one "Blackie Toy." Without probable cause, the agents then proceeded to Blackie Toy's laundry and made an unlawful entry and an unauthorized arrest of Toy. No heroin was found on Toy, but he made statements incriminating himself and one Johnny Yee. The agents then proceeded to Johnny Yee's home, where Yee surrendered heroin to the agents. Toy and Yee then incriminated one "Sea Dog," who was Wong Sun. Wong Sun was then arrested and he and Toy and Yee were arraigned and released on their own recognizance. A few days later, the three defendants appeared at the office of the Narcotic Bureau and, after being warned, made incriminating statements but would not sign the written summaries of their statements. The U.S. Supreme Court reversed the convictions following the trial in which all of the above evidence was used. In reversing and remanding the case, the U.S. Supreme Court held that

> We need not hold that all evidence is 'fruit of the poisonous tree' simply because it would not have come to light *but for the illegal actions* of the police. Rather, the more apt question in such a case is 'whether, granting establishment of the primary illegality, the evidence to which instant objection is made has been come at by exploitation of that illegality or instead by means sufficiently distinguishable to be purged of the primary taint.' ...
>
> ... Wong Sun's unsigned confession was not the fruit of that arrest, and was therefore properly admitted at trial. On the evidence that Wong Sun had been released on his own recognizance after a lawful arraignment, and had returned voluntarily several days later to make the statement, we hold that the connection between the arrest and the statement had "become so attenuated as to dissipate the taint." *Nardone v. United States,* 308 U.S. 338, 341. The fact that the statement was unsigned, whatever bearing this may have upon its weight and credibility, does not render it inadmissible; Wong Sun understood and adopted its substance, though he could not comprehend the English words. The petitioner has never suggested any impropriety in the

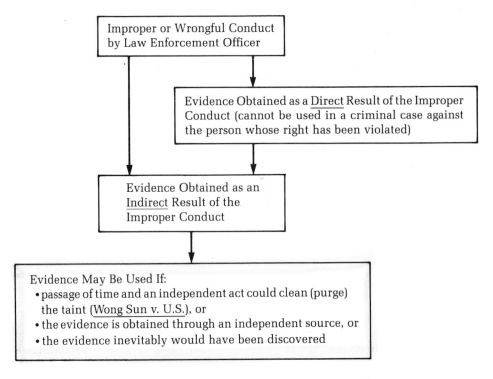

**Figure 8.2   Evidence Obtained Directly or Indirectly
from Improper Police conduct**

interrogation itself which would require the exclusion of this statement.

Would the passage of a couple of hours and the waiver of *Miranda* rights be sufficient to meet the requirements of this exception? The Illinois Supreme Court said yes, but the U.S. Supreme Court said no in the following case:

Brown v. Illinois

Supreme Court of the United States (1975)
422 U.S. 590, 95 S.Ct. 2254

Detectives, investigating a murder in Chicago, suspected the defendant. They broke into his apartment and searched for evidence. When the defendant came home, he was arrested and taken to the police station for questioning without probable cause or a warrant. At the police station, he was given the *Miranda* warnings and within two hours confessed to the murder. In holding that *Miranda* did not break the causal chain between the unlawful arrest and the incriminating statements, the U.S. Supreme Court reversed the defendant's conviction, holding that

> Brown's first statement was separated from his illegal arrest by less than two hours, and there was no intervening event of significance whatsoever. In its essentials, his situation is remarkably like that of James Wah Toy in Wong Sun. We could hold Brown's first statement admissible only if we overrule Wong Sun. We decline to do so. And the second statement was clearly the result and fruit of the first.
>
> The illegality here, moreover, had a quality of purposefulness. The impropriety of the arrest was obvious; awareness of that fact was virtually conceded by the two detectives when they repeatedly acknowledged, in their testimony, that the purpose of their action was "for investigation" or for "questioning" .... The arrest, both in design and in execution, was investigatory. The detectives embarked upon this expedition for evidence in the hope that something might turn up. The manner in which Brown's arrest was effected gives the appearance of having been calculated to cause surprise, fright, and confusion.
>
> We emphasize that our holding is a limited one. We decide only that the Illinois courts were in error in assuming that the Miranda warnings, by themselves, under Wong Sun always purge the taint of an illegal arrest.
>
> The judgment of the Supreme Court of Illinois is reversed and the case is remanded for further proceedings not inconsistent with this opinion.
>
> It is so ordered.

The "Independent Source" Test as an Exception to the Fruit of the Poisonous Tree Doctrine

> When the government learns of evidence "from an independent source," the fruit of the poisonous tree doctrine would not be applied to suppress the evidence. The U.S. Supreme Court held in the 1920 case of *Silverthorne Lumber Co. v. United States*[7] that if "knowledge of (such facts) is gained from an independent source, they may be proved like any other ...". The following case illustrates:

Payne v. United States

U.S. Court of Appeals, District of Columbia Circuit (1961)
294 F.2d 723, review denied by U.S. Supreme Ct. 368 U.S. 883, 82 S.Ct. 131

> The defendant was arrested without warrant as a "flimflam" and con**fidence man. The defendant was properly arrested and evidence was legally obtained in the search incident to the lawful arrest. However, the defendant was not immediately taken before a federal magistrate, as required by the Federal

Rules of Criminal Procedure. During the period of unreasonable detention, the defendant confessed to the crime for which he was arrested and a witness identified him as the perpetrator of the crime. The confession was excluded by the trial court but the witness was permitted to identify the defendant at Payne's trial. In holding that the identification evidence was obtained from an independent source, the Court affirmed the conviction for grand larceny, ruling that

> While we do not condone lengthy detention for the purpose of rounding up complaining witnesses so that they may view a suspect, we must note that here Payne's arrest was based on probable cause, and was proper. The police should have obeyed Rule 5(a): they should have brought Payne before a magistrate for commitment, and filed a complaint based on the events of November 4. But it does not follow that failure to do so vitiates Payne's conviction, since no evidence obtained by interrogation of Payne was introduced at his trial.
>
> The judgment of the District Court will be
> Affirmed.

The "Inevitable Discovery" Rule as an Exception to the Fruit of the Poisonous Tree Doctrine

The vast majority of courts in the United States have recognized the **inevitable discovery rule** as an exception to the fruit of the poisonous tree doctrine. The rule holds that the fruit of the poisonous tree doctrine is not applicable when, in the normal course of police investigation, the evidence in question would have been discovered. The U.S. Supreme Court's first inevitable discovery case is as follows:

Nix v. Williams

Supreme Court of the United States (1984)
467 U.S. 431, 104 S.Ct. 2501

(This case was before the U.S. Supreme Court twice. An account of the first ruling is found in chapter 4 under the case heading of *Brewer v. Williams*.)

Police were seeking to arrest defendant Williams for the abduction (and possible murder) of a ten-year-old girl. The girl disappeared from a YMCA building in Des Moines, Iowa. Williams was seen carrying a large bundle out of the building with the legs of a little girl dangling from the bundle. Williams turned himself into the police in Davenport, Iowa, which is 160 miles east of Des Moines. While two Des Moines detectives were transporting Williams back to Des Moines, they violated Williams' right to an attorney by questioning him by means of the "Christmas speech." Williams then disclosed the location of the little girl's body. Evidence of the body and the condition of the body were allowed in Williams' trial for murder. Williams argued that the challenged evidence violated the Sixth Amendment, whether it would have been inevitably discovered or not. In affirming the murder conviction and in adopting the inevitable discovery rule, the Court held that

> some 200 volunteers ... were searching for the child's body .... The searchers were instructed "to check all the roads, the ditches, any culverts .... If they came upon any abandoned farm buildings, they were instructed to go onto the property and search those abandoned farm buildings or any other places where a small child could be secreted." Ruxlow testified that he marked off highway maps of Poweshiek and Jasper Counties in grid fashion, divided the volunteers into teams of four to six persons, and assigned each team to search specific grid areas. Ruxlow also testified that, if the search had not been suspended because of Williams' promised cooperation, it would have continued into Polk County, using the same grid system .... The search was not resumed once it was learned that Williams had led the police to the body which was found two and one-half miles from where the search had stopped in what would have been the eastern-most grid to be searched in Polk County. There was testimony that it would have taken an additional three to five hours to discover the body if the search had continued; the body was found near a culvert, one of the kinds of places the teams had been specifically directed to search.
>
> On this record it is clear that the search parties were approaching the actual location of the body and we are satisfied, along with three courts earlier, that the volunteer search teams would have resumed the search had Williams not earlier led the police to the body and the body inevitably would have been found. The evidence asserted by Williams as newly discovered, *i.e.,* certain photographs of the body and deposition testimony of Agent Ruxlow made in connection with the federal habeas proceeding, does not demonstrate that the material facts were inadequately developed in the suppression hearing in state court or that Williams was denied a full, fair, and adequate opportunity to present all relevant facts at the suppression hearing.

Means Used to Discourage Improper Police Conduct

One or more of the following procedures could be used to discourage improper police conduct in protecting the rights of suspects:

- Using the exclusionary rule to forbid the use in a criminal case of the evidence obtained in a criminal trial;
- Bringing a civil lawsuit against the offending officers, their department and city, state or county;
- Using departmental discipline against the officers—which could result in a verbal caution, suspension, or dismissal from the department;
- Initiating a criminal action against a police officer (See the case of *State v. O'Neill* in chapter 11, where the chief of a small department was convicted of burglary when he improperly told students to go into a home to recover objects stolen from them. However, the Supreme Court of Wisconsin reversed the conviction blaming the prosecutor.).

Exceptions to the Fruit of the Poisonous Tree Doctrine

The exclusionary rule forbids the use of evidence directly or indirectly obtained as the result of improper police conduct. However, the following are *exceptions* to the exclusionary rule and the fruit of the poisonous tree doctrine:

- **Intervening Independent Act Dissipating the Taint**
  Illegality may be purged by an intervening independent act by the defendant or a third party which breaks the causal chain linking the illegality and the evidence (for an example of an independent act by a third party, see the case of *United States v. Williams*, 436 F.2d 1166, cert. denied 91 S.Ct. 1392).
  Passage of time could be a factor in purging the taint, as in the case of *Wong Sun v. United States*, in which the defendant was released and returned days later to make an oral confession. However, mere passage of time is not sufficient to purge the taint when there is no break in custody.
  Miranda warnings by themselves do not purge the taint. However, proper warnings could be a factor in the case-by-case determination as to whether the taint has been dissipated (see *Brown v. Illinois*).

- **Independent Source**
  If the state obtains the evidence or learns of the evidence from an independent source, the poisonous-tree doctrine is not applicable.

- **Inevitable Discovery Doctrine**
  Under the inevitable discovery doctrine, evidence is admissible if it would have been discovered through legitimate means in the absence of improper or illegal police procedure.
  The state must show that, in the normal course of police investigation, the evidence in question would have been discovered (see *Nix v. Williams* in this chapter).

Table 8.1   Types of Evidence Controlled by the Exclusionary Rule

TYPE OF EVIDENCE	U.S. CONSTITUTIONAL AMENDMENT WHICH CONTROLS THE EVIDENCE	TEST OF ADMISSIBILITY FOR USE OF EVIDENCE
Physical evidence (drugs, weapons, contraband, clothing, fingerprints, etc.)	*Fourth Amendment:* "The right of the people to be secure ... against unreasonable searches and seizures shall not be violated."	The Fourth Amendment requires a search warrant if a right of privacy is involved. If a warrant is not used, the burden is on the officer to show that the search was authorized by one of the well-recognized exceptions to the requirement of a search warrant. (See chapters 10, 11, 12, and 14.)
Confessions, incriminating admissions, and statements	*Fifth Amendment:* "No person ... shall be compelled ... to be a witness against himself." *Sixth Amendment:* "In all criminal prosecutions, the accused shall enjoy the right ... to have the assistance of Counsel for his defense."	The voluntariness test is used for the use of all statements as evidence. The following test may be applicable depending upon the circumstances: ■ *Miranda* requirements and test ■ *Massiah* test *Bruton* requirements (See chapter 5.)
Eyewitness and voice identification	*Fifth and Fourteenth Amendments:* "No person shall be ... deprived of life, liberty, or property, without due process of law." *Sixth Amendment:* "In all criminal prosecutions, the accused shall enjoy the right ... to have the assistance of Counsel for his defense."	Were the procedures used so unnecessarily suggestive and conducive to irreparable mistaken identification as to be a denial of due process of law? (See chapter 13.) Was the accused denied the assistance of counsel at an important and critical stage of the criminal proceedings? (See *Kirby v. Illinois,* 406 U.S. 682.)
Evidence obtained as a result of wiretapping and electronic surveillance	Wiretapping and electronic surveillances are searches controlled by the Fourth Amendment. Title III of the Federal Omnibus Crime Control and Safe Streets Act, and applicable state statutes, control the use of wiretapping and electronic surveillance.	Was the evidence obtained in conformity with the applicable statute (or statutes)? (See chapter 15.)

PROBLEMS

1. Two officers of a lumber company were arrested in their homes early one morning. While they were being held, federal agents "without a shadow of authority went to the office of their company and made a clean sweep of all the books, papers and documents found there." Photographs and copies of material papers were made. The original documents were returned to the defendant but a criminal charge (an indictment) "was framed based upon the knowledge thus obtained."

    Can the indictment stand, and can the evidence be used in criminal proceedings against the defendant corporation? *Silverthorne Lumber Company et al. v. United States,* 251 U.S. 385, 40 S.Ct. 182 (1920).

2. A police officer was visiting in a flower shop when he noticed an envelope on the cash register. The officer picked up the envelope and opened it to find that it contained money and policy slips. He returned the envelope and its contents but reported the discovery to his superiors, which lead them to question the clerk in the shop. The clerk agreed to testify against Ceccolini, the shop's owner and defendant. Ceccolini was summoned before a federal grand jury, where he testified that he had never taken policy bets. The defendant was later indicted and convicted of perjury for that statement.

    Could the police officer testify as to what he saw in the envelope? Can the clerk testify as to the gambling activities of the defendant? Should the conviction be affirmed by the U.S. Supreme Court? *United States v. Ceccolini,* 435 U.S. 268, 98 S.Ct. 1054 (1978).

3. A young man robbed a woman in a woman's restroom at the Washington National Monument. During the robbery, the woman had a good opportunity to see the young man. The woman immediately reported the robbery and described the young man who robbed her. Three days later, a young man (Crews) was improperly and illegally detained. Photographs were taken of the young man and a photographic display (array) was shown to the woman. She immediately identified Crews as the man who robbed her at gunpoint. In a lineup, the woman again identified Crews as the robber. At Crews' trial for armed robbery, the woman appeared as a witness and identified the defendant as the robber. Crews was convicted and appealed, arguing that the in-court identification was the "fruit of the poisonous tree" and should not be used as evidence.

    Should the U.S. Supreme Court affirm Crews' conviction, and should the woman's in-court identification be allowed as evidence? Why? *United States v. Crews,* 445 U.S. 463, 100 S.Ct. 1244 (1980).

4. California police officers improperly arrested Williams in his apartment. Before taking Williams to the police station, arrangements had to be made for the care of Williams' cat and dog. In an attempt to provide for the care of these animals, the officers went to the apartment of a neighbor (Mrs. Lopez) to inquire if she would take care of the animals. Mrs. Lopez told the officers that they should investigate Williams for a recent bank robbery in which the robber had presented his demand in a note threatening that he had nitroglycerin on his person. Mrs. Lopez stated that she was in Williams' apart-

ment on the morning of the robbery and that he was writing a note and had asked her how to spell *nitroglycerin.* The officers had not suspected Williams of the robbery but the investigation which followed produced sufficient evidence to convict the defendant of the bank robbery. An appeal was taken from the conviction arguing among other issues the defense position that the fruit of the poisonous tree doctrine required suppression of the evidence used to convict Williams.

Should the evidence be suppressed or should it be admissible in Williams' trial for armed robbery? Explain. *United States v. Williams,* 436 F.2d 1166 (9th Cir.1970), review denied 402 U.S. 912, 91 S.Ct. 1392 (U.S.Sup.Ct.1971).

5. After a robbery, the defendant shot and killed two police officers and abducted a woman for a short time. Investigating officers had reason to believe that the defendant had fled to his home. No one was on the first floor when the police entered. When the police entered a room on the second floor, the defendant called from a closet in which he was hiding, "Don't shoot, I give up." The officers seized the defendant, handcuffed him, and took him out to a hall, where they gave him the *Miranda* warnings. When he was asked about the gun he used, the defendant stated that it was on a shelf in the closet where he had been hiding. Officers immediately seized the gun, along with six empty shell casings in the cylinder and live ammunition. Because the officers did not testify specifically as to what *Miranda* warnings were given to the defendant, the trial court ruled that the oral statements of the defendant in the hall were inadmissible.

Should any or all of the statements of the defendant be admitted as evidence? Explain. Should the gun and the six empty shell casings be admitted as evidence? *People v. Fitzpatrick,* 346 N.Y.S.2d 793, 300 N.E.2d 139, review denied 414 U.S. 1050, 94 S.Ct. 554 (U.S.Sup.Ct.1973).

6. A few days after the defendant was arrested for murder and was being held in jail, officers were in his neighborhood on other matters. In talking with neighbors of the defendant, the officers were told that the defendant had shot bullets into his front lawn. The defendant had come out of his house and, in front of witnesses, had discharged a revolver into the lawn. The detectives then walked on the public sidewalk, looking at the lawn until they saw two furrows in the lawn in front of the defendant's house. A detective then walked onto the lawn, put his finger into one of the furrows, and overturned the first bullet. The second bullet was obtained when a tenant of the defendant consented to the probing which produced the bullet. The trial judge permitted the bullets and the evidence derived from the bullets to be used in defendant's trial for murder. Defendant was convicted and appealed, arguing error.

Is this a fruit of the poisonous tree case? Was the evidence properly obtained? Should the defendant's conviction be affirmed or reversed? Explain. *People v. Morgan,* 681 P.2d 970 (Colo.Ct.App.1984), certiorari denied 5/21/84.

NOTES

[1] Michigan v. Tucker, 417 U.S. 433, 447, 94 S.Ct. 2357, 2365 (1974).

[2] Weeks v. United States, 232 U.S. 383, 34 S.Ct. 341 (1914), in which federal agents entered the defendant's home without consent and without a search warrant or other authority and obtained evidence used to obtain a conviction.

[3] Mapp v. Ohio, 367 U.S. 643, 81 S.Ct. 1684 (1961), in which police officers forced their way into the defendant's home without consent, and apparently without a search warrant or other authority, and obtained evidence used to convict the defendant.

[4] Judge Warren Burger (former Chief Justice of the U.S. Supreme Court) in his article, "Who Will Watch the Watchman?", 14 *Amer.U.L.Rev.* 1 (1964).

[5] 403 U.S. 388 at 418, 91 S.Ct. 1999 at 2015 (1971).

[6] 242 N.Y. 13, 150 N.E. 585 (1926).

[7] 251 U.S. 385, 40 S.Ct. 182 (1920).

What Is Not a Fourth Amendment Search?

In 1986 the U.S. Supreme Court held that [1]

> The first clause of the Fourth Amendment provides that the "right of the people to be secure in their persons, houses, papers and effects, against unreasonable searches and seizures, shall not be violated ...." This text protects two types of expectations, one involving "searches," the other "seizures." A "search" occurs when an expectation of privacy that society is prepared to consider reasonable is infringed. A "seizure" of property occurs when there is some meaningful interference with an individual's possessory interests in that property. This Court has also consistently construed this protection as proscribing only governmental action; it is wholly inapplicable "to a search or seizure, even an unreasonable one, effected by a private individual not acting as an agent of the Government or with the participation or knowledge of any governmental official."

Therefore, to have a Fourth Amendment violation there would have to be an infringement of a right of privacy by a governmental official that amounted to an "unreasonable search ...".

The exclusionary rule is used to encourage law enforcement officers and other governmental officials to observe and respect not only Fourth Amendment rights, but also all rights given or protected by the U.S. Constitution. The "application of the rule has been restricted to areas where its remedial objectives are thought most efficaciously served." [2]

This chapter attempts to define the scope and extent of the application of the exclusionary rule by listing and illustrating the areas to which the exclusionary rule does not apply.

PRIVATE SEARCHES BY PRIVATE PERSONS

It has always been held that Fourth Amendment protection applies only to government conduct. It does not apply to private persons.

This rule is sometimes called the "Burdeau Rule," going back to the 1921 U.S. Supreme Court case of *Burdeau v. McDowell*.[3] In that case, unknown private persons "drilled the petitioner's (defendant's) private safes, broke the locks upon his private desks, and broke into and abstracted from the files in his office his private papers." Because no governmental official was involved

The Fourth Amendment of the U.S. Constitution

''The right of the people to be secure in their persons, houses, papers, and effects, against unreasonable searches and seizures, shall not be violated, and no Warrants shall issue, but upon probable cause, supported by Oath or affirmation, and particularly describing the place to be searched, and the persons or things to be seized.''

The U.S. Supreme Court and other courts have held that:

- The purpose of the Fourth Amendment is ''to prevent arbitrary and oppressive interference by enforcement officials with privacy and personal security of individuals.'' [1]

- The chief evil against which the ''wording of the Fourth Amendment is physical entry of the home.'' (by enforcement officials).[2]

- ''The ultimate standard set forth in the Fourth Amendment is reasonableness.'' [3]

- The touchstone of the court's analysis under the Fourth Amendment ''is always 'the reasonableness in all the circumstances of the particular governmental invasion of a citizen's personal security.'' [4]

- The Fourth Amendment protects the ''right of the people to be secure in their persons, houses, papers, and effects, against unreasonable searches and seizures.'' [5]

- ''The Fourth Amendment is not a guarantee against all searches and seizures, but only against *unreasonable* searches and seizures.'' [6]

- A basic principle of Fourth Amendment law is ''that searches and seizures inside a home without a warrant are presumptively unreasonable.'' [7]

[1] United States v. Martinez-Fuerte, 428 U.S. 543, 554, 96 S.Ct. 3074, 3081.
[2] Welsh v. Wisconsin, 466 U.S. 740, 748, 104 S.Ct. 2091, 2097 (1984).
[3] Camera v. Municipal Court, 387 U.S. 523, 87 S.Ct. 1727 (1967).
[4] Terry v. Ohio, 392 U.S. 1, 19, 88 S.Ct. 1868, 1878.
[5] Fourth Amendment, United States Constitution.
[6] United States v. Hensley, 469 U.S. 221, 105 S.Ct. 675 (1985).
[7] Payton v. New York, 445 U.S. at 586, 100 S.Ct. at 1380.

in any way in the wrongs done to the defendant, the U.S. Supreme Court held that when such evidence became available to the government, it could be used in the criminal proceedings against the defendant.

The Supreme Court held that the origin and history of the Fourth Amendment ''clearly show that it was intended as a restraint upon the activities of sovereign authority, and was not intended to be a limitation upon other than governmental agencies ....'' The Supreme Court further stated that

In the present case the record clearly shows that no official of the Federal Government had anything to do with the wrongful seizure of the petitioner's property, or had any knowledge thereof until several months after the property had been taken from him. ... We assume that petitioner has an unquestionable right of redress against those who illegally and wrongfully took his private property ... but with such remedies we are not now concerned.

To be a private search or seizure, it must be shown that

- It was conducted by a private citizen; and
- the idea and initiative to conduct the search or seizure originated with a private citizen; and
- the government or its employees had nothing to do with the search and did not participate in the search.

Field Tests for Illegal Drugs, Yes, But Anything Beyond That Requires a Search Warrant

When private persons turn contraband or evidence of a crime over to law enforcement officers, the question before the U.S. Supreme Court in the following cases has been what officers can do without a search warrant, consent, or an emergency. The answer is that they can conduct field tests for illegal drugs under ordinary circumstances, but if they do anything beyond that, they should get a search warrant.

United States v. Jacobsen

Supreme Court of the United States (1984)
466 U.S. 109, 104 S.Ct. 1652

A cardboard box wrapped in brown paper was damaged and torn by a forklift as it was being handled at an airport by Federal Express employees. The employees opened the package in order to examine its contents, as required by a written company policy regarding insurance claims. They observed a white, powdery substance in four plastic bags that had been concealed in a tube inside the package. The employees then notified the Drug Enforcement Administration (DEA). In holding that the field test of the substance did not violate any right of privacy of the defendant, and in affirming the conviction of the defendant of possession of cocaine with intent to distribute, the Court ruled that

When the first federal agent on the scene initially saw the package, he knew it contained nothing of significance except a tube containing plastic bags and, ultimately, white powder. It is not entirely clear that the powder was visible to him before he removed the tube from the box. Even if the white powder was not itself in "plain view" because it was still enclosed in so many containers and covered with papers, there was a virtual certainty that nothing else of significance was in the package and that a manual inspection of the tube and its contents would not tell him anything more than he already had been told. Respondents do not dispute that the Government could utilize the Federal Express employees' testimony concerning the contents of the package. If that is the case, it hardly infringed respondents' privacy for the agents to reexamine the contents of the open package by brushing aside a crumpled newspaper and picking up the tube. The advantage the Government gained thereby was merely avoiding the risk of a flaw in the employees' recollection, rather than in further infringing respondents' privacy. Protecting the risk of misdescription hardly enhances any legitimate privacy interest, and is not protected by the Fourth Amendment. Respondents could have no privacy interest in the contents of the package, since it remained unsealed and since the Federal Express employees had just examined the package and had, of their own accord, invited the federal agent to their offices for the express purpose of viewing its contents. The agent's viewing of what a private party had freely made available for his inspection did not violate the Fourth Amendment . . . .

Similarly, the removal of the plastic bags from the tube and the agent's visual inspection of their contents enabled the agent to learn nothing that had not previously been learned during the private search. It infringed no legitimate expectation of privacy and hence was not a "search" within the meaning of the Fourth Amendment . . . .

While the agents' assertion of dominion and control over the package and its contents did constitute a "seizure," that seizure was not unreasonable. The fact that, prior to the field test, respondents' privacy interest in the contents of the package had been largely compromised, is highly relevant to the reasonableness of the agents' conduct in this respect. The agents had already learned a great deal about the contents of the package from the Federal Express employees, all of which was consistent with what they could see. The package itself, which had previously been opened, remained unsealed, and the Federal Express employees had invited the agents to examine its contents. Under these circumstances, the package could no longer support any expectation of privacy; it was just like a balloon "the distinctive character [of which] spoke volumes as to its contents, particularly to the trained eye of the officer," *Texas v. Brown,* 460 U.S. ___, ___, ...

. . . Such containers may be seized, at least temporarily, without a warrant. Accordingly, since it was apparent that the tube and plastic bags contained contraband and little else, this warrantless seizure was reasonable, for it is well-settled that it is constitutionally reasonable for law enforcement officials to seize "effects" that cannot support a justifiable expectation of privacy without a warrant, based on probable cause to believe they contain contraband.

The question remains whether the additional intrusion occasioned by the field test, which had not been conducted by the Federal Express agents and therefore exceeded the scope of the private search, was an unlawful "search" or "seizure" within the meaning of the Fourth Amendment.

The field test at issue could disclose only one fact previously unknown to the agent—whether or not a suspicious white powder was cocaine. It could tell him nothing more, not even whether the substance was sugar or talcum powder. We must first determine whether this can be considered a "search" subject to the Fourth Amendment—did it infringe an expectation of privacy that society is prepared to consider reasonable?

In sum, the federal agents did not infringe any constitutionally protected privacy interest that had not already been frustrated as the result of private conduct. To the extent that a protected possessory interest was infringed, the infringement was *de minimis* and constitutionally reasonable.

Walter v. United States

Supreme Court of the United States (1980)
447 U.S. 649, 100 S.Ct. 2395

A shipment addressed to Leggs, Inc. was mistakenly delivered to an office of L'Eggs Products, Inc. instead. Employees of the latter company opened the packages to find boxes of 8-millimeter film with descriptions on the covers with explicit statements showing that the films were of male homosexual acts. Instead of calling the private carrier to tell them of their mistake, the employees called the FBI. Because the films could not be viewed with the naked eye, the FBI viewed the films with a projector but without a search warrant. In holding that the filming violated the Fourth Amendment rights of the defendants and that the evidence could not be used, the Court ruled that

> petitioners expected no one except the intended recipient either to open the 12 packages or to project the films. The 12 cartons were securely wrapped and sealed, with no labels or markings to indicate the character of their contents. There is no reason why the consignor of such a shipment would have any lesser expectation of privacy than the consignor of an ordinary locked suitcase. The fact that the cartons were unexpectedly opened by a third party before the shipment was delivered to its intended consignee does not alter the consignor's legitimate expectation of privacy. The private search merely frustrated that expectation in part. It did not simply strip the remaining unfrustrated portion of that expectation of all Fourth Amendment protection. Since the additional search conducted by the FBI—the screening of the films—was not supported by any justification, it violated that Amendment.

The *Claus von Bulow* Case

Rhode Island v. von Bulow

Rhode Island Supreme Court (1984)
475 A.2d 995, review denied 469 U.S. 875, 105 S.Ct. 233 (U.S.Sup.Ct.1984)

This case received extensive public coverage because the attempted murder charges involved wealthy jet-set persons, sex, and intrigue. A Harvard University Medical School professor testified that the two comas Mrs. von Bulow had were the sole result of "external injection of insulin into (her) body." After Mrs.

von Bulow's first coma, her two adult children became suspicious that Claus von Bulow was attempting to murder his wife. They hired a lawyer who brought in a locksmith and got into von Bulow's personal effects. They took drugs and other medical objects which they believed might be evidence of von Bulow's criminal conduct. The results of their private search were turned over to the police, who had them tested at a state toxicology laboratory without first obtaining a search warrant. In holding that the use of the evidence thus obtained violated von Bulow's Fourth Amendment rights, and in reversing the convictions and ordering a new trial, the Court stated that

> "[T]he Government may not exceed the scope of the private search unless it has the right to make an independent search." ... 100 S.Ct. at 2402 ... Consequently, unless the private inspection and testing of the black bag and its contents was so complete as to be virtually coextensive with the State Police search, it only partially frustrated defendant's original expectation of privacy. "It did not ... strip the remaining unfrustrated portion of that expectation of all Fourth Amendment protection." *Walter v. United States,* 447 U.S. at 659, 100 S.Ct. at 2403.
> ...
>
> The facts of this case readily demonstrate that the state's toxicological examination of the contents of the black bag did exceed the scope of the private tests performed by Bio-Science Laboratories at the request of Dr. Stock. In addition to the chemical analysis of both the blue liquid and the white powder performed by Dr. Stock, the state toxicologist chemically analyzed five samples of pills, including three capsules and two tablets, and two samples of ampules that were never tested by Dr. Stock. The state concedes that one of these capsules, a red capsule marked "Lilly F–40," could not have been identified by a simple sight examination.
>
> The state therefore did intrude upon a further expectation of defendant's privacy. The extent of the state's intrusion is significant because, without it, the initial view of the objects tested produced only an inference of criminal conduct by defendant .... In this case, as in *Walter,* the state exceeded the scope of the private search by employing chemical or mechanical means to reveal the hidden nature of these objects. This governmental activity represents a significant expansion of the private search because it positively identified the unknown composition of the pills delivered to the state police .... This additional investigation, being "necessary in order to obtain the evidence which was to be used at trial," *Walter v. United States,* 447 U.S. at 654, 100 S.Ct. at 2400, 65 L.Ed.2d at 416, was an independent search subject to the Fourth Amendment.
>
> Since we hold that the state's subsequent chemical analysis of certain contents of the black bag was a significant expansion of the private search and that there were no exceptions to the warrant requirement, defendant's conviction must be reversed. In a case in which "the authorities have not relied on what is in effect a private search, ... [they] presumptively violate the Fourth Amendment if they act without a warrant." *United States v. Jacobsen,* ___ U.S. at ___, 104 S.Ct. at 1659. The state may not significantly expand the scope of a private search unless it obtains a warrant.

Claus von Bulow had been convicted of two counts of attempted murder in his first trial. In the second trial, the state could not use the evidence obtained in violation of von Bulow's Fourth Amendment rights. The second trial ended in an acquittal (that is, the state failed to carry the burden of proving guilt beyond a reasonable doubt).

THE EXCLUSIONARY RULE DOES NOT APPLY TO EVIDENCE IN CIVIL CASES

The exclusionary rule does not apply to evidence used in civil cases.[4] Therefore, evidence which cannot be used in a criminal case could be used in a civil lawsuit. In the *von Bulow* case, the evidence which could not be used in the attempted murder trial could be used in a civil action against von Bulow. Stepchildren of the Danish-born financier filed a $56-million civil lawsuit against von Bulow, alleging that the "dapper Dane" twice injected his wife with insulin injections, causing by the second injection an irreversible coma. The evidence suppressed for use in the criminal trial of von Bulow can be used in the civil lawsuit.

The following U.S. Supreme Court case illustrates:

United States v. Janis

Supreme Court of the United States (1976)
428 U.S. 433, 96 S.Ct. 3021

Evidence was obtained by Los Angeles police officers under the authority of a search warrant. The search warrant, however, was held to be defective and the evidence excluded from use in California criminal courts. (Today, the evidence which was excluded would most likely be admitted under the new "good faith" rule adopted by the U.S. Supreme Court in 1984. See chapter 14.) The evidence (gambling paraphernalia and cash) was turned over to the federal Internal Revenue Service, which used the evidence to commence a civil action against the defendant. In holding that the evidence could be used in a federal civil proceeding, the U.S. Supreme Court ruled that

> Jurists and scholars uniformly have recognized that the exclusionary rule imposes a substantial cost on the societal interest in law enforcement by its proscription of what concededly is relevant evidence .... And alternatives that would be less costly to societal interests have been the subject of extensive discussion and exploration ....
>
> If the exclusionary rule is the strong medicine that its proponents claim it to be, then its use in the situations in which it is now applied (resulting, for example, in this case in frustration of the Los Angeles police officers' good-faith duties as enforcers of the criminal laws) must be assured to be a substantial and efficient deterrent. Assuming this efficacy, the additional marginal deterrence provided by forbid-

ding a different sovereign from using the evidence in a civil proceeding surely does not outweigh the cost to society of extending the rule to that situation. If, on the other hand, the exclusionary rule does not result in appreciable deterrence, then, clearly, its use in the instant situation is unwarranted. Under either assumption, therefore, the extension of the rule is unjustified.

In short, we conclude that exclusion from federal civil proceedings of evidence unlawfully seized by a state criminal enforcement officer has not been shown to have a sufficient likelihood of deterring the conduct of the state police so that it outweighs the societal costs imposed by the exclusion. This Court, therefore, is not justified in so extending the exclusionary rule.

Probably most states would hold that the exclusionary rule would not be used in sanity commitment hearings (held to commit a person to a mental hospital). In a case involving the brutal murder of a fifteen-year-old girl, former New York State Chief Justice Lumbard pointed this out as follows: [5]

> If it can be shown that Williams is a disturbed person whose freedom is fraught with danger to others, his detention in an appropriate institution would not be for the purpose of punishing him for crime. In that case his detention pursuant to state law would be to protect the public and, indeed, to protect Williams himself from the consequences of further criminal acts. While the use of such evidence in a commitment proceeding would be for the determination of the New York courts in the first instance, I know of no specific federal court case holding which would preclude the state from using Williams' confessions to impose restraints on him in state proceedings which do not seek criminal sanctions.

IF NO RIGHT OF PRIVACY HAS BEEN VIOLATED, NO FOURTH AMENDMENT VIOLATION HAS OCCURRED

The U.S. Supreme Court held in the case of *Katz v. United States* [6] that

> The Fourth Amendment protects people, not places. What a person knowingly exposes to the public, even in his own home or office, is not a subject of Fourth Amendment protection .... But what he seeks to preserve as private, may be constitutionally protected.

"A 'search' occurs when an expectation of privacy that society is prepared to consider reasonable is infringed." [7] A reasonable expectation of privacy exists *only* if

- an individual actually expects privacy, *and*
- his (or her) expectation is reasonable.

The following U.S. Supreme Court cases illustrate:

Dow Chemical Co. v. United States

Supreme Court of the United States (1986)
476 U.S. 227, 106 S.Ct. 1819

When Dow Chemical refused consent for an on-site inspection of a 2,000-acre chemical plant to the Environmental Protection Agency (EPA), the EPA hired a commercial aerial photographer to photograph the plant. Flying within "lawful navigable airspace," the government obtained photographs of the facility. In holding that the evidence was lawfully obtained and was not a search forbidden by the Fourth Amendment, the Court ruled that

> We conclude that the open areas of an industrial plant complex with numerous plant structures spread over an area of 2,000 acres are not analogous to the "curtilage" of a dwelling for purposes of aerial surveillance; such an industrial complex is more comparable to an open field and as such it is open to the view and observation of persons in aircraft lawfully in the public airspace immediately above or sufficiently near the area for the reach of cameras.
>
> We hold that the taking of aerial photographs of an industrial plant complex from navigable airspace is not a search prohibited by the Fourth Amendment.

California v. Ciraolo

Supreme Court of the United States (1986)
476 U.S. 207, 106 S.Ct. 1809

Santa Clara, California police received an anonymous telephone call that marijuana was growing in the defendant's backyard. Because of a six-foot outer fence and a ten-foot inner fence, officers were not able to observe the yard from ground level. Using a private plane, officers flew over the defendant's yard within navigable airspace. Visual observations and photographs confirmed that marijuana was growing in the defendant's yard. Based upon the information obtained, a search warrant was obtained and seventy-three marijuana plants were seized. In holding that the naked-eye aerial observations were not a search within the Fourth Amendment, the Court ruled that

> one who enters a telephone booth is entitled to assume that his conversation is not being intercepted. This does not translate readily into a rule of constitutional dimensions that one who grows illicit drugs in his backyard is "entitled to assume" his unlawful conduct will not be observed by a passing aircraft—or by a power company repair mechanic on a pole overlooking the yard. As Justice Harlan emphasized,
> "a man's home is, for most purposes, a place where he expects privacy, but objects, activities, or statements that he exposes to the

'plain view' of outsiders are not 'protected' because no intention to keep them to himself has been exhibited. On the other hand, conversations in the open would not be protected against being overheard, for the expectation of privacy under the circumstances would be unreasonable." *Katz, supra,* at 361.

One can reasonably doubt that in 1967 Justice Harlan considered an aircraft within the category of future "electronic" developments that could stealthily intrude upon an individual's privacy. In an age where private and commercial flight in the public airways is routine, it is unreasonable for respondent to expect that his marijuana plants were constitutionally protected from being observed with the naked eye from an altitude of 1,000 feet. The Fourth Amendment simply does not require the police traveling in the public airways at this altitude to obtain a warrant in order to observe what is visible to the naked eye.

New York v. Class

Supreme Court of the United States (1986)
475 U.S. 106, 106 S.Ct. 960

(This case is also presented in chapter 12.)

Federal law requires vehicles to carry a vehicle identification number (VIN), which must be visible from outside of the vehicle. After New York police officers stopped the defendant for exceeding the speed limit and driving with a cracked windshield (both are offenses in New York), one of the officers looked for the VIN on the defendant's car. Because some papers were obscuring the area of the dashboard where the VIN should be located, the officer reached in to move the papers. As he did so, he saw the handle of a gun protruding about one inch from under the driver's seat. The officer seized the gun and the defendant was arrested. In holding that law enforcement officers making a lawful stop of a vehicle have a right and duty to inspect the VIN, the Court affirmed the defendant's conviction of criminal possession of a gun, ruling that

We hold that this search was sufficiently unintrusive to be constitutionally permissible in light of the lack of a reasonable expectation of privacy in the VIN and the fact that the officers observed respondent commit two traffic violations. Any other conclusion would expose police officers to potentially grave risks without significantly reducing the intrusiveness of the ultimate conduct—viewing the VIN—which, as we have said, the officers were entitled to do as part of an undoubtedly justified traffic stop.

We note that our holding today does not authorize police officers to enter a vehicle to obtain a dashboard-mounted VIN when the VIN is visible from outside the automobile. If the VIN is in the plain view of someone outside the vehicle, there is no justification for governmental intrusion into the passenger compartment to see it.

Cardwell v. Lewis

Supreme Court of the United States (1974)
417 U.S. 583, 94 S.Ct. 2464

Without a search warrant or any other authority, Ohio police officers investigating a murder, took tire track prints and small paint samples from the defendant's car, which was parked in a public parking lot. The evidence was important evidence in convicting defendant of murder. In holding that there was no violation of the right of privacy, the Court ruled that

> In the present case, nothing from the interior of the car and no personal effects, which the Fourth Amendment traditionally has been deemed to protect, were searched or seized and introduced in evidence. With the "search" limited to the examination of the tire on the wheel and the taking of paint scrapings from the exterior of the vehicle left in the public parking lot, we fail to comprehend what expectation of privacy was infringed. Stated simply, the invasion of privacy, "if it can be said to exist, is abstract and theoretical." *Air Pollution Variance Board v. Western Alfalfa Corp.,* 416 U.S. 861, 865.

Hudson v. Palmer

Supreme Court of the United States (1984)
468 U.S. 517, 104 S.Ct. 3194

> The U.S. Supreme Court stated, "we conclude that prisoners have no legitimate expectation of privacy and that the Fourth Amendment's prohibition on unreasonable searches does not apply in prison cells ...". The plaintiff in this civil action alleged that he had a "reasonable expectation of privacy not to have his cell, locker, personal effects, (and) person invaded for (harassment) purpose(s)."

Controlled Deliveries of Contraband, and Reopening the Container

The U.S. Supreme Court defined *controlled deliveries of contraband* as follows in 1983: [8]

> Controlled deliveries of contraband apparently serve a useful function in law enforcement. They most ordinarily occur when a carrier, usually an airline, unexpectedly discovers what seems to be contraband while inspecting luggage to learn the identity of its owner, or when the contraband falls out of a broken or damaged piece of luggage, or when

the carrier exercises its inspection privilege because some suspicious circumstance has caused it concern that it may unwittingly be transporting contraband. Frequently, after such a discovery, law enforcement agents restore the contraband to its container, then close or reseal the container, and authorize the carrier to deliver the container to its owner. When the owner appears to take delivery he is arrested and the container with the contraband is seized and then searched a second time for the contraband known to be there.

The practice of controlled delivery is used as an alternative to simply seizing contraband and destroying it. Evidence against persons dealing in drugs and other contraband can be developed by controlled deliveries. The following case came before the U.S. Supreme Court in 1983:

Illinois v. Andreas

Supreme Court of the United States (1983)
463 U.S. 765, 103 S.Ct. 3319

A customs inspector at O'Hare Airport in Chicago opened a large locked metal container shipped by air from Calcutta, India. In the box was a wooden table; concealed in the table was marijuana. The Chicago Drug Enforcement Administration (DEA) was notified and an agent came to the airport. He tested the substance and confirmed that it was marijuana. The table and the container were resealed. The next day, the DEA agent put the container in a delivery van and drove to the defendant's building, where he was met by a Chicago detective. The two law enforcement officers entered the apartment building pretending to be delivery men and announced they had a package for the defendant. The defendant came to the lobby and identified himself. When the Chicago detective commented on the weight of the package, the defendant responded that it "wasn't that heavy: that he had packaged it himself, and that it only contained a table." The container was carried to the hallway outside the defendant's apartment. One officer then left to get a search warrant for the defendant's apartment while the other positioned himself to maintain surveillance of the apartment. Before the Chicago detective returned, the defendant came out of his apartment with the container. He was immediately arrested and taken to a police station. There, the container was reopened and the marijuana seized. No search warrant was obtained.

The Illinois courts suppressed the evidence, holding that the defendant had a legitimate expectation of privacy in the contents of the shipping container and that the police had failed to make a "controlled delivery" in that they lost sight of the container while it was in defendant's apartment for thirty to forty-five minutes and, in the court's view, "there is no certainty that the contents of the package were the same before and after the package was brought into the apartment." In holding that "reopening the container did not intrude on any legitimate expectation of privacy and did not violate the Fourth Amendment," the Supreme Court ruled that

The Fourth Amendment protects legitimate expectations of privacy rather than simply places. If the inspection by police does not intrude upon a legitimate expectation of privacy, there is no "search" subject to the Warrant Clause. The threshold question, then, is whether an individual has a legitimate expectation of privacy in the contents of a previously lawfully searched container. It is obvious that the privacy interest in the contents of a container diminishes with respect to a container that law enforcement authorities have already lawfully opened and found to contain illicit drugs. No protected privacy interest remains in contraband in a container once government officers lawfully have opened that container and identified its contents as illegal. The simple act of resealing the container to enable the police to make a controlled delivery does not operate to revive or restore the lawfully invaded privacy rights.

This conclusion is supported by the reasoning underlying the "plain-view" doctrine. The plain-view doctrine authorizes seizure of illegal or evidentiary items visible to a police officer whose access to the object has some prior Fourth Amendment justification and who has probable cause to suspect that the item is connected with criminal activity .... The plain-view doctrine is grounded on the proposition that once police are lawfully in a position to observe an item firsthand, its owner's privacy interest in that item is lost; the owner may retain the incidents of title and possession but not privacy. That rationale applies here; once a container has been found to a certainty to contain illicit drugs, the contraband becomes like objects physically within the plain view of the police, and the claim to privacy is lost. Consequently, the subsequent reopening of the container is not a "search" within the intendment of the Fourth Amendment.

However, the rigors and contingencies inescapable in an investigation into illicit drug traffic often make "perfect" controlled deliveries and the "absolute certainty" demanded by the Illinois court impossible to attain. Conducting such a surveillance undetected is likely to render it virtually impossible for police so perfectly to time their movements as to avoid detection and also be able to arrest the owner and reseize the container the instant he takes possession. Not infrequently, police may lose sight of the container they are trailing, as is the risk in the pursuit of a car or vessel.

During such a gap in surveillance, it is possible that the container will be put to other uses—for example, the contraband may be removed or other items may be placed inside. The likelihood that this will happen depends on all the facts and circumstances, including the nature and uses of the container, the length of the break in surveillance, and the setting in which the events occur. However, the mere fact that the police may be less than 100% certain of the contents of the container is insufficient to create a proteted interest in the privacy of the container .... The issue then becomes at what point after an interruption of control or surveillance, courts should recognize the individual's expectation of privacy in the container as a legitimate right protected by the Fourth Amendment proscription against unreasonable searches.

In fashioning a standard, we must be mindful of three Fourth Amendment principles. First, the standard should be workable for application by rank-and-file, trained police officers .... Second, it should be reasonable; for example, it would be absurd to recognize as legitimate an expectation of privacy where there is only a minimal probability that the contents of a particular container had been changed. Third, the standard should be objective, not dependent on the belief of individual police officers .... A workable, objective standard that limits the risk of intrusion on legitimate privacy interests is whether there is a substantial likelihood that the contents of the container have been changed during the gap in surveillance. We hold that absent a substantial likelihood that the contents have been changed, there is no legitimate expectation of privacy in the contents of a container previously opened under lawful authority.

Applying these principles, we conclude there was no substantial likelihood here that the contents of the shipping container were changed during the brief period that it was out of sight of the surveilling officer. The unusual size of the container, its specialized purpose, and the relatively short break in surveillance combine to make it substantially unlikely that the respondent removed the table or placed new items inside the container while it was in his apartment. Thus, reopening the container did not intrude on any legitimate expectation of privacy and did not violate the Fourth Amendment.

"PLAIN VIEW"

"The plain-view doctrine [9] authorizes seizure of illegal or evidentiary items visible to a police officer whose access to the object has some prior Fourth Amendment justification and who has probable cause to suspect that the item is connected with criminal activity." (U.S. Supreme Court in 1983 case of *Illinois v. Andreas.*)

The most widely quoted explanation of **plain view** can be found in the U.S. Supreme Court case of *Coolidge v. New Hampshire:* [10]

What the "plain view" cases have in common is that the police officer in each of them had a prior justification for an intrusion in the course of which he came inadvertently across a piece of evidence incriminating the accused. The doctrine serves to supplement the prior justification—whether it be a warrant for another object, hot pursuit, search incident to lawful arrest, or some other legitimate reason for being present unconnected with a search directed against the accused—and permits the warrantless seizure. Of course, the extension of the original justification is legitimate only where it is immediately apparent to the police that they have evidence before them; the "plain view" doctrine may not be used to extend a general exploratory search from one object to another until something incriminating at last emerges.

In 1983, the U.S. Supreme Court again reviewed the doctrine of plain view in the following case:

Texas v. Brown

Supreme Court of the United States (1983)
460 U.S. 730, 103 S.Ct. 1535

(This case is also presented in chapter 12.)

The defendant's car was stopped in "a routine driver's license checkpoint" in Fort Worth. Because it was dark, an officer shone his flashlight into the car and saw the defendant drop an opaque, green party balloon to the seat of the car. When the officer asked Brown for his driver's license, Brown opened the glove compartment of the car. As Brown opened the glove compartment, the officer shifted his position outside of the car to obtain a better view of the interior of the glove compartment. The officer saw several small plastic vials, quantities of loose white powder, and an open bag of party balloons. After rummaging through the glove compartment, Brown stated that he had no driver's license. Brown was ordered to get out of the car, after which the officer reached into the car and seized the green balloon on the seat. Brown was then arrested and the officers conducted "an on-the-scene inventory of Brown's car." In affirming Brown's conviction for the possession of heroin, the Supreme Court held that

> if, while lawfully engaged in an activity in a particular place, police officers perceive a suspicious object, they may seize it immediately . . . .
>
> Applying these principles, we conclude that Officer Maples properly seized the green balloon from Brown's automobile. The Court of Criminal Appeals stated that it did not "question . . . the validity of the officer's initial stop of appellant's vehicle as a part of a license check," 617 S.W.2d, at 200, and we agree . . . . It is likewise beyond dispute that Maples' action in shining his flashlight to illuminate the interior of Brown's car trenched upon no right secured to the latter by the Fourth Amendment. The Court said in *United States v. Lee*, 274 U.S. 559, 563, 47 S.Ct. 746, 748, 71 L.Ed. 1202 (1927): "[The] use of a searchlight is comparable to the use of a marine glass or a field glass. It is not prohibited by the Constitution." Numerous other courts have agreed that the use of artificial means to illuminate a darkened area simply does not constitute a search, and thus triggers no Fourth Amendment protection.
>
> Likewise, the fact that Maples "changed [his] position" and "bent down at an angle so [he] could see what was inside" Brown's car is irrelevant to Fourth Amendment analysis. The general public could peer into the interior of Brown's automobile from any number of angles; there is no reason Maples should be precluded from observing as an officer what would be entirely visible to him as a private citizen. There is no legitimate expectation of privacy, . . . shielding that portion of the interior of an automobile which may be viewed from

outside the vehicle by either inquisitive passersby or diligent police officers. In short, the conduct that enabled Maples to observe the interior of Brown's car and of his open glove compartment was not a search within the meaning of the Fourth Amendment ....

With these considerations in mind it is plain that Officer Maples possessed probable cause to believe that the balloon in Brown's hand contained an illicit substance. Maples testified that he was aware, both from his participation in previous narcotics arrests and from discussions with other officers, that balloons tied in the manner of the one possessed by Brown were frequently used to carry narcotics. This testimony was corroborated by that of a police department chemist who noted that it was "common" for balloons to be used in packaging narcotics. In addition, Maples was able to observe the contents of the glove compartment of Brown's car.

The Three Requirements of Plain View

The U.S. Supreme Court has held that the following requirements are necessary for a plain-view seizure of evidence:

First, the police officer must lawfully make an "initial intrusion" or otherwise properly be in a position from which he can view a particular area.

Second, the officer must discover incriminating evidence "inadvertently," which is to say, he may not "know in advance the location of ... evidence and intend to seize it," relying on the plain-view doctrine only as a pretext.

Finally, it must be "immediately apparent" to the police that the items they observe may be evidence of a crime, contraband, or otherwise subject to seizure.[11]

Plain View and the Five Human Senses

Most plain-view cases occur when an officer, who is where he has a right to be, sees evidence or contraband of a crime. However, plain view is not limited to visual observations. Any of the five human senses could provide information that make it "immediately apparent" to the police that the object is evidence of a crime.

- *Plain smell.* In 1948, the U.S. Supreme Court held that odors may be "found to be evidence of the most persuasive character." *Johnson v. United States,* 333 U.S. 10, 13, 68 S.Ct. 367, 368 (1948).

- *Plain hearing.* The "naked ear" or **plain hearing** rule applies to things that are heard without the use of any electronic or mechanical devices. See *United States v. Agapito,* 620 F.2d 324 (2d Cir.1980), *United States v. Mankani,* 738 F.2d 538 (2d Cir.1984), *United States v. Lopez,* 475 F.2d 537 (7th Cir.1973), *United States v. Fisch,* 474 F.2d 1071 (9th Cir.1973).

Would Plain View Justify Moving an Item to Determine If It Is Contraband or Evidence?

THE 1987 U.S. SUPREME COURT CASE OF *ARIZONA v. HICKS*

When a bullet suddenly came through the ceiling of his apartment, the occupant was injured. "Police officers arrived and entered (defendant's) apartment to search for the shooter, for other victims, and weapons. They found and seized three weapons, including a sawed-off rifle, and in the course of their search also discovered a stocking-cap mask."

Expensive stereo equipment was also seen in the defendant's apartment. Because the apartment was furnished with inexpensive furniture, the expensive stereo components seemed out of place. Suspecting that the stereo equipment was stolen, Officer Nelson moved some of the stereo parts to read and record the serial numbers. He then telephoned the numbers in to police headquarters and was informed that a turntable had been taken in a recent armed robbery. Officer Nelson then seized the turntable and later obtained a search warrant to seize other stereo equipment left in the apartment. In holding that the evidence seized could not be used in the armed robbery trial of the defendant, the U.S. Supreme Court ruled that

> Officer Nelson's moving of the equipment, however, did constitute a "search" separate and apart from the search for the shooter, victims, and weapons that was the lawful objective of his entry into the apartment. Merely inspecting those parts of the turntable that came into view during the latter search would not have constituted an independent search, because it would have produced no additional invasion of respondent's privacy interest .... But taking action, unrelated to the objectives of the authorized intrusion, which exposed to view concealed portions of the apartment or its contents, did produce a new invasion of respondent's privacy unjustified by the exigent circumstance that validated the entry. This is why ... the "distinction between 'looking' at a suspicious object in plain view and 'moving' it even a few inches" is much more than trivial for purposes of the Fourth Amendment. It matters not that the search uncovered nothing of any great personal value to the respondent—serial numbers rather than (what might conceivably have been hidden behind or under the equipment) letters or photographs. A search is a search, even if it happens to disclose nothing but the bottom of a turntable.[a]

[a] Arizona v. Hicks, ___ U.S. ___, 107 S.Ct. 1149, 40 CrL 3320 (1987).

- *Plain touch.* If, in making a lawful pat-down, the officer touches what is immediately apparent to be a concealed pistol, **plain touch** has occurred. See also *United States v. Mulligan,* 488 F.2d 732 (9th Cir.1973).
- *Plain taste.* The sense of taste is rarely used to provide information to a law enforcement officer. No reported decisions can be found on this point.

The Use of Flashlights and Binoculars to Aid Vision

The federal rule and the majority rule in the United States is that officers may use binoculars or telescopes as long as they are where they have a right to be.

Flashlights, searchlights, and spotlights are also used to aid vision at night. In the 1927 case of *United States v. Lee,*[12] the U.S. Supreme Court approved of the use of a searchlight, holding that

> Such use of a searchlight is comparable to the use of a marine glass or a field glass. It is not prohibited by the Constitution.

In the 1952 case of *On Lee v. United States,*[13] officers obtained evidence by using binoculars to observe criminal activity in a laundry. In affirming the defendant's conviction, the U.S. Supreme Court held that

> The use of bifocals, field glasses or the telescope to magnify the object of a witness' vision is not a forbidden search or seizure even if they focus without his knowledge or consent upon what one supposes to be private indiscretions .... We find no violation of the Fourth Amendment here.

In the case of *Texas v. Brown,*[14] the U.S. Supreme Court pointed out that because a police officer "changed (his) position" and "bent down at an angle so (he) could see what was inside" the opened glove compartment as the officer stood outside the car "is irrelevant to Fourth Amendment analysis." Another court held that an officer may "crane his neck, bend over, or squat ... so long as what he saw would have been visible to any curious passerby." [15]

"Plain Smell" and the Use of Sniffing Dogs

Not only may a witness testify as to what they smelled, but testimony as to the use of sniffing dogs may be used as evidence in most state courts; upon a proper showing that the breeding, training, performance, and handling of the dog justified an inference that the results obtained from the use of dog were reliable.

In the 1983 case of *United States v. Place,* 462 U.S. 696 at 706, 103 S.Ct. 2637 at 2644, the U.S. Court held that submitting luggage to a "sniff test" by a trained narcotics detection dog was not a search within the meaning of the Fourth Amendment:

> ... we conclude that when an officer's observations lead him reasonably to believe that a traveler is carrying luggage that contains narcotics, the principles of *Terry* and its progeny would permit the officer to detain the luggage briefly to investigate the circumstances that aroused his suspicion, provided that the investigative detention is properly limited in scope.
>
> The purpose for which respondent's luggage was seized, of course, was to arrange its exposure to a narcotics detection dog. Obviously, if this investigative procedure is itself a search requiring probable cause, the initial seizure of respondent's luggage for the purpose of subjecting it to the sniff test—no matter how brief—could not be justified on less than probable cause ....
>
> The Fourth Amendment "protects people from unreasonable government intrusions into their legitimate expectations of privacy." *United States v. Chadwick,* 433 U.S., at 7, 97 S.Ct., at 2481. We have affirmed that a person possesses a privacy interest in the contents of personal luggage that is protected by the Fourth Amendment .... A

"canine sniff" by a well-trained narcotics detection dog, however, does not require opening the luggage. It does not expose noncontraband items that otherwise would remain hidden from public view, as does, for example, an officer's rummaging through the contents of the luggage. Thus, the manner in which information is obtained through this investigative technique is much less intrusive than a typical search. Moreover, the sniff discloses only the presence or absence of narcotics, a contraband item. Thus, despite the fact that the sniff tells the authorities something about the contents of the luggage, the information obtained is limited. This limited disclosure also ensures that the owner of the property is not subjected to the embarrassment and inconvenience entailed in less discriminate and more intrusive investigative methods.

In these respects, the canine sniff is *sui generis* [only one of its own kind: unmatched elsewhere]. We are aware of no other investigative procedure that is so limited both in the manner in which the information is obtained and in the content of the information revealed by the procedure. Therefore, we conclude that the particular course of investigation that the agents intended to pursue here—exposure of respondent's luggage, which was located in a public place, to a trained canine—did not constitute a "search" within the meaning of the Fourth Amendment.

The following cases illustrate other ways, in criminal investigations, that trained dogs may be used in developing evidence:

United States v. Gates

U.S. Court of Appeals, Sixth Circuit (1982)
680 F.2d 1117

Two men committed an armed robbery; in their haste to flee, they each lost a shoe. They also dropped a gun used in the robbery and a bag of money taken in the robbery. Eight months after the robbery, defendant Gates was held in custody for the robbery. A lineup was assembled in a room. A German shepherd with extensive training and experience obtained the scent from the shoe (actually a sandal) and was led into the room where the lineup had been assembled. The dog promptly went to Gates and placed his head on Gates' lap. The Court of Appeals affirmed Gates' conviction for armed robbery and the use of the evidence of the tracking dog used for identification purposes in the lineup. The Court also held that the following instruction to the jury was properly given:

Evidence has been presented in this case that law enforcement authorities conducted portions of their investigation with the aid of a trained dog. Because it is of course not possible for the dog to communicate its findings to us directly, we must rely on the interpretation of the dog's actions provided by the testimony of its trainer, witness John Preston. Because of the nature of this evidence, you are instructed to receive it with caution and not to give it undue weight. It is to be considered as a part of, and along with, all the other evidence in the case in your deliberations.

State v. Roscoe

Supreme Court of Arizona (1984)
145 Ariz. 212, 700 P.2d 1312, 36 CrL 2295

A seven-year-old girl disappeared. Her bicycle was found at the edge of a road, indicating that she might have been taken in a car. The next day, the nude body of the little girl was found in a remote area twelve miles from where her bicycle was found. She had been sexually molested and strangled. Defendant Kevin Roscoe was later convicted of the girl's murder, kidnapping, and molestation. In his appeal to the Supreme Court of Arizona, Roscoe challenged the admission of "dog scenting" evidence of identification tests.

The German shepherd "Harass II" and his trainer were the same dog and trainer used in the preceding *Gates* case. The following identification tests were used. All the tests were run blind—the trainer of the dog was not informed of any of the facts involved.

Test 1:   Five cars were lined up. Harass II was given the victim's scent, obtained from her clothing. The dog picked Roscoe's car, which the dog's trainer stated meant that the girl had been in the car.

Test 2:   The dog was scented on Roscoe's clothing and was taken to the general area where the girl's bike had been found. Harass II "alerted" to the location where the bicycle had been found. The trainer testified that this indicated that Roscoe had been present at that area.

Test 3:   Again, after scenting on Roscoe's clothing, the dog indicated that Roscoe had been in the area where the girl's body was found.

Tests 4 and 5:   Lineups of clothing and bicycles were used. The dog's reaction indicated that Roscoe's scent was present on the clothing the girl wore at the time of her disappearance, and the scent was also on her bike.

In holding that a proper foundation had been presented for the admission of the dog tracing evidence, the Court ruled that

> We hold, therefore, that dog tracking or identification evidence is admissible in Arizona upon a proper foundation showing that the breeding, training, performance and handling of the particular dog warrants an inference that the results obtained from use of that dog are reliable .... We are aware that many of the cases, and at least two involving Harass II, have indicated the advisability of instructing the jury to be cautious in evaluating and using such evidence. We express no opinion on the propriety or advisability of such an instruction, but we do caution trial judges to use care in determining admissibility under Rule 403 of the Rules of Evidence. There is some likelihood that jurors may give such evidence considerable weight; consequently, care should be taken to see that the foundation does indicate that the results from use of the dog are reliable. Demonstra-

tions in the courtroom or on film, to verify the dog's abilities might be advisable.

"STANDING" TO SUPPRESS EVIDENCE AND TO PREVENT ITS USE IN A CRIMINAL TRIAL

A "motion" is an application to a court for an order from the court. In order to prevent evidence from being used against his client, a defense lawyer must make a motion to the court asking the court to suppress the evidence for reasons argued by the defense lawyer.

In order to make a motion in a criminal case to suppress evidence, the defendant must have **standing.** In this sense, *standing* is a legal term meaning the right to stand up in a court and challenge the manner and procedure in which the government obtained the evidence they plan to use against the defendant.

Not all defendants in criminal cases have standing, nor is all illegally or improperly seized evidence forbidden "in all proceedings or against all persons." The U.S. Supreme Court stated the reasoning behind the standing rule in the 1974 case of *United States v. Calandra* [16] as follows:

> Despite its broad deterrent purpose, the exclusionary rule has never been interpreted to proscribe the use of illegally seized evidence in all proceedings or against all persons. As with any remedial device, the application of the rule has been restricted to those areas where its remedial objectives are thought most efficaciously served. The balancing process implicit in this approach is expressed in the contours of the standing requirement. Thus, standing to invoke the exclusionary rule has been confined to situations where the Government seeks to use such evidence to incriminate the victim of the unlawful search .... This standing rule is premised on a recognition that the need for deterrence and hence the rationale for excluding the evidence are strongest where the Government's unlawful conduct would result in imposition of a criminal sanction on the victim of the search.

The following U.S. Supreme Court cases illustrate the present standing rule:

Rakas v. Illinois

Supreme Court of the United States (1978)
439 U.S. 128, 99 S.Ct. 421

After an armed robbery in Illinois, a car was stopped on reasonable suspicion that occupants of the car were involved in the robbery. A box of rifle shells was found in the locked glove compartment and a sawed-off rifle was found under the front passenger seat. The defendants were passengers in the car and admit they did not own the car (the owner of the car was the driver). Nor did

The 1987 Extension of the "Good-Faith" Exception

THE 1987 U.S. SUPREME COURT CASE OF *ILLINOIS v. KRULL*

Krull was arrested when four stolen cars were found in his Chicago junkyard. Detective McNally of the Chicago Police Department discovered the stolen vehicles when he made a routine inspection of the records of the junkyard under an Illinois statute regulating the sale of motor vehicles and vehicular parts. However, the Illinois law authorizing the inspection of the records and premises of junkyards, etc. without a search warrant was declared unconstitutional. In pointing out that the prime purpose of the exclusionary rule "is to deter future unlawful police conduct and thereby effectuate the guarantee of the Fourth Amendment against unreasonable search and seizure," the Supreme Court permitted the use of the evidence against Krull, ruling that

> According to the Illinois Supreme Court, the statute failed to pass constitutional muster solely because the statute "vested State officials with too much discretion to decide who, when, and how long to search." ... Assuming, as we do for purposes of this case, that the Illinois Supreme Court was correct in its constitutional analysis, this defect in the statute was not sufficiently obvious so as to render a police officer's reliance upon the statute objectively unreasonable. The statute provided that searches could be conducted "at any reasonable time during the night or day," and seemed to limit the scope of the inspections to the records the businesses were required to maintain and to the business premises "for the purposes of determining the accuracy of required records." Ill.Rev.Stat. ch. 95½, ¶ 5–401(e) (1981). While statutory provisions that circumscribe officers' discretion may be important in establishing a statute's constitutionality, the additional restrictions on discretion that might have been necessary are not so obvious that an objectively reasonable police officer would have realized the statute was unconstitutional without them. We therefore conclude that Detective McNally relied, in objective good faith, on a statute that appeared legitimately to allow a warrantless administrative search of respondents' business.[a]

The Solicitor General of the United States pointed out that the *Krull* case "is a very important decision because it is the first time that the Supreme Court has extended the good faith exception out of the warrant area." (See the search warrant good-faith exception material in chapter 14 of this text.)

[a] Illinois v. Krull, ___ U.S. ___, 107 S.Ct. 1160, 40 CrL 3327 (1987).

the defendants assert that they owned the rifle or the shells. The defendants were charged and convicted of the armed robbery. The box of shells and the sawed-off rifle were used in evidence against them. The Illinois courts and the U.S. Supreme Court held that the defendants lacked standing to object to what they allege was an unlawful search and seizure. In affirming the convictions, the U.S. Supreme Court held that

> Each time the exclusionary rule is applied it exacts a substantial social cost for the vindication of Fourth Amendment rights. Relevant and reliable evidence is kept from the trier of fact and the search for

truth at trial is deflected .... Since our cases generally have held that one whose Fourth Amendment rights are violated may successfully suppress evidence obtained in the course of an illegal search and seizure, misgivings as to the benefit of enlarging the class of persons who may invoke that rule are properly considered when deciding whether to expand standing to assert Fourth Amendment violations ....

Here petitioners, who were passengers occupying a car which they neither owned nor leased, ... they made no showing that they had any legitimate expectation of privacy in the glove compartment or area under the seat of the car in which they were merely passengers. Like the trunk of an automobile, these are areas in which a passenger *qua* passenger simply would not normally have a legitimate expectation of privacy ....

The Illinois courts were therefore correct in concluding that it was unnecessary to decide whether the search of the car might have violated the rights secured to someone else by the Fourth and Fourteenth Amendments to the United States Constitution. Since it did not violate any rights of these petitioners, their judgment of conviction is
Affirmed.

Rawlings v. Kentucky

Supreme Court of the United States (1980)
448 U.S. 98, 100 S.Ct. 2556

Before the police arrived at a home with a search warrant, the defendant had asked a girl (Vanassa Cox) who he had known for only a few days if she would hold thousands of dollars of illegal drugs for him in her purse. After giving the persons in the home *Miranda* warnings, Cox was asked to empty the contents of her purse on a coffee table. Among the contents was a jar containing 1,800 tablets of LSD and vials of other drugs. The defendant immediately claimed ownership of the controlled substance. The issue before the courts was whether the defendant had a right of privacy in the woman's purse so as to have standing to challenge the lawfulness of the search and seizure. In holding that the defendant did not have standing, the U.S. Supreme Court ruled that

In holding that petitioner could not challenge the legality of the search of Cox's purse, the Supreme Court of Kentucky looked primarily to our then recent decision in *Rakas v. Illinois,* where we abandoned a separate inquiry into a defendant's "standing" to contest an allegedly illegal search in favor of an inquiry that focused directly on the substance of the defendant's claim that he or she possessed a "legitimate expectation of privacy" in the area searched .... In the present case, the Supreme Court of Kentucky looked to the "totality of the circumstances," including petitioner's own admission at the suppression hearing that he did not believe that Cox's purse would be free from governmental intrusion, and held that petitioner "[had] not made a sufficient showing that his legitimate or reasonable expectations of privacy were violated" by the search of the purse ....

We believe that the record in this case supports that conclusion. Petitioner, of course, bears the burden of proving not only that the search of Cox's purse was illegal, but also that he had a legitimate expectation of privacy in that purse .... At the time petitioner dumped thousands of dollars worth of illegal drugs into Cox's purse, he had known her for only a few days. According to Cox's uncontested testimony, petitioner had never sought or received access to her purse prior to that sudden bailment .... Nor did petitioner have any right to exclude other persons from access to Cox's purse .... Cox testified that Bob Stallons, a longtime acquaintance and frequent companion of Cox's, had free access to her purse on the very morning of the arrest had rummaged through its contents in search of a hairbrush. Moreover, even assuming that petitioner's version of the bailment is correct and that Cox did consent to the transfer of possession, the precipitous nature of the transaction hardly supports a reasonable inference that petitioner took normal precautions to maintain his privacy .... In addition to all the foregoing facts, the record also contains a frank admission by petitioner that he had no subjective expectation that Cox's purse would remain free from governmental intrusion, an admission credited by both the trial court and the Supreme Court of Kentucky ....

Petitioner contends nevertheless that, because he claimed ownership of the drugs in Cox's purse, he should be entitled to challenge the search regardless of his expectation of privacy. We disagree. While petitioner's ownership of the drugs is undoubtedly one fact to be considered in this case, *Rakas* emphatically rejected the notion that "arcane" concepts of property law ought to control the ability to claim the protections of the Fourth Amendment .... Had petitioner placed his drugs in plain view, he would still have owned them, but he could not claim any legitimate expectation of privacy. Prior to *Rakas,* petitioner might have been given "standing" in such a case to challenge a "search" that netted those drugs but probably would have lost his claim on the merits. After *Rakas,* the two inquiries merge into one: whether governmental officials violated any legitimate expectation of privacy held by petitioner.

In sum, we find no reason to overturn the lower court's conclusion that petitioner had no legitimate expectation of privacy in Cox's purse at the time of the search.

United States v. Salvucci

Supreme Court of the United States (1980)
448 U.S. 83, 100 S.Ct. 2547

Defendants John Salvucci and Joseph Zackular were charged with the unlawful possession of stolen mail. The federal indictment was based upon twelve checks which police seized during a search of an apartment rented by Zackular's mother. The trial court granted a motion to suppress the evidence, holding that probable cause did not exist to support the search warrant issued to search the apartment. The Supreme Court overruled the 1960 "Automatic Standing Rule" and held that the defendants would have to prove their own Fourth Amendment rights were violated for them to have standing.

ABANDONMENT, OR RELINQUISHING THE RIGHT OF PRIVACY IN PROPERTY

Abandonment or the relinquishment of the right of privacy in property is a matter of <u>intent</u>. This intent may be determined or inferred from words spoken, acts done and other objective facts and circumstances existing at the time of the alleged abandonment. The 5th Circuit Court of Appeals stated in the 1973 case of *United States v. Colbert* (474 F.2d 174) that "one has no standing to complain of a search or seizure of property he has voluntarily abandoned." Abandonment cases can be classified as follows:

- the "throw-away" cases in which the defendant throws, discards, or leaves an object behind.
- the "denial of ownership" cases in which the defendant disclaims interest in the object.
- unattended motor vehicle cases in which by statute or by court ruling, the vehicle is deemed abandoned.

Throw-away Cases

Hester v. United States

Supreme Court of the United States (1924)
265 U.S. 57, 44 S.Ct. 445

> The defendant ran away from revenue officers who were on his property. As the defendant ran in an open field, he threw away a jug and a bottle which broke. The officers then determined that the discarded items contained illegal whiskey. In affirming the conviction of the defendant for the possession of this contraband, the U.S. Supreme Court held that
>
> > It is obvious that even if there had been a trespass, the above testimony was not obtained by an illegal search or seizure. The defendant's own acts, and those of his associates, disclosed the jug, the jar and the bottle—and there was no seizure in the sense of the law when the officers examined the contents of each after it had been abandoned.

Abel v. United States

Supreme Court of the United States (1960)
362 U.S. 217, 80 S.Ct. 683

> In 1957 the famous Russian spy, Colonel Abel, was arrested in a hotel room in New York City. He was told by the arresting officers to dress and pack his bags. After Abel had checked out of his hotel and was taken to jail, FBI agents requested permission from the hotel manager to search his former room. Objects found in a wastebasket in the room were introduced in the criminal trial of the defendant. In affirming the conviction of the defendant, the U.S. Supreme Court ruled that

Police Searches of Trash Barrels

In a two-part article entitled "*Katz* [a] in the Trash Barrel," in the *FBI Law Enforcement Bulletin* (February and March 1979), the following conclusions were presented on the seizure of abandoned personal property:

> Criminals who dispose of contraband and other evidence of criminal offenses in their trash cans are unskilled practitioners. They assume the risk that their discards will be seized by, or turned over to, law enforcement officers for use against them. Such items can be used directly as evidence in a criminal prosecution, or indirectly by forming the basis for issuance of a search warrant.
>
> The following conclusions also can be drawn from an analysis of the Federal and State trash search decisions:
>
> 1. A search warrant is the best assurance that evidence seized from a trash container will not be challenged successfully on constitutional grounds.
> 2. One who disposes of personal property in a trash receptacle placed at curbside for collection, or in a commonly used receptacle, or in a refuse pile accessible to the public, generally is held to have abandoned the property.
> 3. A former possessor retains no reasonable expectation of privacy in abandoned property, and thus has no standing to object to its seizure or inspection.
> 4. Warrantless entry by police or their agents to a constitutionally protected area, such as the yard or garage, in order to gain access to trash, may taint the search or seizure, regardless of the intent of the possessor to abandon; and
> 5. Officers contemplating a warrantless trash inspection should be thoroughly familiar with State as well as Federal principles governing the search or seizure of trash, since State courts may impose under State constitutions more restrictive rules than those announced by Federal courts.

[a] See the case of Katz v. United States in chapter 15.

So far as the record shows, petitioner had abandoned these articles. He had thrown them away. So far as he was concerned, they were *bona vacantia.* There can be nothing unlawful in the Government's appropriation of such abandoned property.

Denial of Ownership in Property as a Form of Abandonment

A person who denies ownership in property to a law enforcement officer relinquishes his right of privacy in that property and cannot later challenge a search or seizure of the property. The following cases illustrate this form of abandonment: [17]

United States v. Colbert

U.S. Court of Appeals, Fifth Circuit (1973)
474 F.2d 174

The two defendants placed two briefcases on a sidewalk when they saw two police officers approach them. They denied ownership of the briefcases to the officers or that they "had any knowledge about them." When they began walking away from the officers and the briefcases, the officers stopped them again. When the officers opened the briefcases, a sawed-off shotgun was found in each briefcase. In affirming the defendants' convictions for the possession of unregistered sawed-off shotguns, the Court held that

> The issue is not abandonment in the strict property-right sense, but whether the person prejudiced by the search had voluntarily discarded, left behind, or otherwise relinquished his interest in the property in question so that he could no longer retain a reasonable expectation of privacy with regard to it at the time of the search.... the government may argue without self-contradiction that a defendant had possession at one time for purposes of conviction, but at a later time lacked sufficient possession to confer standing to object to search and seizure. Accordingly, we do not think the *Jones* rule of standing was intended to prevent the government from showing voluntary pre-search abandonment, if it can, or to apply to a possession prosecution when such abandonment is shown.

United States v. Sanders

U.S. Court of Appeals, Sixth Circuit (1983)
719 F.2d 882

United States v. Tolbert

U.S. Court of Appeals, Sixth Circuit (1982)
692 F.2d 1041

Both of these cases are airport "checked-luggage" cases in which the defendants (both women) were transporting suitcases filled with cocaine. Both defendants were under surveillance when they left the aircraft after arriving at the airport. In both cases, they walked past the baggage claim areas without stopping to pick up their luggage. Sanders was stopped after she left the airport and said that she did not pick up her luggage because she was not going straight home. She refused to consent to a search of her luggage; the court held that she did not abandon her luggage, and that the search by agents without consent or a search warrant was unlawful.

In the *Tolbert* case, the defendant not only walked past the baggage claim area without picking up her luggage, but when questioned by agents she denied having any luggage. The court held that she had not exhibited the necessary expectation of privacy in the suitcase and held that because the suitcase was abandoned, the search by agents did not violate any Fourth Amendment rights.

Under What Circumstances Is a Vehicle Legally Abandoned?

Some states have statutes which determine when a vehicle is legally abandoned. For example, Section 342.30 of the Wisconsin Statutes provides that if a vehicle is left unattended on a public highway or private or public property "under such circumstances as to cause the vehicle to reasonably appear to have been abandoned" for more than 48 hours, "the vehicle is deemed abandoned and constitutes a public nuisance."

In the following case, a court held that a suitcase in a vehicle was abandoned:

United States v. Oswald

U.S. Court of Appeals, Sixth Circuit (1986)
783 F.2d 663

The defendant was transporting $300,000 worth of cocaine north from Florida in a stolen car when the car caught on fire on an interstate highway. Oswald ran from the car in fear that the car would blow up. Oswald did not report the fire or the car on the highway because the car was stolen and had the cocaine in a suitcase in the trunk. Local authorities put out the fire, which extensively damaged the vehicle. Before having the vehicle towed away, a deputy sheriff took the valuables out of the car. After attempting to determine the identity of the owner of the vehicle and why they had not reported the incident, the sheriff (more than an hour and a half later) began to go through the items he had taken from the car. When the sheriff pried open a metal suitcase, the cocaine in the suitcase cleared up the mystery of why no one had claimed the property. In affirming Oswald's conviction, the trial court and the Court of Appeals held that Oswald had abandoned the suitcase when he made no efforts to preserve his right of privacy in the metal suitcase.

A thief has no right of privacy in a stolen object, which in the *Oswald* case was a stolen car. Oswald, therefore, had no standing to challenge the search of the vehicle, just as a burglar would have no standing to challenge the police search of a home he had burglarized.

THE OPEN–FIELD DOCTRINE

The protection of the Fourth Amendment extends to the home and to the "curtilage." The term *curtilage* was defined in 1984 by the U.S. Supreme Court as follows: [18]

> At common law, the curtilage is the area to which extends the intimate activity associated with the "sanctity of a man's home and the privacies of life," *Boyd v. United States,* 116 U.S. 616, 630, 6 S.Ct. 524, 532, 29 L.Ed. 746 (1886), and therefore has been considered part of home itself for Fourth Amendment purposes. Thus, courts have extended Fourth Amendment protection to the curtilage; and they have defined the curtilage, as did the common law, by reference to the factors that determine whether an individual reasonably may expect that an area immediately adjacent to the home will remain private.

In 1987, the U.S. Supreme Court held that

> curtilage questions should be resolved with particular reference to four factors:
> —the proximity of the area claimed to be curtilage to the home,
> —whether the area is included within an enclosure surrounding the home,
> —the nature of the uses to which the area is put,
> —and the steps taken by the resident to protect the area from observation by people passing by.[19]

There is a high degree of privacy in the curtilage (back yard) of a one-family dwelling that is fenced in so as to be protected from observation from people passing by. However, there is a much lesser degree of privacy in the curtilage of a fifty-unit apartment building, because all the occupants of the apartment can use the common area available to them.

But should Fourth Amendment protection extend beyond the curtilage to **open fields?** The U.S. Supreme Court noted in 1974 that the Supreme Court refused in the 1924 case of *Hester v. United States,* 265 U.S. 57, 44 S.Ct. 445 (1924) "to extend the Fourth Amendment to sights seen in the open fields." [20] In the *Hester* case, government agents were trespassing on the defendant's land when they observed the defendant running away from them and throwing contraband to the ground in open fields. In holding that the contraband could be used as evidence to obtain a conviction against the defendant, the U.S. Supreme Court ruled that

> the special protection accorded by the Fourth Amendment to the people in their "persons, houses, papers and effects," is not extended to the open fields. The distinction between the latter and the house is as old as the common law. 4 Bl.Comm. 223, 225, 226.

Table 9.1   Other Areas (or Proceedings) to Which the Exclusionary Rule Does Not Apply (or Only Partially Applies)

TYPE OF SEARCH OR INSPECTION	COURT RULING
Common carriers (airlines, parcel services, truckers, railroads, etc.)	"Common carriers have a common-law right to inspect packages they accept for shipment, based on their duty to restrain from carrying contraband." *Illinois v. Andreas,* 463 U.S. 765 n. 1, 103 S.Ct. 3319 (1983).
U.S. Customs Service	"The U.S. Government has the undoubted right to inspect all incoming goods at a port of entry ... (but like the common carriers) it would be impossible for customs officers to inspect every package." *Illinois v. Andreas,* 463 U.S. 765 n. 1, 103 S.Ct. 3319 (1983).
Grand Jury Proceedings	"... it is unrealistic to assume that application of the rule to grand jury proceedings would significantly further (the) goal (of deterence of police misconduct) .... The grand jury's investigative power must be broad if its public responsibility is adequately to be discharged." *United States v. Calandra,* 414 U.S. 338, 94 S.Ct. 613 (1974).
Probation or Parole Revocation Hearings	"... the overwhelming number of reported cases have held that the fourth amendment's 'exclusionary rule' was not applicable under the circumstances to probation revocation proceedings or qualitatively comparable proceedings to revoke parole ... The only reservation expressed by several courts in denying application of the 'exclusionary rule' to a revocation proceeding might occur in situations where police harassment of probationers is demonstrated." Supreme Court of Illinois in *People v. Dowery,* 62 Ill.2d 200, 340 N.E.2d 529 (1975).
Searches by Probation or Parole Officers	"... based on the nature of probation, we conclude that a probation agent who reasonably believes that a probationer is violating the terms of probation may conduct a warrantless search of a probationer's residence .... A probation agent has a duty to see that a probationer is complying with the terms of his probation." *Wisconsin v. Griffin,* 131 Wis.2d 41, 388 N.W.2d 535 (1986). In June, 1987, the U.S. Supreme Court also affirmed Griffin's conviction for possession of a handgun holding that the "search of Griffin's home satisfied the demands of the Fourth Amendment because it was carried out pursuant to a regulation that itself satisfies the Fourth Amendment reasonableness requirement." __ U.S. __, 107 S.Ct. 3164 (1987).
Military Discharge Proceeding	A military administrative discharge proceeding is a civil proceeding and not a military criminal proceeding. Illegally seized drugs therefore could be used as evidence. The Court held that to force the military to keep a serviceman who uses drugs "is a price which our society cannot afford to pay." *Garrett v. Lehman,* 751 F.2d 997 (9th Cir.1985).

TYPE OF SEARCH OR INSPECTION	COURT RULING
Child Protective Proceedings	"... because a child protective proceeding ... is not punitive in nature ... the State's interest in protecting its children mandates the admissibility of relevant evidence seized during an illegal search." *In re Diane P.*, 110 A.D.2d 354, 494 N.Y.S.2d 881, 38 CrL 2168 (1985).
Searches by School Officials and Teachers	In holding that reasonable suspicion and not probable cause or a search warrant is needed to search a student or his property, the U.S. Supreme Court ruled that "We join the majority of courts that have examined this issue in concluding that the accommodation of the privacy interests of school children with substantial need of teachers and administrators for freedom to maintain order in the school does not require strict adherence to the requirement that searches be based on probable cause to believe that the subject of the search has violated or is violating the law. Rather, the legality of a search of a student should depend simply on the reasonableness under all the circumstances of the search ...". *New Jersey v. T.L.O.*, 469 U.S. 325, 105 S.Ct. 733 (1985).
The "Good Faith" and the "Honest Mistake" Exceptions	For the "Good Faith" and "Honest Mistake" exceptions to search warrants, see chapter 14. The 1987 U.S. Supreme Court case of *Illinois v. Krull* in this chapter states the "good faith" exception adopted for cases in which there is no search warrant. In the 1971 case of *Hill v. California*, 401 U.S. 797, 91 S.Ct. 1106 (1971) police officers with probable cause arrested the wrong man. In holding that the "good faith" arrest based on probable cause was valid, the Supreme Court ruled that "on the record before us the officers' mistake was understandable and the arrest a reasonable response to the situation facing them at the time."
Searches of offices, desks, and file cabinets of public employees by their supervisors	The U.S. Supreme Court held in the 1987 case of *O'Connor v. Ortega*, ___ U.S. ___, 107 S.Ct. 1492, 41 CrL 3001 that public employers have "wide latitude" to search public employees' offices, desks, and files without search warrants or probable cause to believe that the search will uncover evidence of wrongdoing. The Court, however, rejected the government's argument that the Fourth Amendment places no limits on such office searches by public supervisors, either to recover work-related materials or to investigate possible violations of workplace rules. Justice O'Connor in writing the opinion for the Court noted that it might require a greater justification than mere reasonableness for a government employer to search such personal items as "a piece of closed personal luggage, a handbag or a briefcase that happens to be within the employer's business address."

Table 9.2   Tests for Determining the Application of the Exclusionary Rule

	TEST WHICH MAY BE USED	APPLICATION OF THE EXCLUSIONARY RULE
Was the search a police search or private search?	Was it conducted by a private citizen? On his own initiative? Without police participation?	The exclusionary rule is applicable only if the search was a police search (or a search by a governmental official).
Use in a civil case of evidence suppressed for use in criminal cases	Was the trial or hearing (such as sanity hearing) a civil procedure?	The exclusionary rule applies only to criminal and quasi-criminal trials and hearings.
Evidence obtained where no right or expectation of privacy was violated	Did defendant exhibit an actual expectation of privacy? Was the expectation one "that society is prepared to recognize as 'reasonable' "?	Where no right or expectation of the defendant was infringed upon, "a warrantless examination . . . is not unreasonable under the 4th and 14th Amendments." *Cardwell v. Lewis,* 417 U.S. 583, 94 S.Ct. 2464 (1974).
The "plain view" or "plain smell" doctrine	Was the officer lawfully where he could be? Was the discovery inadvertent? Was it immediately apparent that the object was evidence of a crime?	Fourth Amendment protection does not extend to objects perceived (seen, smelled, etc.) in plain view.
Did the defendant have "standing" to make a motion to prevent the evidence from being used against him?	Did the defendant have a legitimate expectation of privacy in the place that was searched?	Without "standing" the defendant cannot make a motion to suppress the evidence which the state seeks to use against him in a criminal trial.
Search or seizure of abandoned property	Did the defendant abandon his right of privacy in the property? Or, did the defendant disclaim any property interest in the object which was searched or seized?	Fourth Amendment protection does not extend to abandoned objects or to objects for which the defendant disclaims any property interest.
The "open field" doctrine	Was the object searched or seized in an open field or was it within the curtilage of the house where the defendant had a right and expectation of privacy?	Fourth Amendment protection does not extend to an open field outside of the curtilage.

The Exclusionary Rule

The exclusionary rule does not apply to:

- private searches by private persons
- civil trials and civil hearings
- situations in which there has been no intrusion into the right and expectation of the defendant's right of privacy
- searches and seizures in an open field
- inspections to determine the ownership of motor vehicles in public places in most instances
- plain view and plain smell evidence which is obtained
- where the defendant has no "standing" to object to the evidence being used against him
- grand jury proceedings
- probation and parole revocation hearings in most instances

The exclusionary rule has been made applicable to:

- the manner in which confession and admission evidence is obtained (see chapter 4)
- the manner in which identification evidence is obtained (see chapter 13)
- evidence obtained by wire tapping and electronic surveillance (see chapter 15)
- the manner in which evidence is obtained by police entry into private premises (see chapter 11)
- the manner in which evidence is obtained in pedestrian and vehicle stops (see chapters 10 and 12)

Police Trespassing to Get to Open Fields Where Marijuana Was Growing

The U.S. Supreme Court also reviewed the open fields doctrine in 1984 in the following case, which is also presented in chapter 11:

Oliver v. United States

Supreme Court of the United States (1984)
466 U.S. 170, 104 S.Ct. 1735

A Kentucky case and a case from Maine were combined. In both cases, police had received reports that marijuana was being grown in rural areas. In both cases, police entered upon private property and went past "no trespassing" signs to get to open fields that were not visible to the public, where the contraband was being grown. In affirming the convictions and the use of the evidence obtained by the police action, the Court held that

It is true, of course, that petitioner Oliver and respondent Thornton, in order to conceal their criminal activities, planted the marijuana upon secluded land and erected fences and no trespassing signs around the property. And it may be that because of such precautions, few members of the public stumbled upon the marijuana crops seized by the police. Neither of these suppositions demonstrates, however, that the expectation of privacy was *legitimate* in the sense required by the Fourth Amendment. The test of legitimacy is not whether the individual chooses to conceal assertedly private activity. Rather, the correct inquiry is whether the government's intrusion infringes upon the personal and societal values protected by the Fourth Amendment. As we have explained, we find no basis for concluding that a police inspection of open fields accomplishes such an infringement.

Nor is the government's intrusion upon an open field a "search" in the constitutional sense because that intrusion is a trespass at common law. The existence of a property right is but one element in determining whether expectations of privacy are legitimate. " '[T]he premise that property interests control the right of the Government to search and seize has been discredited.' " *Katz,* 389 U.S., at 353, 88 S.Ct., at 512 (quoting *Warden v. Hayden*).

. . . "[E]ven a property interest in premises may not be sufficient to establish a legitimate expectation of privacy with respect to particular items located on the premises or activity conducted thereon." *Rakas v. Illinois,* 439 U.S., at 144 n. 12, 99 S.Ct., at 431 n. 12.

The common law may guide consideration of what areas are protected by the Fourth Amendment search by defining areas whose invasion by others is wrongful . . . . The law of trespass, however, forbids intrusions upon land that the Fourth Amendment would not proscribe. For trespass law extends to instances where the exercise of the right to exclude vindicates no legitimate privacy interest. Thus, in the case of open fields, the general rights of property protected by the common law of trespass have little or no relevance to the applicability of the Fourth Amendment.

PROBLEMS

1. A police officer observed a vehicle exceeding the speed limit. While he was attempting to catch the vehicle, the officer heard a police radio dispatch reporting that a theft of motor vehicle parts had occurred in the area he was patrolling. The radio dispatch announced that chrome lug nuts were among the items stolen. The dispatch also provided a description of the two suspects. The officer then saw the speeding vehicle enter a service station, and followed it there for the purpose of issuing a traffic citation to the driver. As the officer approached the car, both occupants stepped out of it and the three persons became involved in a conversation regarding the speeding problem. As the officer stood next to the car, he observed chrome lug nuts and two lug wrenches in the car. The officer then recognized that the two men met the description of the men suspected of stealing motor vehicle parts. He then arrested both men and seized the lug nuts and wrenches.

Were the arrests and seizure of the evidence lawful and proper? Can the evidence be used in the trial of the two men? Why? *Colorado v. Bannister,* 449 U.S. 1, 101 S.Ct. 42 (1980).

2. A police officer stopped a man walking up a freeway on-ramp. The man gave his name as Tony Sedillo, but was unable to produce identification. The officer then noticed an envelope in Sedillo's pocket containing what appeared to be a Treasury check. The name "Mitsuri E. Nagaya" was clearly visible through the transparent window of the envelope. Without asking, the officer pulled the check from Sedillo's pocket. Sedillo stated that he had found the check on the street. When the officer looked at the check, he saw that it had been endorsed. The officer asked Sedillo to sign his name in a notebook. Based upon the similarity of the handwritings, Sedillo was placed under arrest for forgery and given the *Miranda* warnings. A short time later, Sedillo made a full confession.

   Did the officer lawfully seize the check? Give reasons for your answer. Is the confession admissible as evidence? Why? Should any or all of the evidence be suppressed and its use forbidden at Sedillo's trial? Why? *United States v. Sedillo,* 496 F.2d 151 (9th Cir.1974), review denied 419 U.S. 947, 95 S.Ct. 211 (1974).

3. An air quality control inspector walked onto the premises of the defendant corporation. The officer did not have a search warrant or consent to enter the premises, but he walked only where the public was allowed to come and go on the property. The air quality control inspector took readings of the smoke coming from the defendant corporation's smokestacks.

   Was the evidence of violations by the corporation lawfully and properly obtained? Should the evidence be allowed to be used in charges against the defendant corporation? Why? *Air Pollution Variance Board of Colorado v. Western Alfalfa Corp.,* 416 U.S. 861, 94 S.Ct. 2114 (1974).

4. After receiving a complaint that the defendant had regularly been exposing himself in his living room window, the police contacted the neighbor across the street from the defendant's residence. With the neighbor's permission, an officer set up a concealed 35–mm camera equipped with a 135–mm telephoto lens in the neighbor's garage, and focused on the defendant's street-level living room window approximately 100 to 120 feet away. Neither a warrant nor a court order was obtained. During the following week, the defendant was photographed by the officer on at least four occasions. Enlargements of the photographs showed the naked defendant with exposed genitals.

   Were the defendant's Fourth Amendment rights to privacy violated? Should the evidence be allowed to be used in charging the defendant with four counts of public indecency? Why? Should the police have obtained a search warrant? *State v. Louis,* 296 Or. 57, 672 P.2d 708 (1983).

5. As the defendants were fleeing in a car to avoid arrest, they were throwing heroin out of the windows of the car. After arresting the defendants, police officers went back along the streets and picked up (and swept up) heroin.

   Should the heroin picked up from the street be allowed to be used in evidence against the defendants? Why? *Molina v. State,* 53 Wis.2d 662, 193 N.W.2d 874 (1972), Supreme Court of Wisconsin.

NOTES

[1] United States v. Jacobsen, 466 U.S. 109, 104 S.Ct. 1652 (1984); quoting in part Walter v. United States, 447 U.S. 649, 662, 100 S.Ct. 2395, 2404 (1980).

[2] United States v. Calandra, 414 U.S. 338, 94 S.Ct. 613 (1974).

[3] 256 U.S. 465, 41 S.Ct. 574 (1921).

[4] One 1958 Plymouth Sedan v. Pennsylvania, 380 U.S. 693, 85 S.Ct. 1246 (1965).

[5] United States ex rel. Williams v. Fay, 323 F.2d 65 (2d Cir.1963).

[6] 389 U.S. 347, 88 S.Ct. 507 (1967).

[7] See note 1 above.

[8] Illinois v. Andreas, 463 U.S. 765, 103 S.Ct. 3319 (1983) quoting United States v. Bulgier, 618 F.2d 472 (7th Cir.1980), cert. denied, 449 U.S. 843, 101 S.Ct. 125 (1980).

[9] *Plain view* differs from *open view* in that the "Plain view doctrine ... does not occur until a search is in progress" Coolidge v. New Hampshire, 403 U.S. 443, 91 S.Ct. 2022 (1971). Open view can occur at any time. For example, a police car is on an expressway. The wind whips the jacket of a person on a motorcycle open and the police see a pistol hid in the trousers of the person. No search was in progress but because the police car was in such a position that the officers could see evidence of a crime being committed, open view had occurred.

[10] 403 U.S. 443, 91 S.Ct. 2022 (1971).

[11] Texas v. Brown, 460 U.S. 730, 103 S.Ct. 1535 (1983).

[12] 274 U.S. 559, 47 S.Ct. 746 (1927).

[13] 343 U.S. 747, 72 S.Ct. 967 (1952).

[14] See note 12 above.

[15] James v. United States, 418 F.2d 1150, 1151, n. 1 (D.C.Cir.1969) but see Brown v. State, 3 Md.App. 90, 238 A.2d 147 (1968), in which an officer looked over a 5' 5" door to a public toilet booth and observed a known drug addict with narcotic paraphernalia. The Court excluded the evidence, holding that the defendant's Fourth Amendment right of privacy had been violated.

[16] 414 U.S. 338, 94 S.Ct. 613 (1974).

[17] The Wisconsin Supreme Court stated in the 1967 case of Hayes v. State, 39 Wis.2d 125, 158 N.W. 2d 545 (1968) that "there could be no unlawful search of premises in which the defendant disclaims any interest." See also Rossi v. United States, 60 F.2d 955 (7th Cir.1932) affirmed 289 U.S. 89, 53 S.Ct. 532 (1933), Creech v. United States, 97 F.2d 390 (5th Cir.1938) and United States v. Eversole, 209 F.2d 766 (7th Cir.1954), Lurie v. Oberhauser, 431 F.2d 330 (9th Cir.1970).

[18] Oliver v. United States, 466 U.S. 170, 104 S.Ct. 1735 (1984).

[19] United States v. Dunn, ___ U.S. ___, 107 S.Ct. 1913, 40 CrL 3313 (1987). In the *Dunn* case, the Supreme Court used the four factors to resolve the issue as to whether a barn some distance from the defendant's home was within the curtilage or was in an open field. The Court held that

> We do not suggest that combining these factors produces a finely tuned formula that, when mechanically applied, yields a "correct" answer to all extent-of-curtilage questions. Rather, these factors are useful analytical tools only to the degree that, in any given case, they bear upon the centrally relevant consideration—whether the area in question is so intimately tied to the home itself that it should be placed under the home's "umbrella" of Fourth Amendment protection. Applying these factors to respondent's barn and to the area immediately surrounding it, we have little difficulty in concluding that this area lay outside the curtilage of the ranch house.
>
> *First.* The record discloses that the barn was located 50 yards from the fence surrounding the house, and 60 yards from the house itself .... Standing in isolation, this substantial distance supports no inference that the barn should be treated as an adjunct of the house.
>
> *Second.* It is also significant that respondent's barn did not lie within the area surrounding the house that was enclosed by a fence. We noted in *Oliver,* that "for most homes, the boundaries of the curtilage will be clearly marked; and the conception defining the curtilage—as the area around the home to which the activity of home life extends—is a familiar one easily understood from our daily experience." ... Viewing the physical layout of respondent's

ranch in its entirety, . . . it is plain that the fence surrounding the residence serves to demark a specific area of land immediately adjacent to the house that is readily identifiable as part and parcel of the house. Conversely, the barn—the front portion itself enclosed by a fence—and the area immediately surrounding it, stands out as a distinct portion of respondent's ranch, quite separate from the residence.

Third. It is especially significant that the law enforcement officials possessed objective data indicating that the barn was not being used for intimate activities of the home . . . .

Fourth. Respondent did little to protect the barn area from observation by those standing in the open fields. Nothing in the record suggests that the various interior fences on respondent's property had any function other than that of the typical ranch fence; the fences were designed and constructed to corral livestock, not to prevent persons from observing what lay inside the enclosed areas.

The court also held that "there is no constitutional difference between police observations conducted while in a public place and while standing in open fields." Nor does a "naked-eye aerial observation of a home's curtilage . . . violate the Fourth Amendment." Law enforcement officers are not required "to shield their eyes when passing by a home on public thorough-fares." Also, a police officer standing where he has a right to be can shine "his flashlight to illuminate the interior of a car, without probable cause to search the car . . ." Therefore in this case, an officer standing in the open field did not violate the Fourth Amendment by the "use of the beam of a flashlight, directed through the essentially open front of (defendant's) barn . . .".

[20] Air Pollution Variance Board of Colorado v. Western Alfalfa Corp., 416 U.S. 861, 94 S.Ct. 2114 (1974).

Voluntary Conversations, Detentions, and Arrests as Means of Obtaining Evidence

VOLUNTARY CONVERSATIONS

Voluntary conversation and/or observation or surveillance of persons have always been used as investigative techniques by both law enforcement officers and private security personnel.

Conversations with person can often satisfactorily explain what they are doing at that place and time. A motorist parked in an isolated area, a man walking in an alley, a person wandering idly in a public building or department store might have very satisfactory explanations of their presence and their conduct.

A hunch, mere suspicion, or a gut reaction could cause a law enforcement officer or private security person to attempt to engage in voluntary conversation. Or as an alternative, the person could be kept under observation. In 1983, the U.S. Supreme Court held as follows: [1]

> . . . law enforcement officers do not violate the Fourth Amendment by merely approaching an individual on the street or in another public place, by asking him if he is willing to answer some questions, by putting questions to him if the person is willing to listen, or by offering in evidence in a criminal prosecution his voluntary answers to such questions . . . . The person approached, however, need not answer any question put to him; indeed, he may decline to listen to the questions at all and may go on his way . . . . He may not be detained even momentarily without reasonable, objective grounds for doing so; and his refusal to listen or answer does not, without more, furnish those grounds . . . . If there is no detention—no seizure within the meaning of the Fourth Amendment—then no constitutional rights have been infringed.

In 1980, the U.S. Supreme Court held that [2]

> characterizing every street encounter between a citizen and the police as a "seizure," while not enhancing any interest secured by the Fourth Amendment, would impose wholly unrealistic restrictions upon a wide variety of legitimate law enforcement practices. The Court has on other occasions referred to the acknowledged need for police questioning as a tool in the effective enforcement of the criminal laws. "Without such investigation, those who were innocent might be falsely accused, those who were guilty might wholly escape prosecution,

and many crimes would go unsolved. In short, the security of all would be diminished. *Haynes v. Washington,* 373 U.S. 678 . . . .

We conclude that a person has been "seized" within the meaning of the Fourth Amendment only if, in view of all of the circumstances surrounding the incident, a reasonable person would have believed that he was not free to leave. Examples of circumstances that might indicate a seizure, even where the person did not attempt to leave, would be the threatening presence of several officers, the display of a weapon by an officer, some physical touching of the person of the citizen, or the use of language or tone of voice indicating that compliance with the officer's request might be compelled . . . . In the absence of some such evidence, otherwise inoffensive contact between a member of the public and the police cannot, as a matter of law, amount to a seizure of that person.

INVESTIGATIVE DETENTIONS (*TERRY* STOPS OR *TERRY* SEIZURES)

The Free to Leave Test

A conversation between a law enforcement officer and a person could go from a situation in which there is a voluntary verbal exchange to a situation in which "a reasonable person would have believed that he was not free to leave."

The freedom to move freely about is protected by the Fourth Amendment. The U.S. Supreme Court stated in 1968 in regard to this constitutionally protected right that [3]

No right is held more sacred, or is more carefully guarded, by the common law, than the right of every individual to the possession and control of his own person, free from all restraint or interference of others, unless by clear and unquestionable authority of law.

In 1980 the Supreme Court stated that [4]

The Fourth Amendment's requirement that searches and seizures be founded upon an objective justification, governs all seizures of the person, "including seizures that involve only a brief detention short of traditional arrest . . . .

But "[o]bviously, not all personal intercourse between policemen and citizens involves 'seizures' of persons. Only when the officer, by means of physical force or show of authority, has in some way restrained the liberty of a citizen may we conclude that a 'seizure' has occurred." *Terry v. Ohio,* 392 U.S., at 19, n. 16, ...

The test used to determine whether there has been a **seizure** (either a brief or long detention and restriction of freedom of movement) is the **free to leave** test. A seizure has occurred when "a reasonable person would have believed that he was not free to leave."

The Requirement of Reasonable Suspicion to Make an Investigative Detention

To interfere with the freedom of movement of a person, a law enforcement officer must have that amount of information (or evidence) known as reasonable suspicion to believe that the person is committing, has committed, or is about to commit a crime.

The U.S. Supreme Court has held that the police have the authority to undertake "legitimate and restrained investigative conduct ... on the basis of ample factual justification"[5] for situations in which they do not have the authority to arrest or search. The test established for such investigations was stated as follows by the U.S. Supreme Court in 1968:

> [W]ould the facts available to the officer at the moment ... "warrant a man of reasonable caution in the belief" that the action taken was appropriate? *Terry v. Ohio,* 392 U.S. at 21, 22.
>
> ... [I]n determining whether the officer acted reasonably ... due weight must be given, not to his inchoate and unparticularized suspicion or "hunch," but to the specific reasonable inferences which he is entitled to draw from the facts in light of his experience. *Terry v. Ohio,* 392 U.S. at 27.

The *Terry* Case, Which Gave Its Name to the *Terry* Stop

Terry v. Ohio

Supreme Court of the United States (1968)
392 U.S. 1, 88 S.Ct. 1868

While a plainclothes detective was on duty in downtown Cleveland early one afternoon in 1963, he became curious about two men standing on a street corner. The detective, who had thirty-nine years of police service, observed one of the men leave the other and walk past some stores, where he would pause for a moment and look into the window of a particular store. The man would then continue a short distance, turn around, and on his way back to his companion he would again look into the same store window. After the two men conferred for a short time, the second man went through the same series of motions. "The two men repeated this ritual alternately between five and six times apiece—in all roughly a dozen trips." The veteran detective suspected by this time that the two men were "casing a job, a stick-up." When a third man joined the group, the detective approached the men, identified himself as a police officer, and asked for their names. When the men "mumbled something," the officer grabbed the defendant and spun him around so that they were facing the other two men. A pat-down of the three men produced two pistols. In affirming the procedure which was used and the conviction of the defendant for carrying a concealed weapon, the Supreme Court of the United States held that

> Street encounters between citizens and police officers are incredibly rich in diversity. They range from wholly friendly exchanges of

pleasantries or mutually useful information to hostile confrontations of armed men involving arrests, or injuries, or loss of life. Moreover, hostile confrontations are not all of a piece. Some of them begin in a friendly enough manner, only to take a different turn upon the injection of some unexpected element into the conversation. Encounters are initiated by the police for a wide variety of purposes, some of which are wholly unrelated to a desire to prosecute for crime. Doubtless some police "field interrogation" conduct violates the Fourth Amendment. But a stern refusal by this Court to condone such activity does not necessarily render it responsive to the exclusionary rule. Regardless of how effective the rule may be where obtaining convictions is an important objective of the police, it is powerless to deter invasions of constitutionally guaranteed rights where the police either have no interest in prosecuting or are willing to forgo successful prosecution in the interest of serving some other goal . . . .

. . . we deal here with an entire rubric of police conduct—necessarily swift action predicated upon the on-the-spot observations of the officer on the beat—which historically has not been, and as a practical matter could not be, subjected to the warrant procedure. Instead, the conduct involved in this case must be tested by the Fourth Amendment's general proscription against unreasonable searches and seizures . . . .

And in making that assessment it is imperative that the facts be judged against an objective standard: would the facts available to the officer at the moment of the seizure or the search "warrant a man of reasonable caution in the belief" that the action taken was appropriate? . . .

We merely hold today that where a police officer observes unusual conduct which leads him reasonably to conclude in light of his experience that criminal activity may be afoot and that the persons with whom he is dealing may be armed and presently dangerous, where in the course of investigating this behavior he identifies himself as a policeman and makes reasonable inquiries, and where nothing in the initial stages of the encounter serves to dispel his reasonable fear for his own or others' safety, he is entitled for the protection of himself and such persons in an attempt to discover weapons which might be used to assault him.

Such a search is a reasonable search under the Fourth Amendment, and any weapons seized may properly be introduced in evidence against the person from whom they were taken.

Affirmed.

A Drug Courier Profile Case in Which Evidence Was Obtained by a Consent Search

United States v. Mendenhall

Supreme Court of the United States (1980)
446 U.S. 544, 100 S.Ct. 1870

Drug Enforcement Administration (DEA) agents observed the defendant (a young woman) arrive at the Detroit Metropolitan Airport on a flight from Los Angeles. After observing the respondent's conduct, which appeared to the

Loitering and Prowling Statutes and Ordinances

Many states, cities, and counties throughout the United States have enacted loitering and prowling statutes and ordinances. These statutes and ordinances are modeled after or copied almost verbatim from Section 250.6 of the American Law Institute's Model Penal Code. The Omaha, Nebraska ordinance, which is almost identical to the Model Penal Code, reads as follows:

Loitering, Prowling Section 20–171 Prohibited

It shall be unlawful for any person to loiter or prowl in a place, at a time or in a manner not usual for law abiding individuals under circumstances that warrant alarm for the safety of persons or property in the vicinity.

Section 20–172

Among the circumstances which may be considered in determining whether alarm is warranted is the fact that the person takes flight upon appearance of a police officer, refuses to identify himself or endeavors to conceal himself or any object.

Section 20–173

Same—Opportunity to dispel alarm.

Unless flight by the person or other circumstances makes it impracticable a police officer shall, prior to any arrest for an offense under this division, allow the person an opportunity to dispel any alarm which would otherwise be warranted by requesting him to identify himself and explain his presence and conduct.

Section 20–174

Same—Requisites for conviction.

No person shall be convicted of an offense under this provision if the police officer did not comply with the preceding section, or, if it appears at trial that the explanation given by the person, if believed by the police officer at the time, would have dispelled the alarm.

When challenged, courts throughout the United States have sustained the legality of such statutes and ordinances. The Supreme Court of Florida held a similar statute to be valid in the 1985 case of *Watts v. State,* 463 So.2d 205, 36 CrL 2381 (1985). In that case, the defendant fled from a police officer who observed the defendant peering into parked cars in a restaurant parking lot.

agents to be characteristic of persons unlawfully carrying narcotics,[6] the agents approached her as she was walking through the concourse, identified themselves as federal agents, and asked to see her identification and airline ticket. The respondent produced her driver's license, which was in the name of Sylvia Mendenhall, and, in answer to a question of one of the agents, stated that she resided at the address appearing on the license. The airline ticket was issued in the name of "Annette Ford." When asked why the ticket bore a name different from her own, the respondent stated that she "just felt like using that name." In response to a further question, the respondent indicated that she had been in California only two days. Agent Anderson then specifically identified

Court Cases Determining Reasonable Suspicion for Investigative Stops

"The Fourth Amendment does not require a policeman who lacks the precise level of information necessary for probable cause to arrest to simply shrug his shoulders and allow a crime to occur or a criminal to escape. On the contrary, *Terry* recognizes that it may be the essence of good police work to adopt an *intermediate response.* A brief stop of a suspicious individual, in order to determine his identity or to maintain the status quo momentarily while obtaining more information, may be most reasonable in light of the facts known to the officer at the time." (emphasis added) [a]

FACTS WHICH JUSTIFIED A *TERRY* STOP:

- Informant's report that defendant who was in a nearby car was carrying a gun and narcotics. *Adams v. Williams,* 407 U.S. 143, 92 S.Ct. 1920 (1970).
- Occupant of a house was detained while a search warrant for the house was being executed. Held that occupant was sufficiently suspect to justify his temporary detention. *Michigan v. Summers,* 452 U.S. 692, 101 S.Ct. 2587 (1981).
- Where defendants were driving very slowly at 3:30 A.M. through business district which was closed and dark. The slow and aimless wandering of car was in an area victimized by recent burglaries. *United States v. Rickus,* 737 F.2d 360 (3d Cir.1984).
- Italian appearing defendant was near and appeared interested in third party (who had an Italian name) who was meeting with government informant at Houston airport to discuss stolen securities. Third party was known to be involved in criminal wrongdoing. *United States v. Santora,* 619 F.2d 1052 (5th Cir.1980), review denied ___ U.S. ___, (1985).
- Defendant's van swerved on dangerous road normally only used by residents. Van and defendant were strangers to area. *Madison v. State,* 378 So.2d 1311, review denied, 449 U.S. 1124, 101 S.Ct. 940 (1981).
- While police were executing a search warrant for stolen property, defendant walked in. When asked to identify himself, defendant made a 90–degree turn as if to leave. *Terry* stop was proper. *State v. Gobely,* 366 N.W.2d 600 (Minn.1985).
- The past criminal behavior of a person is a factor which can be considered with other facts to determine whether a *Terry* stop and a later pat-down search would be justified. *State v. Brown,* 345 N.W.2d 233 (Minn.1984).
- When the officer, who had reason to believe that defendant was traveling in his camper without any family, saw a child peek over the dashboard momentarily, the officer pulled the camper over in a downtown area. The child seemed nervous and when questioned

himself as a federal narcotics agent and, according to his testimony, the respondent "became quite shaken, extremely nervous. She had a hard time speaking."

After returning the airline ticket and driver's license to her, Agent Anderson asked the respondent if she would accompany him to the airport DEA office for further questions. She did so, although the record does not indicate a verbal response to the request. The office, which was located up one flight of

stated defendant tried to sexually assault him. Court stated that when child abuse or abduction is suspected, *Terry* stop may be based on sketchier facts than in ordinary case. *State v. Parker,* 127 N.H. 525, 503 A.2d 809 (1985).

FACTS WHICH BY THEMSELVES DO NOT JUSTIFY A *TERRY* STOP:

- Only grounds for suspicion was that the occupants of a car near the Mexican border appeared to be of Mexican ancestry. Stop was made to question occupants about their citizenship. *United States v. Brignoni-Ponce,* 422 U.S. 873, 95 S.Ct. 2574 (1975).
- Suspicion that the occupants of a car were violating a city curfew ordinance (minors in a public place after 10 P.M.). *People v. Teresinski,* 30 Cal.3d 822, 180 Cal.Rptr. 617, 642 P.2d 753 (1982).
- Police cruiser turned on its flashing emergency lights and pulled up behind a man sitting in a parked car. The only suspicion was that the area was known to be one where people came to use drugs. Use of flashing lights indicated *Terry* stop. Smell of marijuana and cocaine found in consent search could not be used as evidence. *People v. Bailey,* 176 Cal.App.3d 402, 222 Cal.Rptr. 235 (1985).
- Defendant was walking through a "seedy" neighborhood at an unsteady pace while he constantly looked around. Defendant's raincoat hung lower on one side than the other. *People v. Cornelius,* 113 A.D.2d 666, 497 N.Y.S.2d 16 (1986).
- "... one is not guilty or subject to an unlawful stop and seizure merely because of his associations," 308 So.2d 790 (La.1975) (defendant left house suspect of containing marijuana, 302 So.2d 869 (La.1974)) (defendant left a residence known as a drug outlet, 337 So.2d 441 (La.1976)) Supreme Court Louisiana, 400 So.2d 661 (La.1981).
- Defendant left a plane ahead of another person and occasionally looked back at him as they went through the concourse. Both men arrived in the early morning hours from a city that was a principal place of origin of cocaine sold in the United States (Fort Lauderdale). *Reid v. Georgia,* 448 U.S. 438, 100 S.Ct. 2752 (1980).
- "The inference that people who talk to narcotics addicts are engaged in the criminal traffic of narcotics is simply not the sort of reasonable inference required to support an intrusion by the police upon an individual's security." [b]

[a] U.S. Supreme Court in Adams v. Williams, 407 U.S. 143, 92 S.Ct. 1920 (1972).
[b] Sibron v. New York, 392 U.S. 40, 88 S.Ct. 1889 (1968).

stairs about 50 feet from where the respondent had first been approached, consisted of a reception area adjoined by three other rooms. At the office the agent asked the respondent if she would allow a search of her person and handbag and told her that she had the right to decline the search if she desired. She responded: "Go ahead." She then handed Agent Anderson her purse, which contained a receipt for an airline ticket that had been issued to "F. Bush" three days earlier for a flight from Pittsburgh through Chicago to Los

The *Terry* Stop and the Deadly Drug Trade

Justice Powell, Former Chief Justice Burger, and Justice Blackmun, joining and concurring in the judgment in *United States v. Mendenhall,* 446 U.S. 544, 100 S.Ct. 1870 (1980) and writing as follows:

Terry v. Ohio, 392 U.S. 1, . . . establishes that a reasonable investigative stop does not offend the Fourth Amendment. The reasonableness of a stop turns on the facts and circumstances of each case. In particular, the Court has emphasized (i) the public interest served by the seizure, (ii) the nature and scope of the intrusion, and (iii) the objective facts upon which the law enforcement officer relied in light of his knowledge and expertise . . . .

The public has a compelling interest in detecting those who would traffic in deadly drugs for personal profit. Few problems affecting the health and welfare of our population, particularly our young, cause greater concern than the escalating use of controlled substances. Much of the drug traffic is highly organized and conducted by sophisticated criminal syndicates. The profits are enormous. And many drugs, including heroin, may be easily concealed. As a result, the obstacles to detection of illegal conduct may be unmatched in any other area of law enforcement.

To meet this pressing concern, the Drug Enforcement Administration since 1974 has assigned highly skilled agents to the Detroit Airport as part of a nationwide program to intercept drug couriers transporting narcotics between major drug sources and distribution centers in the United States. Federal agents have developed "drug courier profiles" that describe the characteristics generally associated with narcotics traffickers. For example, because the Drug Enforcement Administration believes that most drugs enter Detroit from one of four "source" cities (Los Angeles, San Diego, Miami, or New York), agents pay particular attention to passengers who arrive from those places . . . . During the first 18 months of the

Angeles. The agent asked whether this was the ticket that she had used for her flight to California, and the respondent stated that it was.

A female police officer then arrived to conduct the search of the respondent's person. She asked the agents if the respondent had consented to be searched. The agents said that she had, and the respondent followed the policewoman into a private room. There the policewoman again asked the respondent if she consented to the search, and the respondent replied that she did. The policewoman explained that the search would require that the respondent remove her clothing. The respondent stated that she had a plane to catch and was assured by the policewoman that if she were carrying no narcotics, there would be no problem. The respondent then began to disrobe without further comment. As the respondent removed her clothing, she took from her undergarments two small packages, one of which appeared to contain heroin, and handed both to the policewoman. The agents then arrested the respondent for possessing heroin.

It was on the basis of this evidence that the District Court denied the respondent's motion to suppress. The court concluded that the agents' conduct in initially approaching the respondent and asking to see her ticket and identi-

program, agents watching the Detroit Airport searched 141 persons in 96 encounters. They found controlled substances in 77 of the encounters and arrested 122 persons .... When two of these agents stopped the respondent in February 1976, they were carrying out a highly specialized law enforcement operation designed to combat the serious societal threat posed by narcotics distribution.

Our cases demonstrate that "the scope of [a] particular intrusion, in light of all the exigencies of the case, [is] a central element in the analysis of reasonableness." *Terry v. Ohio, supra,* 392 U.S., at 18, n. 15, ... The intrusion in this case was quite modest. Two plainclothes agents approached the respondent as she walked through a public area. The respondent was near airline employees from whom she could have sought aid had she been accosted by strangers. The agents identified themselves and asked to see some identification. One officer asked the respondent why her airline ticket and her driver's license bore different names. The agent also inquired how long the respondent had been in California. Unlike the petitioner in *Terry,* ... the respondent was not physically restrained. The agents did not display weapons. The questioning was brief. In these circumstances, the respondent could not reasonably have felt frightened or isolated from assistance.

In reviewing the factors that led the agents to stop and question the respondent, it is important to recall that a trained law enforcement agent may be "able to perceive and articulate meaning in given conduct which would be wholly innocent to the untrained observer." *Brown v. Texas, supra,* at 52, n. 2, 99 S.Ct., at 2641, n. 2. Among the circumstances that can give rise to reasonable suspicion are the agent's knowledge of the methods used in recent criminal activity and the characteristics of persons engaged in such illegal practices. Law enforcement officers may rely on the "characteristics of the area," and the behavior of a suspect who appears to be evading police contact .... "In all situations the officer is entitled to assess the facts in light of his experience." *Id.,* at 885, 95 S.Ct., at 2582.

fication was a permissible investigative stop under the standards of *Terry v. Ohio,* 392 U.S. 1, 88 S.Ct. 1868, 20 L.Ed.2d 889 and *United States v. Brignoni-Ponce,* 422 U.S. 873, 95 S.Ct. 2574, 45 L.Ed.2d 607, finding that this conduct was based on specific and articulable facts that justified a suspicion of criminal activity. The court also found that the respondent had not been placed under arrest or otherwise detained when she was asked to accompany the agents to the DEA office, but had accompanied the agents "voluntarily in a spirit of apparent cooperation." It was the court's view that no arrest occurred until after the heroin had been found. Finally, the trial court found that the respondent "gave her consent to the search [in the DEA office] and ... such consent was freely and voluntarily given."

In affirming the use of the evidence and in affirming the conviction of the defendant, the Supreme Court held that

> We adhere to the view that a person is "seized" only when, by means of physical force or a show of authority, his freedom of movement is restrained. Only when such restraint is imposed is there any foundation whatever for invoking constitutional safeguards. The purpose of the Fourth Amendment is not to eliminate all contact between the

police and the citizenry, but "to prevent arbitrary and oppressive interference by enforcement officials with the privacy and personal security of individuals." *United States v. Martinez-Fuerte,* 428 U.S. 543, 554, 96 S.Ct. 3074, 3081, 49 L.Ed.2d 1116. As long as the person to whom questions are put remains free to disregard the questions and walk away, there has been no intrusion upon that person's liberty or privacy as would under the Constitution require some particularized and objective justification . . . .

On the facts of this case, no "seizure" of the respondent occurred. The events took place in the public concourse. The agents wore no uniforms and displayed no weapons. They did not summon the respondent to their presence, but instead approached her and identified themselves as federal agents. They requested, but did not demand to see the respondent's identification and ticket. Such conduct without more, did not amount to an intrusion upon any constitutionally protected interest. The respondent was not seized simply by reason of the fact that the agents approached her, asked her if she would show them her ticket and identification, and posed to her a few questions. Nor was it enough to establish a seizure that the person asking the questions was a law enforcement official . . . . In short, nothing in the record suggests that the respondent had any objective reason to believe that she was not free to end the conversation in the concourse and proceed on her way, and for that reason we conclude that the agents' initial approach to her was not a seizure.

Our conclusion that no seizure occurred is not affected by the fact that the respondent was not expressly told by the agents that she was free to decline to cooperate with their inquiry, for the voluntariness of her responses does not depend upon her having been so informed . . . . We also reject the argument that the only inference to be drawn from the fact that the respondent acted in a manner so contrary to her self-interest is that she was compelled to answer the agents' questions. It may happen that a person makes statements to law enforcement officials that he later regrets, but the issue in such cases is not whether the statement was self-protective, but rather whether it was made voluntarily . . . .

Counsel for the respondent has also argued that because she was within the DEA office when she consented to the search, her consent may have resulted from the inherently coercive nature of those surroundings. But in view of the District Court's finding that the respondent's presence in the office was voluntary, the fact that she was there is little or no evidence that she was in any way coerced. And in response to the argument that the respondent would not voluntarily have consented to a search that was likely to disclose the narcotics that she carried, we repeat that the question is not whether the respondent acted in her ultimate self-interest, but whether she acted voluntarily.

We conclude that the District Court's determination that the respondent consented to the search of her person "freely and voluntarily" was sustained by the evidence.

An Involuntary Detention Cannot Exceed the Limits Set by the *Terry* Case

Where there is reasonable suspicion to believe that a person is involved in criminal activities, an **investigative detention** may be made to make reasonable inquiries. The *Terry* stop must be brief and many states require by statute that the inquiries be made at the place of the stop. The U.S. Supreme Court held in the following case that the "involuntary detention had exceeded the limited restraint permitted by *Terry*":

Florida v. Royer

Supreme Court of the United States (1983)
460 U.S. 491, 103 S.Ct. 1319

Royer was observed in the Miami, Florida, airport by two Dade County plain-clothes detectives. Royer's appearance, mannerisms, and luggage fit the detectives' drug courier profile. The detectives observed Royer purchase a one-way ticket to New York City and saw him check two suitcases with identification tags bearing the name "Holt". As Royer was making his way to the airline boarding area, the detectives approached him and after identifying themselves, asked Royer if he would speak with them. Royer said he would.

Upon request, Royer produced his airline ticket and his driver's license. The airline ticket (like the baggage identification) bore the name "Holt". The driver's license carried the defendant's correct name, "Royer." Royer became noticeably more nervous when asked about the discrepancy. The detectives then informed Royer that they were in fact narcotics investigators and suspected him of transporting narcotics. They retained Royer's identification and asked him to accompany them to a nearby room some forty feet away. Royer went along without comment while one of the detectives used his baggage claim stubs to retrieve Royer's baggage. When the baggage was brought into the room, Royer consented to a search of his suitcases, both of which contained marijuana. Royer was then told he was under arrest. The entire incident took approximately fifteen minutes.

After Royer's conviction, the Florida Court of Appeal reversed. The U.S. Supreme Court agreed with the Florida Court of Appeal holding:

> The [Florida] District Court of Appeal, sitting en banc, reversed Royer's conviction. The court held that Royer had been involuntarily confined within the small room without probable cause; that the involuntary detention had exceeded the limited restraint permitted by *Terry v. Ohio*, 392 U.S. 1, 88 S.Ct. 1868, 20 L.Ed.2d 889 (1968), at the time his consent to the search was obtained; and that the consent to search was therefore invalid because tainted by the unlawful confinement.

Several factors led the court to conclude that respondent's confinement was tantamount to arrest. Royer had "found himself in a small enclosed area being confronted by two police officers—a situation which presents an almost classic definition of imprisonment." 389 So.2d 1007, 1018 (1980). The detectives' statement to Royer that he was suspected of transporting narcotics also bolstered the finding that Royer was "in custody" at the time the consent to search was given. In addition, the detectives' possession of Royer's airline ticket and their retrieval and possession of his luggage made it clear, in the District Court of Appeal's view, that Royer was not free to leave . . . .

. . . We agree with the Florida District Court of Appeal, . . . that probable cause to arrest Royer did not exist at the time he consented to the search of his luggage. The facts are that a nervous young man with two American Tourister bags paid cash for an airline ticket to a "target city". These facts led to inquiry, which in turn revealed that the ticket had been bought under an assumed name. The proffered explanation did not satisfy the officers. We cannot agree with the prosecutor if this is its position, that every nervous young man paying cash for a ticket to New York City under an assumed name and carrying two heavy American Tourister bags may be arrested and held to answer for a serious felony charge.

How Long May a Person Be Held as Part of an Investigative Detention?

The permissible length of time of a detention was the issue before the U.S. Supreme Court in two 1985 cases. In the *Sharpe* case (which follows), the issue was whether a twenty-minute detention violated the Fourth Amendment. The cases are as follows.

United States v. Sharpe

Supreme Court of the United States (1985)
470 U.S. 675, 105 S.Ct. 1568

A Drug Enforcement Agent (DEA) observed two vehicles traveling in tandem for twenty miles in an area on the Atlantic Coast known to be used by drug traffickers. One of the vehicles was a pickup camper with the windows covered with bed-sheet material rather than curtains. The other vehicle was a Pontiac car. After the DEA agent called for assistance from the South Carolina Highway Patrol, the vehicles began speeding when they saw the marked patrol car. Defendant Sharpe pulled over first in response to the police signals. However, the pickup camper sped away, almost hitting the patrol car. After the camper was stopped down the road and it was determined that probable cause existed to search the vehicle, twenty minutes had elapsed. The drivers of the vehicles were convicted of possession of marijuana with intent to distribute. However, the Federal Court of Appeals held that the investigative stops were unlawful because they "failed to meet the requirement of brevity." In affirming the convictions, the U.S. Supreme Court held that

> In assessing whether a detention is too long in duration to be justified as an investigative stop, we consider it appropriate to examine whether the police diligently pursued a means of investigation that was likely to confirm or dispel their suspicions quickly, during which time it was necessary to detain the defendant . . . .
>
> . . . A court making this assessment should take care to consider whether the police are acting in a swiftly developing situation, and in such cases the court should not indulge in unrealistic second-guessing. . . . A creative judge engaged in *post hoc* evaluation of police conduct can almost always imagine some alternative means by which the objectives of the police might have been accomplished. But "[t]he fact that the protection of the public might, in the abstract, have been accomplished by 'less intrusive' means does not, in itself, render the search unreasonable." *Cady v. Dombrowski,* 413 U.S. 433, 447, . . . The question is not simply whether some other alternative was available, but whether the police acted unreasonably in failing to recognize or to pursue it.
>
> We readily conclude that, given the circumstances facing him, Agent Cooke pursued his investigation in a diligent and reasonable manner. During most of Savage's 20–minute detention, Cooke was attempting to contact Thrasher and enlisting the help of the local police who remained with Sharpe while Cooke left to pursue Officer Thrasher and the pickup. Once Cooke reached Officer Thrasher and Savage, he proceeded expeditiously: within the space of a few minutes, he examined Savage's driver's license and the truck's bill of sale, requested (and was denied) permission to search the truck, stepped on the rear bumper and noted that the truck did not move, confirming his suspicion that it was probably overloaded. He then detected the odor of marihuana.
>
> Clearly this case does not involve any delay unnecessary to the legitimate investigation of the law enforcement officers. Respondents presented no evidence that the officers were dilatory in their investigation. The delay in this case was attributable almost entirely to the evasive actions of Savage, who sought to elude the police as Sharpe moved his Pontiac to the side of the road. Except for Savage's maneuvers, only a short and certainly permissible prearrest detention would likely have taken place. The somewhat longer detention was simply the result of a "graduate[d] . . . respons[e] to the demands of [the] particular situation," *Place, supra,* 462 U.S., at 709, n. 10, 103 S.Ct., at 2646, n. 10.
>
> We reject the contention that a 20–minute stop is unreasonable when the police have acted diligently and a suspect's actions contribute to the added delay about which he complains. The judgment of the Court of Appeals is reversed, and the case is remanded for further proceedings consistent with this opinion.

When an Officer Believes False Identification Is Being Presented, Can Written Identification Be Requested of a Person Lawfully Detained?

The U.S. Supreme Court held in 1972 that

> a brief stop of a suspicious individual, in order to determine his identity or maintain the status quo momentarily while obtaining more information, may be reasonable in light of the facts known to the officer at the time. 407 U.S. 143, 146, 92 S.Ct. 1921, 1923 (1972).

Although a brief investigative stop on reasonable suspicion is lawful, no federal court has directly answered the question as to whether an officer can demand of a lawfully detained person that he produce written identification. The following state courts, however, have been confronted by the issue and have held that an officer may demand written identification under such circumstances:

- In holding that police officers acted properly in removing the wallet of an uncooperative suspect in order to determine his identity, the Supreme Court of Wisconsin ruled in 1979 that

  > To accept [the] contention that the officer can stop the suspect and request identification, but that the suspect can turn right around and refuse to provide it, would reduce the authority of the officer ... recognized by the United States Supreme Court in *Adams* to identify a person lawfully stopped by him to a mere fiction. Unless the officer is given some recourse in the event his request for identification is refused, he will be forced to rely either upon the good will of the person he suspects or upon his own ability to simply bluff that person into thinking that he actually does have some recourse.[a]

- The Supreme Court of New Jersey followed the *Flynn* ruling in 1981 and held that an identification search was proper. When the officer did not believe Wilcox's oral identification and did not believe the false identification produced by Wilcox, the identification search resulted in obtaining Wilcox's true identification. *State v. Wilcox,* 180 N.J.Super. 452, 435 A.2d 569 (1981).

- The California Court of Appeals (6th District) also held that a law enforcement officer may constitutionally request written identification from a person lawfully detained. When the defendant opened his wallet after written identification was requested, the officer saw illegal drugs. The defendant's conviction was affirmed. *People v. Long,* 228 Cal.Rptr. 927, 722 P.2d 210, 40 CrL 2070 (1986).

Because persons wanted for other crimes and persons wanted on arrest warrants will continue to falsely identify themselves, similar cases will continue to be presented to courts in the years to come.

[a] State v. Flynn, 92 Wis.2d 427, 285 N.W.2d 710 (1979).

United States v. Rosa Elvira Montoya De Hernandez

Supreme Court of the United States (1985)
473 U.S. 531, 105 S.Ct. 3304

"Balloon swallowers" are used as a way of smuggling cocaine and heroin into the United States. The swallowers can carry dozens of balloons containing an illegal drug in their stomach. Customs officials often have reasonable suspicion that a person is a balloon swallower, but it is difficult to develop probable cause in order to obtain a court order for x-raying of the person. Customs officials in Los Angeles had reasonable suspicion to believe that the defendant was a balloon swallower. She had arrived on a ten-hour direct flight from Bogota, Colombia. She spoke no English and had no friends and family in the USA. She had $5,000 in cash (mostly $50 bills), with which she said she was going to buy goods for her husband's store. She told Customs officials that she was pregnant but they reasonably suspected that she had a stomach full of balloons. She was given the option of returning to Colombia on the next available flight (which was a wait of many hours), or agreeing to an X ray, or remaining in detention until she produced "a monitored bowel movement" which would confirm or rebut suspicions. She remained in detention for sixteen hours without taking any food or drink and without defecating or urinating. After sixteen hours, a court order was obtained authorizing a pregnancy test, an X ray, and a rectal examination. The rectal exam produced a balloon filled with cocaine. She was then arrested; over the next four days, she passed eighty-eight balloons containing a total of 528 grams of 80 percent pure cocaine. The U.S. Supreme Court affirmed the use of the evidence in her criminal trial and also affirmed her conviction, holding that

> We hold that the detention of a traveler at the border, beyond the scope of a routine customs search and inspection, is justified at its inception if customs agents, considering all the facts surrounding the traveler and her trip, reasonably suspect that the traveler is smuggling contraband in her alimentary canal.
>
> The "reasonable suspicion" standard has been applied in a number of contexts and effects a needed balance between private and public interests when law enforcement officials must make a limited intrusion on less than probable cause. It thus fits well into the situations involving alimentary canal smuggling at the border: this type of smuggling gives no external signs and inspectors will rarely possess probable cause to arrest or search, yet governmental interests in stopping smuggling at the border are high indeed. Under this standard officials at the border must have a "particularized and objective basis for suspecting the particular person" of alimentary canal smuggling . . . .
>
> Respondent's detention was long, uncomfortable, indeed, humiliating; but both its length and its discomfort resulted solely from the method by which she chose to smuggle illicit drugs into this country. In *Adams v. Williams*, 407 U.S. 143 (1972), another *Terry*-stop case, we said that "[t]he Fourth Amendment does not require a policeman

who lacks the precise level of information necessary for probable cause to arrest to simply shrug his shoulders and allow a crime to occur or a criminal to escape." *Id.,* at 145. Here, by analogy, in the presence of articulable suspicion of smuggling in her alimentary canal, the customs officers were not required by the Fourth Amendment to pass respondent and her 88 cocaine-filled balloons into the interior. Her detention for the period of time necessary to either verify or dispel the suspicion was not unreasonable.

Can a Person Being Detained Be Transported from the Place of the Stop to Another Place?

A person who is being detained under a valid *Terry* stop could consent to go to another place, and if the consent was voluntary, the evidence obtained would be admissible. Or, further information could provide enough additional evidence to justify a conclusion that probable cause exists. With probable cause, the person could be transported anywhere that was necessary.

The reason for transporting suspects might be for viewing by witnesses or the victim of a crime such as robbery, rape, purse-snatching, etc. The transporting might be for fingerprinting, footprinting, photographing, etc. The movement to another place might be to talk to the person away from the noise and distractions of the street.

Courts which have suppressed evidence obtained after police forced detained persons to move to a police station on less than probable cause are the Florida Court in the 1985 case of *Hayes v. Florida,* 488 So.2d 77, 36 CrL 3216 (1986); and the U.S. Court of Appeals for the Tenth Circuit in the 1985 cases of *United States v. Recalde,* 761 F.2d 1448, 37 CrL 2172 (1985) and *United States v. Gonzalez,* 776 F.2d 931, 37 CrL 2211 (1985). The Arizona Supreme Court suppressed a murder confession in the following case:

State v. Winegar

Supreme Court of Arizona (1985)
711 P.2d 579

The defendant and her boyfriend were suspects in a murder investigation. Six police officers detained them under a *Terry* stop on a public street, on reasonable suspicion. Winegar was told to keep her hands away from her body and told to step away from her companion. When a pistol was found on the boyfriend, he was arrested. The detectives told the defendant and her boyfriend that they wanted to talk to them at the police station. The two then went with the six officers. She was given the *Miranda* warnings and was twice told that she was not under arrest. She was interrogated and supervised for four hours and was presented with incriminating statements of her companion. The

Supreme Court of Arizona held that the use of the defendant's confession was reversible error, stating that

> We concede that law enforcement authorities can transform *Terry* stops into purely voluntary encounters between citizens and police officers. "When an officer is justified in stopping a suspect for questioning, the stop does not become an arrest if, in the absence of protest or coercion, the officer directs the person to an interview room for questioning." *United States v. Huberts,* ... 637 F.2d at 636; ...
>
> The defendant was surrounded by police officers, deprived of her liberty of movement, and watched her companion be frisked. Defendant was then asked to accompany the officers across the street for further questioning. "These circumstances surely amount to a show of official authority such that 'a reasonable person would have believed he was not free to leave.' " *Florida v. Royer,* ..., 460 U.S. at 501, ... At this point the defendant was under arrest for purposes of Fourth Amendment analysis ....
>
> Despite being told twice that there was no arrest, a reasonable person could not truly believe these statements when they were followed by police actions clearly contradicting the statements. "The mere facts that petitioner was not told he was under arrest, was not 'booked', and would not have had an arrest record if the interrogation had proved fruitless ... obviously do not make petitioner's seizure even roughly analogous to the narrowly defined intrusions involved in *Terry* and its progeny." *Id.,* 442 U.S. at 212–213, 99 S.Ct. at 2256–2257 .... The totality of the circumstances suggests a coercive, police-mediated atmosphere, indicative of arrest.

A New York court came to a different conclusion on facts that were considerably different than those facing the Arizona Supreme Court in the *Winegar* case. The New York case follows:

People v. Hicks

Supreme Court of New York Appellate Division (1986)
116 A.D.2d 150, 500 N.Y.S.2d 449

New York police officers made a *Terry* stop on reasonable suspicion after a factory robbery at four o'clock in the morning. The two men, who fled in a green Pontiac with black trim, were transported back to the scene of the armed robbery, where they were identified by the victims. In holding that "under all the circumstances the limited investigatory detention and transportation were permissible and we affirm the conviction," the court stated that

> An investigative detention is justified at its inception when, based upon the "totality of the circumstances—the whole picture—", the police have a "particularized and objective basis for suspecting the particular person stopped of criminal activity." (*United States v. Cor-*

tez, 449 U.S. 411, . . .) It cannot be seriously questioned that the stop of defendant was justified. Considering the whole picture, Officer Wright had a particularized and objective basis for suspecting that defendant had participated in the robbery at the Worthington factory. The defendant and his accomplice matched the general description of the two robbers as reported by radio. "Critically, the crime and subsequent stop took place at an early morning hour when there was little motor vehicle traffic. This is recognized as a significant factor justifying a stop upon much less comprehensive information than would be adequate were the stop made at midday." Timing and location are of "crucial importance" (*People v. Johnson,* 102 A.D.2d 616, 622–623, 478 N.Y.S.2d 987). Here, defendant was stopped only a short distance from the scene of the robbery, within minutes after it occurred, and as his automobile was travelling away from the place of occurrence.

Although the automobile did not fully match the description given over the radio, nevertheless, the totality of the circumstances supported a reasonable suspicion that the occupants had committed the robbery. As stated by Professor LaFave: "[T]he investigating officers must be allowed to take account of the possibility that some of the descriptive factors supplied by victims or witnesses may be in error." . . . (or the suspects might have changed cars, which is common in planned armed robberies.)

The debatable question is whether the subsequent detention and transportation of defendant were "reasonably related in scope to the circumstances which justified the interference in the first place." As stated in *United States v. Sharpe* . . . (105 S.Ct. at 1575), "[m]uch as a 'bright line' rule would be desirable, in evaluating whether an investigative detention is unreasonable, common sense and ordinary human experience must govern over rigid criteria. * * * In assessing whether a detention is too long in duration to be justified as an investigative stop, we consider it appropriate to examine whether the police diligently pursued a means of investigation that was likely to confirm or dispel their suspicions quickly, during which time it was necessary to detain the defendant." The *Sharpe* court admonished that "[a] court making this assessment should take care to consider whether the police are acting in a swiftly developing situation, and in such cases the court should not indulge in unrealistic second-guessing."

Under the test established by *Sharpe,* the detention was reasonable in duration. By taking the suspects to the Worthington factory a short distance away to determine whether eyewitnesses could identify or exclude the suspects as the perpetrators, the police diligently pursued a means of investigation most likely to confirm or dispel their suspicions quickly. The period of detention was short and it lasted no longer than necessary to accomplish its purposes . . . .

. . . The officers transported the suspects for one purpose only—to be viewed by the victims—and that purpose was clearly likely to "confirm or dispel their suspicions quickly." Moreover, they acted reasonably with complete regard for the rights and dignity of the suspects. There was no harassment, show of force, use of force, or actual physical restraint. The suspects were not handcuffed or mistreated in any way . . . .

Terry Stops in Which the Victim or Witnesses to the Crime are a Short Distance Away

The following alternatives (options) are available for situations in which *Terry* stops are made on less than probable cause and the victim or witnesses to the crime are a short distance away:

- Obtain the consent of the person detained to go to the other place to clear up the matter;
- Bring the victim or witness to the scene of the stop to view the detained person for possible identification;
- Review new evidence and information from other officers and persons to determine whether probable cause does exist in view of the total amount of evidence available.

This problem arises frequently when the crimes of purse-snatching, robbery, rape, or snatch-thief occur.

Courts which have held that the movement of a suspect on reasonable suspicion would not convert the *Terry*-type stop into an unlawful arrest are: *People v. Lippert,* 89 Ill.2d 171, 59 Ill.Dec. 819, 432 N.E.2d 605 (1982), cert. denied 459 U.S. 841, 103 S.Ct. 92 (1982); *United States v. Vanichromanee,* 742 F.2d 340 (7th Cir.1984); and *People v. Hicks,* 116 A.D.2d 150, 500 N.Y.S.2d 449 (1986).

... The officers explained the purpose of the detention and told the suspects they would be free to go if they were not identified. This is not the type of overbearing and illegal police conduct courts have been quick to condemn.

We all fear a police state; yet we desire police protection. A balance must be struck. In striking that balance certain principles have been established that safeguard our liberties and draw the line between reasonable and unreasonable police conduct. Certain police conduct is so intrusive that it is considered to be unreasonable unless founded upon probable cause. Without probable cause we may not be seized for the purpose of interrogation in a custodial setting, nor may our homes, persons or effects be searched. Certain lesser intrusions, however, are considered reasonable when based upon the lesser standard of articulable suspicion.

Can an Investigative Arrest Be Made on Less than Probable Cause?

An investigative detention (*Terry* stop) can be made on less than probable cause. When reasonable suspicion exists, a law enforcement officer may detain (stop) a person and make "reasonable inquiries." The investigative detention must be reasonable in time and "reasonably related in scope to the circumstances which justified the interference in the first place." *United States v. Sharpe,* 470 U.S. at ___, 105 S.Ct. at 1575.

But can an **investigative arrest** or investigative custody be made on less than probable cause? Some European countries permit this as an investigative procedure. The following cases have raised the question before the U.S. Supreme Court:

Dunaway v. New York

Supreme Court of the United States (1979)
442 U.S. 200, 99 S.Ct. 2248

Police investigating a murder of a pizza parlor owner, and the attempted robbery of the shop, received information from an informant that the defendant might have committed the crimes. The information was less than probable cause, but police were ordered to pick up the defendant and bring him in. Defendant was taken into custody and given the *Miranda* warnings at the police station. The defendant waived his right to an attorney and made statements and drew sketches which incriminated him. The majority of the U.S. Supreme Court held that the detention was illegal and that the confession could not be used as evidence. The majority held (former Chief Justice Burger and Chief Justice Rehnquist dissented) that

> No intervening events broke the connection between petitioner's illegal detention and his confession. To admit petitioner's confession in such a case would allow "law enforcement officers to violate the Fourth Amendment with impunity, safe in the knowledge that they could wash their hands in the 'procedural safeguards' of the Fifth."
> Reversed.

Davis v. Mississippi

Supreme Court of the United States (1969)
394 U.S. 721, 89 S.Ct. 1394

A rape occurred when an assailant broke into the victim's home. Finger and palm prints were found on a window sill and the suspect was described as a black youth. The police brought at least twenty-four black youths (including the defendant) to police headquarters for questioning and fingerprinting. Days later, the defendant again was picked up on suspicion. On neither probable cause nor a warrant, the defendant was driven to a city ninety miles away and held overnight in jail. Fingerprints were taken from the defendant again and it was determined that the fingerprints of the defendant matched those found at the crime scene. In holding that the police "round-up" procedures violated the Fourth Amendment, the Supreme Court ruled that

> [T]o argue that the Fourth Amendment does not apply to the investigatory stage is fundamentally to misconceive the purposes of the Fourth Amendment. Investigatory seizures would subject unlimited numbers

of innocent persons to the harassment and ignominy incident to involuntary detention. Nothing is more clear than that the Fourth Amendment was meant to prevent wholesale intrusions upon the personal security of our citizenry, whether these intrusions be termed "arrests" or "investigatory detentions."

Morales v. New York

Supreme Court of the United States (1969)
396 U.S. 102, 90 S.Ct. 291

A brutal murder of an older woman occurred in the elevator of her apartment in the Bronx. There were no eyewitnesses and an extensive police investigation disclosed that narcotics users frequented the building. Morales' mother also lived in the building and Morales was frequently in the building visiting his mother and participating in narcotics activity. Morales disappeared after the murder. Nine days later, Mrs. Morales received a telephone call from her son. She informed him that the police sought to question him and he agreed to meet them at his mother's beauty parlor. When Morales arrived, the police told him that they wished to speak with him. Morales replied, "Yes, I know." He was placed in a police car and driven to a precinct house. After being given the *Miranda* warnings, he confessed within fifteen minutes. Morales was convicted using his confession as evidence.

When this case was appealed to the U.S. Supreme Court, the Court elected "not to grapple with the question of custodial questioning on less than probable cause for a fullfledged arrest." The case was sent back to the trial court for hearings to determine: (1) whether probable cause existed despite the state's admission that it did not; or (2) whether Morales consented to go to the police station with the officers. The trial court held that Morales consented to go to the station with the police and therefore the confession was not the product of an illegal detention (see *People v. Morales,* 42 N.Y.2d 129, 397 N.Y.S.2d 587, 366 N.E.2d 248 (1977).

Detention of Packages and Containers

A drug trafficker who is detained on reasonable suspicion frequently will have in his (or her) possession a container such as a purse, a piece of luggage, or a parcel. If there is probable cause to believe that the container holds contraband drugs, the luggage or parcel may be searched with consent, or a search warrant will be obtained to search the object.

Probable cause to believe the luggage or package contains contraband is usually obtained by use of a narcotics-sniffing dog or from information obtained from an informant.

If consent to search cannot be obtained, a delay will occur until a search warrant is obtained. However, the luggage or package may be detained by law enforcement officers until the arrival of the search warrant (or with telephonic warrants, until a magistrate or judge can be contacted on a telephone).

The 1983 *FBI Law Enforcement Bulletin* article, "Investigative Detention and the Drug Courier: Recent Supreme Court Decisions," makes the following statement regarding the detention of packages:

> In 1970 in *United States v. Van Leeuwen,*[7] the Supreme Court upheld the detention of personal property on the basis of reasonable suspicion alone. For the first time, the Court held that law enforcement officers may "stop" a package in much the same way they may detain a person under *Terry.* Prior to *Van Leeuwen,* with the exception of border searches, a *Terry* stop of a *person* was the only type of limited search and seizure that the Supreme Court found reasonable in the absence of probable cause.

The *Van Leeuwen* case concerned two first-class packages which were being forwarded through the mail. The packages were detained ("stopped") until a search warrant was obtained. The Supreme Court stated that

> Detention for this limited time was, indeed, the prudent act rather than letting the packages enter the mails and then, in case the initial suspicions were confirmed, trying to locate them en route and enlisting the help of distant federal officials in serving the warrant.

In the 1983 case of *United States v. Place,* 462 U.S. 696, 103 S.Ct. 2637 (1983), the U.S. Supreme Court held that a *Terry* stop on reasonable suspicion would not justify holding luggage for ninety minutes. The DEA agents knew when Place was coming into La Guardia airport in New York and should have had the narcotics-detecting dog at La Guardia. They had to take Place's luggage to another airport in New York City (Kennedy), where the dog signalled positively to one of the two bags. The Court held that

> The precise type of detention we confront here is seizure of personal luggage from the immediate possession of the suspect for the purpose of arranging exposure to a narcotics detection dog. Particularly in the case of detention of luggage within the traveler's immediate possession, the police conduct intrudes on both the suspect's possessory interest in his luggage as well as his liberty interest in proceeding with his itinerary. The person whose luggage is detained is technically still free to continue his travels or carry out other personal activities pending release of the luggage. Moreover, he is not subjected to the coercive atmosphere of a custodial confinement or to the public indignity of being personally detained. Nevertheless, such a seizure can effectively restrain the person since he is subjected to the possible disruption of his travel plans in order to remain with his luggage or to arrange for its return. Therefore, when the police seize luggage from the suspect's custody, we think the limitations applicable to investigative detentions of the person should define the permissible scope of an investigative detention of the person's luggage on less than probable cause. Under this standard, it is clear that the police conduct here exceeded the permissible limits of a *Terry*-type investigative stop.

The length of the detention of respondent's luggage alone precludes the conclusion that the seizure was reasonable in the absence of probable cause. Although we have recognized the reasonableness of seizures longer than the momentary ones involved in *Terry, Adams,* and *Brignoni-Ponce,* see *Michigan v. Summers,* 452 U.S. 692, 101 S.Ct. 2587, 69 L.Ed.2d 340 (1981), the brevity of the invasion of the individual's Fourth Amendment interests is an important factor in determining whether the seizure is so minimally intrusive as to be justifiable on reasonable suspicion. Moreover, in assessing the effect of the length of the detention, we take into account whether the police diligently pursue their investigation. We note that here the New York agents knew the time of Place's scheduled arrival at La Guardia, had ample time to arrange for their additional investigation at that location, and thereby could have minimized the intrusion on respondent's Fourth Amendment interests. Thus, although we decline to adopt any outside time limitation for a permissible *Terry* stop, we have never approved a seizure of the person for the prolonged 90–minute period involved here and cannot do so on the facts presented by this case . . . .

Although the 90–minute detention of respondent's luggage is sufficient to render the seizure unreasonable, the violation was exacerbated by the failure of the agents to accurately inform respondent of the place to which they were transporting his luggage, of the length of time he might be dispossessed, and of what arrangements would be made for return of the luggage if the investigation dispelled the suspicion. In short, we hold that the detention of respondent's luggage in this case went beyond the narrow authority possessed by police to detain briefly luggage reasonably suspected to contain narcotics.

We conclude that, under all of the circumstances of this case, the seizure of respondent's luggage was unreasonable under the Fourth Amendment. Consequently, the evidence obtained from the subsequent search of his luggage was inadmissible, and Place's conviction must be reversed. The judgment of the Court of Appeals, accordingly, is affirmed.

It is so ordered.

SEARCHES WHICH MAY BE MADE DURING AN INVESTIGATIVE DETENTION

Consent Searches

Consent searches and protective searches are the only searches which can be made during a *Terry* stop. Consent to search would have to be voluntarily given and would be limited to the area or object consented to be searched.

If there were insufficient facts to justify the stop (an improper or illegal stop), then evidence obtained during that stop (with or without consent) would be the fruit of the illegal stop and not admissible in court.

If the restraints on the person exceeded the limits set by *Terry* and amounted to an arrest (as in the case of *Florida v. Royer*), the consent to search would be "invalid because (it was) tainted by the unlawful confinement." (See the *Royer* case in this chapter.)

Protective Searches

The U.S. Supreme Court pointed out in the *Terry v. Ohio* [8] case that

> We are . . . concerned with more than the governmental interest in investigating crime; . . . there is the more immediate interest of the police officer in taking steps to assure himself that the person with whom he is dealing is not armed with a weapon that could unexpectedly and fatally be used against him. Certainly it would be unreasonable to require that police officers take unnecessary risks in the performance of their duties. American criminals have a long tradition of armed violence, and every year in this country many law enforcement officers are killed in the line of duty, and thousands more are wounded. Virtually all of these deaths and a substantial portion of the injuries are inflicted with guns and knives.
>
> In view of these facts, we cannot blind ourselves to the need for law enforcement officers to protect themselves and other prospective victims of violence in situations where they may lack probable cause for an arrest. When an officer is justified in believing that the individual whose suspicious behavior he is investigating at close range is armed and presently dangerous to the officer or to others, it would appear to be clearly unreasonable to deny the officer the power to take necessary measures to determine whether the person is in fact carrying a weapon and to neutralize the threat of physical harm.

To be "justified in believing . . . that the individual . . . is armed and presently dangerous to the officer or to others," the officer must be able to point to facts which would justify his conclusion that he was concerned (and feared) for his safety or the safety of others.

Reasonable suspicion would justify a protective measure such as a frisk. If the person is carrying a concealed weapon, he could then be arrested and charged with that offense. A defense lawyer could attack the lawfulness of the stop and the authority to make a frisk. The state would have to show reasonable suspicion to make the stop and, in addition, would have to show reasonable suspicion to justify the weapons search.

The following list of factors which may be considered were published by an office of the U.S. Department of Justice: [9]

> a. *Person's appearance:* Do his clothes bulge in a manner suggesting the presence of any object capable of inflicting injury? Do other physical characteristics, like demeanor, suggest the possibility that he may be carrying a weapon?
>
> b. *Person's actions:* Has he made a furtive movement, as if to hide a weapon, as he was approached? Is he nervous during the course of the stop? Are his words or actions threatening?
>
> c. *Prior knowledge:* Does the officer know if the person has an arrest or conviction record for weapons or other potentially violent offenses? Does the person have a reputation in the community for carrying weapons or for assaultive behavior?
>
> d. *Location of incident:* Is the area known for criminal activity—is it a "high crime" area? Is it so isolated that witnesses to an attack on the officer would be unlikely?

e. *Time of day:* Is the incident taking place at night? In the officer's judgment will darkness make an attack more likely, or more difficult to defend?

f. *Police purpose:* Does the officer suspect that the person stopped may have been involved—or be about to become involved—in a serious and violent offense? An armed offense?

g. *Companions:* Has the officer stopped a number of people at the same time? Has a frisk of a companion of the suspect revealed a weapon? Does the officer have sufficient immediately available assistance with regard to the number of subjects he has stopped?

The protective search and a search with consent are the only searches without a search warrant which can be made during a *Terry* stop (investigative detention).

EVIDENCE OBTAINED DURING THE ARREST PROCESS

The search incident to a lawful arrest has always been recognized as one of the well-delineated exceptions to the search warrant requirement of the Fourth Amendment. The authority for the search is based upon the existence of a lawful, custodial arrest made in good faith. In 1973 the U.S. Supreme Court stated in the case of *United States v. Robinson,*[10] that

> A custodial arrest of a suspect based on probable cause is a reasonable intrusion under the Fourth Amendment; that intrusion being lawful, a search incident to the arrest requires no additional justification. It is the fact of the lawful arrest which establishes the authority to search, and we hold that in the case of a lawful custodial arrest a full search of the person is not only an exception to the warrant requirement of the Fourth Amendment, but it is also a "reasonable" search under that Amendment.

What Constitutes an Arrest?

In the case of *People v. Ussery,*[11] the Illinois Appellate Court pointed out that an arrest consists of three elements.[12] In holding that the curbing of a vehicle alone is not an arrest of the driver, the Court ruled that

> An arrest involves three elements: (1) authority to arrest; (2) assertion, of that authority with intention to effect an arrest; and (3) restraint of the person to be arrested . . . . When one is approached by a police officer to be questioned about her identity and actions, this is only an accosting, not an arrest . . . . The act relied on as constituting an arrest must have been performed with the intent to effect an arrest and must have been so understood by the party arrested . . . . In the instant case the defendant's own belief was "Oh, well, he don't want anything of me so I went on." When the defendant was first stopped she did not have reasonable ground to believe that she was under arrest. We conclude that defendant, or a reasonable man, innocent of any crime would not think he had been arrested.

> Unlike an arrest which requires probable cause, in a threshold inquiry of a citizen, aimed at effective crime prevention and detection,

there is "the recognition that a police officer may in appropriate cir- cumstances and in an appropriate manner approach a person for purposes of investigating possible criminal behavior even though there is no probable cause to make an arrest." ... *Terry v. Ohio*, 392 U.S. 1, 22, 88 S.Ct. 1868, 1880, 20 L.Ed.2d 889.

The Requirement of Probable Cause

Probable cause, or **reasonable grounds to believe** that the person has commit- ted a specific crime must exist or there is no authority to make an arrest.

The President's Commission on Crime [13] reported that the federal govern- ment alone has created more than 2,800 crimes and estimates that most states have also created over 2,000 crimes. Arrests are not made for every offense committed. The offender may be warned and cautioned; or may be referred to his school, military service, or parents; or may be ordered to report to the city attorney or district attorney; or other alternatives to arrest may be used.

If there is an intent to make an arrest (which is an essential element of all arrests), there must be authority in the form of probable cause to make the arrest. In the case of *Dunaway v. New York* (see the case in this chapter), Dunaway was picked up and taken into custody on less than probable cause. In holding that the illegal custody and arrest violated Dunaway's Fourth Amendment rights, the U.S. Supreme Court ruled that [14]

The central importance of the probable-cause requirement to the pro- tection of a citizen's privacy afforded by the Fourth Amendment's guarantees cannot be compromised in this fashion. "The requirement of probable cause has roots that are deep in our history." *Henry v. United States,* 361 U.S. 98, 100, ... (1959). Hostility to seizures based on mere suspicion was a prime motivation for the adoption of the Fourth Amendment, and decisions immediately after its adoption af- firmed that "common rumor or report, suspicion, or even 'strong rea- son to suspect' was not adequate to support a warrant for arrest." ..., 80 S.Ct., at 170 .... The familiar threshold standard of probable cause for Fourth Amendment seizures reflects the benefit of extensive expe- rience accommodating the factors relevant to the "reasonableness" requirement of the Fourth Amendment, and provides the relative sim- plicity and clarity necessary to the implementation of a workable rule.

If Law Enforcement Officers Arrest the Wrong Man, Does That Alone Make the Arrest Illegal?

In the case of *Hill v. California* (which follows), law enforcement officers in good faith and with probable cause arrested the wrong man. The question presented to the U.S. Supreme Court was whether the arrest was valid and the evidence obtained admissible:

Hill v. California

Supreme Court of the United States (1971)
401 U.S. 797, 91 S.Ct. 1106

California officers had probable cause to arrest Hill for armed robbery. Having Hill's address and a description of him, the officers went to Hill's apartment without a search or arrest warrant. A man "who fit the description exactly of Archie Hill" answered the door. The officers arrested the man for robbery and he denied that he was Hill and denied any knowledge of where the guns and stolen goods were. Because a pistol and clip of ammunition were lying in plain view on a coffee table, the officers did not believe the man (Miller). A search produced evidence incriminating Hill of the robbery. The trial court admitted the evidence in Hill's trial, holding that the police had probable cause and acted in good faith. In affirming the use of the evidence obtained after the mistaken arrest of Miller, the U.S. Supreme Court held that

> sufficient probability, not certainty, is the touchstone of reasonableness under the Fourth Amendment and on the record before us the officers' mistake was understandable and the arrest a reasonable response to the situation facing them at the time.
>
> Nor can we agree with petitioner that however valid the arrest of Miller, the subsequent search violated the Fourth Amendment. It is true that Miller was not Hill; nor did Miller have authority or control over the premises, although at the very least he was Hill's guest. But the question is not what evidence would have been admissible against Hill (or against Miller for that matter) if the police, with probable cause to arrest Miller, had arrested him in Hill's apartment and then carried out the search at issue. Here there was probable cause to arrest Hill and the police arrested Miller in Hill's apartment, reasonably believing him to be Hill. In these circumstances the police were entitled to do what the law would have allowed them to do if Miller had in fact been Hill, that is, to search incident to arrest and to seize evidence of the crime the police had probable cause to believe Hill had committed. When judged in accordance with "the factual and practical considerations of everyday life on which reasonable and prudent men, not legal technicians, act," *Brinegar v. United States,* 338 U.S. 160, 175 . . . (1949), the arrest and subsequent search were reasonable and valid under the Fourth Amendment.

Must an Officer Obtain an Arrest Warrant Before an Arrest If He Has Time to Do So?

It is a common practice for law enforcement agencies to obtain arrest warrants for persons wanted for serious offenses who have been at large for some time. The advantages are that other law enforcement agencies know when an arrest warrant has been issued that a magistrate (or judge) has reviewed the facts and determined that probable cause exists for the arrest of the wanted person.

Also, there is a presumption of validity as to warrants and the burden of showing they are invalid is on the party challenging the warrant.

But does a law enforcement officer have to obtain an arrest warrant if there is time to obtain one? That was the issue before the U.S. Supreme Court in the following case:

United States v. Watson

Supreme Court of the United States (1976)
423 U.S. 411, 96 S.Ct. 820

A postal inspector arrested the defendant for a felony without an arrest warrant although the officer admitted that he had time to obtain an arrest warrant. The federal Court of Appeals held that the arrest was invalid because of the failure to secure an arrest warrant. In reversing the Court of Appeals, the U.S. Supreme Court held that

> there is nothing in the Court's prior cases indicating that under the Fourth Amendment a warrant is required to make a valid arrest for a felony. Indeed, the relevant prior decisions are uniformly to the contrary. . . .
>
> Watson's arrest did not violate the Fourth Amendment, and the Court of Appeals erred in holding to the contrary

Areas Which May Be Searched Incident to a Lawful Custodial Arrest

In 1969, the case of *Chimel v. California* came before the U.S. Supreme Court. In that case, the defendant was arrested under the authority of an arrest warrant in the front room of his home for the burglary of a coin shop. The arresting officers then searched the entire three-bedroom house, including the attic, the garage, and a small workshop, without the authority of a search warrant and without consent. In excluding the evidence which was obtained as a result of the extensive search and in defining the area which may be searched incident to a lawful custodial arrest, the Court held that

> When an arrest is made, it is reasonable for the arresting officer to search the person arrested in order to remove any weapons that the latter might seek to use in order to resist arrest or effect his escape. Otherwise, the officer's safety might well be endangered, and the arrest itself frustrated. In addition, it is entirely reasonable for the arresting officer to search for and seize any evidence on the arrestee's person in order to prevent its concealment or destruction. And the area into which an arrestee might reach in order to grab a weapon or evidentiary items must, of course, be governed by a like rule. A gun on a table or in a drawer in front of one who is arrested can be as dangerous to the arresting officer as one concealed in the clothing of the person arrested. There is ample justification, therefore, for a search of the arrestee's person and the area "within his immediate

control"—construing that phrase to mean the area from within which he might gain possession of a weapon or destructible evidence.

There is no comparable justification, however, for routinely searching any room other than that in which an arrest occurs—or, for that matter, for searching through all the desk drawers or other closed or concealed areas in that room itself. Such searches, in the absence of well-recognized exceptions, may be made only under the authority of a search warrant. The "adherence to judicial processes" mandated by the Fourth Amendment requires no less. . . .

. . . The scope of the search was, therefore, "unreasonable" under the Fourth and Fourteenth Amendments and the petitioner's conviction cannot stand.

Reversed.

However, an arrest outside of a home, apartment, or motel room will not authorize entrance into the residence to search for evidence. Nor will probable cause to believe that evidence is in the home, apartment, or motel room ordinarily authorize an entrance into the premises. However, an exception to this rule is the **cursory safety check** (also known as the **protective sweep**) which is presented in the following Chart. Also see chapter 11 on Police Entrance Into Private Premises.

What Area Is Within a Person's Immediate Control?

In the *Chimel* decision, the U.S. Supreme Court held that a search could be made "of the arrestee's person and the area 'within his immediate control'—construing that phrase to mean the area from within which he might gain possession of a weapon or destructible evidence."

Since the *Chimel* decision in 1969, there have been many lower-court rulings on the question of what area is within a person's immediate control. Is it the area that an arrested person could lunge, leap, or jump? What if the arrested person were handcuffed; would that limit the area? Should the area be increased if the arrestee is belligerent, uncooperative, or dangerous? If evidence is obtained outside of the area of the arrestee's immediate control, it cannot be used as evidence at the trial.

In 1983, the U.S. Supreme Court stated, "we determined that the lower courts have found no workable definition of 'the area within the immediate control of the arrestee' when that area arguably includes the interior of an automobile and the arrestee is its recent occupant."

The Supreme Court answered this question as to vehicles in the case of *New York v. Belton* (case presented in chapter 12). The Court held that a law enforcement officer "may, as contemporaneous incident of that arrest, search the passenger compartment of that automobile." The Court also held that the police "may also examine the contents of any containers found within the passenger compartment . . ."

The container searched in the *Belton* case incident to the arrest was the zipped-up pocket of a black leather jacket belonging to Belton and lying on the back seat. The Supreme Court held that Belton was properly convicted of the possession of cocaine, based on the evidence of cocaine found in the pocket of the leather jacket.

The Cursory Safety Check, or the Protective Sweep

A law enforcement officer may only search a suspect and the area within the suspect's immediate control incident to an arrest (*Chimel v. California,* 395 U.S. 752). However, a well-recognized exception to this rule exists when there are reasonable grounds to believe that persons in other rooms or elsewhere in the vicinity may jeopardize the safety of the officer or other persons. The "protective sweep," or the "cursory safety check," was defined as follows:

> Arresting officers have a right to conduct a quick and cursory check of the arrestee's lodging immediately subsequent to arrest—even if the arrest is near the door but outside the lodging—where they have reasonable grounds to believe that there are other persons present inside who might present a security risk.[a]

Examples of cases reviewing the safety-check exception:

- *United States v. Kolodziej,* 706 F.2d 590 (5th Cir.1983). A "security sweep" was not justified where it was believed that the arrested defendant occasionally carried a pistol and there was a possibility that a man named Barney might be in the home. Penalty: Marijuana found in plain view could not be used in evidence for new charge.

- *McGeehan v. Wainwright,* 526 F.2d 397 (5th Cir.1976), review denied 425 U.S. 997, 96 S.Ct. 2214 (U.S.Sup.Ct.1976). When seven armed robbery suspects surrendered from a trailer but did not surrender their weapons, it was feared other suspects were still inside with weapons. "Safety check" of the trailer was proper.

- *United States v. Cravero,* 545 F.2d 406 (5th Cir.1976), review denied 430 U.S. 983, 97 S.Ct. 1679 (U.S.Sup.Ct.1977). A security sweep was justified when two suspects were arrested in possession of a loaded pistol and suspicious noises were heard in an adjoining room.

- *United States v. Looney,* 481 F.2d 31 (5th Cir.1973), review denied 414 U.S. 1070, 94 S.Ct. 581 (U.S.Sup.Ct.1973). Arrest for attempted assassination of a federal judge late at night in a house in an unfamiliar rural area. Two loaded rifles were seen in plain view. The protective sweep of the house was proper.

- *United States v. Jackson,* 700 F.2d 181 (5th Cir.1983). Officers were told that at least two armed men committed the offense. When two suspects were apprehended outside their motel room, a cursory safety check of the motel room was proper because the officers had no way of knowing that the two suspects were the persons involved in the crime.

[a] United States v. Sheikh, 654 F.2d 1057 (5th Cir.1981), review denied 455 U.S. 991, 102 S.Ct. 1617 (U.S.Sup.Ct.1982).

The Authority to Make A Full, Intensive Search under the Federal *Robinson-Gustafson* Rule

When the *Robinson* and *Gustafson* cases came before the U.S. Supreme Court, the Court held that full, intensive searches could be made of objects within the immediate control of an arrestee immediately after an arrest. Some states, however, have limited such searches either by state statutes or by court decisions. The limitation could be a requirement that the search be limited to evidence of the crime for which the person is arrested, plus weapons and objects which could aid in escape. Therefore in such states, in a drunk driving arrest case, the search could be only for evidence of the drunk driving (alcoholic beverages) and not for drugs, as were found in both the *Robinson* and *Gustafson* cases:

United States v. Robinson

Supreme Court of the United States (1973)
414 U.S. 218, 94 S.Ct. 467

Gustafson v. Florida

Supreme Court of the United States (1973)
414 U.S. 260, 94 S.Ct. 488

Because these cases are vehicle arrest cases, they are also presented in chapter 12.

The defendants in both cases were arrested while driving an automobile. Robinson was arrested for driving after the revocation of his driver's license and Gustafson for driving without a valid driver's license. In the searches after the arrests, evidence of other crimes were discovered in both cases. In the *Robinson* case, the officer came upon a "crumpled up cigarette package" in the defendant's pocket. The officer testified, "I could feel objects in the package but I couldn't tell what they were ... I knew they weren't cigarettes." The officer opened the package and found fourteen capsules, which he believed to be heroin (they were later proved to be heroin). In the *Gustafson* case, marijuana cigarettes were found in a cigarette box. In both cases, the evidence found in the searches incident to the arrests was used in additional criminal charges against the defendants. In affirming the use of the new evidence and the convictions of both defendants, the Court held in the *Robinson* case that

> The search of respondent's person conducted by Officer Jenks in this case and the seizure from him of the heroin, were permissible under established Fourth Amendment law. While thorough, the search partook of none of the extreme or patently abusive characteristics which were held to violate the Due Process Clause of the Fourteenth Amendment in Rochin v. California, 342 U.S. 165, ... (1952). Since it is the fact of custodial arrest which gives rise to the authority to search, it is of no moment that Jenks did not indicate any subjective fear of the respondent or that he did not himself suspect that respondent was armed. Having in the course of a lawful search come upon the crumpled package of cigarettes, he was entitled to inspect it; and when his inspection revealed the heroin capsules, he was entitled to seize them

as "fruits, instrumentalities, or contraband" probative of criminal conduct.

The Mechanics of an Arrest

Search of the Person of an Arrestee

In large police and sheriff departments, a person who has been arrested will be handled by different officers who have different jobs to do. Many departments require that when an officer takes custody of an arrested person, they immediately search that person. The mechanics and administrative process of an arrest are illustrated by the following example:

- A burglar is apprehended at the scene of a crime by two uniformed officers. The officers arrest the burglar and search the man for weapons and evidence.

- Two detectives arrive at the scene and take custody of the burglar, because they wish to interrogate him. Upon taking custody of the burglar, they immediately search him as required by their department.

- A police wagon arrives to transport the prisoner to the police department. When the wagon officers take custody of the burglar, they also immediately search him, as required by department regulations.

- The wagon officers turn the arrested person over to booking officers upon arrival at the station. The booking officers also immediately search the prisoner.

- When the booking officers have finished their job, they then turn the arrested person over to jailers. The jailers will then make a search of the person before placing the person in a cell.

All the above searches of the person of the arrestee are proper and lawful searches in the arrest process.

Search of Containers

Containers (purses, suitcases, boxes, bags, etc.) in the possession or in the immediate control of an arrested person can be searched under the *Robinson-Gustafson* rule immediately after the arrest. As illustrated by the *Robinson* and *Gustafson* cases, containers can be searched and, if evidence of a crime is discovered, the evidence is lawfully obtained and can be used in the criminal trial of the defendant.

However, if the police take "exclusive dominion (control)" of the container or property and "there is no danger that the arrestee might gain access to the property to seize a weapon or destroy evidence, a search of that property is no longer an incident of the arrest." *United States v. Chadwick,* 433 U.S. 1, 97 S.Ct. 2476 (1977).

Therefore, to search a container after the police have taken exclusive control cannot be done incident to the lawful arrest. If the police seek evidence of a crime from the container, they must obtain a search warrant or consent to go into the container.

U.S. Supreme Court Cases Controlling Searches in the Arrest Process

Search of the Person of an Arrestee

United States v. Edwards

Supreme Court of the United States (1974)
415 U.S. 800, 94 S.Ct. 1234

Just before midnight, the defendant was arrested and placed in jail for attempting to break into the post office in Lebanon, Ohio. There were no eyewitnesses to the attempted entry into the post office, which had been made by forcing a wooden window with a pry bar. Because the police needed additional evidence, the next day (June 1) they purchased a pair of trousers and a T-shirt for Edwards. They told him to put on the new clothing and took his old clothes from him. When the old clothes were sent to a crime lab, it was discovered that paint and wood chips found on clothes matched samples taken from the post office window. The trial court permitted the clothing to be used as evidence and permitted an expert witness to testify as to the similarity of the wood and paint chips. In affirming the use of the evidence and the defendant's conviction, the U.S. Supreme Court held that

> This was and is a normal incident of a custodial arrest, and reasonable delay in effectuating it does not change the fact that Edwards was no more imposed upon than he could have been at the time and place of the arrest or immediately upon arrival at the place of detention. The police did no more on June 1 than they were entitled to do incident to the usual custodial arrest and incarceration . . . .
>
> . . . When it became apparent that the articles of clothing were evidence of the crime for which Edwards was being held, the police were entitled to take, examine, and preserve them for use as evidence, just as they are normally permitted to seize evidence of crime when it is lawfully encountered . . . .
>
> . . . once the accused is lawfully arrested and is in custody, the effects in his possession at the place of detention that were subject to search at the time and place of his arrest may lawfully be searched and seized without a warrant even though a substantial period of time has elapsed between the arrest and subsequent administrative processing, on the one hand, and the taking of the property for use as evidence, on the other. This is true where the clothing or effects are immediately seized upon arrival at the jail, held under the defendant's name in the "property room" of the jail, and at a later time searched and taken for use at the subsequent criminal trial. The result is the same where the property is not physically taken from the defendant until sometime after his incarceration.

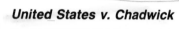

Searches of Containers

United States v. Chadwick

Supreme Court of the United States (1977)
433 U.S. 1, 97 S.Ct. 2476

Law enforcement officers in Boston had probable cause to believe that Chadwick was bringing a 200–pound footlocker filled with marijuana into Boston on an Amtrak train from San Diego. Instead of arresting Chadwick when a dog confirmed the presence of a controlled substance in the footlocker, they watched Chadwick and another person place the footlocker into the trunk of a waiting automobile. Chadwick and his companions were then arrested and taken to the federal building in Boston. The car with the large footlocker sticking out of the trunk was driven to the federal building by an officer. More than an hour after the footlocker was seized, it was searched without a warrant or consent while Chadwick was being held in custody. In holding that the evidence was obtained from the improper search of the footlocker, the Supreme Court ruled that

> When a custodial arrest is made there is always some danger that the person arrested may seek to use a weapon, or that evidence may be concealed or destroyed. To safeguard himself and others, and to prevent the loss of evidence, it has been held reasonable for the arresting officer to conduct a prompt, warrantless "search of the arrestee's person and the area 'within his immediate control'—construing that phrase to mean the area from within which he might gain possession of a weapon or destructible evidence." *Chimel v. California*, 395 U.S., at 763, ...
>
> Such searches may be conducted without a warrant, and they may also be made whether or not there is probable cause to believe that the person arrested may have a weapon or is about to destroy evidence. The potential dangers lurking in all custodial arrests make warrantless searches of items within the "immediate control" area reasonable without requiring the arresting officer to calculate the probability that weapons or destructible evidence may be involved . . . . However, warrantless searches of luggage or other property seized at the time of an arrest cannot be justified as incident to that arrest either if the "search is remote in time or place from the arrest." *Preston v. United States*, 376 U.S., at 367, 84 S.Ct., at 883, or no exigency exists. Once law enforcement officers have reduced luggage or other personal property not immediately associated with the person of the arrestee to their exclusive control, and there is no longer any danger that the arrestee might gain access to the property to seize a weapon or destroy evidence, a search of that property is no longer an incident of the arrest.
>
> Here the search was conducted more than an hour after federal agents had gained exclusive control of the footlocker and long after respondents were securely in custody; the search therefore cannot be

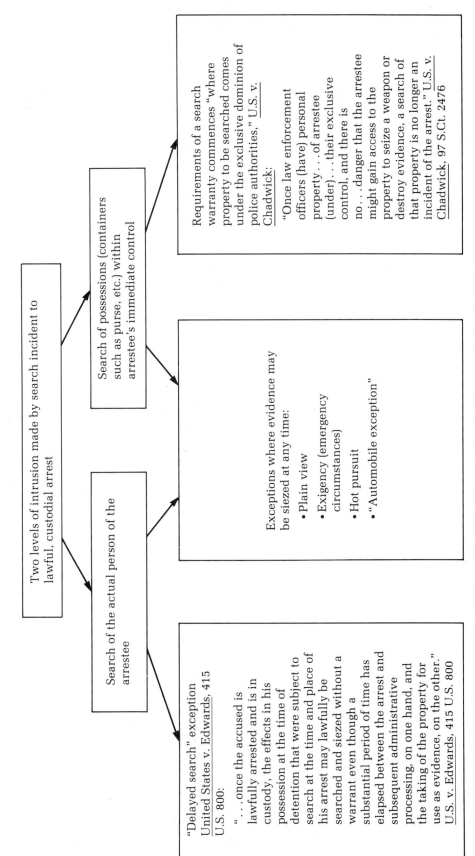

Figure 10.1 Searches Incident to Lawful Custodial Arrests

viewed as incidental to the arrest or as justified by any other exigency. Even though on this record the issuance of a warrant by a judicial officer was reasonably predictable, a line must be drawn. In our view, when no exigency is shown to support the need for an immediate search, the Warrant Clause places the line at the point where the property to be searched comes under the exclusive dominion of police authority. Respondents were therefore entitled to the protection of the Warrant Clause with the evaluation of a neutral magistrate, before their privacy interests in the contents of the footlocker were invaded.

EVIDENCE OBTAINED BY INVENTORY SEARCHES

The U.S. Supreme Court listed the following reasons and needs for inventorying property belonging to other persons which is being held by the police:

1. The protection of the owner's property while it remained in police custody.
2. The protection of the police against claims or disputes over lost or stolen property.
3. The protection of the police from potential danger.[16]

Inventory searches are therefore not searches for incriminating evidence. They are a common and sensible police procedure to determine what the law enforcement agency is responsible for. They are "not an independent legal concept but rather an incidental administrative step following arrest and preceding incarceration." [17]

In the following case, the U.S. Supreme Court answers the question as to whether evidence discovered in an inventory search can be used in a criminal case.

Illinois v. LaFayette

Supreme Court of the United States (1983)
462 U.S. 640, 103 S.Ct. 2605

When the police arrived at a theatre in Kankakee, Illinois, they found the defendant involved in a fight with the theatre manager. They arrested the defendant, put him in handcuffs, and took him to the police station. In the booking room, defendant was told to empty the contents of his pockets on a counter. Defendant had a purse-type shoulder bag from which he took a package of cigarettes and put the bag on the counter. An officer found ten amphetamine pills inside the plastic wrap of a cigarette package. The new evidence caused the defendant to be charged with a violation of the Illinois Controlled Substance Act. However, the evidence was suppressed. Review was then granted by the U.S. Supreme Court. In holding that the evidence was obtained by a valid inventory search, the Court ruled that

Table 10.2 Investigative Procedures Which May Be Used by Law Enforcement Officers

VOLUNTARY CONVERSATION AND/OR OBSERVATION/ SURVEILLANCE	INVESTIGATIVE STOP OR *TERRY* STOP	CUSTODY OR ARREST
Can be used for investigative purposes and do not require a showing of "reasonable suspicion" or "probable cause." (See *Weber v. Cedarburg*, 125 Wis.2d 22, 370 N.W.2d 791 (1985), in which the Supreme Court of Wisconsin affirmed a ruling that the defendant had no civil cause of action for surveillance without reason to suspect wrongdoing. Police followed Weber to bars, sporting events, etc. and made notes of his activities.)	Police must have reasonable suspicion to make a *Terry* stop (investigative detention). A detention is made and a *Terry* stop has occurred when a "reasonable person would have believed that he was not free to leave." *U.S. v. Mendenhall.* The free-to-leave test determines when a police encounter is no longer a voluntary conversation. The detention (*Terry* stop) "must be temporary and last no longer than is necessary" (*Florida v. Royer*). In the 1985 case of *United States v. Sharpe,* the Supreme Court held that a twenty-minute stop was not unreasonable "when the police have acted diligently and a suspect's actions contributed to the added delay about which he complains." 470 U.S. at ___, 105 S.Ct. at 1576.	Probable cause (also known as reasonable grounds to believe) must exist to hold a person in custody or make an arrest. Incident to a lawful, custodial arrest, a search may be made of the person and the area under the person's immediate control. Under the "delayed search" exception of *United States v. Edwards,* searches of the arrestee's person may be made at later times. But if police take control of property of a container, they may only search it at the time of arrest. Under *U.S. v. Chadwick* a warrant or consent is required to obtain evidence at a later time.

Officer Mietzner testified that he examined the bag's contents because it was standard procedure to inventory "everything" in the possession of an arrested person .... He testified that he was not seeking and did not expect to find drugs or weapons when he searched the bag, and he conceded that the shoulder bag was small enough that it could have been placed and sealed in a bag, container, or locker for protective purposes ....

... A so-called inventory search is not an independent legal concept but rather an incidental administrative step following arrest and preceding incarceration. To determine whether the search of respondent's shoulder bag was unreasonable we must "balanc[e] its intrusion on the individual's Fourth Amendment interests against its promotion of legitimate governmental interests." *Delaware v. Prouse,* 440 U.S. 648 (1979) ....

Authority to Make a Search

Before making a search, an officer should ask himself whether he has the authority to make the search. The U.S. Supreme Court has repeatedly stated that the "burden (to show justification for a search) is on those seeking the exemption to show the need for it" (see *Coolidge v. New Hampshire,* 403 U.S. 443, 91 S.Ct. 2022, 29 L.Ed.2d 564 (1971)). Therefore, in order to use evidence obtained as a result of a search, one of the following justifications must be shown by the state in criminal cases:

- That the search was made under the authority of a search warrant or wiretap order issued by a judge or magistrate.
- That the search was made incident to a lawful, custodial arrest.
- That probable cause existed to believe that a motor vehicle, aircraft, or watercraft contained evidence of a crime and that a warrantless search was justified under the Carroll Rule (also known as the "automobile exception").
- That consent was voluntarily given to make the search by a person who has such "mutual use" or "joint access or control" of the property searched so as to authorize the search.
- That the search was justified by a valid concern of the officer for his safety or the safety of others so as to authorize a "frisk" or "protective sweep."
- That an exigency (emergency) existed which justified the search or that an "urgent need" existed which justified the seizure of evidence before the evidence was destroyed or moved to an unknown place.
- That the search was made under the common law right to make a jailhouse search or that the search was made during the mechanics of an arrest.
- That the search was a valid inventory search or inspection of property lawfully in the custody of a law enforcement agency.

An arrested person is not invariably taken to a police station or confined; if an arrestee is taken to the police station, that is no more than a continuation of the custody inherent in the arrest status. Nonetheless, the factors justifying a search of the person and personal effects of an arrestee upon reaching a police station but prior to being placed in confinement are somewhat different from the factors justifying an immediate search at the time and place of arrest.

The governmental interests underlying a station house search of the arrestee's person and possessions may in some circumstances be even greater than those supporting a search immediately following arrest. Consequently, the scope of a station house search will often vary from that made at the time of arrest. Police conduct that would be impractical or unreasonable—or embarrassingly intrusive—on the street can more readily—and privately—be performed at the station. For example, the interests supporting a search incident to arrest would hardly justify disrobing an arrestee on the street, but the practical necessities of routine jail administration may even justify taking a prisoner's clothes before confining him, although that step would be rare. This was made clear in *United States v. Edwards,* 415 U.S. 800, 804 ... (1974): "With or without probable cause, the authorities were entitled [at the station house] not only to search [the arrestee's] clothing but also to take it from him and keep it in official custody."

At the station house, it is entirely proper for police to remove and list or inventory property found on the person or in the possession of an arrested person who is to be jailed. A range of governmental interests supports an inventory process. It is not unheard of for persons employed in police activities to steal property taken from arrested persons; similarly, arrested persons have been known to make false claims regarding what was taken from their possession at the station house. A standardized procedure for making a list or inventory as soon as reasonable after reaching the station house not only deters false claims but also inhibits theft or careless handling of articles taken from the arrested person. Arrested persons have also been known to injure themselves—or others—with belts, knives, drugs, or other items on their person while being detained. Dangerous instrumentalities—such as razor blades, bombs, or weapons—can be concealed in innocent-looking articles taken from the arrestee's possession. The bare recital of these mundane realities justifies reasonable measures by police to limit these risks—either while the items are in police possession or at the time they are returned to the arrestee upon his release. Examining all the items removed from the arrestee's person or possession and listing or inventorying them is an entirely reasonable administrative procedure. It is immaterial whether the police actually fear any particular package or container; the need to protect against such risks arises independently of a particular officer's subjective concerns. ... Finally, inspection of an arrestee's personal property may assist the police in ascertaining or verifying his identity .... In short, every consideration of orderly police administration benefiting both police and the public points toward the appropriateness of the examination of respondent's shoulder bag prior to his incarceration.
...

Applying these principles, we hold that it is not "unreasonable" for police, as part of the routine procedure incident to incarcerating an arrested person, to search any container or article in his possession, in accordance with established inventory procedures.

PROBLEMS

1. A police officer patrolling in downtown New York City saw the defendant "continually from the hours of 4:00 P.M. to 12:00 midnight." The officer saw the defendant talking to six or eight persons, who the officer knew from experience were narcotic addicts. The officer did not overhear any of the conversations, nor did he see anything pass between the defendant and the persons. Later in the evening, the officer saw the defendant enter a restaurant and speak to three more known addicts inside the restaurant. Once

again, nothing was overheard and nothing was seen to pass between persons. The defendant ordered pie and coffee in the restaurant and as he was eating, the officer approached him "and told him to come outside." Outside, the officer said to the defendant, "You know what I am after." The defendant "mumbled something and reached into his pocket." The officer also thrust his hand into the same pocket of the defendant and came out with several glassine envelopes, which contained heroine.

Was the heroin lawfully obtained in an authorized search? Explain. Can the heroin be used as evidence in charging the defendant with possession of heroin? Explain. Should the U.S. Supreme Court affirm the defendant's conviction? *Sibron v. New York,* 392 U.S. 40, 88 S.Ct. 1899 (1968).

2. An off-duty police officer was drying himself after a shower in his apartment when he heard a noise at his door. However, the telephone then rang and he answered the telephone. When he looked out of the peephole in his front door into the hall, he saw two men tiptoeing toward the stairway. The officer called the police, put on some clothes, and armed himself with his service revolver. Looking out of the peephole again, he saw the men continuing to tiptoe. The officer had lived in the apartment building for twelve years but did not recognize either of the men as tenants. Believing that the men were attempting to burglarize an apartment, the officer opened the door, stepped out into the hall, and slammed the door loudly behind him. The men immediately ran down the stairs from the sixth floor. The officer caught defendant Peters between the fourth and fifth floors. With Peters in tow, the officer tried to catch the other man but could not. Peters said he was in the building to visit a girl friend but because she was a married woman, he would not give her name. The officer patted Peters down for weapons and discovered a hard object in his pocket. The officer testified that the object did not feel like a gun, but because the object might have been a knife, he removed it from Peters' pocket. It was an opaque plastic envelope containing burglar's tools.

Was the stop and search lawful and proper? Explain. Did the Supreme Court permit the use of the evidence in Peters' trial for possessing burglary tools? Why? *Peters v. New York,* 392 U.S. 40, 88 S.Ct. 1899 (1968).

3. Detectives first noticed the defendant at a ticket counter in the Miami airport. Their attention was drawn to the defendant because he and his two companions behaved in an unusual manner as they left the counter. The other two men talked to one another but not to the defendant. When one of the men saw the detectives who were following the three men, he turned and talked to the other man. When the second man saw the detectives as the men were getting off an escalator, he turned to the defendant and said, "Let's get out of here." He repeated in a lower voice, "Get out of here." The defendant then saw the detectives. A detective testified that the defendant attempted to move away, but his "legs were pumping up and down very fast and not covering much ground, but his legs were as if the person were running in place." Finding that he was not leaving the presence of the detectives, defendant turned to a detective and uttered a vulgar expression.

A detective then showed his badge to the defendant and asked if they might talk. Defendant agreed and the detective suggested they move a short distance to where the other two men and the other detective stood. Both detectives had been identified to all of the men and as they stood in the public area of the airport, the defendant was asked for identification and if he had an airline ticket. When a ticket was produced by one of the other men, the officers asked for consent to search the defendant's luggage. Defendant handed the officer a key to the luggage and three bags of cocaine were found in a suit bag.

Was the procedure used by the officers proper and lawful? Explain. Can the evidence obtained be used in the trial of the three men? Should they be charged with possession with intent to deliver? *Florida v. Rodriguez,* 469 U.S. 1, 105 S.Ct. 308 (U.S.Sup.Ct.1984).

4. Police officers were investigating the robbery of a grocery store and other robberies in the Montgomery, Alabama area. A man held in jail on an unrelated charge told a police officer that "he had heard that Omar Taylor was involved in the (grocery store) robbery." The man did not tell the police where he heard the information, did not provide any details of the crime, and had never provided information to the police before.

Police officers arrested Omar Taylor, and upon arrival at the police station, gave him the *Miranda* warnings. Taylor was fingerprinted, questioned, and placed in a lineup. When victims of the robbery were unable to identify Taylor, he was told that his fingerprints matched those found on objects at the crime scene. After Taylor had a short visit with his girlfriend and a male companion, he signed a waiver-of-rights form and executed a written confession. The form and confession were admitted into evidence.

Were the procedures used by the police lawful and proper? Why? Was the form and confession properly used as evidence? Why? Should the Supreme Court affirm the use of the evidence and Taylor's conviction? *Taylor v. Alabama,* 457 U.S. 687, 102 S.Ct. 2664 (1982).

5. A police officer observed the defendant riding a bicycle slowly through a residential area in the very early morning hours. The officer stopped the petitioner and asked him his name and what he was doing in the area. During this conversation the officer became cognizant of a strong odor of marijuana and saw a clear plastic bag containing a brown substance protruding from petitioner's shirt pocket. Petitioner was thereupon arrested and the contraband seized.

Was the stop of the defendant lawful and proper? Was the evidence obtained properly? Should the defendant be charged and convicted of the possession of marijuana? *Mullins v. Florida,* 366 So.2d 1162 (Fla.Sup.Ct.1978).

6. Portland, Oregon police officers were investigating the strangulation murder of the defendant's wife in her home. The defendant was not living with his wife and voluntarily came into the police station with an attorney for questioning. The defendant was not arrested but probable cause to arrest him existed on the following facts:
   - The fact that there were no signs of a struggle, break-in, or robbery at the scene of the crime "tended to indicate a killer known to the victim rather than a burglar or other stranger."

- "The decedent's son, the only other person in the house that night, did not have fingernails which could have made the lacerations observed on the victim's throat."
- "The defendant and his deceased wife had a stormy marriage and did not get along well."
- The defendant admitted being at the home of his wife on the night of the murder but claimed that he drove back to central Oregon without entering the house or seeing his wife.
- The defendant "volunteered a great deal of information without being asked, yet expressed no concern or curiosity about his wife."

While the defendant and his attorney were in the police station, officers noticed dark spots on the defendant's finger and under his fingernails. The police asked Murphy if they could take a sample of scraping from under his fingernails. Murphy refused and put his hands in his pockets, and was attempting to clean his nails with objects in his pockets.

Was there any way that the police could get samples of scrapings from under Murphy's nails before he destroyed what might be important evidence of the murder? Explain. *Cupp v. Murphy,* 412 U.S. 291, 93 S.Ct. 2000 (1973).

7. The defendant was a resident of Florida. When he arrived at an airport in Puerto Rico, he appeared nervous and kept looking at an armed, uniformed officer standing in the airport. Other than this, there was no reason to suspect that he was carrying contraband. After the defendant claimed his baggage, two police officers stopped him and took him to an office in the airport. Over the defendant's objections, his bags were searched. Marijuana and $250,000 were found.

Because Puerto Rico is part of the United States and is similar to Alaska and Hawaii, was the evidence against the defendant obtained in a lawful and proper manner? Explain. *Torres v. Puerto Rico,* 442 U.S. 465, 99 S.Ct. 2425, 25 CrL 3157 (U.S.Supreme Court, 1979).

NOTES

[1] Florida v. Royer, 460 U.S. 491, 103 S.Ct. 1319 (1983).

[2] United States v. Mendenhall, 446 U.S. 544, 100 S.Ct. 1870 (1980).

[3] Terry v. Ohio, 392 U.S. 1, 88 S.Ct. 1868 (1968).

[4] United States v. Mendenhall, 446 U.S. 544, 100 S.Ct. 1870 (1980).

[5] See note 3 above.

[6] The agent testified that the respondent's behavior fit the so-called drug courier profile—an informally compiled abstract of characteristics thought typical of persons carrying illicit drugs. In this case the agents thought it relevant that (1) the respondent was arriving on a flight from Los Angeles, a city believed by the agents to be the place of origin for much of the heroin brought to Detroit; (2) the respondent was the last person to leave the plane, "appeared to be very nervous," and "completely scanned the whole area where [the agents] were standing"; (3) after leaving the plane the respondent proceeded past the baggage area without claiming any luggage; and (4) the respondent changed airlines for her flight out of Detroit.

[7] 397 U.S. 249, 90 S.Ct. 1029 (1970).

[8] 392 U.S. 1, 88 S.Ct. 1868 (1968).

[9] Advanced Prosecutor Training Program (U.S. Attorney's Office for the District of Columbia and the Institute for Law and Social Research, Washington, D.C.).

[10] 414 U.S. 218, 94 S.Ct. 467 (1973).

[11] 24 Ill.App.3d 864, 321 N.E.2d 718 (1974).

[12] See Howell v. State, 271 Md. 378, 318 A.2d 189 (1974) in which it was stated that "... It is said that four elements must ordinarily coalesce to constitute a legal arrest: (1) an intent to arrest; (2) under a real or pretended authority; (3) accompanied by a seizure or detention of the person; and (4) which is understood by the person arrested. 6A C.J.S. Arrest § 42 (1975) ...".

[13] "The Challenge of Crime in a Free Society," (1966) p. 18.

[14] 442 U.S. at 214, 99 S.Ct. at 2257.

[15] 395 U.S. 752, 89 S.Ct. 2034 (1969).

[16] South Dakota v. Opperman, 428 U.S. 364, 96 S.Ct. 3092 (1976).

[17] Illinois v. LaFayette, 462 U.S. 640, 103 S.Ct. 2605 (1983).

11

Obtaining Evidence by Police Entry Into Private Premises

ENTRY INTO THE HOME OR PREMISES

Each person in the United States has a right of privacy in their home and residence. The Fourth Amendment of the U.S. Constitution protects this right. The U.S. Supreme Court held that an illegal or improper police "physical entry of the home is the chief evil against which the wording of the Fourth Amendment is directed." [1]

The right of privacy in the home has deep roots in Anglo-Saxon law. The U.S. Supreme Court quoted the following statement attributed to William Pitt in 1763:

> The poorest man may in his cottage bid defiance to all the forces of the Crown. It may be frail—its roof may shake—the wind may blow through it—the storm may enter—the rain may enter—but the King of England cannot enter—all his force dares not cross the threshold of the ruined tenement! [2]

Authorities Which Justify Governmental Entry into Private Premises

The Fourth Amendment of the U.S. Constitution forbids "unreasonable searches and seizures" and requires a search warrant unless it can be shown that a court-recognized exception to the warrant requirement of the Fourth Amendment exists. The following are the authorities which would justify entry of law enforcement officers into private premises:

- A search warrant
- Consent to enter given by a person capable of giving consent
- **Exigency** (emergency)
- To arrest a suspect in his own home or residence "for Fourth Amendment purposes, an arrest warrant founded on probable cause implicitly carries with it the limited authority to enter a *dwelling in which the suspect lives* when there is reason to believe the suspect is within." (emphasis added) (The U.S. Supreme Court in *Preston v. United States.*[3])

Fourth Amendment of the U.S. Constitution

The right of the people to be secure in their persons, houses, papers, and effects, against unreasonable searches and seizures, shall not be violated, and no Warrant shall issue, but upon probable cause, supported by Oath or affirmation, and particularly describing the place to be searched, and the persons or things to be seized.

Probable Cause Alone Will Not Justify an Entry into a Home or Residence

Courts throughout the United States have required that governmental officials (including law enforcement officers) respect the right of privacy of homes of suspects. If evidence is obtained without a showing by the government that authority to enter existed, the evidence will be suppressed and cannot be used in a criminal trial.

Probable cause alone will not authorize an entry into a private residence. The following cases illustrate:

Vale v. Louisiana

Supreme Court of the United States (1970)
399 U.S. 30, 90 S.Ct. 1969

The defendant was properly arrested on the front steps of his home after he had just completed a narcotic sale. The officers had probable cause to believe there were further illegal narcotics in the home and proceeded into the home and seized the narcotics. The U.S. Supreme Court held that the entry into the home and the seizure of the narcotics in the home were improper and suppressed the evidence obtained in the home. The Court quoted other Supreme Court decisions, holding that

> "Belief, however well founded, that an article sought is concealed in a dwelling house furnishes no justification for a search of that place without a warrant." *Agnello v. United States,* 269 U.S. 20, 46 S.Ct. 4 (1925). That basic rule "has never been questioned in this Court." *Stoner v. California,* 376 U.S. 483, at 487 n. 5, 84 S.Ct., at 892 n. 5 ....
>
> There is no suggestion that anyone consented to the search. The officers were not responding to an emergency. They were not in hot pursuit of a fleeing felon. The goods ultimately seized were not in the process of destruction. *Schmerber v. California,* 384 U.S. 757, 770–771, 86 S.Ct. at 1835–1836. Nor were they about to be removed from the jurisdiction. *Chapman v. United States,* 365 U.S. 610, 81 S.Ct. 776 (1961).

Riddick v. New York

Supreme Court of the United States (1980)
445 U.S. 573, 100 S.Ct. 1371

Payton v. New York

Supreme Court of the United States (1980)
445 U.S. 573, 100 S.Ct. 1371

These cases were heard together before the Supreme Court because both cases concern entry into private premises without either arrest or search warrants.

After two days of intensive investigation, New York detectives assembled evidence amounting to probable cause to believe that Payton had murdered the manager of a gas station. Six officers went to Payton's apartment in the Bronx, intending to arrest him. Lights were on and music could be heard, but no one responded to knocks on the metal door. When the police forced their way in, no one was in the apartment. In plain view, however, was a 30-caliber shell casing, which was used in the murder case against Payton after he later turned himself in. The question before the Court was whether the entry was lawful and the evidence properly obtained.

Riddick was wanted for two armed robberies. When the police learned of his address, they obtained neither an arrest nor a search warrant. Four officers knocked on his door in Queens at about noon. When his young son opened the door, the police could see Riddick sitting in bed covered by a sheet. The police entered and arrested him. Before permitting him to dress, they opened a chest of drawers near the bed to search for weapons. They found narcotics which were used as evidence in narcotic criminal charges against Riddick.

The U.S. Supreme Court held that the evidence in both cases was improperly obtained and could not be used in the criminal trials of the two men. The Court ruled that

> It is true that an arrest warrant requirement may afford less protection than a search warrant requirement, but it will suffice to interpose the magistrate's determination of probable cause between the zealous officer and the citizen. If there is sufficient evidence of a citizen's participation in a felony to persuade a judicial officer that his arrest is justified, it is constitutionally reasonable to require him to open his doors to the officers of the law. Thus, for Fourth Amendment purposes, an arrest warrant founded on probable cause implicitly carries with it the limited authority to enter a dwelling in which the suspect lives when there is reason to believe the suspect is within.
>
> Because no arrest warrant was obtained in either of these cases, the judgments must be reversed and the cases remanded to the New York Court of Appeals for further proceedings not inconsistent with this opinion.
>
> It is so ordered.

Steagald v. United States

Supreme Court of the United States (1981)
451 U.S. 204, 101 S.Ct. 1642

Ricky Lyons was a federal fugitive with a six-month-old arrest warrant. Drug Enforcement Administration (DEA) officers in the Detroit area obtained information as to the residence Lyons would be at for a day in Atlanta, Georgia. Without a search warrant, DEA officers in Atlanta went to the address. The defendant (who lived there), his wife, and another man were present. Ricky Lyons, however, was not in the premises but narcotics were seen in plain view. A search warrant was obtained and a search of the premises uncovered forty-three pounds of cocaine. The defendant was charged and convicted of federal drug charges. The Court held that the evidence could not be used since the arrest warrant would authorize only an entry of the suspect's own residence "where there is reason to believe the suspect is within." In reversing the conviction, the Court ruled that

> The inconvenience of obtaining such a warrant does not increase significantly when an outstanding arrest warrant already exists. In this case, for example, Agent Goodowens knew the address of the house to be searched two days in advance, and planned the raid from the federal courthouse in Atlanta where, we are informed, three full time magistrates were on duty. In routine search cases such as this, the short time required to obtain a search warrant from a magistrate will seldom hinder efforts to apprehend a felon. Finally, if a magistrate is not nearby, a telephonic search warrant can usually be obtained. See Fed.Rule Crim.Proc. 41(c)(1), (2).
>
> Whatever practical problems remain, however, cannot outweigh the constitutional interests at stake. Any warrant requirement impedes to some extent the vigor with which the Government can seek to enforce its laws, yet the Fourth Amendment recognizes that this restraint is necessary in some cases to protect against unreasonable searches and seizures. We conclude that this is such a case. The additional burden imposed on the police by a warrant requirement is minimal. In contrast, the right protected—that of presumptively innocent people to be secure in their homes from unjustified, forcible intrusions by the Government—is weighty. Thus, in order to render the instant search reasonable under the Fourth Amendment, a search warrant was required.

To make search warrants easier to obtain, an increasing number of states have enacted statutes similar to the federal code, which permits telephonic search warrants (search warrants obtained by telephoning a judge or magistrate).

EXIGENCIES WHICH JUSTIFY POLICE ENTRY INTO HOMES AND PREMISES

Former Chief Justice Warren Burger wrote the following of the "emergency search doctrine" (also known as "exigent circumstances") in 1963: [4]

A warrant is not required to break down a door to enter a burning home to rescue occupants or extinguish a fire, to prevent a shooting or to bring emergency aid to an injured person. The need to protect or preserve life or avoid serious injury is justification for what would be otherwise illegal absent an exigency or emergency. Fires or dead bodies are reported to police by cranks where no fires or bodies are to be found. Acting in response to reports of "dead bodies," the police may find the "bodies" to be common drunks, diabetics in shock, or distressed cardiac patients. But the business of policemen and firemen is *to act*, not to speculate or meditate on whether the report is correct. People could well die in emergencies if police tried to act with the calm deliberation associated with the judicial process. Even the apparently dead often are saved by swift police response. A myriad of circumstances could fall within the terms "exigent circumstances" ... e.g., smoke coming out a window or under a door, the sound of gunfire in a house, threats from the inside to shoot through the door at police, reasonable grounds to believe an injured or seriously ill person is being held within.

Situations which would fall under the **exigency** (emergency) search doctrine may be classified as follows:

- When an officer has reason to believe that a life may be in jeopardy.
- When an officer is in hot pursuit of a person who has committed a crime.
- "Now-or-never" situations in which evidence or contraband such as drugs will be destroyed or moved to another place before a search warrant can be obtained.

If an entry into premises by a law enforcement officer is lawful and proper, the officer then has the right to be where he is. What the officer then sees in plain view (and unexpectedly) comes under the plain-view doctrine and can be seized if there is reason to believe it is evidence of a crime.

When There Is Reason to Believe That a Life May Be Endangered

Exigency entries by police occur every day in American cities. The concern for the safety of persons (usually the elderly) is the usual reason. When a person has not been seen or heard from in some time, there is a normal concern that the person may be ill, have become incapacitated, or have died. Entry into homes may reveal any of these problems, or it may disclose a crime scene and a dead (or injured) victim.

Probably the courts of every state have had dozens of "life-endangered" exigency cases appealed within them. Some of these cases are presented in other chapters of this text. The *Patrick* case is presented here because of the attention it has received over the years:

Patrick v. State

Supreme Court of Delaware (1967)
227 A.2d 486

When an employee did not show up for work, his employer went to his house and found the man's body. The employer immediately called the police and told them of the crime scene and that the man might be dead. Acting on that information, the police entered the dwelling, found the body, and later removed various physical evidence. In holding that the entry was lawful without a search warrant or consent, the Court ruled that

> As a general rule, we think, an emergency may be said to exist, within the meaning of the "exigency" rule, whenever the police have credible information that an unnatural death has, or may have, occurred. And the criterion is the reasonableness of the belief of the police as to the existence of an emergency, not the existence of an emergency in fact.
> . . .
> Applying these tenets to the instant case, we have no doubt that the entry of the police was reasonable under the circumstances. The officers were informed by Larrimore that Woods was dead or dying from a head wound. Clearly, the police had good reason to believe that a life was in balance and that emergency aid might be needed. Under the circumstances, it was the duty of the police to act forthwith upon the report of the emergency—not to speculate upon the accuracy of the report or upon legal technicalities regarding search warrants. It follows that the entry by the police was reasonable and lawful.
> After the entry, there was no further search by the officers. All articles taken were in open view in the room in which the body was found. The seizure of evidence in open view upon a lawful entry violates no right of privacy. *Wayne v. United States, supra.* That which is in open view is not the product of a search.

Arizona v. Hicks

Supreme Court of the United States (1987)
___ U.S. ___, 107 S.Ct. 1149, 40 CrL 3320

(This case is also presented in chapter 9.)
When a man was injured by a bullet which came through the ceiling of his apartment, the police were called. When police officers arrived, they entered the defendant's "apartment to search for the shooter, for other victims and for weapons. They found and seized three weapons, including a sawed-off rifle, and in the course of their search also discovered a stocking-cap mask." The defendant and the courts agreed "that the initial entry and search (by the police), although warrantless, were justified by the exigent (emergency) cir-

cumstances of the shooting." The Court quoted the 1978 U.S. Supreme Court case of *Mincey v. Arizona,* holding that

> a warrantless search must be "strictly circumscribed by the exigency which justifies its initiation."

When an Officer Is in Hot Pursuit of a Person Who Has Committed a Crime

Warden, Md. Penitentiary v. Hayden

Supreme Court of the United States (1967)
387 U.S. 294, 87 S.Ct. 1642

Immediately after the defendant robbed a Baltimore cab company, his flight was observed by two cab drivers who reported that he entered a nearby home. Within minutes, police arrived at the home. Having been given a description of the defendant, they requested entrance and when Mrs. Hayden offered no objections, the police began a search of the home for the defendant. Before finding the defendant, the officers seized a shotgun, a pistol, and clothing similar to the type worn by the fleeing felon. In affirming the use of this evidence and the conviction of the defendant, the U.S. Supreme Court held that

> They (the police) acted reasonably when they entered the house and began to search for a man of the description they had been given and for weapons which he had used in the robbery or might be used against them. The Fourth Amendment does not require police officers to delay in the course of an investigation if to do so would gravely endanger their lives or the lives of others. Speed here was essential and only a thorough search of the house for persons and weapons could have insured that Hayden was the only man present and that the police had control of all weapons which could be used against them or to effect an escape . . . .
> . . . The permissible scope of search must, therefore, at the least, be as broad as may reasonably be necessary to prevent the dangers that the suspect at large in the house may resist or escape.

United States v. Santana

Supreme Court of the United States (1976)
427 U.S. 38, 96 S.Ct. 2406

After the defendant sold heroin and had marked money in her possession, police officers had probable cause to arrest her. The officers identified themselves to the defendant as she stood in the doorway of her home. The defendant retreated into the house and the officers followed and caught her in the vestibule of the home. In holding that the arrest and the evidence obtained in the search incident to the arrest were lawful, the U.S. Supreme Court reversed the lower court's ruling, and held that

> The only remaining question is whether her act of retreating into her house could thwart an otherwise proper arrest. We hold that it could not. In *Warden v. Hayden,* 387 U.S. 294, 87 S.Ct. 1642 (1967), we recognized the right of police, who had probable cause to believe that an armed robber had entered a house a few minutes before, to make a warrantless entry to arrest the robber and to search for weapons. This case, involving a true "hot pursuit," is clearly governed by *Warden;* the need to act quickly here is even greater than in that case while the intrusion is much less. The District Court was correct in concluding that "hot pursuit" means some sort of a chase, but it need not be an extended hue and cry "in and about [the] public streets." The fact that the pursuit here ended almost as soon as it began did not render it any the less a "hot pursuit" sufficient to justify the warrantless entry into Santana's house. Once Santana saw the police, there was likewise a realistic expectation that any delay would result in destruction of evidence .... Once she had been arrested the search, incident to that arrest, which produced the drugs and money was clearly justified.
>
> We thus conclude that a suspect may not defeat an arrest which has been set in motion in a public place, and is therefore proper under *Watson,* (see *United States v. Watson* in chapter 10) by the expedient of escaping to a private place. The opinion of the Court of Appeals is
> Reversed.

Welsh v. Wisconsin

Supreme Court of the United States (1984)
466 U.S. 740, 104 S.Ct. 2091

> Welsh's car was observed weaving dangerously back and forth on a busy highway. He then lost control and the vehicle swerved off the road into an open field. Other motorists stopped and told Welsh that police were being called. When Welsh heard this, he left his car and walked away. Upon arrival, the police were told that Welsh was either very inebriated or sick. A check of the license plate of the car showed that Welsh lived only a few blocks away. When the police rang the doorbell of Welsh's home, Welsh's step-daughter answered the door and, in response to a police question as to whether Welsh was in, answered, "Yes, he just stumbled in." The police then entered the house, found Welsh in bed, and arrested him for drunken driving.
>
> The U.S. Supreme Court reversed Welsh's conviction, holding that the police entry without a warrant or consent was illegal. The Court rejected

public safety arguments, holding that there was little threat that Welsh would get another car and drive in his intoxicated condition. The state also argued a need to obtain evidence of Welsh's blood-alcohol level, but this was also rejected. The focus of the Supreme Court holding was on the fact that in Wisconsin at the time of Welsh's arrest, first offense drunken driving was a civil offense punishable in civil court. No imprisonment was possible for the noncriminal, civil forfeiture offense.

People v. Hampton [5]

California Court of Appeals, First District (1985)
164 Cal.App.3d 27, 209 Cal.Rptr. 905

Most states make first offense drunken driving a criminal offense and punish the conduct as a misdemeanor. In the *Hampton* case, Ms. Hampton was stopped two blocks from her home for drunken driving. She was escorted to her home and told not to drive until she sobered up. After the officer left, Ms. Hampton was seen within a short time driving her car. The police officer lost sight of her car and went to her apartment. When she answered the door she appeared more intoxicated than before. When she backed into her apartment, the officer followed her and arrested her. During the booking search at the jail, cocaine was found in her pocket. In holding that the police procedure was lawful and proper and that the evidence obtained should be used in the drunken driving and possession of cocaine charges, the Court ruled that

> (U.S. Supreme Court) Justice Blackmun emphasized his deep concern with what he perceived to be the nation's unwillingness to do something about drunk drivers, and expressed amazement that Wisconsin still classifies a first offense of driving while intoxicated as a civil violation. (At pp. ___ –___, 104 S.Ct. at pp. 2100–2101.)
>
> California, however, is not so lenient on those who drink and drive. The penalty which attaches to a first conviction of drunk driving in this state indicates that California has a far greater interest in arresting persons suspected of committing such an offense than does Wisconsin. A first offense of driving under the influence in this state is a criminal offense . . . .
>
> . . . In light of *Welsh* and the differences between California and Wisconsin law, we consider the fact that the offense was a misdemeanor rather than a felony as of no significance, and conclude that the warrantless entry was justified to prevent the dissipation or destruction of evidence . . . .
>
> . . . this is an even stronger case than *Santana;* here respondent was actually placed under arrest while at the threshold, i.e., in a public place, whereas in *Santana* the police merely "set in motion" the arrest (by shouting "police") while the defendant was in a public place.

"Now or Never" as an Exigency

Ker v. California

Supreme Court of the United States (1963)
374 U.S. 23, 83 S.Ct. 1623

Having reasonable grounds to believe that Ker had narcotics in his possession, officers followed his car. The officers, however, lost his car when Ker eluded them by a furtive turn. The officers then obtained the address of Ker's apartment from his automobile license number. When Ker's car was found parked at his apartment, the officers obtained a key to his apartment from the apartment manager. Believing that evidence would be destroyed if they made an entry by knocking, the officers made a "no-knock" entry into Ker's apartment by use of the key. In holding that the officer's testimony sustained an exception to the California "knock" requirement, the U.S. Supreme Court affirmed the defendant's conviction and the use of the narcotics seized as evidence in Ker's trial, holding that [6]

> Here, ..., the criteria under California law clearly include an exception to the notice requirement where exigent circumstances are present ....
>
> ... Here justification for the officers' failure to give notice is uniquely present. In addition to the officers' belief that Ker was in possession of narcotics, which could be quickly and easily destroyed, Ker's furtive conduct in eluding them shortly before the arrest was ground for the belief that he might well have been expecting the police. We therefore hold that in the particular circumstances of this case the officers' method of entry, sanctioned by the law of California, was not unreasonable under the standards of the Fourth Amendment as applied to the States through the Fourteenth Amendment.

WHEN CONSENT WOULD JUSTIFY A POLICE ENTRY INTO PRIVATE PREMISES

A person may waive his or her Fourth Amendment rights by consenting to a search of their home or other property in which they have **mutual use** and **joint access or control**. The U.S. Supreme Court and other courts have repeatedly held that when the government seeks to use evidence which was obtained by a "consent search," the government "has the burden of proving that the consent was, in fact, freely and voluntarily given." [7]

Consent to enter a home or apartment is not consent to search. If a law enforcement officer seeks consent to search, they should ask for consent. *Miranda*-type warnings informing the person they have a right to refuse are not required but this would be a factor in determining whether the consent was given voluntarily and intelligently. The U.S. Supreme Court held that "the

"Urgent Need" as Defined by the Dorman Case in Justifying Exigency Entry

Most federal courts and many state courts have recognized the "urgent need" exception as defined by the 1970 case of *Dorman v. United States,* 435 F.2d 385 (D.C.Cir.1970). After robbing a men's clothing store, Harold Dorman left a copy of his monthly probation report, containing his name, in the store. Victims identified a photo of Dorman as one of the robbers. Attempts to obtain an arrest warrant failed because detectives were unable to locate a magistrate. After 10 P.M. officers went to his mother's home. She answered the door and said that neither Dorman nor anyone else was in the home. While officers were talking to the mother, they heard a noise of someone in a back room. The officers rushed by the mother in the doorway, thinking that Dorman was in the home. The noise was made by a boyfriend of the mother. However, in searching for Dorman the officers came upon a new blue suit with unhemmed cuffs, which was stolen in the robbery of the men's store. The officers seized the suit; after Dorman was apprehended, the suit was used as evidence in Dorman's trial for armed robbery. An eight-judge federal appeals court affirmed Dorman's conviction and the use of the suit as evidence. The entry into the home and the search was held to be lawful under the following *Dorman* factors:

- The offense was a grave offense, involving violence.
- The suspect was believed to be armed and dangerous.
- There was reasonably trustworthy evidence of Dorman's guilt beyond a minimal showing of probable cause.
- There was good reason to believe Dorman was on the premises which were entered.
- There was a likelihood Dorman would escape if not apprehended immediately.
- The officers had first attempted to enter by peaceful means and had identified themselves and their purpose.

subject's knowledge of a right to refuse is a factor to be taken into account, the prosecution is not required to demonstrate such knowledge as a prerequisite to establishing a voluntary consent." [8] The following U.S. Supreme Court cases concerned entry into private premises:

Bumper v. North Carolina

Supreme Court of the United States (1968)
391 U.S. 543, 88 S.Ct. 1788

A sixty-six-year-old black grandmother, who lived in a house located in a rural area at the end of an isolated mile-long dirt road, allowed four white law enforcement officers to search her home after they asserted they had a search warrant to search the house. The officers were seeking and obtained evidence which was used in the rape trial of the woman's grandson. There is no statement in the case to indicate that a search warrant ever existed. The State of

---

FBI Articles on Emergency Search of Premises

Commencing in the March 1987 issue of the *FBI Law Enforcement Bulletin* is a series of articles entitled "Emergency Searches of Premises." A few highlights of the articles follow.

- "Courts commonly recognize three threats as providing justification for emergency warrantless action—danger to life, danger of escape, and danger of destruction or removal of evidence."

- "Officers acting without a warrant to neutralize a suspected threat to human life must limit that action to what is necessary to eliminate the danger."

- Quoting the U.S. Supreme Court from the case of *Washington v. Chrisman,* 455 U.S. 1, 102 S.Ct. 812 (1982), holding that ". . . it is not 'unreasonable' under the Fourth Amendment for a police officer, as a matter of routine, to monitor the movements of an arrested person, as his judgment dictates, following the arrest." In the *Chrisman* case, a police officer waited at the door of a dorm room while a student the officer had arrested went into his dorm room to obtain identification. The U.S. Supreme Court held that the officer lawfully entered the room when he observed a marijuana pipe and seeds in the room.

The articles present many cases and extensive discussions of this area of the law.

North Carolina then argued that the alleged consent given by the grandmother was the authority for the search and the justification for the admission of the evidence obtained in the search. In holding the alleged consent to be invalid, the U.S. Supreme Court ruled that

> [w]hen a law enforcement officer claims authority to search a home under a warrant, he announces in effect that the occupant has no right to resist the search. The situation is instinct with coercion—albeit colorably lawful coercion. Where there is coercion there cannot be consent.

Johnson v. United States

Supreme Court of the United States (1948)
333 U.S. 10, 68 S.Ct. 367

> (This case is a favorite of many experienced defense lawyers, some of whom have memorized the citation and parts of the decision for use in oral arguments in courts.)
>
> When officers went to a Seattle hotel to investigate a report that opium was being used, they smelled burning opium in the hotel. When they knocked on the door of the hotel room from which the smell seemed to be originating, a voice asked who was there. "Lieutenant Balland," was the reply. There was a slight delay, some "shuffling or noise," and the door was then opened by the defendant. The officer said, "I want to talk to you a little bit." The defendant then, as the officer described it, "stepped back acquiescently and admitted us."

The officer then said, "I want to talk to you about this opium smell in the room here." The defendant denied that there was such a smell. The officer then told the defendant, "I want you to consider yourself under arrest because we are going to search the room." A search then turned up incriminating opium and smoking apparatus, the latter still warm from recent use. The U.S. Supreme Court, while holding that odors may be "found to be evidence of most persuasive character," ruled that consent did not exist for the entry into the room, stating that

> Entry to defendant's living quarters, which was the beginning of the search, was demanded under color of office. It was granted in submission to authority rather than as an understanding and intentional waiver of a constitutional right.

Chapman v. United States

Supreme Court of the United States (1961)
365 U.S. 610, 81 S.Ct. 776

> The U.S. Supreme Court held that a landlord did not have the authority to consent to the entry and search of a tenant's house by the police, even when there is probable cause to believe that the house is being used for criminal activity (bootlegging).

Stoner v. California

Supreme Court of the United States (1964)
376 U.S. 483, 84 S.Ct. 889

> When a person rents a hotel or motel room they, in most instances, imply their consent to the entry of maids to clean the room and make the bed. The U.S. Supreme Court ruled that this, however, did not authorize hotel or motel employees to consent to police searches of such rooms. In holding that a hotel clerk had no authority to consent to a search of Stoner's room, the Court stated that
>
> > Our decisions make clear that the rights protected by the Fourth Amendment are not to be eroded by strained applications of the law of agency or by unrealistic doctrines of "apparent authority."

Abel v. United States

Supreme Court of the United States (1960)
362 U.S. 217, 80 S.Ct. 683

The defendant was arrested as a Russian spy in his New York hotel room. After the search incident to the arrest, the FBI agents ordered the defendant to get dressed and pack his bags. The defendant then paid his hotel bill and was taken to jail after he checked out of the hotel. FBI agents then obtained permission from the hotel manager to search the defendant's former room. Evidence found in a wastebasket was used in the trial of the defendant. The U.S. Supreme Court affirmed the conviction of the defendant and the use of the evidence, stating that

> at the time of the search petitioner had vacated the room. The hotel then had the exclusive right to its possession, and the hotel management freely gave its consent that the search be made. Nor was it unlawful to seize the entire contents of the wastepaper basket, even though some of its contents had no connection with crime. So far as the record shows, petitioner had abandoned these articles. He had thrown them away. So far as he was concerned, they were *bona vacantia.* There can be nothing unlawful in the Government's appropriation of such abandoned property.

Coolidge v. New Hampshire

Supreme Court of the United States (1971)
403 U.S. 443, 91 S.Ct. 2022

Because there was mutual use and joint access or control, the Supreme Court held that

> where a wife surrendered to the police guns and clothing belonging to her husband, we found nothing constitutionally impermissible in the admission of that evidence at trial since the wife had not been coerced.

United States v. Matlock

Supreme Court of the United States (1974)
415 U.S. 164, 94 S.Ct. 988

The defendant was arrested by FBI agents for bank robbery as he stood in the front yard of a house where he lived with a woman who was not his wife. Three of the agents then went to the door of the house and were admitted into the house by the woman (Mrs. Graff). The agents told Mrs. Graff that they were looking for money from the robbery and a gun, and asked consent to search the house. The trial court found that Mrs. Graff consented to the search (although at the trial of the defendant, she denied that she consented). The agents found $4,995 taken in the robbery in a dirty diaper bag in the closet of the bedroom shared by the defendant and Mrs. Graff.

In affirming the conviction of the defendant, the Supreme Court held that Mrs. Graff had mutual use and joint access or control so as to consent to the search, holding that

> Common authority is, of course, not to be implied from the mere property interest a third party has in the property. The authority which justifies the third-party consent does not rest upon the law of property, with its attendant historical and legal refinements, see *Chapman v. United States,* 365 U.S. 610, . . . (landlord could not validly consent to the search of a house he had rented to another), *Stoner v. California,* 376 U.S. 483, . . . (night hotel clerk could not validly consent to search of customer's room) but rests rather on mutual use of the property by persons generally having joint access or control for most purposes, so that it is reasonable to recognize that any of the co-inhabitants has the right to permit the inspection in his own right and that the others have assumed the risk that one of their number might permit the common area to be searched.

ARRESTS AT THE DOOR OF A HOME OR RESIDENCE

Can law enforcement officers arrest a person for a felony as the person is at the door of a home when the officers do not have a warrant and an exigency does not exist? This question has come before many courts. The better course of action would be, if there is time, to obtain an arrest or search warrant.

If a warrant has not been obtained, then an alternative would be to ask the person to step outside the home or residence, or to ask permission and consent for the police to step inside the home. Arrests made outside the home, or where consent has been given for the police to enter the home, would not violate the Fourth Amendment right of privacy of the home.

The following cases concern arrests at or near the door of a home or residence:

Byrd v. State

Supreme Court of Florida (1985)
481 So.2d 468, 38 CrL 2205

The defendant and his wife, Debra, managed a motel in Tampa. On 13 October 1981, Debra was found murdered in the motel office. A resident of the motel, Robert Sullivan, was arrested and charged with the murder. After interviewing

Sullivan, the police determined that they had probable cause to arrest the defendant. At 2:30 A.M. on October 28, the police arrived at the defendant's residence at the motel. Without a warrant, one of the officers knocked on the defendant's door and identified himself to the defendant through a window. The officer stated that he had previously spoken to the defendant regarding his wife's death. After a few seconds, the defendant opened the door and stepped back. The detective then took a step inside, placed the defendant under arrest for the murder of his wife, and advised him of his rights. The defendant was convicted of first-degree murder and sentenced to death. Defendant appealed, arguing that his confession was the fruit of his illegal arrest and should not have been admitted as evidence. The Supreme Court of Florida affirmed the conviction and use of the confession, holding that

> There is no question that if appellant had been asked to step outside and had complied, the warrantless arrest outside the room would have been proper and Payton would not apply. A significant question arises, however, when a warrantless arrest occurs at or just within the threshold of a residence. We find that the arrest of appellant at the threshold of his residence was the result of a consensual entry. The appellant knew the arresting officer, who had identified himself and requested admission. Appellant voluntarily opened the door and stepped back to admit the officers, at which point he was arrested at the threshold. There is no evidence of deception or forced entry on the part of the police officers. In our view, the appellant consented to the law enforcement officers' entry into the threshold area by voluntarily opening the door, stepping back, and standing in the threshold after knowing who was present; therefore, this was a valid warrantless arrest. In so holding, we choose to accept the view of those courts which have found entries to be consensual where there is no forced entry or deception, and when the defendant knows who is asking for admission and then opens the door. In our opinion, an entry under those circumstances is consensual, at least with respect to the area immediately surrounding the threshold or vestibule entrance of the residence, particularly where the defendant makes no objection. See *United States v. Griffin*, 530 F.2d 739 (1976); *United States v. Sheard*, 473 F.2d 139 (D.C.Cir.1972) cert. denied, 412 U.S. 943, 93 S.Ct. 2784, 37 L.Ed.2d 404 (1973); *Robbins v. Mackinzie*, 364 F.2d 45 (1st Cir.), cert. denied, 385 U.S. 913, 87 S.Ct. 215, 17 L.Ed.2d 140 (1966); *Jones v. State*, 409 N.E.2d 1254 (Ind.App.1980); *State v. McLain, 367 A.2d 213 (Me. 1976).*
>
> There is also a line of cases which have held, in situations analogous to that presented here, that an arrest at or in the threshold of a residence does not involve an entry and therefore, does not implicate Payton considerations. These cases have characterized the threshold area as a public place wherein a warrant is not required to effectuate a valid arrest. See *United States v. Mason*, 661 F.2d 45 (5th Cir.1981); *People v. Morgan*, 113 Ill.App.3d 543, 69 Ill.Dec. 590, 447 N.E.2d 1025 (1983); *People v. Haynes*, 89 Ill.App.3d 231, 44 Ill.Dec. 510, 411 N.E.2d 876 (1980); *State v. Patricelli*, 324 N.W.2d 351 (Minn.1982). (Other cases are: *United States v. Botero*, 589 F.2d 430 (9th Cir.1978) cert. denied, 441 U.S. 944, 99 S.Ct. 2162, 60 L.Ed.2d 1045 (1979) [in response to DEA agents' knock, defendant opens door and is arrested; no war-

rantless entry issue, since agents did not enter to arrest]; *United States v. Mason* (5th Cir.1981) 661 F.2d 45 [arrest at door of home permissible].)

State v. Peters

Missouri Court of Appeals (1985)
695 S.W.2d 140, 37 CrL 2278

Police went to the home of the defendant to arrest him for rape, based upon the complaint of a woman who stated that a "Bill" had raped her at the defendant's address. The defendant answered the door in response to the police knock. When the defendant stated his name was Bill, the police informed him that he was under arrest for rape. Defendant made no resistance but stepped back somewhat. The police then "swarmed into the house" and handcuffed defendant. On a table nearby lay a handgun, some green leafy substance in clear plastic bags, and another container with six folded packets. The police searched these containers and the entire house. The court reversed the defendant's conviction for possession of a controlled substance, holding that

> In the circumstances of a home arrest, it is the location of the person arrested, and not of the arresting officer, that determines whether the arrest occurred in the home. U.S. v. Johnson, 626 F.2d 753, 28 CrL 2065 (CA9 1980). The prosecutor argues, however, that when the defendant answered the door to his home, he relinquished any expectation of privacy due a dweller, and hence the arrest was a public event ....
>
> In U.S. v. Johnson, federal agents acting without a warrant knocked on a suspect's door, confronted him in the doorway with weapons drawn (they outside and he inside the home), and were told to enter. The court determined that the arrest was consummated while the suspect was physically inside the home and was therefore unlawful under Payton because executed without a warrant or exigent circumstances. Santana was distinguished because the suspect there was standing within the frame of her doorway when the officers approached and so was exposed to public view.
>
> We determine that the seizure of the defendant was an in-home, and not a public, arrest, and hence unlawful in the absence of a warrant or exigent circumstances ....
>
> The conviction rests on an illegal arrest, an illegal search, and illegal evidence. The defendant is discharged.

People v. LeVan

New York Court of Appeals (1984)
62 N.Y.2d 139, 476 N.Y.S.2d 101, 464 N.E.2d 469, 35 CrL 2188

Defendant was identified by a witness several days after a Manhattan shooting as the killer. Several times during the following week, police went to defendant's apartment but did not find him home. When a neighbor telephoned to tell police defendant was home, six officers went to the apartment. Neither an arrest warrant nor a search warrant had been obtained during the week. The police waited in the hall for the defendant to come out of his apartment. When a neighbor rang the doorbell and the defendant answered the door, the police rushed the defendant and entered the apartment. Defendant was frisked and handcuffed. When an officer saw the defendant glancing at shoes in a nearby closet, the officer looked inside the shoes and found a handgun which at trial was shown to be the gun used in the killing. The defendant was found not guilty of murder and manslaughter, but was convicted of criminal possession of a weapon. In reversing that conviction, the court held that

[It is clear that in this case defendant was arrested in his apartment and that the police forcibly entered without a warrant and without consent. The fact that the police may have been able to see defendant when he opened his door in response to his neighbor's knock does not affect the constitutional prohibition against such entry. In *Riddick v. New York,* 445 U.S. 573, 100 S.Ct. 1371, 63 L.Ed.2d 639 supra, the companion case to Payton, the police prior to entering Riddick's apartment observed Riddick through a door opened by another occupant to the apartment. The Supreme Court did not find that fact to be significant, and found that the police had no more authority to enter Riddick's apartment to arrest him than they did Payton's.

United States v. Santana, 427 U.S. 38, 96 S.Ct. 2406, 49 L.Ed.2d 300 supra, ... relied upon by the majority below and by the People, concerned a different situation. There, the defendant was seen by the police while outside her home, holding what they believed to be destructible evidence. As the police approached, she retreated into the vestibule of her home and the police, in hot pursuit, followed her in and arrested her there. The court noted that "a suspect may not defeat an arrest which has been set in motion in a public place, and is therefore proper under Watson [*United States v. Watson,* 423 U.S. 411, 96 S.Ct. 820, 46 L.Ed.2d 598] by the expedient of escaping to a private place." (427 U.S. p. 43.) Santana furnishes no support for the actions of the police in this case, given the Supreme Court's pronouncement in Payton that "the Fourth Amendment has drawn a firm line at the entrance to the house. Absent exigent circumstances, that threshold may not reasonably be crossed without a warrant." (445 U.S. p. 590, 100 S.Ct., p. 1382).

The error in failing to suppress the gun seized in the search incident to defendant's unlawful arrest was not harmless . . . .

The arrest of defendant was improper. The police had neither a warrant nor consent to enter defendant's apartment. There was an affirmed finding that no exigent circumstances existed; the police themselves cannot by their own conduct create an appearance of exigency. The gun seized in defendant's apartment and testimony as to its discovery there, as fruits of that unlawful arrest, should have been suppressed, and their admission was not harmless error.

State v. Holeman

Court of Appeals of Washington (1984)
37 Wash.App. 283, 679 P.2d 422

[On April 27, 1982, two Seattle police officers went to Holeman's home to question (David Holeman) about the theft of a bicycle. The officers had no warrant for Holeman's arrest. David's father, Clarence Holeman, met the officers at the door, called David to the door, and a discussion followed. During the discussion, David's father became angry, causing the officers to believe they should question David at the police station. They then advised David of his *Miranda* rights, and that they were going to take him down to the station to continue the questioning. When one of the officers reached through the doorway to take David by the arm, David's father grabbed a crowbar and raised it above his head in a position indicating a threat to use it as a weapon against the officers. In response, the police officers drew their guns and entered the house to disarm Clarence Holeman and place him under arrest.

David and his older brother attempted to prevent their father's arrest and were both formally arrested for obstructing a public servant. At the police station, David was again advised of his *Miranda* rights, which he waived in writing. He then gave Officer Pike an oral confession and directed the officer to the location where the missing bicycle was hidden. David then signed a typewritten statement for Officer Pike.

The Court of Appeals affirmed the convictions, holding that

[David contends that his typewritten statement should have been suppressed because his warrantless arrest inside his home violated his rights under the fourth amendment of the United States Constitution, citing *Payton v. New York,* 445 U.S. 573, 100 S.Ct. 1371, 63 L.Ed.2d 639 (1980). We do not agree.

We agree that when the officers advised David of his *Miranda* rights and attempted to take him into their physical custody while he was standing inside the threshold of his home, they were attempting to make an unlawful arrest . . . . There were no exigent circumstances justifying that arrest.

Clarence Holeman was not justified, however, in threatening the officers with the crowbar . . . .

The assault was not justified by the fact that his actions were in response to an attempted invalid arrest of his son because David was never in actual danger of physical injury. Therefore, Clarence Holeman's arrest was legal.

It is immaterial that all the arrests arose out of the officers' initial attempt to unlawfully arrest David . . . .

Because Clarence Holeman's arrest was legal, David's arrest for obstructing was valid. It follows that the trial court was correct in denying his motion to suppress the voluntary statement he gave to the police officer following that valid arrest.

Judgment affirmed.

ARE HALLWAYS AND STAIRS IN APARTMENT BUILDINGS, ETC., PART OF A SUSPECT'S HOME UNDER THE PAYTON RULE?

Does a suspect who lives in an apartment building have the same right of privacy in the apartment hallway that he has in his apartment? Would an arrest in an apartment hallway be held to be an arrest in a public place or an arrest in the suspect's home? This was the issue in the following case:

United States v. Holland

United States Court of Appeals, Second Circuit (1985)
755 F.2d 253, review denied 471 U.S. 1125, 105 S.Ct. 2657 (U.S.Sup.Ct.1985)

On February 4, 1983, Deputy Sheriff James Robinson, who was participating with other officers in a drug bust, rang the bell for appellee's apartment at the ground floor entranceway to the common hallway. Appellee and Robinson were friends, or at least acquaintances, and appellee knew that Robinson was a police officer. When Robinson rang the bell, appellee left his second floor apartment, walked down a flight of stairs to the first floor, then down another flight of stairs to a hallway or vestibule leading to the outer door. Recognizing Robinson, he opened the door to him. The district court found that appellee was not induced to open the door as the result of police deception or coercion.

When the door was opened, Robinson drew his gun, displayed his badge and said, "Doc, this is business." From that time on, appellee's liberty of movement was restricted, and he could not reasonably have believed that he was free to leave. He was under arrest.

In holding that the arrest was lawful and that evidence obtained as a result of the arrest could be used, the Court stated that

We see no need to treat this as a "threshold" case. Assuming that appellee's arrest took place in the vestibule or hallway, it nevertheless did not take place in appellee's "home".

Although the Supreme Court has accorded apartments and hotel rooms status as "homes" for Fourth Amendment purposes, it has never given the same status to adjoining common hallways . . . .

Moreover, we never have held that the common areas must be accessible to the public at large nor have we required a quantified amount of daily traffic through the area as a basis for determining that a common area is beyond an individual's protected zone of privacy . . . .

This rule gives tenants the benefit of much-needed police protection in common hallways, while it preserves for them the privacy of their actual places of abode, their apartments. It also lays down a clearly-defined boundary line for constitutionally permissible police action . . . .

. . . In addition to protecting the public against the untoward effect of a "constable's blunder", it protects the "constable" against potential civil liability under 42 U.S.C. § 1983 resulting from an erroneous determination as to whether the door to a tenant's "home" is his apartment door or a door at the other end of a common hallway. We see no reason why the rule should not be applied in the instant case.

In passing along the common ways in his building on any given day, including the day of his arrest, appellee reasonably might expect to meet the landlord or his agents, the occupants of the first floor apartment, deliverymen, tradesmen, or one or more visitors to the first floor apartment . . . . He had no right to exclude them from the common hallway, and there is no indication that he ever tried to do so.

ORDERING SUSPECTS OUT OF PREMISES

If law enforcement officers have authority to enter premises (exigency, consent, arrest or search warrant), they could then order a suspect out of premises. If they do not have the authority to enter, they do not have the authority to order out. For example, homeowners come back to their residence to discover a burglar in their home. The suspect is still in the home when the police arrive. The burglar is illegally in the premises and has no lawful right of privacy in the home. The police order the man out (to which the homeowners tacitly approve). The arrest would be lawful and any evidence obtained (confession, concealed weapon, drugs, etc.) could be used against him under ordinary circumstances.

The following cases illustrate:

People v. Trudell

California Court of Appeals, First District (1985)
173 Cal.App.3d 122, 219 Cal.Rptr. 679, 38 CrL 2188

Police had probable cause to arrest the defendant for kidnapping and rape. They had neither an arrest warrant nor a search warrant when they were told by the defendant's mother that the defendant was in his brother's house. In a telephone conversation with a police dispatcher, the defendant agreed to step out of the house. When he did not do this and when he did not answer the doorbell and calls to him, the police used a loudspeaker and ordered him out of the house by name. In holding that the police procedure was proper, the court ruled that

Here, the officers were investigating a recent violent offense—the forcible kidnap and rape of a 14-year-old child; the defendant was thought to be armed and violent; his accomplice had just been arrested and had implicated him; the defendant had no fixed address; he knew that he was wanted for a violent crime; and the officers knew that he had just learned about their interest in him. Given the gravity of the underlying offense and the other attending circumstances, the officers reasonably believed that an immediate arrest was necessary to ensure public safety and prevent the defendant from escaping. Moreover, there was sufficient exigency to excuse the warrant requirement.

United States v. Morgan

United States Court of Appeals, Sixth Circuit (1984)
744 F.2d 1215, review denied U.S. Supreme Court 37 CrL 4034

An unknown bystander informed a law enforcement officer that the defendant had a trunkful of automatic weapons in his car and that the defendant and his friends had threatened to kill anyone who tried to arrest them. The officer had seen five or six persons loading guns into the trunk of a blue Cadillac. In the next hour to two hours, law enforcement officers were assembled but no effort was made to obtain a search warrant. Police then surrounded the defendant's home. The show of force—spotlights, a bullhorn ordering defendant out of the house, and the blocking of the defendant's car—was held to constitute an arrest of the defendant in his home. The only weapon violation was a .45-caliber pistol found inside the door of the defendant's home. All other weapons were lawful. In suppressing the evidence and holding that no exigency existed, the court ruled that

Absent exigent circumstances, police officers may not enter an individual's home or lodging to effect a warrantless arrest or search. *Payton v. New York.* .... Moreover, the burden is on the government to demonstrate exigency .... Also, a district court's factual finding on the existence of exigent circumstances will not be disturbed unless clearly erroneous .... [T]he critical time for determining whether exigency exists "is the moment of the warrantless entry by the officers" onto the premises of the defendant. *U.S. v. Killebrew,* 560 F.2d 729 (CA6 1977).

The record here reveals no exigency sufficient to justify the warrantless entry of the home and arrest of Morgan. None of the traditional exceptions justifying abandonment of the warrant procedure are present here. The officers involved were not in hot pursuit of a fleeing suspect .... Chief Alcorn specifically testified that he and his officers had sufficient time to assemble at a local coffee shop where they "assessed the situation" and waited for Sheriff Reynolds' arrival before proceeding to the Morgan home ....

The United States argues no warrant was required because the police conduct constituted a "cursory safety check," which is a recognized exception to the warrant requirement. See *U.S. v. Kolodziej,* 706 F.2d 590, 596–97, 33 CrL 2461 (5th Cir.1983) (and cases cited therein). We disagree. To satisfy the cursory safety check exception "the government must show that there was 'a serious and demonstrable potentiality for danger.' " ... As found by the district court, the evidence "shows that the occupants of the [Morgan] house were peaceful until startled by Officer Alcorn's car coming up their driveway in a clandestine manner." Moreover, Morgan's prior contact with police officials had been friendly and cooperative. There was no substantiated evidence that Morgan was dangerous or that a grave offense or crime of violence had occurred or was even threatened ....

Finally, there can be no claim that immediate police action was needed to prevent the destruction of vital evidence or thwart the escape of known criminals ....

In sum, there were no exigent circumstances justifying the warrantless intrusion by the police onto the Morgan property. As Chief Alcorn testified, Morgan's arrest was a planned occurrence, rather than the result of an ongoing field investigation .... Therefore, a warrant should have been obtained before proceeding to the Morgan home....

As an alternative justification for its actions, the United States argues that the facts here, "at the very least," provided the reasonable suspicion of a weapons violation necessary to support a brief investigatory stop of Morgan and his group. See *Terry v. Ohio,* 392 U.S. 1 (1968). The government then contends that once Morgan appeared at the door holding a weapon in plain view, the police were justified in immediately arresting him and seizing the weapon. Even assuming the validity of this legal theory, the police conduct outside of the Morgan home cannot be characterized as a brief investigatory stop. On the contrary, the record provides ample proof that, "as a practical matter, [Morgan] was under arrest," *Florida v. Royer,* 460 U.S. 491, 32 CrL 3095 (1983), as soon as the police surrounded the Morgan home, and therefore, the arrest violated Payton because no warrant had been secured. The police show of force and authority was such that a "reasonable person would have believed he was not free to leave." *U.S. v. Mendenhall,* 446 U.S. 544, 554–55, 27 CrL 3127 (1981). To describe the encounter between the police and Morgan as a "brief investigatory stop" ignores the facts of this case .... Viewed objectively, Morgan was placed under arrest, without the issuance of a warrant, at the moment the police encircled the Morgan residence.

USING TRICK, RUSE, OR SUBTERFUGE TO GAIN ENTRANCE TO PREMISES OR TO LURE SUSPECTS OUT

The leading case on gaining entrance to a person's home by deception is that of *Lewis v. United States,* in which an undercover police officer using a false name was invited into Lewis' home so that Lewis could sell the officer narcotics. That case and other cases in which tricks or deceptions were used follow:

Lewis v. United States

Supreme Court of the United States (1966)
385 U.S. 206, 87 S.Ct. 424

When a stranger telephoned "Duke" Lewis and asked about the possibility of purchasing drugs, Lewis invited him to his home after the man stated that a mutual friend recommended him. The man arrived at Duke's home and Duke sold him marijuana. Another sale was made in Lewis' home at a later date, at which time Lewis was arrested and charged with the violation of the narcotic statutes. The stranger whom Lewis had invited into his home was not "Jimmy the Pollack," as he had stated, but was a law enforcement officer. The U.S. Supreme Court noted that Lewis did not use entrapment as a defense "as he could not on the facts of this case." The defense argument was that the deception used by the officer violated the Fourth Amendment. In affirming Lewis' conviction, the Supreme Court held that

> Were we to hold the deceptions of the agent in this case constitutionally prohibited, we would come near to a rule that the use of undercover agents in any manner is virtually unconstitutional *per se*. Such a rule would, for example, severely hamper the Government in ferreting out those organized criminal activities that are characterized by covert dealings with victims who either cannot or do not protest. A prime example is provided by the narcotics traffic.
>
> The fact that the undercover agent entered petitioner's home does not compel a different conclusion. Without question, the home is accorded the full range of Fourth Amendment protections .... But when, as here, the home is converted into a commercial center to which outsiders are invited for purposes of transacting unlawful business, that business is entitled to no greater sanctity than if it were carried on in a store, a garage, a car, or on the street. A government agent, in the same manner as a private person, may accept an invitation to do business and may enter upon the premises for the very purposes contemplated by the occupant. Of course, this does not mean that, whenever entry is obtained by invitation and the locus is characterized as a place of business, an agent is authorized to conduct a general search for incriminating materials; a citation to the *Gouled* case,[9] ... is sufficient to dispose of that contention.

People v. Porras

California Court of Appeal, 1st Div. (1979)
99 Cal.App.3d 874, 160 Cal.Rptr. 627

Police did not have authority to enter an apartment, but did have information from an informant as to continuous narcotic activities for over two months. When the informant stated that the occupants of the apartment were then manicuring marijuana on the kitchen table and that they kept the LSD, the amphetamines, and the proceeds from the drug sales in a silver-gray metal tool box in the apartment, a police officer made a telephone call to the apartment. Without identifying himself, he told the occupants that he had been arrested after purchasing narcotics in the apartment. The officer informed the occupants that they should "get rid of the dope" because the police were coming with a search warrant and would be at the apartment in twenty minutes. Within a short time, men came running out of apartment. The defendant was carrying the tool box. When the police ordered him to stop, he continued to run. Defendant tripped and dropped the tool box, which he left behind. Police opened the box and found the contraband. Defendant was apprehended later. The Court of Appeal affirmed defendant's conviction. The Court quoted another California appellate court, holding that

> Many cases have held that the mere fact that a suspect is led to incriminate himself by use of some ruse or stratagem does not make the evidence thus obtained inadmissible. We cite, merely for illustration: *Hoffa v. United States* (1966) 385 U.S. 293, 87 S.Ct. 408, 17 L.Ed.2d 374; *Lewis v. United States* (1966) 385 U.S. 206, 87 S.Ct. 424, 17 L.Ed.2d 312; *People v. Ramirez* (1970) 4 Cal.App.3d 154, 84 Cal.Rptr. 104; *People v. Tambini* (1969) 275 Cal.App.2d 757, 762, 80 Cal.Rptr. 179; *People v. Boulad* (1965) 235 Cal.App.2d 118, 126, 45 Cal.Rptr. 104. As the Attorney General points out, were we to accept the defense argument made in the cases at bench, all under-cover activity would likewise be proscribed. Where the ruse does no more than to cause a defendant, activated by his own decision, to do an incriminating act—whether that act be a sale to an undercover agent or a jettisoning of incriminating material—no illegality exists.

State v. Myers

Washington Supreme Court (1984)
102 Wash.2d 548, 689 P.2d 38, 36 CrL 2047

Police officers had a valid search warrant to search for heroin in the defendant's home, but they knew that Myers had a double front door with the first door made of cast iron grill. Myers would open the inner normal door to speak to callers and keep the iron grill door locked. The officers also believed that Myers opened the inner door with a handgun in his possession or nearby.

For these reasons, the officers developed a ruse to get Myers to open the iron door. They prepared a fictitious arrest warrant for a traffic offense in Myers' name and signed with the name of a phony judge. As several officers waited a block away, two detectives knocked on Myers' door. When he opened the inside door, they showed him the arrest warrant. When Myers replied that a mistake had been made, the officers asked to use the phone to clear the matter up. Myers agreed and invited the detectives in. At that point, testimony of Myers and the officers diverged. The officers testified that the detectives summoned the other officers, advised Myers they had a search warrant, and entered in response to his statement that they could enter and that he had nothing to hide. The search produced heroin, paraphernalia, and a large amount of cash.

Myers testified that the officers forced their way in at gunpoint as soon as he opened the iron gate and that he was not told the true purpose of the entry until 45 or 50 minutes later. The trial court believed the officers.

The Court affirmed the use of the evidence obtained and the defendant's conviction, holding that

> The general rule is that entry by ruse is permissible if no force is used. See Annot., What Constitutes Compliance With Knock-And-Announce Rule in Search of Private Premises—State Cases, 70 ALR3d 217 (1976), § 10.5, at 12 (Supp.1983) (state cases); Annot., What Constitutes Violation at 18 USCS § 3109 Requiring Federal Officer to Give Notice of His Authority and Purpose Prior to Breaking Open Door or Window or Other Part of House to Execute Search Warrant, 21 ALR Fed. 820, §§ 11, 13 (1974) (federal cases). Although the U.S. Supreme Court has not yet clearly spoken on the issue, language in some of its cases tends to support the majority rule. See *Lewis v. United States,* 385 U.S. 206, 87 S.Ct. 424, 17 L.Ed.2d 312 (1966), in which the Supreme Court seemed to approve of "covert dealings" and "the use of decoys" in narcotics cases.

> Washington courts have been more specific in their approval. In *State v. Huckaby,* 15 Wash.App. 280, 549 P.2d 35 (1976), the court stated: "The use of deception to gain entry to a premises, as long as no force is involved, has long been considered proper police practice, and in such cases law enforcement officers need not announce their identity, authority, and purpose under the 'knock and announce' rule . . . .

> In short, it seems that since an occupant cannot deny entry to police in possession of a search warrant, he loses nothing in terms of privacy when the officers fail to state their actual authority and purpose, but rather obtain permission to enter by means of a trick or ruse . . . .

> Our refusal to apply the exclusionary rule in this case should in no way be read to condone the use of a bogus judicial warrant . . . . Repeated use of fictitious warrants invites disobedience and confrontation . . . .

State v. Ahart

Iowa Supreme Court (1982)
324 N.W.2d 317, 32 CrL 2125

Two officers in plain clothes parked an unmarked police car in front of defendant's home and acted as if the car had engine trouble. One of the officers knocked at defendant's door and told the person who answered the door that his car had broken down and asked to use the telephone. The officer was allowed to enter and pretended to place a credit card call and to talk to someone. While doing this, the officer looked around and observed marijuana and drug paraphernalia in the room. The officer then went back to his car and left the area. Several days later a search warrant was issued on this information. As a result of the search, evidence was obtained to charge and convict the defendant of the possession of marijuana. In holding that the evidence could not be used and in reversing the conviction, the court ruled that

> We hold that if the police effect a ruse to obtain entry to a home based only on conjecture of criminal activity, incriminating evidence seen in plain view in the home does not provide probable cause to issue a subsequent search warrant. [*End Text*]

A warrantless entry gained by ruse is legitimate if the officer-agent had some rational basis to suspect criminal activity before he effected a ruse to gain entry into a defendant's home or motel room. However, we also recognize that the security of one's home against arbitrary intrusion by the police is at the core of the Fourth Amendment.

It is our conclusion that consent given to a warrantless entry to a private home is invalid if the police, absent a show of cause, obtain entry by ruse .... [T]his cause may be based on the officer's participation with the consentor in an illegal transaction or it may be grounded on a reasonable belief that criminal activity is afoot. The consent is clearly invalid, however, when there is no reason shown for selecting a particular home to enter. We hold that a search is patently unreasonable as an arbitrary intrusion when it is based upon consent obtained by deception unless there is a justifiable and reasonable basis for the deception.

In this case, however, we are unable to determine whether the police had any reason whatsoever to believe that criminal activity was afoot in the Ahart home. The officers failed to articulate any cause for the ruse and the record is devoid of any indicia of logical connection between the ruse and legitimate law enforcement. We are forced to conclude that the intrusion was based on mere conjecture or idle curiosity. Police intrusion into a home based on mere conjecture suggests that officers are entering homes randomly in hope of discovering incriminating evidence.

Commonwealth v. Poteete

Pennsylvania Superior Court (1980)
274 Pa.Super. 490, 418 A.2d 513, 26 CrL 2445

To get into a burglary suspect's home, a Pennsylvania officer used the ruse that he wanted to ask some questions about a car previously reported as stolen. When the officer saw that furniture in the home fit the description of the stolen property, the officer informed the defendant that he was a suspect in the burglaries and advised him of his *Miranda* warnings. When the defendant refused to allow the officer to examine the furniture more closely, the officer left and returned two hours later with a search warrant. Photographs were then taken of the furniture, and used as evidence in the defendant's criminal trial. In holding that the photographs should not have been used as evidence, the court reversed the defendant's conviction, ruling that

Courts have permitted police officers to use ruses and concealment of their identities to investigate crimes which cannot be effectively investigated without such techniques, such as violations of vice, liquor, narcotics and racketeering laws. See *Hoffa v. United States,* 385 U.S. 293, 87 S.Ct. 408, 17 L.Ed.2d 374 (1966); *Commonwealth v. Weimer,* 262 Pa.Super. 69, 396 A.2d 649 (1978). Courts, however, have held invalid consents to searches of the home where officers, having identified themselves, misrepresent their purpose in seeking entry ....

This case is not one of vice, racketeering or any of the other crimes which, by their nature, police need often investigate by ruses and deceptions .... Nor is this case one in which appellant mistakenly placed his confidence in an individual who, contrary to fact, appeared unconnected to police agencies .... Rather, it is one in which an officer misrepresented his purpose in order to gain entrance to a home. In the circumstances of this case, the misrepresentation rendered involuntary appellant's consent.

Denying the police use of such deception does not add any extra burden to their task of investigating crimes. Rather, to allow use of such deception would authorize police conduct otherwise impermissible. There is no reason why Westcott, simply because he was engaged in investigating another, unrelated matter concerning appellant, should have been able to conduct an investigation into appellant's involvement in the burglaries by means otherwise denied him.

"KNOCK" OR "NO-KNOCK" REQUIREMENTS FOR POLICE ENTRY INTO PRIVATE PREMISES

Law enforcement agents who have authority to enter private premises are obligated to knock, identify themselves, state their purpose, and await a refusal or silence before entering. There are two good reasons for imposing these requirements and forbidding unannounced police entries into private premises:

- *Possibility of mistake.* "... cases of mistaken identity are surely not novel in the investigation of crime. The possibility is very real that the police may be misinformed as to the name or address of a suspect, or as to other material information .... Innocent citizens should not suffer the shock, fright or embarrassment attendant upon an unannounced police intrusion." U.S. Supreme Court in *Ker v. California* (see case in this chapter).

- *Protection of the officers.* "... (It) is also a safeguard for the police themselves who might be mistaken for prowlers and be shot down by a fearful householder." U.S. Supreme Court in *Miller v. United States* (see case in this section).

Although "knock-and-announce" entries are the most usual type of police entry, a "no-knock" entry would be justified if one or more of the following conditions can be shown:

- Such notice would be likely to endanger the life or the safety of the officer or another person; or

- Such notice would be likely to result in the evidence subject to seizure being easily and quickly destroyed or disposed of (see *Ker v. California* in this chapter); or

- Such notice would be likely to enable the escape of a party to be arrested; or

- Such notice would be a useless gesture.

In order to justify a no-knock entry when no prior notice was given, the officer would have to point to evidence which would give him the authority to enter without announcement.

The following U.S. Supreme Court cases illustrate entry problems:

Miller v. United States

Supreme Court of the United States (1958)
357 U.S. 301, 78 S.Ct. 1190

In a "buy-and-bust" operation, narcotic officers provided an informant with $100 in marked currency to purchase heroin from the defendant. After the buy was made, the informant did not have the marked money on his person but did have heroin purchased from the defendant. Narcotic officers without an arrest or search warrant then went to the defendant's apartment at 3:45 A.M. to arrest the defendant and obtain evidence of the criminal transaction. The officers knocked and when a voice within the apartment asked, "Who's there?", the officer responded in a low voice, "Police." The defendant opened the door with an attached door chain and asked what the officers were doing there. Before the officers could answer, the defendant attempted to close the door. The officers then forced their way into the apartment, arrested the defendant, and obtained the marked money, which was used as evidence. In holding that the use of deception and then force was not a lawful police entry, the Supreme Court ruled that

> The single fact known to the officers upon which the Government relies is the "split-second" occurrence in which the petitioner evinced "instantaneous resistance to their entry," an "almost instinctive attempt to bar their entry after they [the officers] had identified themselves as police ...." It is argued that this occurrence "certainly points up that he knew their purpose immediately ... [and], at once, realized that he had been detected and that the officers were there to arrest him"; that "[i]t would be wholly unrealistic to say that the officers had not made their purpose known because they did not more formally announce that they were there to arrest him."
>
> But first, the fact that petitioner attempted to close the door did not of itself prove that he knew their purpose to arrest him. It was an ambiguous act. It could have been merely the expected reaction of any citizen having this experience at that hour of the morning, particularly since it does not appear that the officers were in uniform, and the

answer "Police" was spoken "in a low voice" and might not have been heard by the petitioner so far as the officers could tell.

Second, petitioner's reaction upon opening the door could only have created doubt in the officers' minds that he knew they were police intent on arresting him. On the motion to suppress, agent Wilson testified that "he wanted to know what we were doing there." This query, which went unanswered, is on its face inconsistent with knowledge . . . .

. . . Every householder, the good and the bad, the guilty and the innocent is entitled to the protection designed to secure the common interest against unlawful invasion of the house. The petitioner could not be lawfully arrested in his home by officers breaking in without first giving him notice of their authority and purpose. Because the petitioner did not receive that notice before the officers broke the door to invade his home, the arrest was unlawful, and the evidence seized should have been suppressed.

Sabbath v. United States

Supreme Court of the United States (1968)
391 U.S. 585, 88 S.Ct. 1755

William Jones was detained at the Mexico-California border and admitted to transporting cocaine from Mexico into California. He agreed to cooperate and delivered the cocaine to the defendant's apartment in Los Angeles. The customs agents waited outside for five to ten minutes. They then went to the apartment door. One officer knocked, waited a few seconds, and after receiving no response, opened the unlocked door and entered the apartment with his gun drawn. The defendant was arrested after he was seen placing cocaine under a cushion. In holding that the entry was unlawful, the Court ruled that

this record does not reveal any substantial basis for excusing the failure of the agents here to announce their authority and purpose. The agents had no basis for assuming petitioner was armed or might resist arrest, or that Jones was in any danger. Nor, as to the former, did the agents make any independent investigation of petitioner prior to setting the stage for his arrest with the narcotics in his possession.

POLICE ENTRY ONTO PRIVATE LAND

There is no right of privacy in open fields by the owner or any other person (see the open-field cases in chapter 9). Law enforcement officers may enter open fields without a warrant or court order, but there would be no authority to dig holes or to do other damage to such property without a court order or consent by the owner.

There is a right of privacy to the "curtilage," which has been defined as "that area near the dwelling itself which a person has a right to close off from public traffic."[10]

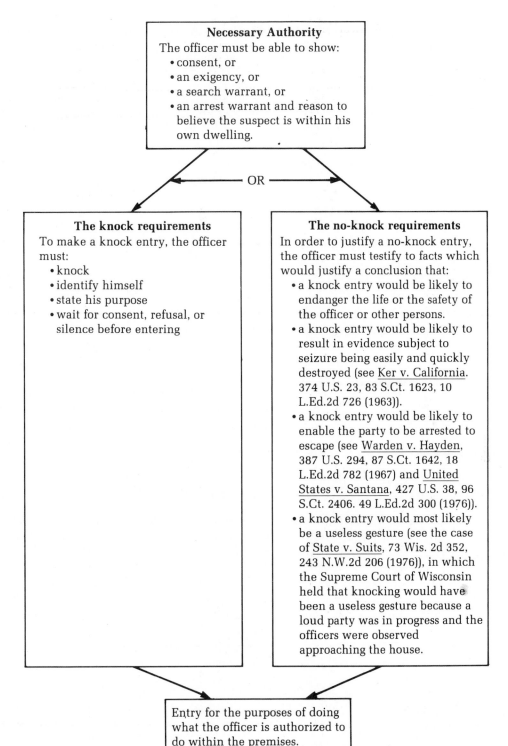

Figure 11.1 Police Entry into Private Premises

Police Entry onto Private Land to Make an Arrest or to Investigate Criminal Activity

The Restatement (Second) of Torts, sec. 204 at p. 381 provides that

> The privilege to make an arrest for a criminal offense carries with it the privilege to enter land in the possession of another for the purpose of making such an arrest, if the person sought to be arrested is on the land or if the actor reasonably believes him to be there.

The following case illustrates the privilege of law enforcement to go onto private land for the purposes of investigating criminal activity:

Prahl v. Brosamle

Wisconsin Court of Appeals (1981)
98 Wis.2d 130, 295 N.W.2d 768

A Wisconsin sheriff's department received a report that shots were fired at four boys biking in the area of the Prahl property. Because it was believed that the shots came from the Prahl property, officers properly entered onto Prahl's land to investigate the incident. However, the court held that a sheriff lieutenant had no authority to give consent to a TV crew entering the land for filming purposes. Prahl filed a civil lawsuit for whatever damages he could prove resulted from the trespass of the TV crew. Because the sheriff lieutenant participated in the trespass by consenting, he was also a party to the trial which was ordered.

Police Entry onto Private Land for Other Legitimate Purposes

Many legitimate purposes exist to justify the entry of law enforcement officers onto private land to contact the owner or resident. The officers could be serving civil or criminal papers on the occupants; they might be checking voting registration lists; they may be investigating a complaint from a neighbor (or want to talk to the occupant regarding the complaint); they may be notifying the occupant of an ordinance or state law violation (such as failure to clear sidewalks of snow and ice, or a weed problem). They may seek information from the occupant regarding a vehicle parked in front of their premises, or whether they had any information regarding a criminal incident or a missing person or child. The following cases further illustrate:

Avenson v. Zegart

U.S. District Court, Eastern District of Minnesota (1984)
577 F.Supp. 958

Because there was neither a gate nor a no-trespassing sign, a deputy sheriff and a humane society director could enter onto property to inform owners of complaints against their business of dog breeding. When nobody answered the door, the two men walked toward the barn, where they observed a number of diseased dogs. This evidence was held to be properly obtained to be used to justify the issuance of a search warrant.

United States v. Messerly

United States District Court of Montana (1982)
530 F.Supp. 751

After receiving descriptions of items which were allegedly stolen, law enforcement officers went to the residence of the defendant. The owner of the stolen property had stated that he saw one of the stolen items near the residence of the defendant. When the officers were on the defendant's property, they saw items matching the description of the stolen property. The defendant's wife then appeared and refused the officers' request to search the premises. The officers then obtained two search warrants on the basis of their information and observations to search defendant's premises and his vehicle. In affirming the use of the evidence obtained and in affirming the defendant's conviction, the court held that

> the plain view doctrine does not require that an officer's presence at a vantage point from which he observes evidence must be justified by warrant to search or by "hot pursuit" or the search incident to arrest rationale; rather, a legitimate reason for the officer's presence unconnected with a search against a defendant will suffice to legitimize the officer's presence at the vantage point .... Thus, the "plain view" doctrine has been applied where a police officer is not searching but nonetheless inadvertently comes across an incriminating object ....
>
> In determining the propriety of the application of the "plain view" doctrine to the factual situation now before this court, it must first be determined whether the initial intrusion of Chief Halver and Agent Wixson upon the property of the defendant was justified or whether it was tantamount to a search.
>
> It is firmly established that a police officer who in the performance of his duty enters upon private property to ask preliminary questions of the occupants thereof does not commit an illegal search. *United States v. Hersh,* 464 F.2d 228 (9th Cir.1972); *Davis v. United States,* 327 F.2d 301 (9th Cir.1964) ....
>
> A review of the surrounding circumstances leading to the entry of the defendant's property in the present case, convinces this court that the entry was legitimate. The entry was in a reasonable manner for the purpose of asking investigatory questions and not with the intent to search or make an arrest. The fact that certain stolen objects fell within the plain view of the officers does not serve to make this legitimate entry an unlawful search. In this context, it is clear that the evidence which was in plain view should not be regarded as having been discovered through a search.

United States v. Ventling

United States Court of Appeals, Eighth Circuit (1982)
678 F.2d 63

Roadblocks in the form of boulders were found on roads in a national forest. A U.S. Forest Service employee, in an attempt to determine who had created the roadblocks, followed tractor-tire tracks to the Ventling residence. The employee drove into Ventling's driveway and went to the front door of the house. From where he stood he could see more tire tracks in the yard, and further up in the yard, he saw a tractor equipped with a backhoe and a front-end loader. After a brief conversation with Mrs. Ventling, the employee was refused permission to inspect the tractor and was asked to leave the premises. Before leaving, the Forest Service employee photographed some of the tractor tracks along the side of Ventling's driveway. Mrs. Ventling objected again, and again asked the employee to leave the property. A search warrant was obtained and Ventling was convicted of blocking or interfering with the use of a U.S. Forest Service road. In affirming his conviction, the Court held that

> Ventling maintains that the photographs and observations made were within the curtilage area and should be suppressed since he had a reasonable expectation of privacy for that area. He argues that this expectation was further reinforced by the fact that he had clearly posted the entrance of his driveway with no trespassing signs. The transcript reveals conflicting testimony as to the placement of the signs and their degree of obviousness. Ventling testified that the signs were posted on his property and were immediately noticeable to anyone entering the drive. Sutton testified that some signs had been posted on Forest Service property near the entrance to Ventling's drive and that he had removed them. The trial court found and the district court agreed that the signs were posted on Forest Service property ....
>
> The standard for determining when the search of an area surrounding a residence violates Fourth Amendment guarantees no longer depends on outmoded property concepts, but whether the defendant has a legitimate expectation of privacy in that area. *United States v. John Bernard Industries,* 589 F.2d 1353, 1362 (8th Cir.1979).
>
> Ventling's assertions of expectations of privacy with regard to the driveway and yard seem unreasonable under the circumstances here. We have in some instances found such expectations reasonable with regard to property located out of public view on a defendant's land. *United States v. Knotts,* 662 F.2d 515, 518 (8th Cir.1981) .... The extension of Ventling's expectations of privacy to the driveway and that portion of the yard in front of the house do not, under these circumstances, appear reasonable.

Police Trespassing to Get to Open Fields Where Marijuana Was Growing

See the 1984 U.S. Supreme Court case of *Oliver v. United States,* 466 U.S. 170, 104 S.Ct. 1735 (1984) in chapter 9. In that case, law enforcement officers trespassed to get to an open field area where marijuana was growing illegally. In affirming the conviction and the use of the evidence, the Supreme Court held that "the general rights of property protected by the common law of trespass have little or no relevance to the application of the Fourth Amendment."

POSSIBLE PENALTIES FOR ILLEGAL ENTRY INTO PRIVATE PREMISES

The penalties which could be inflicted for an improper or illegal entry by a law enforcement officer into private premises are

- *Suppression and exclusion of evidence.* The evidence which could be suppressed and forbidden for use in a criminal trial could be:

  Evidence directly obtained as a result of the wrong

  Evidence indirectly obtained as a result of the wrong (this is known as derivative evidence and is controlled by the fruit-of-the-poisonous-tree doctrine, also known as the derivative evidence rule)

- *A civil lawsuit brought either in state or federal court.* The lawsuit could be brought by the person or persons who were wronged by the wrongful police action against:

  The officer (see *Rollins by Agosta v. Farmer,* 731 F.2d 533 (8th Cir.1984) in which the federal appellate court held that a law enforcement officer could be held individually liable in a civil court for entering a home to make an arrest without either a warrant or consent of the occupants

  The employer of the officer (city, county, state or federal government)

- *Discipline by the officer's department.* Discipline could include a verbal or written reprimand, loss of pay or suspension for a period of days or weeks, demotion in rank or loss of promotion opportunity, and/or loss of job.

- *Criminal charges against the officer or officers.* Charges could be trespass, criminal damage to property, burglary, misconduct in public office, or other charges. The following unusual case occurred in Wisconsin.

State v. O'Neill

Supreme Court of Wisconsin (1984)
121 Wis.2d 300, 359 N.W.2d 906

Chief O'Neill was the chief of a university campus police department and was investigating reports of thefts of property from students. A student who did not want his or her name used (unidentified informant) told the chief where some of the property was located off-campus in a house. The chief twice requested that the district attorney of that county obtain a search warrant for him. Both requests were denied because the student informant's name was not disclosed. (The officer could have gone right to a judge himself and requested a search warrant.)

Chief O'Neill then went to the house with victims who had lost property. He knocked on the door and the door swung open; no one was present in the house. The chief told the students to go into the house and find their property. The victims did this and were able to recover some of their property. Other property was returned anonymously to O'Neill's office. The district attorney charged the chief with burglary and two felony counts of misconduct in public office. The misconduct in public office charges were dismissed and only the burglary charge was submitted to the jury. The jury returned a guilty verdict, which was appealed to the Wisconsin Supreme Court. The Supreme Court dismissed the conviction, holding that the district attorney should have obtained a search warrant, as twice requested by the chief. The court stated that

> The availability of a charge of burglary is not necessary to deter officers from conducting overzealous entries and searches of premises. In addition to the charge of misconduct in public office, other types of discipline are available. The exclusionary rule, which makes illegally seized evidence inadmissible in court, has been recognized as a principal means of discouraging unlawful police conduct. *Terry v. Ohio,* 392 U.S. 1, 12, 88 S.Ct. 1868, 1875, 20 L.Ed.2d 887 (1968). Civil actions for damages may be brought against officers who conduct unreasonable entries or searches. Officers conducting unreasonable searches may be subject to suits brought under 42 U.S.C. sec. 1983 (1982). See *Monroe v. Pape,* 365 U.S. 167, 81 S.Ct. 473, 5 L.Ed.2d 492 (1961); *Terry v. Kolski,* 78 Wis.2d 475, 254 N.W.2d 704 (1977). Officers who exceed the scope of their authority may also be subject to administrative disciplinary action. If a police review board concludes that an officer exceeded his authority in conducting a search, the officer could be suspended or dismissed, subjected to a monetary penalty, or have an entry of misconduct noted in his personnel record.

PROBLEMS

1. A police officer in plain clothes entered an adult bookstore and looked over magazines offered for sale. He purchased two of the magazines, paid for them with a $50 bill, and received $38 in change. After leaving the store, the officer examined the magazines and concluded that they were obscene. He then went back to the store and, after arresting the clerk, recovered the $50 bill but did not return the change. The clerk was convicted of selling obscene material. At the trial the magazines, but not the $50 bill, were used as evidence.

   Was the police officer's entry into the store a search in violation of the Fourth Amendment? Was the purchase of the magazines a seizure in violation of the Fourth Amendment? Explain. *Maryland v. Macon,* 472 U.S. 463, 105 S.Ct. 2778 (U.S.Sup.Ct.1985).

2. A campus police officer observed the defendant on the campus carrying a half-gallon bottle of gin. The defendant did not appear to be twenty-one years of age and, because state law forbade possession of alcohol by persons under twenty-one, the officer asked the defendant for his identification. The university also forbade alcohol on their property. Defendant stated his identification was in his dormitory room and the officer stated that he would have to accompany him to get it. When the defendant went into his dormitory room, the officer stood in the open doorway. From where he stood, the officer could see on a desk a small pipe and some seeds, which led the officer to suspect were from marijuana. The officer stepped into the room, seized the seeds and the pipe, and asked for consent to search the room. Consent was given and LSD and additional marijuana were found.

   Was the entry of the police officer into the room lawful? Should the marijuana seen in plain view be used as evidence against the defendant? Should the LSD and marijuana obtained in the consent search be permitted to be used as evidence? Give reasons for your answers. *Washington v. Chrisman*, 455 U.S. 1, 102 S.Ct. 812 (U.S.Sup.Ct.1982).

3. A woman in Tucson, Arizona called the police for help, excitedly stating that her son was after her with a knife. Five police officers responded to the call. When the police arrived at the home, the husband and other sons met the officers, telling the police that "everything was all right." The husband asked the police to leave but the officers insisted on seeing the woman to verify that everything was all right. The family stated that the woman was resting and they did not want her disturbed. When officers tried to enter the yard of the house, the husband and sons grabbed the lead officers and a struggle resulted.

   Who is right, and why? Should the police insist on seeing the woman? Should the husband and sons be arrested? Why? *State v. Sainz*, 18 Ariz.App. 358, 501 P.2d 1199 (1972).

4. Police were called to a Las Vegas hotel. They found that a violent struggle had occurred in Room 83, and on the floor was a "blood-drenched corpse, with its throat cut and multiple stab wounds." All of the occupants of the nearby rooms were in the hall and police were interviewing them, seeking information. Only one room on the floor was not open, and that was Room 82 next to the crime scene. The police knocked at the door but there was no response.

   Should the police order the hotel manager to open the door to Room 82, which was occupied by a hotel guest? Why? *State v. Hardin*, 90 Nev. 10, 518 P.2d 151 (Nevada Sup.Ct., 1974).

5. "Having some information that [the petitioner here] was selling narcotics, three deputy sheriffs of the County of Los Angeles, on the morning of July 1, 1949, made for the two-story dwelling house in which Rochin lived with his mother, common-law wife, brothers and sisters. Finding the outside door open, they entered and then forced open the door to Rochin's room on the second floor. Inside they found petitioner sitting partly dressed on the side of the bed, upon which his wife was lying. On a 'night stand' beside the bed the deputies spied two capsules. When asked 'Whose stuff is this?' Rochin seized the capsules and put them in his mouth. A struggle ensued, in the

course of which the three officers 'jumped upon him' and attempted to extract the capsules. The force they applied proved unavailing against Rochin's resistance. He was handcuffed and taken to a hospital. At the direction of one of the officers a doctor forced an emetic solution through a tube into Rochin's stomach against his will. This 'stomach pumping' produced vomiting. In the vomited matter were found two capsules which proved to contain morphine."

Was the entry into Rochin's home a lawful entry? Was the evidence obtained in a lawful and proper procedure? Explain. Should the U.S. Supreme Court affirm Rochin's conviction? *Rochin v. California*, 342 U.S. 165, 72 S.Ct. 205 (1952).

6. Almost two weeks after a cocaine sale, police went late at night to the apartment of a woman to arrest her for the crime. The police had neither an arrest nor a search warrant. They rang the doorbell of the woman's apartment at about midnight and her five-year-old son answered the door. The child said that his mother was not at home and admitted the police to the apartment. The officers watched television until the woman arrived some time later. The police then arrested the woman.

Was the police entry into the apartment lawful? Was the arrest lawful? Explain your answers. *Laasch v. State*, 84 Wis.2d 587, 267 N.W.2d 278 (Wisconsin Sup.Ct.1978).

7. Two employees of a doctor were subpoenaed as witnesses to testify against him before a grand jury investigating welfare fraud. After the employees failed to appear, capiases (arrest orders) were issued by a court to compel the appearance of the subpoenaed witnesses. Deputy sheriffs attempted to serve the capiases at the doctor's clinic but the doctor refused to allow the officers to enter the clinic. After the county prosecutor told the deputy sheriffs "to go in and get" the witnesses, city police officers and deputy sheriffs chopped the door to the clinic down.

Was the entry lawful, and is the county liable in a civil action for damages? *Pembaur v. Cincinnati*, 473 U.S. 932, 106 S.Ct. 26 (U.S.Sup.Ct.1985).

8. The following problem is taken from the *FBI Law Enforcement Bulletin* article "Emergency Searches of Premises" in the March 1987 issue:

A bank robbery by two men armed with handguns is reported to the police. Within minutes, the first patrolmen on the scene have obtained descriptions of the robbers and caused this information to be broadcast to fellow officers. A suspect matching the description of one of the robbers is detained on a sidewalk at the door to a residence less than a mile from the bank. The detainee is frisked, but no weapons are located. Suspecting that the second robber is inside the residence, officers kick open the door and search the house for additional suspects. The bank robbery loot is found stacked on a table in the living room.

Was the entry into the residence lawful and proper? Can the money taken in the bank robbery (the loot) be used as evidence in the criminal trial of the men? Explain your answers.

NOTES

[1] Payton v. New York, 445 U.S. 573, 585, 100 S.Ct. 1371–1379 (1980).

[2] In the 1958 case of Miller v. United States, 357 U.S. 301, 78 S.Ct. 1190 (1958), the U.S. Supreme Court quoted from the Oxford Dictionary of Quotations (2nd ed., 1953), attributing the statement to William Pitt in 1763. The U.S. Supreme Court traces the history of the Fourth Amendment in the case of Stanford v. Texas, 379 U.S. 476, 85 S.Ct. 506 (1965).

[3] See note 1 above.

[4] The material quoted from former Chief Justice Burger was written in the 1963 case of Wayne v. United States, 318 F.2d 205 (1963), cert. denied 375 U.S. 860, 84 S.Ct. 125 (1963) while the Chief Justice was a judge in that court.

[5] *Welsh v. Wisconsin* holds that violation of a civil offense (such as speeding or jay walking) will not authorize entry into private premises without consent by a law enforcement officer. However, state cases such as People v. Hampton demonstrate that most (if not all) states will authorize hot pursuit entries for misdemeanors which threaten public safety such as drunken driving. But would a 50¢ shoplifting justify a police entry in hot pursuit of private premises?

[6] Footnote 12 in the Ker case reads as follows:

A search of the record with the aid of hindsight may lend some support to the conclusion that, contra the reasonable belief of the officers, petitioners may not have been prepared for an imminent visit from the police. It goes without saying that in determining the lawfulness of entry and the existence of probable cause we may concern ourselves only with what the officers had reason to believe *at the time of their entry*. Johnson v. United States, 333 U.S. 10, 17, 68 S.Ct. 367, 370–371 (1948). As the Court said in United States v. Di Re, 332 U.S. 581, 595, 68 S.Ct. 222, 229 (1948), "a search is not to be made legal by what it turns up. In law it is good *or bad* when it starts and does not change character from" what is dug up subsequently. (Emphasis added.)

[7] *Bumper v. North Carolina,* 391 U.S. 543, 88 S.Ct. 1788 (1968).

[8] *Schneckloth v. Bustamonte,* 412 U.S. 218, 93 S.Ct. 2041 (1973).

[9] The U.S. Supreme Court held in the case of Gouled v. United States, 255 U.S. 298, 41 S.Ct. 261 (1961), that "a business acquaintance of the (defendant), acting under orders of federal officers, obtained entry into the petitioner's office by falsely representing that he intended only to pay a social visit. In the petitioner's absence, however, the intruder secretly ransacked the office and seized certain private papers of an incriminating nature. This Court had no difficulty concluding that the Fourth Amendment had been violated by the secret and general ransacking, notwithstanding that the initial intrusion was occasioned by a fraudulently obtained invitation rather than by force or stealth."

[10] United States v. Blank, 251 F.Supp. 166 (N.D. Ohio, 1966).

12

Obtaining Evidence by Vehicle Stops and Searches

DOES A PERSON HAVE THE SAME RIGHT OF PRIVACY IN A VEHICLE THAT HE HAS IN HIS HOME?

Studies show that motor vehicles are involved in some manner in over 75 percent of the crimes committed in the United States. More than one million vehicles are stolen every year in this country. Not only are many crimes committed in vehicles but illegally driven vehicles present a serious safety hazard on American highways, as demonstrated by the over forty thousand deaths caused by vehicle accidents every year in the United States.

The U.S. Supreme Court pointed out that in "discharging their varied responsibilities for ensuring public safety, law enforcement officials are necessarily brought into frequent contact with automobiles," and that most of the contact is "noncriminal in nature."[1]

Because of the mobility of motor vehicles and the fact that vehicles travel "public thoroughfares where both the occupants and its contents are in plain view," a person traveling in a vehicle "has a lesser expectation of privacy in a motor vehicle because its function is transportation and it seldom serves as one's residence or as the repository of personal effects."[2] Fourth Amendment protection of persons traveling in vehicles is therefore less in some respects since the United States Supreme Court held as follows:

> This Court has traditionally drawn a distinction between automobiles and homes or offices in relation to the Fourth Amendment. Although automobiles are "effects" and thus within the reach of the Fourth Amendment, ... warrantless examinations of automobiles have been upheld in circumstances in which a search of a home or office would not.[3]

CAN LAW ENFORCEMENT OFFICERS STOP VEHICLES WITH NO REASON?

A vehicle stop may be made by a law enforcement officer for many valid reasons: the driver may be speeding or may have violated other sections of the traffic code; there may be an equipment violation, such as a headlight out; there may be probable cause or reasonable suspicion to arrest or question the driver or a passenger in the vehicle. But can a vehicle be stopped with no reason? That question was before the U.S. Supreme Court in the case of

---

Most Traffic Stops are Temporary, Brief, and Public

In pointing out that most traffic stops are temporary, brief, and public, the U.S. Supreme Court stated in footnote 26 of *Berkemer v. McCarty*, 82 L.Ed.2d at 333 that ''no state requires that a detained motorist be arrested unless he is accused of a specified serious crime, refuses to promise to appear in court, or demands to be taken before a magistrate.''

However, a motorist who fails to furnish satisfactory self-identification or an out-of-state motorist who is unable to post bail or to pay a traffic fine or a citation is likely to be detained until the matter is cleared.

Delaware v. Prouse.[4] In that case, the officer making the vehicle stop testified, "I saw the car in the area and wasn't answering any complaints, so I decided to pull them off." In holding that such stops are unreasonable under the Fourth Amendment, the Court ruled that

> we hold that except in those situations in which there is at least articulable and reasonable suspicion that a motorist is unlicensed or that an automobile is not registered, or that either the vehicle or an occupant is otherwise subject to seizure for violation of law, stopping an automobile and detaining the driver in order to check his driver's license and the registration of the automobile are unreasonable under the Fourth Amendment.

Although a traffic stop significantly interferes with the freedom of movement, not only of the vehicle driver but also of the passengers, most traffic stops are temporary, brief, and public police stops. In the 1984 case of *Berkemer v. McCarty,*[5] the U.S. Supreme Court pointed out the consequences to a motorist of failing to obey a law enforcement officer's signal to stop:

> It must be acknowledged at the outset that a traffic stop significantly curtails the "freedom of action" of the driver and the passengers, if any, of the detained vehicle. Under the law of most States, it is a crime either to ignore a policeman's signal to stop one's car or, once having stopped, to drive away without permission . . . .
> . . . Certainly few motorists would feel free either to disobey a directive to pull over or to leave the scene of a traffic stop without being told they might do so. Partly for these reasons, we have long acknowledged that "stopping an automobile and detaining its occupants constitute a 'seizure' within the meaning of [the Fourth] Amendmen[t], even though the purpose of the stop is limited and the resulting detention quite brief." *Delaware v. Prouse,* 440 U.S. 648, 653.

PLAIN VIEW REQUIREMENTS

If a proper vehicle stop is made, then what a law enforcement officer sees, hears, or smells is ordinarily held to be in plain view. Plain view is not a search. In the 1983 case of *Texas v. Brown*,[6] the U.S. Supreme Court held that if, while lawfully engaged in an activity in a particular place, police officers perceive (see, hear or smell) a suspicious object, they may seize it immediately .... This rule merely reflects an application of the Fourth Amendment's central requirement of reasonableness to the law governing seizure of property.

The U.S. Supreme Court has held that the "plain view" doctrine permits the warrantless seizure by police of private possession where three requirements are satisfied.

First, the police officer must lawfully make an "initial intrusion" or otherwise properly be in a position from which he can view a particular area.

Second, the officer must discover incriminating evidence "inadvertently" which is to say, he may not "know in advance the location of ... evidence and intend to seize it," relying on the plain-view doctrine only as a pretext.

Finally, it must be "immediately apparent" to the police that the items they observe may be evidence of a crime, contraband, or otherwise subject to seizure.[7]

The following U.S. Supreme Court cases illustrate these requirements:

Delaware v. Prouse

Supreme Court of the United States (1979)
440 U.S. 648, 99 S.Ct. 1391

After a Delaware police officer stopped a vehicle for no reason other than that the officer had nothing else to do, the officer smelled marijuana smoke and seized marijuana which was in plain view on the car floor. The Supreme Court affirmed the suppression of the evidence because the car stop violated the Fourth Amendment. The Court held that

An individual operating or traveling in an automobile does not lose all reasonable expectation of privacy simply because the automobile and its use are subject to government regulation. Automobile travel is a basic, pervasive, and often necessary mode of transportation to and from one's home, workplace, and leisure activities. Many people spend more hours each day traveling in cars than walking on the streets. Undoubtedly, many find a greater sense of security and privacy in traveling in an automobile than they do in exposing themselves by pedestrian or other modes of travel. Were the individual subject to unfettered governmental intrusion every time he entered an automobile, the security guaranteed by the Fourth Amendment would be seriously circumscribed. As *Terry v. Ohio* recognized, people are not shorn of all Fourth Amendment protection when they step from their homes onto the public sidewalks. Nor are they shorn of those interests when they step from the sidewalks into their automobiles.

Texas v. Brown

Supreme Court of the United States (1983)
460 U.S. 730, 103 S.Ct. 1535

A "routine driver's license checkpoint" was set up on a summer evening in Fort Worth, Texas. Around midnight, the defendant's car was stopped and he was asked for his driver's license. Officer Maples shone a flashlight into the car as Brown was withdrawing his right hand from his pocket. "Caught between the two middle fingers of the hand was an opaque, green party balloon, knotted about one-half inch from the tip. Brown let the balloon fall to the seat beside his leg, and then reached across the passenger seat and opened the glove compartment."

Officer Maples then shifted his position in order to obtain a better view of the interior of the glove compartment. He saw that the glove compartment contained several small plastic vials, quantities of loose white powder, and an open bag of party balloons. After looking in the glove compartment, Brown stated to the officer that he had no driver's license in his possession. Brown was then instructed to get out of the car. The officer then picked up the green balloon from the floor of the car, because he believed that it contained illegal narcotics. When the officer saw that the balloon contained a powdery substance, Brown was placed under arrest. An "on-the-scene inventory of Brown's car" was conducted and other containers believed to contain heroin were seized. In affirming Brown's conviction for the possession of heroin, the Supreme Court held that

> if, while lawfully engaged in an activity in a particular place, police officers perceive a suspicious object, they may seize it immediately....
>
> Applying these principles, we conclude that Officer Maples properly seized the green balloon from Brown's automobile. The Court of Criminal Appeals stated that it did not "question ... the validity of the officer's initial stop of appellant's vehicle as a part of a license check," 617 S.W.2d, at 200, and we agree .... It is likewise beyond dispute that Maples' action in shining his flashlight to illuminate the interior of Brown's car trenched upon no right secured to the latter by the Fourth Amendment. The Court said in *United States v. Lee,* 274 U.S. 559, 563, 47 S.Ct. 746, 748, 71 L.Ed. 1202 (1927): "[The] use of a searchlight is comparable to the use of a marine glass or a field glass. It is not prohibited by the Constitution." Numerous other courts have agreed that the use of artificial means to illuminate a darkened area simply does not constitute a search, and thus triggers no Fourth Amendment protection.
>
> Likewise, the fact that Maples "changed [his] position" and "bent down at an angle so [he] could see what was inside" Brown's car ... is irrelevant to Fourth Amendment analysis. The general public could peer into the interior of Brown's automobile from any number of angles; there is no reason Maples should be precluded from observing

as an officer what would be entirely visible to him as a private citizen. There is no legitimate expectation of privacy ... shielding that portion of the interior of an automobile which may be viewed from outside the vehicle by either inquisitive passersby or diligent police officers. In short, the conduct that enabled Maples to observe the interior of Brown's car and of his open glove compartment was not a search within the meaning of the Fourth Amendment ....

With these considerations in mind it is plain that Officer Maples possessed probable cause to believe that the balloon in Brown's hand contained an illicit substance. Maples testified that he was aware, both from his participation in previous narcotics arrests and from discussions with other officers, that balloons tied in the manner of the one possessed by Brown were frequently used to carry narcotics. This testimony was corroborated by that of a police department chemist who noted that it was "common" for balloons to be used in packaging narcotics. In addition, Maples was able to observe the contents of the glove compartment of Brown's car.

CONSENT TO SEARCH A VEHICLE

A person who has lawful use of a vehicle, or who has "mutual use" and "joint access and control," can consent to the search of a vehicle. The U.S. Supreme Court pointed out that as a practical matter "where the police have some evidence of illicit activity, but lack probable cause to arrest or search, a search authorized by a valid consent may be the only means of obtaining important and reliable evidence." [8]

As the following cases illustrate, consent may be obtained from a person already arrested or in custody, or can be obtained when law enforcement officers suspect criminal conduct.

Schneckloth v. Bustamonte

Supreme Court of the United States (1973)
412 U.S. 218, 93 S.Ct. 2041

A California police officer stopped a car at 2:40 in the morning because one headlight was burned out and the car's license plate light was not functioning. When the driver could not produce a driver's license and only one of the five passengers had any evidence of identification, the officer requested the six men to step out of the car. Two additional officers had then arrived at the scene and the original officer asked the driver if he could search the car. "Sure, go ahead" was the response and in the following search, the driver actually helped by opening the trunk and glove compartment of the car. The search produced three stolen checks which were used in evidence in obtaining the conviction of one of the passengers (Bustamonte) for possessing a check with

The Use of Roadblocks in the United States

Stopping a motor vehicle and detaining its occupant is a seizure within the meaning of the Fourth Amendment of the U.S. Constitution. The U.S. Supreme Court, in the case of *Delaware v. Prouse*, 440 U.S. 648, 99 S.Ct. 1391 (1979), held that

> This holding does not preclude the State of Delaware and other states from developing methods for spot checks that involve less intrusion or that do not involve the unconstrained exercise of discretion. Questioning of all on-coming traffic at roadblock-type stops is one possible alternative. We hold only that persons in automobiles on public roadways may not for that reason alone have their travel and privacy interfered with at the unbridled discretion of police officers.

Many states have now approved of roadblocks. The defendant in the case of *Texas v. Brown* (see cases) was stopped at midnight for a "routine driver's license checkpoint" when heroin was seen in plain view. The Supreme Court of Florida joined other state courts in approving "drunk driver" roadblocks in the case of *State v. Jones*, 483 So.2d 433 (1986). The Florida Supreme Court stated that

> This balancing test involves three considerations: (1) the gravity of the public concern that the seizure serves; (2) the degree to which the seizure advances the public interest; and (3) the severity of the interference with individual liberty . . . . As with all warrantless searches and seizures, courts determine the constitutionality of DUI roadblocks by balancing the legitimate government interests involved against the degree of intrusion on the individual's Fourth Amendment rights.

The Florida Supreme Court held that advance publicity on roadblocks is *not* necessary and that "in our view roadblocks need not stop every car in order to avoid running afoul of *Prouse.*" The critical considerations reviewed by the Florida Supreme Court in establishing roadblocks are

> . . . (1) whether the law enforcement agency conducted the roadblock pursuant to a plan which supervisory personnel formulated and which substantially restricted the discretion of field officers as to both operating procedures and the selection of vehicles; (2) whether the roadblock procedures assured the safety of motorists through the use of proper means such as adequate lighting, warning signs or signals, and clearly identifiable police officers; (3) the degree of intrusion upon motorists and the length of the detention of each motorist; and (4) whether the roadblock procedures proved significantly more effective in combating an egregious law enforcement problem than other available less intrusive means.

intent to defraud. In affirming the conviction and holding that "Miranda-type" warnings were not required in order to obtain valid and voluntary consent, the Court ruled that

> Our decision today is a narrow one. We hold only that when . . . the State attempts to justify a search on the basis of his consent, the Fourth and Fourteenth Amendments require that it demonstrate that the consent was in fact voluntarily given, and not the result of duress or coercion, express or implied. Voluntariness is a question of fact to be determined from all the circumstances, and while the subject's

knowledge of a right to refuse is a factor to be taken into account, the prosecution is not required to demonstrate such knowledge as a prerequisite to establishing a voluntary consent.

United States v. Watson

Supreme Court of the United States (1976)
423 U.S. 411, 96 S.Ct. 820

(This case is also presented in chapter 10.)

After the defendant was arrested and was given the *Miranda* warnings, a search of his person revealed no stolen credit cards. The postal inspector then asked the defendant if he could look inside of Watson's car which was standing within view. "Watson said, 'Go ahead,' and repeated these words when the inspector cautioned that '(i)f I find anything, it is going to go against you.' Using keys furnished by Watson, the inspector entered the car and found under the floor mat an envelope containing two cards in the names of other persons." In holding that the credit cards were properly used as evidence, the U.S. Supreme Court reversed the Court of Appeal's ruling that the Fourth Amendment prohibited the use of the cards as evidence, holding that

the fact of custody alone has never been enough in itself to demonstrate a coerced confession or consent to search. Similarly, under *Schneckloth,* the absence of proof that Watson knew he could withhold his consent, though it may be a factor in the overall judgment, is not to be given controlling significance. There is no indication in this record that Watson was a newcomer to the law, mentally deficient or unable in the face of a custodial arrest to exercise a free choice. He was given *Miranda* warnings and was further cautioned that the results of the search of his car could be used against him. He persisted in his consent.

In these circumstances, to hold that illegal coercion is made out from the fact of arrest and the failure to inform the arrestee that he could withhold consent would not be consistent with *Schneckloth* and would distort the voluntariness standard that we reaffirmed in that case.

In consequence, we reverse the judgment of the Court of Appeals.

REASONABLE SUSPICION AS AN AUTHORITY TO STOP AND DETAIN

Evidence Obtained During Investigative Stops

The U.S. Supreme Court held in *Terry v. Ohio* [9] that a police officer who observes suspicious circumstances may stop an individual or a vehicle briefly to investigate the circumstances, provided the officer is "able to point to specific and articulable facts which, taken together with rational inferences from those facts, reasonably warrant that intrusion." *Terry v. Ohio* at p. 21.

The reasonable suspicion required to make a stop and investigative detention is less than that amount of information and evidence known as probable cause.

To determine whether an investigative stop is justified, "the totality of the circumstances—the whole picture—must be taken into account. Based upon the whole picture the detaining officers must have a particularized and objective basis for suspecting the particular person stopped of criminal activity." [10]

The following case illustrates the authority of Border Patrol officers to stop a vehicle on reasonable suspicion:

United States v. Cortez

Supreme Court of the United States (1981)
449 U.S. 411, 101 S.Ct. 690

Border Patrol officers found footprints in the Arizona desert, indicating that illegal border crossing was occurring almost weekly during the night. They calculated that the illegal aliens would walk thirty miles, arriving at a highway where they would be picked up by a vehicle such as a camper. Officers waited on a night when such a crossing and pickup would most likely occur. They watched the few vehicles which came from the east and then, after the pickup, returned east on the highway. By noting license numbers, only one vehicle fit into this pattern. The officers turned on their police light and stopped the camper driven by the defendant. The officers identified themselves and told the defendant and his passenger that they were conducting an immigration check. When they asked if defendant was carrying any passengers in the camper, Cortez stated that he had picked up some hitchhikers and opened the back of the camper. Six illegal aliens were in the back of the camper. In affirming the conviction of the defendant, the Court held that

> The Fourth Amendment applies to seizures of the person, including brief investigatory stops such as the stop of the vehicle .... An investigatory stop must be justified by some objective manifestation that the person stopped is, or is about to be, engaged in criminal activity ....
>
> Courts have used a variety of terms to capture the elusive concept of what cause is sufficient to authorize police to stop a person. Terms like "articulable reasons" and "founded suspicion" are not self-defining; they fall short of providing clear guidance dispositive of the myriad factual situations that arise. But the essence of all that has been written is that the totality of the circumstances—the whole picture—must be taken into account. Based upon that whole picture the detaining officers must have a particularized and objective basis for suspecting the particular person stopped of criminal activity ....
>
> The limited purpose of the stop in this case was to question the occupants of the vehicle about their citizenship and immigration status and the reasons for the round trip in a short timespan in a virtually

deserted area. No search of the camper or any of its occupants occurred until after respondent Cortez voluntarily opened the back door of the camper; thus, only the stop, not the search is at issue here. The intrusion upon privacy associated with this stop was limited and was "reasonably related in scope to the justification for [its] initiation," *Terry v. Ohio,* 392 U.S., at 29, 88 S.Ct., at 1883.

We have recently held that stops by the Border Patrol may be justified under circumstances less than those constituting probable cause for arrest or search. *United States v. Brignoni-Ponce,* 422 U.S., at 880, 95 S.Ct., at 2579. Thus, the test is not whether Officers Gray and Evans had probable cause to conclude that the vehicle they stopped would contain "Chevron" and a group of illegal aliens. Rather the question is whether, based upon the whole picture, they, as experienced Border Patrol officers, could reasonably surmise that the particular vehicle they stopped was engaged in criminal activity. On this record, they could so conclude.

United States v. Brignoni-Ponce

Supreme Court of the United States (1975)
422 U.S. 873, 95 S.Ct. 2574

A vehicle stop was made because the occupants of the vehicle appeared to be of Mexican ancestry. Because no other reason for the vehicle stop was given, the Supreme Court held that this factor alone does not justify stopping all Mexican-Americans to ask if they are aliens. The Court stated that

> Any number of factors may be taken into account in deciding whether there is reasonable suspicion to stop a car in the border area. Officers may consider the characteristics of the area in which they encounter a vehicle. Its proximity to the border, the usual patterns of traffic on the particular road, and previous experience with alien traffic are all relevant .... They also may consider information about recent illegal border crossings in the area. The driver's behavior may be relevant, as erratic driving or obvious attempts to evade officers can support a reasonable suspicion .... Aspects of the vehicle itself may justify suspicion. For instance, officers say that certain station wagons, with large compartments for fold-down seats or spare tires, are frequently used for transporting concealed aliens .... The vehicle may appear to be heavily loaded, it may have an extraordinary number of passengers, or the officers may observe persons trying to hide .... The Government also points out that trained officers can recognize the characteristic appearance of persons who live in Mexico, relying on such factors as the mode of dress and haircut ....
>
> ... In all situations the officer is entitled to assess the facts in light of his experience in detecting illegal entry and smuggling ....
>
> In this case the officers relied on a single factor to justify stopping respondent's car: the apparent Mexican ancestry of the occupants. We cannot conclude that this furnished reasonable grounds to believe that the three occupants were aliens. At best the officers had only a fleeting glimpse of the persons in the moving car, illuminated by head-

lights. Even if they saw enough to think that the occupants were of Mexican descent, this factor alone would justify neither a reasonable belief that they were aliens, nor a reasonable belief that the car concealed other aliens who were illegally in the country. Large numbers of native-born and naturalized citizens have the physical characteristics identified with Mexican ancestry, and even in the border area a relatively small proportion of them are aliens. The likelihood that any given person of Mexican ancestry is an alien is high enough to make Mexican appearance a relevant factor, but standing alone it does not justify stopping all Mexican-Americans to ask if they are aliens.

Investigative Stops for Completed Crimes

Investigative detentions based upon reasonable suspicion may be made not only when a law enforcement officer reasonably suspects that a person is committing a crime or is about to commit one, but also after the suspect has already committed a crime.

After a serious crime such as an armed robbery or a rape, there is often a radio alert or a lookout for the getaway vehicle. If the description of the vehicle is specific enough to single out the one vehicle "probably" used in committing the crime, then probable cause would authorize the stop of the vehicle.

If the description of the vehicle was general (year, make, color) and highway or street traffic was such as to expect several vehicles of that type on the highways or streets, the stop could then be on the "possibility" that this was the getaway car if the information available to the police amounted to reasonable suspicion.

"Wanted Flyer" Based Upon Reasonable Suspicion

Wanted flyers are generally issued upon probable cause, which would authorize another law enforcement agency to arrest and hold a suspect for the department that issued the flyer. The following U.S. Supreme Court case involves a situation in which a wanted flyer was issued on reasonable suspicion (less than probable cause):

United States v. Hensley

Supreme Court of the United States (1985)
469 U.S. 221, 105 S.Ct. 675

After an armed robbery in St. Bernard, Ohio (a suburb of Cincinnati), police obtained information amounting to reasonable suspicion that Hensley had driven the getaway car during the robbery. A "wanted flyer" was issued to other police departments in the area "to pick up and hold Hensley ... in the event he were located." Twelve days later, police in another suburb saw

Hensley driving a white Cadillac convertible. The vehicle was stopped on the basis of the wanted flyer and the two men in the car were instructed to step out of the car. After the men left the vehicle, the butt of a revolver was observed protruding from underneath the passenger seat. The passenger was then arrested and the car searched. A second handgun was found wrapped in a jacket in the middle of the front seat and a third handgun in a bag in the back seat. Hensley was also then arrested. After the state handgun possession charges against Hensley were dropped, Hensley was indicted for being a convicted felon in possession of firearms. Hensley moved to suppress the use of the handguns as evidence on the grounds that the police stop of his vehicle was in violation of the Fourth Amendment. The Supreme Court affirmed the conviction, holding that

> law enforcement agents may briefly stop a moving automobile to investigate a reasonable suspicion that its occupants are involved in criminal activity . . . . (within United States borders, Government interest in preventing illegal entry of aliens permits a *Terry* stop on reasonable suspicion that particular vehicle contains aliens). Although stopping a car and detaining its occupants constitutes a seizure within the meaning of the Fourth Amendment, the governmental interest in investigating an officer's reasonable suspicion, based on specific and articulable facts, may outweigh the Fourth Amendment interest of the driver and passengers in remaining secure from the intrusion . . . .

> This is the first case we have addressed in which police stopped a person because they suspected he was involved in a completed crime. In our previous decisions involving investigatory stops on less than probable cause, police stopped or seized a person because they suspected he was about to commit a crime, . . . or was committing a crime at the moment of the stop . . . where police have been unable to locate a person suspected of involvement in a past crime, the ability to briefly stop that person, ask questions, or check identification in the absence of probable cause promotes the strong government interest in solving crimes and bringing offenders to justice. Restraining police action until after probable cause is obtained would not only hinder the investigation, but might also enable the suspect to flee in the interim and to remain at large. Particularly in the context of felonies or crimes involving a threat to public safety, it is in the public interest that the crime be solved and the suspect detained as promptly as possible. The law enforcement interests at stake in these circumstances outweigh the individual's interest to be free of a stop and detention that is no more extensive than permissible in the investigation of imminent or ongoing crimes.

> We need not and do not decide today whether *Terry* stops to investigate all past crimes, however serious, are permitted. It is enough to say that, if police have a reasonable suspicion, grounded in specific and articulable facts, that a person they encounter was involved in or is wanted in connection with a completed felony, then a *Terry* stop may be made to investigate that suspicion . . . .

> The justification for a stop did not evaporate when the armed robbery was completed. Hensley was reasonably suspected of involvement in a felony and was at large from the time the suspicion arose

until the stop by the Covington police. A brief stop and detention at the earliest opportunity after the suspicion arose is fully consistent with the principles of the Fourth Amendment.

Turning to the flyer issued by the St. Bernard police, we believe it satisfies the objective test announced today. An objective reading of the entire flyer would lead an experienced officer to conclude that Thomas Hensley was at least wanted for questioning and investigation in St. Bernard. Since the flyer was issued on the basis of articulable facts supporting a reasonable suspicion, this objective reading would justify a brief stop to check Hensley's identification, pose questions, and inform the suspect that the St. Bernard police wished to question him. As an experienced officer could well assume that a warrant might have been obtained in the period after the flyer was issued, we think the flyer would further justify a brief detention at the scene of the stop while officers checked whether a warrant had in fact been issued. It is irrelevant whether the Covington officers intended to detain Hensley only long enough to confirm the existence of a warrant, or for some longer period; what matters is that the stop and detention that occurred were in fact no more intrusive than would have been permitted an experienced officer on an objective reading of the flyer.

To be sure, the St. Bernard flyer at issue did not request that other police departments briefly detain Hensley merely to check his identification or confirm the existence of a warrant. Instead, it asked other departments to pick up and hold Hensley for St. Bernard. Our decision today does not suggest that such a detention, whether at the scene or at the Covington police headquarters, would have been justified. Given the distance involved and the time required to identify and communicate with the department that issued the flyer, such a detention might well be so lengthy or intrusive as to exceed the permissible limits of a *Terry* stop . . . .

The length of Hensley's detention from his stop to his arrest on probable cause was brief. A reasonable suspicion on the part of the St. Bernard police underlies and supports their issuance of the flyer. Finally, the stop that occurred was reasonable in objective reliance on the flyer and was not significantly more intrusive than would have been permitted the St. Bernard police. Under these circumstances, the investigatory stop was reasonable under the Fourth Amendment, and the evidence discovered during the stop was admissible.

Protective Measures Which May Be Taken During a Vehicle Stop

Unless there exists probable cause or consent, a search for contraband or evidence of a crime would not generally be authorized during a vehicle stop. Protective measures such as those illustrated in the following cases would be authorized:

Pennsylvania v. Mimms

Supreme Court of the United States (1977)
434 U.S. 106, 98 S.Ct. 330

> The facts are not in dispute. While on routine patrol, two Philadelphia police officers observed respondent Harry Mimms driving an automobile with an expired license plate. The officers stopped the vehicle for the purpose of issuing a traffic summons. One of the officers approached and asked respondent to step out of the car and produce his owner's card and operator's license. Respondent alighted, whereupon the officer noticed a large bulge under respondent's sports jacket. Fearing that the bulge might be a weapon, the officer frisked respondent and discovered in his waistband a .38-caliber revolver loaded with five rounds of ammunition. The other occupant of the car was carrying a .32-caliber revolver. Respondent was immediately arrested and subsequently indicted for carrying a concealed deadly weapon and for unlawfully carrying a firearm without a license. His motion to suppress the revolver was denied; and, after a trial at which the revolver was introduced into evidence, respondent was convicted on both counts.

In holding that the officers properly ordered the defendant out of the car and upon seeing the "bulge" properly made a pat-down for weapons, the Court stated that

> it appears "that a significant percentage of murders of police officers occurs when the officers are making traffic stops." . . .
> The hazard of accidental injury from passing traffic to an officer standing on the driver's side of the vehicle may also be appreciable in some situations. Rather than conversing while standing exposed to moving traffic, the officer prudently may prefer to ask the driver of the vehicle to step out of the car and off onto the shoulder of the road where the inquiry may be pursued with greater safety to both.
> Against this important interest we are asked to weigh the intrusion into the driver's personal liberty occasioned not by the initial stop of the vehicle, which was admittedly justified, but by the order to get out of the car. We think this additional intrusion can only be described as *de minimis*. The driver is being asked to expose to view very little more of his person than is already exposed. The police have already lawfully decided that the driver shall be briefly detained; the only question is whether he shall spend that period sitting in the driver's seat of his car or standing alongside it. Not only is the insistence of the police on the latter choice not a "serious intrusion upon the sanctity of the person," but it hardly rises to the level of a " 'petty indignity.' " *Terry v. Ohio, supra,* 392 U.S. at 17, 88 S.Ct. at 1877. What is at most a mere inconvenience cannot prevail when balanced against legitimate concerns for the officer's safety.
> There remains the second question of the propriety of the search once the bulge in the jacket was observed. We have as little doubt on

this point as on the first; the answer is controlled by *Terry v. Ohio, supra.* In that case we thought the officer justified in conducting a limited search for weapons once he had reasonably concluded that the person whom he had legitimately stopped might be armed and presently dangerous. Under the standard enunciated in that case— whether "the facts available to the officer at the moment of the seizure or the search 'warrant a man of reasonable caution in the belief' that the action taken was appropriate"—there is little question the officer was justified. The bulge in the jacket permitted the officer to conclude that Mimms was armed and thus posed a serious and present danger to the safety of the officer. In these circumstances, any man of "reasonable caution" would likely have conducted the "pat down."

Michigan v. Long

Supreme Court of the United States (1983)
463 U.S. 1032, 103 S.Ct. 3469

Deputies Howell and Lewis were on patrol in a rural area one evening when, shortly after midnight, they observed a car traveling erratically and at excessive speed. The officers observed the car turning down a side road, where it swerved off into a shallow ditch. The officers stopped to investigate. Long, the only occupant of the automobile, met the deputies at the rear of the car, which was protruding from the ditch onto the road. The door on the driver's side of the vehicle was left open.

Deputy Howell requested Long to produce his operator's license, but he did not respond. After the request was repeated, Long produced his license. Long again failed to respond when Howell requested him to produce the vehicle registration. After another repeated request, Long, who Howell thought "appeared to be under the influence of something," . . . turned from the officers and began walking toward the open door of the vehicle. The officers followed Long and both observed a large hunting knife on the floorboard of the driver's side of the car. The officers then stopped Long's progress and subjected him to a *Terry* protective patdown, which revealed no weapons.

Long and Deputy Lewis then stood by the rear of the vehicle while Deputy Howell shined his flashlight into the interior of the vehicle, but did not actually enter it. The purpose of Howell's action was "to search for other weapons." . . . The officer noticed that something was protruding from under the armrest on the front seat. He knelt in the vehicle and lifted the armrest. He saw an open pouch on the front seat, and upon flashing his light on the pouch, determined that it contained what appeared to be marihuana. After Deputy Howell showed the pouch and its contents to Deputy Lewis, Long was arrested for possession of marihuana. A further search of the interior of the vehicle, including the glovebox, revealed neither more contraband nor the vehicle registration.

The U.S. Supreme Court upheld the use of the evidence of marijuana obtained from the passenger compartment of the car. (However, another 75 pounds of marijuana were found in the trunk after the officers impounded the car and opened the trunk. The issue of the legality of this search was returned to the Supreme Court of Michigan for their determination.)

> ... Just as a *Terry* suspect on the street may, despite being under the brief control of a police officer, reach into his clothing and retrieve a weapon, so might a *Terry* suspect in Long's position break away from police control and retrieve a weapon from his automobile .... In addition, if the suspect is not placed under arrest, he will be permitted to reenter his automobile, and he will then have access to any weapons inside .... Or, as here, the suspect may be permitted to reenter the vehicle before the *Terry* investigation is over, and again, may have access to weapons. In any event, we stress that a *Terry* investigation, such as the one that occurred here, involves a police investigation "at close range," ... when the officer remains particularly vulnerable in part *because* a full custodial arrest has not been effected, and the officer must make a "quick decision as to how to protect himself and others from possible danger...". In such circumstances, we have not required that officers adopt alternative means to ensure their safety in order to avoid the intrusion involved in a *Terry* encounter.

Adams v. Williams

Supreme Court of the United States (1972)
407 U.S. 143, 92 S.Ct. 1921

> (This case is given more completely in chapter 3.)
> In commenting on *Adams v. Williams* in the 1981 case of *Michigan v. Summers*, the U.S. Supreme Court stated at 452 U.S. at 708, 101 S.Ct. at 2597 that

> > Similarly, in *Adams v. Williams*, 407 U.S. 143, 92 S.Ct. 1921, 32 L.Ed.2d 612, the officer had received an informant's tip, not amounting to probable cause, that Williams was carrying narcotics and a gun. The Court held that the officer acted legally in reaching into the car and intruding on Williams' person to see if Williams indeed was in possession of a lethal weapon. In so holding, the Court made clear that what justified this intrusion on Williams' person was not the possibility of finding contraband narcotics, but rather the officer's need to protect himself from harm by seizing the suspected gun: "The purpose of this limited search is not to discover evidence of crime, but to allow the officer to pursue his investigation without fear of violence...". *Id.*, at 146, 92 S.Ct., at 1923, accord, *Pennsylvania v. Mimms*, 434 U.S. 106, 110, 98 S.Ct. 330, 333, 54 L.Ed.2d 331. See *Ybarra v. Illinois*, 444 U.S. 85, 93, 100 S.Ct. 338, 343, 62 L.Ed.2d 238.

The U.S. Supreme Court held in *Adams v. Williams* that

In *Terry* this Court recognized that "a police officer may in appropriate circumstances and in an appropriate manner approach a person for purposes of investigating possibly criminal behavior even though there is no probable cause to make an arrest." The Fourth Amendment does not require a policeman who lacks the precise level of information necessary for probable cause to arrest to simply shrug his shoulders and allow a crime to occur or a criminal to escape. On the contrary, *Terry* recognizes that it may be the essence of good police work to adopt an intermediate response. A brief stop of a suspicious individual, in order to determine his identity or to maintain the status quo momentarily while obtaining more information, may be most reasonable in light of the facts known to the officer at the time.

EVIDENCE OBTAINED IN SEARCHES INCIDENT TO LAWFUL ARRESTS

If a lawful arrest is made, an officer may make a search incident to that arrest. The search has to be made at the time of the arrest and must be made at the place of the arrest. The search is limited to the person of the suspect and the area under his (or her) immediate control. The following U.S. Supreme Court cases concern the extent of the scope of the search which may be made:

United States v. Robinson

Supreme Court of the United States (1973)
414 U.S. 218, 94 S.Ct. 467

The defendant was at first arrested for driving after the revocation of his driver's license; the officer then made a search incident to the arrest. The officer came upon a "crumpled up cigarette package." The officer testified that "I could feel objects in the package but I couldn't tell what they were ... I knew they weren't cigarettes." The officer opened the package and found fourteen capsules, which he believed to be heroin and which were later proved to be heroin. The trial court permitted the heroin to be used as evidence and the U.S. Supreme Court affirmed the defendant's conviction for the possession of heroin, holding that

It is well settled that a search incident to a lawful arrest is a traditional exception to the warrant requirement of the Fourth Amendment. This general exception has historically been formulated into two distinct propositions. The first is that a search may be made of the *person* of the arrestee by virtue of the lawful arrest. The second is that a search may be made of the area within the control of the arrestee.

Examination of this Court's decisions in the area show that these two propositions have been treated quite differently. The validity of the search of a person incident to a lawful arrest has been regarded as settled from its first enunciation, and has remained virtually unchallenged until the present case. The validity of the second proposition, while likewise conceded in principle, has been subject to differing interpretations as to the extent of the area which may be searched.

. . .

. . . Since it is the fact of custodial arrest which gives rise to the authority to search, it is of no moment that Jenks did not indicate any subjective fear of the respondent or that he did not himself suspect that respondent was armed. Having in the course of a lawful search come upon the crumpled package of cigarettes, he was entitled to inspect it; and when his inspection revealed the heroin capsules, he was entitled to seize them as "fruits, instrumentalities, or contraband" probative of criminal conduct.

Gustafson v. Florida

Supreme Court of the United States (1973)
414 U.S. 260, 94 S.Ct. 488

The defendant was arrested and taken into custody for driving without a valid driver's license. In the search incident to the arrest, the officer found marijuana cigarettes in a cigarette box. In affirming the use of the evidence obtained and the defendant's conviction for the possession of marijuana, the U.S. Supreme Court held that

We hold therefore that upon arresting petitioner for the offense of driving his automobile without a valid operator's license, and taking him into custody, Smith was entitled to make a full search of petitioner's person incident to that lawful arrest. Since it is the fact of custodial arrest which gives rise to the authority to search, it is of no moment that Smith did not indicate any subjective fear of the petitioner or that he did not himself suspect that the petitioner was armed. Having in the course of his lawful search come upon the box of cigarettes, Smith was entitled to inspect it; and when his inspection revealed the homemade cigarettes which he believed to contain an unlawful substance, he was entitled to seize them as "fruits, instrumentalities or contraband" probative of criminal conduct . . . . The judgment of the Supreme Court of Florida is therefore
Affirmed.

The *Robinson-Gustafson* rule is a federal rule followed by many (but not all) states. The Rule holds that a full and thorough search may be made incident to an arrest. Some states limit such a search to weapons and evidence relating to the arrest which was made, but the *Robinson-Gustafson* rule does not impose such limitations. As can be seen from the cases, which are arrests for traffic offenses, a search can be made for evidence of other crimes and contraband.

What Is "the Area Within the Immediate Control of the Arrestee"?

In 1983, the U.S. Supreme Court explained, "we determined that the lower courts 'have found no workable definition of the area within the immediate control of the arrestee' when that area arguably includes the interior of an automobile and the arrestee is its recent occupant." [11] The Court answered this question in the following case of *New York v. Belton:*

New York v. Belton

Supreme Court of the United States (1981)
453 U.S. 454, 101 S.Ct. 2860

On April 9, 1978, Trooper Douglas Nicot, a New York State policeman driving an unmarked car on the New York Thruway, was passed by another automobile traveling at an excessive rate of speed. Nicot gave chase, overtook the speeding vehicle, and ordered its driver to pull it over to the side of the road and stop. There were four men in the car, one of whom was Roger Belton, the respondent in this case. The policeman asked to see the driver's license and automobile registration, and discovered that none of the men owned the vehicle or was related to its owner. Meanwhile, the policeman had smelled burnt marihuana and had seen on the floor of the car an envelope marked "Supergold" that he associated with marihuana. He therefore directed the men to get out the car, and placed them under arrest for the unlawful possession of marihuana. He patted down each of the men and "split them up into four separate areas of the Thruway at this time so they would not be in physical touching area of each other." He then picked up the envelope marked "Supergold" and found that it contained marihuana. After giving the arrestees the warnings required by *Miranda v. Arizona,* 384 U.S. 436, ... the state policeman searched each one of them. He then searched the passenger compartment of the car. On the back seat he found a black leather jacket belonging to Belton. He unzipped one of the pockets of the jacket and discovered cocaine. Placing the jacket in his automobile, he drove the four arrestees to a nearby police station.

In affirming Belton's conviction for the possession of cocaine and the use of the cocaine as evidence in Belton's trial, the Court held that

we hold that when a policeman has made a lawful custodial arrest of the occupant of an automobile, he may, as a contemporaneous incident of that arrest, search the passenger compartment of that automobile.

It follows from this conclusion that the police may also examine the contents of any containers found within the passenger compartment, for if the passenger compartment is within reach of the arrestee, so also will containers in it be within his reach .... Such a container may, of course, be searched whether it is open or closed, since the justification for the search is not that the arrestee has no privacy interest in the container, but that the lawful custodial arrest justifies the infringement of any privacy interest the arrestee may have. Thus, while the Court in *Chimel* held that the police could not search all the drawers in an arrestee's house simply because the police had arrested him at home, the Court noted that drawers within an arrestee's reach could be searched because of the danger their contents might pose to the police ....

It is true, of course, that these containers will sometimes be such that they could hold neither a weapon nor evidence of the criminal conduct for which the suspect was arrested. However, in *United States v. Robinson,* the Court rejected the argument that such a container—there a "crumpled up cigarette package"—located during a search of Robinson incident to his arrest could not be searched: "The authority to search the person incident to a lawful custodial arrest, while based upon the need to disarm and to discover evidence, does not depend on what a court may later decide was the probability in a particular arrest situation that weapons or evidence would in fact be found upon the person of the suspect. A custodial arrest of a suspect based on probable cause is a reasonable intrusion under the Fourth Amendment; that intrusion being lawful, a search incident to the arrest requires no additional justification."

EVIDENCE OBTAINED BY SEARCHES UNDER THE AUTOMOBILE EXCEPTION OR THE CARROLL RULE

Over the years since motor vehicles have been used as means of transportation, the courts have consistently noted the constitutional difference between motor vehicles and fixed structures such as homes and other types of buildings.[12] In the 1976 case of *South Dakota v. Opperman,*[13] the U.S. Supreme Court stated that

> This Court has traditionally drawn a distinction between automobiles and homes or offices in relation to the Fourth Amendment. Although automobiles are "effects" and thus within the reach of the Fourth Amendment, ... warrantless examinations of automobiles have been upheld in circumstances in which a search of a home or office would not.

The U.S. Supreme Court then stated the following two reasons for "this well-settled distinction":

> (1) First, the inherent mobility of automobiles creates circumstances of such exigency that, as a practical necessity, rigorous enforcement of the warrant requirement is impossible .... But the Court has also upheld warrantless searches where no immediate danger was presented that the car would be removed from the jurisdiction.
>
> (2) Besides the element of mobility, less rigorous warrant requirements govern because the expectation of privacy with respect to one's automobile is significantly less than that relating to one's home or

office. In discharging their varied responsibilities for ensuring the public safety, law enforcement officials are necessarily brought into frequent contact with automobiles. Most of this contact is distinctly noncriminal in nature .... Automobiles, unlike homes, are subjected to pervasive and continuing governmental regulation and controls, including periodic inspection and licensing requirements. As an every-day occurrence, police stop and examine vehicles when license plates or inspection stickers have expired, or if other violations, such as exhaust fumes or excessive noise, are noted, or if headlights or other safety equipment are not in proper working order.

The expectation of privacy as to autos is further diminished by the obviously public nature of automobile travel. Only two Terms ago, the Court noted:

> "One has a lesser expectation of privacy in a motor vehicle because its function is transportation and it seldom serves as one's residence or as the repository of personal effects. It travels public thoroughfares where both its occupants and its contents are in plain view." *Cardwell v. Lewis,* 417 U.S., at 590, 94 S.Ct. 2464, 41 L.Ed.2d 325, 69 Ohio Ops.2d 69.

The Automobile Exception

The **Carroll rule,** or the **probable cause rule,** is a simple one. It authorizes a law enforcement officer who has probable cause to believe a vehicle contains evidence of a crime to search the vehicle and to seize the evidence. Probable cause alone will not get a law enforcement officer into a home to make an arrest or a search for evidence. However, probable cause alone will authorize entry into a vehicle to seize evidence. The rule which originated during Prohibition in the 1925 case of *Carroll v. United States* is stated by the following cases:

Carroll v. United States

Supreme Court of the United States (1925)
267 U.S. 132, 45 S.Ct. 280

Officers had probable cause to believe that Carroll's roadster had intoxicating liquor in violation of the National Prohibition Act. A search without a warrant discovered sixty-eight bottles of gin and whisky. The Court affirmed the use of the evidence and conviction, holding that

> On reason and authority the true rule is that if the search and seizure without a warrant are made upon probable cause, that is, upon a belief, reasonably arising out of circumstances known to the seizing officer, that an automobile or other vehicle contains that which by law is subject to seizure and destruction, the search and seizure are valid. The Fourth Amendment is to be construed in the light of what was deemed an unreasonable search and seizure when it was adopted, and in a manner which will conserve public interests as well as the interests and rights of individual citizens.

Dyke v. Taylor Implement Mfg. Co.

Supreme Court of the United States (1968)
391 U.S. 216, 88 S.Ct. 1472

> Automobiles, because of their mobility, may be searched without a warrant upon facts not justifying a warrantless search of a residence or office .... The cases so holding have, however, always insisted that the officers conducting the search have "reasonable or probable cause" to believe that they will find the instrumentality of a crime or evidence pertaining to a crime before they begin their warrantless search. The record before us does not contain evidence that Sheriff Kirkpatrick, Deputy Sheriff Powers, or the officers who assisted in the search had reasonable or probable cause to believe that evidence would be found in petitioners' car.

Automobile Exception Searches Made Later at the Station House

> In the 1926 *Carroll* case, the roadster was searched for whiskey at the roadside immediately following the car stop. But when armed robbery suspects are apprehended late at night, wouldn't it be safer to put them in jail before searching their car for evidence? This question was before the U.S. Supreme Court in the case of *Chambers v. Maroney*, in which the officers moved the vehicle to the station house and then searched for evidence without a warrant. The U.S. Supreme Court has repeatedly held that the evidence of such a search is admissible, as illustrated by the following two cases. However, not all state courts have gone along with this rule and have held that a search warrant is necessary in such cases.

Chambers v. Maroney

Supreme Court of the United States (1970)
399 U.S. 42, 90 S.Ct. 1975

> After an armed robbery of a gasoline service station, Pennsylvania police officers arrested four men in a blue compact station wagon. Two of the men matched descriptions of the robbers. After the men were arrested, the station wagon was driven to the police station where a thorough search of the vehicle was made and incriminating evidence obtained. Additional evidence was obtained in a search of the defendant's home under the authority of a search warrant. In affirming the defendant's conviction and the search of the station wagon under the automobile exception, the U.S. Supreme Court held that

On the facts before us, the blue station wagon could have been searched on the spot when it was stopped since there was probable cause to search and it was a fleeting target for a search. The probable-cause factor still obtained at the station house and so did the mobility of the car unless the Fourth Amendment permits a warrantless seizure of the car and the denial of its use to anyone until a warrant is secured. In that event there is little to choose in terms of practical consequences between an immediate search without a warrant and the car's immobilization until a warrant is obtained. The same consequences may not follow where there is unforeseeable cause to search a house. Footnote 10 of *Chambers v. Maroney* states, "It was not unreasonable in this case to take the car to the station house. All occupants in the car were arrested in a dark parking lot in the middle of the night. A careful search at that point was impractical and perhaps not safe for the officers, and it would serve the owner's convenience and the safety of his car to have the vehicle and the keys together at the station house."

Texas v. White

Supreme Court of the United States (1975)
423 U.S. 67, 96 S.Ct. 304

Per Curiam.

Respondent was arrested at 1:30 p.m. by Amarillo, Tex., police officers while attempting to pass fraudulent checks at a drive-in window of the First National Bank of Amarillo. Only 10 minutes earlier, the officers had been informed by another bank that a man answering respondent's description and driving an automobile exactly matching that of respondent had tried to negotiate four checks drawn on a nonexistent account. Upon arrival at the First National Bank pursuant to a telephone call from that bank, the officers obtained from the drive-in teller other checks that respondent had attempted to pass there. The officers directed respondent to park his automobile at the curb. While parking the car, respondent was observed by a bank employee and one of the officers attempting to "stuff" something between the seats. Respondent was arrested and one officer drove him to the station house while the other drove respondent's car there. At the station house, the officers questioned respondent for 30 to 45 minutes and, pursuant to their normal procedure, requested consent to search the automobile. Respondent refused to consent to the search. The officers then proceeded to search the automobile anyway. During the search, an officer discovered four wrinkled checks that corresponded to those respondent had attempted to pass at the first bank. The trial judge, relying on *Chambers v. Maroney,* 399 U.S. 42, 90 S.Ct. 1975, 26 L.Ed.2d 419 (1970), admitted over respondent's objection the four checks seized during the search of respondent's automobile at the station house. The judge expressly found probable cause both for the arrest and for the search of the vehicle, either at the scene or at the station house. Respondent was convicted after a jury trial of knowingly attempting to pass a forged instrument. The Texas Court of Criminal Appeals, in a 3–2 decision, reversed respondent's conviction on the ground that the evidence of the four wrinkled checks was obtained without a warrant in violation of respondent's Fourth Amendment rights. 521 S.W.2d 255, rehearing denied, 521 S.W.2d 258 (1975). We reverse.

In *Chambers v. Maroney* we held that police officers with probable cause to search an automobile on the scene where it was stopped could constitutionally do so later at the station house without first obtaining a warrant. There, as here, "[t]he probable cause factor" that developed on the scene "still obtained at the station house." 399 U.S., at 52, 90 S.Ct., at 1981. The Court of Criminal Appeals erroneously excluded the evidence seized from the search at the station house in light of the trial judge's finding, undisturbed by the appellate court, that there was probable cause to search respondent's car.

The Scope and Extent of the Carroll Rule Search

The extent and scope of a Carroll rule search was determined by the U.S. Supreme Court in the case of *United States v. Ross*, in which the Court held that

> [i]f probable cause justifies the search of a lawfully stopped vehicle, it justifies the search *of every part of the vehicle* and its contents that may conceal the object of the search. [Emphasis added].

The case follows.

United States v. Ross

Supreme Court of the United States (1982)
456 U.S. 798, 102 S.Ct. 2157

Police officers had probable cause to believe that the defendant was selling heroin out of the trunk of his car on the streets in Washington, D.C. They stopped the defendant's car and told him to get out. After they found a pistol in the glove compartment, they arrested the defendant and handcuffed him. Because the police had probable cause to believe that there was heroin in the trunk of the car, they took Ross' keys and opened the trunk. They opened a brown paper bag found in the trunk and discovered a number of glassine bags containing a white powder. They then closed the trunk and drove the car to headquarters, where additional evidence was found and it was determined that the powder in the paper bag was heroin. Ross was convicted of possession of heroin with intent to distribute. In affirming the use of the evidence and the conviction, the Court held that

> Contraband goods rarely are strewn across the trunk or floor of a car; since by their very nature such goods must be withheld from public

Table 12.1 "Can the Police Do That?" Vehicle Stops and Searches

YES, THE FOLLOWING POLICE ACTIONS WITHOUT A SEARCH WARRANT ARE JUSTIFIED:

Authority	Requirements	Comments
Plain view (plain smell)	■ If the vehicle stop was proper and/or the officer is where he has a right to be; and ■ The incriminating evidence is discovered "inadvertently"; and ■ It is "immediately apparent" that the item may be evidence of a crime, the officer may seize the evidence.	U.S. Supreme Court Chief Justice Rehnquist stated in *Texas v. Brown*, "Whatever may be the final disposition of the 'inadvertence' element of 'plain view', it is clearly no bar to seizure (in that case)."
Consent to search	A person who has lawful use or "mutual use" and "joint access and control" of a vehicle can consent to a search if the consent is voluntarily given.	
Reasonable suspicion would justify: ■ An investigative stop ■ A frisk or search for weapons if there was justifiable concern for safety	There must be reasonable suspicion to believe a crime has been, is being, or will be committed. The detaining officer "must have a particularized and objective basis for suspecting the particular person stopped of criminal activity."	Many states have statutes governing the authority to make an investigative stop and the separate authority to take a protective action.
If a lawful custodial arrest is made	The officer may, at the time of the arrest and the place of the arrest: ■ Search the "passenger compartment of that automobile" and also ■ Search opened or closed containers within the reach of the arrested person.	Some states have statutes which limit this authority.
The "automobile exception" (or the Carroll rule or probable cause rule)	Probable cause to believe that a vehicle contains evidence of a crime. A search of "a lawfully stopped vehicle" can then be made. The search can be "of every part of the vehicle and its contents that may conceal the object of the search." U.S. Supreme Court in *United States v. Ross* (see case in this chapter).	
Authority to inventory property in lawful custody of a law enforcement agency	An inventory is a search but it is *not* a search for evidence to incriminate a suspect. The purpose of an inventory is to: ■ Protect the owner's property ■ Protect police against claims or disputes over property ■ Protect police from potential danger.	
Community caretaking function	A community caretaking function is a task or job which has to be done or which should be done in the best interests of the community. The officer is not looking for evidence of a crime, but while he (or she) is performing the community caretaking function, he comes upon evidence of a crime. For example, an accident blocks traffic lanes on a busy street. To open the street to traffic, an officer gets into one of the cars and moves it to the curb. While in the vehicle, the officer sees contraband. See the U.S. Supreme Court case of *Cady v. Dombrowski*.	

view, they rarely can be placed in an automobile unless they are enclosed within some form of container .... The luggage carried by a traveler entering the country may be searched at random by a customs officer; the luggage may be searched no matter how great the traveler's desire to conceal the contents may be. A container carried at the time of arrest often may be searched without a warrant and even without any specific suspicion concerning its contents. A container that may conceal the object of a search authorized by a warrant may be opened immediately; the individual's interest in privacy must give way to the magistrate's official determination of probable cause.

In the same manner, an individual's expectation of privacy in a vehicle and its contents may not survive if probable cause is given to believe that the vehicle is transporting contraband. Certainly the privacy interests in a car's trunk or glove compartment may be no less than those in a movable container. An individual undoubtedly has a significant interest that the upholstery of his automobile will not be ripped or a hidden compartment within it opened. These interests must yield to the authority of a search, however, which—in light of *Carroll*—does not itself require the prior approval of a magistrate. The scope of a warrantless search based on probable cause is no narrower—and no broader—than the scope of a search authorized by a warrant supported by probable cause. Only the prior approval of the magistrate is waived; the search otherwise is as the magistrate could authorize.

The scope of a warrantless search of an automobile thus is not defined by the nature of the container in which the contraband is secreted. Rather, it is defined by the object of the search and the places in which there is probable cause to believe that it may be found ....

... We hold that the scope of the warrantless search authorized by that exception is no broader and no narrower than a magistrate could legitimately authorize by warrant. If probable cause justifies the search of a lawfully stopped vehicle, it justifies the search of every part of the vehicle and its contents that may conceal the object of the search.

Aircraft and Watercraft as Mobile Vehicles

Because aircraft and watercraft are mobile vehicles capable of swiftly carrying evidence out of a jurisdiction, they are included under the automobile exception. In the following case, evidence obtained in a search without a warrant of an airplane was held to be admissible by the Supreme Court of Iowa.

State v. McReynolds

Supreme Court of Iowa (1972)
195 N.W.2d 102, 11 CrL 2011

Viewing the problem confronting the officers from the standpoint of practical law enforcement rather than with the benefit of the hindsight which we now possess, we think the officers did not act in an unconstitutional manner. They set up surveillance by the owner of Midwest Aviation. When that individual saw defendant loading the plane, he notified the officers. The articles which defendant loaded—the duffle bag and the garbage cans—might have looked sufficiently suspicious, taken with the informer's tips, to justify the issuance of a search warrant. But that question we need not decide. When the officers got the message from Strunk, the situation was exigent indeed. They went into action. Actually, the officers did not have hard evidence that defendant had narcotics until defendant nodded affirmatively when Sergeant McElroy said he understood defendant had narcotic drugs on board. The situation was quite similar to the one in *Husty v. United States,* 282 U.S. 694, 701, 51 S.Ct. 240, 242, 75 L.Ed. 629, 632–633 .... We think exigent circumstances existed here.

As to probable cause, when Sergeant McElroy arrived at the plane, he did not demand entry into the plane, nor did he search it. He stated to defendant he understood defendant had narcotic drugs aboard. Defendant nodded and mumbled "yes." At that point the sergeant not only had probable cause but very strong cause to believe the plane contained contraband, from defendant's own lips. The sergeant could lawfully proceed with a search and seizure. Here the case is quite similar to *Scher v. United States,* 305 U.S. 251, 253–255, 59 S.Ct. 174, 176, 83 L.Ed. 151, 154–155: .... We think Sergeant McElroy had probable cause in the case at bar.

EVIDENCE OBTAINED WHEN PROPERTY IN THE CUSTODY OF A LAW ENFORCEMENT AGENCY IS INVENTORIED

Law enforcement agencies can obtain the custody of property of other persons in any of the following manners:

- Property which has been lost, stolen, or abandoned.
- Property seized as evidence of crimes.
- Temporary custody of property of persons who have been arrested or who are incapacitated.
- Property which has been impounded or which has been seized for forfeiture proceedings.

It is standard police procedure to inventory such property before storing the property for safekeeping. The U.S. Supreme Court listed the following reasons and needs for inventorying impounded property: [14]

1. "The protection of the owner's property while it remained in police custody."
2. "The protection of the police against claims or disputes over lost or stolen property."
3. "The protection of the police from potential danger."

The Court held that "(t)he practice has been viewed as essential to respond to incidents of theft or vandalism . . . . In addition, police frequently attempt to determine whether a vehicle has been stolen and thereafter abandoned."

With lost, stolen, and valuable property which appears to be abandoned, an effort would be made to determine the identity of the owner. This would require examining and inventorying the property. Law enforcement agencies recommend that property likely to be stolen (TV sets, etc.) should be marked with the owner's driver's license number. The name and address of the owner can then be obtained by use of the state computer system.

The following U.S. Supreme Court case states the majority ruling in the United States on vehicle inventories:

South Dakota v. Opperman

Supreme Court of the United States (1976)
428 U.S. 364, 96 S.Ct. 3092

The defendant's vehicle was observed at approximately 3 A.M., parked illegally on a Vermillion, South Dakota street. A parking ticket was issued warning that the vehicle could be "towed away from the area." Another ticket was issued at approximately 10 A.M. and after the car was inspected, the vehicle was towed to the city impound lot. At the impound lot, a police officer observed a watch on the dashboard and other items of personal property in the car. The vehicle was then unlocked and, before storing the defendant's valuables for safekeeping, the officer inventoried the contents of the car "using a standard inventory form pursuant to standard police procedure." Marijuana was found in the unlocked glove compartment and the defendant was charged with the possession of marijuana. After a motion to suppress failed, the defendant was found guilty after a jury trial and was sentenced to a fine of $100 and fourteen days incarceration in the county jail. After the Supreme Court of South Dakota reversed the conviction, the matter was appealed to the U.S. Supreme Court. In reversing the judgment of the South Dakota Supreme Court and holding that the evidence was properly obtained, the U.S. Supreme Court ruled that

> The decisions of this Court point unmistakably to the conclusion reached by both federal and state courts that inventories pursuant to standard police procedures are reasonable. . . .
>
> The Vermillion police were indisputably engaged in a caretaking search of a lawfully impounded automobile. . . . The inventory was conducted only after the car had been impounded for multiple parking violations. The owner, having left his car illegally parked for an extended period, and thus subject to impoundment, was not present to make other arrangements for the safekeeping of his belongings. The inventory itself was prompted by the presence in plain view of a number of valuables inside the car. As in Cady, (*Cady v. Dombrowski,* 413 U.S. 433, 93 S.Ct. 2523, 37 L.Ed.2d 706 (1973)) there is no suggestion whatever that this standard procedure, essentially like that

Authorities Which Would Justify a Search by a Law Enforcement Officer

SEARCHES UNDER THE EMERGENCY SEARCH DOCTRINE

The state must show that an officer reasonably believed

- that a life was endangered, or
- that a "hot pursuit" was justified, or
- that evidence to be seized is in the process of being destroyed, or
- that evidence to be seized is about to be moved to an unknown place or out of the jurisdiction.

INVENTORY SEARCHES OF PROPERTY IN THE CUSTODY OF A LAW ENFORCEMENT AGENCY

- The property must have been lawfully impounded or is properly in the custody of the police.
- The inventory search must be made in good faith for the purposes of inventorying the vehicle or property.
- The scope and extent of the search must comply with the court rulings of the officer's jurisdiction.

JAIL OR STATION HOUSE SEARCHES

- There is no right of privacy in a jail or station house. (*Lanza v. New York,* 370 U.S. 139, 82 S.Ct. 1218, 8 L.Ed.2d 384 (1962)).
- "... once the accused is lawfully arrested and is in custody, the effects in his possession at the place of detention that were subject to search at the time and place of his arrest may lawfully be searched and seized without a warrant even though a substantial period of time has elapsed ...". *United States v. Edwards,* 415 U.S. 800, 94 S.Ct. 1234, 39 L.Ed.2d 771 (1974) unless otherwise modified in your jurisdiction.

SEARCHES UNDER THE AUTOMOBILE EXCEPTION OR CARROLL RULE

An officer must have probable cause (or reasonable grounds to believe) that a motor vehicle, aircraft, or watercraft contains evidence of a crime or contraband which may be seized.

followed throughout the country, was a pretext concealing an investigatory police motive.

On this record we conclude that in following standard police procedures, prevailing throughout the country and approved by the overwhelming majority of courts, the conduct of the police was not "unreasonable" under the Fourth Amendment.

SEARCH INCIDENT TO AN ARREST

- There must be a lawful, custodial arrest.

- The search must be at the time and place of the arrest.   (*Preston v. United States,* 376 U.S. 364, 84 S.Ct. 881, 11 L.Ed.2d 777 (1964)).

- The search is limited to the area within the arrestee's "immediate control."

- A full, intensive search may be made unless the *Robinson-Gustafson* rule has been limited in your jurisdiction.

SEARCHES MADE FOR THE PROTECTION OF THE OFFICER OR ANOTHER PERSON

- The "stop" or other action taken by the officer prior to search must be lawful.

- "Reasonable suspicion" must exist to justify the "frisk" or the "protective sweep" and in some jurisdictions, the officer must testify as to his fear for his safety or the safety of another person.

- The frisk must be limited to a search for weapons while the protective sweep is limited to a search for persons in or about the premises.

SEARCH WARRANTS

- The search warrant must be in writing and signed by a judge or magistrate.

- It must direct a law enforcement officer to search a specifically described person, place, or object for the purpose of seizing specifically described evidence of a crime.

- The warrant must be based upon a finding of probable cause by the judge or magistrate.

- Probable cause may be established by firsthand knowledge known to law enforcement officers or by hearsay information which has been shown to be reliable.

CONSENT SEARCHES

- The consent to search must be voluntarily given ...

- by the defendant, or another person who had such "joint access or control" and "mutual use" of the property so as to have authority to consent to the search.

The judgment of the South Dakota Supreme Court is therefore reversed and the case is remanded for further proceedings not inconsistent with this opinion.

Reversed and remanded.

State v. Opperman

Supreme Court of South Dakota (1976)
247 N.W.2d 673

> After the U.S. Supreme Court held that the inventory search of the defendant's glove compartment was reasonable under the U.S. Constitution, the case was appealed to the Supreme Court of South Dakota. The South Dakota Supreme Court held that under the South Dakota Constitution, the search was unreasonable. The evidence therefore could not be used and the case would be dismissed.

Obtaining Lawful Custody of Vehicles or Other Property

The Supreme Court of Kansas stated in the 1975 case of *State v. Boster* [15] that

> An inventory search cannot be valid unless the police initially obtain lawful custody of the vehicle .... The impoundment of a vehicle by the police at the station house or other place of safekeeping is lawful if authorized by statute or ordinance. In the absence of such express authority, it has been held that police may still be considered to have lawful custody of a vehicle when there are "reasonable grounds" for impoundment.

The Supreme Court of Kansas then quoted the State of Washington Court of Appeals as to "what might be considered reasonable grounds for impoundment: [16]

> Reasonable cause for impoundment may, for example, include the necessity for removing (1) an unattended-to car illegally parked or otherwise illegally obstructing traffic; (2) an unattended-to car from the scene of an accident when the driver is physically or mentally incapable of deciding upon steps to be taken to deal with his property, as in the case of the intoxicated, mentally incapacitated or seriously injured driver; (3) a car that has been stolen or used in the commission of a crime when its retention as evidence is necessary; (4) an abandoned car; (5) a car so mechanically defective as to be a menace to others using the public highway; (6) a car impoundable pursuant to ordinance or statute which provides therefor as in the case of forfeiture. The mere commission of one or more of the 27 bailable traffic offenses listed in JTR T2.03(m) does not necessarily provide reasonable cause for impoundment .... There is even case support for the view that if the driver cannot present his driver's license when arrested on a traffic violation, impoundment on that account is not required.

Situations in Which Impoundment Has Been Held to Be Improper

In the following cases, courts have suggested or held that impoundments by law enforcement officers were improper:

- When the driver can take reasonable steps to safeguard his car at the time of arrest. *United States v. Lawson*, 487 F.2d 468 (8th Cir.1973).

- If other passengers in the vehicle could have taken the responsibility for the car. *Virgil v. Superior Court*, 268 Cal.App.2d 127, 73 Cal.Rptr. 793 (1968).

- If the arrestee's friend could have removed the vehicle from the precinct station within a few hours. *United States v. Pannell*, 256 A.2d 925 (D.C. App.1969).

- When reasonable alternatives to impoundment exist. *State v. Bales*, 15 Wash.App. 834, 552 P.2d 688 (1976).

- When the defendant would be absent from the car for only a brief time to post bond. *State v. Singleton*, 9 Wash.App. 327, 511 P.2d 1396 (1973).

- When another officer could have driven the vehicle to a nearby parking area where it would have been reasonably safe. *People v. Nagel*, 17 Cal. App.3d 492, 95 Cal.Rptr. 129 (1971).

- When the location of the vehicle does not create a traffic hazard or nuisance and the owner or operator chooses not to have his car impounded. *State v. Jenkins*, 319 So.2d 91 (Fla.App.1975).

The U.S. Supreme Court pointed out that the justification for the impoundment in the case of *South Dakota v. Opperman* was that the car had been "illegally parked for an extended period" and that "(t)he owner (Opperman) ... was not present to make other arrangements for the safekeeping of his belongings."

The Requirement That the Inventory Be Bona Fide and Made in Good Faith

In the 1975 case of *State v. Jenkins*,[17] the Court of Appeal of Florida stated the requirement that the inventory be made in good faith as follows:

> The foregoing cases support the proposition that a search conducted for the purpose of making an inventory of the contents of an automobile is not "unreasonable" within the proscription of the Fourth Amendment if the totality of the circumstances demonstrate that the search is a bona fide inventory made in the ordinary course of police procedures. The general standard to be applied is reasonableness. An "inventory" search will be unreasonable if it is utilized as a pretext to conduct an "exploratory" search in order to hunt for incriminating evidence. Whether or not an inventory search is unreasonable and has been misused will depend upon the particular facts and circumstances of each case.

The Supreme Court of Arizona stated the requirement of good faith as follows in the 1973 case of *In re One 1965 Econoline, I.D. No. EI6JH 702043 Arizona License No. EC–7887*:[18]

> A second requirement according to many cases is that the police must have acted in good faith in conducting the inventory and must not have used the inventory procedure as a subterfuge for a warrantless search. For example, in *Pigford v. United States*, 273 A.2d 837 (D.C. App.1971), it was stated:

The Law Having to Do With the Search of Containers

All persons carry personal property in containers. A container could be a purse, wallet, briefcase, suitcase, etc. The Fourth Amendment recognized the right of privacy which persons have in containers by stating that the "right of the people to be secure in their persons, houses, papers and effects ... shall not be violated ...". A right of privacy exists in containers whether the container is a "worthy" container (an expensive purse, wallet, or briefcase) or an "unworthy" container (such as a dirty paper bag or battered cardboard box). Authority for a law enforcement search of a container could be:

Consent

The government must show by "clear and convincing" [1] evidence that consent was, in fact, freely and voluntarily given by a person who has exclusive use of the container or by a person with "mutual use" and "joint access or control" so as to have authority to give consent. See *Frazier v. Cupp*, 394 U.S. 731, 89 S.Ct. 1420 (1969), in which valid consent was obtained from the defendant's cousin who was a "joint user" of a duffel bag with the defendant.

Incident to an Arrest

At the time and place of a lawful, custodial arrest, a law enforcement officer may search the arrestee's person and any container within the immediate control of the arrested person. If the arrested person is in a motor vehicle, the officer "may, as contemporaneous incident of that arrest, search the passenger compartment of that automobile" and "also examine the contents of any containers found within the passenger compartment ...". *New York v. Belton.*[2] Some states, however, have limited this authority. (see chapter 10.)

Exigency (Emergency) Circumstances

Police may search containers under the following exigency circumstances:

- *The Automobile Exception or the Carroll Rule.* If a law enforcement officer has probable cause to believe that a motor vehicle contains evidence of criminal activity, he (or she) may then search the vehicle and all items or containers located in the vehicle, including the trunk. (See chapter 12.)

"These circumstances, we think, militate strongly against any conclusion that the search of the car was for inventory purposes; rather, they are persuasive that the search was 'exploratory and therefore forbidden.' We hold the purported inventory search and seizure illegal." *Pigford v. United States, supra,* 273 A.2d at 840.

COMMUNITY CARETAKING FUNCTIONS

The term **community caretaking functions** has been used in recent years by the U.S. Supreme Court and other courts in describing functions by governmental officials in performing duties other than seeking evidence of a crime or criminal intent. The U.S. Supreme Court described this function as follows in the 1973 case of *Cady v. Dombrowski*[19]:

- *Where a life is endangered.* In poisoning and attempted suicide cases, law enforcement officers would be justified in seizing and opening containers in an effort to provide doctors with samples of the drug or poison. (See chapter 11.)

Inventory

When a container is properly in the custody of a law enforcement agency, an inventory is a procedure used to identify valuables the agency is responsible for. Inventorying the property of a person to be placed in jail is an example. The U.S. Supreme Court held in the case of *Illinois v. Lafayette* [3] that it was reasonable prior to "incarcerating an arrested person, to search any container or article in his possession, in accordance with established inventory procedures." (See chapter 10.)

Search Warrant

Where probable cause exists to believe that evidence of criminal activity is concealed in a container, a search warrant may be obtained to search and seize the container. (See chapter 14.)

WHEN A CONTAINER IS THE "TARGET" AND THE CONTAINER IS IN A MOTOR VEHICLE

If probable cause exists to believe that a container holds evidence of criminal activity and the container is in a motor vehicle, the police may seize and hold the container, but must obtain a search warrant prior to opening the container. In this type of situation, it is the container which is the target, not the motor vehicle. Consent or a search warrant would authorize the opening of the container. (See *United States v. Chadwick,* 433 U.S. 1, 97 S.Ct. 2476 (1977) and *Arkansas v. Sanders,* 442 U.S. 753, 99 S.Ct. 2586 (1979).)

[1] Bumper v. North Carolina, 391 U.S. 543, 88 S.Ct. 1788 (1968).
[2] 453 U.S. 454, 101 S.Ct. 2860 (1981).
[3] 462 U.S. 640, 103 S.Ct. 2605 (1983).

As a result of our federal system of government ... state and local police officers, unlike federal officers, have much more contact with vehicles for reasons related to the operation of vehicles themselves. All States require vehicles to be registered and operators to be licensed. States and localities have enacted extensive and detailed codes regulating the condition and manner in which motor vehicles may be operated on public streets and highways.

Because of the extensive regulation of motor vehicles and traffic, and also because of the frequency with which a vehicle can become disabled or involved in an accident on public highways, the extent of police-citizen contact involving automobiles will be substantially greater than police-citizen contact in a home or office. Some such contacts will occur because the officer may believe the operator has violated a criminal statute, but many more will not be of that nature. Local police officers, unlike federal officers, frequently investigate vehicle accidents in which there is no claim of criminal liability and engage in what, for want of a better term, may be described as community caretaking functions, totally divorced from the detection, investigation, or acquisition of evidence relating to the violation of a criminal statute.

The three U.S. Supreme Court cases from which the community caretaking function concept has emerged are as follows:

Harris v. United States

Supreme Court of the United States (1968)
390 U.S. 234, 88 S.Ct. 992

The U.S. Supreme Court described the *Harris* case as follows in *Cady v. Dombrowski:*

In *Harris,* petitioner was arrested for robbery. As petitioner's car had been identified leaving the site of the robbery, it was impounded as evidence. A regulation of the District of Columbia Police Department required that an impounded vehicle be searched, that all valuables be removed, and that a tag detailing certain information be placed on the vehicle. In compliance with this regulation, and without a warrant, an officer searched the car and, while opening one of the doors, spotted an automobile registration card, belonging to the victim, lying face up on the metal door stripping. This item was introduced into evidence at petitioner's trial for robbery. In rejecting the contention that the evidence was inadmissible, the Court stated:
"Once the door had lawfully been opened, the registration card ... was plainly visible. It has long been settled that objects falling in the plain view of an officer who has a right to be in the position to have that view are subject to seizure and may be introduced in evidence." 390 U.S., at 236, 88 S.Ct., at 993.

Cooper v. California

Supreme Court of the United States (1967)
386 U.S. 58, 87 S.Ct. 788

The U.S. Supreme Court described the *Cooper* case as follows in *Cady v. Dombrowski:*

In *Cooper,* the petitioner was arrested for selling heroin, and his car impounded pending forfeiture proceedings. A week later, a police officer searched the car and found, in the glove compartment, incriminating evidence subsequently admitted at petitioner's trial. This

Court upheld the validity of the warrantless search and seizure with the following language:

> "This case is not *Preston,* nor is it controlled by it. Here the officers seized petitioner's car because they were required to do so by state law. They seized it because of the crime for which they arrested petitioner. They seized it to impound it and they had to keep it until forfeiture proceedings were concluded. Their subsequent search of the car—whether the State had 'legal title' to it or not—was closely related to the reason petitioner was arrested, the reason his car had been impounded, and the reason it was being retained. The forfeiture of petitioner's car did not take place until over four months after it was lawfully seized. It would be unreasonable to hold that the police, having to retain the car in their custody for such a length of time, had no right, even for their own protection, to search it." 386 U.S., at 61–62, 87 S.Ct., at 791.

Cady v. Dombrowski

Supreme Court of the United States (1973)
413 U.S. 433, 93 S.Ct. 2523

The defendant called a sheriff's department in Wisconsin and reported that he had wrecked his car on a highway. Two officers went to the scene of the accident, took the defendant to a hospital, and arranged to have the severely damaged vehicle towed to a private garage. At the hospital, the officers became aware of how intoxicated the defendant was and arrested him. Because the defendant had stated that he was an off-duty Chicago police officer, one of the arresting officers then went to the private garage in search of the defendant's police service revolver, which he assumed was in the wrecked vehicle. Upon opening the trunk of the defendant's car, the officer came upon blood-splattered items which the officer seized. The evidence found in the defendant's car trunk was later used in a trial in which the defendant was convicted of first-degree murder. The officer making the search knew nothing of the murder until the body of the victim was found the following day. In affirming the murder conviction and holding that the search for the revolver was reasonable, the Supreme Court ruled that

> We believe that the instant case is controlled by principles that may be extrapolated from *Harris v. United States,* supra, and *Cooper v. California,* supra . . . .
>
> In *Harris* the justification for the initial intrusion into the vehicle was to safeguard the owner's property, and in *Cooper* it was to guarantee the safety of the custodians. Here the justification, while different, was as immediate and constitutionally reasonable as those in *Harris* and *Cooper:* concern for the safety of the general public who might be endangered if an intruder removed a revolver from the trunk of the vehicle . . . .
>
> Where, as here, the trunk of an automobile, which the officer reasonably believed to contain a gun, was vulnerable to intrusion by

vandals, we hold that the search was not "unreasonable" within the meaning of the Fourth and Fourteenth Amendments . . . .

PROBLEMS

All of the following problems are U.S. Supreme Court Cases.

1. Police in Newport, Kentucky received a telephone complaint at 3 A.M. that "three suspicious men acting suspiciously" had been sitting in a car in a business district since 10 P.M. the evening before. Four officers immediately went to the scene. They asked the men who they were and what they were doing there, but the men gave answers which the officers testified were unsatisfactory and evasive. All of the men admitted they were unemployed. Together they had only 25¢, and none of them had the title to the car. The men said that they were in Newport to meet a truck driver who would pass through town that night, but they did not know at what time; they did not know the name of the trucking company, or what type of truck the man would be driving. The men were arrested for vagrancy, searched for weapons, and taken to the police station. The car was driven to the police station by an officer and then towed to a garage. After the men were booked, officers went to the garage and in a search of the car found two loaded revolvers in the glove compartment. They were unable to get into the trunk and when they went back to the police station were told to go back to the garage and make another effort to get into the trunk. After forcing their way in through the rear seat, the officers found caps, women's stockings (one with mouth and eye holes), rope, pillow slips, an illegally manufactured license plate equipped to be snapped over another plate, and other items. After the search, one of the men confessed that there was a plan to rob a bank in a town fifty miles away. The matter was turned over to the FBI and the three men were convicted of conspiracy to rob a federally insured bank.

   Was the first search of the car lawful? Was the second search of the car lawful? Explain.

   Preston v. United States, 376 U.S. 364, 84 S.Ct. 881 (1964).

2. The defendant let an unlicensed fourteen-year-old boy drive his car. Police stopped the vehicle for failure to signal a left turn. As the officers approached the car, defendant was bent forward so that his head was at or below the level of the dashboard. An opened bottle of beer was on the floor between the two occupants of the car. The defendant was arrested for possession of an open intoxicant in a motor vehicle. The defendant and the boy were taken to the squad car and a truck was called to tow the car. One of the officers then searched the car pursuant to a departmental policy that impounded vehicles be searched before being towed. Two bags of marijuana were found in the open glove compartment. In a careful search, a loaded .38-caliber revolver was found by opening an air vent under the dashboard. The Michigan Court of Appeals reversed the defendant's conviction for

possession of a concealed weapon, holding that the search violated the defendant's Fourth Amendment rights.

Was the search reasonable and lawful under the Fourth Amendment? Should the U.S. Supreme Court affirm the conviction holding the search was lawful? Why?

Michigan v. Thomas, 458 U.S. 259, 102 S.Ct. 3079 (1982).

3. Police in Boston were alerted by San Diego railroad officials that defendant Chadwick was arriving by train with a 200-pound footlocker which was believed to contain marijuana. When Chadwick arrived in Boston, officers had probable cause to believe the footlocker contained marijuana. The probable cause was based upon the information provided them, and by a trained dog who signaled that the footlocker contained marijuana. Instead of arresting Chadwick in the railroad station, the officers waited until the footlocker was loaded into the trunk of a car. Chadwick was then arrested and taken to the federal building in Boston. The car with the footlocker sticking out of the trunk was also driven to the federal building. An hour after arriving at the federal building, the footlocker was opened and was found to contain marijuana.

Was the opening of the footlocker without a search warrant or consent lawful and proper? Can the evidence be used in convicting Chadwick of possession of marijuana? Should the U.S. Supreme Court affirm Chadwick's conviction? Explain. *United States v. Chadwick,* 433 U.S. 1, 97 S.Ct. 2476 (1977).

4. Five days after a murder, defendant Lewis was asked to come to an Ohio police department to answer questions in regard to the crime. Defendant arrived with two attorneys and although the police had a warrant to arrest him, they did not inform him that he was arrested until late in the afternoon. When he was arrested, the keys to his car and a parking lot claim check for the car were released to the police. Without a warrant and without consent, the police went to the nearby parking lot and had the car towed to a police impoundment lot. The next day, a crime lab technician took prints of the tires of the car and found that the right rear tire impression matched a track found at the scene of the crime. As the murder victim and his car were pushed over an embankment by another car, paint samples were taken from Lewis' car. At Lewis' murder trial, an expert witness testified that foreign paint found on the victim's car was no different in color, texture, or order of layering than the paint samples taken from Lewis' car.

Was the evidence from Lewis' car obtained lawfully? Should it be allowed to be used as evidence to convict Lewis of murder? Should the U.S. Supreme Court affirm Lewis' murder conviction? Why?

Cardwell v. Lewis, 417 U.S. 583, 94 S.Ct. 2464 (1974).

5. Police officers were investigating the rape and murder of a teenage babysitter. They had probable cause to arrest Coolidge, which they did in the front room of his home. They had a search warrant for Coolidge's car, which was parked in his driveway. They seized the car and drove it to police property where, days and weeks later, intensive crime laboratory tests of the interior of the car produced important evidence for the state of the rape and murder. However, unknown to the police, the search warrant was seriously defec-

tive. Because the case was heard before the U.S. Supreme Court in 1971 and the "good faith" exception to defective search warrants was not adopted until 1985, the evidence obtained could not be used unless the state could justify authority in another way.

The U.S. Supreme Court held that the automobile exception (Carroll rule) would not justify the search of the car days and weeks later. But what about plain view? Would that authorize the use of the evidence? Would the seizure of the evidence be justified as a search and seizure incident to Coolidge's lawful arrest? Why? *Coolidge v. New Hampshire,* 403 U.S. 443, 91 S.Ct. 2022 (1971).

6. Law enforcement officers had uncorroborated information that a Dodge Mini Motor Home parked in a lot in downtown San Diego was being used to exchange marijuana for sex with teenage boys. An officer watched defendant Charles Carney approach a youth in the neighborhood. The youth then went with Carney to the Dodge Mini Home. All of the window shades in the motor home were then closed while the two persons were in the home for an hour and a quarter. Agents followed the youth when he left and, after they stopped the youth, he told the agents that he had received marijuana in return for allowing Carney sexual contacts.

> At the officers' request, the youth returned to the motor home and knocked on its door; Carney stepped out. The agents identified themselves as law enforcement officers. Without a warrant or consent, one agent entered the motor home and observed marijuana, plastic bags, and a scale of the kind used in weighing drugs on a table. Agent Williams took Carney into custody and took possession of the motor home. A subsequent search of the motor home at the police station revealed additional marijuana in the cupboards and refrigerator.

Carney was charged with possession of marijuana for sale.
Was the entry into the Mini Motor Home lawful without a search warrant or consent? Is this a home or a motor vehicle in the eyes of the Court? Should the evidence be used to convict the defendant? Explain. *California v. Carney,* 471 U.S. 386, 105 S.Ct. 2066 (1985).

7. U.S. Customs officers investigating a drug smuggling operation near the Mexican border followed pickup trucks to a remote airstrip near the border. When two small aircraft landed, the trucks approached the planes. After the second plane departed, officers approached the trucks, where they could smell marijuana and see packages wrapped as "smuggled marijuana is commonly packaged". The men in the trucks were arrested but the trucks were not searched at that time. The trucks were driven to Tucson, where the packages were placed in a DEA warehouse. Three days after the packages were seized from the trucks, some of the packages were opened without a search warrant. Samples were tested and proved to be marijuana.

Was the delayed search without a warrant lawful? May the evidence be used in the trial of the defendants? Should the U.S. Supreme Court reverse defendant's conviction for drug smuggling? Explain. *United States v. Johns,* 469 U.S. 478, 105 S.Ct. 881 (1985).

8. Officers had probable cause to believe that a car contained contraband and evidence of criminal activity. When they stopped the car, two of the three occupants fled. A search resulted in criminal evidence being seized, but the defendants were not arrested until later.

   Can the evidence obtained before their arrest be used in their criminal trials? Should the U.S. Supreme Court affirm their conviction?
   Husty v. United States, 282 U.S. 694, 51 S.Ct. 240 (1931).

9. The defendant was properly and lawfully arrested for driving his van while under the influence of alcohol (drunk driving). After the defendant (Bertine) was taken into custody, but before a tow truck arrived to tow Bertine's truck to an impoundment lot, another officer inventoried the contents of the van. The inventory was conducted in accordance with local police procedures, which required a detailed inspection and inventory of impounded vehicles. Directly behind the front seat of the van, the officer saw a backpack. The officer went into the backpack and found a nylon bag. In the nylon bag were metal canisters which contained a substantial amount of cocaine, cocaine paraphernalia, other contraband, and cash.

   Was the evidence lawfully and properly obtained? Should the defendant's conviction for the unlawful possession of cocaine with intent to dispense, sell, and distribute be affirmed? State reasons for your answer. *Colorado v. Bertine,* ___ U.S. ___, 107 S.Ct. 738, 40 CrL 3175 (U.S. Sup.Ct. 1987).

NOTES

[1] South Dakota v. Opperman, 428 U.S. 364, 96 S.Ct. 3092 (1976).

[2] Cardwell v. Lewis, 417 U.S. 583, 94 S.Ct. 2464 (1974).

[3] South Dakota v. Opperman, supra (See note 1 above).

[4] 440 U.S. 648, 99 S.Ct. 1391 (1979).

[5] 468 U.S. 420, 104 S.Ct. 3138 (1984).

[6] 460 U.S. 730, 103 S.Ct. 1535 (1983).

[7] Texas v. Brown, supra (See note 6 above).

[8] Schneckloth v. Bustamonte, 412 U.S. 218, 93 S.Ct. 2041 (1973).

[9] 392 U.S. 1, 88 S.Ct. 1868 (1968).

[10] United States v. Cortez, 449 U.S. 411, 417, 101 S.Ct. 690, 695 (1981).

[11] Michigan v. Long, 463 U.S. 1032, 103 S.Ct. 3469 (1983).

[12] The automobile exception is also known as the probable cause rule in some states.

[13] 428 U.S. 364, 96 S.Ct. 3092 (1976).

[14] South Dakota v. Opperman, 428 U.S. 364, 96 S.Ct. 3092 (1976).

[15] 217 Kan. 618, 539 P.2d 294 (1975).

[16] State v. Singleton, 9 Wash.App. 327, 511 P.2d 1396 (1973).

[17] 319 So.2d 91 (Fla.App.1975).

[18] 109 Ariz. 433, 511 P.2d 168 (1973).

[19] 413 U.S. 433, 93 S.Ct. 2523 (1973).

13

Identification Evidence

After presenting corpus delicti evidence proving that a crime has been committed, the state must then present sufficient evidence proving beyond a reasonable doubt that it was the defendant who committed the crime charged. The identification of the defendant as the person who committed the crime (or as a party to the crime) may be accomplished by a showing of one or more of the following:

- Identification by the victim of the crime.
- Identification by an eyewitness to the crime or by a person who can place the defendant in or near the crime scene (for example, a person who saw the defendant fleeing the scene immediately after the crime was committed).
- Confessions, admissions, or incriminating statements by the defendant or his associates showing that the defendant committed the crime or was a party to the crime.
- Fingerprints, footprints, tire tracks, etc. which place the defendant at the scene of the crime.
- Other physical evidence left at the scene of the crime, or obtained later by the police, which implicate the defendant as the perpetrator of the crime (for example, the gun which killed the victim is found in the defendant's possession the day after the crime was committed).
- Photographs taken as the defendant committed the crime (bank surveillance cameras, for example).
- Voice identification or, if admissible, voiceprints (spectrographic) evidence which identifies the defendant as the perpetrator of the crime or as a party to the crime.

Although this chapter presents a discussion of the rules governing the admissibility of identification evidence, it must be remembered that it is the trier of facts (the jury or the judge) who determines whether the evidence the state has presented proves beyond a reasonable doubt that the defendant has committed the crime he is charged with.

THE PROBLEM OF INCORRECT EYEWITNESS IDENTIFICATION AND TESTIMONY

Some knowledgeable observers of the criminal justice system argue that incorrect eyewitness identification and testimony has led to more miscarriages of justice than any other single cause. Mistaken identification could occur

- If a "look-alike" situation occurred between an innocent person and the person who actually committed a crime.
- If a suspect's story and claim of innocence is not carefully checked out.
- If other leads are not carefully checked out. Such leads could be fingerprints, blood, sperm, alibi stories, etc.

Cases of mistaken identification which have received national attention include:

- A young aerospace engineer named Lenell Geter served sixteen months in a Dallas prison after being wrongfully identified by five witnesses of robbing a Taco Bell and Kentucky Fried Chicken restaurant. Discrepancies were pointed out by friends and the "60 Minutes" CBS show. In 1987, CBS presented the TV movie "Guilty of Innocence: The Lenell Geter Story," which told the story of the wrongful imprisonment.
- Father Bernard Pagano, a Roman Catholic priest, was accused of robbing six Delaware stores in 1979 until a man fourteen years younger than the balding priest confessed to the crimes.
- William Jackson of Ohio served four-and-a-half years for two rapes until Dr. Edward Jackson, a prominent physician, was arrested and charged with thirty-six counts of rape and other charges. The two Jacksons are not related, but bear a striking resemblance to each other. It was determined that Dr. Jackson committed the offenses, not William Jackson.
- Douglas Forbes, a Tennessee mailman, was convicted of two rapes and served five years until a look-alike truck driver confessed to the rapes.
- A Wisconsin man served nine years for the attempted murder and rape of a fifteen-year-old girl. Neither the police, the prosecutor, nor the defense lawyer had the semen found on the victim's clothing tested. When it was tested, it showed that the attacker had type B blood and the man in prison for the crime had type A blood. The man sued his defense lawyer and recovered $500,000 in a settlement.

Not only is there a problem of mistaken identification, but there is also a possibility that a supposed victim falsely stated that a crime was committed. The 1985 Gary Dotson case received national attention as Dotson was serving his sixth year in an Illinois prison for rape.

The woman who accused Dotson of raping her recanted and stated in a Chicago courtroom that she falsely accused Dotson of rape. However, based upon the evidence presented, the trial judge upheld the original conviction. A three-day televised hearing was then held before the Illinois Prisoner Review Board. As chairperson of the Board, Illinois Governor James R. Thompson conducted the hearing, which was televised throughout the Midwest. After the hearings the governor concluded that the evidence did not confirm the woman's altered story, and would not pardon Dotson. Dotson's sentence was commuted to the time served, however, and Dotson was released; the governor stated that he believed Dotson had been adequately punished for his crime.

SEEKING IDENTIFICATION OF AN OFFENDER IMMEDIATELY AFTER A CRIME HAS BEEN COMMITTED

Immediately after offenses are committed, law enforcement officers and private persons seek to determine, if possible, the identity of the offender. The following case illustrates:

Simmons v. United States

Supreme Court of the United States (1968)
390 U.S. 377, 88 S.Ct. 967

FBI agents investigating the robbery of a Chicago savings and loan association obtained snapshots of two of the three men suspected of the crime from a relative of one of the suspects. When these snapshots were shown to five bank witnesses, each identified one of the defendants. In affirming the identification procedures used, the U.S. Supreme Court stated that

> A serious felony had been committed. The perpetrators were still at large. The inconclusive clues which law enforcement officials possessed led to Andrews and Simmons. It was essential for the FBI agents swiftly to determine whether they were on the right track, so that they could properly deploy their forces in Chicago and, if necessary, alert officials in other cities ....
> ... there was in the circumstances of this case little chance that the procedure utilized led to misidentification of Simmons. The robbery took place in the afternoon in a well-lighted bank. The robbers wore no masks. Five bank employees had been able to see the robber later identified as Simmons for periods ranging up to five minutes. Those witnesses were shown the photographs only a day later, while their memories were still fresh. At least six photographs were displayed to each witness. Apparently, these consisted primarily of group photographs, with Simmons and Andrews each appearing several times in the series. Each witness was alone when he or she saw the photographs. There is no evidence to indicate that the witnesses were told anything about the progress of the investigation, or that the FBI agents in any other way suggested which persons in the pictures were under suspicion.

"SHOWUPS" AND OTHER SCENE–OF–THE–CRIME IDENTIFICATION PROCEDURES

A **showup** differs from a lineup in that in a showup law enforcement officers permit witnesses or the victim of a crime to view a suspect in police custody singly instead of as part of a group. In commenting on showups in 1967, the U.S. Supreme Court stated that "(t)he practice of showing suspects singly to persons for the purposes of identification and not as part of a lineup, has been widely condemned." [1]

Showups, therefore, are suggestive and should not be used by law enforcement officers unless they are necessary under the circumstances. However, suggestiveness alone would not justify a ruling by a court that there has been a violation of the defendant's due process rights. In order to rule that the defendant's due process rights have been violated, there must have been impermissible suggestiveness to such a degree as to make the identification unreliable as a matter of law and resulting in a possible miscarriage of justice.

The U.S. Supreme Court has repeatedly held that the question of whether there has been a violation of the defendant's due process rights must be determined "on the totality of the circumstances." [2] In using the totality of the circumstances test, the U.S. Supreme Court and other courts have held that showups do not violate the due process rights of defendants when

- The showup was held a short time after the crime was committed in a scene-of-the-crime, on-the-spot, or short detour confrontation and viewing. Courts have approved of such showups because the memory of the witness is very fresh and officers can make an immediate determination as to whether they have taken the right person into custody. For example, a woman's purse is snatched. Witnesses to the incident chase the purse-snatcher and after several blocks catch the person. A police officer immediately brings the man and the recovered purse back to ask the victim if the purse was hers and if the man in custody is the man who snatched the purse.

- Though showups are generally held a short time after the crime and are generally held at or near the crime scene, they have also been approved under the following circumstances by the U.S. Supreme Court:

When the showup was necessary because the victim or witness was in critical condition and could die at any time. In the case of *Stovall v. Denno* (which follows), one victim was dead and his wife was in critical condition because of eleven stab wounds.

When the suspect has in his (or her) possession property recently stolen from a victim. In the case of *Kirby v. Illinois* (which follows), the defendant was arrested in downtown Chicago with traveler's checks and a social security card taken from a man who had been robbed the day before.

When the showup did not create a very substantial likelihood of irreparable misidentification which could result in a possible miscarriage of justice. For example, if an independent basis of identification exists because the victim of the crime had previously known the assailant, or if the witness had given the police such a specific description of the suspect as to clearly identify the suspect from other persons. The important case of *Neil v. Biggers* (which follows) illustrates the factors established by the U.S. Supreme Court in determining whether a "substantial likelihood of misidentification" existed.

Stovall v. Denno

Supreme Court of the United States (1967)
388 U.S. 293, 87 S.Ct. 1967

In the commission of the crime charged, the victim's husband was killed and the victim was in critical condition because of eleven stab wounds. Two days after the offense, the defendant was taken in handcuffs into the hospital room, where the victim identified him. The victim lived and was able to testify at the trial, where she again identified the defendant as the perpetrator of the crime. The U.S. Supreme Court affirmed the conviction, holding that

> The practice of showing suspects singly to persons for the purpose of identification, and not as part of a lineup, has been widely condemned. However, a claimed violation of due process of law in the conduct of a confrontation depends on the totality of the circumstances surrounding it, and the record in the present case reveals that the showing of Stovall to Mrs. Behrendt in an immediate hospital confrontation was imperative. The Court of Appeals, *en banc,* stated, 355 F.2d at 735,
>> "Here was the only person in the world who could possibly exonerate Stovall. Her words, and only her words, 'He is not the man' could have resulted in freedom for Stovall . . . ."

Kirby v. Illinois

Supreme Court of the United States (1972)
406 U.S. 682, 92 S.Ct. 1877

The day after a robbery in Chicago, two men were arrested when it was found that they had three traveler's checks and a social security card, all bearing the victim's name, in their possession.

The arrested men were taken to a police station and a police car was dispatched to bring the victim to the police station. When the victim entered the room where the arrested men were seated at a table, the victim positively identified them as the men who had robbed him. The U.S. Supreme Court affirmed the convictions for robbery, holding that the defendants' right to an attorney for identification procedures did not commence until after a defendant was charged or indicted for a crime. The Court stated that

> In this case we are asked to import into a routine police investigation an absolute constitutional guarantee historically and rationally applicable only after the onset of formal prosecutorial proceedings. We decline to do so.

Neil v. Biggers

Supreme Court of the United States (1972)
409 U.S. 188, 93 S.Ct. 375

The victim was assaulted in the doorway to her kitchen. When the victim screamed, her twelve-year-old daughter came into the room and also began to scream. Brandishing a butcher knife, the assailant "directed the victim to 'tell her (the daughter) to shut up, or I'll kill you both.' She did so, and was then walked at knifepoint about two blocks along a railroad track, taken into a woods, and raped there. She (the victim) testified that 'the moon was shining brightly, full moon.' After the rape, the assailant ran off, and she returned home, the whole incident having taken between 15 minutes and half an hour."

During the next seven months, the victim viewed suspects in lineups, and others in showups, and was also shown thirty to forty photographs. She did not identify any of the suspects as the offender. After seven months, the defendant was taken into custody on another offense. Because of his similarity to the description given by the victim, officers attempted to make up a lineup, but could find no one fitting the defendant's "unusual physical description." When the victim appeared at the police station, a showup was used. After having the defendant repeat "shut up or I'll kill you," the victim identified the defendant as her assailant. After his conviction for rape, the defendant appealed to the federal courts, arguing that the station-house identification was so suggestive as to violate due process. The U.S. Supreme Court reversed the finding of the U.S. District Court and affirmed the Supreme Court of Tennessee's finding that the identification evidence was properly used to convict the defendant. The Court held that

It is, first of all, apparent that the primary evil to be avoided is "a very substantial likelihood of irreparable misidentification." *Simmons v. United States,* 390 U.S., at 384, 88 S.Ct., at 971 . . . .

. . . It is the likelihood of misidentification which violates a defendant's right to due process . . . . Suggestive confrontations are disapproved because they increase the likelihood of misidentification, and unnecessarily suggestive ones are condemned for the further reason that the increased chance of misidentification is gratuitous. But as *Stovall* makes clear, the admission of evidence of a showup without more does not violate due process . . . .

We turn, then, to the central question, whether under the "totality of the circumstances" the identification was reliable even though the confrontation procedure was suggestive. As indicated by our cases, the factors to be considered in evaluating the likelihood of misidentification include the opportunity of the witness to view the criminal at the time of the crime, the witness' degree of attention, the accuracy of the witness' prior description of the criminal, the level of certainty demonstrated by the witness at the confrontation, and the length of time between the crime and the confrontation. Applying these factors, we disagree with the District Court's conclusion . . . .

We find that the District Court's conclusions on the critical facts are unsupported by the record and clearly erroneous. The victim spent a considerable period of time with her assailant, up to half an hour. She was with him under adequate artificial light in her house and under a full moon outdoors, and at least twice, once in the house and later in the woods, faced him directly and intimately. She was no casual observer, but rather the victim of one of the most personally humiliating of all crimes. Her description to the police, which included the assailant's approximate age, height, weight, complexion, skin texture, build, and voice, might not have satisfied Proust but was more than ordinarily thorough. She had "no doubt" that respondent was the person who raped her. In the nature of the crime, there are rarely witnesses to a rape other than the victim, who often has a limited opportunity of observation. The victim here, a practical nurse by profession, had an unusual opportunity to observe and identify her assailant. She testified at the habeas corpus hearing that there was something about his face "I don't think I could ever forget."

There was, to be sure, a lapse of seven months between the rape and the confrontation. This would be a seriously negative factor in most cases. Here, however, the testimony is undisputed that the victim made no previous identification at any of the showups, lineups, or photographic showings. Her record for reliability was thus a good one, as she had previously resisted whatever suggestiveness inheres in a showup. Weighing all the factors, we find no substantial likelihood of misidentification. The evidence was properly allowed to go to the jury.

LINEUPS

"The Primary Evil to Be Avoided ... A Very Substantial Likelihood of Irreparable Misidentification"

Proper lineups should be used whenever possible, not only to minimize suggestiveness but also to increase the reliability of the identification evidence.

Lineups are used to test recognition in a manner that avoids suggestiveness. The National Council of Judges provides the following rules for the lineup procedure:

- Reasonable notice of the proposed lineup shall be given to the suspect and his counsel, and both shall be informed that the suspect may have his attorney present at the lineup. If the suspect is not represented by counsel, he shall be advised of his right to have counsel assigned without charge. He may waive in writing the presence of his attorney.

- The lineup should consist of at least six persons, approximately alike in age, size, color, and dress; and none of them, other than possibly the suspect, shall be known to the witness.

- Persons in the lineup may be requested to speak certain words, identical for each person, for purposes of voice identification.

- Neither directly nor indirectly shall any police officer indicate or allow anyone but the witness to indicate in any way any person in the lineup as

Neil v. Biggers ᵃ Tests Used to Determine Reliability of Eyewitness Identification

- What was the witness' opportunity to observe the criminal at the time of the crime?

    Length of time of the encounter—distance between the witness and the suspect—lighting conditions—was the witness' view unobstructed?—What was the witness' state of mind?

- Was the witness a casual observer or did the witness show a high degree of attention?

    A witness who observed a man hurry down a hall or a street might be a very casual observer and may not be able to accurately describe or identify the man a short time later. On the other hand, the victim of a rape or a robbery would ordinarily have a very high degree of attention which could result in a more accurate and more reliable identification of the perpetrator of the crime.

- How accurate was the witness' prior description of the criminal?

    How accurate was the description recorded by the investigating officers? Did it record unusual features such as scars, moles, birthmarks, tatoos, distinctive clothing, etc. which could establish an independent basis of identification and make the identification highly reliable?

    How well did the testimony of the witness in court stand up under cross-examination? Was the witness able to explain why she (or he) identified the defendant as the person who committed the crime? Any discrepancies between the prior identification and the actual appearance of the defendant would ordinarily be brought out in cross-examination.

- What was the level of certainty demonstrated by the witness at the confrontation?

    Did the witness immediately identify the suspect? Was there hesitancy? Was there a misidentification?

- What time element elapsed between the commission of the crime and identification of the suspect as the perpetrator of the crime?

    Did the identification occur ten minutes after the crime, or ten hours, ten days, or ten months? This factor, when combined with the other factors, would determine the basis of reliability upon which the decision by the trial judge as to whether to submit the identification evidence to a jury would be determined.

ᵃ Tests developed by the U.S. Supreme Court and stated in the case of Neil v. Biggers, 409 U.S. 188, 93 S.Ct. 375 (1972).

the suspect or defendant. Any instructions shall be given to all as a group, not individually.

- The lineup shall be viewed by only one witness at a time, others being excluded from the room and not permitted to discuss the lineup or descriptions of the suspect.

The following U.S. Supreme Court cases of the 1960s reflect why the judge's rules on lineups were drafted:

United States v. Wade

Supreme Court of the United States (1967)
388 U.S. 218, 87 S.Ct. 1926

Wade was arrested for robbery of a bank in Texas. A lineup was conducted in the courtroom of a local courthouse without first informing Wade's attorney. The Supreme Court ordered a new hearing before excluding the identification at the trial of Wade by the bank witnesses because of the failure to notify the lawyer. At the hearing, the government was given an opportunity to establish by clear and convincing evidence that the in-court identifications were based upon observations of the suspect other than the lineup identification. The Court further held that

We think it follows that the proper test to be applied in these situations is that quoted in *Wong Sun v. United States,* 371 U.S. 471, 488, ... "[W]hether, granting establishment of the primary illegality, the evidence to which instant objection is made has been come at by exploitation of that illegality or instead by means sufficiently distinguishable to be purged of the primary taint." ·

Application of this test in the present context requires consideration of various factors; for example, the prior opportunity to observe the alleged criminal act, the existence of any discrepancy between any pre-lineup description and the defendant's actual description, any identification prior to lineup of another person, the identification by picture of the defendant prior to the lineup, failure to identify the defendant on a prior occasion, and the lapse of time between the alleged act and the lineup identification. It is also relevant to consider those facts which, despite the absence of counsel, are disclosed concerning the conduct of the lineup.

Gilbert v. California

Supreme Court of the United States (1967)
388 U.S. 263, 87 S.Ct. 1951

Gilbert was arrested for the robbery of a savings and loan association and the murder of a police officer during the robbery. Gilbert was also charged with other robberies. A lineup was held without notifying Gilbert's lawyer. The lineup was held on a stage with "upwards of 100 persons in the audience", each an eyewitness to one of the robberies charged to Gilbert. Bright lights prevented the persons in the lineup from seeing the audience. Persons in the audience would call out the number of the man they could identify in the lineup. It is not known whether the audience talked to one another during the lineup, but they did talk to each other after the lineup. In holding that the lineup was illegal, the Court stated that

The admission of the in-court identifications without first determining that they were not tainted by the illegal lineup but were of independent origin was constitutional error. *United States v. Wade, supra.* We there held that a post-indictment pretrial lineup at which the accused is exhibited to identifying witnesses is a critical stage of the criminal prosecution; that police conduct of such a lineup without notice to and in the absence of his counsel denies the accused his Sixth Amendment right to counsel and calls in question the admissibility at trial of the in-court identifications of the accused by witnesses who attended the lineup. However, as in *Wade,* the record does not permit an informed judgment whether the in-court identifications at the two stages of the trial had an independent source. Gilbert is therefore entitled only to a vacation of his conviction pending the holding of such proceedings as the California Supreme Court may deem appropriate to afford the State the opportunity to establish that the in-court identifications had an independent source, or that their introduction in evidence was in any event harmless error.

USING PHOTOGRAPHS FOR IDENTIFICATION PURPOSES

Photographs are often used for identification purposes in criminal investigations. In the case of *Simmons v. United States* (see excerpt earlier in this chapter), photos from a family album were used to identify Simmons as one of the men who robbed a Chicago Savings and Loan. The U.S. Supreme Court noted in the *Simmons* case that "Each witness was alone when he or she saw the photographs. There is no evidence to indicate that the witnesses were told anything about the progress of the investigation, or that the FBI agents in any other way suggested which persons in the picture were under suspicion."

The Metropolitan Police Department of the District of Columbia (Washington, D.C.) issued the following instructions in regard to the use of photographs: [3]

1. The use of photographs for identification purposes prior to an arrest is permissible provided the suspect's photograph is grouped with at least eight other photographs of the same general description.

2. Adequate records of the photographs shown to each witness must be kept so that the exact group of photographs from which an identification was made can be presented in court at a later date to counteract any claim of undue suggestion and enhance the reliability of the in-court identification. This information shall be recorded in the statement of facts of the case.

3. Each witness shall view the photographs independently, out of the immediate presence of the other witnesses.

Failure to preserve the photographs used to make an identification creates serious problems. The court cannot then determine whether due process was complied with and identification was made without excessive suggestiveness. In the 1980 case of *Branch v. Estelle,*[4] the Federal Court of Appeals for the 5th

Circuit held that "in situations where the police fail to preserve the photographic array, there shall exist a presumption that the array is impermissibly suggestive."

Using "Mug Shot" Photographs as Evidence

Files of **mug shot** pictures are maintained by probably all law enforcement agencies. The purposes of these photographs are for identification, and to acquaint law enforcement officers with known suspects and persons who have criminal records. Victims and witnesses to crimes often view police mug shots in efforts to identify the perpetrators of crimes.

Mug shots are seldom used as evidence in a criminal trial because (1) there is rarely a need for this type of photograph as evidence, and (2) using mug shots of the defendant in a criminal trial could easily cause members of a jury to believe that the defendant had a prior criminal record or has had prior trouble with the law. This could deny a defendant his right to a fair trial.

"It is well established that evidence of other offenses and prior trouble with the law is inadmissible in a criminal prosecution as part of the government's case against the defendant." [5] The U.S. Supreme Court stated in the 1948 case of *Michelson v. United States* [6] that

> The state may not show defendant's prior trouble with the law, specific criminal acts, or ill name among his neighbors, even though such facts might logically be persuasive that he is by propensity a probable perpetrator of the crime. The inquiry is not rejected because character is irrelevant; on the contrary, it is said to weigh too much with the jury and to so overpersuade them as to prejudge one with a bad general record and deny him a fair opportunity to defend against a particular charge. The overriding policy of excluding such evidence, despite its admitted probative value, is the practical experience that its disallowance tends to prevent confusion of issues, unfair surprise and undue prejudice.

The only time a defendant's past criminal record may be shown by the government in a criminal trial is for impeachment purposes after the defendant has appeared as a witness in his own behalf. In the 1973 case of *United States v. Harrington* [7] a federal prosecutor was surprised and "probably seriously injured" when a government witness failed to make an in-court identification of the defendant as expected. The federal prosecutor was then permitted to introduce into evidence mug shot photographs of the defendant. The Second Circuit Court of Appeals established the following tests for determining whether mug shots may be used in a criminal trial:

1. The prosecutor must show a demonstrable need to introduce the photographs; and

2. The photographs, if shown to the jury, must not imply that the defendant has a prior criminal record; and

3. The introduction at trial does not draw particular attention to the source or implications of the photographs.

In holding that the government failed to pass tests 2 and 3, the case was reversed and remanded for a new trial with the Court, suggesting that we think that the preferable course of action when mug shots are to be introduced would be to produce photographic duplicates of the mug shots. These copies would lack any incriminating indicia—i.e., inscriptions or identification numbers, and they could also avoid use of the juxtaposed full face and profile photographic display normally associated with "mug shots."

References by Government Witnesses to Police Photographs (Mug Shots)

Identifications of the perpetrators of crimes are often made (or affirmed) through the use of police photographs, or mug shots. References to police photographs or mug shots by a government witness while testifying in a criminal trial before a jury could indicate to members of the jury that the defendant had a past criminal record, had previously been arrested, or had been in trouble with the police.

In the case of *Commonwealth v. Allen,*[8] the Supreme Court of Pennsylvania discusses four cases in which that Court reversed conviction "because of references to police photographs" before juries. The best practice by law enforcement officers and prosecutors would be to caution witnesses for the government not to make any references to police photographs or mug shots unless a defense lawyer asked questions in cross-examination which required such a reference.

Does a Suspect Have a Right to Have an Attorney Present During the Showing of Photos?

When robbery, rape, or burglary suspects are arrested and there is reason to believe that the person has committed other similar offenses, it is common practice to check descriptions given by witnesses and victims. If the person in custody fits a description given of an offender who has committed another crime, putting together a photographic array of photos would be a practical procedure. Witnesses and victims could then view the photos to determine whether the suspect in custody has committed other offenses.

Would law enforcement officers be obligated to inform the suspect's attorney of the photographic display and give him (or her) an opportunity to be present during the showing? This issue was presented to the U.S. Supreme Court in the following case:

United States v. Ash

Supreme Court of the United States (1973)
413 U.S. 300, 93 S.Ct. 2568

When the trial date for the defendant was finally set almost three years after the crime, the prosecutor decided to use a photographic display to determine whether the witnesses would be able to make in-court identifications. Five colored photographs were shown to four witnesses and three of the witnesses selected the picture of Ash as the armed robber of the bank. In affirming the conviction and holding that a defendant has no right to have an attorney present during photographic identification, the United States Supreme Court stated that

> We are not persuaded that the risks inherent in the use of photographic displays are so pernicious that an extraordinary system of safeguards is required.

SKETCHES BY ARTISTS OR IDENTI-KITS

Many large law enforcement departments either have artists on their staff or professionals who can be called upon to do sketches of the likenesses of suspects for "wanted" posters. Many other departments can make drawings of suspects without an artist by using an Identi-Kit, which was invented by a police officer in 1957. The Identi-Kit has hundreds of facial components (noses, eyes, chins, hairlines, hair, etc.) which can be built into a likeness of a person.

Sketches may not look exactly like a suspect who is believed to have committed a crime, but it is hoped that a sketch will present a lot of information about the person. The public may use the information to contact the police. Investigators can use the information to further limit the number of suspects and narrow the focus of the investigation.

The witness is the key to a good sketch. Some witnesses are able to provide accurate and specific information about the appearance of a suspect. Showing a witness mug shots could lead to an identification, or it could lead to a "look-alike" which could assist in making a sketch by modifying and altering features. Some witnesses will use mug shots or Identi-Kit transparencies to describe features such as eyes, hairlines, and other likenesses of suspects.

If descriptions and sketches closely resemble a defendant charged with a crime, law enforcement officers and prosecutors can use such evidence to demonstrate the reliability of the identification evidence. If there is very little resemblance between the description given by the victim or the sketch, the defense lawyer can use this to demonstrate and argue that the state or government has not identified the defendant beyond a reasonable doubt as the person who committed the crime.

IDENTIFICATION BY VOICE AND OTHER MEANS

Criminals are not only recognized by their physical appearances, but they are also recognized and identified by the clothing they wear, by the motor vehicle they use, by their voices, and in some instances by the manner in which they walk and conduct themselves.

Knowledgeable criminals could attempt to discard or change clothing. They could do this after being arrested or while in jail. They could trade jackets, sweaters, and hats with other prisoners. Clothing with unusual features and items such as sunglasses could be identified by a victim or witness,

Rights of a Defendant as to Identification Evidence

It is the Reliability of Identification Evidence That Primarily Determines its Admissibility. U.S. Supreme Court in *Manson v. Brathwaite*, 432 U.S. 98, 113–114, 97 S.Ct. 2243, (1977).

Reliability is determined by the tests stated in the U.S. Supreme Court case of *Neil v. Biggers*, 409 U.S. 188, 93 S.Ct. 375 (1972). Defense lawyers "can both cross-examine the identification witnesses and argue in summation as to factors causing doubts as to the accuracy of the identification—including reference to both any suggestibility in the identification procedure and any countervailing testimony such as alibi." *Watkins v. Sowders*, 449 U.S. 341, 101 S.Ct. 654, 28 CrL 3037 (1981).

The Primary Evil to Be Avoided . . . A Very Substantial Likelihood of Irreparable Misidentification. U.S. Supreme Court in *Neil v. Biggers*, 409 U.S. 188, 93 S.Ct. 375 (1972) and *Simmons v. United States*, 390 U.S. 384.

Identification evidence could be denied admission for use as evidence in a trial if the evidence was not reliable, or if the evidence was obtained in a manner that was so impermissibly suggestive as to cause a "very substantial likelihood of irreparable misidentification."

The right to an attorney for identification procedures commences:

- After a defendant is charged or indicted for a crime (see U.S. Supreme Court case of *Kirby v. Illinois*, 406 U.S. 682, 92 S.Ct. 1877 (1972)).

- If a defendant is included in a lineup (see *United States v. Wade*, 388 U.S. 218, 87 S.Ct. 1926 (1967) and *Gilbert v. California*, 388 U.S. 263, 87 S.Ct. 1951 (1967)).

- There is no right to have an attorney present during identification by use of photographs (see *United States v. Ash*, 413 U.S. 300, 93 S.Ct. 2568 (1973)).

and could be very incriminating. Such items could be very important evidence for use in the identification of the person who committed the crime.

Voice identification evidence has always been accepted by courts. In many instances, the victim or the witness not only identifies the defendant by his physical appearances and his clothing but is also able to testify that they recognize the defendant by his voice. In other cases involving telephone threats, bomb threats, etc., the primary means of identifying a defendant may be by voice identification because the witness has not seen the defendant at the time of the crime. It has long been held that voice identification evidence alone may be sufficient to sustain a conviction if the evidence presented carries the burden of proving the defendant guilty beyond a reasonable doubt. The Supreme Court of Minnesota reflected this rule of law when the Court ruled in the case of *City of St. Paul v. Caulfield* [9] that

It is the rule in this state that the foundation for admission of testimony as to the identity of the voice of a telephone caller is sufficient when it appears that the witness to whom the telephone call is made testifies that he is reasonably certain as to the voice of such caller and can identify it.

Using Spectrograms (Voiceprints) in Identification

The voices of persons involved in the crimes of kidnapping, murder plots, extortion, bomb threats, false alarms, and other crimes are sometimes recorded on tape when a telephone message is used as part of the criminal act. When a suspect is arrested or ordered to do so by a court or a grand jury, samples of his voice may be obtained and used by experts to compare to the original tape by means of spectrograms (voiceprints).

The Supreme Court of Rhode Island defined voice spectrograms in the 1985 case of *State v. Wheeler* [10] as

> visual representations of the sound produced by the human voice broken down into factors of time, frequency, and energy. The basic scientific theory involved is that every human voice is unique and that the qualities of uniqueness can be electronically reduced to visual representation, that is, voice spectrograms, through a voice spectrograph. Proponents of the theory of voice identification through voice spectrographs claim that a person properly trained in the recognition of these qualities can render an opinion about whether two or more voice spectrograms were made by the same person. A practical description of the spectrograph and its operation is found in *Reed v. State of Maryland*, 283 Md. 374, 391 A.2d 364 (1978).
> "The process involves the use of a machine known as a spectrograph. This machine analyzes the acoustic energy of the human voice into three components—time, frequency, and intensity—and graphically displays these components by generating, through an electric stylus, a series of closely spaced light and dark lines, varying in position, on a sheet of electrically sensitive paper. The resulting graphic representation is what is called a spectrogram or 'voiceprint.' It reveals certain patterns or 'formats' which correspond to the sounds which are analyzed." *Id.* at 377–78, 391 A.2d at 366.

In pointing out that the Supreme Judicial Courts of Massachusetts and Maine have approved spectrograph-voice-identification evidence, the Rhode Island Court also affirmed the admission of such evidence, holding that

> On the record before us, it is clear from the well-reasoned decision of the trial justice ordering the admission of the evidence of the voice spectrographic identification that he carefully considered all of the criteria under our settled case law and reached a correct conclusion. At trial the attorneys for defendants had the opportunity to cross-examine the experts and question the correctness of their conclusions. And it remained for the jury to reject the voice-identification evidence for any number of reasons, including the view that the spectrographic-voice-identification techniques were either unreliable or misleading. *State v. Williams,* 4 Ohio St.3d at 59, 446 N.E.2d at 448. We conclude, therefore, that the trial justice properly admitted the evidence of voice identification.

Identification of Eyewitnesses

TESTS USED TO DETERMINE THE ADMISSIBILITY OF EYEWITNESS IDENTIFICATION EVIDENCE

- Were the defendant's Fifth Amendment due process rights violated by identification procedures which were so unnecessarily suggestive so as to cause "a very substantial likelihood of irreparable misidentification"? (*Simmons v. United States,* 390 U.S. at 384, 88 S.Ct. at 971, 19 L.Ed.2d 1247 (1968)).

- Was the defendant's Sixth Amendment right to an attorney observed and complied with during identification proceedings after the defendant was charged (or indicted)? However, defendants have no right to an attorney during any photographic identification proceedings (*United States v. Ash,* 413 U.S. 300, 93 S.Ct. 2568, 37 L.Ed.2d 619 (1973)), unless your state courts have held otherwise.

THE ONE-TO-ONE "SHOWUP"

1. Showups are suggestive but not necessarily in violation of the Fifth Amendment due process requirement.

2. The propriety of a showup is determined by the "totality of the circumstances surrounding" the identification. (U.S. Supreme Court in *Stovall v. Denno*)

3. The suggestiveness inherent in the one-to-one showup can be outweighed by the following policy considerations:

   - The reliability due to the nearness in time of the identification to the crime committed.

   - The reliability of a witness, as demonstrated in *Neil v. Biggers,* in which the U.S. Supreme Court stated, "Her record for reliability was thus a good one, as she had previously resisted whatever suggestiveness inheres in a showup."

   - The expeditious and immediate release of a suspect who is innocent.

Not all courts, however, allow expert testimony concerning voice spectrography. The Supreme Court of Indiana held in the 1983 case of *Cornett v. State*[11] that the expert witnesses for voice spectrograms are a limited few who appear "again and again" as expert witnesses in courts throughout the United States. The court found this to be proof that spectrographic analysis has not been generally accepted by the relevant scientific community. See chapter 20 on the application of the test for the admissibility of scientific evidence in courts which follow the test established in *Frye v. United States,* 293 Fed. 1013 (D.C.Cir.1923).

COURTROOM IDENTIFICATION BY A WITNESS DURING A TRIAL

In criminal trials, the state must carry the burden of identifying the defendant beyond a reasonable doubt as the person who committed the crime (or crimes)

- An emergency condition exists, such as in *Stovall v. Denno,* in which two days after a murder, the only witness was in critical condition in a hospital. The U.S. Supreme Court held in *Stovall v. Denno* that "immediate hospital confrontation was imperative."

PHOTOGRAPHIC IDENTIFICATION

- The propriety of pretrial photographic identification is determined by the "totality of the circumstances surrounding" the identification and will be set aside "only if the photographic identification was so impermissibly suggestive as to give rise to a very substantial likelihood of irreparable misidentification." (*Simmons v. United States,* 390 U.S. 377, 88 S.Ct. 967, 19 L.Ed.2d 1247 (1968)).

- The suspect's photograph should be grouped with a sufficient number of other photographs of the same general description and shown to witnesses separately. The exact group of photographs should be preserved so that they may be presented to the court at a later date to counteract any claim of undue suggestiveness and to enhance the reliability of the in-court identification.

- A suspect has no right to have an attorney present during a photographic identification proceeding (*United States v. Ash,* 413 U.S. 300, 93 S.Ct. 2568, 37 L.Ed.2d 619 (1973)), unless your state courts have held otherwise.

- A single photograph identification procedure is suggestive but is not per se impermissibly suggestive. The burden would be on the state to show that the identification was sufficiently reliable to be used as evidence in view of the "totality of the circumstances surrounding" the identification procedure used.

being charged. This is ordinarily done when the prosecutor asks the witness to describe the person who committed the crime or who was seen fleeing from the crime scene. The witness is then asked whether that person is in the courtroom. When the witness answers yes, the witness is then asked to point out the person.

Because the defendant is ordinarily seated next to his attorney at the defense table,[12] the witness will then point him out to the court and the jury.[13] In order to clearly establish that the witness has identified the defendant as the person who committed the crime, the witness is then ordinarily requested to further identify the defendant by one or more of the following methods:

- By asking the witness to describe what the defendant is wearing in court and to specifically describe where he (or she) is sitting, or

- By asking the defendant to stand and asking the witness whether this is the person who committed the crime or was seen fleeing from the crime scene, or

- By requesting the witness to step down from the stand and to touch the person who committed the crime or who was seen fleeing from the crime scene.

The prosecutor will then request that the court record show that the witness has identified the defendant (name given) as the person who was seen committing the crime or was seen fleeing from the crime scene.

Because many jurisdictions permit testimony by eyewitnesses as to prior out-of-court identification, the witness may then be asked if he (or she) had previously identified the defendant as the person who assaulted them or committed the crime being charged. Such testimony can be technically considered hearsay, but it is important and meaningful because it gives the jury and judge a full picture of the identification process which was used. Such testimony also buttresses the ritualized in-court identification against possible attack in cross-examination and shows to the jury and the judge the extent of the investigation and deliberation before the decision to bring the defendant to trial was made.

The Importance of Obtaining Prior Descriptions of Offenders

It is very important that investigating officers have the witnesses give them as detailed a description of the offender as is possible soon after the crime is reported. The officer should assist the victim and the witness in searching their memories (without being in any way suggestive) for details of physical appearances and clothing, no matter how insignificant such details may seem to appear. Such prior descriptions are important in that

- They will authorize stops in the neighborhood and elsewhere for investigative detentions of persons reasonably matching these descriptions.
- The descriptions may be compared to descriptions given by victims and witnesses of other crimes and further aid in the apprehension of the offender.
- Detailed descriptions which match defendants can significantly increase the reliability of identifications made later by victims and witnesses.
- Testimony by the investigating officers in court as to prior descriptions provides important evidence for juries and judges in the determination of the issue of guilt or innocence.

PROBLEMS

1. Connecticut State Trooper Glover was working as an undercover officer in narcotics. He and an informer went to an apartment building in Hartford, where Glover knocked on the door of one of the apartments. A man (the defendant in this case) opened the door and in a five- to seven-minute period sold $20 worth of heroin to Glover. Glover had never seen the defendant before, and did not know the defendant's proper name. Upon leaving the building, Trooper Glover described the man to Officer D'Onofrio, who had been backing him up outside the building. From the description, Officer D'Onofrio suspected that the seller was the defendant. D'Onofrio obtained a single photograph of the defendant and left the picture at Trooper Glover's

office. Two days later (May 7), Glover viewed the single picture and identified the defendant as the man who sold him the heroin. Based upon this information, the defendant was arrested. Without defense objection, the picture was used as evidence and Trooper Glover made a positive in-court identification of the defendant.

What improper procedure was used by the officers which caused defense lawyers to appeal this case to the U.S. Supreme Court? Should the evidence of the in-court identification be allowed, and should the defendant's conviction for selling heroin be affirmed? Why? *Manson v. Brathwaite,* 432 U.S. 98, 97 S.Ct. 2243 (1977).

2. After three men robbed a Western Union office, one of the men surrendered to the police and implicated Foster (who had gone into the office with him) and another man. Foster was placed in a three-man lineup for viewing by the only witness (the manager of the office). Foster was about six feet tall, while the other two men in the lineup were about five feet six inches tall. Foster wore a leather jacket, which the night manager said he saw the robber wear under coveralls. After viewing the lineup, the night manager of the Western Union office could not positively identify Foster as one of the robbers. The manager was not sure but he thought Foster was one of the robbers. The manager then asked to speak with Foster, who was taken into an office and sat at a table across from the manager. No one else was in the room except prosecuting officials. The manager still could not positively identify Foster. About ten days after the first lineup, the night manager viewed a second lineup. Of the five men in the lineup, Foster was the only person who had been in the first lineup. This time, the manager was "convinced" that Foster was one of the robbers.

Should the identification evidence be permitted to be used in Foster's trial? Should the U.S. Supreme Court affirm Foster's conviction for armed robbery? Why? *Foster v. California,* 394 U.S. 440, 89 S.Ct. 1127 (1969).

3. A young man robbed a woman in a woman's restroom at the Washington National Monument. During the robbery, the woman had a good opportunity to see the young man. The woman immediately reported the robbery and described the young man who robbed her. Three days later, a young man (Crews) was improperly and illegally detained. Photographs were taken of the young man and a photographic display (array) was shown to the woman. She immediately identified Crews as the man who robbed her. In a lineup, the woman again identified Crews as the man who robbed her. At Crews' trial for armed robbery, the woman appeared as a witness and identified the defendant as the robber. Crews was convicted and appealed, arguing that the in-court identification was the "fruit of the poisonous tree" and should not be used as evidence.

Should the woman's in-court identification be allowed to be used as evidence, and should the U.S. Supreme Court affirm Crews' conviction? Why? *United States v. Crews,* 445 U.S. 463, 100 S.Ct. 1244 (1980).

NOTES

[1] Stovall v. Denno, 388 U.S. 293, 87 S.Ct. 1967 (1967).

2 Stovall v. Denno and Neil v. Biggers, 409 U.S. 188, 93 S.Ct. 375 (1972).

3 "Procedures for Obtaining Pretrial Eyewitness Identification" Series 304, No. 7.

4 631 F.2d 1229, 28 CrL 2396 (5th Cir.1980).

5 United States v. Hines, 470 F.2d 225 (3d Cir.1972).

6 335 U.S. 469, 69 S.Ct. 213 (1948).

7 490 F.2d 487 (2d Cir.1973).

8 448 Pa. 177, 292 A.2d 373 (1972).

9 254 Minn. 142, 144, 94 N.W.2d 263, 264 (1959).

10 496 A.2d 1382 (R.I.Sup.Ct.1985).

11 450 N.E.2d 498 (Ind.Sup.Ct.1983).

12 In a few instances, defense lawyers have had persons who look similar to the defendant sit next to them at the defense table with the defendant sitting elsewhere in the courtroom during the trial. If the court is not informed of this situation, contempt charges could result against the defense attorney and the look-alike. In the 1973 case of Duke v. State, 260 Ind. 638, 298 N.E. 453, the decoy sitting next to the defense lawyer was convicted and temporarily jailed in place of the defendant. In that case, Justice DuBruler of the Indiana Supreme Court wrote in a concurring opinion that

> The trial judge had a duty at the beginning of a trial to satisfy himself that the person on trial was present in the courtroom and prepared for trial. The presence of the defendant in court should be made to clearly appear on the record. The trial judge should leave nothing to chance in this matter, but should personally address the defendant and require that the defendant identify himself to the court. The court may then determine the state of preparedness of the defendant. This personal identification procedure familiarizes the judge with the accused and permits the trial judge to quickly determine for the record, the presence of the defendant upon resumption of proceedings following recesses in the trial. It is the duty of the judge to conduct the trial in the presence of the defendant and to make the record reflect such fact. The modern rule is that an accused must personally present himself to the court for trial and that the trial judge may require him also to personally identify himself. Kivette v. United States, 230 F.2d 749 (5th Cir.1956); Swingle v. United States, 151 F.2d 512 (10th Cir.1945).

13 See the 1984 case of *United States v. Archibald,* 734 F.2d 938 (2d Cir.1984) in which the defendant was charged with robbing a New York bank. A lineup had not been conducted in the case and prosecution witnesses had identified the defendant only from a photographic display. The defendant was the only black person in the courtroom when the case was called. The defendant requested to be removed from his place at the defense table next to his lawyer and to be placed among men his approximate age and skin color. The trial court refused and the in-court identification was conducted with the defendant sitting at the defense table.

> The Court of Appeals held that the trial court should have complied with the defendant's request. The court was not obligated to provide a lineup in the courtroom. The Court of Appeals affirmed the conviction of the defendant, however, holding that the "impermissible" identification procedure was harmless error because of the other evidence which supported the defendant's conviction.

Search Warrants as a Means of Obtaining Evidence

A search warrant is an order signed by a judge or magistrate directing a law enforcement officer to conduct a search of a specifically described person, place, or object for the purpose of seizing specifically described evidence of a crime. The Fourth Amendment of the U.S. Constitution provides that

> no warrants shall issue, but upon probable cause, supported by Oath, or affirmation, and particularly describing the place to be searched, and the person or things to be seized.

Search warrants must be in writing. They must be issued by a judicial official authorized to issue such a warrant. The search warrant must be directed to a law enforcement officer. The warrant must be based upon a finding that probable cause exists. The showing of probable cause can be made by sworn oral testimony before the judge or magistrate or may be made in a sworn affidavit. Information from a number of persons may be pooled to provide the issuing judge with sufficient evidence from which it can be independently determined that probable cause exists.

THE PROBABLE CAUSE REQUIREMENT

Sources of Information Used to Establish Probable Cause

In the article entitled "Search Warrants," [1] published in *The Police Chief* magazine, the authors point out that "in 95 percent of the cases the (search) warrant and affidavit are quite routine and involve fairly common situations. Examples include: hand-to-hand buys of narcotics, direct observations by officers who have been to the location and seen the material involved, solid factual information supplied by reliable informants, and so forth."

Information to establish probable cause could come from any of the following (or any combination of the following):

- Law enforcement officers (or departments)
- Private citizens or persons
- Informants (or informers) who are receiving (or are hopeful of receiving) something in return for their information

In addition, information from an anonymous letter or telephone call when corroborated and affirmed as extensively as was done in the U.S. Supreme Court case of *Illinois v. Gates* (which follows in this chapter) could establish probable cause.

Probable Cause to Arrest Is Not Necessarily Probable Cause Required for a Search Warrant

To issue a search warrant, probable cause must exist to believe that contraband or evidence of a crime is at the place (or on the person) to be searched. Probable cause to arrest a suspect does not necessarily establish probable cause to obtain a search warrant. The following example illustrates: Two days after a theft or a burglary, the offender is arrested and taken into custody. However, the stolen objects are not recovered. It is *possible* that the suspect may have the objects in his home, or they may be in his car, or at his office, or they may be at his girl friend's home. *Possibility* alone would not authorize a search warrant.

Possibility is not the same as *probability*. To search the suspect's home for the stolen objects, law enforcement officers must obtain sufficient information that when pooled together would amount to *probability* to believe that the stolen objects are at the place authorized to be searched under the authority of the search warrant.

Certainty or absolute certainty is not required. Probable cause could exist and the object (or objects) which are searched for are not found in the place that is searched under a search warrant. In the example given, probable cause to arrest the suspect would not authorize searches of places where the contraband might *possibly* be unless evidence establishing *probability* can be shown or another authority (such as consent) exists.

Illinois v. Gates and the Test for Probable Cause to Issue a Search Warrant

Before 1983, not only was probable cause required to authorize a search warrant, but when the information was from an informant, the rigid "two-pronged test" was also applied. The 1983 case of *Illinois v. Gates* (which follows) gave the U.S. Supreme Court an opportunity to establish the totality-of-the-circumstances test. Stating that the old "*Aguilar-Spinelli* two-pronged test" was "hypertechnical"[2] and used "artificial standards," the U.S. Supreme Court rejected the two-pronged test.

Illinois v. Gates

Supreme Court of the United States (1983)
462 U.S. 213, 103 S.Ct. 2317

The police department in the Chicago suburb of Bloomingdale, Illinois received by mail the following anonymous handwritten letter:

This letter is to inform you that you have a couple in your town who strictly make their living on selling drugs. They are Sue and Lance Gates, they live on Greenway, off Bloomingdale Rd. in the condominiums. Most of their buys are done in Florida. Sue his wife drives their car to Florida, where she leaves it to be loaded up with drugs, then Lance flys down and drives it back. Sue flys back after she drops the car off in Florida. May 3 she is driving down there again and Lance will be flying down in a few days to drive it back. At the time Lance drives the car back he has the trunk loaded with over $100,000.00 in drugs. Presently they have over $100,000.00 worth of drugs in their basement.

They brag about the fact they never have to work, and make their entire living on pushers.

I guarantee if you watch them carefully you will make a big catch. They are friends with some big drugs dealers, who visit their house often.

    Lance & Susan Gates

    Greenway

    In Condominiums

Bloomingdale officers and federal agents, in following the leads, were able to develop the following: The Gates lived at the address given. On May 5, L. Gates flew from Chicago to West Palm Beach, Florida and took a taxi to a nearby Holiday Inn, where he spent the night with Susan Gates. At 7:00 A.M., the two left for Chicago in a Mercury with license plates registered to a Hornet station wagon owned by Gates. This information and the anonymous letter were presented in an affidavit in an application for an Illinois search warrant. When Lance Gates and his wife arrived at their Illinois home 36 hours after Lance had left Illinois, police officers were waiting with a search warrant. A search of the trunk of the Mercury uncovered approximately 350 pounds of marijuana. A search of the Gates' home revealed marijuana, weapons, and other contraband. The Illinois courts suppressed all of the evidence, holding that the two-pronged test had not been satisfied and that there was not a showing that probable cause existed to support the search warrant. In holding that probable cause did exist, the U.S. Supreme Court ruled that

> We agree with the Illinois Supreme Court that an informant's "veracity," "reliability," and "basis of knowledge" are all highly relevant in determining the value of his report. We do not agree, however, that these elements should be understood as entirely separate and independent requirements to be rigidly exacted in every case, which the opinion of the Supreme Court of Illinois would imply. Rather, as detailed below, they should be understood simply as closely intertwined issues that may usefully illuminate the commonsense, practical question whether there is "probable cause" to believe that contraband or evidence is located in a particular place.
>
> This totality-of-the-circumstances approach is far more consistent with our prior treatment of probable cause than is any rigid demand that specific "tests" be satisfied by every informant's tip. Perhaps the central teaching of our decisions bearing on the probable-cause standard is that it is a "practical, nontechnical conception." *Brinegar v. United States,* 338 U.S. 160, 176, 69 S.Ct. 1302, 1311, 93 L.Ed. 1879

(1949). "In dealing with probable cause, . . . as the very name implies, we deal with probabilities. These are not technical; they are the factual and practical considerations of everyday life on which reasonable and prudent men, not legal technicians, act." at 175, 69 S.Ct., at 1310. Our observation in *United States v. Cortez,* 449 U.S. 411, 418, . . . (1981), regarding "particularized suspicion," is also applicable to the probable-cause standard:

"The process does not deal with hard certainties, but with probabilities. Long before the law of probabilities was articulated as such, practical people formulated certain common-sense conclusions about human behavior; jurors as factfinders are permitted to do the same—and so are law enforcement officers. Finally, the evidence thus collected must be seen and weighed not in terms of library analysis by scholars, but as understood by those versed in the field of law enforcement."

As these comments illustrate, probable cause is a fluid concept—turning on the assessment of probabilities in particular factual contexts—not readily, or even usefully, reduced to a neat set of legal rules. Informants' tips doubtless come in many shapes and sizes from many different types of persons. As we said in *Adams v. Williams,* 407 U.S. 143, 147, . . . (1972): "Informants' tips, like all other clues and evidence coming to a policeman on the scene, may vary greatly in their value and reliability." Rigid legal rules are ill-suited to an area of such diversity. "One simple rule will not cover every situation."

Moreover, the "two-pronged test" directs analysis into two largely independent channels—the informant's "veracity" or "reliability" and his "basis of knowledge." . . . There are persuasive arguments against according these two elements such independent status. Instead, they are better understood as relevant considerations in the totality-of-the-circumstances analysis that traditionally has guided probable-cause determinations: a deficiency in one may be compensated for, in determining the overall reliability of a tip, by a strong showing as to the other, or by some other indicia of reliability. . . .

For all these reasons, we conclude that it is wiser to abandon the "two-pronged test" established by our decisions in *Aguilar* and *Spinelli.* In its place we reaffirm the totality-of-the-circumstances analysis that traditionally has informed probable-cause determinations. The task of the issuing magistrate is simply to make a practical, common-sense decision whether, given all the circumstances set forth in the affidavit before him, including the "veracity" and "basis of knowledge" of persons supplying hearsay information, there is a fair probability that contraband or evidence of a crime will be found in a particular place. And the duty of a reviewing court is simply to ensure that the magistrate had a "substantial basis for . . . conclud[ing]" that probable cause existed. *Jones v. United States,* 362 U.S., at 271, 80 S.Ct., at 736. We are convinced that this flexible, easily applied standard will better achieve the accommodation of public and private interests that the Fourth Amendment requires than does the approach that has developed from *Aguilar* and *Spinelli.* . . .

In addition, the judge could rely on the anonymous letter, which had been corroborated in major part by Mader's efforts—just as had occurred in *Draper.* The Supreme Court of Illinois reasoned that *Draper* involved an informant who had given reliable information on previous occasions, while the honesty and reliability of the anonymous informant in this case were unknown to the Bloomingdale police. While this distinction might be an apt one at the time the Police Department received the anonymous letter, it became far less significant after Mader's independent investigative work occurred. The corroboration of the letter's predictions that the Gateses' car would be in Florida, that Lance Gates would fly to Florida in the next day or so, and that he would drive the car north toward Bloomingdale all indicated, albeit not with certainty, that the informant's other assertions also were true. "[B]ecause an informant is right about some things, he is more probably right about other facts," *Spinelli,* 393 U.S., at 427, . . . including the claim regarding the Gateses' illegal activity. This may well not be the type of "reliability" or "veracity" necessary to satisfy some views of the "veracity prong" of *Spinelli,* but we think it suffices for the practical, common-sense judgment called for in making a probable cause determination. It is enough, for purposes of assessing probable-cause, that "[c]orroboration through other sources of information reduced the chances of a reckless or prevaricating tale," thus providing "a substantial basis for crediting the hearsay." *Jones v. United States,* 362 U.S., at 269, 271, 80 S.Ct., at 735, 736.

Finally, the anonymous letter contained a range of details relating not just to easily obtained facts and conditions existing at the time of the tip, but to future actions of third parties ordinarily not easily predicted. The letterwriter's accurate information as to the travel plans of each of the Gateses was of a character likely obtained only from the Gateses themselves, or from someone familiar with their not entirely ordinary travel plans. If the informant had access to accurate information of this type a magistrate could properly conclude that it was not unlikely that he also had access to reliable information of the Gateses' alleged illegal activities. Of course, the Gateses' travel plans might have been learned from a talkative neighbor or travel agent; under the "two-pronged test" developed from *Spinelli,* the character of the details in the anonymous letter might well not permit a sufficiently clear inference regarding the letterwriter's "basis of knowledge." But, as discussed previously, . . . probable cause does not demand the certainty we associate with formal trials. It is enough that there was a fair probability that the writer of the anonymous letter had obtained his entire story either from the Gateses or someone they trusted. And corroboration of major portions of the letter's predictions provides just this probability. It is apparent, therefore, that the judge issuing the warrant had a "substantial basis for . . . conclud[ing]" that probable cause to search the Gateses' home and car existed. The judgment of the Supreme Court of Illinois therefore must be
Reversed.

Not all states have adopted the totality-of-the-circumstances test established in *Illinois v. Gates.* In interpreting their state constitutions, a few states have rejected the *Gates* test and continue to use the two-pronged *Aguilar-Spinelli* test. Among the states declining to adopt the *Gates* totalities test are

Alaska in the case of *State v. Jones* [3] and the state of Washington in the case of *State v. Jackson.* [4]

THE GOOD FAITH EXCEPTION

If a law enforcement officer executes a search warrant which he (or she) believes in good faith is a valid warrant, but is later determined to be invalid, should the rule of exclusion of evidence be applied and the evidence forbidden for use in a criminal trial? In 1984 the U.S. Supreme Court held that if an officer reasonably relied upon a search warrant issued by a detached and neutral magistrate, the evidence would not be suppressed under the exclusionary rule. This significant change is stated in the following case:

United States v. Leon

Supreme Court of the United States (1984)
468 U.S. 897, 104 S.Ct. 3405

"An experienced and well-trained (California) narcotics investigator prepared an application to search" a specific home and specific cars for items relating to the defendants' drug-trafficking activities. The "extensive application was reviewed by several Deputy District Attorneys," and a search warrant was issued which produced large quantities of drugs. The defendants were charged with conspiracy to possess and distribute cocaine and other charges. The trial court, however, held that while the "case was a close one," the affidavit was insufficient to establish probable cause and suppressed the evidence. The Court of Appeals affirmed the suppression order which prevented the use of the evidence against the defendants. In reversing and ordering that the seized evidence could be used, the U.S. Supreme Court held that

> Because a search warrant "provides the detached scrutiny of a neutral magistrate, which is a more reliable safeguard against improper searches than the hurried judgment of a law enforcement officer 'engaged in the often competitive enterprise of ferreting out crime,'" *United States v. Chadwick*, 433 US 1, 9, . . . we have expressed a strong preference for warrants and declared that "in a doubtful or marginal case a search under a warrant may be sustainable where without one it would fail." *United States v. Ventresca*, 380 US 102, 106, . . . Reasonable minds frequently may differ on the question whether a particular affidavit establishes probable cause, and we have thus concluded that the preference for warrants is most appropriately effectuated by according "great deference" to a magistrate's determination. *Spinelli v. United States*, 393 U.S., at 419 . . . .
> Deference to the magistrate, however, is not boundless. It is clear, first, that the deference accorded to a magistrate's finding of probable cause does not preclude inquiry into the knowing or reckless falsity of the affidavit on which that determination was based. . . . Second, the courts must also insist that the magistrate purport to "perform his

'neutral and detached' function and not serve merely as a rubber stamp for the police." *Aguilar v. Texas*, supra, at 111 . . . A magistrate failing to "manifest that neutrality and detachment demanded of a judicial officer when presented with a warrant application" and who acts instead as "an adjunct law enforcement officer" cannot provide valid authorization for an otherwise unconstitutional search. . . .

Third, reviewing courts will not defer to a warrant based on an affidavit that does not "provide the magistrate with a substantial basis for determining the existence of probable cause." *Illinois v. Gates*, . . . 76 L.Ed.2d 527, 103 S.Ct. 2317. "Sufficient information must be presented to the magistrate to allow that official to determine probable cause; his action cannot be a mere ratification of the bare conclusions of others." See *Aguilar v. Texas*, supra at 114–115 . . . Even if the warrant application was supported by more than a "bare bones" affidavit, a reviewing court may properly conclude that, notwithstanding the deference that magistrates deserve, the warrant was invalid because the magistrate's probable-cause determination reflected an improper analysis of the totality of the circumstances . . . or because the form of the warrant was improper in some respect.

Only in the first of these three situations, however, has the Court set forth a rationale for suppressing evidence obtained pursuant to a search warrant; in the other areas, it has simply excluded such evidence without considering whether Fourth Amendment interests will be advanced. To the extent that proponents of exclusion rely on its behavioral effects on judges and magistrates in these areas, their reliance is misplaced. First, the exclusionary rule is designed to deter police misconduct rather than to punish the errors of judges and magistrates. Second, there exists no evidence suggesting that judges and magistrates are inclined to ignore or subvert the Fourth Amendment or that lawlessness among these actors requires application of the extreme sanction of exclusion.

Third, and most important, we discern no basis, and are offered none, for believing that exclusion of evidence seized pursuant to a warrant will have a significant deterrent effect on the issuing judge or magistrate. Many of the factors that indicate that the exclusionary rule cannot provide an effective "special" or "general" deterrent for individual offending law enforcement officers apply as well to judges or magistrates. And, to the extent that the rule is thought to operate as a "systemic" deterrent on a wider audience, it clearly can have no such effect on individuals empowered to issue search warrants. Judges and magistrates are not adjuncts to the law enforcement team; as neutral judicial officers, they have no stake in the outcome of particular criminal prosecutions. The threat of exclusion thus cannot be expected significantly to deter them. Imposition of the exclusionary sanction is not necessary meaningfully to inform judicial officers of their errors, and we cannot conclude that admitting evidence obtained pursuant to a warrant while at the same time declaring that the warrant was somehow defective will in any way reduce judicial officers' professional incentives to comply with the Fourth Amendment, encourage them to repeat their mistakes, or lead to the granting of all colorable warrant requests. . . .

In the absence of an allegation that the magistrate abandoned his detached and neutral role, suppression is appropriate only if the officers were dishonest or reckless in preparing their affidavit or could not have harbored an objectively reasonable belief in the existence of probable cause. Only respondent Leon has contended that no reasonably well-trained police officer could have believed that there existed probable cause to search his house; significantly, the other respondents advance no comparable argument. Officer Rombach's application for a warrant clearly was supported by much more than a "bare bones" affidavit. The affidavit related the results of an extensive investigation and, as the opinions of the divided panel of the Court of Appeals make clear, provided evidence sufficient to create disagreement among thoughtful and competent judges as to the existence of probable cause. Under these circumstances, the officers' reliance on the magistrate's determination of probable cause was objectively reasonable, and application of the extreme sanction of exclusion is inappropriate.

Accordingly, the judgment of the Court of Appeals is reversed.

THE DEFENDANT'S RIGHT TO A NEUTRAL AND DETACHED JUDGE

In the case of *United States v. Leon* (just presented), the U.S. Supreme Court stated that "the courts must also insist that the magistrate purport to 'perform his neutral and detached function and not serve merely as a rubber stamp for the police.' "

The two tests which a magistrate or judge must meet are (1) that he (or she) be "neutral and detached" and (2) that he (or she) be capable of determining whether probable cause exists to issue the arrest or search warrant. The following cases illustrate these requirements:

Coolidge v. New Hampshire

Supreme Court of the United States (1971)
403 U.S. 443, 91 S.Ct. 2022

Under New Hampshire statutes, the state attorney general could issue a search warrant. The state attorney general took charge of the investigation of the murder of a teenaged girl in this case. When he needed a search warrant, he applied to himself and issued one. In commenting on this case a year later (see following case), the Supreme Court stated that they

voided (the) search warrant issued by the state attorney general "who was actively in charge of the investigation and later was to be chief prosecutor at trial."

Shadwick v. Tampa

Supreme Court of the United States (1972)
407 U.S. 345, 92 S.Ct. 2119

Municipal court clerks in the City of Tampa were authorized by the city charter to issue warrants for the arrest of persons charged with breach of municipal ordinances. In affirming the validity of the practice and holding that a warrant must be issued by a magistrate who meets the two tests required by the Court, the Court ruled as follows:

He must be neutral and detached, and he must be capable of determining whether probable cause exists for the requested arrest or search. This Court long has insisted that inferences of probable cause be drawn by "a neutral and detached magistrate instead of being judged by the officer engaged in the often competitive enterprise of ferreting out crime." *Johnson v. United States, supra*, at 14 of 333 U.S., ... In *Coolidge v. New Hampshire, supra*, the Court last Term voided a search warrant issued by the state attorney general "who was actively in charge of the investigation and later was to be chief prosecutor at trial." *Id.*, at 450 of 403 U.S., at 2029 of 91 S.Ct. If, on the other hand, detachment and capacity do conjoin, the magistrate has satisfied the Fourth Amendment's purpose.

The requisite detachment is present in the case at hand. Whatever else neutrality and detachment might entail, it is clear that they require severance and disengagement from activities of law enforcement. There has been no showing whatever here of partiality, or affiliation of these clerks with prosecutors or police. The record shows no connection with any law enforcement activity or authority which would distort the independent judgment the Fourth Amendment requires. Appellant himself expressly refused to allege anything to that effect. The municipal court clerk is assigned not to the police or prosecutor but to the municipal court judge for whom he does much of his work. In this sense, he may well be termed a "judicial officer." ...

The clerk's neutrality has not been impeached: he is removed from prosecutor or police and works within the judicial branch subject to the supervision of the municipal court judge.

Appellant likewise has failed to demonstrate that these clerks lack capacity to determine probable cause. The clerk's authority extends only to the issuance of arrest warrants for breach of municipal ordinances. We presume from the nature of the clerk's position that he would be able to deduce from the facts on an affidavit before him whether there was probable cause to believe a citizen guilty of impaired driving, breach of peace, drunkenness, trespass, or the multiple other common offenses covered by a municipal code. There has been no showing that this is too difficult a task for a clerk to accomplish. Our legal system has long entrusted nonlawyers to evaluate more complex and significant factual data than that in the case at hand. Grand juries daily determine probable cause prior to rendering indictments, and trial juries assess whether guilt is proved beyond a reasonable doubt. The significance and responsibility of these lay judgments

The "Honest Mistake" Exception

THE 1987 U.S. SUPREME COURT CASE OF
MARYLAND v. GARRISON

Baltimore police officers obtained a warrant to search the person and apartment of Law-rence McWebb. When the police applied for the warrant and when they conducted the search under the warrant, they reasonably believed that there was only one apartment on the third floor of the building where McWebb lived. Before the police became aware that there were two apartments on the third floor, they discovered heroin, cash, and drug paraphernalia in the apartment of Garrison (the defendant in this case). The U.S. Supreme Court held that the search warrant was valid because validity is judged in light of the information available to the officers at the time they obtained the warrant. In holding that the evidence obtained could be used under the "honest mistake" exception, the Supreme Court ruled that

> We have no difficulty concluding that the officers' entry into the third-floor common area was legal; they carried a warrant for those premises, and they were accompa-nied by McWebb, who provided the key that they used to open the door giving access to the third-floor common area. If the officers had known, or should have known, that the third floor contained two apartments before they entered the living quarters on the third floor, and thus had been aware of the error in the warrant, they would have been obligated to limit their search to McWebb's apartment. Moreover, as the officers recognized, they were required to discontinue the search of respondent's apartment as soon as they discovered that there were two sepa-rate units on the third floor and therefore were put on notice of the risk that they might be in a unit erroneously included within the terms of the warrant. The officers' conduct and the limits of the search were based on the information available as the search proceeded. While the purposes justifying a police search strictly limit the permissible extent of the search, the Court has also recognized the need to allow some latitude for honest mistakes that are made by officers in the dangerous and difficult process of making arrests and executing search warrants.
>
> In *Hill v. California,* 401 U.S. 797 (1971), we considered the validity of the arrest of a man named Miller based on the mistaken belief that he was Hill. The police

betray any belief that the Tampa clerks could not determine probable cause for arrest.

We decide today only that clerks of the municipal court may consti-tutionally issue the warrants in question. We have not considered whether the actual issuance was based upon an adequate showing of probable cause ....

The single question is whether power has been lawfully vested, not whether it has been constitutionally exercised ....

What we do reject today is any *per se* invalidation of a state or local warrant system on the ground that the issuing magistrate is not a lawyer or judge. Communities may have sound reasons for delegating the responsibility of issuing warrants to competent personnel other than judges or lawyers. Many municipal courts face stiff and unrelent-

had probable cause to arrest Hill and they in good faith believed that Miller was Hill when they found him in Hill's apartment. As we explained:

"The upshot was that the officers in good faith believed Miller was Hill and arrested him. They were quite wrong as it turned out, and subjective good-faith belief would not in itself justify either the arrest or the subsequent search. But sufficient probability, not certainty, is the touchstone of reasonableness under the Fourth Amendment and on the record before us the officers' mistake was understandable and the arrest a reasonable response to the situation facing them at the time." *Id.,* at 803–804.

While *Hill* involved an arrest without a warrant, its underlying rationale that an officer's reasonable misidentification of a person does not invalidate a valid arrest is equally applicable to an officer's reasonable failure to appreciate that a valid warrant describes too broadly the premises to be searched. Under the reasoning in *Hill,* the validity of the search of respondent's apartment pursuant to a warrant authorizing the search of the entire third floor depends on whether the officers' failure to realize the overbreadth of the warrant was objectively understandable and reasonable. Here it unquestionably was. The objective facts available to the officers at the time suggested no distinction between McWebb's apartment and the third-floor premises.

For that reason, the officers properly responded to the command contained in a valid warrant even if the warrant is interpreted as authorizing a search limited to McWebb's apartment rather than the entire third floor. Prior to the officers' discovery of the factual mistake, they perceived McWebb's apartment and the third-floor premises as one and the same; therefore their execution of the warrant reasonably included the entire third floor. Under either interpretation of the warrant, the officers' conduct was consistent with a reasonable effort to ascertain and identify the place intended to be searched within the meaning of the Fourth Amendment.[a]

[a] *Maryland v. Garrison,* ___ U.S. ___, 107 S.Ct. 1013, 40 CrL 3288 (1987).

ing caseloads. A judge pressured with the docket before him may give warrant applications more brisk and summary treatment than would a clerk. All this is not to imply that a judge or lawyer would not normally provide the most desirable review of warrant requests. But our federal system warns of converting desirable practice into constitutional commandment. It recognizes in plural and diverse state activities one key to national innovation and vitality. States are entitled to some flexibility and leeway in their designation of magistrates, so long as all are neutral and detached and capable of the probable-cause determination required of them.

We affirm the judgment of the Florida Supreme Court.

Affirmed.

AREAS WHICH MAY BE SEARCHED UNDER A
SEARCH WARRANT

The U.S. Supreme Court stated in the 1982 case of *United States v. Ross* as to searches under the authority of a search warrant that

> A lawful search of fixed premises generally extends to the entire area in which the object of the search may be found and is not limited by the possibility that separate acts of entry or opening may be required to complete the search. Thus, a warrant that authorizes an officer to search a home for illegal weapons also provides authority to open closets, chests, drawers, and containers in which the weapon might be found. A warrant to open a footlocker to search for marihuana would also authorize the opening of packages found inside. A warrant to search a vehicle would support a search of every part of the vehicle that might contain the object of the search. When a legitimate search is under way, and when its purpose and its limits have been precisely defined, nice distinctions between closets, drawers, and containers, in the case of a home, or between glove compartments, upholstered seats, trunks, and wrapped packages, in the case of a vehicle, must give way to the interest in the prompt and efficient completion of the task at hand.

A search warrant which would authorize the search of premises for stolen truck tires or stolen 21″ television sets would authorize a search of areas where such objects may be. Many search warrants, however, are for illegal drugs or for other objects that could be concealed in drawers and in small boxes and containers. Searches for illegal drugs and other small objects would justify entry into and search of all areas and containers within a premise or within a vehicle.

Plain-View Seizures When Executing a
Valid Search Warrant

A search warrant is issued to search X's apartment for stolen jewelry taken in a burglary. While the officers are executing the valid search warrant, they find one pound of heroin in a dresser drawer. The authority to seize the evidence which the police did not expect to find is stated in the U.S. Supreme Court case of *Coolidge v. New Hampshire,* 403 U.S. at 468, 91 S.Ct. at 2039:

> Where, once an otherwise lawful search is in progress, the police inadvertently come upon a piece of evidence, it would often be a needless inconvenience, and sometimes dangerous—to the evidence or to the police themselves—to require them to ignore it until they have obtained a warrant particularly describing it.

But could the police go into the dresser drawer after they have found all of the stolen jewelry described in the search warrant? The answer is no.[5] If the warrant authorized a search for a stolen horse, could the police go into the dresser drawer? The answer is no.

Law enforcement officers may remain on premises for as long as is necessary to conduct a thorough search for the objects named in a warrant. Some searches would only take a few minutes, since a search for a large object would not authorize opening containers in which the object could not be concealed. Other searches (drugs, for example) could possibly take long periods of time.

DETAINING THE OCCUPANTS OF PREMISES TO BE SEARCHED UNDER A SEARCH WARRANT

A search warrant is sometimes issued where there is not probable cause to arrest the person whose premises are to be searched. In 1981, the question of whether such a person may be detained until after the police searched the premises was presented to the U.S. Supreme Court in the following case:

Michigan v. Summers

Supreme Court of the United States (1981)
452 U.S. 692, 101 S.Ct. 2587

> As Detroit police officers were about to execute a warrant to search a house for narcotics, they encountered (defendant) descending the front steps. They requested his assistance in gaining entry and detained him while they searched the premises. After finding narcotics in the basement and ascertaining that (defendant) owned the house, the police arrested him, searched his person, and found in his coat pocket an envelope containing 8.5 grams of heroin.

Defendant was also charged with the possession of the heroin found on his person. The trial judge and later the Supreme Court of Michigan held that the heroin found on his person was the product of an illegal search in violation of the Fourth Amendment and suppressed the evidence. In reversing, the U.S. Supreme Court held that the search was lawful and that the evidence could be used against the defendant, ruling that

> Of prime importance in assessing the intrusion is the fact that the police had obtained a warrant to search respondent's house for contraband. A neutral and detached magistrate had found probable cause to believe that the law was being violated in that house and had authorized a substantial invasion of the privacy of the persons who resided there. The detention of one of the residents while the premises were searched, although admittedly a significant restraint on his liberty, was surely less intrusive than the search itself. Indeed, we may safely assume that most citizens—unless they intend flight to avoid arrest—would elect to remain in order to observe the search of their possessions ....
>
> In *Payton v. New York,* 445 U.S. 573, ... we held that police officers may not enter a private residence to make a routine felony arrest without first obtaining a warrant. In that case we rejected the suggestion that only a search warrant could adequately protect the privacy interests at stake, noting that the distinction between a search warrant and an arrest warrant was far less significant than the interposi-

tion of the magistrate's determination of probable cause between the zealous officer and the citizen:

"It is true that an arrest warrant requirement may afford less protection than a search warrant requirement, but it will suffice to interpose the magistrate's determination of probable cause between the zealous officer and the citizen. If there is sufficient evidence of a citizen's participation in a felony to persuade a judicial officer that his arrest is justified, it is constitutionally reasonable to require him to open his doors to the officers of the law. Thus, for Fourth Amendment purposes, an arrest warrant founded on probable cause implicitly carries with it the limited authority to enter a dwelling in which the suspect lives when there is reason to believe the suspect is within." *Id.,* at 602–603, 100 S.Ct., at 1388.

That holding is relevant today. If the evidence that a citizen's residence is harboring contraband is sufficient to persuade a judicial officer that an invasion of the citizen's privacy is justified, it is constitutionally reasonable to require that citizen to remain while officers of the law execute a valid warrant to search his home. Thus, for Fourth Amendment purposes, we hold that a warrant to search for contraband founded on probable cause implicitly carries with it the limited authority to detain the occupants of the premises while a proper search is conducted.

Because it was lawful to require respondent to re-enter and to remain in the house until evidence establishing probable cause to arrest him was found, his arrest and the search incident thereto were constitutionally permissible. The judgment of the Supreme Court of Michigan must therefore be reversed.

It is so ordered.

SEARCHES WHICH MAY BE MADE OF PERSONS ON PREMISES WHILE SEARCH WARRANTS ARE BEING EXECUTED

If probable cause exists, a search warrant may authorize the search of a specific person. If a law enforcement agency has probable cause to believe that a person has committed a crime, that person could be arrested and a search could be made incident to the lawful arrest (see chapter 10).

But can a person present on premises being searched under the authority of a search warrant be searched when probable cause does not exist? This was the question presented to the U.S. Supreme Court in the following case:

Ybarra v. Illinois

Supreme Court of the United States (1979)
444 U.S. 85, 100 S.Ct. 338

A valid search warrant was issued to search an Aurora, Illinois tavern and a bartender named Greg in the tavern. The warrant authorized a search for "heroin, contraband, other controlled substances, money, instrumentalities and narcotics ...". Late in the afternoon of the day the warrant was issued, officers proceeded to the tavern to execute the warrant. Nine to thirteen customers were present, who were informed that the officers were going to conduct a "cursory search for weapons." Ybarra was one of the customers. In the first pat-down of Ybarra, the officer felt what he described as "a cigarette pack with objects in it." However, the officer moved on and minutes later came back to Ybarra again. The officer again located the object and removed it from Ybarra's pants pocket. Inside were six tinfoil packets containing heroin. Ybarra was charged and convicted of the possession of heroin. The Illinois courts held that the search producing the evidence was lawful under the authority of an Illinois statute. In reversing the conviction and holding that the search violated the Fourth Amendment, the U.S. Supreme Court stated that

> It is true that the police possessed a warrant based on probable cause to search the tavern in which Ybarra happened to be at the time the warrant was executed. But, a person's mere propinquity to others independently suspected of criminal activity does not, without more, give rise to probable cause to search that person .... Where the standard is probable cause, a search or seizure of a person must be supported by probable cause particularized with respect to that person. This requirement cannot be undercut or avoided by simply pointing to the fact that coincidentally there exists probable cause to search or seize another or to search the premises where the person may happen to be. The Fourth and Fourteenth Amendments protect the "legitimate expectations of privacy" of persons, not places. See *Rakas v. Illinois,* 439 U.S. 128, 138–143, ...
>
> Each patron who walked into the Aurora Tap Tavern on March 1, 1976, was clothed with constitutional protection against an unreasonable search or an unreasonable seizure. That individualized protection was separate and distinct from the Fourth and Fourteenth Amendment protection possessed by the proprietor of the tavern or by "Greg." Although the search warrant, issued upon probable cause, gave the officers authority to search the premises and to search "Greg," it gave them no authority whatever to invade the constitutional protections possessed individually by the tavern's customers.
>
> Notwithstanding the absence of probable cause to search Ybarra, the State argues that the action of the police in searching him and seizing what was found in his pocket was nonetheless constitutionally permissible. We are asked to find that the first patdown search of Ybarra constituted a reasonable frisk for weapons under the doctrine of *Terry v. Ohio,* 392 U.S. 1, ... If this finding is made, it is then possible to conclude, the State argues, that the second search of Ybarra was constitutionally justified. The argument is that the patdown yielded probable cause to believe that Ybarra was carrying narcotics, and that this probable cause constitutionally supported the second search, no warrant being required in light of the exigencies of the situation coupled with the ease with which Ybarra could have disposed of the illegal substance.
>
> We are unable to take even the first step required by this argument. The initial frisk of Ybarra was simply not supported by a reasonable belief that he was armed and presently dangerous, a belief which this

Court has invariably held must form the predicate to a patdown of a person for weapons .... When the police entered the Aurora Tap Tavern ... the lighting was sufficient for them to observe the customers. Upon seeing Ybarra, they neither recognized him as a person with a criminal history nor had any particular reason to believe that he might be inclined to assault them. Moreover, as Police Agent Johnson later testified, Ybarra, whose hands were empty, gave no indication of possessing a weapon, made no gestures or other actions indicative of an intent to commit an assault, and acted generally in a manner that was not threatening. At the suppression hearing, the most Agent Johnson could point to was that Ybarra was wearing a ¾-length lumber jacket, clothing which the State admits could be expected on almost any tavern patron in Illinois in early March. In short, the State is unable to articulate any specific fact that would have justified a police officer at the scene in even suspecting that Ybarra was armed and dangerous.

The *Terry* case created an exception to the requirement of probable cause, an exception whose "narrow scope" this Court "has been careful to maintain." Under that doctrine a law enforcement officer, for his own protection and safety, may conduct a patdown to find weapons that he reasonably believes or suspects are then in the possession of the person he has accosted .... Nothing in *Terry* can be understood to allow a generalized "cursory search for weapons" or indeed, any search whatever for anything but weapons. The "narrow scope" of the *Terry* exception does not permit a frisk for weapons on less than reasonable belief or suspicion directed at the person to be frisked, even though that person happens to be on premises where an authorized narcotics search is taking place ....

For these reasons, we conclude that the searches of Ybarra and the seizure of what was in his pocket contravened the Fourth and Fourteenth Amendments. Accordingly, the judgment is reversed, and the case is remanded to the Appellate Court of Illinois, Second District, for further proceedings not inconsistent with this opinion.

It is so ordered.

OTHER DEFENSES WHICH COULD BE USED IN ATTACKS ON THE VALIDITY OF SEARCHES UNDER SEARCH WARRANTS

The job of a defense lawyer is to attack the possible use of evidence against his client. In addition to the defenses listed in this chapter, a defense lawyer could also attack the validity of searches made under search warrants in the following manner.

That the Life of the Warrant Ceased

An otherwise valid search warrant could "die" (cease to be a valid warrant) when

- Probable cause supporting the warrant vanishes, or

- The period fixed by state or federal statute expires, or
- The time period fixed by the warrant itself (if this is made a part of the warrant) expires, or
- Under the case law of that state, there is an unreasonable delay.

That the Warrant Was Improperly Executed at Night

Most state search warrants, and non-drug federal warrants, direct that they shall be served only in the daytime. However, the issuing judge could find reasonable cause for a night search and could insert permission in the warrant to make a night search. (Federal Rules of Court Procedure, Rule 41(c).)

Federal drug warrants can authorize a nighttime search without any special showing that a nighttime search is necessary. (21 U.S.C. 879(a); also *Gooding v. United States,* 416 U.S. 430, 94 S.Ct. 1780 (1974).)

Staleness as a Challenge to the Validity of a Search Warrant

If too great a length of time elapsed between the reported information and the issuance of the warrant, probable cause could vanish with the passage of time. For example, officers receive reliable information that X has a substantial amount of heroin in his home. However, it is X's practice to have the heroin out on the street within a matter of hours. This practice is known to the police. In this example, a search warrant issued a day later could be challenged as being issued on stale information.

Violation of the Byars Doctrine

A city police officer has a valid search warrant to search X's home in an attempt to recover fur coats taken in the burglary of a fur coat store. The officer has a tip that X is also involved in drugs and asks a federal drug agent to accompany the local officers and assist in the execution of the search warrant. The local officers want the experience and knowledge of the federal drug officer. But if the search is conducted in this manner, the officer will have extended and expanded the search beyond the authorized scope of the warrant. The U.S. Supreme Court forbade this practice in the 1927 case of *Byars v. United States,* 273 U.S. 28, 47 S.Ct. 248 (1927).

The "Knock" or "No-Knock" Requirements Were Violated

As pointed out in chapter 11, law enforcement officers must knock, identify themselves, state their purpose, and await a refusal or silence before entering private premises. The reasons for these requirements are stated in chapter 11.

An unannounced (no-knock) entry can be made if it is specifically authorized by the search warrant, or if it can be shown that such notice (knocking) is likely to (a) endanger the life or the safety of the officer or another person; or (b) result in the evidence subject to seizure being easily and quickly destroyed or disposed of; or (c) enable the party to be arrested or searched to escape; or (d) be a useless gesture.

"Searches ... Without Prior Approval by Judge or Magistrate, Are ... Unreasonable ..." Unless ...

The most basic constitutional rule in this area is that "searches conducted outside the judicial process, without prior approval by judge or magistrate, are per se unreasonable under the Fourth Amendment—subject only to a few specifically established and well-delineated exceptions." The exceptions are "jealously and carefully drawn," and there must be "a showing by those who seek exemption ... that the exigencies of the situation made that course imperative." "[T]he burden is on those seeking the exemption to show the need for it." [a]

[a] U.S. Supreme Court in Coolidge v. New Hampshire, 403 U.S. 443, 91 S.Ct. 2022 (1971).

That the Search Exceeded the Scope of the Warrant

In the case of *Ybarra v. Illinois* (in this chapter), officers searched a tavern customer for drugs. Because probable cause did not exist to authorize the search, the search exceeded the scope of the search warrant. Going into a desk drawer when a search warrant authorizes only a search for stolen truck tires would also exceed the scope of the warrant.

Many courts (but not all) consider vehicles parked upon the curtilage to be part of the premises.[6] It would be a better practice to have the search warrant include a vehicle, because defense lawyers will attack the use of evidence obtained from such a search unless authority can be shown to justify the search.

OBTAINING A SEARCH WARRANT IN TWELVE MINUTES BY USE OF A TELEPHONE

Probably all states have statutes governing the issuance of search warrants in that state. These statutes are enacted by the legislative body of that state, and the manner in which search warrants are issued and executed would have to be in conformity with the statutes.

California (in 1970) and Arizona (in 1971) led the way in enacting statutes authorizing oral procedures for the issuance of search warrants. Other states and the federal government have since adopted the procedure whereby a search warrant may be obtained using a telephone, radio, or other similar means of communication.

Under such statutes, a law enforcement officer may telephone or radio a judge or magistrate and apply for a search warrant. Statements of the officer and the judge must be recorded and the officer must be placed under oath. If probable cause to issue a search warrant is shown and other requirements are satisfied, the judge may authorize the officer to fill in a search warrant form, which the officer would have to have available. The judge would then authorize the officer to sign his (the judge's) name to the warrant form.

Obtaining Evidence by Means of Entry into Private Premises

When evidence is obtained as a result of a law enforcement officer's entry into private premises, it must be shown that

- The officer had authority to enter (existence of a search warrant, an emergency, or consent).

- The entry requirements were complied with in that

  consent to enter can be shown, or

  a showing that the "knock" requirements were complied with, or

  a showing that conditions existed which justified a "no-knock" entry, or

  entry was obtained by ruse (trick) which involved no breaking (see *Lewis v. United States,* 385 U.S. 206, 87 S.Ct. 424, 17 L.Ed.2d 312 (1966), in which an undercover officer gained entry to the defendant's home by not disclosing his true identity).

Unless the statutory or common law of your jurisdiction directs otherwise, the following are the requirements for knock and no-knock entries:

To make a knock entry, the officer must:

- Knock.
- Identify himself.
- State his purpose.
- Wait for consent, refusal, or silence before entering.

In order to justify a no-knock entry, the officer must testify to facts which would justify a conclusion that:

- A knock entry would be likely to endanger the life or the safety of the officer or other persons.

- A knock entry would be likely to result in evidence subject to seizure being easily and quickly destroyed (see *Ker v. California,* 374 U.S. 23, 83 S.Ct. 1623, 10 L.Ed.2d 726 (1963)).

- A knock entry would be likely to enable the party to be arrested to escape (see *Warden v. Hayden,* 387 U.S. 294, 87 S.Ct. 1642, 18 L.Ed.2d 782 (1967) and *United States v. Santana,* 427 U.S. 38, 96 S.Ct. 2406, 49 L.Ed.2d 300 (1976)).

- A knock entry would likely be a useless gesture (see the case of *State v. Suits,* 73 Wis.2d 352, 243 N.W.2d 206 (1976)), in which the Supreme Court of Wisconsin held that knocking would have been a useless gesture because a loud party was in progress and the officers were observed approaching the house.

The following California case illustrates the use of such procedure to obtain a search warrant within a very short period of time:

People v. Aguirre

Court of Appeals of California (1972)
26 Cal.App.3d Supp. 7, 103 Cal.Rptr. 153

A California police officer telephoned a duty judge at his home at 9:46 P.M. and related information which amounted to probable cause for the issuance of a search warrant. The officer was placed under oath and the statements of the officer and the judge were recorded. The officer was then authorized by the judge to sign the judge's name to the search warrant after filling out the form. The officer then inquired as to whether the warrant was authorized for night service, based upon the statements which he had made. The judge stated, "Any time of Day or Night service." The Appellate Court pointed out that the entire telephone conversation "lasted a mere 12 minutes." In affirming the conviction of the defendants and the use of the evidence obtained in the search of their premises under the authority of the search warrant, the California Court held that

> Therefore, it is the opinion of this court that the language of Penal Code section 1526, subdivision (b) is sufficiently broad to allow a telephone statement, providing it is recorded, which this was, as the basis for the issuance of a search warrant; and administering the oath following the statement, together with the judge's inquiry as to the truth of the statement just made is not prejudicial error.

Courts throughout the United States have urged law enforcement officers to make greater use of search warrants. Studies over the years have concluded that search warrants are underused. In states where telephonic warrants are authorized, the procedure is very simple. Warrants can now be obtained in the middle of the night and on holidays and weekends without difficulty, since most warrants are routine and involve fairly common situations.

PROBLEMS

1. Police officers in Yarmouth, Massachusetts were investigating a series of burglaries. A search warrant was obtained to search the motel room used by Richard Kelleher. Some items (credit cards) taken in two burglaries were recovered but other items (jewelry, silver, and gold) which the police were looking for were not recovered.

   A few hours after recovering the credit cards, an unidentified woman telephoned the police, stating that the stolen jewelry, silver, and gold could be found in a motor home parked in Yarmouth. She stated that the motor home was owned by George Upton and that Upton had purchased the stolen items from Kelleher. She stated that because Kelleher's motel room had been raided, Upton was going to move his motor home. The woman stated that she had seen the stolen items and that the "motor home (was) full of stolen stuff." The woman would not identify herself because she stated that Upton would "kill me."

The police officer talking to the woman on the telephone then told the woman that the officer had met her at Upton's repair shop in Yarmouthport four months earlier. The woman stated that she was surprised that the officer knew who she was. Upton had identified the woman as being his girlfriend and the woman stated that she had broken up with George Upton and wanted to "burn him." The woman would not give her name or her telephone number but stated she would contact the officer in the future "if need be."

The officer then checked and confirmed that a motor home was parked on the property and behind a home owned by George Upton and his mother. While other officers watched the premises, an application for a search warrant was prepared, setting out all of the information above in an affidavit. Also attached were reports on the two prior burglaries with lists of the stolen property. A search warrant was issued and the stolen property and other incriminating evidence was obtained. The use of the evidence led to Upton's conviction of multiple counts of burglary, receiving stolen property, and related crimes.

Under federal standards, what test would be used to determine today whether probable cause existed to issue the search warrant? What facts increase the "reliability," "basis of knowledge," and "veracity" of the woman informant's report? How much deference (consideration) should an appellate court give to the local judge's decision that probable cause does (or does not) exist in a case such as this? Should the U.S. Supreme Court affirm the use of the evidence and the conviction of Upton? Why? *Massachusetts v. Upton,* 466 U.S. 727, 104 S.Ct. 2085 (1984).

2. "The badly burned body of Sandra Boulware was discovered in a vacant lot in the Roxbury section of Boston at approximately 5 A.M., Saturday, May 5, 1979. An autopsy revealed that Boulware had died of multiple compound skull fractures caused by blows to the head. After a brief investigation, the police decided to question one of the victim's boyfriends, Osborne Sheppard. Sheppard told the police that he had last seen the victim on Tuesday night and that he had been at a local gaming house (where card games were played) from 9 P.M. Friday until 5 A.M. Saturday. He identified several people who would be willing to substantiate the claim."

Officers then contacted the other persons who had been at the gaming house and learned that Sheppard had borrowed a car and had been gone from 3 A.M. to 5 A.M. The officers then contacted the owner of the car and obtained consent to inspect the vehicle.

Bloodstains and pieces of hair were found on the rear bumper and within the trunk compartment. In addition, the officers noticed strands of wire in the trunk similar to wire strands found on and near the body of the victim. The owner of the car told the officers that when he last used the car on Friday night, shortly before Sheppard borrowed it, he had placed articles in the trunk and had not noticed any stains on the bumper or in the trunk.

An affidavit for a search warrant was then prepared, seeking to obtain evidence linking Sheppard to the murder of Ms. Boulware. A detective (O'Malley) showed the affidavit to the district attorney, to the first assistant of the D.A., and to a police sergeant, who all concluded that the affidavit set forth probable cause for a search of Sheppard's home and also Sheppard's arrest.

However, because it was Sunday and the court was closed, the only search warrant form which could be found was one for the search of drugs (controlled substance). Detective O'Malley made some changes in the form but did not cross out and delete "controlled substance" in the main body of the warrant itself. The affidavit and the warrant form were then taken to the judge's home. After the judge made the decision to issue and sign the search warrant,

> Detective O'Malley offered the warrant form and stated that he knew the form as presented dealt with controlled substances. He showed the judge where he had crossed out the subtitles. After unsuccessfully searching for a more suitable form, the judge informed O'Malley that he would make the necessary changes so as to provide a proper search warrant. The judge then took the form, made some changes on it, and dated and signed the warrant. However, he did not change the substantive portion of the warrant, which continued to authorize a search for controlled substances; nor did he alter the form so as to incorporate the affidavit. The judge returned the affidavit and the warrant to O'Malley, informing him that the warrant was sufficient authority in form and content to carry out the search as requested. O'Malley took the two documents and, accompanied by other officers, proceeded to Sheppard's residence. The scope of the ensuing search was limited to the items listed in the affidavit, and several incriminating pieces of evidence were discovered. Sheppard was then charged with first degree murder.

After Sheppard was convicted, he appealed to the Supreme Judicial Court of Massachusetts, arguing the evidence obtained as a result of the search warrant should be suppressed because the warrant was defective. The Massachusetts Supreme Court agreed and the case was appealed to the U.S. Supreme Court.

In view of the purpose of the exclusionary rule (see chapter 8), would reversing Sheppard's conviction and ordering a new trial without use of the evidence serve the purpose of the exclusionary rule? *Massachusetts v. Sheppard,* 468 U.S. 981, 104 S.Ct. 3424 (1984).

3. In the 1978 case of *Massachusetts v. White,* 439 U.S. 280, 99 S.Ct. 712, 24 CrL 3023, (1978) an equally divided U.S. Supreme Court affirmed the judgment of the Supreme Judicial Court of Massachusetts that a statement taken from a defendant in violation of *Miranda v. Arizona* (see chapter 10) may not be used to establish probable cause for the issuance of a search warrant. In view of the purpose of the exclusionary rule (see chapter 8), does this ruling serve the purpose of the exclusionary rule? Give reasons for your answer.

NOTES

[1] December 1975 issue of *The Police Chief*. Written by Robert R. Dempsey and Robert W. Wennerholm, former police officers and legal advisers to the Dade County Public Safety Department.

[2] See Massachusetts v. Upton, 466 U.S. 727, 104 S.Ct. 2085 (1984).

[3] 706 P.2d 317, 38 CrL 2042 (Alaska Sup.Ct.1985).

[4] 102 Wash.2d 432, 688 P.2d 136, 35 CrL 2445 (Wash.Sup.Ct.1984).

[5] See United States v. Odland, 502 F.2d 148 (7th Cir.1974); United States v. Feldman, 366 F.Supp. 356 (D.Hawaii 1973); United States v. Highfill, 334 F.Supp. 700 (E.D.Ark.1971).

[6] See 47 ALR 2d 1444 and Joyner v. State, 303 So.2d 60 (Fla.App., 1974).

15

Evidence Obtained by Wiretapping and Electronic Surveillance

CHAPTER OUTLINE

Attempting to obtain evidence by means of mechanical or electronic eavesdropping is in most instances a search, while the obtaining of such evidence is a seizure within the meaning of the Fourth Amendment. In pointing out that the Fourth Amendment protects the privacy of conversations against unreasonable governmental intrusions, the U.S. Supreme Court stated in the 1967 case of *Katz v. United States* [1]

> the Fourth Amendment protects people, not places. What a person knowingly exposes to the public, even in his own home or office, is not a subject of Fourth Amendment protection .... But what he seeks to preserve as private, even in an area accessible to the public, may be constitutionally protected.

In the *Katz* case, evidence was obtained when FBI agents attached an electronic listening and recording device to the outside of the public telephone booth which the defendant was using to transmit gambling information to cities in other states. The trial court permitted this evidence to be used in the trial, which resulted in the conviction of the defendant. Because the federal statutes at that time contained neither provisions for a court order nor a search warrant for such activity, the FBI agents had no court order. In reversing the defendant's conviction, the U.S. Supreme Court held that

> The Government's activities in electronically listening to and recording the petitioner's words violated the privacy upon which he justifiably relied while using the telephone booth and thus constituted a "search and seizure" within the meaning of the Fourth Amendment. The fact that the electronic device employed to achieve that end did not happen to penetrate the wall of the (telephone) booth can have no constitutional significance.

THE 1968 FEDERAL WIRETAPPING AND ELECTRONIC SURVEILLANCE ACT

In the year following the 1967 case of *Katz v. United States,* the Congress of the United States enacted the 1968 Federal Wiretapping and Electronic Surveillance Act. [2] This federal act, which was followed by similar legislation in many states, made the following important changes in the law of wiretapping and electronic surveillance:

The 1986 Federal "Electronic Privacy" Act

Many new communication technologies have been developed since the 1968 Federal Wiretapping and Electronic Surveillance Act was enacted. Congress enacted a new "Electronic Privacy" Act in October 1986 to apply the U.S. Constitution's Fourth Amendment privacy protections to almost all forms of communications. The Act protects the new forms of communication, regardless of how they are transmitted. These include mobile cellular telephones, electronic mail, and other data transmission systems. Violations are punishable by penalties from fines up to prison terms.

ELECTRONIC COMMUNICATIONS

Electronic Communications is defined as "any transfer of signs, signals, writing, images, sounds, data, or intelligence of any nature" that may be transmitted wholly or partly by wire, radio, electromagnetic, photo-electronic, or photo-optical systems.

EXCEPTIONS THE LEGISLATION DOES NOT PROTECT:

- Radio signals and communications which are readily accessible to the general public. These signals can be protected, however, if they are scrambled or put into code.
- Cordless telephones can also be easily picked up by the general public and also have a lower expectation of privacy than owners of conventional equipment. These signals, also, can be protected by scrambling or transforming conversations into code during transmission.

- It authorizes court orders permitting wiretapping and electronic surveillance by law enforcement officers in much the same manner as search warrants are issued.
- The act makes wiretapping and electronic surveillance done in violation of the act a felony. The distribution, possession, and advertising of mechanical and electronic devices used for wiretapping and electronic surveillance is also made a felony (see Section 2513 of the Act).

SITUATIONS IN WHICH COURT ORDERS ARE NOT REQUIRED

Conversations Overheard Without the Use of Mechanical or Electronic Devices

Law enforcement officers may use artificial means of aiding their vision such as bifocals, binoculars, or telescopes, but they may not use mechanical or electronic listening devices which intrude and violate the privacy of another person without a court order.

Persons who are talking about criminal activity sometimes become careless and do not exercise a right of privacy. Persons overhearing such conversations may testify as to what they have heard as long as they have a right to be where they were. The following examples illustrate:

- A few years ago, an FBI agent was waiting to be picked up at the airport in Milwaukee. Because he had a half-hour wait before his ride would appear, the agent went to the coffee shop and ordered a cup of coffee. In the next booth at the restaurant, a group of men were discussing criminal activity in which they had engaged. The agent listened to the conversation and observed the men for identification purposes. What the agent heard and saw was used as evidence in the trial of the men for criminal charges.

- In many cases, officers testified as to what they overheard from adjacent hotel or motel rooms, or while the officers were in hallways. The following appellate cases held that such evidence was properly admitted for use: *United States v. Fisch,* 474 F.2d 1071 (9th Cir.1973), review denied 412 U.S. 921, 93 S.Ct. 2472, 37 L.Ed.2d 148 (1973); *United States v. Llanes,* 398 F.2d 880 (2d Cir.1968); *United States v. Jackson,* 588 F.2d 1046 (5th Cir.1979), and *Ponce v. Craven,* 409 F.2d 621 (9th Cir.1969).

The following U.S. Supreme Court cases illustrate other situations in which the Court held that officers may testify as to what they heard and saw:

Lewis v. United States

Supreme Court of the United States (1966)
385 U.S. 206, 87 S.Ct. 424

> An undercover federal narcotic officer was invited into the defendant's home, where the defendant sold the officer narcotics. In affirming the defendant's conviction and in holding that testimony as to what the defendant said and did was properly used as evidence, the U.S. Supreme Court ruled that
>
>> A government agent, in the same manner as a private person, may accept an invitation to do business and may enter upon the premises for the very purposes contemplated by the occupant. Of course, this does not mean that, whenever entry is obtained by invitation and the locus is characterized as a place of business, an agent is authorized to conduct a general search for incriminating materials ....

Hoffa v. United States

Supreme Court of the United States (1966)
385 U.S. 293, 87 S.Ct. 408

> The former union official, James Hoffa, made incriminating statements in the presence of a paid government informer. Testimony as to what Hoffa said was permitted as evidence in Hoffa's trial on criminal charges. The U.S. Supreme Court affirmed the defendant's conviction, holding that there was no violation

of Hoffa's Sixth Amendment right to confer privately with his attorneys out of the presence of government agents and informers.

However, if an officer or agent is not where he has a right to be, then what he hears or sees may not be used as evidence. The following cases illustrate situations in which officers heard and observed criminal activity in private premises while the officer was outside of the premises.

State of Texas v. Gonzales

United States Court of Appeals, Fifth Circuit (1968)
388 F.2d 145

Law enforcement officers sneaked into the defendant's yard at night to listen to conversations in the house and to observe activity. Evidence obtained in this manner led the officers to believe that the defendants were engaged in criminal activity. The Court held that the conduct of the officers violated the Fourth Amendment, because the defendants (and all other persons) have a right of privacy in the curtilage, which is the yard and area around a home. (The word *eavesdropping* is an old English word meaning to sneak under the eaves of a home and listen to the conversations within the home. This conduct was forbidden under old English common law, and is forbidden under present law.)

Where Mechanical or Electronic Devices Are Used But There Is No Violation of Defendant's Rights and Expectation of Privacy

Undercover officers, police agents, or informants sometimes attempt to make narcotic purchases or to make contacts with suspects for the purposes of obtaining evidence. It is common practice to wire such persons with small microphones and radio transmitters for any or all of the following reasons:

- To alert nearby officers should the undercover officer or the police agent be endangered and need assistance.
- To keep nearby officers informed as to what is being said and the events which are occurring.
- After listening to (and in some instances recording) such conversations, the officers may then testify as to what they have heard by means of the radio transmitters.

The following U.S. Supreme Court cases illustrate the use of such means of obtaining evidence without the use of prior court orders:

Important U.S. Supreme Court Cases on Electronic Surveillance

Katz v. United States, 389 U.S. 347, 88 S.Ct. 507 (1967)

Wiretapping was brought under the Fourth Amendment when the Court overruled other cases. The test used to determine whether the Fourth Amendment was violated is: Did the person demonstrate an expectation of privacy, and is the expectation of privacy "one that society is prepared to recognize as 'reasonable' "? If a right of privacy is to be intruded upon, a warrant is required with particularization and probable cause shown for the suspect, the crime, the telephone, and the time.

United States v. Miller, 425 U.S. 435, 96 S.Ct. 1619 (1976)

The Court ruled that a bank customer's financial record is the property of the bank, and that the customer has no legitimate "expectation of privacy" in these records.

United States v. New York Telephone Co., 434 U.S. 159, 98 S.Ct. 364 (1977)

The Court held that to be covered by Title III of the 1968 Federal Wiretapping and Electronic Surveillance Act, a communication must be capable of being overheard.

Smith v. Maryland, 442 U.S. 735, 99 S.Ct. 2577 (1979)

The Court held that the use of a pen register did not violate the Fourth Amendment.

United States v. Knotts, 460 U.S. 276, 103 S.Ct. 1081 (1983)

The Court held that listening to a beeper, which was placed in a container of chloroform before it was sold to a suspect, was not a search and seizure. Narcotics agents believed that the chloroform was being used in the manufacture of illegal drugs. The agents used the beeper signals and visual observations to follow the suspect's vehicle. Based upon the information obtained, the agents were able to obtain a search warrant for defendant's home. It was held that there was no reasonable expectation of privacy since the vehicle's movements, which were tracked, were public.

United States v. Karo, 468 U.S. 705, 104 S.Ct. 3296 (1984)

The Court held that using a beeper to trail a container of ether into a house and "to keep in touch with it (the container) inside the house" did violate the Fourth Amendment. The ether was being used to extract cocaine from clothing that had been imported into the United States.

On Lee v. United States

Supreme Court of the United States (1952)
343 U.S. 747, 72 S.Ct. 967

Federal narcotics agents wired an undercover agent with a small microphone and radio transmitter. The agent then purchased a pound of opium from the

Important Federal Electronic Surveillance Statutes [a]

Section 605 of the Communications Act of 1934 provided that "No person not being authorized by the sender shall intercept any communication and divulge . . . the contents . . .".

Title III of the 1968 Omnibus Crime Control and Safe Streets Act is designed to protect the privacy of wire and oral communications and also to allow evidence to be obtained for "certain types of major offenses." Law enforcement electronic surveillance of conversations is thus prohibited except under a court order, which a judge may issue after being convinced that the following procedural requirements have been met:

1. application by a high-ranking prosecutor;

2. surveillance for one of the crimes specified in Title III; [b]

3. probable cause to believe that a crime has occurred, that the target of the surveillance is involved, and that the evidence of that crime will be obtained by the surveillance;

4. a statement indicating that other investigative procedures are ineffective; and

5. an effort to minimize the interception.

Crime Control Act of 1973 requires that State criminal justice information systems, developed with Federal funds, be protected by measures to ensure the privacy and security of information.

Privacy Act of 1974 requires agencies to comply with fair information practices in their handling of personal information, including the following: records must be necessary, lawful, current, and accurate; records must be used only for purpose collected except with an individual's consent or where exempted; no record of an individual's exercise of first amendment rights is to be kept unless authorized by statute; information cannot be sold or rented for mailing list use. The following are exempted: CIA records; records maintained by law enforcement agencies; Secret Service records; Federal testing materials; etc.

Foreign Intelligence Surveillance Act of 1978 establishes legal standards and procedures for the use of electronic surveillance to collect foreign intelligence and counter-intelligence within the United States. This was the first legislative authorization for wiretapping and other forms of electronic surveillance (including radio intercepts, microphone eavesdropping, closed circuit television, beepers, and oth-

defendant, after conducting conversations with the defendant in his laundry and on the streets in New York City. The undercover agent did not testify at the defendant's trial, but one of the federal narcotic agents who overheard the conversations by means of the radio transmitter was permitted to testify as to what he heard and saw. In affirming the defendant's conviction and the use of this evidence, the U.S. Supreme Court held that

> No good reason of public policy occurs to us why the Government should be deprived of the benefit of On Lee's admissions because he made them to a confidante of shady character.

er monitoring techniques). It created the Foreign Intelligence Surveillance Court, composed of seven Federal District Judges, to review and approve surveillance capable of monitoring U.S. persons (defined as U.S. citizens, lawfully admitted permanent resident aliens, and domestic organizations or corporations that are not openly acknowledged to be directed and controlled by foreign governments) in the United States. The procedural requirements of FISA apply only to electronic surveillance for foreign intelligence purposes, but the criminal penalties appear to apply more broadly to include law enforcement surveillance.

Right to Financial Privacy Act of 1978 provides bank customers with some privacy regarding their records held by banks and other financial institutions, and provides procedures whereby Federal agencies can gain access to such records.

Electronic Funds Transfer Act of 1980 provides that any institution providing EFT or other bank services must notify its customers about third-party access to customer accounts.

Privacy Protection Act of 1980 prohibits Government agents from conducting unannounced searches of press offices and files if no one in the press room is suspected of a crime.

Cable Communications Policy Act of 1984 requires the cable service to inform the subscriber of: the nature of personally identifiable information collected and the nature of the use of such information; the disclosures that may be made of such information; the period during which such information will be maintained; and the times during which an individual may access such information. Also places restrictions on the cable services' collection and disclosures of such information. The act creates a subscriber right to privacy against Government surveillance.

The Child Protection Act of 1984 amends the 1968 Federal Electronic Eavesdropping Statute (18 U.S.C. 2510–20) to include sexual exploitation of children among those offenses that may be investigated by use of wiretaps and electronic surveillance. It is hoped that this will be helpful in identifying cults that exchange child pornography.

[a] Much of this material is taken from pp. 25–26 of the 1985 publication titled "Electronic Surveillance and Civil Liberties" of the Congressional Office of Technology Assessment, published by the U.S. Government Printing Office.

[b] Crimes included are kidnapping, robbery, murder, extortion, bribery of public officials, gambling, counterfeiting offenses, narcotic violations, violations of the Atomic Energy Act, espionage, sabotage, treason, and riots.

United States v. White

Supreme Court of the United States (1971)
401 U.S. 745, 91 S.Ct. 1122

Federal narcotics agents overheard conversations between the defendant and a governmental informer, who was wired with a concealed radio transmitter. At the time of the defendant's trial, the informer could not be located to testify and the narcotics agents were permitted to testify as to what they heard. The

U.S. Supreme Court affirmed the defendant's conviction and the use of the officer's testimony as evidence, holding that

> Concededly a police agent who conceals his police connections may write down for official use his conversations with a defendant and testify concerning them, without a warrant authorizing his encounters with the defendant and without otherwise violating the latter's Fourth Amendment rights . . . . For constitutional purposes, no different result is required if the agent instead of immediately reporting and transcribing his conversations with defendant, either (1) simultaneously records them with electronic equipment which he is carrying on his person, . . . (2) or carries radio equipment which simultaneously transmits the conversations either to recording equipment located elsewhere or to other agents monitoring the transmitting frequency. *On Lee v. United States* [343 U.S. 747 . . . .] If the conduct and revelations of an agent operating without electronic equipment do not invade the defendant's constitutionally justifiable expectations of privacy, neither does a simultaneous recording of the same conversations made by the agent or by others from transmissions received from the agent to whom the defendant is talking and whose trustworthiness the defendant necessarily risks.

Recording of Face-to-Face Conversations

In situations where an attempt is made to bribe a law enforcement or other person, there often is no other evidence available other than the statements of the person complaining of the matter. In many situations the testimony of the person who was offered the bribe would be sufficient to sustain a conviction, for example, when a motorist attempts to bribe a law enforcement officer in an attempt to avoid being issued a traffic citation.

However, in other situations the testimony of one witness would not be sufficient evidence to sustain a conviction where the defendant denies attempting to make a bribe. In such cases it is common practice to obtain additional evidence either in the form of another witness or by means of a pocket tape recorder. The following U.S. Supreme Court case illustrates this practice:

United States v. Caceres

Supreme Court of the United States (1979)
440 U.S. 741, 99 S.Ct. 1465

The defendant was having federal tax problems and offered to bribe a federal tax agent to fix his tax audits. Unknown to the defendant, three of his face-to-face conversations with the Internal Revenue Service agent were recorded by means of a radio transmitter concealed on the agent's person. However, IRS regulation required that prior authorization be obtained before taping and the tax agent did not obtain the required permission. The U.S. Supreme Court held that the evidence was admissible despite the federal tax agency requirement. The Court referred to and quoted a very similar case (*Lopez v. United States*), and stated that

> Nor does the Constitution protect the privacy of individuals in respondent's position. In *Lopez v. United States,* 373 U.S. 427, 439, 83 S.Ct. 1381, 1388, 10 L.Ed.2d 462, we held that the Fourth Amendment provided no protection to an individual against the recording of his statements by the IRS agent to whom he was speaking. In doing so, we repudiated any suggestion that the defendant had a "constitutional right to rely on possible flaws in the agent's memory, or to challenge the agent's credibility without being beset by corroborating evidence that is not susceptible of impeachment," concluding instead that "the risk that petitioner took in offering a bribe to [the IRS agent] fairly included the risk that the offer would be accurately reproduced in court, whether by faultless memory or mechanical recording."

The Case in Which a Murder Victim Tape Recorded His Own Murder

The following case received a great deal of national attention because the principal evidence against the defendant was a tape recording of a murder made by the victim of the murder. In holding that the tape recording was admissible as evidence, the Supreme Court of Florida followed the principle of law stated by the U.S. Supreme Court in the *On Lee, White,* and *Caceres* cases found in this chapter.

State v. Inciarrano

Supreme Court of Florida (1985)
473 So.2d 1272

Florida police investigating the murder of a psychologist who was shot five times in his office thought at first they had a hard case to solve. There were no witnesses, nor did anyone hear the shots. But to their surprise, the police found that the psychologist had tape recorded the business meeting between himself and the defendant. The sounds of the two men quarreling, a gun being cocked, five shots, groans by the victim, gushing of blood, and the victim falling to the floor could be heard on the tape. But Florida, like twelve other states, has a law forbidding the tape recording of private conversations unless all parties consent. The trial court allowed the tape to be used as evidence but the Florida court of appeals held that the tape could not be used.

In reversing the court of appeals and holding that the tape was properly used as evidence in the murder trial of the defendant, the Supreme Court of Florida affirmed the defendant's conviction, ruling that

To prevail Inciarrano must not only have had a subjective expectation of privacy, but also his expectation under the circumstances must have been one that society is prepared to recognize as reasonable. Assuming he had a subjective expectation of privacy, we conclude that such expectation, under the circumstances, was not justified. Without a reasonable expectation of privacy, Inciarrano's "oral communications" were not protected under section 934.03, and the trial court properly denied his motion to suppress. Inciarrano went to the victim's office with the intent to do him harm. He did not go as a patient. The district court, in the present case, correctly stated:

> One who enters the business premises of another for a lawful purpose is an invitee. At the moment that his intention changes, that is, if he suddenly decides to steal or pillage, or murder, or rape, then at that moment he becomes a trespasser and has no further right upon the premises. Thus, here, if appellant ever had a privilege, it dissolved in the sound of gunfire.

447 So.2d at 389.

Accordingly, we hold that because Inciarrano had no reasonable expectation of privacy, the exclusionary rule of section 934.06 does not apply.

The Few States That Do Not Follow the Law Established in the U.S. Supreme Court Cases of *On Lee*, *White*, and *Caceres*

Most states hold that if there was no violation of a person's right of privacy, then tape recordings of such conversations may be used as evidence. Most states also hold that if one of the parties to a conversation (telephone or by other means) consent to a tape recording of the conversation, the tape may be used as evidence. But not all states follow the federal and majority rule. The following murder case illustrates:

State v. Lucas

Supreme Court of Minnesota (1985)
372 N.W.2d 731

Minnesota law enforcement officers were investigating the murder of a husband in Minnesota. They had evidence that the defendant was having an affair with the victim's wife and suspected that he was a party to the murder. As an alibi, the defendant stated that he spent the night of the murder at the apartment of a woman in Wisconsin. When Minnesota investigators talked to the woman in Wisconsin, she did not corroborate the alibi the defendant had given the police, but instead provided a different alibi for the defendant. When an officer stated that he did not believe her, the woman began crying and stated that the defendant had told her that the defendant and the victim's wife planned to kill the victim for insurance money and offered to pay her $1,000.00 to provide an alibi for the defendant. The woman then agreed to make tele-

The Difference Between Wiretapping and Bugging

In footnote 1 of the case of *Dalia v. United States*, 441 U.S. 238, 99 S.Ct. 1682 (1979) the U.S. Supreme Court stated the difference between wiretapping and bugging as follows:

> [1] All types of electronic surveillance have the same purpose and effect: the secret interception of communications. As the Court set forth in *Berger v. New York,* 388 U.S. 41, 45–47 (1967), however, this surveillance is performed in two quite different ways. Some surveillance is performed by "wiretapping," which is confined to the interception of communication by telephone and telegraph and generally may be performed from outside the premises to be monitored .... At issue in the present case is the form of surveillance commonly known as "bugging," which includes the interception of all oral communication in a given location. Unlike wiretapping, this interception typically is accomplished by installation of a small microphone in the room to be bugged and transmission to some nearby receiver.

Can a Person Legally Tape Record His (or Her) Telephone Call?

A person may make notes (either during or after) a telephone call. Under federal law and in most states, a person may also tape record his (or her) telephone calls. In the majority of the states, telephone conversations may be tape recorded by the police or other persons with the consent of one of the parties even when the other party (or parties) are unaware of the tapping. Under federal law and in most states, such tapes may be used as evidence in either criminal or civil trials if the tapes are relevant and material to the issues before the court.

The taping of personal telephone calls received wide attention in the United States in November 1986. One of Wall Street's most prominent speculators, Ivan Boesky, admitted using inside information in stock trading for his personal gain. This conduct is illegal. To help himself, Mr. Boesky cooperated with government investigators and tape recorded telephone conversations which he had with other speculators. These tapes could be used as evidence in federal courts and most states (including New York).

Illegal Use of Cellular Telephones

Persons who have illegally altered chips installed in cellular telephones could find themselves arrested and their phones confiscated for use as evidence. The altered chips cause other persons to be charged for phone calls made on the illegal phones.

After eighteen persons were arrested in New York City in 1987, an FBI agent stated that the persons arrested were going to have one more telephone call that day (referring to the call an arrested person is permitted to make), "but that call is not going to be made through a cellular telephone." (See 27 March 1987 *New York Times* article, "18 Arrested in Illegal Use of Cellular Phones.")

phone calls to the defendant and the victim's wife without informing them that the police were listening and were taping the telephone conversations. Incriminating statements were obtained in the tape recordings. The use of such tapes (obtained without a court order) is forbidden in Wisconsin but they were permitted for use at defendant's murder trial in Minnesota. In holding that the incriminating statements on the tapes were properly used as evidence, the Minnesota Supreme Court stated that

> Defendant argues that the trial court should have applied the Wisconsin rule of exclusion, because the telephone calls and the tapes were made in Wisconsin, and that the trial court's failure to do so was prejudicial.
>
> It is clear that evidence obtained in another state in violation of the Federal Constitution is subject to the same rule of exclusion that would apply if the evidence had been obtained in this state. *Mapp v. Ohio,* 367 U.S. 643 .... There is, however, no requirement that evidence obtained in another state be excluded in this state merely because it would be inadmissible if the prosecution were in that other state. 1 W. LaFave, Search and Seizure § 1.3(c) at 51–52 ....
>
> ... Taking into account the several policy reasons underlying the exclusionary rule, we readily conclude that in this case the trial court correctly refused to suppress the evidence. Neither the Wisconsin police who taped Baker's conversations with defendant and (victim's wife) nor the Minnesota police who suggested that Baker make the calls and who participated in the taping violated the laws of either Wisconsin or Minnesota. Hence, exclusion of the tapes would not serve to deter misconduct by police officers of either Minnesota or Wisconsin. On the other hand, admission of the tapes does not compromise judicial integrity and does not have the effect of permitting Minnesota to profit from any wrongdoing.

INSTALLING ELECTRONIC EAVESDROPPING DEVICES

Authority to enter private premises to install an electronic eavesdropping device was the issue before the United States Supreme Court in the following case.

Dalia v. United States

Supreme Court of the United States (1979)
441 U.S. 238, 99 S.Ct. 1682

Three dissenting justices (Stevens, Brennan, and Marshall) described the case as follows:

> At midnight on the night of April 5–6, 1973, three persons pried open a window to petitioner's business office and secretly entered the prem-

Categories of Behavior Subject to Electronic Surveillance

1. *Movements*—where someone is. Individuals can be tracked electronically via beepers as well as by monitoring computerized transactional accounts in real time.

2. *Actions*—what someone is doing or has done. Electronic devices to monitor action include: monitoring of keystrokes on computer terminals, monitoring of telephone numbers called with pen registers, cable TV monitoring, monitoring of financial and commercial computerized accounts, and accessing computerized law enforcement or investigatory systems.

3. *Communications*—what someone is saying or writing, and hearing or receiving. Two-way electronic communications can be intercepted whether the means be analog or digital communication via wired telephones, communication via cordless or cellular phones, or digital electronic mail communication. Two-way nonelectronic communication can be intercepted via a variety of microphone devices and other transmitters.

4. *Actions and communications*—the details of what someone is doing or saying. Electronic visual surveillance, generally accompanied by audio surveillance, can monitor the actions and communications of individuals in both private and public places, in daylight or darkness.

5. *Emotions*—the psychological and physiological reactions to circumstances. Polygraph testing, voice stress analyzers, breath analyzers, and brain wave analyzers attempt to determine an individual's reactions.

Source: U.S. Office of Technology Assessment.

ises. During the next three hours they moved freely about the building, eventually implanting a listening device in the ceiling. Several weeks later, they again broke into the office at night and removed the device.

The perpetrators of these break-ins were agents of the Federal Bureau of Investigation. Their office, however, carries with it no general warrant to trespass on private property. Without legislative or judicial sanction, the conduct of these agents was unquestionably "unreasonable" and therefore prohibited by the Fourth Amendment. Moreover, that conduct violated the Criminal Code of the State of New Jersey unless it was duly authorized.

However, the majority on the U.S. Supreme Court affirmed the defendant's conviction and rejected the defendant's contention that separate court authorization was necessary to enter defendant's office as done by the FBI. The Court stated that

Petitioner contends, nevertheless, that the April 5th order was insufficient under the Fourth Amendment for its failure to specify that it would be executed by means of a covert entry of his office. Nothing in the language of the Constitution or in this Court's decisions interpreting that language suggests that, in addition to the three requirements discussed above, search warrants also must include a specification of

---

Dimensions for Balancing Civil Liberty Interest v. Government Investigative Interest

CIVIL LIBERTY INTEREST:

1. *Nature of information:* The more personal or intimate the information that is to be gathered about a target, the more intrusive the surveillance technique and the greater the threat to civil liberties.

2. *Nature of place or communication:* The more "private" the area or type of communication to be placed under surveillance, the more intrusive the surveillance and the greater the threat to civil liberties.

3. *Scope of surveillance:* The more people and activities that are subject to surveillance, the more intrusive the surveillance and the greater the threat to civil liberties.

4. *Surreptitiousness of surveillance:* The less likely it is for the individual to be aware of the surveillance and the harder it is for the individual to detect it, the greater the threat to civil liberties.

5. *Pre-electronic analogy:* Pre-electronic analogies are often considered in determining intrusiveness, but with widely varying interpretations.

GOVERNMENT INVESTIGATIVE INTEREST:

1. *Purpose of investigation:* Importance ranked as follows: national security, domestic security, law enforcement, and the proper administration of Government programs.

2. *Degree of individualized suspicion:* The lower the level of suspicion, the harder it is to justify the use of surveillance devices.

3. *Relative effectiveness:* More traditional investigative techniques should be used and proven ineffective before using technologically sophisticated techniques.

Source: U.S. Office of Technology Assessment.

---

the precise manner in which they are to be executed. On the contrary, it is generally left to the discretion of the executing officers to determine the details of how best to proceed with the performance of a search authorized by warrant—subject of course to the general Fourth Amendment protection "against unreasonable searches and seizures."

PROBLEMS

1. Lopez was having federal tax problems and attempted to bribe an Internal Revenue agent. After the IRS agent reported the matter to his superior, he was instructed to keep an appointment with Lopez. However, at the second meeting the IRS agent had a tape recorder in his pocket and recorded the

conversation, in which Lopez again attempted to bribe the agent to fix his tax problems with the federal government. Lopez was then charged with attempted bribery and at his trial took the witness stand in his own behalf. After Lopez denied under oath that he attempted to bribe the tax agent, the tape recorder was introduced into evidence to show that Lopez had not told the truth under oath.

Should the U.S. Supreme Court hold that the evidence of the tape recorder was properly used in the federal trial of Lopez? Should the U.S. Supreme Court affirm Lopez's conviction for bribery? Why? *Lopez v. United States,* 373 U.S. 427, 83 S.Ct. 1381 (1963).

2. Chandler and another man conducted a conversation using walkie-talkies (handie-talkies). During their open-air conversation, the two men made many statements linking them to a burglary. A tape recording was made of the conversation.

Could the tape recording be used as evidence in your state if the incident occurred in your state? Could persons overhearing the conversation by means of walkie-talkies testify as to what they heard? Give reasons for your answers. *Chandler v. State,* 366 So.2d 64 (Fla.App.1978), review denied 376 So.2d 1157 (1979), affirmed 449 U.S. 560, 101 S.Ct. 802 (1981).

3. Two hospital police officers and the associate director of the hospital overheard the defendant talking to a hospital social worker. They heard him confess that he beat a child. The social worker was not acting for the police nor did the social worker exert any physical or psychological pressure on the defendant.

Should the persons who overheard defendant's statements be permitted to testify as to what they heard? Explain. *Commonwealth v. Roberts,* 6 Mass.App.Ct. 891, 376 N.E.2d 895 (1978).

4. A police officer made a proper stop of a vehicle, having reasonable suspicion to believe the driver was driving while intoxicated. The officer, who was in full uniform, talked with the defendant (driver). The defendant did not know that the officer was tape recording the conversation and made statements incriminating himself.

Would the tape recording be admissible as evidence in your state in a trial for drunken driving? Explain. *City and Borough of Juneau v. Quinto,* 684 P.2d 127 (Alaska Sup.Ct.1984). Would a videotaping of the defendant after he was arrested for drunken driving be admissible as evidence? *Palmer v. State,* 604 P.2d 1106 (Alaska 1979).

5. Cordless telephones are short-range radio transmitters whose signals can sometimes be picked up by ordinary radio receivers. Could a person (ordinary citizen or law enforcement officer) who overheard telephone conversations in this manner testify as to what they heard? Would tape recordings made of such conversations be admissible as evidence?

NOTES

[1] 389 U.S. 347, 88 S.Ct. 507 (1967).

[2] Title 18, Chapter 119 of the Omnibus Crime Control and Safe Streets Act of 1968.

PART FOUR

Physical and Demonstrative Evidence

Physical Evidence and Evidence Obtained from the Crime Scene

REAL OR PHYSICAL EVIDENCE

Physical Evidence Generally

The term **evidence** was defined in chapter 3 as that which gives proof or tends to give proof for or against a fact in issue during a trial or other court hearing. In layman's terms, evidence can also be defined as that which gives information. Using the latter definition in a legal sense, evidence would consist of information accepted for use in a trial or other official proceeding.

Physical evidence (or real evidence, as it is sometimes called) is just one type of evidence used in court proceedings. The testimony of witnesses is also evidence. Public records, business records, and demonstrative devices can be used as evidence. Judicial notice (or knowledge of the court) is another form of evidence.

Physical evidence differs from other types of evidence in that physical evidence often speaks for itself. Whereas the testimony of a witness may be inaccurate, exaggerated or biased, it has been stated by writers that physical evidence cannot lie. Nor may physical evidence be impeached as the testimony of a witness may be impeached. As a general rule, juries and judges like physical evidence because they can see what has been stated in oral testimony. For these reasons, criminal courts tend to give greater weight to scientific tests and physical evidence which speaks for itself.

The U.S. Department of Justice report entitled "An Analysis of the Physical Evidence Recovery Process" lists the following categories of physical evidence as those usually found in criminal investigations of crime scenes:

- toolmarks
- fingerprints and palmprints
- organic material
- glass and plastic fragments
- tracks and impressions
- paint
- clothing
- wood fragments

The Greatest Advantage of Trace Evidence

Perhaps the greatest single advantage of trace evidence relates to the fact that there must usually have been contact for an exchange of trace material to have occurred between persons or things. Thus, the problem of identification is considerably simplified when microscopic evidence linking the suspect with the crime scene is detected.

Evidence standards assume their highest importance with respect to trace materials. Without such standards, the trace materials collected from the suspect or the crime scene have little value.

TRACE EVIDENCE ASSOCIATED WITH CLOTHING

The clothing of the suspect is a prime accumulator of trace evidence. For this reason, his clothing should be collected as soon as possible after the arrest and submitted to the laboratory for examination. Such collection is particularly important when the clothing is believed to be the same worn when the crime was committed. Before removing the clothing from the suspect, a cursory examination should be made of each item to avoid overlooking an obvious piece of evidence. The location of an item may be as important as what it is.

Because of the critical importance of identifying the origin of trace materials and insuring that they are not contaminated, the suspect's clothing should never be allowed to come in contact with or even close to the victim or his clothing. The suspect should never be brought to the scene of the crime until after the scene and his person have been searched. The reason for this precaution relates to the possibility that the suspect may claim that hairs, fibers, or other trace materials used to identify him and place him at the scene of the crime were actually transferred or deposited at the time he was brought on the scene by the police—not during the commission of the crime itself.

- dust
- cigarettes, matches, and ashes
- paper
- soil
- fibers
- tools and weapons
- grease and oil
- construction and packing material
- documents
- containers
- metal fragments
- hair
- blood
- inorganic and mineralogical material

There may arise situations in which it is impossible or undesirable to confiscate the clothing of the suspect. If so, the items of clothing may be temporarily removed from the suspect and swept with a vacuum. The sweepings from each of the clothing items must be placed in separate containers. Similarly, the sweepings from each pocket and pants cuff must be separately processed and packaged. The labeling of these packages must specifically identify the source of the material.

RECOVERY OF THE CLOTHING OF A VICTIM

Trace materials on the clothing of victims or suspects are particularly susceptible to contamination or loss at a hospital. Medical personnel are naturally concerned only with providing immediate treatment to the injured person and, therefore, cut away clothing from the body in order to save time. Frequently, the garments are thrown in a pile on the floor and, if not recovered quickly by the police, may even be destroyed. The investigator should make an immediate effort to have the injured person's clothing recovered for examination. In recovering such items he should use caution to prevent further damage and contamination of the evidence. However, if garments have been recovered in a pile, it is normally useless to separate them—and they may be wrapped together. When the victim's clothing has been brushed or cleaned by hospital personnel, an effort should still be made to recover them for laboratory examination. The laboratory would still be able to collect standards for comparison; and the recesses of the clothing may contain valuable trace materials.

Source: U.S. Dept. of Justice, *Crime Scene Search and Physical Evidence Handbook.*

Trace Evidence [1]

When two objects come into contact, there will frequently be a transfer of small amounts of the material from one to the other. This is nearly always the case when fabrics come in contact with a rough surface. Therefore when a suspect comes in contact with the victim and objects at the crime scene, he frequently leaves behind traces of himself and takes with him traces of the things he has touched. Materials transferred in this way are normally referred to as trace evidence. The term trace evidence is usually very loosely defined; however, it most often is applied to minute or microscopic bits of materials that are not immediately apparent to even a trained investigator. Thus, trace evidence is usually in the hard-to-find category. Because trace materials resulting from exchange are less likely to excite the attention of the criminal, or even to be apparent to him, there is far less probability that they will be deliberately eliminated by him than is the case with larger items of evidence or latent prints.

The following hypothetical situation illustrates the potential for the exchange of physical evidence during a series of fairly typical criminal actions.

The criminal crosses the back porch of a residence and steps on a brown paper bag lying on the floor. To gain entry, he breaks a small glass pane in the back door and reaches in to unlock the door. After gaining entry, he is surprised by the homeowner and a struggle follows. During the struggle the victim's nose begins to bleed. The suspect flees the scene.

In a situation of this type, the following exchanges of materials are entirely possible:

- The suspect's shoe print to the brown paper bag on the back porch.
- Fibers from the suspect's clothing to the edge of the broken pane of glass in the back door (or blood on the glass from a cut on the suspect's arm).
- Fingerprints to the glass on the back door, and possibly to other surfaces along the suspect's route of entry.
- Fibers from the suspect's clothing to the victim's clothing during the struggle, and vice versa.

The following (transferred) evidence may be found on or in possession of the suspect:

- Glass fragments or small paint chips on the outer garments of the suspect from the back door window pane and frame.
- Blood or hair from the victim to the suspect's clothing.
- Bruises or lacerations suffered by the suspect in the struggle with the victim.
- Fibers from the rug or furniture at the crime scene on the shoes or garments of the suspect.

It is apparent from this example that the possibilities for exchanges of trace materials are great. Even if the shoe prints and fingerprints are excluded from the array of physical evidence potential, there are still abundant opportunities to link the suspect with the crime scene, if proper collections are made at the scene and from the person of the suspect.

PROVING THAT REAL EVIDENCE IS GENUINE AND AUTHENTIC

To use physical (or real) evidence in a criminal or civil trial, the party offering the object has the burden of proving the evidence is genuine and authentic. They must show that the object is what they claim it is.

Professor McCormick states this requirement as follows in his book, *McCormick on Evidence:* [2] "When real evidence is offered (at a trial), an adequate foundation for admission will require testimony first that the object *is the object* which was involved in the incident, and further that the condition of the object is substantially unchanged." Federal Rule of Evidence 901(a) also states the same requirement (see appendix B of this text).

For example, a handgun is recovered by police at the scene of a murder. The defendant's fingerprints are found on the gun and ballistic tests show that the gun is the murder weapon. Because there were no eyewitnesses to the crime, the handgun is very important evidence. To use the handgun as evidence, the state must show that

- the weapon was the one used to commit the crime; and
- the gun is the one found at the crime scene and the condition of the evidence has not been altered or changed.

The state must therefore show that the fingerprints have not been altered or tampered with and that the gun is otherwise "substantially unchanged."

To prove that evidence is genuine and authentic and to show that the object is what it is claimed to be, a witness would have to be able to

- Testify as to where and how the object was obtained.
- Identify the object by a serial number if a serial number is on the object. In the example above, a serial number would probably be on the handgun and it would be identified in this manner.
- Identify the object based upon personal knowledge and observations. That is, the object must be "readily identifiable." [3]
- Establish and show a "chain of custody" for the object. In the example given, a chain of custody should be shown for the handgun to prove that the gun has not been tampered with in such a way as would affect the fingerprints or the ballistic test results.

The object may also be identified because a law enforcement officer has marked the object with his (or her) initials or in some other manner to identify the evidence. In the above example, it would be a recommended practice for a law enforcement officer to scratch his name or initials on such evidence.

Each of the above methods which are used to prove real evidence to be genuine and authentic is discussed in the following material.

Using Serial Numbers to Prove Evidence to Be Genuine and Authentic

Serial numbers can be found on guns, money, bicycles, motor vehicles, and other objects. Property such as TV sets and other items likely to be stolen are often marked by their owners with the driver's license number of the owner.[4] In the event of a theft, burglary, or robbery, the property can be identified by such numbers.

Serial numbers and other markings for identification purposes are therefore important in recovering stolen property and in the prosecution of theft, burglary, and robbery cases. If the stolen property is large and bulky, it is not brought into a courtroom during a trial but instead is specifically described by a witness and is (if possible) identified by a serial number or other identification marking. For example, a stolen motorcycle which has been recovered would not be brought into a courtroom as evidence in the criminal trial of the person charged with theft of the motorcycle.

Scratching Initials and Dates on Objects to Make Them Readily Identifiable Evidence

Police training manuals and directives recommend that objects that are likely to be used as evidence be identified by having the collecting officer scratch his (or her) initial or name and date on the object if practical. The officer can then readily identify the object as the evidence which was recovered at the crime scene (or other place). Firearms, spent cartridges, bullets, clothing, currency, and many other objects have been identified and authenticated as genuine in this manner. Weapons used in the commission of a felony are ordinarily identified not only by the serial number but also by initials (and date) scratched on the object by a law enforcement officer.

If the weapon is also to be used as the basis for evidence such as fingerprints or ballistic reports, a chain of custody must then be established and used to show that the evidence has not been altered or tampered with.

The Evidence Is "Readily Identifiable" Because a Witness Has Personal Knowledge of the Object

Many objects have unique characteristics which the owner of the property or other persons may be able to use to positively identify the object. Clothing, for example, may have such unique features that it may readily be identified. Other clothing items, however, may not have identifiable features to distinguish the object from other similar type clothing.

In rape and sexual assault cases, clothing of the victim or the suspect is often sent to a crime lab for testing. In these cases identification by the victim that the clothing was hers is not sufficient because it does not assure that the evidence of the blood, sperm, or pubic hair was not tampered with or substituted. The following case illustrates the problem:

Robinson v. Commonwealth

Supreme Court of Virginia (1971)
212 Va. 136, 183 S.E.2d 179

In a rape case, vital links in the "chain of possession" of the victim's panties, blouse, and pubic hair were not shown. The victim appeared as a witness and identified the panties and blouse as the garments she was wearing at the time of the crime. But the state did not introduce evidence showing what was done with these objects during time periods after the crime and before trial. Because semen and blood stains on the panties were used as evidence which linked the defendant to the crime and wool fiber on the blouse was similar to fiber in a sweater worn by the defendant, the evidence seriously incriminated the defendant. In reversing the defendant's conviction and ordering a new trial, the Supreme Court of Virginia stated that

> In the case at bar the Commonwealth failed to establish a chain of possession of the panties, blouse and pubic hair. It is not reasonably certain from the testimony presented that these exhibits were in the same condition when analyzed as they were when taken from the victim. Furthermore, it was not shown that the pubic hair taken from the victim was the same pubic hair that was analyzed.

A vital link in the chain of possession of these exhibits was the treatment they received from the time they were taken from the victim until delivered to Officer Thompson. Yet, the Commonwealth failed to establish this vital link in the chain of possession. We cannot assume that these exhibits were properly handled. Without an unbroken chain of possession of the panties, blouse and pubic hair, they were not admissible as evidence insofar as they supplied a basis for the opinion testimony of the FBI agents, who had examined them. Thus, the opinions of the FBI agents were also not admissible.

It is true that the blouse and panties were identified at the trial by the victim as a part of the clothes she was wearing when attacked. The Commonwealth contends that they were properly admitted because the victim identified them. If they had been admitted only to establish what the victim was wearing when attacked, then we would agree with the Commonwealth's position. But the blouse and the panties were also admitted to supply a basis for the opinion testimony of the FBI agents. The mere fact the blouse and the panties were identified did not prove the chain of possession necessary to validate the FBI analysis of them.

The error in admitting the exhibits as a basis for the testimony of the FBI agents was not harmless. In his closing argument before the jury, the Commonwealth's Attorney stressed the importance of this evidence. He referred to it as "scientific proof to back up that young lady's story that this man is the one."

For the reasons stated, the judgment appealed from is reversed and the case remanded for a new trial.

Reversed and remanded.

Other criminal cases in which courts held that the government sufficiently authenticated the evidence and showed that it was not tampered with or substituted are as follows:

United States v. Howard–Arias

U.S. Court of Appeals, Fourth Circuit (1982)
679 F.2d 363, review denied 459 U.S. 874, 103 S.Ct. 165 (U.S.Sup.Ct.)

Approximately 240 bales of marijuana were salvaged from a fishing trawler before it sank off the Virginia coast. The defendant was one of the crew of the vessel and was charged with the crimes of possession of marijuana on the high seas with intent to distribute, and possession with intent to import into the United States. In proving a chain of custody, the Coast Guard officer who seized the marijuana and two DEA agents testified. There was, however, a break in the chain of custody because a third DEA agent involved in the transfer and testing of the marijuana did not testify. In affirming the conviction of the defendant, the Court of Appeals stated that

The "chain of custody" rule is but a variation of the principle that real evidence must be authenticated prior to its admission into evidence. *See* Fed.R.Evid. 901; McCormick, *Handbook on the Law of Evidence* § 213 (2d ed. E. Cleary ed. 1972). The purpose of this threshold requirement is to establish that the item to be introduced, *i.e.,* marijuana, is what it purports to be, *i.e.,* marijuana seized from the "Don Frank." Therefore, the ultimate question is whether the authentication testimony was sufficiently complete so as to convince the court that it is improbable that the original item had been exchanged with another or otherwise tampered with .... Contrary to the appellant's assertion, precision in developing the "chain of custody" is not an iron-clad requirement, and the fact of a "missing link does not prevent the admission of real evidence, so long as there is sufficient proof that the evidence is what it purports to be and has not been altered in any material aspect." *United States v. Jackson,* 649 F.2d 967 (3d Cir.), cert. denied, 454 U.S. 871, 1034, ... Resolution of this question rests with the sound discretion of the trial judge, and we cannot say that he abused that discretion in this case.

United States v. Briddle

U.S. Court of Appeals, Eighth Circuit (1971)
443 F.2d 443

The defense lawyer argued that the government failed to prove the chain of evidence required for the admission of physical or real evidence. The object admitted for evidence was a unique button found at the scene of the burglary and traced to the defendant's coat. The officer who found the button at the scene of the burglary described it as follows: "It had a whale on the front of it. It was leather .... (I)t was a dark color .... The tail (of the whale) was up in the air Split. And I believe it was the left eye of the animal that was up." In holding that the button was properly admitted into evidence, the Court ruled that

> Given the uniqueness of the buttons on Briddle's coat, we think this identification evidence established that exhibit 2–V was the button top found at the scene of the burglary. Accordingly, we conclude that the trial court properly rejected appellants' request to strike the exhibit from evidence.

People v. Sansone

Illinois Court of Appeals (1976)
42 Ill.App.3d 512, 1 Ill.Dec. 101, 356 N.E.2d 101

The defendant was arrested for the theft of twenty-six record albums from a department store. The store security manager then counted the records, placed the date, his initials, and the defendant's name on the label of each record and made a list of the records and their value. The security man (Baier) then bound the records with twine and placed the records in the store's "evidence room and locked them up." In affirming the defendant's conviction and holding that a proper foundation for the use of the records as evidence had been made by the state, the Illinois Appellate Court held that

> The rule is well established that a foundation for the admission in evidence of an object may be laid either through its identification by a witness or through establishment of a chain of possession .... To require both identification of the object by a witness and establishment of a chain of possession would impose an unnecessary burden and would not assure a fairer trial to the accused ....
>
> Baier identified the bundle of albums in question, including the manner in which it was tied and knotted, and each of the records bore Baier's initials, the date and the defendant's name. Baier's identifying marks enabled him to make a positive identification of the record albums as the ones which were taken by the defendant. There is not the slightest proof in the record of any substitution or any form of tampering with them. The prosecution was not required under the circumstances to exclude all possibility of tampering. All that is required is that there be only the reasonable probability that the article has not been changed in any important respect .... It is clear, therefore, that the State laid a proper foundation for the introduction into evidence of the albums.

Using Chain of Custody to Show That Evidence Has Not Been Altered or Substituted

Some physical or real evidence is very susceptible to contamination, tampering, substitution, or mistake. To provide a foundation for the introduction of such evidence, a chain of custody, chain of possession, or chain of evidence must be shown. The Supreme Court of Indiana held in the case of *Graham v. State,*[5] that

> The danger of *tampering, loss, or mistake* with respect to an exhibit is greatest where the exhibit is small and is one which has physical characteristics fungible in nature and similar in form to substances familiar to people in their daily lives. The white powder in this case could have been heroin, or it could have been for example, baking powder, powdered sugar, or even powdered milk. The burden on the state in seeking to admit such evidence is clear. Unless the state can show by producing records or testimony, the continuous whereabouts of the exhibit at least between the time it came into their possession until it was laboratory tested to determine its composition, testimony of the state as to the laboratory's findings is inadmissible ....
>
> We believe the rule announced here can be summarized as follows: *where as in the case of seized or purchased narcotics, the object offered in evidence has passed out of the possession of the original receiver and into the possession of others, a chain of possession must*

be established to avoid any claim of substitution, tampering or mistake, and failure to submit such proof may result in the exclusion of the evidence or testimony as to its characteristics. Where such evidence or testimony is improperly introduced and is prejudicial to the party against whom it is directed, then the judgment of the trial court should be reversed.

Officers who recover evidence which is susceptible to tampering, contamination, substitution, or mistake must therefore establish a chain of custody of the evidence. In such situations, it is best that as few persons as possible have custody of the evidence. Chains of possession involving many persons usually require the calling of all of the persons who have had custody as witnesses in order to establish the necessary foundation for the admission of the evidence.

USING PROPERTY OF A VICTIM AS EVIDENCE

Stolen property which is recovered after the crimes of burglary, theft, and robbery is often taken to a police property room to be held as evidence until the trial of the defendant. Victims of these crimes often become very annoyed over the loss of the use of their property. One witness whose color TV set had been stolen complained that the defendant had his TV set for only two days but the court kept the set for five months.[6]

Such common complaints from victims of property crimes can be heard not only from persons losing personal property but also from business people whose office equipment and other business property had been taken. A study done by the Sacramento (California) Police Department reported that there was no legal reason which required the retention of victim property "except in the case of contraband or of substances whose composition was itself an issue in the case ...."

In order to promptly return property to victims, procedures have been developed in some American jurisdictions. The following methods could be used for cases in which the property and the owner of property can be clearly identified:

- A photograph of the property can be taken and used as evidence at the trial. The victim and officer or person recovering the property would testify at the trial as to the essential elements of the crime charged. This procedure has been held to suffice for evidentiary and identification purposes in jurisdictions using this practice.[7]

- Parol evidence (oral or verbal evidence) also could be sufficient to prove all of the essential elements of the crime charged if the property taken can be specifically identified by the owner in a theft. For example, stolen automobiles and motorcycles are never brought into a courtroom when there is a theft of these objects. Parol evidence is used to identify the stolen property and to establish all of the essential elements of the crime charged.

- In addition to the procedures used in the two items above, the following procedure can also be used. If the property stolen can be easily transported, the victim could bring the property which was stolen into court and testify as to the identity of the property and the "chain of custody" of the property after it was recovered following the theft, burglary or robbery.

LOSS OR DESTRUCTION OF PHYSICAL EVIDENCE PRIOR TO TRIAL

The loss of important physical evidence before a trial could seriously weaken a state's case. For example, loss of heroin or cocaine prior to lab testing and prior to trial would require the dropping of the charges against a defendant charged with possession of those substances.

In the following murder case, the state of Colorado was penalized for failure to preserve evidence but found that the remaining evidence was sufficient to obtain a conviction.

People v. Morgan

Supreme Court of Colorado (1980)
199 Colo. 237, 606 P.2d 1296

Police found the severed fingertip of the defendant at the scene of a murder. A fingerprint and blood samples were obtained from the fingertip which were found to match the defendant, but someone at the police department threw the fingertip away. Because the fingertip was not available for examination by the defense, the trial court suppressed and excluded for use as evidence "the fingertip and all evidence relating thereto, of whatever kind or nature." This included the fingerprint, blood samples, and any reference to the fact that the defendant was missing a fingertip. However, the state was able to obtain a conviction of first-degree murder and conspiracy to commit first-degree murder by the use of other evidence available to the state.

(Another aspect of the "case of the missing fingertip" is used as a problem at the end of chapter 1.)

Parol (verbal) evidence may be used to describe and identify motor vehicles which have been stolen. The stolen motor vehicle is never brought into a court and introduced as physical evidence. The vehicle may or may not have been recovered and returned to the owner. In the following case, parol evidence was used in a shoplifting case to describe the items shoplifted. The stolen items (evidence) were either lost or misplaced while they were in the police property locker.

People v. Bendix

Court of Appeals of Michigan (1975)
58 Mich.App. 276, 227 N.W.2d 316

A shoplifter was apprehended with a box of stolen merchandise as she left a drug store. The evidence was stored in the property locker at a police station. But at the time of trial, the evidence could not be located. A store security officer and a police officer described the stolen property and a copy of a report written by the security officer was introduced as evidence. The defendant was convicted of shoplifting and appealed. In affirming the defendant's conviction, the court of appeals stated that

> The production of the stolen goods would have added nothing to the proofs already elicited at trial. Such production could not have increased or decreased the evidence of defendant's guilt or innocence. The testimony at trial is undisputed: defendant placed certain paper plates and household goods in a box and left the store with them. The security officer for the store and the defendant agree as to those facts. The only question in dispute is whether or not the defendant stole those goods. Under the facts, there is no additional evidentiary value which could attach to the actual production of the box of goods.
>
> The nature, appearance and condition of the goods was proved by parol evidence and the production of the goods themselves is merely cumulative. *Francis v. United States*, 239 F.2d 560, 562 (10th Cir.1956).
>
> In the case at bar there was no showing of any intentional suppression of the evidence by the police or the prosecution .... In the context of the facts presented, the unintentional loss of such well-described evidence did not constitute deliberate suppression of evidence, is not reversible error, and does not require overturning the conviction. The trier of the facts found the defendant guilty. There was no showing of negligent failure on the part of the prosecution, as is indicated by *United States v. Bryant*, 439 F.2d 642 (D.C.Cir.1971).
>
> Affirmed.

OBTAINING EVIDENCE FROM A CRIME SCENE

When law enforcement officers are called to the scene of a crime, they are expected to immediately commence an investigation. Authority to enter and search a crime scene is often given by the victim or a family member. In some instances, the crime scene is a public place where officers may come and go as they wish.

Chapter 11 presents cases and material on obtaining evidence by police entry into private premises. Authority to enter private premises could be by consent, the existence of an exigency (emergency), or by use of a search warrant. Chapter 14 presents cases and material on search warrants as a means of obtaining evidence. Additional cases and material on obtaining evidence from a crime scene are presented in the following pages.

There Is No "Murder Scene" Exception to the Fourth Amendment

Cases and material in chapter 11 point out that when law enforcement officers have reliable information as to shooting, serious injuries, or life-threatening situations within private premises, they may enter the premises under the exigency (emergency) doctrine. The question as to how long law enforcement officers may stay in and on the premises, and to what extent may they search such premises, was presented to the U.S. Supreme Court in the following case:

Mincey v. Arizona

Supreme Court of the United States (1978)
437 U.S. 385, 98 S.Ct. 2408

In a drug raid of Mincey's apartment in Tucson, Arizona, Officer Headricks was shot and later died. Arizona police officers seized the apartment and held it for four days, during which they searched the entire apartment. In reversing the conviction of the defendant and holding that the "murder scene exception" created by the Arizona Supreme Court violated the Fourth Amendment of the U.S. Constitution, the U.S. Supreme Court ruled that

The first question presented is whether the search of Mincey's apartment was constitutionally permissible. After the shooting, the narcotics agents, thinking that other persons in the apartment might have been injured, looked about quickly for other victims. They found a young woman wounded in the bedroom closet and Mincey apparently unconscious in the bedroom, as well as Mincey's three acquaintances (one of whom had been wounded in the head) in the living room. Emergency assistance was requested, and some medical aid was administered to Officer Headricks. But the agents refrained from further investigation, pursuant to a Tucson Police Department directive that police officers should not investigate incidents in which they are involved. They neither searched further nor seized any evidence; they merely guarded the suspects and the premises.

Within 10 minutes, however, homicide detectives who had heard a radio report of the shooting arrived and took charge of the investigation. They supervised the removal of Officer Headricks and the suspects, trying to make sure that the scene was disturbed as little as possible, and then proceeded to gather evidence. Their search lasted four days, during which period the entire apartment was searched, photographed, and diagrammed. The officers opened drawers, closets, and cupboards, and inspected their contents; they emptied clothing pockets; they dug bullet fragments out of the walls and floors; they pulled up sections of the carpet and removed them for examination. Every item in the apartment was closely examined and inventoried, and 200 to 300 objects were seized. In short, Mincey's apartment was subjected to an exhaustive and intrusive search. No warrant was ever obtained.

The petitioner's pretrial motion to suppress the fruits of this search was denied after a hearing. Much of the evidence introduced against him at trial (including photographs and diagrams, bullets and shell casings, guns, narcotics, and narcotics paraphernalia) was the product of the four-day search of his apartment. On appeal, the Arizona Supreme Court reaffirmed previous decisions in which it had held that the warrantless search of the scene of a homicide is constitutionally permissible. It stated its ruling as follows:

"We hold a reasonable, warrantless search of the scene of a homicide—or of a serious personal injury with likelihood of death where there is reason to suspect foul play—does not violate the Fourth Amendment to the United States Constitution where the law enforcement officers were legally on the premises in the first instance. ... For the search to be reasonable, the purpose must be limited to determining the circumstances of death and the scope must not exceed that purpose. The search must also begin within a reasonable period following the time when the officials first learn of the murder (or potential murder)." 115 Ariz., at 482, 566 P.2d, at 283.

Since the investigating homicide detectives knew that Officer Headricks was seriously injured, began the search promptly upon their arrival at the apartment, and searched only for evidence either establishing the circumstances of death or "relevant to motive and intent or knowledge (narcotics, e.g.)," *id.,* at 483, 566 P.2d, at 284, the court found that the warrantless search of the petitioner's apartment had not violated the Fourth and Fourteenth Amendments.

We cannot agree. The Fourth Amendment proscribes (forbids) all unreasonable searches and seizures, and it is a cardinal principle that "searches conducted outside the judicial process, without prior approval by judge or magistrate, are *per se* unreasonable under the Fourth Amendment—subject only to a few specifically established and well-delineated exceptions." *Katz v. United States,* 389 U.S. 347, 357 .... The Arizona Supreme Court did not hold that the search of the petitioner's apartment fell within any of the exceptions to the warrant requirement previously recognized by this Court, but rather that the search of a homicide scene should be recognized as an additional exception ....

In sum, we hold that the "murder scene exception" created by the Arizona Supreme Court is inconsistent with the Fourth and Fourteenth Amendments—that the warrantless search of Mincey's apartment was not constitutionally permissible simply because a homicide had recently occurred there.[9]

[Footnote 9 states:

"To what extent, if any, the evidence found in Mincey's apartment was permissibly seized under established Fourth Amendment standards will be for the Arizona courts to resolve on remand."]

How Long Should Law Enforcement Officers Be Permitted to Remain in Private Premises to Investigate a Crime?

A defendant would have to have "standing" (see chapter 9) to challenge police entry and presence on a crime scene. In the case of *Mincey v. Arizona*, Mincey had standing to challenge the four-day presence of police officers in his apartment. If the apartment had not belonged to Mincey, he would not have had standing to move to suppress the evidence obtained during the four-day stay of police officers.

To be lawful under the Fourth Amendment, searches and seizures must be reasonable. Cases in chapter 11 and the following cases further define what would be reasonable searches of premises under the Fourth Amendment:

Michigan v. Tyler

Supreme Court of the United States (1978)
436 U.S. 499, 98 S.Ct. 1942

On January 21, Michigan fire fighters were called to a fire in a Detroit-area furniture store. After fighting the fire for a number of hours, the fire fighters found evidence of arson and notified fire investigators. When fire investigators entered the burning building, they found that heat, darkness, steam, and smoke made the criminal investigation very difficult. They left the building at 4 A.M. on January 22 and returned again at 8 A.M. of the same day. In holding that this entry was valid and lawful but that entries made more than twenty-seven days after the fire were not lawful, the U.S. Supreme Court stated that

> On the facts of this case, we do not believe that a warrant was necessary for the early morning re-entries on January 22. As the fire was being extinguished, Chief See and his assistants began their investigation, but visibility was severely hindered by darkness, steam, and smoke. Thus they departed at 4 a.m. and returned shortly after daylight to continue their investigation. Little purpose would have been served by their remaining in the building, except to remove any doubt about the legality of the warrantless search and seizure later that same morning. Under these circumstances, we find that the morning entries were no more than an actual continuation of the first, and the lack of a warrant thus did not invalidate the resulting seizure of evidence.
>
> The entries occurring after January 22, however, were clearly detached from the initial exigency and warrantless entry. Since all of these searches were conducted without valid warrants and without consent, they were invalid under the Fourth and Fourteenth Amendments, and any evidence obtained as a result of those entries must, therefore, be excluded at the respondents' retrial.
>
> In summation, we hold that an entry to fight a fire requires no warrant, and that once in the building, officials may remain there for a reasonable time to investigate the cause of the blaze. Thereafter,

additional entries to investigate the cause of the fire must be made pursuant to the warrant procedures governing administrative searches .... Evidence of arson discovered in the course of such investigations is admissible at trial, but if the investigating officials find probable cause to believe that arson has occurred and require further access to gather evidence for a possible prosecution, they may obtain a warrant only upon a traditional showing of probable cause applicable to searches for evidence of crime.

People v. Neulist

Supreme Court of New York, Appellate Division (1973)
43 A.D.2d 150, 350 N.Y.S.2d 178

Police were called to the defendant's house and found the defendant's wife in a pool of blood. Medical examiners tentatively set the cause of death as natural. Investigating officers left with the body after posting guards at the room where the body was found. After an autopsy determined the cause of death to be foul play, officers returned to the crime scene within an hour after they had left. Evidence obtained in the following search of the room was suppressed by the trial court. In holding that the search of the room was lawful and also holding, in dictum, that the police would have been authorized to search the entire house, the New York Court of Appeals ruled that

> The posting of a police guard at the bedroom door served not only to prevent the destruction or removal of any potential evidence but also to establish a continued and legally proper police presence on the scene. The fact that the detectives involved in the initial investigation left the house at about 2:40 P.M., when the body was removed for the purposes of autopsy, did not in any way signify that the investigation had been completed or that the police had quit the scene. It was clear to the police at the time the body was removed that the diagnosis of the cause of death was merely tentative and, in the light of the excessive blood loss suffered by the decedent, that foul play was a distinct possibility .... The crucial elements are the posting of the guard, thereby establishing a continuing police presence on the scene, and the relatively brief lapse of time between the removal of the body and the continuation of the investigation ....
>
> Additionally, in dealing with a homicide the police should be accorded a greater leeway both in terms of the element of time and in the permissible scope of their investigation. In the context of this case, the police were not limited to an examination and search of the immediate area where the body was found (i.e., the bedroom). On the contrary, they had the right, indeed the duty, to examine the "crime scene", which should be deemed to include the entire house. There was here no more than the "legitimate and restrained investigative conduct undertaken on the basis of ample factual justification" (*Terry v. Ohio*, 392 U.S. 1, 15, 88 S.Ct. 1868, 1876, 20 L.Ed.2d 889). Therefore, that branch of the order of the County Court which suppressed the

items taken by the police after their return to the premises should be reversed and the defendant's motion in that respect denied.

What May Law Enforcement Officers Search for (Scope of Search) When the Crime Scene Is in Private Premises?

In the case of *Mincey v. Arizona,* the police seized 200 to 300 objects during the four days they held the apartment. If Mincey had consented to this "exhaustive and intrusive search" into all of Mincey's drawers, closets, and cupboards it would then have been lawful. But the search was not made under the authority of consent.

It would be very unusual for a search warrant to authorize such an extensive search; in the *Mincey* case, there was no search warrant. In the following exigency (emergency) cases, the courts state the extent and scope of the searches which were justified:

Warden, Md. Penitentiary v. Hayden

Supreme Court of the United States (1967)
387 U.S. 294, 87 S.Ct. 1642

(This case is also presented in chapter 11.)
After the defendant robbed a taxi cab company, he was seen entering a house (which the police found later was his home). In affirming the entry and search of the home, the U.S. Supreme Court held that

> Speed here was essential, and only a thorough search of the house for persons and weapons could have insured that Hayden was the only man present and that the police had control of all weapons which could be used against them or to effect an escape .... The permissible scope of search must, therefore, at the least, be as broad as may reasonably be necessary to prevent the dangers that the suspect at large in the house may resist or escape.

Hayden's shotgun and a pistol were found in a toilet flush tank in Hayden's house. Ammunition for the pistol was found under the mattress of Hayden's bed and ammunition for the shotgun was found in a bureau drawer in Hayden's room. Other evidence was found in plain view.

People v. Williams

Supreme Court of Colorado (1976)
192 Colo. 249, 557 P.2d 399

After Claudine Longet (Mrs. Andy Williams) shot her lover, professional skier "Spider" Sabich, she was arrested and taken to the sheriff's office. Because the shooting occurred in the house which Ms. Longet and her three children had shared with Sabich for some time, a search was made of the house. After the gun used in the shooting was recovered and photographs of the crime scene were taken, a further search revealed a diary. The trial court held that the diary had been inside a closed dresser drawer and suppressed its use as evidence since it was obtained without consent or a search warrant. In affirming the suppression of the diary for use as evidence, the Supreme Court of Colorado held that

> Under the circumstances, with the defendant gone and the house secured, there was no justification for not seeking a warrant from one of the locally available judges before proceeding with the search. There was no indication of any risk that evidence at the house might have been lost or destroyed while a warrant was being obtained.
>
> The People, claiming that "exigent circumstances" justified dispensing with the warrant requirement, have cited cases from other jurisdictions which have condoned searches at homicide scenes. Most of these cases involved limited searches for guns, knives, or other instrumentalities of crime. One involved a limited investigation to learn the cause of a death. Others involved seizure of items in plain view. These authorities do not support the contention that, in situations comparable to this case, exigent circumstances justify a warrantless general search.
>
> Further, the evidence here would not support a finding of exigent circumstances based on a reasonable belief that, without an immediate search, other persons might be harmed, a dangerous criminal might escape, or evidence might be lost or destroyed. We conclude that no exigent circumstances existed to justify the police failure to obtain a warrant before conducting the general search.

State v. Davidson

Supreme Court of Wisconsin (1969)
44 Wis.2d 177, 170 N.W.2d 755

> The murdered body of the defendant's wife was found in the basement of her home. The police entered the premises when they observed blood on the back porch and a broken window. The court held that it was "reasonable for the (police) to conclude that the perpetrator of the crime was lurking or hiding in the house," and therefore a sweep of the whole house was proper.

Thompson v. Louisiana

Supreme Court of the United States (1984)
469 U.S. 17, 105 S.Ct. 409

> The defendant (petitioner) shot her husband in their home and then took a drug overdose in a suicide attempt. She then changed her mind and called

her daughter, who contacted the police. The daughter admitted the police to the home and directed them to the rooms containing her dead father and unconscious mother. The mother (defendant) was immediately taken to a hospital and the crime scene secured. In the following two hours, the police conducted what they stated was a "general exploratory search for evidence of a crime." When the defendant (petitioner) was charged with second-degree murder of her husband, she moved to suppress three items of evidence discovered during the two-hour search: (1) a pistol found inside a chest of drawers in the same room as the deceased's body, (2) a torn-up note found in a wastepaper basket in an adjoining bathroom, and (3) another letter (alleged to be a suicide note) found folded up inside an envelope containing a Christmas card on top of a chest of drawers. The Louisiana Supreme Court held all of the evidence to be admissible. The U.S. Supreme Court reversed this ruling, holding that

> Although the homicide investigators in this case may well have had probable cause to search the premises, it is undisputed that they did not obtain a warrant. Therefore, for the search to be valid, it must fall within one of the narrow and specifically delineated exceptions to the warrant requirement. In *Mincey v. Arizona,* 437 U.S. 385, 98 S.Ct. 2408, 57 L.Ed.2d 290 (1978), we unanimously rejected the contention that one of the exceptions to the warrant clause is a "murder scene exception." Although we noted that police may make warrantless entries on premises where "they reasonably believe that a person within is in need of immediate aid," *id.,* at 392, and that "they may make a prompt warrantless search of the area to see if there are other victims or if a killer is still on the premises," *ibid.,* we held that "the 'murder scene exception' . . . is inconsistent with the Fourth and Fourteenth Amendments—that the warrantless search of Mincey's apartment was not constitutionally permissible simply because a homicide had recently occurred there." *Id.,* at 395. *Mincey* is squarely on point in the instant case . . . .
>
> The Louisiana Supreme Court attempted to distinguish *Mincey* in several ways. The court noted that *Mincey* involved a four-day search of the premises, while the search in this case took only two hours and was conducted on the same day as the murder . . . . Although we agree that the scope of the intrusion was certainly greater in *Mincey* than here, nothing in *Mincey* turned on the length of time taken in the search or the date on which it was conducted. A two-hour general search remains a significant intrusion of petitioner's privacy and therefore may only be conducted subject to the constraints—including the warrant requirement—of the Fourth Amendment.
>
> The Louisiana Court also believed that petitioner had a "diminished" expectation of privacy in her home, thus validating a search that otherwise would have been unconstitutional. The court noted that petitioner telephoned her daughter to request assistance. The daughter then called the police and let them in to the residence. These facts, according to the court, demonstrated a diminished expectation of privacy in petitioner's dwelling and therefore legitimated the warrantless search.
>
> Petitioner's attempt to get medical assistance does not evidence a diminished expectation of privacy on her part. To be sure, this

action would have justified the authorities in seizing evidence under the plain view doctrine while they were in petitioner's house to offer her assistance. In addition, the same doctrine may justify seizure of evidence obtained in the limited "victim-or-suspect" search discussed in *Mincey*. However, the evidence at issue here was not discovered in plain view while the police were assisting petitioner to the hospital, nor was it discovered during the "victim-or-suspect" search that had been completed by the time the homicide investigators arrived. Petitioner's call for help can hardly be seen as an invitation to the general public that would have converted her home into the sort of public place for which no warrant to search would be necessary. Therefore, the Louisiana Supreme Court's diminished expectation of privacy argument fails to distinguish this case from *Mincey*.

The State contends that there was a sufficient element of consent in this case to distinguish it from the facts of *Mincey*. The Louisiana Supreme Court's decision does not attempt to validate the search as consensual, although it attempts to support its diminished expectation of privacy argument by reference to the daughter's "apparent authority" over the premises when she originally permitted the police to enter .... Because the issue of consent is ordinarily a factual issue unsuitable for our consideration in the first instance, we express no opinion as to whether the search at issue here might be justified as consensual. However, we note that both homicide investigators explicitly testified that they had received no consent to search. Any claim of valid consent in this case would have to be measured against the standards of *United States v. Matlock,* 415 U.S. 164, 94 S.Ct. 988, 39 L.Ed.2d 242 (1974) and *Schneckcloth v. Bustamonte,* 412 U.S. 218, 93 S.Ct. 2041, 36 L.Ed.2d 854 (1973) ....

... the judgment of the Louisiana Supreme Court is reversed, and the cause is remanded for further proceedings not inconsistent with this opinion.

It is so ordered.

PROTECTION AND SEARCH OF A CRIME SCENE

Many States Hold That a Crime Scene Is Evidence Itself

Many states (but not all) hold that the scene of a crime is itself evidence.[8] Testimony of a trained police officer concerning observations and findings at an unchanged crime scene is vitally important to the successful clearance of the case. Improper protection of the crime scene will usually result in the contamination, loss, or unnecessary movement of physical evidence items, any one of which is likely to render the evidence useless. Therefore, the first officer to arrive at the scene of the crime automatically incurs the serious and critical responsibility of securing the crime scene from unauthorized intrusions. Even though the officer who arrives first will also search it for physical evidence, the necessity to immediately take precautions to protect it remains unchanged.

Dimensions of a Crime Scene

Obviously, there is no definite rule or set of rules that can be applied to defining the dimensions of the scene of a crime. However, the best physical evidence is normally found at or near the site of the most critical action that was taken by the criminal against property or the victim. Thus, it is more likely to find important physical evidence in the immediate area surrounding the body in a homicide case than at some distance away. Similarly, the site of forcible entry into a building, or the area immediately surrounding a cracked safe, normally have the greatest potential for yielding evidence. While it is entirely possible that the dimensions of a crime scene will be large, there will usually be apparent to the investigative priority areas that should be given immediate protection. On the other hand, valuable evidence may be discarded or inadvertently deposited by the criminal at some distance from the (apparent) immediate scene of the crime. Thus, the area to be protected may eventually be considerably expanded beyond the limits of that considered to have the highest priority.

Legal and Scientific Requirements

To satisfy the legal requirements concerning physical evidence the investigator must be able to:

- Identify each piece of evidence, even months after he collected it.
- Describe the exact location of the item at the time it was collected.
- Prove that from the moment of its collection until it was presented in court, the evidence was continuously in proper custody.
- Describe changes that may have occurred in the evidence between the time of its collection and its introduction as evidence in court.

Scientific requirements in the handling and processing of physical evidence are basically that the evidence be protected from change or modification. Biological materials will always undergo some change, and the weather or other unavoidable circumstances may induce change in other types of materials. Therefore, the practical objective of the investigator in satisfying scientific requirements is to take every precaution to minimize change. Examples of the type of changes that must be avoided are the use of unclean containers that would introduce chemical or bacterial contamination to a sample; the use of containers that allow spillage, evaporation, or seepage of a sample; or alteration of an item by accidentally scratching, bending, or even touching it, or cross-exchange, such as placing the suspect tool to be examined for paint in intimate contact with the painted wood frame from the scene.

The Preliminary Examination of the Crime Scene

Aside from any other consideration, the investigator should consider the crime scene as highly dynamic, that is, undergoing change; and fragile, in the sense that the evidence value of items it contains can be easily downgraded. Usually, there is only one opportunity to search the scene properly. Making a good preliminary survey of the layout helps to use that opportunity to best advantage.

The investigator should first take into account all the information and opinions that have been accumulated by persons preceding him on the scene. The apparent physical focal point or points of the crime are of particular interest in this information exchange, as are the perceptions of other officers as to items or material having potential evidentiary value.

Preferably without entering the more critical areas of the scene, the investigator should, in this preliminary examination, assimilate the items, conditions, and locations that seem to have the greatest importance to him. The key words at this stage of the search are *observation* and *recording,* rather than action. The relative position of items, one to the other and to the victim, if any, can be as important to the investigator as an item itself. Notes concerning these matters should be taken. It is useful to photograph the scene at this time, providing that doing so does not require traversing areas before the preliminary survey is completed.

Statements of witnesses should be considered, as well as background information that can be gathered concerning any victims involved. The descriptions of witnesses of things they observed should be amplified, whenever possible, by photographs taken by the investigator. Such photographs should take the perspective the witnesses had and notations should be made as to the lighting conditions and measurements which may tend to support or disprove the witnesses' statements.

If the search will be a lengthy one, the investigator should choose an area close by, but not in a critical area, which he designates as a collection point for trash generated in the search, and the place where police and other official personnel may smoke. Equipment not in immediate use should be placed in this area. Such a "headquarters" can significantly reduce the chance that the scene will be contaminated.

When the initial survey of the scene is completed, the investigator should have noted the obvious items of evidence to be collected; decided in what order he will collect them; concluded what should be searched for; and decided how the tasks and area are to be divided, if more than one investigator is employed or if the scene is unusually large.

The Importance of the Investigator's Experience and Insight

A crime scene search is greatly aided by procedures such as those just outlined. However, the success of any investigation is always the function of the intellect and experience of the officer. He must develop an hypothesis that will serve as the initial framework for the investigation. That hypothesis, based on the first survey of the scene, is simply a set of reasoned assumptions concerning how the crime was committed and the general sequence of acts that were involved.

The hypothesis must be constantly reassessed in light of each new fact or lead that is uncovered. There is a common tendency to make contradictory information fit a set of assumptions already made. For example, if the investigator has substantial evidence that a murder was committed where the body was discovered, he may be tempted to ignore a fact or lead that does not fit the framework of that idea. Such inflexibility must always be avoided in the crime scene search. The investigator must be willing to modify, or change altogether, his initial ideas concerning the commission of the crime. It is only through such a process of reassessment that the full value of the investigator's experience can be realized.

Recording the Crime Scene

It is sufficient to note here the importance to the successful outcome of the case of the written, photographic and perhaps the audio record of the scene compiled by the investigator. The point was made earlier that one of the principal legal requirements in introducing physical evidence in court is the ability of the person who collected it to later identify it and accurately report the circumstances of its collection and custody. An adequate record of the crime scene aids considerably in this identification process. But just as important is the support the written and photographic record of the scene gives to the furtherance of the investigation and examination of the physical evidence by laboratory experts. Finally, the investigator's notes provide him with an immediate reference as to the actions taken during the search and with a ready means of doublechecking on the thoroughness of those actions before leaving the scene of the crime. The amount of detail involved in a major case is usually so large that very few investigators can successfully rely on their memories.

Barring unusual circumstances, the crime scene is recorded before any objects are collected or removed from it. This statement does not, of course, apply to injured persons, and does not necessarily apply to the bodies of deceased persons, as will be discussed later.

A Recommended General Method of Crime Scene Search

Although the circumstances of the case must always govern the investigator's actions in processing the crime scene, experience has shown that the following general rules are useful in helping to systematize the search and to prevent error.

- If there is evidence that is being significantly deteriorated by time or the elements, these have first priority. Otherwise—

- All of the major evidence items are examined, photographed, recorded and collected, as appropriate, taking them in the order that is most logical, considering the requirement to conserve movement. Making casts and lifting latent prints from objects to be moved from the scene is done as necessary. Items should not be moved until they have been examined for trace evidence. Fingerprints should be taken, or at least developed and covered with tape, before the object is moved.

- When an (obviously) deceased person is involved, the evidence items lying between the point of entry to the scene and the body are processed; then the detailed search of the deceased is conducted. After that search, the body should be removed, and the processing of obvious evidence continued as noted above.

- After processing the more obvious evidence, the search for and collection of additional trace material is commenced. Trace evidence should be searched for and collected before any dusting for fingerprints is done.
- After the trace materials have been collected, other latent prints are lifted.
- When sweeping or vacuuming, surface areas should be segmented, the sweepings from each area packaged separately, and the location of their point of recovery noted.
- Normally, elimination fingerprints and physical evidence standards are collected after the above actions have been completed.

Note Taking

The investigating officer's notes are his personal and most readily available record of the search. It is common to rely on the memory of associated events to give cryptic notes or single words their full meaning. No rule can be expressed concerning the detail the investigator's notes should reflect. However, the objective should always be to make notes that will remain fully meaningful even months after the event. Very often, a note that is completely clear to the writer a short time after being made later becomes unintelligible.

The notes should begin with the investigator's assignment to the case and continue through the completion of the investigation. They should, of course, be supplemented by photographs, sketches, and scale drawings, as applicable. Notes are recorded in the order that the observations they pertain to are made. Thus, the sequence of the investigator's notes will not necessarily be in logical order. At this stage of the recording process, it is important only that the notes are complete. The investigator will later reorganize the information during the writing of his formal report.

Sketching the Crime Scene

Sketches properly prepared may be used during the questioning of persons, in preparing the report of investigation, and in presenting information in court. The sketch complements the photographs and notes made during the crime scene search. The sketch combines the inherent communications advantage of any illustration with the additional advantage that unnecessary detail can be eliminated in order to portray the most essential elements of the crime scene and their relationships. There are several techniques that may be used to establish the location of evidence and other important items on a sketch. However, it is important to remember that the purpose of the sketch is to portray the information accurately not necessarily artistically. It is therefore not required that the investigator have any artistic ability in order to construct an adequate sketch of a crime scene.

U.S. SUPREME COURT CASES HAVING TO DO WITH OBTAINING EVIDENCE FROM THE PERSON OF SUSPECTS

The American Highway Problem and the Case of *Schmerber v. California*

The U.S. Supreme Court noted the American highway problem in the 1957 case of *Breithaupt v. Abram,* 352 U.S. 432, 77 S.Ct. 408 (1957), stating that

> The increasing slaughter on our highways, most of which should be avoidable, now reaches the astounding figures only heard of on the battlefield. The States, through safety measures, modern scientific methods, and strict enforcement of traffic laws, are using all reasonable means to make automobile driving less dangerous.

Because the blood alcohol evidence of drunken driving is quickly destroyed by the body and does not allow enough time for law enforcement officers to obtain a search warrant, the ruling in the following case was critical in providing public safety on the highways.

Schmerber v. California

Supreme Court of the United States (1966)
384 U.S. 757, 86 S.Ct. 1826

The defendant in this case was arrested after a car accident for driving a vehicle while under the influence of alcohol. Blood was then obtained from his body by a physician despite his objections and without the authority of a search warrant. The resulting evidence of intoxication was admitted for use at the defendant's trial in obtaining a conviction. In his appeal to the U.S. Supreme Court, the defendant argued that this procedure violated the following rights:

- Denial of due process of law.
- Violation of his privilege against self-incrimination under the Fifth Amendment.
- His right to counsel under the Sixth Amendment.
- His right not to be subjected to unreasonable searches and seizures in violation of the Fourth Amendment.

The U.S. Supreme Court held that the procedures used did not violate any of the above rights and privileges. The Court held that the "minor intrusion" into the defendant's right to the privacy of his body was justified under the circumstances:

> That we today hold that the Constitution does not forbid the States *minor intrusions* into an individual's body under stringently limited

conditions *in no way indicates* that it permits more *substantial intrusions* or intrusions under other conditions. [Emphasis added]

Cases Holding Body Intrusions to Be Unconstitutional

Rochin v. California

Supreme Court of the United States (1952)
342 U.S. 165, 72 S.Ct. 205

In 1949 three officers improperly and illegally entered Rochin's home and forced open the door to his bedroom on the second floor. They saw Rochin seize two capsules which were on a nightstand and place them in his mouth. The officers tried to recover the capsules by force; when that failed, they placed Rochin in handcuffs and took him to a hospital, where they directed a doctor to pump Rochin's stomach. The capsules proved to contain morphine and Rochin was convicted for the possession of the capsules recovered from his stomach. The U.S. Supreme Court reversed the conviction, stating that

> Coerced confessions offend the community's sense of fair play and decency. So here, to sanction the brutal conduct which naturally enough was condemned by the court whose judgment is before us, would be to afford brutality the cloak of law. Nothing would be more calculated to discredit law and thereby to brutalize the temper of a society.
> On the facts of this case the conviction of the petitioner has been obtained by methods that offend the Due Process Clause. The judgment below must be reversed.
> Reversed.

Winston v. Lee

Supreme Court of the United States (1985)
470 U.S. 753, 105 S.Ct. 1611

The owner of a store was wounded in an attempted robbery of his store. But the storekeeper also wounded the other man. Twenty minutes after the attempted robbery, the defendant was found eight blocks from the shootings with a gunshot wound to his left chest area. The store owner identified him as the man who attempted to rob him. The defendant, however, stated that he was the victim of an attempted robbery. The trial judge granted a motion by the State of Virginia ordering surgery to obtain the bullet in the defendant's chest to be used as evidence. The U.S. Supreme Court held that surgery under general anesthetic for the bullet in this case would be a procedure of "more substantial intrusion," which was cautioned against by the Supreme Court in

Schmerber v. California. The Court held that the surgery would violate defendant's (petitioner's) right to be secure in his person guaranteed by the Fourth Amendment. The Court stated that

> We noted in *Schmerber* that a blood test is "a highly effective means of determining the degree to which a person is under the influence of alcohol." *Id.,* at 771, 86 S.Ct., at 1836. Moreover, there was "a clear indication that in fact [desired] evidence [would] be found" if the blood test were undertaken. *Id.,* at 770, 86 S.Ct., at 1835. Especially given the difficulty of proving drunkenness by other means, these considerations showed that results of the blood test were of vital importance if the State were to enforce its drunken driving laws. In *Schmerber,* we concluded that this state interest was sufficient to justify the intrusion, and the compelled blood test was thus "reasonable" for Fourth Amendment purposes ....
>
> The Commonwealth claims to need the bullet to demonstrate that it was fired from Watkinson's gun, which in turn would show that respondent was the robber who confronted Watkinson. However, although we recognize the difficulty of making determinations in advance as to the strength of the case against respondent, petitioners' assertions of a compelling need for the bullet are hardly persuasive. The very circumstances relied on in this case to demonstrate probable cause to believe that evidence will be found tend to vitiate the Commonwealth's need to compel respondent to undergo surgery. The Commonwealth has available substantial additional evidence that respondent was the individual who accosted Watkinson on the night of the robbery. No party in this case suggests that Watkinson's entirely spontaneous identification of respondent at the hospital would be inadmissible. In addition, petitioners can no doubt prove that Watkinson was found a few blocks from Watkinson's store shortly after the incident took place. And petitioners can certainly show that the location of the bullet (under respondent's left collarbone) seems to correlate with Watkinson's report that the robber "jerked" to the left. The fact that the Commonwealth has available such substantial evidence of the origin of the bullet restricts the need for the Commonwealth to compel respondent to undergo the contemplated surgery ....
>
> ... although the bullet may turn out to be useful to the Commonwealth in prosecuting respondent, the Commonwealth has failed to demonstrate a compelling need for it. We believe that in these circumstances the Commonwealth has failed to demonstrate that it would be "reasonable" under the terms of the Fourth Amendment to search for evidence of this crime by means of the contemplated surgery .... when the State seeks to intrude upon an area in which our society recognizes a significantly heightened privacy interest, a more substantial justification is required to make the search "reasonable." Applying these principles, we hold that the proposed search in this case would be "unreasonable" under the Fourth Amendment.

PROBLEMS

1. After shooting her husband with a .22–caliber semiautomatic rifle, Mrs. Jolley (defendant) dialed a telephone operator and requested help. Rescue squad members arrived first and began emergency procedures. Law enforcement officers then arrived, and as they observed the rescue team working on the victim, an officer observed a .22 rifle leaning against a chair about six feet from the victim. The officer also saw the defendant kneeling on the floor in the kitchen, sobbing.

   When the officer secured the crime scene and sealed it off with a rope and sign, could he seize the rifle, spent cartridges, and shells seen in the house? Police officers stayed in the house for six hours. Should the police have obtained a search warrant? (*State v. Jolley,* 312 N.C. 296, 321 S.E.2d 883, 36 CrL 2150, North Carolina Sup.Ct. (1984)).

2. Ms. Claudine Longet (Mrs. Andy Williams) was arrested after she shot and killed her lover, professional skier "Spider" Sabich. The officer in charge of the investigation was informed that Ms. Longet had been seen in a bar earlier in the day. After Ms. Longet was in custody, the officer noticed a faint smell of liquor coming from her person. He then ordered that Ms. Longet be taken to a hospital for blood and urine tests. Other officers and a hospital technician stated that she did not appear to be under the influence of alcohol or drugs. Ms. Longet objected to the tests, but the body fluids were obtained over her objections.

   Should the trial court and the Supreme Court of Colorado permit the results of the urine and blood tests to be used as evidence? Give reasons for your answer. *People v. Williams,* 192 Colo. 249, 557 P.2d 399 (Colorado Sup. Ct. (1976).

3. After the assassination of President Kennedy in 1963, Dallas police officers found a rifle which they believed was the murder weapon in the School Book Depository Building. The rifle was not moved until after photographs were taken of the rifle and the surrounding area. After a live shell was ejected from the rifle, a police officer scratched his name and date on the rifle (his initials and date on the shell). The serial number on the rifle was C–2566.

   With the serial number and the officer's name and date scratched on the rifle, should any other procedure be used in anticipation of the possibility of use of the rifle as evidence in a criminal or other type of proceeding? In the weeks which followed, the rifle was in a FBI laboratory in Washington D.C. and was also returned to the police department in Dallas. What evidence must the government produce to show that the rifle (and evidence associated with the rifle) is genuine and authentic? Give reasons for your answers.

NOTES

[1] The material on trace evidence was taken from pages 9 and 10 of the U.S. Department of Justice Law Enforcement Assistance Administration book entitled *Crime Scene Search and Physical Evidence Handbook.*

2 *McCormick on Evidence,* p. 527 (emphasis in original).

3 *McCormick on Evidence,* p. 527.

4 Law enforcement departments recommend that driver's license numbers be placed on objects because the owner's name and address can then be easily obtained from the state computer system.

5 253 Ind. 525, 255 N.E.2d 652 (1970).

6 See the article, "The Witness: Forgotten Man," *Reader's Digest,* November 1974, p. 22; and the article, "Returning the Loot," *Newsweek,* January 6, 1975, p. 35.

7 See the article "Returning the Loot," *Newsweek,* January 6, 1975, p. 35; and see "An Invitation to a Challenge," June 1974, a report (draft) submitted by Louis P. Benson, in conjunction with the LEAA-aided Crime Victims Consultation Project, under a grant from the New York City Criminal Justice Coordinating Council. See also Chicago Crime Commission, "Dismissed for Want of Prosecution," March 13, 1974.

8 Much of the following material in this chapter is taken from the U.S. Department of Justice Law Enforcement Assistance Administration book entitled *Crime Scene Search and Physical Evidence Handbook.*

17

Fingerprints as Evidence

OBTAINING FINGERPRINTS AS EVIDENCE

Obtaining Fingerprints From an Arrested Person

"Fingerprints are perhaps the most common form of physical evidence, and certainly one of the most valuable. They relate directly to the ultimate objective of every criminal investigation ... the identification of the offender .... Since a print of one finger has never been known to exactly duplicate another fingerprint (even of the same person or identical twin) it is possible to identify an individual with just one impression ... a person's fingerprints have never been known to change. The unchanging pattern thus provides a permanent record of the individual throughout life." [1]

The U.S. Supreme Court stated in the case of *Davis v. Mississippi* [2] that "... fingerprinting is an inherently more reliable and effective crime-solving tool than eyewitness identification or confessions and is not subject to such abuses as the improper lineup and the 'third-degree.' "

In holding that a person in lawful custody may be fingerprinted, former U.S. Supreme Court Chief Justice Burger held in *Smith v. United States* [3] that

> it is elementary that a person in lawful custody may be required to submit to photographing ... and fingerprinting.

Chief Judge Aldrich, speaking for the 1st Circuit Court of Appeals in the case of *Napolitano v. United States*,[4] held that fingerprints taken before the defendant was released on bail were admissible in evidence:

> Taking of fingerprints in such circumstances is universally standard procedure, and no violation of constitutional rights.

The Federal Court in the case of *United States v. Laub Baking Company* [5] held that a person charged with a misdemeanor in Ohio must submit to fingerprinting, stating that

> There is a legitimate governmental interest in knowing for an absolute certainty the identity of the person charged with the crime. The Government also has an interest in knowing whether the accused is wanted in other jurisdictions, and in ensuring his identification in the event

487

he flees prosecution. To satisfy these interests, the Government routinely takes the fingerprints of the accused.

Obtaining Fingerprints Without Probable Cause, Consent, or a Court Order

Law enforcement officers have no authority to compel persons who are not in lawful custody to submit to fingerprinting. Such persons could voluntarily consent to being fingerprinted, or in some instances courts may order fingerprinting "under narrowly defined circumstances ... found to comply with the Fourth Amendment even though there is no probable cause in the traditional sense." (U.S. Supreme Court in *Davis v. Mississippi.*)

Fingerprint files found in state central identification bureaus and the FBI Identification Division are compiled from prints taken of arrested persons, persons who have served in the military forces of the United States, and from persons who are or have been employed in certain types of occupations.

When investigating officers at the scene of a crime find fingerprints or palmprints that they have reason to believe may belong to the perpetrator of the crime, the prints are ordinarily forwarded to the state's central identification bureau or to the FBI Identification Division. Because such agencies have hundreds of thousands of fingerprints on file, a positive identification might result.

In 1986, it was reported that the FBI Identification Division had over 83 million cards representing over 22 million persons. However, not all persons have their fingerprints on file in Washington or with a state agency. Identification problems could also occur if only a palmprint (or partial fingerprint) were found at the scene of a crime. The following cases illustrate:

Davis v. Mississippi

Supreme Court of the United States (1969)
394 U.S. 721, 89 S.Ct. 1394

A rape occurred in the victim's home on December 2, 1965. Finger- and palmprints were found on the window sill where the police believed that entry was made. Because the victim's only description of her assailant was that he was a "Negro youth," at least twenty-four black youths were taken to police headquarters, where they were questioned, fingerprinted, and then released without charge. The defendant was one of the youths fingerprinted on December 3. Then on December 12, the defendant, who was fourteen years old, was taken into custody and held. On December 14 he was fingerprinted a second time. The defendant was convicted of rape, with the fingerprints used as evidence at his trial. On appeal, the State admitted that probable cause to authorize the defendant's detention did not exist. Holding that the fingerprints obtained on December 3 "were not validly obtained," the U.S. Supreme Court reversed the defendant's conviction, ruling that "(d)etention for the sole purpose of obtaining fingerprints are ... subject to the constraints of the Fourth Amendment." The Court further stated that

It is arguable, however, that because of the unique nature of the fingerprinting process, such detentions might under narrowly defined circumstances, be found to comply with the Fourth Amendment even though there is no probable cause in the traditional sense. See *Camara v. Municipal Court,* 387 U.S. 523, 87 S.Ct. 1727, 18 L.Ed.2d 930 (1967). Detention for fingerprinting may constitute a much less serious intrusion upon personal security than other types of police searches and detentions. Fingerprinting involves none of the probing into an individual's private life and thoughts that marks an interrogation or search. Nor can fingerprint detention be employed repeatedly to harass any individual, since the police need only one set of each person's prints. Furthermore, fingerprinting is an inherently more reliable and effective crime-solving tool than eyewitness identifications or confessions and is not subject to such abuses as the improper line-up and the "third degree." Finally, because there is no danger of destruction of fingerprints, the limited detention need not come unexpectedly or at any inconvenient time.

Hayes v. Florida

Supreme Court of the United States (1985)
470 U.S. 811, 105 S.Ct. 1643

The defendant generally fit the description of a man committing a series of burglaries and rapes in Punta Gorda, Florida. Because police had fingerprints from one of the crime scenes, the defendant was told that if he did not go with police to the station for fingerprinting, he would be arrested. The U.S. Supreme Court reaffirmed *Davis v. Mississippi* and held that taking the defendant to the police station on reasonable suspicion and without probable cause, consent, or a court order violated the Fourth Amendment.

However, when the case of *Hayes v. Florida* was sent back to the Florida court, the Florida court reaffirmed the defendant's conviction on the basis of the "inevitable discovery" doctrine (see chapter 9). The Florida court held that the "taking of the (finger)prints was not held to be a Fourth Amendment violation in itself .... Moreover, compelling a suspect to submit to fingerprinting does not involve unconstitutional 'testimonial' compulsion. Thus, so long as the defendant is subject to trial, his fingerprints would be available for comparison with the latent prints discovered at the crime scene ... (this) defendant's fingerprints would be available from a variety of sources, such as his stint in military service, were he to be retried. It was just a matter of time ... until identification evidence uncovered by investigators would have led them to make a valid arrest of the defendant. Therefore, the victim's identification of the defendant and the fingerprint comparison evidence that could be produced would be so attenuated that any taint resulting from the illegal arrest would be dissipated." (*Hayes v. State,* ___ So.2d ___, 38 CrL 2417, Fla.App., 1986).

THE IMPORTANCE OF FINGERPRINTS AS PHYSICAL EVIDENCE [6]

Fingerprints of the offender are frequently found at the scene of a crime, and they may take more than one form. However, in all cases, the prints are fragile and susceptible to complete destruction by the first careless act. They are also, in many cases, difficult to find.

With but a few exceptions, everyone has fingerprints. This universal character is a prime factor in the establishment of a standard of identification. Since a print of one finger has never been known to exactly duplicate another fingerprint (even of the same person or identical twin) it is possible to identify an individual with just one impression. The relative ease with which a set of inked fingerprints can be taken as a means of identification is a further basis for using this standard. Despite such factors as aging and a variety of environmental influences, a person's fingerprints have never been known to change. The unchanging pattern thus provides a permanent record of the individual throughout life.

Although there are many different filing systems for fingerprints, each is based on classification of common characteristics. The classification system works to readily categorize a set of fingerprints, as well as to provide quick access to a set of prints with a given characteristic.

Definition of Fingerprints

A direct or inked fingerprint is an impression of the ridge detail of the underside of the fingers, palms, toes, or the soles of the feet. This is contrasted with a latent print, which is an impression caused by the perspiration through the sweat pores on the ridges of the skin being transferred to some surface. Fingerprints also occur as residues when the finger ridges have been contaminated with such materials as oil, dirt, blood, and grease.

Basis of Identification of Fingerprints

The ridge detail of fingerprints including ends of ridges, their separations, and their relationship to each other constitute the basis for identification of fingerprints . . . . In checking for similarity, most experts require from 10 to 12 points although there is no specific number required. However, regardless of the points of similarity, should an unexplainable difference appear, positive identification cannot be made.

There is no set print size requirement for positive identification. The only requirement is that the print be large enough to contain at least 10 to 12 points. This requirement count may be met by an area as small as the end of a pencil. As a general rule, if the investigator develops an area which appears to have several ridges, regardless of the size of the area, it should be lifted, marked, and submitted to the laboratory.

Some investigators believe that the points used for identification of the fingerprint occur only in the pattern area of the finger. This is not true. All the different types occur outside of the pattern area on the finger as well as on the first and second joint of the finger and the entire palm of the hand. They are also present on the toes and the entire sole of the foot. In fact, they may be found in any area where friction ridges occur.

People v. Gomez

Supreme Court of Colorado (1975)
189 Colo. 91, 537 P.2d 297

Fingerprint evidence was permitted to be used despite the fact that the State was unable to establish the twelve-point comparison used by the FBI. In holding that the fingerprint evidence was properly admitted, the Supreme Court of Colorado stated that

> Entry into the liquor store with the intent to commit the crime of theft was proven by fingerprints. The defendant's fingerprint was located on a section of a liquor carton which could only be reached by a person reaching in through the broken window and which was not readily accessible to in-store traffic.
>
> Expert testimony established that the fingerprint which was removed from the liquor carton was the thumb print of the defendant Gomez. Experiments conducted with identical liquor cartons were admitted to prove that the fingerprint was placed on the liquor carton at about the same time that the break-in at the liquor store occurred. A proper foundation was laid for the admission of the fingerprint, and the weight to be afforded the fingerprint evidence was for the trier of the fact ....
>
> The inability of the prosecution to establish the twelve-point comparison used by the Federal Bureau of Investigation went to the weight to be given the fingerprint identification, but not to the admissibility of the evidence ....
>
> Moreover, counsel did not object to the experiments which were offered to show the time that the fingerprint was impressed on the liquor carton ....
>
> Accordingly, the fingerprint evidence was properly admitted.

Limitations of Latent Prints

Even though latent prints are invaluable in the course of investigative work, there are certain limitations as to what information these prints can be expected to provide. It is impossible, for example, to determine the age of the latent print because there are a number of factors other than time that change the appearance of the developed latent. It is sometimes possible, however, to estimate the age of the print in relation to certain events. For example, prints appearing on an object thoroughly cleaned during a recent housecleaning can be dated as occurring after that event.

Likewise, it is not possible to determine, from the examination of the print alone, the age or sex of the person leaving the print. Even though a rough correlation does exist between age and sex and such characteristics as size of the ridge or pattern, individual variations occur.

Prints cannot be used to identify the race of a suspect, nor can occupational groups be determined with an accepted degree of accuracy on the basis of fingerprints. It is true that many occupations, such as bricklaying, cause certain characteristic damage to the skin of the fingers and hands. However, any conjecture as to occupation of a suspect made on this basis should be considered only as an investigative lead and not as substantive evidence.

Conditions Which Affect Latent Prints

The quality of latent fingerprints is affected by such conditions as the type of surface material, the manner in which the print was transferred, nature and quantity of the substance (perspiration, oils, blood, etc.) which covered the ridge surfaces, weather conditions, and, to some extent, the physical or occupational defects of the person transferring the print . . . .

The nature and the condition of the surface on which the latent print is deposited are very important. The surface must be fairly clean and smooth or the ridge detail of the finger will be lost. Such surfaces as coarse cloth, unfinished wood, grained leather, etc., are very poor surfaces for fingerprints.

Another important consideration is the manner in which the object was touched or released. The ridges on fingers are very close together. Should the finger move just the distance between two ridges when touching or releasing an object, most of the ridge detail will be lost. This condition explains why most latents which are developed are smeared in the pattern area and only their ridges outside the pattern area have enough detail for identification.

There are conditions which occur that cause the friction surfaces to become completely covered with perspiration or other materials. When such materials cover not only the ridge surface of the skin, but fill the valleys as well, no ridge detail can be recorded. Prints of this type generally develop very dark and appear about the same as a print that was developed with too much powder.

The weather affects the latent print in a number of ways. The print may be dried out or washed away. Humidity will cause latent prints on paper to become smudged or even disappear. Because of the sponge nature of paper, moisture enters it from all directions and causes the ridge detail to diffuse to the extent that it will not be recognized as a print.

The more oil that is deposited with perspiration, the longer the print will last. Since perspiration is mostly water, the oil that is deposited with it will float on the surface and reduce its evaporation rate. After the water evaporates, the oil remains and becomes quite tacky. This condition results in better development of the ridge detail when using fingerprint powder. Body oil is present on the friction ridges of the fingers as contamination from the hairy parts of the body and, therefore, may not be present in the latent print at all. When no oils are present, the water content of the deposited material is subject to the same evaporation rate as any like amount of water under the same conditions and the print will be less tacky.

Responsibility of the Crime Scene Investigator in Collecting Fingerprints

Latent prints are such valuable evidence that extraordinary efforts should be made to recover them. The investigator is strongly urged to adopt a positive attitude toward this aspect of the search, regardless of any apparent problems.

It is absolutely imperative that the crime scene investigator make a thorough search of all surface areas in and around the scene of the crime that have the potential of retaining finger or palm prints. Particular attention should be paid to the less obvious places, such as the undersides of toilet seats, table tops and dresser drawers, the surface of dinner plates, filing cabinets, the backs of chairs, rearview mirrors (both the glass and frame) and the trunk lids of automobiles. Heavily handled objects, such as door knobs or telephones, may not yield good prints. However, they are objects that are quite likely to be touched and should always be processed.

The investigator should not assume that the offender took precautions against leaving prints or that he destroyed those he did leave. A person committing a criminal offense is usually under some stress and may be prone to oversight. If he wore gloves he may have removed them for some operation, or they may have been torn.

It is helpful to attempt to view the scene as the criminal did. Hence, such conditions as time of day, weather, and physical layout may suggest that certain surface areas should be closely examined. In conducting the examination for latent prints in a burglary case, for example, it is suggested that the investigation begin at the point of entry. For other crimes, such as rape, the point of entry takes on less importance as a source of latent prints. Whatever the nature of the crime and the particular circumstances, its reconstruction by the investigator is intended to give practical direction to the search.

Valuable aid in obtaining latent print leads may be solicited from a person who is familiar with the usual physical layout of the crime scene, such as the owner of the building or the usual occupant of an apartment. That person should be allowed to observe at least a part of the preliminary investigation and be encouraged to point out items which appear out of place or to identify objects that may have been brought in by the suspect.

Things which have permanent serial numbers attached to them, such as automobiles, weapons, and machinery require special attention. In addition to checking such items for latent prints, it is good policy to make a lift of the serial number (using fingerprint tape), as well as prints and attach both to the same fingerprint card. Such direct lifts of serial numbers prove invaluable for latter reference, particularly as evidence in court.

Prints Which Require No Further Developing

There are two basic types of latent prints that the crime scene examiner will likely encounter which do not need developing. The first of these is the visible type created after the suspect's hand has come in contact with blood, ink, paint, grease, dirt, etc., and the print transferred to some surface area. Prints made from these substances are usually distinct and should stand out to the investigator. The procedure to be used in collecting the print is to first photograph and then cover it with protective tape. The surface on which the print rests must then be transported to the crime laboratory. Common sense must rule the decision as to just how much damage is justifiable in collecting items or surface areas where prints are found.

The second type of print which requires no further developing is an *impression* in a soft substance such as putty, clay, or fresh paint. Again, the procedure is to first photograph the impression, then transport the object or a section containing it to the crime laboratory. If a physical transfer of the impression is not possible, it should be sprayed with shellac and a cast prepared of silicone rubber. The cast should then be identified and sent to the laboratory in place of the actual imprint.

LAW ENFORCEMENT OFFICERS AS FINGERPRINT EXPERTS

State v. Cox

Court of Appeals of Missouri (1975)
527 S.W.2d 448

In holding that a police officer was properly qualified to appear as an expert fingerprint witness, the Missouri Court of Appeals ruled that

> The well established rule is that the qualification of an expert witness in a criminal case is a matter resting primarily in the sound discretion of the trial court and is not reversible on appeal absent a clear showing of abuse of that discretion.... We find no such abuse of discretion here. Since no exact standard by which to determine the qualifications of an expert witness exists, much is necessarily left to the discretion of the trial court.... The testimony of Officer Ratermann was limited to an explanation of the procedure utilized in the development and removal of appellant's latent palm print from the surface of the refrigerator door. The state did not attempt to elicit an opinion from Officer Ratermann regarding identification or comparison of the latent print. Rather, Officer Ratermann's testimony established the procedure of fingerprint removal and the transfer of custody of the palm print exhibit to Officer Salamone....
>
> The state showed that Officer Ratermann had attended a two-week formal training course in the procedure of fingerprint removal followed by several weeks of "on the job" training. Moreover, he had worked in the Evidence Technicians Unit for more than a year, during which time he had "lifted" at least a thousand fingerprints.
>
> It is argued by appellant that, notwithstanding his practical experience, the extent of Officer Ratermann's formal education in the field of latent fingerprint "removal and retention" was insufficient to quali-

fy him as an expert. There is no requirement that an expert be a technical scientist or a college graduate.... The test of expert qualification is whether he has knowledge from education or experience which will aid the trier of fact in forming an opinion on the subject matter of the inquiry.... We hold that Officer Ratermann's training and experience in the field of latent fingerprint development was sufficient to enable him to testify on the particular procedure followed with respect to the retrieval of appellant's latent palm print. His testimony was confined to the scope of the procedure followed and was necessary as a prerequisite to the comparison testimony of Officer Salamone....

We find no merit in appellant's point, and we conclude that the trial court did not err or abuse its discretion (1) in admitting the testimony of Officer Ratermann regarding the procedure followed in obtaining the latent print, and (2), in permitting Officer Ratermann to testify "as an expert in fingerprint removal and retention."

THE CHAIN OF CUSTODY REQUIREMENT FOR FINGERPRINT EVIDENCE

State v. Burrell

Court of Appeals of North Carolina (1975)
27 N.C.App. 61, 217 S.E.2d 751

In affirming the defendant's conviction for the felony of breaking or entering with the intent to commit larceny, the Court of Appeals of North Carolina held that

The State offered the following evidence with respect to the chain of custody of Exhibit 1. On 4 February 1974 Fred Stewart, owner of a property protection company, and Carl Zachary, a deputy sheriff of Macon County, went to the home of John Ritchie to investigate the break-in. Stewart lifted the fingerprint (Exhibit 1) from the door knob of the basement door and retained possession of it until 17 February 1974. During this period of time, the fingerprint was stored in a lock box at Stewart's place of business. On 17 February 1974 Stewart delivered Exhibit 1 to George Moses, Sheriff of Macon County. Sheriff Moses placed Exhibit 1 in an envelope addressed to the Latent Evidence Section of the SBI and sealed the envelope. He personally deposited the envelope in the mail on either 17 February 1974 or on the morning of 18 February 1974. Stephen Jones received an envelope containing Exhibit 1 from Sheriff Moses by first class mail at his office in Raleigh on 19 February 1974. Jones retained possession of the fingerprint until trial.

In our opinion, the foregoing evidence reveals a complete chain of custody of Exhibit 1. Consequently, Jones' testimony was based upon examination of a fingerprint lifted from the crime scene and was properly admitted into evidence. This assignment of error is overruled.

PALMPRINTS AS ADMISSIBLE EVIDENCE

State v. Inman

Supreme Judicial Court of Maine (1976)
350 A.2d 582

After the trial of the defendant for murder, the trial judge instructed the jury. At the conclusion of the instructions, the trial judge stated that

> I indicated that I would ask you to take judicial notice of one thing. I now say that I have taken judicial notice that fingerprinting, which includes palmprinting, is the most accurate present means of identification, and that it is universally used in cases of this kind, but I also say to you that fingerprint and palmprint analysis requires greater skill than that which the ordinary witness has.
>
> And in this connection, you are to assume that I have taken judicial notice and hand it to you that the fingerprint method of identification is accurate and no two sets of fingerprints or palmprints are exactly alike.

In affirming the defendant's conviction and holding that there was no error, the Supreme Judicial Court of Maine cited California, Mississippi, Michigan, Illinois, North Carolina, and Vermont courts, ruling that

> The infallibility of fingerprints as a method of identification is now too widely accepted to require citation of authority. We further acknowledged in *Inman* that there is little or no difference between the methods used in the comparison of fingerprints and in the comparison of palm prints. The reliability of palm prints as evidence that a person was in the place where the palm print was found is now so well accepted that we know of no courts who hold such evidence to be incompetent. In fact, since the learned and comprehensive analysis of their attributes by the Nevada Court in *State v. Kuhl,* 42 Nev. 185, 175 P. 190, 3 A.L.R. 1694 (1918), palm prints have been adjudged no less reliable than fingerprints in jurisdictions where the issue has arisen....
>
> While the Justice took judicial notice of the scientific principle of the *capacity* for identification by comparison of two sets of palm prints, he properly left to the jury to decide what confidence they should place in the securing and preservation of the print on the floor and the defendant's prints which were used for comparison and the process of comparison *as conducted by these officers,* the competence

and reliability of the expert witness and the credibility of the witnesses. He did not take from the jury the essential decision of whether the print on the floor near the victim's shoulder was or was not made by the defendant's palm. In language of undoubted clarity, the Justice discussed the manner in which opinions of experts may be considered by the jury and concluded:

"If you should decide that the opinion of an expert witness is not based upon sufficient education and experience, or if you should conclude that the reasons given in support of the opinion are not founded, or that the opinion is outweighed by other evidence in the case, you may disregard the opinion in whole or in part."

"THE MOST SIGNIFICANT TECHNOLOGICAL INNOVATION IN LAW ENFORCEMENT IN DECADES ..."

A 1986 article in the *FBI Law Enforcement Bulletin*[7] commenced with the following statements:

Time Magazine reported that 3 minutes after receiving its first assignment, (in 1985) Los Angeles' new automated fingerprint system identified a suspect in the "Night Stalker" killer case that had terrorized the city for months.[8] In a recent issue of the *FBI Law Enforcement Bulletin*, two police chiefs wrote:

"... the automation of fingerprints for classification and matching ... [is] the most significant technological innovation in law enforcement in decades....[9]

The FBI Identification Division has been the center for the Nation's fingerprint records since 1934. Because of the millions of fingerprint files, automation by computer was commenced in 1963.

Since 1983, states that can access the Interstate Identification Index can now make on-line requests for records from the FBI's Identification Division and receive them back on-line.

Major cities throughout the United States have recently (or will in the near future) automated their local fingerprint files with computers. National automation of the nation's fingerprint files and local automation of the files of states and cities is the "most significant technological innovation in law enforcement in decades."

Before automation, the manual search of fingerprint files in an attempt to match fingerprints was slow and, in many instances, unsuccessful. Backlogs of work grew to months and sometimes years. Low-priority offenses, such as misdemeanor thefts and even burglaries, would have to wait for long periods of time. Los Angeles' new automated system became operational in 1985 and demonstrated the ability of the new system by identifying the "Night Stalker" in three minutes. The new automated systems will provide a much more efficient and reliable fingerprint identification system for the nation.

IDENTIFICATION BY FOOTPRINTS

Before the turn of the century, the art of identification by fingerprints was little known, and was viewed with skepticism in the United States. Mark Twain's 1894 novel about a Missouri murder trial, *Pudd'nhead Wilson,* opened the American public eyes to the potential use of fingerprints for identification purposes.

Today, fingerprint identification procedures are accepted as being reliable by courts and are generally known by the American public. Some experts in the American criminal justice system look upon identification by footprints as being in the early development stage that fingerprinting was at the turn of the last century. They point out that people may wear gloves, but it is very difficult to get in and out of a crime scene without using their feet.

The leading American expert on identification by footprints is a fifty-year-old anthropology professor at the University of North Carolina (Greensboro), Dr. Louise Robbins. Dr. Robbins has testified in murder cases as a forensic expert in California, Oklahoma, Pennsylvania, Florida, and North Carolina. In the following murder case, the Supreme Court of North Carolina held that her testimony as a physical anthropologist was admissible on the issue of footprint identification, even though she is apparently the only person using the method in question in this country and has had no formal training in footprint identification.

State v. Bullard

Supreme Court of North Carolina (1984)
312 N.C. 129, 322 S.E.2d 370

This case involved a bare footprint found at a murder scene. In affirming the defendant's conviction for murder and in holding that the trial court properly admitted Dr. Robbins' testimony on the footprint identification which linked the defendant to the crime scene, the Court stated that

> The method of comparison employed by Dr. Robbins does not involve ridge detail as does traditional fingerprint analysis. Instead, she relies upon a technique of comparison pertaining to the size and shape of the footprint in four areas: namely, the heel, arch, ball, and toe regions. The footprint size and shape reflect the size and shape of the internal bone structure of the foot, so the bones indirectly play a major part in the analysis of the footprint, according to Dr. Robbins. Dr. Robbins explains that since each person's foot size and shape are unique, she can identify a footprint represented by a clearly definable print of whatever part of the foot touches the ground. By examining the sides, front, and rear ends of each region of the foot, Dr. Robbins explains that she can compare known footprints with unknown footprints and determine if they are made by the same person....
>
> ... the trial judge is afforded wide latitude of discretion when making a determination about the admissibility of expert testimony. Justice Moore stated in *State v. King,* 287 N.C. 645, 215 S.E.2d 540

(1975), *death sentence vacated,* 428 U.S. 903, 96 S.Ct. 3208, 49 L.Ed.2d 1209 (1976):

> Whether the witness has the requisite skill to qualify him as an expert is chiefly a question of fact, the determination of which is ordinarily within the exclusive province of the trial judge....
>
> A finding by the trial judge that the witness possesses the requisite skill will not be reversed on appeal unless there is no evidence to support it....

Dr. Robbins was clearly in a superior position and better qualified to compare the bloody bare footprint found on the bridge with those of the defendants. The expertise to make the comparisons involved a certain knowledge which was beyond the realm of that of the average juror. Her testimony indicated that there were unusual and distinct features observed by Dr. Robbins when she examined the photograph of the bloodstained footprint on the bridge, the crime scene. In examining the footprints, Dr. Robbins made acetate overlays by tracing the photographed footprints. She made visual comparisons by observing these footprints with her naked eye and with a magnifying glass. After Dr. Robbins had observed the footprints and prepared the acetate tracing overlays, she used the tracings of the left and right footprints in the photographs to compare them with the footprints made by the defendant on several rolls of brown paper....

Certainly, Dr. Robbins' testimony assisted the jury in making certain inferences about the footprints on the bridge, which could not have been made without the testimony of someone with the qualifications of Dr. Robbins. Even though Dr. Robbins has no formal training in footprint identification, she testified at length concerning her independent study and research which spanned the last fourteen years. In addition, she is an expert in the field of physical anthropology and has received extensive formal training in this area....

She explained the number of footprints she had collected to justify why she believed each footprint is unique, just as the expert (in another case) explained how he had examined the teeth of thousands of people and believed that each person possessed an individual and unique dentition. All of the foregoing factors relative to an expert's testimony based on a novel scientific method have been accepted by this Court as cogent to its determination that the expert's method was reliable and his testimony admissible. We also have determined that Dr. Robbins' unique scientific method is reliable because of her explanatory testimony, professional background, independent research, and use of established procedures to make her visual comparisons of bare footprints.

PROBLEMS

1. The semi-nude "beaten, lifeless" body of a woman was found in her apartment. A latent palmprint impression was found on the floor next to the body. Suspicion focused on the defendant because: (1) he had known the victim and had previously rented an apartment in the building, (2) the

"crime, including its sexual overtones, was strikingly similar to a crime for which" the defendant had been previously indicted, (charged) (3) the defendant had fresh scratches on his hands, neck, and face, and abrasions on his elbows "of the type ... which a woman under sexual attack might inflict." The police wanted palmprints from the defendant. What procedures could they use to obtain palmprints from the defendant after it was determined that there were none on file at either the state or federal governments? To obtain palmprints, police officers followed the defendant's automobile. When he was observed speeding, he was then arrested and prints were obtained at that time. The defendant's lawyer argued that the State should not be permitted to use the palmprints as evidence because they were obtained from a "sham" arrest.

Did the Supreme Judicial Court of Maine permit the use of this evidence? (*State v. Inman*, 301 A.2d 348 (Maine Sup.Jud.Ct.1973)).

2. One shoeprint of a gym shoe (sneaker) was found in a gas station which had been vandalized. The police officer investigating the criminal damage to property and the burglary observed the shoeprint. The officer then observed the defendant hitchhiking several miles away and observed that the defendant was wearing a popular brand of running shoes. There was no evidence that the defendant was fleeing or acting in a suspicious manner. The officer then arrested the defendant and later developed other evidence used in charging and convicting the defendant of the offense.

Was the arrest lawful? Should the conviction be affirmed? (*State v. Reynolds*, 453 A.2d 1319, New Hampshire Sup.Ct. 1982).

3. A law enforcement officer investigating a burglary asked the victim if she suspected anyone. The victim replied that the defendant was the only one she could think of. The officer then contacted the defendant, who was on parole for another offense, and arranged for a meeting. At the meeting, the officer falsely told the defendant that his fingerprints were found at the scene of the burglary. The defendant, after a few minutes of silence, admitted that he had committed the burglary.

Should the officer's false statement as to the fingerprints cause the court to rule that the confession of the defendant could not be used as evidence? Explain. (*Oregon v. Mathiason*, 429 U.S. 492, 97 S.Ct. 711, U.S. Sup.Ct. 1977).

NOTES

[1] *Crime Scene Search and Physical Evidence Handbook,* published by the U.S. Dept. of Justice Law Enforcement Assistance Administration National Institute of Law Enforcement (U.S. Gov't. Printing Office, 1973), p. 47.

[2] 394 U.S. 721, 89 S.Ct. 1394 (1969).

[3] 324 F.2d 879, 882 (D.C.Cir.1963).

[4] 340 F.2d 313, 314 (1st Cir.1965).

[5] 283 F.Supp. 217 (N.D.Ohio 1968).

[6] The material in this subsection (with the exception of the case of *People v. Gomez*) is reprinted from the U.S. Department of Justice Law Enforcement Assistance Administration book entitled *Crime Scene, Search and Physical Evidence Handbook.*

[7] "Fingerprint Automation: Progress in the FBI Identification Division" March 1986 issue of the *FBI Law Enforcement Bulletin.*

[8] *Time,* October 14, 1985, p. 96.

[9] Col. Carroll D. Buracker and William K. Stover, "Automated Fingerprint Identification: Regional Application of Technology," *FBI Law Enforcement Bulletin,* August 1984, p. 1.

Photographs and Other Demonstrative Evidence

USING DEMONSTRATIVE EVIDENCE AND EXHIBITS

Physical evidence (or real evidence) is the object itself. **Demonstrative** evidence demonstrates to a jury and court the presence elsewhere of a real object. In a murder case, photographs of the victim would be demonstrative evidence. Diagrams, models, or sketches of the crime scene would also be demonstrative evidence.

Demonstrative Evidence and Exhibits as "Silent Witnesses"

Demonstrative evidence is frequently used in both criminal and civil cases. It is a form of evidence which demonstrates and serves as a visual aid to juries and judges. Such evidence is sometimes called a "silent witness," which sometimes speaks loudest to a jury.

When words alone are inadequate to explain facts or when it is difficult to understand the situation out of which the case arose, the use of demonstrative evidence and exhibits should be seriously considered. With the use of demonstrative evidence or exhibits, the judge and jury are not only able to hear the testimony of a witness but they are also able to see the facts as they are presented. Demonstrative evidence and exhibits can not only assist a jury and judge in better understanding a witness' testimony, but they can also aid in preventing confusion or misunderstanding.

To create demonstrative evidence and exhibits, some material and some artistic skill is required to create the evidence which is desired. Just as a skillful teacher uses teaching aids to present facts and information, witnesses (particularly expert witnesses) may use demonstrative evidence or exhibits to testify in a more effective manner.

Because most demonstrative evidence and exhibits are used in aiding juries and judges in better understanding the testimony of witnesses, the exhibits in many instances are not ordinarily offered as having been involved in or as depicting some aspect of the crime involved. However, proper foundations must be laid for the use of demonstrative evidence and exhibits. In most instances, the statement of a witness that the exhibit will assist him in his testimony will normally be sufficient to permit the use of such evidence.

Demonstrative evidence should consist of neat, clear, and authoritative presentations of the facts sought to be presented. The witness should be thoroughly familiar with the charts, diagrams, etc. which will be used and must be prepared to present sufficient information so that the jury and judge can understand the demonstrative evidence and the reason for its use. Because the testimony of the witness and the demonstrative evidence will be subjected to cross-examination, any discrepancies or inaccuracies which become apparent could cause the probative value of the evidence to diminish considerably.

Demonstrative evidence and exhibits, like other evidence, should be concealed from the eyes of a jury until they are ready for use. The evidence should be well packaged and conveniently available until needed. Large pieces of demonstrative evidence may be prominently located in the courtroom but should be covered to conceal the nature of the evidence and display. This should ordinarily heighten the jury's curiosity and fascination until the evidence is unveiled. Such procedures will also ordinarily assure greater dramatic impact and a higher degree of attention when the evidence is presented.

Demonstrative evidence and exhibits should always be handled with great dignity, care, and respect in order to assure that the evidence will receive the degree of attention and weight it deserves. Handling such evidence in an indifferent and careless manner could cause a jury to view it with indifference and to minimize or ignore whatever probative value the evidence has. A witness or prosecutor who is not able to find demonstrative evidence when it is needed could lose some of the dramatic impact which can be obtained by swiftly and effectively producing and presenting the evidence at the appropriate time.

Unless the demonstrative evidence is a shocking or gruesome display, it may be used to serve valuable purposes at all stages of a trial. When charts, diagrams, etc. are critical to an understanding of the case, such evidence could be used during the opening statement by the prosecutor. It is often stated that education of a jury should begin at the earliest possible time and if demonstrative evidence can enable the jury to evaluate the testimony which will follow in the light of a favorable factual theory, the use of demonstrative evidence during the opening statements should be considered and their availability should be made known to the prosecutor.

Once demonstrative evidence such as charts, diagrams, models, etc. are used to assist a jury in understanding a witness' testimony, it can ordinarily remain on display for the remainder of the trial. However, overexposure of demonstrative evidence which is shocking or gruesome is likely to diminish its impact, and such evidence should be removed or covered.

Examination of Physical Evidence, Demonstrative Evidence, and Exhibits by the Jury and Judge

The grim realities of a crime are particularly impressed upon the minds of juries and judges when physical evidence of the crime is passed to them for their further inspection. Bullets and other small objects may be placed in small boxes with transparent tops so that they may easily be passed among the jurors, who may then closely examine the evidence without actually touching the object. Weapons, such as guns and knives, may also be placed in similar boxes or may be mounted on small display boards. Photographs may be passed as they are.

Experienced trial lawyers recommend that demonstrative and physical evidence be passed to jurors whenever possible. By personally examining tangible evidence, judges and jurors may perceive additional facts. If the trial judge shows a particular interest in the evidence, this often tends to influence the jury to believe that the evidence is indeed important.

Because many jurors understand what they see better than what they hear, it always pays to have exhibits which can be passed to jurors and judges. These silent witnesses speak loudest when jurors and judges can personally examine the evidence. The initiative and responsibility for preparing evidence so that it may be passed to the jury and the judge for their personal examination often rests upon the officer who will bring the evidence into the courtroom.

Courtroom Demonstrations

Courtroom demonstrations can also be very effective in communicating to a jury and judge. Some witnesses can demonstrate what they saw and the events which occurred much better than they can describe it. This is particularly true of poorly educated witnesses.

The trial judge's discretion as to courtroom demonstrations is very broad. Simple demonstrations are usually permitted. When a witness is testifying poorly in response to questions, a simple demonstration in the courtroom might present very vividly the events which occurred. For example, in an assault, the prosecutor could act the part of the victim and the witness could take the part of the person committing the crime.

USING PHOTOGRAPHS AS EVIDENCE

Photographs are a special type of demonstrative evidence. Because of their importance to law enforcement agencies as a means of identification and because of their importance as evidence in both civil and criminal trials, they are given special attention in the study of criminal evidence. The Court of Appeals of Texas made the following statement regarding the use of photographs as evidence:

> Photographs are admissible in evidence on the theory that they are pictorial communications of a witness who uses them instead of, or in addition to, some other method of communication. Thus, they are admissible on the same grounds and for the same purposes as are diagrams, maps, and drawings of objects or places, and the same rules of admissibility applicable to objects connected with the crime apply to photographs of such objects. This is true whether they are originals or copies, black and white or colored. So, a photograph, proved to be a true representation of the person, place, or thing which it purports to represent, is competent evidence of those things of which it is material and relevant for a witness to give a verbal description.[1]

When speaking of the admissibility of photographs for use as evidence, courts and lawyers use the terms of accuracy, verification, evidentiary value, and identification rather than the terms of competency, relevancy, and materiality which are ordinarily used for other types of evidence. The admissibility of a photograph is based upon what is pictured. If the object, place, or person shown in the photograph is not in itself admissible, then it ordinarily cannot be made admissible by picturing it in a photograph.

INTRODUCING PHOTOGRAPHS INTO EVIDENCE

The Requirement of an Authenticating or Verifying Witness

In order to introduce a photograph into evidence, a foundation must be laid by a witness who can testify from firsthand knowledge that the photograph accurately portrays and represents the object, place, or person shown in the picture. The extent that the verifying witness would have to testify as to the accuracy of a photograph might vary somewhat depending upon the importance of each photograph to the issues before the court. Some photographs might be admitted by stipulation (agreement between the parties) or with no challenge, while other photographs might be sharply contested and challenged. A photograph which is very incriminating to a defendant is more likely to be contested and would therefore require more testimony as to verification. On the other hand, minimal proof of accuracy may be sufficient for a photograph illustrating something which is not seriously contested.

It is not always necessary to have the person who actually took the picture as the authenticating and verifying witness, although in most instances the photographer is the witness who verifies the accuracy of the photograph. When the photographer is the verifying witness, he can testify from firsthand knowledge as to when the photograph was taken, the type of camera used, the film or other equipment used, lens opening and shutter speed, etc. if this is required. Many law enforcement agencies have developed photographic data forms with this information being placed on the back of the photograph or attached to the photograph.

The Requirement of Relevancy and Essential Evidentiary Value

All evidence sought to be admitted for use in a criminal or civil trial must be relevant to at least one of the issues before that court. In determining the admissibility of a photograph as evidence, the trial judge must determine that the picture has probative value (essential evidentiary value) and tends to prove or disprove some issue in dispute. The Texas Court of Appeals stated in the case of *Terry v. State* [2] that

> the admission in evidence of photographs must necessarily rest largely in the discretion of the trial judge, who determines whether they serve a proper purpose in the jury's enlightenment, and his action will not be disturbed in the absence of a showing of an abuse of discretion.

In the case of *Terry v. State*, the defendant was convicted of the murder without malice of her one month-old son. In approving of the use of three pictures and an X ray, the Court held that

The first three pictures, though gruesome, are admissible as they corroborate the verbal description and bring visibly to the jury the details of the crime by showing the location, nature and extent of the wounds or injuries to the body of the deceased child. Their probative value far outweighs any probable prejudicial effect on the jury. This is especially true since the appellant testified to a single, unintentional act of dropping the child and the pictures show what the jury could reasonably conclude to have been a continual assault.

The X ray showing the broken arm is admissible. It bears on the degree of the atrociousness of the crime. Such proves a relative issue and enables the jury to better understand the testimony.

But other pictures, taken of parts of the baby's body after an autopsy, were held to be "at most, only remotely connected with the crime" and "served to inflame the minds of the jury." For this reason, the case was reversed and remanded for a new trial.

When the Inflammatory Effect of Photographs on a Jury Outweighs Their Evidentiary Value

It is well established that the admission of photographs is ordinarily within the sound discretion of the trial court. The Florida Court of Appeals held in the case of *Young v. State* [3] that

The fact that the photographs are offensive to our senses and might tend to inflame the jury is insufficient by itself to constitute reversible error, but the admission of such photographs, particularly in large numbers must have some relevancy, either independently or as corroborative of other evidence....

The very number of photographs of the victim in evidence here, especially those taken away from the scene of the crime, cannot but have had an inflammatory influence on the normal fact-finding process of the jury. The number of inflammatory photographs and resulting effect thereof was totally unnecessary to a full and complete presentation of the state's case. The same information could have been presented to the jury by use of the less offensive photographs whenever possible and by careful selection and use of a limited number of the more gruesome ones relevant to the issues before the jury.

In the case of *Leach v. State*, [4] the Florida Court of Appeals held that

Where there is an element of relevancy to support admissibility then the trial judge in the first instance and this Court on appeal must determine whether the gruesomeness of the portrayal is so inflammatory as to create an undue prejudice in the minds of the jury and detract them from a fair and unimpassioned consideration of the evidence.

Identification of the Photograph

Officers are ordinarily urged to take as many pictures as possible during the investigation of a crime because of the possibility that a picture may be found that contains some significant information which may have been overlooked.

Photographs are taken of the crime scene, the victim, and the evidence obtained. Having several photographs also permits the officer and the prosecutor a wider selection to choose pictures of good quality to prove facts in issue and to complement the testimony of witnesses presented in court.

After verifying the accuracy of a photograph, the officer may then be asked to state how he knows that the photograph is the one he took. The witness may show identification of the photograph by testimony showing any one or more of the following:

- That he had sole continuous possession of the photograph from the time of the taking up through the presentation of the photograph in court.
- A chain of possession for the period of time between the taking of the photograph and the presentation in court.
- The presence of an identifiable object in the picture which the officer placed at the scene before taking the photograph. The identifiable object could be an information data board or a measuring device with the initials of the officer and the date and place that the photograph was taken.

MUG SHOTS

Using Mug Shot Photographs as Evidence

Files of **mug shot** pictures are maintained by probably all law enforcement agencies. These photographs are for identification purposes and to acquaint law enforcement officers with known suspects and persons who have criminal records. Victims and witnesses to crimes often view police mug shots in efforts to identify the perpetrators of crimes.

Mug shots are seldom used as evidence in a criminal trial because (1) there is rarely a need for use of this type of photograph as evidence, and (2) the use of mug shots of the defendant in a criminal trial could easily cause members of a jury to believe that the defendant had a prior criminal record or has had prior trouble with the law. This could deny a defendant his right to a fair trial.

"It is well established that evidence of other offenses and prior trouble with the law is inadmissible in a criminal prosecution as part of the government's case against the defendant." [5] The U.S. Supreme Court stated in the 1948 case of *Michelson v. United States* [6] that

> The state may not show defendant's prior trouble with the law, specific criminal acts, or ill name among his neighbors, even though such facts might logically be persuasive that he is by propensity a probable perpetrator of the crime. The inquiry is not rejected because character is irrelevant; on the contrary, it is said to weigh too much with the jury and to so overpersuade them as to prejudge one with a bad general record and deny him a fair opportunity to defend against a particular charge. The overriding policy of excluding such evidence, despite its admitted probative value, is the practical experience that its disallowance tends to prevent confusion of issues, unfair surprise and undue prejudice.

The only time that a defendant's past criminal record may be shown by the government in a criminal trial is for impeachment purposes after the defendant has appeared as a witness in his own behalf. In the case of *United States v. Harrington* [7] a federal prosecutor was surprised and "probably seriously injured" when a government witness failed to make an in-court identification of the defendant as expected. The federal prosecutor was then permitted to introduce into evidence mug shot photographs of the defendant. The Second Circuit Court of Appeals established the following tests for determining whether mug shots may be used in a criminal trial:

1. The prosecutor must show a demonstrable need to introduce the photographs; and

2. the photographs, if shown to the jury, must not imply that the defendant has a prior criminal record; and

3. the introduction at trial must not draw particular attention to the source or implications of the photographs.

In holding that the government failed to pass tests 2 and 3, the case was reversed and remanded for a new trial, with the Court suggesting that

> we think that the preferable course of action when mug shots are to be introduced would be to produce photographic duplicates of the mug shots. These copies would lack any incriminating indicia—i.e., inscriptions or identification numbers, and they could also avoid use of the juxtaposed full face and profile photographic display normally associated with "mug shots."

References by Government Witnesses to Police Photographs

Identifications of the perpetrators of crimes are often made (or affirmed) through the use of police photographs, or mug shots. References to police photographs, or mug shots, by a government witness while testifying in a criminal trial before a jury could indicate to members of the jury that the defendant had a past criminal record, had previously been arrested, or had been in trouble with the police.

In the case of *Commonwealth v. Allen,* [8] the Supreme Court of Pennsylvania discusses four cases in which that court reversed conviction "because of references to police photographs" before juries. The best practice by law enforcement officers and prosecutors would be to caution witnesses for the government not to make any references to police photographs, or mug shots, unless a defense lawyer asked questions in cross-examination which required such a reference.

X RAY FILMS, VIDEOTAPES, AND MOTION PICTURES

Rule 1001 of the Federal Rules of Evidence defines photographs as includ(ing) still photographs, X ray films, videotapes, and motion pictures. Therefore X ray films, videotapes, and motion pictures are introduced into evidence upon the same basis and principles as still photographs.

X ray Films

X ray films (radiographs, roentgenograms, and skiagrams) are different from the ordinary type of photographs in the following respects:

- An untrained person may take a photograph, but a trained technician or a doctor must take an X ray. Therefore, the photographer of the X ray must testify in court unless the defense stipulates (agrees) to the admission of the X ray film.

- Unlike most photographs, X ray films require an expert to explain and interpret them. Therefore, in most situations a licensed physician who has had experience with X rays would have to be qualified as an expert witness to testify as to what he has learned from the X ray film.

- Since no witness is capable of testifying that he has actually seen the injury depicted by the X ray, the picture must be admitted as original evidence in order to provide the basis for the opinion of the expert trained in the interpretation of X rays.

Videotapes and Motion Pictures

If motion pictures and videotapes are relevant to a case and can be authenticated as accurately portraying the action shown, they generally can be admitted as evidence. Their use to show a robbery of a bank or other business place is frequent. They could be used to show a crime scene or the injuries inflicted upon a victim. Their use in drunken driving cases has caused many defendants to plead guilty because the defendants appeared very intoxicated. However, some intoxicated drivers do not appear drunk, and the movie or videotape in such cases could be helpful as evidence to the defense lawyer.

The visual portions of movies and videotapes have been looked upon by courts as a series of still photographs. Therefore, the rules governing the admissibility of photographs as evidence are frequently applied to movies and videotapes.

The audio portion (sound) is not as easily authenticated for use as evidence as is the picture. Because magnetic sound recordings can easily be altered with little chance of detection, this method of recording sound is not admissible when proper objections are made to its use as evidence. Optic sound tracks, however, cannot be erased or altered without detection and generally are admissible if shown to be genuine and relevant.

The Use of Closed-Circuit TV or Video in Child Sex Crime Cases

An article appearing in the May 14, 1984 issue of *Newsweek* magazine states that "between 100,000 and 500,000 American children will be (sexually) molested (in 1984)." The article also refers to a study "showing that 19% of all American women and 9% of all men were sexually victimized as children."

Defendants in all criminal cases have a Sixth Amendment right "to be confronted with the witness against him" which includes the right to cross-examine witnesses for the state (see the Bill of Rights in appendix A).

But in child sex crime cases, children are often upset by testifying in an open courtroom. A child can also be further traumatized and intimidated by being compelled to appear in the presence of the adult who violated their person and to repeat under such circumstances the events which have deeply hurt them. The child incest victim can find that appearing as a witness is even more difficult. "Her confusion and sense of guilt at her involvement is ... potentially far greater than other victims' experience." [9]

Because of the harm which could be caused to a child witness, some states have enacted legislation permitting children to testify through the use of video equipment or by means of closed-circuit television. It is generally required that a showing be made that the child would be further traumatized or intimidated by testifying in open court. Then, guidelines must be followed to ensure that the defendant's rights are infringed upon as little as possible.

Courts in the following cases held that such statutes are valid despite the lack of eye contact between the witness and the defendant:

State v. Sheppard

Superior Court of New Jersey (1984)
197 N.J.Super. 411, 484 A.2d 1330

State v. Warford

Supreme Court of Nebraska (1986)
223 Neb. 368, 389 N.W.2d 575, 39 CrL 2305

In the *Sheppard* case, a ten-year-old victim was permitted to testify as to a sexual assault through the use of video equipment. The Superior Court of New Jersey held that the defendant waived his right of confrontation by making threats against the child. The Court stated that

> The use of videotaped testimony of the child victim in this case will be permitted because:
> (a) It will not unduly inhibit the defendant's right of confrontation and therefore does not violate our constitutional provisions.
> (b) The testimony of a child victim in a child sexual abuse case may be presented by videotape as an exception to the confrontation requirement.
> (c) The use of the video technique is a permissible restriction of cross-examination.
> (d) The defendant in this case has waived his right of confrontation.

The Supreme Court of Nebraska upheld the use of videotape or televised testimony under the Nebraska statute. The *Warford* case involved a 4½-year-old victim. The court stated that

> Concern about the proper way to present the testimony of child victims in sex abuse cases is not new. Some jurisdictions are expanding

the hearsay exceptions to accommodate the special problems involved in child sex abuse cases. See *Symposium Issue: Child Abuse and the Law,* 89 Dickinson Law Review 3 (Spring 1985)....

In the eighteenth and nineteenth centuries, live testimony was the only way that a jury could observe the demeanor of a witness. The use of video tapes does not represent a significant departure from that tradition because the goal of providing a view of the witness' demeanor to the jury is still achieved.

However, a new trial was ordered because the trial court did not require the state to stay within the minimal constitutional guidelines and "denied the defendant his rights under the due process and confrontation clauses."

CRIME SCENE AND FIELD PHOTOGRAPHY [10]

The hackneyed statement that "a picture is worth one thousand words" may or may not be true. However, it is certain that photography, properly performed, can be one of the most valuable aids to the police investigation. Good crime scene photography can be properly done without great expertise. This section presents a summary of the techniques and considerations bearing on comprehensive crime scene photographic coverage. The techniques involved in operating cameras and associated equipment is, however, outside the scope of this handbook.

Investigative Photographs

These are simply any photographs made to record an object or event, or to clarify a point that is relative to a matter under investigation. Many investigative photographs are made in the photographic laboratory. However, this chapter is concerned with those taken on the crime scene.

Admissibility of Photographs as Evidence

Photographs are admissible in court if the investigator can testify that they accurately depict the area he observed. The accuracy of the photograph always relates to the degree it represents the appearance of the subject matter as to form, tone, color (if applicable), and scale. Thus, the use of a lens that will record with accuracy all objects and areas in focus may not portray correct distances between objects, nor reproduce them with the proper perspective, when they are out of focal range. In such situations, the crime scene sketch and the investigator's notes play strong supporting roles.

Usually a photographic negative is considered sufficient proof to refute any allegation that a photograph has been altered. However, if enlarged photographs are made for presentation in court, a contact print without borders should also be made.

Because of the importance of scale, distances, and perspective in interpreting the photographs taken at crime scenes, it is good procedure to include a ruler or other scale measurement in the photograph, when this is practicable.

However, because some courts have not allowed even this minor modification to the scene, an identical photograph without the scale indicator should also be taken.

If the photograph is to have the highest quality as evidence, it must depict the scene, persons, or objects precisely as they were found. Photography must therefore be an *exclusive* function of the crime scene search—that is, no people should be working within the scene at the time it is photographed nor should extraneous objects, such as police equipment, be included in the pictures.

Identification of Photographs

The photograph must be precisely identified, and the identifying data must be noted as each shot is taken.

The information relative to the technical history of a photograph will be recorded in the investigator's notes, which become part of the permanent record of the case.

Custody of Photographs

Custody of investigative photographs should be carefully maintained. When the film is sent by mail to a commercial processor, registered mail with return receipt should be used.

General Considerations in Field Photography

Time is an essential factor. Photography frequently will preempt other aspects of the investigation. Objects cannot be moved or examined with thoroughness until they have been photographed from all necessary angles. Because there are situations in which the object of interest undergoes significant change with the passage of time, it is very important that photographic equipment be in a constant state of readiness.

All camera positions should be recorded on the crime scene sketch. This can be done by measuring the distance from immovable objects to a vertical line extending downward from the camera lens. Photographs of interior scenes, intended to depict the area as a whole, should be taken as overlapping segments in one direction around the room or area. In making such photographs, it is best to keep the camera at about eye level, unless a tripod is used.

The most important element in police photography is maintaining perspective. Proper photographic perspective produces the same impression of relative position and size of visible objects as the actual objects do when viewed from a particular point. Any significant distortion in the perspective will reduce, or destroy altogether, its evidentiary value.

As a second rule, natural perspective can best be maintained by shooting pictures with the camera aimed so that a 90° angle is formed with opposite walls, or if outdoors, with fixed objects such as trees or the landscape.

Other Types of Photography Used in The Preservation and Collection of Evidence

Photography is a widely used and important tool in the collection and preservation of evidence. Photographs must accurately portray the object or scene represented. Absolute honesty is required and retouching is prohibited. Some of the other types of photography used are as follows:

- *Snapshots (family album and group photos).* In the U.S. Supreme Court case of *Simmons v. United States* (see chapter 13), the Court held that due process was not violated when identification of the offender was obtained by the use of snapshots. The group photos were not used as evidence in the criminal trial and were used only for out-of-court identification.

- *Surveillance Photographs.* Many banks, savings and loans, and other businesses have installed surveillance cameras which either automatically take photographs or can be activated by means of a hidden footswitch in the event of a holdup or other trouble. Photographs taken under such circumstances are routinely used for out-of-court identification and as evidence in criminal trials.

- *Night Surveillance Photographs.* By use of special equipment, photographs accurately portraying subjects have been obtained and used as evidence.

- *Special Photographic Techniques.* In order to make details visible to the naked eye, one or more of the following special photographic techniques could be used (a) infrared photography, (b) ultraviolet photography, (c) filters and other techniques.

Critical Photographic Requirements

- Approaches to the scene.
- Surrounding areas (the yard of a house in which the homicide occurred, the general area surrounding an outdoor crime scene, and so forth).
- Close-up photographs should be taken of the entrance and exit to the scene, or those most likely to have been used if these are not obvious.
- A general scenario shot showing the location of the body and its position in relation to the room or area in which it was found.
- At least two photographs of the body at 90° angles to each other. Camera should be placed as high as possible pointing downward toward the body.
- As many close-ups of the body should be taken as needed to show wounds or injuries, weapons lying near the body, and the immediate surroundings.
- After the body is moved, and after the removal of each item of evidence, the area underneath them should be photographed if there is any mark, stain or other apparent change.
- All fingerprints which do not need further development or cannot be lifted should be photographed. Areas in which fingerprints were discovered are photographed to show the location if this area was not included in other photographs.

- Bloodstains, including locations. Color film is desirable, although not absolutely necessary. Black and white pictures must also be taken.

Photographing the Arson Scene

When photographing the arson scene, complete coverage of the damage is important. But perhaps of even greater importance are objects or areas that are suspected to have been the point or points of initiation of the fire. Close-up photographs should be made of all such objects or areas. In addition, there are several other critical points or items of interest in an arson scene that should be photographed:

- Exterior views of all structures involved in the fire.
- Interior views that give a complete representation of the damaged areas and any undamaged areas immediately adjacent.

Photographing the Burglary Scene

The photographic requirements already cited for the homicide scene apply to the burglary situation. In addition, particular attention should be paid to:

- The interior and exterior of the building.
- Damaged areas, particularly those around the points of entry and exit used by the criminal.
- Close-ups of damaged containers that were the target of the burglar—safes, jewel boxes, strong boxes, etc.
- Tool marks both close up and from a perspective that will allow the position of the mark with respect to the general scene to be noted.
- Fingerprints. Although fingerprints are of major interest to all type investigations, they are of particular value in a burglary investigation. Fingerprints are photographed only when they are visible without development and when they cannot be lifted after they have been developed.

Photographing the Vehicle Accident

The accident scene should be photographed as soon as possible after the incident. Normally, except when photographing vehicles, the lenses should be of a normal focal length. If any lenses of an unusual length are used, considerable distortion will occur in the relative width of roads, distances between points, and so forth. Therefore, if special lenses were used, the record of the search should note the fact, and their description.

The following are the more critical aspects of interest to be photographed:

- The overall scene of the accident—from both approaches to the point of impact.
- The exact positions of the vehicles, injured persons, and objects directly connected to the accident.
- All points of impact, marks of impact, and damage to real property.

- All pavement obstructions and defects in the roadways.
- Close-ups of damage to vehicles. One photograph should show the front and one side, and another should show the rear and other side of the vehicle.
- Skid marks. If possible, photographs should be taken before the vehicle has been removed and again after it has been moved.
- Tire tracks, glass, and other associated debris.

Photographing Deceased Persons

The evidentiary value of a photograph of a deceased person is often considerably reduced by the inclusion of views that can be later alleged to be deliberately inflammatory. The unnecessary exposure of the sexual organs is a frequent case in point.

When photographing a body that is lying in a horizontal position, the camera should be placed directly over the victim's head at a height of no less than 5 feet.

Close-up photographs taken of injured parts of the body are most effective if in color, but black and white pictures must also be taken.

If the presence of wounds, blood, or other discoloration on the corpse may affect identification, the use of a lens filter may create more lifelike tones and thus aid in identification.

Photographing Live Victims and Suspects

Photographs that show areas of the body which usually are not visible when the person is clothed should be taken only under the direct supervision of the examining physician whose testimony the photographs are intended to illustrate. Thus, it is unusual that this type of photograph will be taken on the crime scene.

Before photographing any part of the female body normally covered by clothing, written consent of the subject must be obtained. If the subject is a minor, the written consent of the parent is needed and the photography must be done with witnesses present.

Photographing Fingerprints

To this point, the general requirement for close-up photographs of latent prints has been considered; however, it is important to consider also the uses that can be made of photography in the preparation and presentation of fingerprint evidence.

Fingerprints found at crime scenes may frequently be photographed and an enlargement produced that can be very useful in studying the print and comparing it with others. Fingerprints that can be seen without the aid of dusting powder should be photographed prior to dusting. There is always danger of damaging the print during the dusting process.

PROBLEMS

1. The defendant had reservations to fly out of the Los Angeles International Airport. He approached the pre-boarding inspection station and placed two briefcases on the conveyor belt of the X-ray machine. The security agent operating the machine observed a "dark object with what looked to be lines in it" in one of the briefcases. The agent suspected that the object might be a bomb and asked another agent if she could determine what the object was. When the second agent could not identify the object, a supervisor was called. The supervisor thought the lines were wires which indicated a bomb. When the defendant was asked what was in the briefcase, he answered, "clothes." The briefcase was run through the X-ray machine a second time and then the briefcase was opened for a visual and hand inspection. The airport agents found 2138 grams of cocaine in the briefcase and the defendant was arrested.

   Did the inconclusive X-ray scan establish probable cause to arrest the defendant and search the briefcase? Or was there consent or implied consent from the defendant to search the briefcase? Should the cocaine be permitted to be used as evidence against the defendant? Give reasons for your answer. *United States v. Pulido–Baquerizo*, 800 F.2d 899, 40 CrL 2030 (9th Cir.1986).

2. After a truck hijacking, FBI agents showed the driver of the stolen truck (Medina), photographs of Baker (defendant in this case). At the first identification session (before Baker's arrest), Medina was shown a series of fifteen pictures, one at a time. One photograph of Baker was included and Medina tentatively identified Baker. At the second identification session, Medina was shown a group of eleven photographs, including two of Baker. Again, Medina tentatively identified Baker as the gunman in the hijacking. Medina had ample opportunity to view the offender at the time of the crime. At Baker's criminal trial, Medina identified Baker as the hijacker with a gun.

   Were the photographic identification procedures "so impermissibly suggestive as to give rise to a very substantial likelihood of irreparable misidentification"? What are the requirements for showing groups of photographs to a witness (or witnesses)? What should law enforcement officers and private security persons do to show that photographic identifications were not "impermissibly suggestive"? *United States v. Baker*, 419 F.2d 83 (2nd Cir.1969), review denied 397 U.S. 971, 90 S.Ct. 1086 (U.S.Sup.Ct.1970).

3. Federal Alcohol, Tobacco and Firearms agents set up a "sting" operation in Michigan. The undercover officers used a storefront operation and pretended to be fences willing to buy stolen property. A videotape was made of the defendant selling stolen property to the agents in the storefront operation.

   Should the videotape (which was material and relevant to the criminal charges against the defendant) be permitted to be used as evidence against the defendant? *People v. Barker*, 101 Mich.App. 599, 300 N.W.2d 648 (1980).

4. An elderly woman was the victim of a "pigeon-drop" scheme ("flimflam" operation, or "con game"). The elderly woman was persuaded to withdraw $26,000 from her bank and turn it over to the defendant, believing that she would share in money which the defendant falsely told the elderly woman

had been found. Police officers investigating the crime requested bank surveillance photographs and were able to identify the defendant as the woman who accompanied the elderly woman into the bank to withdraw the money. Because the bank camera also photographed a clock and calendar, the time and date of the photographs could be determined. At the defendant's criminal trial, a bank officer testified as to the source of the photographs and to the fact that the photographs showed the interior of the bank.

Was this a sufficient foundation to permit the use of the photographs as evidence? *State v. Pulphus,* 465 A.2d 153 (R.I.Sup.Ct.1983).

5. Detroit fire fighters responded to a fire in a home, arriving at about 5:42 A.M. The fire was extinguished and all of the fire persons and police left the premises at 7:04 A.M. Because arson was suspected, fire investigators were instructed to investigate the fire. The fire investigators, however, did not arrive at the burned home until 1:00 P.M. that day. A neighbor told them that the owners of the home were out of town on a camping trip but had been contacted by telephone and had arranged through their insurance agent to have a boarding crew secure the house. The crew was working as the fire investigators arrived. The fire investigators went into the damaged home. After they found evidence of arson, the investigators called in a photographer to take pictures throughout the house.

Were the photographs and other incriminating evidence obtained in a manner that did not violate the right of privacy of the owners of the home? Can the evidence be used to support criminal charges against the home owners? Should the fire investigators have obtained a search warrant or consent before going into the building? Could the neighbor have given them consent and authority to go into the house? Explain. *Michigan v. Clifford,* 464 U.S. 287, 104 S.Ct. 641 (U.S.Sup.Ct.1984).

6. In problem 5, photographic and other evidence was obtained which showed that the Clifford home was deliberately burned (arson). If this evidence could not be used in a criminal case against the Cliffords, could it be used by their insurance company as a defense if the Cliffords sued the insurance company to collect the fire insurance money on the house? Give reasons for your answer.

NOTES

[1] The Court of Appeals of Texas in the case of Terry v. State, 491 S.W.2d 161 (Tex.Crim.App.1973).

[2] See note 1 above.

[3] 234 So.2d 341 (Fla.1970).

[4] 132 So.2d 329 (Fla.1961).

[5] United States v. Hines, 470 F.2d 225 (3d Cir.1972).

[6] 335 U.S. 469, 69 S.Ct. 213 (1948).

[7] 490 F.2d 487 (1973). The Court in the case of United States v. Harrington stated that

... the introduction of photographs of a defendant may well be equivalent to the introduction of direct evidence of a prior criminal conviction has been articulated in a number of recent opinions which have recognized that the introduction of certain photographs may result in getting before the jury the fact that the defendant has a prior record, and so has deprived the defendant of his right to a fair trial.

See also State v. Cauthen, 18 N.C.App. 591, 197 S.E.2d 567 (1973), where the Court of Appeals of North Carolina held that it was error to admit into evidence a photograph which contained information indicating that it was a prison photograph. However, the Court held that the error was harmless where the trial court instructed the jury to disregard any writing on the photograph and it was not shown that a different result would likely have resulted had the photograph been excluded.

[8] 448 Pa. 177, 292 A.2d 373 (1972).

[9] "Proving Parent-Child Incest: Proof at Trial Without Testimony in Court by the Victim," 15 *U. of Mich. Journal of Law Reform* 131 (1981).

[10] The material in this section has been taken from *Crime Scene Search and Physical Evidence Handbook*, prepared by the U.S. Department of Justice Law Enforcement Assistance Administration National Institute of Law Enforcement and Criminal Justice.

Documents and Writings as Evidence

PROVING THAT DOCUMENTS AND WRITINGS ARE GENUINE AND AUTHENTIC

Documents and writings are used frequently as evidence in civil cases, but are not used as often in criminal cases. Confessions and written admissions are probably the most frequent writings used as evidence in criminal cases. Writings would also be very important in bad check and forgery cases, and in kidnapping and robbery cases in which demand notes were used.

The party seeking to use a document or writing as evidence must carry the burden of showing that the document or writing is not only relevant and material but is also genuine and authentic evidence. Some documents and evidence can prove their own authentication. Federal Rule of Evidence 902 (see appendix B) provides that public documents, certified copies of public records, newspapers and periodicals, and other writings and documents fall within this group.

In all cases, the opposing party could challenge the proposed use of documents or writings as evidence. The challenge could be on the grounds that the writing or document is not relevant, or not material, or not genuine or authentic.

Although a document or writing may be shown to be authentic and genuine, this is not proof as to statements and assertions made in the document or writing. For example, a newspaper may be shown to be genuine and authentic and accepted for use in evidence as such. However, a jury or judge could find that statements made in the newspaper were not true.

Using Direct Evidence to Prove That Documents and Writings Are Authentic and Genuine

Documents and writings may be proved to be genuine and authentic [1] by any of the following forms of direct evidence:

- By the testimony of a witness who observed the signing or the writing of the document. For example, an officer who observed the defendant write or sign the consent form or a confession.

- By the testimony of the person who wrote or signed the document acknowledging that the writing was genuine and authentic.

- Regularly kept business records may be authenticated by witnesses who are custodians or supervisors of such records and who can testify that the writing which is offered for use in evidence is actually part of the records of the business. In such cases, the custodian or supervisor may not have actually seen the writing or document written or signed. However, the trustworthiness of the writing may be established with testimony that the writing was a regularly kept business record. The "regularly kept business record exception" is also sometimes referred to as the "shopbook rule." (See chapter 7 on "Regularly Kept Records" as a major exception to the hearsay rule.)

- Testimony establishing proof of handwriting by a witness who is

  An expert witness qualified to testify as to the identity of the writer of the document or writing. For example, an expert could testify as to the identity of the writer of a check, a demand note in a robbery case, or a threat found in a writing sent to a victim.

  A person who is not a handwriting expert but is well acquainted with the handwriting of the signer or writer of the document or writing. This could be a member of the family, a friend, or other person who had seen the handwriting of the writer frequently.

- By the contents of the document or writing. For example, a demand note or a check may be easily recognized by the contents and form of the writing.

Proving That Documents and Writings Are Authentic and Genuine by Circumstantial Evidence

The great majority of documents and writings introduced for use as evidence in criminal trial are proved authentic and genuine by direct evidence, or by the contents of the document or writing itself. If the document or writing cannot be proved to be authentic and genuine by these means, circumstantial evidence may be used. The types of circumstantial evidence which may be used include

- Circumstantial evidence such as the fact that the writing was in the custody of defendant, the victim, or the deceased; or that the defendant, victim, or deceased acted in response to the writing; or that the defendant, victim, or deceased referred to the document or writing in oral or written communications with other persons; or that the document or writing did not appear to be forged or have any other suspicious appearance.

- The "ancient documents rule" which permits the use of circumstantial evidence where the document has been in existence for a number of years (twenty years under the Federal Rules of Evidence).[2]

- Circumstantial evidence derived from the fact that the document or writing was in the custody of a public official. Statements made in a will, an income tax return, a bill of sales, or a deed could be used in evidence. If there was any question as to the authenticity or genuineness of such documents, circumstantial evidence could be used.

- The "reply doctrine" permits the use of circumstantial evidence to show that a writing was in response to other communication. Writings which are in response to other communications often indicate this in the contents of the writing. The following case illustrates a situation in which the writing was shown to be a reply communication.

Case Illustrating the "Reply Doctrine"

Winel v. United States

U.S. Court of Appeals, Eighth Circuit (1966)
365 F.2d 646

In holding that a postcard was properly admitted for use in evidence in a mail fraud case, the Court held that

It has long been recognized that one of the principal situations where the authenticity of a letter is provable by circumstantial evidence arising out of the letter's context, other than proof of handwriting or the business records exception, is where it can be shown that the letter was sent in reply to a previous communication....

... In the instant case the inherent nature of the communication makes it absolutely certain that it is a reply communication. The only question that can then arise with respect to its admissibility would be whether there was proof of its mailing and receipt. This is clearly answered by the record....

... It is not necessary that there be direct testimony of placing in the mails or removing from the mails if there is a full showing of the customs and usage relating to this type of communication.

Cases Illustrating That the Contents of a Writing Can Be Used to Identify the Writer and to Prove the Genuineness of the Writing

United States v. Sutton

U.S. Court of Appeals (D.C.Cir., 1969)
426 F.2d 1202

Four handwritten notes were found on the body of a murdered woman. The government argued that three of the unsigned notes were written by the defendant, since the notes revealed knowledge identifying and incriminating the defendant. The Court held that the contents of the notes alone could establish that they were genuine and authentic, and that

we recognize the general proposition that authorship of writings may be shown by circumstantial evidence, among the components of which the contents of the writing may play a significant role. Circumstances be-

---

Terms Used in the Examination of Documents and Writings

- *Questioned document.* A writing or a document which is believed to be forged, or is not genuine and authentic.

- *Questioned document examiner.* A person with special training and experience necessary to examine questioned documents to determine the author or the genuineness of the document. To make this determination, the questioned document is often compared with one or more other documents.

- *Graphologist.* A person who studies one or more documents written by a known person and concludes from the writing or penmanship personality traits of the writer of the document. Because graphology is not recognized by courts as a reliable science, such evidence would not be admissible.

- *Indented writings.* A person writing on a note pad or telephone pad may leave indented writing on one or more of the sheets under the paper upon which he (or she) is writing. Indented writing could provide valuable information in the investigation of a crime.

- *Charred document.* A writing or document which has been partially or completely burned. If the document can be preserved (or is left undisturbed), the written contents can generally be determined by a document examiner.

- *Linguistics analyst.* A study of language usage; could be used to determine the genuineness of a document, or could be used in an effort to determine who wrote the document. (The defense in the Patty Hearst case used linguistic evidence of writings and tape recordings in an attempt to prove that she did not participate voluntarily in the bank robbery. See *United States v. Hearst*, 412 F.Supp. 893 (N.D.Cal.1976).)

---

yond the four corners of a document may point with sufficient certitude to the person whose pen created it. Moreover, in special circumstances, where the contents reveal a *knowledge* or other trait peculiarly referable to a single person, the contents alone may suffice, and where a document, purportedly that of a particular person, makes reference to facts peculiarly known to him, the manifest probabilities that the document is his permit a logical conclusion that in actuality he is in fact the composer. The receipt of otherwise unauthenticated writings in evidence under such conditions adequately safeguards the policy considerations underlying the broad rule disfavoring authentication of writings solely on the basis of what they contain.

State v. Milum

Supreme Court of Kansas (1968)
202 Kan. 196, 447 P.2d 801

The Supreme Court of Kansas held that

Proof of the genuineness of a letter may be established when the contents themselves reveal knowledge peculiarly referable to a certain person or the contents are of such nature that the letter could not have passed between persons other than the purported writer and the person to whom it was delivered.... For that matter, any relevant writing may be admitted when, from its contents or other circumstances in evidence, it is reasonably inferable that the author is the person sought to be charged. Whether or not the authenticity of a writing is sufficiently established to render it admissible in evidence is a matter largely within the discretion of the trial court.... *State v. Huffman*, 141 W.Va. 55, 87 S.E.2d 541.

In State v. Huffman, supra, which was a rape prosecution, notes allegedly written by the defendant to the prosecuting witness while both were incarcerated in jail were introduced into evidence. The notes referred to the rape charge, were signed with the initials of the defendant, and urged the prosecutrix not to testify against him. The court held the notes were admissible on the basis their contents, together with the circumstances under which they were written and delivered to the prosecutrix, sufficiently established authorship by the defendant.

Computer Printouts as Evidence

Sears, Roebuck & Co. v. Merla

Superior Court of New Jersey (1976)
142 N.J.Super. 205, 361 A.2d 68

The Superior Court of New Jersey held that

We hold that as long as a proper foundation is laid, a computer printout is admissible on the same basis as any other business record

. . . .

Computerized bookkeeping has become commonplace. Because the business records exception is intended to bring the realities of the business world into the courtroom, a record kept on computer in the ordinary course of business qualifies as competent evidence. This result is in accordance with that reached in other jurisdictions.... Of course, if the computer printout at issue here is admitted at trial, it will constitute only prima facie evidence of an account stated. Defendant will have the opportunity to refute plaintiff's evidence.

United States v. De Georgia

U.S. Court of Appeals, Ninth Circuit (1969)
420 F.2d 889

After documentary proof was used to establish that the vehicle was owned by a car rental agency, the security manager of the rental agency testified that he had consulted the company's master computer control office. Because all rent-al and lease information was routinely fed to the company computer and the computer reported no lease or rental to the defendant, the security manager testified that this indicated that the vehicle was stolen. The Court held that this was sufficient evidence to corroborate the defendant's confession. (See the section on "Corroboration in the Use of Confessions ... as Evidence" in chapter 5.)

THE "BEST EVIDENCE," OR THE "ORIGINAL DOCUMENT" RULE

The famous English lawyer and writer, Blackstone, wrote in the 1760s that [3]

> the best evidence the nature of the case will admit of shall always be required, if possible to be had; but if not possible then the best evi-dence that can be had shall be allowed.

It is generally held today that the best evidence rule applies only to documents, writings, and recordings. In the case of *Munsford v. State*,[4] the defendants were convicted of armed robbery. A police officer appeared as one of the witnesses and testified that a track found at the scene of the crime matched the tennis shoe of one of the defendants. A photograph of the track was admitted into evidence but the tennis shoe was not used in evidence. In holding that this procedure did not violate the best evidence rule and in affirming the defen-dant's convictions, the Supreme Court of Georgia quoted an earlier Georgia case, ruling that

> The rule ("best evidence") has nothing to do with evidence generally, but is restricted to writings alone.

Because the best evidence rule today almost exclusively applies only to docu-ments, writings, and recordings, the rule is more accurately described as the original document rule. The terms *writings* and *recordings* are defined in Rule 1001 of the Federal Rules of Evidence, found in appendix B. Federal Rules of Evidence 1002 through 1006 (see appendix B) provide for the admissibility of documents, writings, and recordings as evidence.

Reasons for the Best Evidence, or Original Document Rule

Carbon or photographic copies of an original document or writing are "second-ary" evidence of the original. The requirement that the original be offered as evidence is an ancient requirement which originated in English law prior to the American Revolution. Some writers state that the reason for the rule was the prevention of fraud. Most modern writers, however, state that the primary purpose of the rule was to assure the most accurate written version, which is the original document or writing.

The rule requires that the best evidence available be used. This preference for the original of any document or writing is a common-sense attempt to minimize possibilities of errors (or fraud) in seeking the truth. Possibilities of errors certainly existed years ago when all of the copies of original documents were hand-copied. With modern copy machines, the margin of error has been minimized but still exists. The rule, which originated centuries ago, continues to require that the best available evidence be used.

Documents or Writings "Not Closely Related to a Controlling Issue"

Federal Rule of Evidence 1004(4) provides that the "original is not required . . . if . . . (the) writing . . . is not closely related to a controlling issue." This rule permits the trial judge the discretion not to impose the original document rule when no good purpose is served in demanding the use of original writing or document.

Just what matters are collateral (auxiliary or indirectly related to the principal issues) would have to be decided by the trial judge. The original document rule would certainly apply to a written confession, a demand note in a robbery case, and to a check in a check forgery case. Probably in very few instances would writings used in evidence in criminal cases "not (be) closely related to a controlling issue." If the writing is easily available, the most practical procedure would be to submit the original for use in evidence.

QUESTIONED DOCUMENTS [5]

The term *questioned* documents is used here to include altered, forged, or otherwise suspect documents. A document may be the sole basis for an investigation, such as a forged check, or it may be the prime evidence in another case, such as a murder or kidnapping.

When a questioned document comes to the attention of the investigator, he should take steps at once to protect it from damage, contamination, or alteration. The document should be placed in a transparent container as soon as it is received, taking care not to add folds.

Preliminary Examination of Documents

Documents may be examined from the standpoint of identifying physical characteristics (type paper, marks, and indentations), chemical properties (quality of paper, inks used), or handwriting (and thereby, the author). However, the investigator should limit himself to only the physical examination, focusing attention on color of inks or pencils used, the type of paper, and handwriting. Evidence of erasures or other apparent alterations of what appeared to be the original document are of particular interest when quantities of goods and money are involved.

The type of writing instrument (apparently) used and the physical characteristics of the paper should be given close attention. The paper's overall quality, color, texture, weight, and the presence of watermarks are useful characteristics to include in the investigator's case report. Such characteristics may identify a special manufacturing process or a particular supplier or pur-

---

The Use of Writings or Documents as Evidence

Documents and Writings May Be Admissible for Use as Evidence If:

- The document or writing is shown to be:
  genuine and authentic.

- The evidence contained in the document or writing is
  relevant
  material
  and competent.

- The document or writing does not contain:
  inadmissible hearsay (parts of the writing may be held to be inadmissible for this reason).

- The requirements of the "best evidence," or "original doctrine" rule are complied with.

After the Writing or Document Has Been Admitted for Use as Evidence, the Factfinder (Jury or Judge) Would Then Determine:

- The author and person who wrote the writing if this question and issue was unresolved.
- The truth and credibility of the statements and assertions made in the document or writing.
- The weight to be given to the statements and assertion made in the document or writing.
- The issue of guilt or innocence of each of the charges made against the defendant.

---

chaser, or they may be used for comparison with standards collected during the investigation.

Alterations of Documents

An *alteration* of a document is the writing over of previous writing. Common examples of alterations include changing a one to a seven or adding one or more zeros to an amount that has been expressed numerically.

- An *obliteration* is the intentional destruction of some part of an original writing by marking through or over it. If this is done with the same material as was used to write the original material, recovery of the writing is difficult, if not impossible.

- Erasures on documents may be accomplished by either chemically or mechanically removing marks on the paper. Chemical erasures are used most often on documents written with ink. The chemical does not remove the ink, but renders it colorless. Mechanical erasures remove the written material and disturb the fibers of the paper. When the writing is thoroughly removed with a mechanical eraser, it may be impossible to determine what was written originally, although the erasure may be quite evident.

The discovery of a torn document or a fragment of a document during an investigation should spark an attempt to find all of the remaining pieces. The laboratory will first chemically process the document fragments for latent prints and then attempt to restructure them.

If a document fragment has been partially or completely burned, it should be handled with the greatest care because of its brittle character. If the ash is not disturbed, it may still be possible to read writing on it and to reconstitute all or part of the document by physical and chemical means. If the ash is discovered in a container which can be transported, the container should be covered and then carefully removed to the laboratory, making no attempt to remove the contents. If the material is in an area that cannot be transported (such as a fireplace), the investigator should carefully slide a board or other thin, firm material under the ash and place that board in a cardboard box for transport to the laboratory....

The investigator should be alert for indented writing left on a paper pad after a top sheet has been removed. Writing of this type can be read by passing light over the paper at a very low angle. The indentions which receive less light than the original writing will appear as shadows and likely be discernible. Carbon paper, particularly relatively new sheets, may often reveal similar information, although no special lighting is required.

Mechanical Writing Devices

The most common mechanical writing devices the investigator will encounter are typewriters, check protectors, adding machines, cash registers, and rubber stamps. An attempt should be made to establish the make and model of the instrument used to print a suspect document, or to find the particular machine used to generate it. The investigator may be able to develop significant leads in his work through the various factors or conditions which serve to individualize any mechanical writing instrument.

A slight variation, such as an off center key built into a typewriter at the time of manufacture, may later serve as a valuable means of individualizing a machine. Every writing instrument is subject to normal wear, damage from improper use, and accumulation of debris on the type face. The resulting variations in printing may prove valuable in identifying a particular instrument. In some cases, dirty type faces may be useful in dating a document that was written on the instrument, if machine maintenance records are available.

Document Standards

Standards (samples of documents of known authorship or origin) are critically important to the expert examiner. In many cases, without both the document in question and a standard of reference, the laboratory examiner is limited as to the number of analyses he can perform. For example, a fragmented page of a telephone directory found in the possession of a suspect is not incriminating in itself. But if the fragment can be matched with a page of a directory found at the crime scene, the evidence takes on dramatically increased significance.

Analysis of the paper in a sample and a standard may determine that the composition of the paper is identical, thus providing a missing link in the case. Paper standards can also provide information used to identify the manufacturer of the paper and watermarks can establish that the paper in the questioned document and the standard were manufactured at the same time. The expert examiner can also determine if an indented impression appearing in a standard was made by the writing on the original questioned document. Thus, he can establish that the standard was underneath the original document at the time it was written. He can also ascertain whether the standard and sample have undergone similar stress or strain pressures, indicating that they were close at some time. A primary purpose of document comparison is to identify alterations of original documents, whether accomplished by mechanical or chemical means. Documents which are frequently altered include checks, receipts, affidavits, discharge papers, etc. Whenever a paper standard is available for submission with a questioned document (such as a blank check with a suspected forged check), both should be sent to the laboratory. Alterations of original documents are much easier to observe if a standard is available for reference.

Handwriting comparisons of a document with a standard may determine whether the document was written by one or by several persons, that a signature on a document is genuine, or that additions or deletions were made after an original was made.

Typewriter material comparisons can identify changes in document context made by a different typewriter, inconsistencies in the date of manufacture of a typewriter and the date of the document, the common origin of two or more documents (same machine used), or the specific typewriter used in preparing a particular document.

Collection of Document Standards

Following are the general requirements of the crime laboratory for document standards. However, if the standard is not available, the investigator should still submit a document for examination.

- An envelope that apparently "matches" the stationery on which a suspect document was prepared.
- The tablet from which a sheet of paper in question may have been torn.
- A blotter that may have been under the questioned document.
- A sample of a similar type paper of known age, if the age of the suspect document is important.
- The pen suspected to have been used to write the material in question.
- Pencils of the same lead type as believed used in writing on the questioned document.
- Material written in the hand of a suspect. (Comparisons are then conducted between writings of know authorship (the standard) and documents submitted in the case.)

- Typewriter standards.

Collected for the purpose of determining whether a questioned document was written on a particular machine.

Typewriter standards may be collected during an investigation or the typewriter may be submitted to the laboratory. If the investigator does not choose to submit the typewriter as evidence, he may obtain the typewriter standards himself.

The document in question should be reproduced on the standard typewriter unless it is excessively lengthy, in which case, only the first paragraph need be reproduced.

In addition to typing the content of the questioned material, each character on the typewriter should be reproduced, both in shift and nonshift positions with a space between each.

A separate sheet of paper should be used for each standard (if more than one machine is involved).

The same relative intensity used in typing the questioned document should be used in preparing the standard.

The name of the person making the standard, the date and place it was made, the manufacturer of the machine, and serial and model number should be typed on the front of each sheet.

Handwriting Identification and Handwriting Samples

This section deals briefly with the factors that affect the acquisition of handwriting skill and characteristics, and with the proper means of collecting handwriting standards.

The child learns to write by attempting to draw a character that will match a standard he is given. However, that initial handwriting skill is soon increased and changed as he matures and acquires experience in the nerve-muscle responses that are involved. These responses become habitual and his writing becomes more an automatic process to him, taking on highly individual aspects.

There are some who theorize that personality manifests itself in the subject's handwriting. However, there is sharp disagreement among experts as to just how personality may affect this process. In any event, it is certain that such factors as the pressures of business, the way a person consistently uses his hands, a conscious attempt at "style" (such as deliberate rearward slanting of the characters), muscular development, and physical disabilities can cause an individual's handwriting to change. Such change is usually a slow process; however, most individuals exhibit sufficiently consistent character formation, spacing, slant, and pressure characteristics to make it probable that their writing can be identified by an expert.

The police investigator collecting a sample of handwriting from a subject should be aware of the several possibilities of introducing variables that could significantly alter the usual style of the subject's writing. The more important of these are:

- *Shock or fear.* If the individual is badly shaken, as a suspect in a criminal investigation or a victim of recent criminal action may easily be, a quaver or other characteristic may show in the standard that is abnormal to the individual's style.

- *Unfamiliar writing materials.* Generally, those furnished for writing the standard should be as alike as possible to those apparently used in writing the questioned document. An individual unaccustomed to a fluid type fountain pen, as are many Americans today, may write somewhat different with such a pen, than with the more familiar ball point. The way the paper is ruled, or the fact that it is unruled may also affect the handwriting of persons who have become particularly accustomed to one type or the other.

- *Unfamiliar physical position or adverse conditions.* The subject should be allowed to sit down and be comfortable to write the standard. He should not be made to write on an irregular surface, under poor lighting, around loud noises or other obvious distractions. If there is some reason to suspect that the questioned document was written in some particular way such as standing, using a clip board, it may be advisable to take an additional standard written under those same conditions.

- *Writing without glasses that are normally worn.* The point needs no amplification. However, it is one for the investigator to check before taking a handwriting sample.

- *Taking an insufficient sample.* It is always good practice to have the subject write several full pages. The subject matter is not particularly important, however, there should be provision to have him repeat the same words or characters that are in question. There is danger, in taking a short, specific-type standard, that the subject will successfully alter his handwriting, or be so nervous or distraught during the writing that it will not be representative. Writing a several page sample will offer opportunity for him to unconsciously relax any deception he may be attempting, or simply to calm down.

As opposed to requested exemplars, constituting handwritten samples written by the subject with knowledge that the sample will be used in a police investigation, nonrequested samples can, and should, be sought from a variety of sources . . . .

Nonrequested exemplars offer two principal advantages. The first is that the writing is almost certain to be free of any conscious attempt at disguise or distortion by the subject. Such attempts must always be considered a possibility when taking requested examples. The second advantage is that nonrequested examples can often be found that date comparably to the time of the incident or offense under investigation which involved the suspect's writing. For example, a note figuring in the investigation of a homicide occurring 3 years previous could possibly be matched to a business letter handwritten by the suspect dated about the same time, together with canceled checks and other documents. Although handwriting styles normally undergo comparatively slow change, the ability to make both a style and temporal comparison of a subject's handwriting adds powerfully to any conclusions reached concerning identity.

The investigator should record and report to the expert who will examine the questioned document and the standard, the conditions under which a handwriting sample was taken. The apparent state of mind of the subject is also of interest in this regard.

OBTAINING HANDWRITING EXEMPLARS (SAMPLES)

A **questioned document** is any document or writing for which there is a question as to who wrote, typed, or made the marking on the document. The document or writing could be a check which the State is alleging was forged. The writing could be a demand note used in a robbery or kidnapping.

To determine who wrote or altered a questioned document, samples (exemplars) of genuine writings must be obtained. Handwriting samples could be obtained by the following means:

- Voluntary cooperation of the suspect
- Business transactions (renting a car, bank transaction, hotel, motel, etc.)
- Letters suspect wrote to other persons
- Job applications
- Business licenses (tavern, bartender, etc.)
- Grand jury or John Doe used to obtain handwriting
- Writings made as part of suspect's job
- Writings from a school or used in the military
- Legal papers on file (affidavits, wills, mortgages, etc.)
- Hospital or library records
- Handwriting samples found in wallets and on the person of an arrested suspect

WRITINGS AND DOCUMENTS WHICH ARE PROTECTED BY THE FOURTH AND FIFTH AMENDMENTS OF THE U.S. CONSTITUTION

Fourth Amendment Protection of Documents, Writings, and Records

The Fourth Amendment provides that "The right of the people to be secure in their persons, houses, papers and effects, against unreasonable searches and seizures, shall not be violated ...." Therefore, law enforcement officers and other governmental officials cannot intrude into a "zone of privacy" of a person to seize documents, writings, or records without a showing of proper authority. For example, law enforcement officers enter the home of an arrested person without a search warrant or consent and seize documents and writings which incriminate the defendant. This evidence cannot be used against the defendant as the evidence was obtained in a manner which violated the defendant's Fourth Amendment rights.

However, papers and documents exposed to public view have no right of privacy and therefore are not protected by the Fourth Amendment. Also, handwriting and the tone quality of a person's voice is exposed to the public and also is not protected by the Fourth Amendment, because there is no right of privacy. The following U.S. Supreme Court cases illustrate:

United States v. Mara

Supreme Court of the United States (1973)
410 U.S. 19, 93 S.Ct. 774

United States v. Dionisio

Supreme Court of the United States (1973)
410 U.S. 1, 93 S.Ct. 764

The Supreme Court held in these cases that handwriting, like speech, is a characteristic which is continually on display to the public and that there can be no greater expectation of privacy to the writing of an individual than there is to the tone quality of his voice. A grand jury can therefore order persons to submit samples of their handwriting just as a person can be requested to talk for identification purposes.

United States v. Miller

Supreme Court of the United States (1976)
425 U.S. 435, 96 S.Ct. 1619

The defendant was charged with various federal offenses. Microfilms of checks, deposit slips, and other records were obtained by the government by means of subpoenas duces tecum served upon officials of two banks where the defendant had accounts. The U.S. Supreme Court held that these documents and records were properly used as evidence in the defendant's trial because

- The evidence was business records of the banks and was not private papers of the defendant.
- The defendant had no legitimate "expectation of privacy" in the original checks and deposit slips because these writings were not confidential communications but negotiable instruments which were used in commercial transactions.

The U.S. Supreme Court ruled that

The depositor takes the risk, in revealing his affairs to another, that the information will be conveyed by that person to the government.... This Court has held repeatedly that the Fourth Amendment does not prohibit the obtaining of information revealed to a third party and conveyed by him to government authorities, even if the information is revealed on the assumption that it will be used only for a limited purpose and the confidence placed in the third party will not be betrayed.

Fifth Amendment Protection of Writings, Documents, and Records

The Fifth Amendment of the U.S. Constitution provides that "No person shall ... be compelled in any criminal case to be a witness against himself." The Fifth Amendment would therefore forbid demanding that a suspect write out a confession or otherwise incriminate himself by producing a writing. The U.S. Supreme Court stated the Fifth Amendment privilege against self-incrimination as follows:

> ... the constitutional privilege against self-incrimination ... is designed to prevent the use of legal process to force from the lips of the accused individual the evidence necessary to convict him or to force him to produce and authenticate any personal documents or effects that might incriminate him. *Bellis v. United States*, 417 U.S. at 88, 94 S.Ct. at 2183.

Although the government cannot force a suspect to produce a document which would incriminate the suspect, this does not mean that the government cannot seize a document lawfully which would incriminate the defendant. U.S. Supreme Court Justice Holmes stated this principle of law in 1913 as follows:

> A party is privileged from producing the evidence but not from its production. *Johnson v. United States*, 228 U.S. 457, 458, 33 S.Ct. 572 (1913).

The following U.S. Supreme Court case illustrates:

Andresen v. Maryland

Supreme Court of the United States (1976)
427 U.S. 463, 96 S.Ct. 2737

The defendant, an attorney who practiced alone, was convicted of real estate fraud. Business records were obtained from the defendant's office under the authority of a search warrant. The trial court permitted these records to be used as evidence, holding that the defendant had not been compelled to do anything which incriminated himself. At the trial, the records were authenticated by prosecution witnesses and not by the defendant. In affirming the defendant's conviction, the U.S. Supreme Court held that

There is no question that the records seized from petitioner's offices and introduced against him were incriminating. Moreover, it is undisputed that some of these business records contain statements made by petitioner....

This case thus falls within the principle stated by Mr. Justice Holmes: "A party is privileged from producing the evidence but not from its production." *Johnson v. United States*, 228 U.S. 457, 458, 33 S.Ct. 572, 57 L.Ed. 919 (1913). This principle recognizes that the protection afforded by the self-incrimination clause of the Fifth Amendment "adheres basically to the person, not to information that may incriminate him." *Couch v. United States*, 409 U.S., at 328, 93 S.Ct. at 611. Thus, although the Fifth Amendment may protect an individual from complying with a subpoena for the production of his personal records in his possession because the very act of production may constitute a compulsory authentication of incriminating information, ... a seizure of the same materials by law enforcement officers differs in a crucial respect—the individual against whom the search is directed is not required to aid in the discovery, production, or authentication of incriminating evidence....

Accordingly, we hold that the search of an individual's office for business records, their seizure, and subsequent introduction into evidence does not offend the Fifth Amendment's prescription that "[n]o person ... shall be compelled in any criminal case to be a witness against himself."

PROBLEMS

1. The defendant, Colonel Abel, was the highest-ranking Soviet spy taken into custody. Colonel Abel was arrested in a New York hotel room in the middle of the night. He was ordered to dress, pack, and then check out of his room. After Abel was taken to jail, FBI agents received consent from the hotel management to search the room. False identity papers and a coded message found in the room were used as evidence to convict Abel.

   Did the use of these documents violate Abel's Fifth Amendment rights? Are papers treated in a manner different from other property in the law of criminal evidence? Explain. *Abel v. United States*, 362 U.S. 217, 80 S.Ct. 683 (U.S. Sup.Ct.1960).

2. The defendant (Gouled) was a businessman who had contracts for supplies with the U.S. government. Army officers suspected him of defrauding the Army through the contracts. They sent a U.S. Army private who had known Gouled to visit Gouled, pretending to make a friendly call. While visiting Gouled and while Gouled was out of the room, the private searched Gouled's personal property and took several papers which were used to convict Gouled of criminal fraud.

   Should the papers be permitted to be used as evidence against Gouled? Explain. Could the papers be used in a civil action by the government against Gouled? Explain. *Gouled v. United States*, 255 U.S. 298, 41 S.Ct. 261 (U.S. Sup.Ct.1921).

NOTES

[1] Under the old common law, it was required that the signer or writer of the document or writing had to be produced. This requirement has generally been abolished except for proof of wills, for which an attesting witness is still required in some states. (See Rule 903 of the Federal Rules of Evidence in appendix B.)

[2] Federal Rule of Evidence 901(b)(8) and also the Uniform Rules of Evidence provide that the following evidence is "sufficient to support a finding that the matter in question is what its proponents claim":

(8) **Ancient documents or data compilation.** Evidence that a document or data compilation, in any form, (A) is in such condition as to create no suspicion concerning its authenticity, (B) was in a place where it, if authentic, would likely be, and (C) has been in existence 20 years or more at the time it is offered.

[3] 3 Blackstone, Commentaries 368.

[4] 235 Ga. 38, 218 S.E.2d 792 (1975).

[5] The material in this subsection is reprinted from the U.S. Department of Justice Law Enforcement Assistance Administration book, entitled *Crime Scene Search and Physical Evidence Handbook*.

Obtaining and Using Scientific Evidence

Scientific evidence is the product of many different sciences. A few of the sciences and skills used are chemistry, physics, mathematics, and medical and dental science. Crime laboratories with sophisticated equipment are often used. Highly skilled arts and specialized training are often required. Experts with skills, knowledge, and extensive experience are often called upon.

Scientific evidence has been discussed in previous chapters. Chapter 17 discusses the use of fingerprints as evidence, which requires skills, training, and calls on several different sciences. Photography is discussed in chapter 18. Photography is a skill and art which uses the science of chemistry and other sciences. The examination of questioned documents (chapter 19) requires knowledge, experience, and the use of the sciences of microscopy, chemistry, and photography.

THE IMPORTANCE OF SCIENTIFIC EVIDENCE

Experienced law enforcement officers state that most crimes are solved through the use of common sense and hard work. An officer who is investigating a crime may obtain enough information to identify the perpetrator of the offense but may find that he (or she) has insufficient evidence to charge and obtain a conviction. In such situations, the use of scientific techniques may provide the additional evidence necessary to carry the burden of proving guilt beyond a reasonable doubt.

In other situations, no other evidence is available to the investigating officer other than that evidence obtained from crime laboratories. In such situations, scientific evidence may be the starting point providing the link which leads to the solution of the crime.

For these reasons, it has been stated that scientific evidence has become one of the strongest weapons available for the successful prosecution of criminal offenders. However, judges and juries may overestimate the reliability of scientific evidence. This problem caused the Supreme Judicial Court of Massachusetts to state that

> We are aware that scientific proof may in some instances assume "a posture of mystic infallibility in the eyes of a jury of laymen." [1]

THE USE OF SCIENTIFIC EVIDENCE

Scientific evidence and expert testimony by scientists have become indispensible in criminal investigations and in criminal trials. During criminal investigations, scientific evidence could:

- Provide a lead (or leads) to head a criminal investigation in the right direction.

- Provide information eliminating a suspect as the offender (for example, blood or sperm found at a crime scene could show that the offender had blood group A, thus eliminating a suspect who had a different blood group).

- Establish that a crime had been committed or corpus delicti (scientific evidence could show that a fire was deliberately started (arson) or that death was caused by poisoning (murder or suicide)).

- Provide the independent corroborative evidence necessary to support a confession (see chapter 5), or it could corroborate and support other evidence presented by the prosecutor or the defense lawyer.

- Establish a link between the crime scene and the suspect, or the suspect and the victim of the crime.

- Prove one of the essential elements of the crime being investigated.

- Affirm or disprove an alibi.

- Establish the innocence of persons not involved in the crime.

- Encourage or induce a person to make a confession or an incriminating admission when the person is confronted with scientific evidence which incriminates them (if such a person were being held in custody, *Miranda* warnings would have to be given before the confrontation).

- By itself, scientific evidence could amount to:

  reasonable suspicion (for an investigative stop)

  probable cause (to make an arrest, obtain a search warrant, etc.)

  or could by itself be sufficient to establish proof beyond a reasonable doubt (necessary for a criminal conviction).

JUDICIAL NOTICE BY A COURT OF THE RELIABILITY OR "GENERAL ACCEPTANCE" OF A SCIENTIFIC PRINCIPLE

Before a court will permit expert witnesses to testify and present scientific evidence in a trial, there could be a showing (or the court could take judicial notice) that the scientific test or principle has received widespread scientific recognition in its field. The **general acceptance test** is the oldest method used to determine whether scientific evidence should be admissible for use in a court trial. The test was stated for the first time in the 1923 case of *Frye v. United States*,[2] when a Federal Court of Appeals held that

> Just when a scientific principle or discovery crosses the line between the experimental and demonstrable stages is difficult to define. Somewhere in this twilight zone the evidential force of the principle must

be recognized, and while courts will go a long way in admitting expert testimony deduced from a well-recognized scientific principle or discovery, the thing from which the deduction is made must be sufficiently established *to have gained general acceptance in the particular field in which it belongs.*

In the years since the 1923 *Frye* case, less emphasis has been placed by courts upon general acceptance of scientific discoveries and more emphasis has been placed upon the reliability of scientific techniques, tests, and procedures. The broad language of Rule 702 of the Federal Rules of Evidence now presents greater latitude and flexibility in the admission of scientific evidence:

> Rule 702: If scientific, technical, or other specialized knowledge will assist the trier of fact (jury or judge) to understand the evidence or to determine a fact in issue, a witness qualified as an expert by knowledge, skill, experience, training, or education, may testify thereto in the form of an opinion or otherwise.

MICROANALYSIS

The microscope was one of the earliest tools used for the development of scientific evidence. By microanalysis, the scientist is able to examine physical evidence under magnifications that would not be possible with the naked eye. Ordinarily, the field investigator collects and preserves the trace evidence or other objects for examination by the microanalyst, who is the scientist working in the laboratory. The microanalyst could have a wide variety of microscopes available to him (or her).

The comparison microscope is an invaluable improvement over the ordinary microscope. The comparison microscope permits the examination and comparison of two objects at the same time. For example, the bullet which killed a victim may be compared with a bullet fired from the defendant gun with a comparison microscope. Both bullets may be positioned in the comparison microscope to compare markings and pattern configurations.

Other instruments available to the microanalyst could be the phase, interference, and dark field microscopes, emission spectrography, infrared and ultraviolet spectrophotometry, atomic absorption spectrophotometry, electron microprobe X-ray analysis, X-ray diffraction and gas chromatrography, and the scanning electron microscope (SEM). The SEM is an expensive piece of electronic equipment. It permits observations of the surface of materials at magnifications up to 140 thousand times the original size. It also permits an elemental analysis of any portion of material in concentrations as low as one part per million. This would mean, for example, that arsenic or lead could be detected in a single red blood cell. It is estimated that it would take four thousand red blood cells laid end to end to equal one inch.

Microanalysis may be made of any physical evidence. Drugs may be observed and identified. Examinations may be made of trace evidence, hair, weapons, tools, metals, fibers, glass, debris, soil, paint, cloth, bullets, semen, etc. The following types of evidence are among the many which have been obtained by microanalysis:

"Justice is truth in action, and any instrumentality, which aids justice in the ascertaiment of truth, should be embraced without delay." Supreme Court of North Carolina in 1981 case of State v. Temple, 273 S.E. 2d 273.

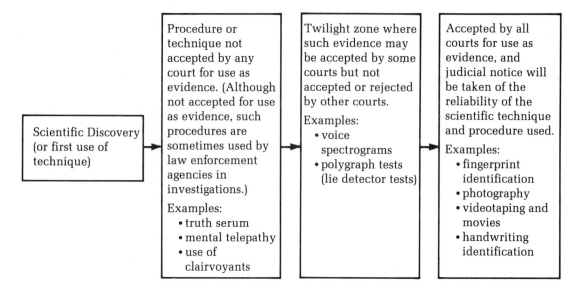

Figure 20.1   Development of Scientific Techniques, Tests, and Procedures

- Identification of cutting tools or burglarious tools from markings made by the tools.
- Matching of paint and metal scrapings from the scene of hit-and-runs.
- Analysis of glass fragments from break-ins and other sources.
- Identification of counterfeit money.
- Presence of trace material on fibers and clothing to establish environment or occupation.
- Identification of soil and other material on the shoes or clothing of a person to determine whether he was at the scene of the crime.
- Hair can only in unusual cases be identified as coming from a particular person. However, hair can be identified as either human or animal; as head, pubic, or body hair; and as to its color. The sex and the race of the person can also generally be determined.
- Wood can be identified by the matching of the wood grain; by whether it was sawed, chipped, or broken; and by the comparisons of the paint on the wood. If the wood evidence is large enough, it can be identified by type or species.
- Dust and soil are said to be present at practically all crime scenes. Soil (clay, sand, dirt, building and plant material) could be important evidence at an outdoor crime scene, or at an indoor crime scene where the material is

tracked in or is on the shoes of a victim or the suspect. Dust and soil are also often found on the floor mats of vehicles which could be linked to a crime scene or the person committing the crime.

- Fibers are identified in manners similar to hair. In the Atlanta murders case, Wayne Williams was charged with two of twenty-eight murders of blacks in 1982. Over sixty fiber comparisons were presented as evidence which linked the defendant to the two murders he was charged with, and ten other murders. Animal hair was linked to the defendant's dog. The microanalyst who testified for the State said it was "virtually impossible" for the fibers found on the victim to come from any source other than Williams. The Supreme Court of Georgia pointed out in the 1983 case of *Williams v. State* [3] that

> Part of the evidence used by the state to connect appellant with these crimes consisted of comparisons of fibers and hairs discovered on the victims' clothing, and bodies, and on items used in the recovery of their bodies, with fibers and hairs removed from appellant, his home and cars, and his German Shepherd dog. These comparisons were conducted by three state's experts—FBI Agent Harold Deadman, GBI employee Larry Peterson, and Royal Canadian Mounted Police employee Barry Gaudette.
>
> To compare the hairs and fibers found in the appellant's environment with those found on the victims, the state's experts used a variety of microscopes. In this regard, Agent Deadman, a microanalyst, described as follows the microscopes which can be used to compare fibers: 1) a stereobinocular microscope, which can magnify a single fiber about seventy times, and which is used to visually compare fibers; 2) a compound microscope, which can magnify a single fiber approximately 400 to 500 times, and which, like the stereobinocular microscope, is used to visually compare fibers; 3) a comparison microscope, which can magnify two fibers side by side, and which is used to compare the microscopic and optical properties of the two fibers; 4) a microspectrophotometer . . .; 5) a polarizing light microscope, which is used to examine the optical properties of fibers in a more discriminating fashion than that provided by a comparison microscope; and 6) a flourescence microscope, which is used to determine the type of light a fiber emits after it has been illuminated with a certain type of light. Additionally, a scanning electron microscope was used occasionally by the state's experts. From the transcript it is difficult to discern which of these microscopes were used to conduct each particular fiber comparison; however, Larry Peterson implied that the stereobinocular microscope, the comparison microscope, and the polarizing light microscope were used to conduct all of the comparisons. It is also apparent that several of the other microscopes, in particular the microspectrophotometer and the florescence microscope, were used to compare some selected fibers.

SPECTROGRAPHIC ANALYSIS

Whenever large or small quantities of unknown substances are made available to crime laboratories, it is necessary to perform some type of analysis either for identification or comparison. Spectrographic analysis is particularly useful in many situations. In comparing and identifying small amounts and smears, microanalysis may also be used.

Spectrographic analysis is a very common laboratory procedure used to compare two substances and to establish the identity of a questioned substance. Not only is chemical analysis by means of a spectrograph a practical and rapid method of identifying and comparing substances, but it has the additional advantage of providing a permanent photographic record of the finding which is made.

Scientists have known for many years that different substances burn at different temperatures and with different characteristic colors. In spectrographic analysis, the light emitted by the questioned substance on burning is passed through a prism in the spectrograph and a photographic record is made. In comparing a suspected substance with a known substance, photographic analysis of the two substances can be made for comparisons.

Through the use of a laboratory spectrograph, small amounts and smears of paint, inks, lipstick, dirt, metal, and other material may be analyzed precisely. The photographic record of the chemical analysis is then very valuable as evidence in court. An expert witness who is testifying as to an identification which was made can use the photograph as evidence to demonstrate the results of the procedure used. Examples of the use of spectrographic analysis are as follows:

- Small smears of lipstick, eyeshade, or other cosmetics found on the clothing or body of a suspect may be compared with those used by a female victim to determine whether they are identical.

- Small amounts of paint found on the clothing or body of a hit-and-run victim can be compared to paint taken from the vehicle of a suspect.

- Traces of material on tools and shoes may be compared to material at the crime scene to determine the source of the material on the tools or shoes.

NEUTRON ACTIVATION ANALYSIS EVIDENCE

The **Neutron Activation Analysis (NAA) technique** is a method used for the analysis of many types of very small particles of physical evidence. However, the forensic use of NAA for evidence in criminal courts is limited to gunshot residue analysis and a few others.

The NAA technique is reported to be far more reliable than the old "paraffin" test, and other tests used in an attempt to obtain evidence as to whether a suspect has recently fired a gun. Special facilities and highly skilled persons are needed to operate the expensive equipment. The following "hand swabbing" cases describe the process and procedures used in NAA:

State v. Toney

Court of Appeals of Missouri (1976)
537 S.W.2d 586

Neutron activation analysis evidence was used in the defendant's trial, which resulted in his conviction on two counts of murder, two counts of assault with intent to kill, and two counts of robbery with a deadly weapon. The Missouri Court of Appeals affirmed the convictions and the use of the neutron activation analysis evidence, holding that

On March 18, 1972, after appellant was in custody at the Maplewood Police Department, Robert Roither, a criminologist employed by the St. Louis County Police Department, processed the hands of appellant for the purpose of providing material for a neutron activation analysis to determine whether or not appellant's hands bore gunshot residue. Using a kit supplied by the University of Missouri Research Reactor Facility, Roither made separate swabs of the back and front of appellant's hands with Q-Tip cotton swabs dipped in diluted nitric acid. The four Q-Tips so used, along with a fifth which had, for control purposes, been only dipped in the acid solution, were replaced in separate vials, sealed and eventually delivered to the Research Reactor Facility on the campus of the University of Missouri at Columbia.

Dr. Matthew Eichor, a radio chemist at the Research Reactor Facility, received the swabs and testified to the procedures followed and the results obtained in their neutron activation analysis. Appellant's assignment of error on this appeal relates primarily to the admission of Doctor Eichor's testimony to the results of the analysis and, although numerous grounds of error in the admission of such testimony are argued in the brief, the one made at the trial and therefore properly preserved for review is that Doctor Eichor did not himself perform all of the steps involved in the analysis and that he had no personal knowledge pertaining to the steps performed by others.

The purpose of the analysis here involved was to ascertain the presence of antimony and barium on the hands of the person from whom the materials subjected to analysis have been taken. Barium and antimony are used in the primer-material of American made ammunition. The presence of such materials on the hand of a person may indicate that such person has recently handled or fired a weapon.

Such elements appear in gunshot residue in minute quantities, and neutron activation analysis is a procedure which has been developed for the determination of whether or not such elements are found in a test sample and the quantity thereof found. As explained by Doctor Eichor, the process here employed involved placing each of the swabs in a separate plastic container which is then placed in a nuclear reactor where it is subjected to atomic radiation. Various trace elements in the sample become radioactive as they absorb neutrons. The test sample is then removed from the reactor and processed chemically for the separation of the radioactive barium and antimony. In this process the swabs which were employed are destroyed. The radioactive barium and antimony are then placed in a detector with a multi-channel analyzer which analyzes and records the gamma rays emitted by the radioactive elements in the sample. The detector records an electrical pulse when gamma ray is detected in a crystal. A print-out supplies the number of pulses detected in the detector. Such results are compared with those for known amounts of radioactive barium and antimony and the ratio permits a mathematical calculation of the quantity of the respective elements, expressed in micrograms, present in the test sample. These results are then compared with results of similar testing of material taken from the hands of persons known not to have recently fired a gun and from persons known to have fired guns.

United States v. Bridges

U.S. Court of Appeals Seventh Circuit (1974)
499 F.2d 179

The defendant was convicted of unlawfully possessing and using an unregistered dynamite bomb to damage a building. After the defendant was arrested, his hands were swabbed and the evidence obtained was used in the criminal trial. The hand swabbing was done without his consent and without a search warrant. The Court held that

We think that swabbing, like drawing the defendant's blood in *Schmerber v. California,* 384 U.S. 757, 86 S.Ct. 1826, 16 L.Ed.2d 908 (1966), was not a violation of that Amendment's protection against self-incrimination, since the swabbing did not "provide the state with evidence of a testimonial or communicative nature ...." Id. at 761.

Neither did the Court err in denying the motion on the Fourth Amendment ground.

In *Schmerber* the Court held that the warrantless intrusion into Schmerber's body for blood was reasonable in light of the exigent circumstances therein; the blood was drawn to determine its alcoholic content which diminishes rapidly in time.

The Second Circuit, in *United States v. D'Amico,* 408 F.2d 331, 333 (2d Cir.1969), held that admission into evidence of clippings of D'Amico's hair did not violate his Fourth Amendment right....

It is apparent that had the agents not swabbed Bridges' hands at the time, the opportunity may not have knocked again, especially if Bridges washed his hands. Accordingly, we find that the intrusion upon Bridges was similar to that in *Schmerber* and *D'Amico.* The swabbing was no more offensive to Bridges' person than fingerprinting or photographing him.... We hold that the swabbing was not an unreasonable search, and affirm the district court's ruling.

United States v. Love

U.S. Court of Appeals Fifth Circuit (1973)
482 F.2d 213

The defendants were convicted for maliciously destroying a building by means of an explosive and possessing an unregistered firearm. Without their consent and without a search warrant, officers swabbed their hands, and the evidence obtained was used in their criminal trial.

In response to the argument that the defendant had the right to have his attorney present during the hand swabbing, the Court held that

> Oglesby's Sixth Amendment contention proceeds on the assertion from *United States v. Wade,* 388 U.S. 218, 87 S.Ct. 1926, 18 L.Ed.2d 1149 (1967), that counsel is required at critical stages of the criminal process, and, in his view, what could be more critical than the removal of swabbings. There is no doubt that defendants were validly arrested and that the swabbings were a search and seizure incident to that arrest.... But·the presence of counsel at the taking of the samples was not constitutionally required.

After reviewing the U.S. Supreme Court cases of *Cupp v. Murphy* (obtaining material from under Murphy's fingernails) and *Schmerber v. California* (obtaining blood for alcohol testing),[4] the Court held that

> The nitrate on Oglesby's hands was even more likely to vanish than the materials lodged under Murphy's fingernails, or the alcohol in Schmerber's blood. The first vigorous scrubbing of the hands would have destroyed Murphy's material, but merely rubbing the hands would have destroyed the nitrate oils. Moreover, since Oglesby could testify whether the swabbings were actually taken and sealed, counsel could perform no service justifying invocation of constitutional principles.

FORENSIC PATHOLOGY

The television series "Quincy" popularized the role of the medical examiner or coroner in the use of science and skill in determining the cause of death and obtaining evidence. Many medical examiners may also conduct hearings, called inquests, for which witnesses may be subpoenaed and placed under oath to obtain their testimony.

Do the Dead Tell Tales?

When the old saying, "Dead men tell no tales" was quoted to a prominent medical examiner recently, he disagreed and quoted William Shakespeare as saying, "Murder, though it has no tongue, will speak with most miraculous organ."

The dead do tell tales, in that an autopsy will most often provide information as to the cause of death, the time of death, and sometimes the identity of the deceased (if this is not already known).

Proof of the Cause of Death

In a criminal homicide case, the State must prove beyond reasonable doubt that (1) the deceased died as the result of a criminal act, and (2) that the defendant was a party to the criminal act causing the death of the deceased.

Under the law, there is a presumption that death was due to natural causes.[5] Police investigation and investigations by a medical examiner are made to determine whether death was the result of homicide, suicide, accident, or natural causes.

If a criminal homicide is charged, the State must overcome the presumption that the death was due to natural causes by the testimony of an expert witness (either a medical doctor or a pathologist). Proof that death was caused by a criminal act is known as corpus delicti.

In proving corpus delicti, the pathologist will often testify as to the autopsy conducted on the body of the deceased. The cause of death must be specifically identified and proven. Expert witnesses for the defense could contradict a witness for the State and could testify that the deceased died of natural causes or in a manner other than what the State is seeking to prove.

In proving the cause of death, witnesses for the State will ordinarily also testify as to the time of death, which could be a critical element in the State's case against the defendant. Other injuries and the condition of the body of the deceased could provide evidence of the events which occurred before (or after) the criminal homicide.

Identity of a Deceased

When a body is badly decomposed, charred, or dismembered, identity of the body could be a problem. Fingerprints or dental work could specifically identify a deceased if such evidence is available. Examination of the bones by an anthropologist can produce information as to the sex, age, race, body size, and sometimes cause of death, health, and occupation of the deceased.

The forensic anthropologist with expert analytical skills can often provide considerable information obtained by the examination of skeletal remains. To law enforcement officers, the forensic anthropologist is an aid and tool in crime detection. Anthropologists also provide an understanding of society by studies of remains of persons who lived in ancient societies hundreds and sometimes thousands of years ago.

When fingerprints and dental information are not available, and the forensic anthropologist is unable to obtain evidence sufficient for identification from the skeletal remains, a few options remain for investigators. Facial reconstruction is a procedure generally not used until all else fails.

After the Chicago homosexual serial killer, John Wayne Gacy, was taken into custody, the remains of over thirty young men were found. When some of these young men could not be identified, facial reconstruction was used. Measurement of the remains were used to determine body height, size, and other proportions. An internationally recognized expert, Mr. Clyde Snow of the University of Oklahoma, with the help of a medical illustrator and sculptor, created heads with facial features.

Mr. Snow states that reconstructions cannot be used for positive identifications, but can often create "a good enough resemblance" to enable someone to identify the deceased. Snow also worked on the identification of the skeleton remains of Nazi war criminal Josef Mengele.

SCIENTIFIC EVIDENCE OF SPEEDING VIOLATIONS

Excessive speed on highways is a factor causing many deaths, injuries, and property damage on American highways and streets. Law enforcement officers have always been able to testify that they "clocked" the suspect by using the speedometer of the police vehicle. Visual observation of the officer may also be used as evidence.[6] The following equipment is now also used by law enforcement agencies to detect violations of speed limits:

- Radar speed detection devices (the word *radar* is an acronym for Radio Detection and Ranging. The term *radar* is applied both to the technique and the equipment used.)
- VASCAR (Visual Average Speed Computer and Record) See the case of *State v. Finkle*[7] as an example of a court taking judicial notice of the scientific reliability of VASCAR.

Though judicial notice by courts of the scientific reliability of such devices is necessary in order for evidence of speed violations to be admissible, statutes in some states have recognized the scientific reliability of radar evidence. The usual foundation for the introduction of such evidence is proof that

- The operator of the equipment was properly trained and was qualified.
- The equipment had been checked, tested, and was operating accurately.
- The officer observed the defendant's vehicle as the vehicle was violating the speed limit.
- The defendant was the operator of the vehicle identified as violating the speed limit.

FIREARM EVIDENCE

Law enforcement officers testifying in cases in which firearms were used or will be introduced as evidence should be prepared to testify as to the following:

- Location of the firearm at the time it was recovered for use as evidence by the officer. If the weapon contained live ammunition, the exact position of the ammunition in the firearm.

- Identification of the person in possession of the weapon before or at the time of the crime, if such information is available.

- Type of firearm (revolver, semiautomatic pistol, rifle, shotgun, etc.). The caliber or the gauge of the weapon.

- Condition and appearance of the weapon at the time of recovery. What was the position of the hammer and safety of the weapon at the time of recovery? Was there evidence that the weapon had been fired?

- The number and location of spent cartridges. Were there reports from witnesses as to the number of shots fired?

- The number and location of spent bullets. What were the number of shots fired? What injury or death was caused by the shooting? Which of the spent bullets are accounted for and which are not?

- The name of the person who fired the weapon. What was his position at the crime scene each time the weapon was fired?

- Efforts made to obtain additional evidence, such as fingerprints and trace evidence from the weapon; hand swabbing for neutron activation analysis, etc.

At the crime laboratory, the firearm would again be examined for any evidence linking the weapon to a suspect. This would be followed by an examination of the interior of the barrel and chamber of the weapon. After the weapon was thoroughly examined, it would then be checked for its general operating condition. The triggerpull and the operating condition of the safety would be tested. Information obtained regarding the operation of the weapon might determine a defense that the firearm accidently discharged.

If the weapon had previously been fired, it must be fired again for further tests which will be conducted. Crime laboratories have firing boxes into which a weapon may be discharged in such a manner that the spent bullet or projectile can be easily recovered.

The spent bullet and the cartridge casing from the test firing are then examined under a microscope for individual characteristics and pattern configurations. Comparisons are then made with spent bullets and cartridge casings from the crime scene being investigated, or from other crime scenes or killings. As a result of this study and comparisons, the laboratory scientist can then come to one of the following conclusions or opinions:

- That because the spent bullets and/or cartridge casings which were compared have such identical markings and pattern configurations, it can be positively concluded that the weapon of the defendant fired the bullet found at the scene of the crime.

- That because the comparisons did not show identical markings and pattern configurations, the weapon of the defendant did not fire the bullet found at the scene of the crime.

- That the results of the comparisons are inconclusive because the spent bullet found at the scene of the crime was fragmented or distorted in such a way that an opinion cannot be reached by the laboratory scientist.

Because no formula exists by which laboratory scientists can match patterns and count lines in comparing spent bullets and cartridge casings, the field of firearms identification is therefore primarily a skill and an art rather than a science.

DRUG TESTS AS SCIENTIFIC EVIDENCE

For many years, drug abuse has been a terrible problem in our society. The extent of this problem, which is growing rather than diminishing, is illustrated by the following 1986 estimates of the U.S. National Institute of Justice:

- Twenty-five percent of all general hospital admissions arise from drug abuse, illustrating the terrible costs in human lives and misery.
- Forty percent of hospital admissions from accidents are drug related.
- Half of the national cost of accidents (estimated at $81 billion) is directly attributable to drug abuse.
- A few years ago, deaths from cocaine overdose were at a rate of twenty-five per year. The rate in 1986 was twenty-five per week.
- Drug addiction of newborn babies is now a serious public health concern.
- Urinalysis testing of fourteen thousand persons arrested in Washington D.C. and New York City in 1986 showed that more than half had been using dangerous drugs such as cocaine, PCP, or heroin.
- Nearly a third of the drug-using arrestees in New York City and almost two-fifths of those in Washington had evidence of the use of more than one drug at the time of their arrest.

Not only is the national cost of drug abuse staggering, but drug abuse substantially increases crime rates, thus increasing many people's fear and anxiety of becoming crime victims.

The national strategy against drugs works on two fronts: (1) to reduce the supply of drugs, and (2) to reduce the demand for drugs. The 1986 Comprehensive Drug Control Bill, passed by the Congress of the United States, provides additional funds and authority to achieve these goals.

Evidence of Death Caused by Drugs

As the number and complexity of drugs available for use both legally and illegally in our chemical society increases, the problem of identification of drugs in the body has also increased. Some drugs are devastating in such tiny quantities that it may be impossible to detect them, even by the most advanced techniques known to scientists at this time.

For these reasons, the observations and the information which law enforcement officers might be able to obtain has become more important to doctors attempting to save lives or attempting to determine the cause of death. The following might be important evidence and information:

- The appearance of the body of the person.
- Bottles, vials, and other containers on or near the body.

A Not-So-Trivial Question:

What do John Belushi, Len Bias, and Janis Joplin have in common?

Answer: They used drugs and they're dead.

Source: State of New York State Education Department (Substance Abuse) pamplet.

- Information from relatives, friends, and neighbors of the person. For example, information that a child was sampling a prescription of his mother's would in most cases be very useful, particularly when the drug caused no observable change in the child's body.
- Suicide notes which might disclose the type of drug used.
- Information as to whether other suicide attempts were made.

Identification of Illegal Drugs as Evidence in Criminal Trials

In all criminal trials for possession, sale, or manufacture of illegal drugs, the government must present evidence proving that the drugs which were seized are contraband. Not only must expert witnesses positively identify the drugs, but they must also testify as to the methods and tests used.

Expert witnesses will often testify that a screening test was used first, to eliminate the possibility that the drug was some other substance. The expert witness will go on to testify that a verification test was then used, and that the results caused the expert to conclude that the substance is the illegal drug which the state charges in its complaint against the defendant.

Some drugs can be identified under a microscope. Other drugs can be identified by use of one or more of the many tests used in laboratories. For example, the Duquenois-Levine test is commonly used to identify marijuana. Marijuana may also be identified by microscopic tests. Many of the tests used are color tests that cause the substance tested to turn a known color when solutions are added.

Urine tests are the best-known chemical tests used to determine the presence of narcotics in persons. Different urine tests are used to test for various drugs. Urine tests are more sensitive than the Nalline test. Nalline, which is a narcotic itself, is injected into a person to detect the presence (or absence) of other narcotics.

Drug Testing by Employers

In 1986, the Attorney General of the United States urged employers not only to test employees for drugs, but also to inspect lockers, watch parking lots closely, and if necessary, spy on nearby taverns. Persons who urge drug testing in the workplace point to some of the following alarming statistics:

- Anywhere from 10 percent to 23 percent of workers use drugs on the job.

- Accident rates on the job are up.
- Lost productivity due to alcohol and drugs is close to $100 billion per year.

Polls show that the public believes the government should spend more money fighting drugs, and that there should be more testing for drug use.

About a third of the large corporations in the United States test job applicants for drug use prior to employment. In 1986, about 18 percent of the firms responding to questions stated that they test employees for drugs if supervisors suspect intoxication because of an accident or the worker's behavior.

In 1986, drug screening and testing for employers was a $60-million-a-year business, and was expected to grow within the next few years to a $200-million-a-year business. It is also reported that another $60 million worth of drug-testing products are sold annually.

EVIDENCE OF ALCOHOLIC INTOXICATION

Alcohol is the most widely abused and misused drug in America, and in the world. Evidence of intoxication is often necessary in many criminal trials to prove an essential element of the crime charged. Evidence of intoxication can also be relevant evidence in other criminal cases such as homicide or rape.

Evidence of intoxication can consist of testimony by witnesses as to what they saw and smelled. After describing the appearance, the conduct, the movements, the speech, and the smell of a defendant, ordinary witnesses may also testify as to their opinion of whether a defendant or other person was intoxicated or not.

Chemical tests used to determine intoxication include analysis of blood, urine, and breath. Although blood tests are believed to be the most reliable, the most commonly used evidence presented in court trials is chemical tests of the breath. Equipment used to obtain this evidence is commercially known as the Drunkometer, Breathalyzer, Intoximeter, and the Intoxilyzer. Law enforcement officers qualified to administer these tests ordinarily appear as witnesses to testify as to the procedures used and the results of the tests. The officers may also testify as to the appearance of the defendant, his speech, and his smell. The officer may also testify to give his opinion, based upon his observations, as to whether the defendant was intoxicated.

Chemical tests used to determine intoxication in corpses include direct analysis of brain tissue and spinal fluid analysis. Blood tests may be used in determining intoxication in hospitalized persons just as they may be used with corpses.

Implied Consent and the Crime of Refusal to Submit to a Chemical Test

State statutes provide that a person who drives or operates a motor vehicle on the highways of that state shall be deemed to have given consent to one or more tests of his or her breath, blood, or urine for the purposes of determining the presence or quantity of alcohol or a controlled substance. This is known as **implied consent.**

When a law enforcement officer has probable cause to believe that a person is driving or operating a vehicle on a public highway under the influence of alcohol or a controlled substance, the officer may request the person to submit to a chemical test as required by the statutes of that state. Refusal to submit to a chemical test as requested by a law enforcement officer under the statutes of the state is a crime separate from the crime of driving under the influence. The following 1983 U.S. Supreme Court case illustrates:

South Dakota v. Neville

Supreme Court of the United States (1983)
459 U.S. 553, 103 S.Ct. 916

South Dakota police officers stopped the defendant's car after he failed to stop at a stop sign. When the defendant was asked to get out of his car, he staggered and fell against the car to support himself. The defendant smelled of alcohol and did not have a driver's license because it had been revoked after a previous driving-while-intoxicated conviction. After the defendant failed field sobriety tests, he was placed under arrest and read his *Miranda* rights. The defendant acknowledged that he understood his rights and agreed to talk without a lawyer present. When the police officer requested that the defendant take a test to determine his blood-alcohol level, the defendant refused, stating, "I'm too drunk, I won't pass the test." Two further requests were made but the defendant refused, continuing to state that he was too drunk to pass the test. Evidence of the defendant's refusal to take a test to determine blood-alcohol level was suppressed because of the officer's failure to advise the defendant that the refusal could be used against him at trial. In holding that it was not necessary for the officers to warn the defendant, the U.S. Supreme Court ruled that

> The carnage caused by drunk drivers is well documented and needs no detailed recitation here. This Court, although not having the daily contact with the problem that the state courts have, has repeatedly lamented the tragedy .... ("The increasing slaughter on our highways, most of which should be avoidable, now reaches the astounding figures only heard of on the battlefield"); ... (deploring "traffic irresponsibility and the frightful carnage it spews upon our highways"); ... ("The slaughter on the highways of this Nation exceeds the death toll of all our wars"); ... (recognizing the "compelling interest in highway safety").
>
> As part of its program to deter drinkers from driving, South Dakota has enacted an "implied consent" law .... This statute declares that any person operating a vehicle in South Dakota is deemed to have consented to a chemical test of the alcoholic content of his blood if arrested for driving while intoxicated. In *Schmerber v. California,* 384 U.S. 757, ... this Court upheld a state-compelled blood test against a claim that it infringed the Fifth Amendment right against self-incrimination, made applicable to the States through the Fourteenth Amendment. We recognized that a coerced blood test infringed to some degree the "inviolability of the human personality" and the "requirement that the State procure the evidence against an accused 'by its

Alcohol is not a stimulant but has a depressing effect upon body functions

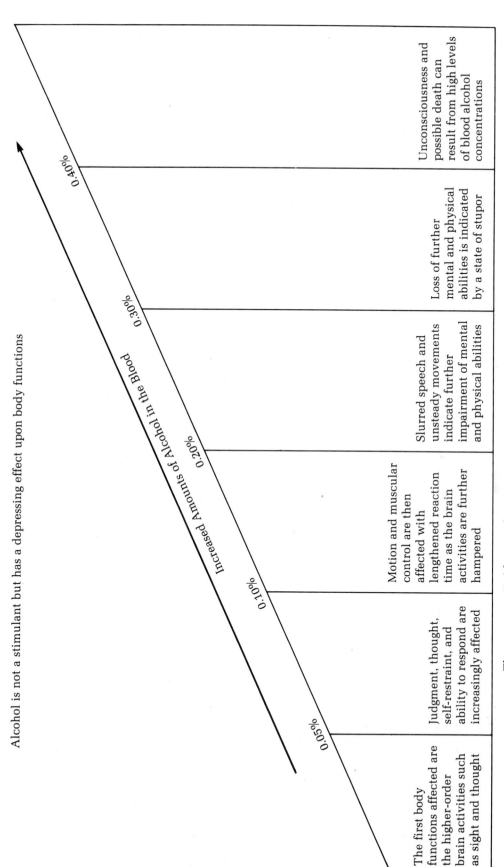

Increased Amounts of Alcohol in the Blood

0.05%

0.10%

0.20%

0.30%

0.40%

The first body functions affected are the higher-order brain activities such as sight and thought

Judgment, thought, self-restraint, and ability to respond are increasingly affected

Motion and muscular control are then affected with lengthened reaction time as the brain activities are further hampered

Slurred speech and unsteady movements indicate further impairment of mental and physical abilities

Loss of further mental and physical abilities is indicated by a state of stupor

Unconsciousness and possible death can result from high levels of blood alcohol concentrations

Figure 20.2   Evidence of Intoxication and Effects on Bodily Functions

own independent labors,' " but noted the privilege has never been given the full scope suggested by the values it helps to protect .... We therefore held that the privilege bars the State only from compelling "communications" or "testimony." Since a blood test was "physical or real" evidence rather than testimonial evidence, we found it unprotected by the Fifth Amendment privilege.

In contrast to these prohibited choices, the values behind the Fifth Amendment are not hindered when the State offers a suspect the choice of submitting to the blood-alcohol test or having his refusal used against him. The simple blood-alcohol test is so safe, painless, and commonplace, see *Schmerber,* 384 U.S., at 771, ... that respondent concedes, as he must, that the State could legitimately compel the suspect, against his will, to accede to the test. Given, then, that the offer of taking a blood-alcohol test is clearly legitimate, the action becomes no *less* legitimate when the State offers a second option of refusing the test, with the attendant penalties for making that choice. Nor is this a case where the State has subtly coerced respondent into choosing the option it had no right to compel, rather than offering a true choice. To the contrary, the State wants respondent to choose to take the test, for the inference of intoxication arising from a positive blood-alcohol test is far stronger than that arising from a refusal to take the test.

We recognize, of course, that the choice to submit or refuse to take a blood-alcohol test will not be an easy or pleasant one for a suspect to make. But the criminal process often requires suspects and defendants to make difficult choices .... We hold, therefore, that a refusal to take a blood-alcohol test, after a police officer has lawfully requested it, is not an act coerced by the officer, and thus is not protected by the privilege against self-incrimination ....

... It is true the officers did not inform respondent of the further consequence that evidence of refusal could be used against him in court, but we think it unrealistic to say that the warnings given here implicitly assure a suspect that no consequences other than those mentioned will occur. Importantly, the warning that he could lose his driver's license made it clear that refusing the test was not a "safe harbor," free of adverse consequences.

While the State did not actually warn respondent that the test results could be used against him, we hold that such a failure to warn was not the sort of implicit promise to forgo use of evidence that would unfairly "trick" respondent if the evidence were later offered against him at trial. We therefore conclude that the use of evidence of refusal after these warnings comported with the fundamental fairness required by due process.

BLOOD AND OTHER BODY FLUIDS AS EVIDENCE

Blood is sometimes found at the scene of crimes of violence such as sex offenses, homicides, or assaults. It could also be found at the scene of a nonviolent offense such as burglary. If the blood or other body fluid is that of the victim, the evidence will not provide a lead or link to the perpetrator of the offense.

Blood from the offender could be found on the clothing of the victim, or under the fingernails of the victim, or splattered on the ground, floor, or some other object. Blood splatter patterns could show the direction in which the person was moving, where a crime occurred, and the height that the blood fell.

Approximately 40 percent of the population in the United States has type A blood; 43 percent has type O; 14 percent has type B; and 3 percent has type AB. Blood can be identified as being of one of these types, and it can also be identified by blood groups.

Blood groups are found not only in blood. Approximately 80 percent of the population are secretors, and have blood group substances present in their perspiration, saliva, tears, semen, vaginal fluids, and mucus. Therefore, semen found at the scene of a rape would likely provide the blood type of the offender. If a suspect does not have a blood type which matches the type obtained from the evidence, this would be very strong evidence eliminating him as the offender.

The use of blood types and blood grouping techniques is used not only in criminal cases but also in civil hearings. The use of such evidence is used in paternity disputes. Expert witnesses would be needed to introduce and use such scientific evidence.

EXPERT TESTIMONY AS TO MENTAL DISEASE, DEFECTS, AND INCOMPETENCY

All persons are inferred to be sane and to intend the natural and probable consequences of their deliberate acts. The question of insanity or incompetency because of mental disease or defect is usually brought before criminal courts at one of the following stages of the criminal proceedings:

- When there is reason to doubt a defendant's competency to proceed with the trial. A defendant who as a result of mental disease or defect is unable to understand the proceedings against him, or is unable to assist in his own defense, cannot be tried and convicted.

- When the defense enters a plea of not guilty because of mental disease or defect.

In order to determine whether a defendant is competent to stand trial or to determine whether the defendant was mentally responsible at the time he committed the crime, expert witnesses are needed to assist the court and the factfinder. After medical experts have examined the defendant, they may testify as to their findings and conclusions. After listening to the testimony and opinions of the expert witnesses, judges and juries make the determination as to whether the defendant was competent or criminally responsible at the time the crime was committed.[8]

After many defendants are convicted of such sex crimes as rape, they are also examined by medical experts for possible mental and physical aberrations and defects. Should the examining doctors recommend specialized treatment for mental or physical aberrations which are found, the trial court would hold a hearing to consider commitment of the defendant for such treatment.

In the 1985 case of *Ake v. Oklahoma,* 470 U.S. 68, 105 S.Ct. 1087 (1985), the U.S. Supreme Court made the following observations regarding psychiatrists as expert witnesses:

Failure to Have Lab Tests Done ... Could Result in the Conviction of Innocent Persons

Failure to have lab tests done on body fluid samples obtained after sexual assaults resulted in convictions of innocent persons in the following cases:

- In 1986 a New Jersey man, sentenced to life in prison plus fifty years, was freed when tests of vaginal fluids taken at the time of the crime showed that the man did not commit the crimes. The rape, sodomy, and kidnapping occurred in 1974 but the fluids obtained as evidence at the time of the crime were not tested until October 1986.

- A Wisconsin man served nine years of a sentence for the attempted murder and rape of a fifteen-year-old girl. Neither the police, the prosecutor, nor the defense lawyer had the semen found on the victim's clothing tested. When it was tested in 1984, the lab tests showed that the attacker had type B blood and the man in prison for the crime had type A blood. The man sued his defense lawyer and recovered $500,000 in a settlement.

Psychiatry is not ... an exact science, and psychiatrists disagree widely and frequently on what constitutes mental illness, on the appropriate diagnosis to be attached to given behavior and symptoms, on cure and treatment, and on likelihood of future dangerousness. Perhaps because there often is no single, accurate psychiatric conclusion on legal insanity in a given case, juries remain the primary factfinders on this issue, and they must resolve differences in opinion within the psychiatric profession on the basis of the evidence offered by each party. When jurors make this determination about issues that inevitably are complex and foreign, the testimony of psychiatrists can be crucial and "a virtual necessity if an insanity plea is to have any chance of success." By organizing a defendant's mental history, examination results and behavior, and other information, interpreting it in light of their expertise, and then laying out their investigative and analytic process to the jury, the psychiatrists for each party enable the jury to make its most accurate determination of the truth on the issue before them. It is for this reason that States rely on psychiatrists as examiners, consultants, and witnesses, and that private individuals do as well, when they can afford to do so. In so saying, we neither approve nor disapprove the widespread reliance on psychiatrists but instead recognize the unfairness of a contrary holding in light of the evolving practice.

The foregoing leads inexorably to the conclusion that, without the assistance of a psychiatrist to conduct a professional examination on issues relevant to the defense, to help determine whether the insanity defense is viable, to present testimony, and to assist in preparing the cross-examination of a State's psychiatric witnesses, the risk of an inaccurate resolution of sanity issues is extremely high. With such assistance, the defendant is fairly able to present at least enough information to the jury, in a meaningful manner, as to permit it to make a sensible determination.

Table 20.1 Lost Evidence and the Duty of the Government to Preserve Evidence

For a defendant to show that a constitutional violation has occurred, it must be shown that

- The evidence was material so as to affect the outcome of the defendant's case; and that

- The evidence was favorable to the defendant.

EVIDENCE INVOLVED	CASE	REMEDY
Failure to preserve the deceased victim's hands in a condition suitable for scientific testing to determine whether she had been holding a gun.	*People ex rel. Gallagher ...* 656 P.2d 1287 (Colo.1983). The defendant claimed his wife attacked him with a gun which discharged and killed her when he defended himself. The defense lawyer requested a "trace metal test," but no test was conducted because, as a standard embalming practice, morticians scrubbed the victim's hands with a chemical solution preventing any test.	The Supreme Court of Colorado reduced defendant's conviction from first- to second-degree murder, holding that the hands should have been in a preserved condition suitable for scientific testing.
The government deported two aliens before the defense lawyer could question them as potential witnesses.	*United States v. Valenzuela–Bernal,* 458 U.S. 858, 102 S.Ct. 3440 (1982). The defendant was convicted of knowingly transporting illegal aliens into the United States after being arrested with three illegal aliens. The government deported two of the aliens after it was determined they possessed no evidence material to the defendant's case.	The U.S. Supreme Court held that no violation of the defendant's Fifth or Sixth Amendment rights had occurred. Defendant's conviction was affirmed.
Police failed to preserve breath samples taken to test for drunk driving. California police do not save breath samples, although it is possible to do so.	*California v. Trombetta,* 467 U.S. (1984). Because the accuracy of Intoxilyzers is checked regularly by the State, and since testing procedures ensure the accuracy of the test results, the breath samples which would be preserved would simply confirm defendant's high blood-alcohol concentration at the time of his arrest.	The U.S. Supreme Court affirmed defendant's conviction, holding that his due process rights were not violated.

EVIDENCE INVOLVED	CASE	REMEDY
Sperm was found in the vaginal fluid sample taken from a rape victim. Defense lawyer requested the evidence, but a sperm sample was not made available for testing by defense.	*Hilliard v. Spalding*, 719 F.2d 1443 (9th Cir.1983). Since 80 percent of the male population secrete blood into their semen, the test could possibly show defendant did not commit rape. Sample was material and should have been produced for defendant.	A hearing was ordered to determine if prosecutor knew the sample had been taken, and had control of sample and whether a request from the defense would have been successful.
Drug urinalysis sample was inadvertently destroyed before it could be independently tested by the defense.	*Frost v. United States*, 22 M.J. 95 (1986), review denied by U.S. Supreme Ct. ___ U.S. ___, 40 CrL 4057 (U.S.Sup.Ct.1986). The defendant's conviction of the possession of marijuana was affirmed by the U.S. Air Force Court of Military Review in view of *California v. Trombetta* (see above).	Review denied by the U.S. Supreme Court.

PROBLEMS

1. A murder occurred as the victim was sitting in the back seat of a yellow 1974 Mercury sedan. The defendant (Gerald) and his brother (Harold) were charged with the murder. The car belonged to Gerald. During the murder trial, an expert witness for the State testified that he had found "hairs inside the yellow Mercury which were microscopically similar to sample hairs taken from Gerald and Harold." However, before the trial the prosecutor for the State failed to provide the defense with samples of the hair found in the car.

   Should a new trial be ordered for the failure to provide samples of the hair to the defense? Give reasons for your answer. *State v. Tillinghast*, 465 A.2d 191 (Rhode Island Sup.Ct.1983).

2. Police received a report from a motel manager that money had been stolen from coin-operated machines in the motel. The police officer investigating the theft put fluorescent powder and paste onto and around the coin box of a vending machine in an effort to identify the thief. Within a short time, money was again taken from the machine. Because coins with fluorescent powder were found in the motel cash register, suspicion then focused on motel employees who had access to the keys of the vending machines. All of these employees were told to assemble and to place their hands under an ultraviolet light. Police were then able to determine that traces of powder and paste were on the hands of the defendant. The defendant had not been

asked to consent to the procedure, but had done so without making any objections.

May the evidence obtained be used in a criminal trial of the defendant? Did the defendant have a reasonable expectation of privacy in substances on his hands whose incrimination nature was not visible to the naked eye? Explain. *Colorado v. Santistevan,* 715 P.2d 792 (1986), review denied ___ U.S. ___, 40 CrL 4089 (U.S.Sup.Ct.1986).

3. Police found the body of a woman in her home. The woman was severely beaten and lying in a large pool of blood. Many broken mason jars were near the body, and there was broken glass and blood throughout the house. The woman was separated from her husband. She had commenced an annulment action against him. After the body was found, a police officer telephoned the husband and asked him to drive to the house to identify the body. The husband entered the house and identified his wife. The husband then returned to his car, where he became sick and was driven by a police officer to a doctor. The next day a search warrant was issued to search the car, and the following items were seized: a horn rim with what appeared to be a bloodstain on it, a pair of rubbers, sweepings from the floor of the car.

Can the bloodstains on the horn rim and blood and small glass fragments found on the floor of the car be successfully used as evidence to show that the husband (defendant) was in the home at the time of the murder? Give reasons for your answer. *State v. Davidson,* 44 Wis.2d 177, 170 N.W.2d 755 (Wisconsin Sup.Ct.1969).

NOTES

[1] Commonwealth v. Lykus, 367 Mass. 191, 327 N.E.2d 671 (1975) quoting United States v. Addison, 498 F.2d 741 (D.C.Cir.1974).

[2] 293 Fed. 1013 (1923). In the *Frye* case, the court refused to admit the results of a polygraph test showing that Frye was telling the truth when he stated that he did not commit the murder. Frye was convicted and served three years of his sentence before another man confessed to the crime. Frye was then freed.

[3] 251 Ga. 749, 312 S.E.2d 40 (1983).

[4] Both of these U.S. Supreme Court cases are presented in this text.

[5] See 41 C.J.S. Homicide sec. 312(d)(1).

[6] Heacox v. Polce, 392 Pa. 415, 141 A.2d 229 (Pa.Sup.Ct.1958), Hastings v. Serleto, 61 Cal.App.2d 672, 143 P.2d 956 (1943).

[7] 128 N.J.Super. 199, 319 A.2d 733 (N.J.Sup.Ct.1974).

[8] Tests used in most American jurisdictions to determine guilt or innocence because of mental disease or defect are: (1) the M'Naughten "Right and Wrong" test, or (2) the American Law Institute "Substantial Capacity" test. For a discussion of these tests and other tests, see *Criminal Law: Principles and Cases,* 3d Ed., Gardner (West Publishing Co., 1985).

Appendix A

APPLICABLE SECTIONS OF THE U.S. CONSTITUTION
Ratified in 1788

PREAMBLE

WE THE PEOPLE of the United States, in Order to form a more perfect Union, establish Justice, insure domestic Tranquility, provide for the common defence, promote the general Welfare, and secure the Blessings of Liberty to ourselves and our Posterity, do ordain and establish this CONSTITUTION for the United States of America.

Article I

Section 1   All legislative Powers herein granted shall be vested in a Congress of the United States, which shall consist of a Senate and House of Representatives. . . .

Article II

Section 1   The executive Power shall be vested in a President of the United States of America. . . .

Article III

Section 1   The judicial Power of the United States, shall be vested in one supreme Court, and in such inferior Courts as the Congress may from time to time ordain and establish. . . .

Article IV

Section 4   The United States shall guarantee to every State in this Union a Republican Form of Government, and shall protect each of them against Invasion; and on Application of the Legislature, or of the Executive (when the Legislature cannot be convened) against domestic Violence. . . .

Article VI

This Constitution, and the Laws of the United States which shall be made in Pursuance thereof; and all Treaties made, or which shall be made, under the Authority of the United States, shall be the supreme Law of the Land; and the Judges in every State shall be bound thereby, any Thing in the Constitution or Laws of any State to the Contrary notwithstanding. . . .

American Bill of Rights
Ratified 1791

Amendment I

Congress shall make no law respecting an establishment of religion, or prohibiting the free exercise thereof; or abridging the freedom of speech or of the press; or the right of the people peaceably to assemble and to petition the Government for a redress of grievances.

Amendment II

A well regulated Militia, being necessary to the security of a free State, the right of the people to keep and bear Arms, shall not be infringed.

Amendment III

No Soldier shall, in time of peace be quartered in any house, without the consent of the Owner, nor in time of war, but in a manner to be prescribed by law.

Amendment IV

The right of the people to be secure in their persons, houses, papers, and effects, against unreasonable searches and seizures, shall not be violated, and no Warrants shall issue, but upon probable cause, supported by Oath, or affirmation, and particularly describing the place to be searched and the persons or things to be seized.

Amendment V

No person shall be held to answer for a capital, or otherwise infamous crime, unless on a presentment or indictment of a Grand Jury, except in cases arising in the land or naval forces, or in the Militia, when in actual service in time of War or public danger; nor shall any person be subject for the same offence to be twice put in jeopardy of life or limb; nor shall be compelled in any criminal case to be a witness against himself, nor be deprived of life, liberty, or property, without due process of law; nor shall private property be taken for public use, without just compensation.

Amendment VI

In all criminal prosecutions, the accused shall enjoy the right to a speedy and public trial, by an impartial jury of the State and district wherein the crime shall have been committed, which district shall have been previously ascertained by law, and to be informed of the nature and cause of the accusation; to be confronted with the witnesses against him; to have compulsory process for obtaining witnesses in his favor, and to have the Assistance of Counsel for his defence.

Amendment VII

In suits at common law, where the value in controversy shall exceed twenty dollars, the right of trial by jury shall be preserved, and no fact tried by jury, shall be otherwise reexamined in any Court of the United States, than according to the rules of the common law.

Amendment VIII

Excessive bail shall not be required, nor excessive fines imposed, nor cruel and unusual punishments inflicted.

Amendment IX

The enumeration in the Constitution, of certain rights, shall not be construed to deny or disparage others retained by the people.

Amendment X

The powers not delegated to the United States by the Constitution, nor prohibited by it to the States, are reserved to the States respectively, or to the people....

14th Amendment
Ratified 1868

Amendment XIV

Section 1. All persons born or naturalized in the United States, and subject to the jurisdiction thereof, are citizens of the United States and of the State wherein they reside. No State shall make or enforce any law which shall abridge the privileges or immunities of citizens of the United States; nor shall any State deprive any person of life, liberty, or property, without due process of law; nor deny to any person within its jurisdiction the equal protection of the laws....

Appendix B

FEDERAL RULES OF EVIDENCE

(effective 1982)

ARTICLE I.   GENERAL PROVISIONS

Rule 101.   Scope

These rules govern proceedings in the courts of the United States and before United States magistrates, to the extent and with the exceptions stated in rule 1101.

Rule 102.   Purpose and Construction

These rules shall be construed to secure fairness in administration, elimination of unjustifiable expense and delay, and promotion of growth and development of the law of evidence to the end that the truth may be ascertained and proceedings justly determined.

Rule 103.   Rulings on Evidence

(a) Effect of erroneous ruling.—Error may not be predicated upon a ruling which admits or excludes evidence unless a substantial right of the party is affected, and

(1) Objection.—In case the ruling is one admitting evidence, a timely objection or motion to strike appears of record, stating the specific ground of objection, if the specific ground was not apparent from the context; or

(2) Offer of proof.—In case the ruling is one excluding evidence, the substance of the evidence was made known to the court by offer or was apparent from the context within which questions were asked.

(b) Record of offer and ruling.—The court may add any other or further statement which shows the character of the evidence, the form in which it was offered, the objection made, and the ruling thereon. It may direct the making of an offer in question and answer form.

(c) Hearing of jury.—In jury cases, proceeding shall be conducted, to the extent practicable, so as to prevent inadmissible evidence from being suggested to the jury by any means, such as making statements or offers of proof or asking questions in the hearing of the jury.

(d) Plain error.—Nothing in this rule precludes taking notice of plain errors affecting substantial rights although they were not brought to the attention of the court.

Rule 104.   Preliminary Questions

(a) Questions of admissibility generally.—Preliminary questions concerning the qualification of a person to be a witness, the existence of a privilege, or the admissibility of evidence shall be determined by the court, subject to the provisions of subdivision (b). In making its determination it is not bound by the rules of evidence except those with respect to privileges.

(b) Relevancy conditioned on fact.—When the relevancy of evidence depends upon the fulfillment of a condition of fact, the court shall admit it upon, or subject to, the introduction of evidence sufficient to support a finding of the fulfillment of the condition.

(c) Hearing of jury.—Hearings on the admissibility of confessions shall in all cases be conducted out of the hearing of the jury. Hearings on other preliminary matters shall be so conducted when the interests of justice require or, when an accused is a witness, if he so requests.

(d) Testimony by accused.—The accused does not, by testifying upon a preliminary matter, subject himself to cross-examination as to other issues in the case.

(e) Weight and credibility.—This rule does not limit the right of a party to introduce before the jury evidence relevant to weight or credibility.

Rule 105. Limited Admissibility

When evidence which is admissible as to one party or for one purpose but not admissible as to another party or for another purpose is admitted, the court, upon request, shall restrict the evidence to its proper scope and instruct the jury accordingly.

Rule 106. Remainder of or Related Writings or Recorded Statements

When a writing or recorded statement or part thereof is introduced by a party, an adverse party may require him at that time to introduce any other part or any other writing or recorded statement which ought in fairness to be considered contemporaneously with it.

ARTICLE II.   JUDICIAL NOTICE

Rule 201.   Judicial Notice of Adjudicative Facts

(a) Scope of rule.—This rule governs only judicial notice of adjudicative facts.

(b) Kinds of facts.—A judicially noticed fact must be one not subject to reasonable dispute in that it is either (1) generally known within the territorial jurisdiction of the trial court or (2) capable of accurate and ready determination by resort to sources whose accuracy cannot reasonably be questioned.

(c) When discretionary.—A court may take judicial notice, whether requested or not.

(d) When mandatory.—A court shall take judicial notice if requested by a party and supplied with the necessary information.

(e) Opportunity to be heard.—A party is entitled upon timely request to an opportunity to be heard as to the propriety of taking judicial notice and the tenor of the matter noticed. In the absence of prior notification, the request may be made after judicial notice has been taken.

(f) Time of taking notice.—Judicial notice may be taken at any stage of the proceeding.

(g) Instructing jury.—In a civil action or proceeding, the court shall instruct the jury to accept as conclusive any fact judicially noticed. In a criminal case, the court shall instruct the jury that it may, but is not required to, accept as conclusive any fact judicially noticed.

ARTICLE III.   PRESUMPTIONS IN CIVIL ACTIONS AND PROCEEDINGS

Rule 301.   Presumptions in General in Civil Actions and Proceedings

In all civil actions and proceedings not otherwise provided for by Act of Congress or by these rules, a presumption imposes on the party against whom it is directed the burden of going forward with evidence to rebut or meet the presumption, but does not shift to such party the burden of proof in the sense of the risk of nonpersuasion, which remains throughout the trial upon the party on whom it was originally cast.

Rule 302. Applicability of State Law in Civil Actions and Proceedings

In civil actions and proceedings, the effect of a presumption respecting a fact which is an element of a claim or defense as to which State law supplies the rule of decision is determined in accordance with State law.

ARTICLE IV. RELEVANCY AND ITS LIMITS

Rule 401. Definition of "Relevant Evidence"

"Relevant evidence" means evidence having any tendency to make the existence of any fact that is of consequence to the determination of the action more probable or less probable than it would be without the evidence.

Rule 402. Relevant Evidence Generally Admissible; Irrelevant Evidence Inadmissible

All relevant evidence is admissible, except as otherwise provided by the Constitution of the United States, by Act of Congress, by these rules, or by other rules prescribed by the Supreme Court pursuant to statutory authority. Evidence which is not relevant is not admissible.

Rule 403. Exclusion of Relevant Evidence on Grounds of Prejudice, Confusion, or Waste of Time

Although relevant, evidence may be excluded if its probative value is substantially outweighed by the danger of unfair prejudice, confusion of the issues, or misleading the jury, or by considerations of undue delay, waste of time, or needless presentation of cumulative evidence.

Rule 404. Character Evidence Not Admissible To Prove Conduct; Exceptions; Other Crimes

(a) Character evidence generally.—Evidence of a person's character or a trait of his character is not admissible for the purpose of proving that he acted in conformity therewith on a particular occasion, except:

(1) Character of accused.—Evidence of a pertinent trait of his character offered by an accused, or by the prosecution to rebut the same;

(2) Character of victim.—Evidence of a pertinent trait of character of the victim of the crime offered by an accused, or by the prosecution to rebut the same, or evidence of a character trait of peacefulness of the victim offered by the prosecution in a homicide case to rebut evidence that the victim was the first aggressor;

(3) Character of witness.—Evidence of the character of a witness, as provided in rules 607, 608, and 609.

(b) Other crimes, wrongs, or acts.—Evidence of other crimes, wrongs, or acts is not admissible to prove the character of a person in order to show that he acted in conformity therewith. It may, however, be admissible for other purposes, such as proof of motive, opportunity, intent, preparation, plan, knowledge, identity, or absence of mistake or accident.

Rule 405. Methods of Proving Character

(a) Reputation or opinion.—In all cases in which evidence of character or a trait of character of a person is admissible, proof may be made by testimony as to reputation or by testimony in the form of an opinion. On cross-examination, inquiry is allowable into relevant specific instances of conduct.

(b) Specific instances of conduct.—In cases in which character or a trait of character of a person is an essential element of a charge, claim, or defense, proof may also be made of specific instances of his conduct.

Rule 406. Habit; Routine Practice

Evidence of the habit of a person or the routine practice of an organization, whether corroborated or not and regardless of the presence of eyewitnesses, is relevant to prove that the conduct of the person or organization on a particular occasion was in conformity with the habit or routine practice.

Rule 407. Subsequent Remedial Measures

When, after an event, measures are taken which, if taken previously, would have made the event less likely to occur, evidence of the subsequent measures is not admissible to prove negligence or culpable conduct in connection with the event. This rule does not require the exclusion of evidence of subsequent measures when offered for another purpose, such as proving ownership, control, or feasibility of precautionary measures, if controverted, or impeachment.

Rule 408. Compromise and Offers to Compromise

Evidence of (1) furnishing or offering or promising to furnish, or (2) accepting or offering or promising to accept, a valuable consideration in compromising or attempting to compromise a claim which was disputed as to either validity or amount, is not admissible to prove liability for or invalidity of the claim or its amount. Evidence of conduct or statements made in compromise negotiations is likewise not admissible. This rule does not require the exclusion of any evidence otherwise discoverable merely because it is presented in the course of compromise negotiations. This rule also does not require exclusion when the evidence is offered for another purpose, such as proving bias or prejudice of a witness, negativing a contention of undue delay, or proving an effort to obstruct a criminal investigation or prosecution.

Rule 409. Payment of Medical and Similar Expenses

Evidence of furnishing or offering or promising to pay medical, hospital, or similar expenses occasioned by an injury is not admissible to prove liability for the injury.

Rule 410. Inadmissibility of Pleas, Plea Discussions, and Related Statements

Except as otherwise provided in this rule, evidence of the following is not, in any civil or criminal proceeding, admissible against the defendant who made the plea or was a participant in the plea discussions:

(1) a plea of guilty which was later withdrawn;

(2) a plea of nolo contendere;

(3) any statement made in the course of any proceedings under Rule 11 of the Federal Rules of Criminal Procedure or comparable state procedure regarding either of the foregoing pleas; or

(4) any statement made in the course of plea discussions with an attorney for the prosecuting authority which do not result in a plea of guilty or which result in a plea of guilty later withdrawn.

However, such a statement is admissible (i) in any proceeding wherein another statement made in the course of the same plea or plea discussions has been introduced and the statement ought in fairness be considered contemporaneously with it, or (ii) in a criminal proceeding for perjury or false statement if the statement was made by the defendant under oath, on the record and in the presence of counsel.

(As amended Dec. 12, 1975; Apr. 30, 1979, eff. Dec. 1, 1980.)

Rule 411.   Liability Insurance

Evidence that a person was or was not insured against liability is not admissible upon the issue whether he acted negligently or otherwise wrongfully. This rule does not require the exclusion of evidence of insurance against liability when offered for another purpose, such as proof of agency, ownership, or control, or bias or prejudice of a witness.

Rule 412.   Rape Cases; Relevance of Victim's Past Behavior

(a) Notwithstanding any other provision of law, in a criminal case in which a person is accused of rape or of assault with intent to commit rape, reputation or opinion evidence of the past sexual behavior of an alleged victim of such rape or assault is not admissible.

(b) Notwithstanding any other provision of law, in a criminal case in which a person is accused of rape or of assault with intent to commit rape, evidence of a victim's past sexual behavior other than reputation or opinion evidence is also not admissible, unless such evidence other than reputation or opinion evidence is—

(1) admitted in accordance with subdivisions (c)(1) and (c)(2) and is constitutionally required to be admitted; or

(2) admitted in accordance with subdivision (c) and is evidence of—

(A) past sexual behavior with persons other than the accused, offered by the accused upon the issue of whether the accused was or was not, with respect to the alleged victim, the source of semen or injury; or

(B) past sexual behavior with the accused and is offered by the accused upon the issue of whether the alleged victim consented to the sexual behavior with respect to which rape or assault is alleged.

(c)(1) If the person accused of committing rape or assault with intent to commit rape intends to offer under subdivision (b) evidence of specific instances of the alleged victim's past sexual behavior, the accused shall make a written motion to offer such evidence not later than fifteen days before the date on which the trial in which such evidence is to be offered is scheduled to begin, except that the court may allow the motion to be made at a later date, including during trial, if the court determines either that the evidence is newly discovered and could not have been obtained earlier through the exercise of due diligence or that the issue to which such evidence relates has newly arisen in the case....

ARTICLE V.   PRIVILEGES

Rule 501.   General Rule

Except as otherwise required by the Constitution of the United States or provided by Act of Congress or in rules prescribed by the Supreme Court pursuant to statutory authority, the privilege of a witness, person, government, State, or political subdivision thereof shall be governed by the principles of the common law as they may be interpreted by the courts of the United States in the light of reason and experience. However, in civil actions and proceedings, with respect to an element of a claim or defense as to which State law supplies the rule of decision, the privilege of a witness, person, government, State, or political subdivision thereof shall be determined in accordance with State law.

ARTICLE VI.   WITNESSES

Rule 601.   General Rule of Competency

Every person is competent to be a witness except as otherwise provided in these rules. However, in civil actions and proceedings, with respect to an element of a claim or defense as to which State law supplies the rule of decision, the competency of a witness shall be determined in accordance with State law.

Rule 602. Lack of Personal Knowledge

A witness may not testify to a matter unless evidence is introduced sufficient to support a finding that he has personal knowledge of the matter. Evidence to prove personal knowledge may, but need not, consist of the testimony of the witness himself. This rule is subject to the provisions of rule 703, relating to opinion testimony by expert witnesses.

Rule 603. Oath or Affirmation

Before testifying, every witness shall be required to declare that he will testify truthfully, by oath or affirmation administered in a form calculated to awaken his conscience and impress his mind with his duty to do so.

Rule 604. Interpreters

An interpreter is subject to the provisions of these rules relating to qualification as an expert and the administration of an oath or affirmation that he will make a true translation. . . .

Rule 607. Who May Impeach

The credibility of a witness may be attacked by any party, including the party calling him.

Rule 608. Evidence of Character and Conduct of Witness

(a) Opinion and reputation evidence of character.—The credibility of a witness may be attacked or supported by evidence in the form of opinion or reputation, but subject to these limitations: (1) the evidence may refer only to character for truthfulness or untruthfulness, and (2) evidence of truthful character is admissible only after the character of the witness for truthfulness has been attacked by opinion or reputation evidence or otherwise.

(b) Specific instances of conduct.—Specific instances of the conduct of a witness, for the purpose of attacking or supporting his credibility, other than conviction of crime as provided in rule 609, may not be proved by extrinsic evidence. They may, however, in the discretion of the court, if probative of truthfulness or untruthfulness, be inquired into on cross-examination of the witness (1) concerning his character for truthfulness or untruthfulness, or (2) concerning the character for truthfulness or untruthfulness of another witness as to which character the witness being cross-examined has testified.

The giving of testimony, whether by an accused or by any other witness, does not operate as a waiver of his privilege against self-incrimination when examined with respect to matters which relate only to credibility.

Rule 609. Impeachment by Evidence of Conviction of Crime

(a) General rule.—For the purpose of attacking the credibility of a witness, evidence that he has been convicted of a crime shall be admitted if elicited from him or established by public record during cross-examination but only if the crime (1) was punishable by death or imprisonment in excess of one year under the law under which he was convicted, and the court determines that the probative value of admitting this evidence outweighs its prejudicial effect to the defendant, or (2) involved dishonesty or false statement, regardless of the punishment.

(b) Time limit.—Evidence of a conviction under this rule is not admissible if a period of more than ten years has elapsed since the date of the conviction or of the release of the witness from the confinement imposed for that conviction, whichever is the later date, unless the court determines, in the interests of justice, that the probative value of the conviction supported by specific facts and circumstances substantially outweighs its prejudicial effect. However, evidence of a conviction more than 10 years old as calculated herein, is not admissible unless the proponent gives to the adverse party sufficient advance written notice of intent to use such evidence to provide the adverse party with a fair opportunity to contest the use of such evidence.

(c) Effect of pardon, annulment, or certificate of rehabilitation.—Evidence of a conviction is not admissible under this rule if (1) the conviction has been the subject of a pardon, annulment, certificate of rehabilitation, or other equivalent procedure based on a finding of the rehabilitation of the person convicted, and that person has not been convicted of a subsequent crime which was punishable by death or imprisonment in excess of one year, or (2) the conviction has been the subject of a pardon, annulment, or other equivalent procedure based on a finding of innocence.

(d) Juvenile adjudications.—Evidence of juvenile adjudications is generally not admissible under this rule. The court may, however, in a criminal case allow evidence of a juvenile adjudication of a witness other than the accused if conviction of the offense would be admissible to attack the credibility of an adult and the court is satisfied that admission in evidence is necessary for a fair determination of the issue of guilt or innocence.

(e) Pendency of appeal.—The pendency of an appeal therefrom does not render evidence of a conviction inadmissible. Evidence of the pendency of an appeal is admissible.

Rule 610. Religious Beliefs or Opinions

Evidence of the beliefs or opinions of a witness on matters of religion is not admissible for the purpose of showing that by reason of their nature his credibility is impaired or enhanced.

Rule 611. Mode and Order of Interrogation and Presentation

(a) Control by court.—The court shall exercise reasonable control over the mode and order of interrogating witnesses and presenting evidence so as to (1) make the interrogation and presentation effective for the ascertainment of the truth, (2) avoid needless consumption of time, and (3) protect witnesses from harassment or undue embarrassment.

(b) Scope of cross-examination.—Cross-examination should be limited to the subject matter of the direct examination and matters affecting the credibility of the witness. The court may, in the exercise of discretion, permit inquiry into additional matters as if on direct examination.

(c) Leading questions.—Leading questions should not be used on the direct examination of a witness except as may be necessary to develop his testimony. Ordinarily leading questions should be permitted on cross-examination. When a party calls a hostile witness, an adverse party, or a witness identified with an adverse party, interrogation may be by leading questions.

Rule 612. Writing Used To Refresh Memory

Except as otherwise provided in criminal proceedings by section 3500 of title 18, United States Code, if a witness uses a writing to refresh his memory for the purpose of testifying, either—

(1) while testifying, or
(2) before testifying, if the court in its discretion determines it is necessary in the interests of justice,

an adverse party is entitled to have the writing produced at the hearing, to inspect it, to cross-examine the witness thereon, and to introduce in evidence those portions which relate to the testimony of the witness. If it is claimed that the writing contains matters not related to the subject matter of the testimony the court shall examine the writing in camera, excise any portions not so related, and order delivery of the remainder to the party entitled thereto. Any portion withheld over objections shall be preserved and made available to the appellate court in the event of an appeal. If a writing is not produced or delivered pursuant to order under this rule, the court shall make any order justice requires, except that in criminal cases when the prosecution elects not to comply, the order shall be one striking the testimony or, if the court in its discretion determines that the interests of justice so require, declaring a mistrial.

Rule 613. Prior Statements of Witnesses

(a) Examining witness concerning prior statement.—In examining a witness concerning a prior statement made by him, whether written or not, the statement need not be shown nor its contents disclosed to him at that time, but on request the same shall be shown or disclosed to opposing counsel.

(b) Extrinsic evidence of prior inconsistent statement of witness.—Extrinsic evidence of a prior inconsistent statement by a witness is not admissible unless the witness is afforded an opportunity to explain or deny the same and the opposite party is afforded an opportunity to interrogate him thereon, or the interests of justice otherwise require. This provision does not apply to admissions of a party-opponent as defined in rule 801(d)(2).

Rule 614. Calling and Interrogation of Witnesses by Court

(a) Calling by court.—The court may, on its own motion or at the suggestion of a party, call witnesses, and all parties are entitled to cross-examine witnesses thus called.

(b) Interrogation by court.—The court may interrogate witnesses, whether called by itself or by a party.

(c) Objections.—Objections to the calling of witnesses by the court or to interrogation by it may be made at the time or at the next available opportunity when the jury is not present.

Rule 615. Exclusion of Witnesses

At the request of a party the court shall order witnesses excluded so that they cannot hear the testimony of other witnesses, and it may make the order of its own motion. This rule does not authorize exclusion of (1) a party who is a natural person, or (2) an officer or employee of a party which is not a natural person designated as its representative by its attorney, or (3) a person whose presence is shown by a party to be essential to the presentation of his cause.

ARTICLE VII.   OPINIONS AND EXPERT TESTIMONY

Rule 701. Opinion Testimony by Lay Witnesses

If the witness is not testifying as an expert, his testimony in the form of opinions or inferences is limited to those opinions or inferences which are (a) rationally based on the perception of the witness and (b) helpful to a clear understanding of his testimony or the determination of a fact in issue.

Rule 702. Testimony by Experts

If scientific, technical, or other specialized knowledge will assist the trier of fact to understand the evidence or to determine a fact in issue, a witness qualified as an expert by knowledge, skill, experience, training, or education, may testify thereto in the form of an opinion or otherwise.

Rule 703.   Bases of Opinion Testimony by Experts

The facts or data in the particular case upon which an expert bases an opinion or inference may be those perceived by or made known to him at or before the hearing. If of a type reasonably relied upon by experts in the particular field in forming opinions or inferences upon the subject, the facts or data need not be admissible in evidence.

Rule 704.   Opinion on Ultimate Issue

(a) Except as provided in subdivision (b), testimony in the form of an opinion or inference otherwise admissible is not objectionable because it embraces an ultimate issue to be decided by the trier of fact.

(b) No expert witness testifying with respect to the mental state or condition of a defendant in a criminal case may state an opinion or inference as to whether the defendant did or did not have the mental state or condition constituting an element of the crime charged or of a defense thereto. Such ultimate issues are matters for the trier of fact alone.

(As amended Oct. 12, 1984.)

Rule 705.   Disclosure of Facts or Data Underlying Expert Opinion

The expert may testify in terms of opinion or inference and give his reasons therefor without prior disclosure of the underlying facts or data, unless the court requires otherwise. The expert may in any event be required to disclose the underlying facts or data on cross-examination.

ARTICLE VIII.   HEARSAY

(See chapter 7 for material on hearsay.)

ARTICLE IX.   AUTHENTICATION AND IDENTIFICATION

Rule 901.   Requirement of Authentication or Identification

(a) General provision.—The requirement of authentication or identification as a condition precedent to admissibility is satisfied by evidence sufficient to support a finding that the matter in question is what its proponent claims.

(b) Illustrations.—By way of illustration only, and not by way of limitation, the following are examples of authentication or identification conforming with the requirements of this rule:

(1) Testimony of witness with knowledge.—Testimony that a matter is what it is claimed to be.

(2) Nonexpert opinion on handwriting.—Nonexpert opinion as to the genuineness of handwriting, based upon familiarity not acquired for purposes of the litigation.

(3) Comparison by trier or expert witness.—Comparison by the trier of fact or by expert witnesses with specimens which have been authenticated.

(4) Distinctive characteristics and the like.—Appearance, contents, substance, internal patterns, or other distinctive characteristics, taken in conjunction with circumstances.

(5) Voice identification.—Identification of a voice, whether heard firsthand or through mechanical or electronic transmission or recording, by opinion based upon hearing the voice at any time under circumstances connecting it with the alleged speaker.

(6) Telephone conversations.—Telephone conversations, by evidence that a call was made to the number assigned at the time by the telephone company to a particular person or business, if (A) in the case of a person, circumstances, includ-

ing self-identification, show the person answering to be the one called, or (B) in the case of a business, the call was made to a place of business and the conversation related to business reasonably transacted over the telephone.

(7) Public records or reports.—Evidence that a writing authorized by law to be recorded or filed and in fact recorded or filed in a public office, or a purported public record, report, statement, or data compilation, in any form, is from the public office where items of this nature are kept.

(8) Ancient documents or data compilation.—Evidence that a document or data compilation, in any form, (A) is in such condition as to create no suspicion concerning its authenticity, (B) was in a place where it, if authentic, would likely be, and (C) has been in existence 20 years or more at the time it is offered.

(9) Process or system.—Evidence describing a process or system used to produce a result and showing that the process or system produces an accurate result.

(10) Methods provided by statute or rule.—Any method of authentication or identification provided by Act of Congress or by other rules prescribed by the Supreme Court pursuant to statutory authority.

Rule 902. Self-authentication

Extrinsic evidence of authenticity as a condition precedent to admissibility is not required with respect to the following:

(1) Domestic public documents under seal.—A document bearing a seal purporting to be that of the United States, or of any State, district, Commonwealth, territory, or insular possession thereof, or the Panama Canal Zone, or the Trust Territory of the Pacific Islands, or of a political subdivision, department, office, or agency thereof, and a signature purporting to be an attestation or execution.

(2) Domestic public documents not under seal.—A document purporting to bear the signature in his official capacity of an officer or employee of any entity included in paragraph (1) hereof, having no seal, if a public officer having a seal and having official duties in the district, or political subdivision of the officer or employee certifies under seal that the signer has the official capacity and that the signature is genuine....

(4) Certified copies of public records ...

(5) Official publications—books, etc. issued by public authority ...

(6) Newspapers and periodicals ...

(7) Trade inscriptions and the like ...

(8) Acknowledged documents ...

(9) Commercial papers and related documents ...

ARTICLE X.   CONTENTS OF WRITINGS, RECORDINGS, AND PHOTOGRAPHS
   ...

Rule 1002.   Requirement of Original

To prove the content of a writing, recording, or photograph, the original writing, recording, or photograph is required, except as otherwise provided in these rules or by Act of Congress.

Rule 1003.   Admissibility of Duplicates

A duplicate is admissible to the same extent as an original unless (1) a genuine question is raised as to the authenticity of the original or (2) in the circumstances it would be unfair to admit the duplicate in lieu of the original.

Rule 1004.   Admissibility of Other Evidence of Contents

The original is not required, and other evidence of the contents of a writing, recording, or photograph is admissible if—

(1) Originals lost or destroyed.—All originals are lost or have been destroyed, unless the proponent lost or destroyed them in bad faith; or

(2) Original not obtainable.—No original can be obtained by any available judicial process or procedure; or

(3) Original in possession of opponent.—At a time when an original was under the control of the party against whom offered, he was put on notice, by the pleadings or otherwise, that the contents would be a subject of proof at the hearing, and he does not produce the original at the hearing; or

(4) Collateral matters.—The writing, recording, or photograph is not closely related to a controlling issue.

Rule 1005.   Public Records

The contents of an official record, or of a document authorized to be recorded or filed and actually recorded or filed, including data compilations in any form, if otherwise admissible, may be proved by copy, certified as correct in accordance with rule 902 or testified to be correct by a witness who has compared it with the original. If a copy which complies with the foregoing cannot be obtained by the exercise of reasonable diligence, then other evidence of the contents may be given.

Rule 1006.   Summaries

The contents of voluminous writings, recordings, or photographs which cannot conveniently be examined in court may be presented in the form of a chart, summary, or calculation. The originals, or duplicates, shall be made available for examination or copying, or both, by other parties at reasonable time and place. The court may order that they be produced in court.

Rule 1007.   Testimony or Written Admission of Party

Contents of writings, recordings, or photographs may be proved by the testimony or deposition of the party against whom offered or by his written admission, without accounting for the nonproduction of the original.

Rule 1008.   Functions of Court and Jury

When the admissibility of other evidence of contents of writings, recordings, or photographs under these rules depends upon the fulfillment of a condition of fact, the question whether the condition has been fulfilled is ordinarily for the court to determine in accordance with the provisions of rule 104. However, when an issue is raised (a) whether the asserted writing ever existed, or (b) whether another writing, recording, or photograph produced at the trial is the original, or (c) whether other evidence of contents correctly reflects the contents, the issue is for the trier of fact to determine as in the case of other issues of fact.

Index